D1503827

# INTERNATIONAL RETAILING

## second edition

## Brenda Sternquist

### Michigan State University

**FAIRCHILD PUBLICATIONS**

**NEW YORK**

Director of Sales and Acquisitions: Dana Meltzer-Berkowitz
Executive Editor: Olga T. Kontzias
Senior Development Editor: Jennifer Crane
Development Editor: Barbara A. Chernow
Art Director: Adam B. Bohannon
Production Manager: Ginger Hillman
Senior Production Editor: Elizabeth Marotta
Production Editor: Chernow Editorial Services, Inc.
Copyeditor: Susan Norton
Cover Design: Kristina Berberich
Cover Art: Corbis
Text Design: Susan Day
Cartography: Carto-Graphics

Copyright © 2007 Fairchild Publications, Inc.
Fairchild Fashion Group
A Division of Condé Nast Publications

Library of Congress Catalog Card Number: 2006939041

ISBN: 978-1-56367-490-7

GST R 133004424

Printed in the United States of America

To my Retailing 465 students,
and my son, Gavin Witter.

## BRIEF CONTENTS

# CONTENTS

# PREFACE

A popular best-seller in 2006 is *The World Is Flat* by Thomas Friedman. The point he makes, which I think it is very true, is that the combination of technology and events have allowed India and China, as well as other countries, to become part of the global supply chain for goods and services. The result has been an explosion of middle-class wealth in these two countries with large populations. Countries can no longer contain trade within their borders; it is a worldwide system.

When I wrote the first edition of *International Retailing* in 1998, it was one of only two books with this title. Nearly 10 years later, there are still only a couple of books with this title. In these 10 years, retailers have become more aggressive in moving into foreign markets. In most parts of the world, two or three of the major multinationals are setting the pace for price wars. Some companies have found that they can not be competitive in foreign markets. Both Wal-Mart and Carrefour have exited from Korea. These companies are developing a portfolio of knowledge about how to do business in other countries.

A new breed of retailer, the born global company, expands almost from the beginning of its existence. Companies such as Zara and Mango have set a blistering pace of internationalization and have reinvented the expectation of how quickly inventory can be turned. This concept of quick fashion is a difficult to duplicate differential advantage.

One of the most important changes since the first edition of this book was published is the enlargement of the European Union to include countries that had been part of the Soviet Union. Most of these countries have underdeveloped retail systems and booming consumer demand, providing an excellent expansion vehicle for Western European retailers. *International Retailing* is based on more than 20 years of original research conducted in foreign countries. I have done research in each of the countries included, except a few of the Central/Eastern European countries.

This book is organized into five parts. Part I introduces the international retail environment and lays the groundwork for understanding retailing in specific countries; it provides a theoretical context for what follows. Chapter 1 deals with internationalization of retailing as a phenomenon. Chapter 2 presents a theoretical framework, with research propositions that can be used to predict where, when, and why retailers internationalize. Chapter 3 analyzes how location affects retailing. Chapter 4 deals focuses on the relationship between international culture and human behavior. Chapter 5 discusses the retail environment in developing countries and how it changes as a country develops economically. Licensing, franchising and strategic alliances are the focus of Chapter 6. The final chapter in Part I is about retailing in multinational markets and the phenomenon of several countries entering into trade agreements, such as the North American Free Trade Agreement (NAFTA).

Parts II, III, and IV focus on retiling in particular areas of the world. Part II covers the Americas, with a look at retailing in the United States (Chapter 8), Mexico and Canada (Chapter 9), and South America (Chapter 10). Part II covers retailing in Europe. The chapters in this unit are divided into the geographical and cultural bands of northern Europe (Chapter 11), Germany and France (Chapter 12), southern Europe (Chapter 13) and retailing in central and Eastern Europe (Chapter 14). Not every country considered a part of Europe is included. This is because some countries do not have distinguishing retail characteristics or major retailers that have expanded internationally. The selection of countries for inclusion was based on whether an overview of that country could be used to generalize about other countries. For example, the concentration of retailing in German department stores is unmatched, with two retail companies controlling 90% of the department store industry. This characteristic enables me to explain how such a concentration affects market mix variables, such as price. If the reader encounters a similar situation in another country, he or she should be able to compare it with the German retail environment. In fact this is the case with Australian retailing, where just two companies dominate the food industry.

Part IV is devoted to retailing in Asia, where I have conducted most of my research. I know Shanghai and Hong Kong better than I know Chicago or Detroit. Chapter 15 looks at retailing in Japan, the first foreign retail market I studied beginning in 1984. When I went to do my first series of interviews, I felt unable to ask an intelligent question. Although I had read everything I could find, it did not prepare me for understanding just how much Japanese culture influences how the Japanese sell goods. To explain the difference to students, I usually start by stretching my arms out as wide as I can. Then I tell that one hand is the United States, the other is Japan; retailing in every other country falls somewhere in the middle. Knowing about retailing in the United States and Japan will enable students to analyze retailing anywhere else in the world. Chapter 16 is about the overseas Chinese markets of Hong Kong and Taiwan. Chapter 17 is about retailing in the People's Republic of China (PRC), or mainland China. This is a particularly exciting time to be studying China because it is undergoing a major change to becoming a free market. From the 1950s until the late 1980s, the Chinese market was a planned economy. All retail stores were state owned or cooperatives (owned by work units). It was not until 1992 that China allowed any foreign joint ventures in retailing. As a part of joining the World Trade Organization (WTO), China has opened the retail sector at a very rapid rate. Timing is everything. My first trip to China was in 1987. Since then, I have returned almost every year. I have seen the retail industry go from dark, dusty distribution facilities to shiny chrome shopping centers with big screen televisions.

The next three chapters have something in common. They were either written by someone else or in conjunction with someone else. Byoungho Jin, from Oklahoma State University, was a visiting scholar at Michigan State University. Since that time we have collaborated on research and have written several articles on retailing in Korea. Chapter 18, Retailing in South Korea, benefits from her voice as someone who has experienced Korean retailing her whole life. The next chapter, Chapter 19, Retailing in India, was coauthored with Payal Dutta. Payal came to Michigan State University as a graduate student after spending years working in the Indian retail industry. After conducting research in India, I became interested in the similarities between China's retail modernization and that of India. India, like China, had a ban on foreign direct investment in retailing. The government has lifted the restriction slightly, by allowing retailers that sell only a private label product produced in India to also open retail stores. Otherwise, foreign ownership is still banned. Foreign competition generally ignites the modernization of the retail industry, and we can see this influence in China, but not yet in India. The last chapter in this section, Chapter 20, Retailing in Australia, was written by Patricia Huddleston, one of my Michigan State University colleagues. She spent a sabbatical leave in Australia studying their retail system and therefore has some special insight into the characteristics of that market.

Part V has only one chapter, which I wrote. It is a "Prognosis for the Future." In this chapter, I reintroduce the Strategic International Retail Expansion model from Chapter 2. It contains a review of the various theories that help explain the internationalization of retailers. The chapter reinforces the propositions presented in Chapter 2 and gives examples of retailers who fit the propositions.

Each chapter in this second edition of *International Retailing* begins with a list of learning objectives and concludes with a summary, a list of key terms, a series of discussion questions, and a list of endnotes.

Six company cases are included in the book. These cases were written by students in my undergraduate International Retailing class. Their major assignment was to complete a research project on a company's internationalization strategy and then to evaluate the propositions presented in Chapter 2 to determine if they fit the predicted pattern. If the company does not fit the predicted pattern, students are invited to stipulate their own propositions for explaining the company's international movement. I have selected the most outstanding papers. After much scrutiny and editing, they appear in this book along with their authors' names.

Technical terms used in the text are boldfaced at their first occurrence in the text and are boldfaced in the index for easy identification. This enables the index to function as a glossary

I hope you enjoy *International Retailing*. It was a labor of love to write.

# ACKNOWLEDGMENTS

The second edition of *International Retailing* still benefits from the helpful insight of those who reviewed the first edition. They are Holly Bastow-Shoop, Marianne Bickle, Kitty Dickerson, Carl Dyer, Fay Gibson, Jan Hathcote, Richard Hise, Cynthia Jasper, Rita Kean, Sherri Lotz, Martha Moran, Soyeon Shim, Bart Weitz, and Sarah Wise. They provided many helpful suggestions.

Leigh Sparks (UK) responded to my request that he review the UK chapter by sending me about 300 pages of papers to read. I did, and I hope the result satisfies him.

My retailing colleagues at Michigan State University are always a source of inspiration and support. I can not thank Linda Good, Patricia Huddleston, Dawn Pysarchik, and Nan Kwon enough for being part of our team.

I also want to thank the students in my undergraduate and graduate international retailing courses for contributing cases and challenging insights. Brandye Vanderploeg, one of my undergraduate teaching assistants, put a great deal of work into the franchising chapter and updating the franchising table. Ying Huang, one of my doctoral students, was very helpful in finding updated information, particularly for the chapter on retailing in developing countries.

Conducting international retailing research is expensive. Funding sources that have made this process possible include: College of Human Ecology Travel Grants, Michigan State University Research Initiation Grants, Michigan State University Foreign Travel Fund, Michigan State University Agriculture Experiment Station, United States Department of Agriculture Challenge Grants, Isetan Department Store (Japan), Marui Department Store (Japan), Hoso Bunko Foundation (Japan), Japan Telecommunications Advancement Foundation (Japan), MSU-CIBER grants, MSU-CASID grants, and United States Department of Agriculture Research Initiative Grant.

As much as money, it is the people you know that help foster international research. I would like to thanks colleagues who are simply too numerous to mention for their assistance in arranging interviews. I would also like to thank the hundreds of business executives who have agreed to talk with me.

As always I would like to thank my son, Gavin Witter. With humor, curiosity, and encouragement, he has been my research assistant in Asia, South America and Europe, and even though he no longer lives at home, is a constant source of support.

# PART I

# Overview

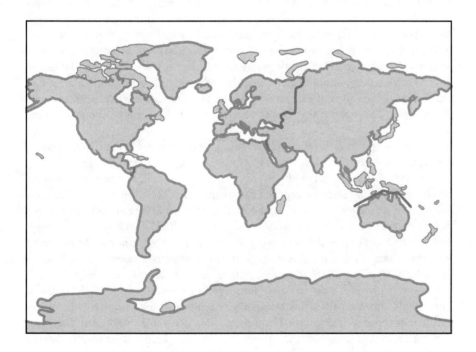

The chapters in Part I of this book provide an introduction to the international retailing environment, laying the groundwork for understanding the retail environment in specific countries around the world. Chapter 1 begins with an overview of issues related to the internationalization of retailing and a discussion of how international retailing differs from international marketing. Retailing is geographically tied. Although manufacturers have the option of producing their product in one location and then exporting that product, to be a retailer, one must operate within a given country. The retail function is the direct-to-consumer link; thus, retailers must have a physical presence in the market. This presence may differ for various types of retailers. For instance, a mail-order company's presence may be a catalog and distribution facilities, rather than a retail store. Both approaches, however, constitute a physical presence. In Chapter 1, I discuss why a retailer might internationalize. In Chapter 2, I tie the reasons into several theories that help to explain the internationalization decision. This chapter presents research propositions that can explain the internationalization process, Strategic International Retail Expansion Model SIRE2.

Factors of production (land, labor, capital, and entrepreneurship) influence a country's comparative advantage. These factors can be used to understand a retailer's comparative advantage. Chapter 3 focuses on location. Dunning's theory of the eclectic firm (presented in Chapter 2) concentrates on three types of advantages a company might use to decide whether it should internationalize, and the attractiveness of various expansion alternatives. The macro-marketing environment is an environment that the retailer cannot control. Retailers monitor and evaluate this environment for company decision-making.

Chapter 4 focuses on international culture and human behavior, and highlights the ways in which people from different societies are taught to understand space, possessions, friendships, agreements, and time. Each person becomes acculturated to his or her particular culture through aspects of everyday society: material elements, social institutions, human interaction, aesthetics, and language. In this chapter, I discuss findings from Hofstede's study of culture, which identified four major dimensions of difference that can be used to generalize about groups of countries. Throughout this chapter, I adapt Hofstede's ideas to convey retailing concepts.

In Chapter 5, I look at retailing in developing countries. Certain characteristics are typical of retailing in less developed countries. Consumers bargain for prices, there is little use of formal credit, product choice is limited, and retailers compete by virtue of having a scarce product rather than through strategic or price considerations. As a country develops, the market changes from a seller's market to a buyer's market. Power changes from the suppliers (sellers) to the consumers (buyers). The last part of this chapter looks at Samiee's theory of economic development and retail change. I will use this framework later to discuss changes in the People's Republic of China as it moved from a planned to a free market economy.

Chapter 6 provides a discussion of licensing, franchising, and strategic alliances. This chapter begins with a theoretical explanation of franchising and then looks at different types of international franchisers. Retailers have a particularly difficult decision in determining whether or not to franchise. Franchising means sharing one's company secrets with others. Those outside the company can easily exploit these advantages. Franchising can be helpful in achieving rapid expansion, but the long-term effects on a company's proprietary knowledge can be harmful. The final part of this chapter includes a discussion of international strategic alliances. Buying alliances have been popular and successful for international retailers. European retailers have been particularly successful participating in buying alliances. Other types of strategic alliances go further than just buying associations. Strategic alliances are a powerful means for international expansion, but they have their own problems.

The world is becoming segregated not by countries, but by trading groups. Chapter 7, the concluding chapter in Part I, focuses on multinational markets. In addition to discussing the advantages and disadvantages of multinational markets,

I also provide a discussion of multinational market levels. There is a hierarchical development of markets based on the control countries give to the market integration.

The chapters in Part I provide a theoretical framework for understanding the country-specific chapters that follow. By reading Chapter 5, on retailing in developing countries, you will be able to identify the importance of informal markets in a country such as Mexico. By understanding the hierarchy behind formal multinational markets described in Chapter 7, you will better understand Europe's problem with monetary unification. Finally, throughout the book, the theme of retail internationalization will emerge.

# 1

# INTERNATIONALIZATION OF RETAILING

## After reading this chapter, you should understand

> Concepts that make international retailing different from international marketing.

> Entry strategies available to international retailers and how these strategies affect retailer market exposure and long-term potential for internationalization.

> Why retailers engage in international expansion.

> How the four factors of production help to explain the theory of comparative advantage and how they help apply Dunning theory of the eclectic firm to retail internationalization.

> Why the macro-marketing environments affect a retailer decision to enter foreign markets.

This chapter presents concepts and theories necessary for understanding international retailing. I begin by exploring the ways in which international retailing differs from international marketing. Next, I outline reasons why companies decide to pursue INTERNATIONALIZATION and analyze the types of firms that expand into foreign markets.

## › GEOGRAPHY OF RETAILING

The focus of this book is international retail markets. My intent is to discuss concepts and theories that will help you to understand differences in various countries' retail markets and the process of retail internationalization. Retailing is geographically tied. To conduct a retailing business in a foreign market, a company must have a physical presence there. Although manufacturers can produce a product at home and then export it throughout the world, retailers must be physically present wherever they are doing business. Each country in the world has different rules and regulations for retailing. To operate in such disparate environments requires both knowledge and experience. If a manufacturer wants to sell a product in the European Union (EU), for example, that manufacturer needs only to make sure that the product meets ISO 9000 regulations—product standards that apply to every country in the EU. The regulations of all the European countries are thus harmonized into one standard. However, a retailer wishing to operate in the EU needs to meet a different set of regulatory requirements for each country being considered.

When we think of geography, we often think in terms of physical geography; that is, where things are. When I went to school, geography was synonymous with learning the capitals of all of the states and countries. Today real geographers know that this science includes the study of both cultural geography and economic geography. In the United States and other countries, different regions reflect CULTURAL GEOGRAPHY, how people live their lives in different regions of the country or world. The pattern of life in the deep South is very different from life in New England. Americans who live on the East Coast are very different from those who live on the West Coast.

ECONOMIC GEOGRAPHY relates to the distribution of industrialization or wealth. The designation "G7" is used by economists when referring to the seven most developed countries in the world. This designation applies to the United States, Japan, Germany, France, the United Kingdom, Italy, and Canada. These countries are not all located next to each other, yet their level of economic development makes consumption practices similar. "G8" refers to the "G7" plus Russia.

Economic geography affects retailing both within individual countries and throughout the world. We have geographically based wealth. Consumers who are geographically adjacent may be vastly different economically. Consider the example of Malaysia and Singapore. Retailing in Singapore is sophisticated and diverse while retailing in adjacent Malaysia is less developed. Cultural and economic borders determine rates of retail growth.

Retailing activity is tied to economic activity. Later in the book (Chapter 5), I will discuss how retailing changes with economic activity. Retailing advancement depends on infrastructures such as transportation, communication, and packaging.

Companies that produce products can become international nearly effortlessly. Most manufacturers begin their international operations when a foreign consumer approaches them, wanting to buy their product. At this point, it is not the marketer that is international, it is the customer.

The major issue for international marketing is one of standardization versus adaptation. Some products are global products, meaning they can be sold in foreign markets with virtually no adaptation. This is what is meant by STANDARDIZATION. Most products, however, need some changes in the product or promotion strategy to fit new markets. This is what is meant by ADAPTATION. In retailing, the product is the retail business. Even if the retailer operates using a standard format throughout the world, the company is placed in the middle of a culturally different surrounding.

Manufacturers who become involved in foreign markets have several alternatives for getting their product to users. They may choose the least involvement, exporting their product to a foreign country through a distributor. Because they have a distributor in the foreign country, these manufacturers may incur few of the financial risks or headaches involved in international sales. Retailers do not have this option. They sell products to the ultimate user; they need to be geographically located where the ultimate user lives. Retailers must have a physical presence in the markets where they want sales.

Mail-order retailers have a presence in the market, not as a store, but through a medium, such as a catalog. It is as difficult to decide a strategy for distribution of catalogs as it is to set retail store location strategy. The catalog is the retailer's physical presence in the market. Mail-order retailers must also have a behind-stage presence, such as a distribution center.

You might think that electronic retailers do not have a location problem, but their concerns are similar to those of catalog retailers. Their website is their physical presence in the market. They need to overcome problems related to shipping merchandise across countries, collecting sales tax if the country requires it, and making sure their website speaks to customers in the countries they target. You see evidence of this challenge by observing Amazon.com, a successful electronic retailer with different websites in different regions of the country.

A retailer's required physical presence in the market also presents problems different from those encountered by international marketers. In particular, the element of culture is a more important variable for retailers than for manufacturers.

Retailers fall far behind manufacturers in internationalization efforts. Of the top 100 retail companies in the world, only 56 operate outside their home markets. Only 5 of those retailers generate more than 50 percent of their sales in foreign markets. Ikea, the Scandinavian home furnishings specialty store that has moved into 18 countries, generated the largest proportion of revenues, 89 percent, from global operations.[1]

Wal-Mart Stores, Inc., the giant discount department store chain, dominates the list of 250 largest retail companies (Chapter 1, Appendix). If Wal-Mart were a nation, its revenue ($258,681,000) would be equal to the 34th largest economy, just behind that of Greece. However, even Wal-Mart's exposure to international markets is small. The company generates only 14 percent of its sales from international operations in 10 countries. Three of these countries are the North American Free Trade Agreement (NAFTA) partners: the United States, Canada, and Mexico. Wal-Mart's other international operations are in Argentina, Brazil, China, Japan, Puerto Rico, the United Kingdom, and Central America. Wal-Mart withdrew from Germany and South Korea in 2006.

## Internationalization Choices

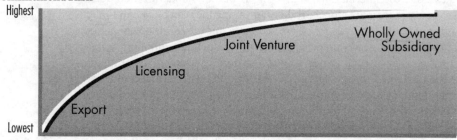

**International Alternatives for Manufacturers**

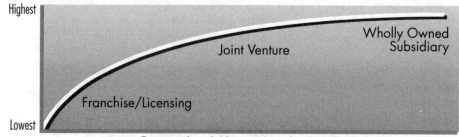

**International Alternatives for Retailers**

**Figure 1.1**
For manufacturers, the export alternative carries the least amount of risk when internationalizing. For retailers, who must have presence in the market in order to internationalize, the least risky option is to franchise or license; the downside to this strategy, however, is that they lose control of their concept.

> **ENTRY STRATEGY**

When a manufacturer is interested in expanding internationally, certain choices will determine its level of involvement and financial commitment (Figure 1.1). The lowest level of involvement is to EXPORT, shipping a product to a foreign country. When a manufacturer exports merchandise, it incurs a limited level of risk, but it also has limited exposure to the market. This means that the manufacturer does not learn how to conduct business in that market; someone else, generally a distributor, is handling the details. A second level of exposure for a manufacturer is to LICENSE the product or company name. When a company licenses its name, it allows another company to produce a product under that company name. With licensing, a manufacturer places itself at risk of losing control of product quality and distribution in the foreign country. The financial risk with licensing, as with exporting, is small. Like exporting, licensing does not give the company exposure to the foreign market, and no significant learning takes place. The third level of involvement for a manufacturer is to enter a JOINT VENTURE with a company in the destination country. Joint ventures exist when two companies join together to form a new business entity. This type of international involvement offers the company knowledge of the new market. The last level of involvement is to open a WHOLLY OWNED SUBSIDIARY, the manufacturer's own company, in the foreign market. In effect, the manufacturer sets up a facility in the foreign country, produces the product, and sells the product there. This offers the greatest exposure to the foreign market, and it also provides the greatest opportunity to learn about the new market.

Retailers have different international expansion choices. The lowest level of involvement for a retailer is through a licensing or franchising arrangement. LICENSING arrangements for retailers, like those for manufacturers, allow a foreign company to use the licensing company's name. For example, Carrefour, the French hypermarket chain, licenses its name in Taiwan. Retailers sacrifice control in this type of arrangement, and it is unusual in retailing. Generally, retail companies use FRANCHISING. Through the franchise arrangement, the franchisor gives imitators the right to use the retailer's name; the retailer, in turn, gives the franchisee the training needed to run the business. Every franchise agreement is different, but each gives some elements of distinctive retail format to the franchisee. If a retailer has a distinctive retail format and it provides this format to franchisees, the retailer is selling its trade secrets. Franchising may thus be good for short-term profitability, but it makes it difficult for the retailer to enter the market later as a wholly owned subsidiary. This is an important consideration, because although franchisees are very popular and have been successful in foreign markets, their presence can block future expansion opportunities. Fast-food businesses in the United States have successfully entered international markets using franchisees. McDonald's, for one, expands internationally using franchisees exclusively. Other companies, such as Benetton and The Body Shop, have used a combination of licensing, franchising, and wholly owned subsidiaries for their international expansion. We will discuss franchising and licensing in more detail in Chapter 6.

The second level of international involvement for a retailer is a joint venture with a foreign company. As with franchising, this type of expansion involves sharing company secrets. If the joint venture partner is knowledgeable about the target country, the joint venture can be mutually beneficial. Retailers who can change their retail format from country to country will find a joint venture even more helpful. For example, Wal-Mart's joint venture with CIFRA, the major Mexican retailer, was called a superb example of successful retail joint ventures by industry analysts. Wal-Mart had not focused on food before this joint venture and Cifra was Mexico's major food retailer. In contrast, when Isetan, a major Japanese department store chain, entered a joint venture with Barney's, a New York specialty chain, the results were disastrous. Barney's hoped to have an infusion of funds; Isetan viewed Barney's as a key retail signature. In the end neither got what they expected.

The third level of international involvement for retailers is to start a wholly-owned subsidiary in the new market. This is the only method that does not sacrifice company secrets. Companies that transfer their retail format in a standardized form are more likely to benefit from this alternative. The less important it is for a retailer to modify its product and retail format offerings, the more attractive this alternative is. Ikea's international expansion has been through wholly owned stores, except where host governments prohibit this type of ownership.

## > REASONS FOR INTERNATIONALIZING

Retailers engage in international expansion for a variety of reasons. Among these are (1) the desire to reach beyond a mature home market with low growth potential,

(2) a need to diversify their investment, (3) a situation in which expansion at home is blocked by legislation, (4) the possession of a unique market format, (5) intense competition at home, (6) an economic downturn at home, or (7) the desire to secure first-mover advantages.

American retailers have been slow to internationalize because they have a big home market. National retail chains were a new idea in the United States and until retailers saturated their home market, there was little motivation for them to expand elsewhere. Other countries, such as the Netherlands, are so small that retailers who want to grow are forced into international markets.

## Mature Home Market—Low Growth Potential

Retail formats, like new products, go through four stages: introduction, growth, maturity, and decline. Retail formats that have reached the maturity stage do not continue to show growth in sales. However, retail formats that are not considered innovative or exciting in the home market may be viewed as new and interesting in a foreign market. For instance, warehouse clubs peaked in popularity in the United States in the late 1980s, but these formats are now entering Asian and South American markets with great pizzazz. Toys "Я" Us began expanding into Asia and Europe because it had already opened stores in most of the U.S. locations that seemed appropriate for its format. The hard discount format, looks like a warehouse club but which is the size of a convenience store, began in Europe but it is proving successful in the United States.

Often retailers view the expansion into a foreign market, using their existing retail format, as less risky than staying at home and adapting to a new retail format. Those who expand, therefore, are generally large-scale retailers, and their expansion

This Toys "Я" Us store is located in Saudi Arabia. Toys "Я" Us is a global retailer; the format is recognizable wherever the stores are located. *Courtesy of Amal Aswailem.*

is to less developed countries. Wal-Mart's expansion into Mexico seems to fit this model.

## Need to Diversify Investment

The old adage "Don't put all your eggs in one basket" is true in business investment. During the 1970s, Delhaize, a family-owned Belgian food retailer, decided it did not want to have all of its investments in Europe. The company concluded that having some investments in the United States would be a prudent move, and it acquired the Food Lion supermarket chain. However, Delhaize did not take over day-to-day operation and management of Food Lion. Purchasing this business was not a part of a retail format diversification strategy. It was part of a financial portfolio diversification strategy.

Some countries are more attractive to retailers than others. The United States is an attractive investment area because of its stable political climate and the low level of government involvement in business operations. However, it is also one of the most over-stored countries, making competition great. OVER-STORED means that a country has too much retail space per consumer. The United States may have as much as 30 percent too much retail space. As a result, domestic cannibalization—obtaining sales at one store, at the expense of another store—is continuing at a rapid rate.

## Expansion at Home Blocked by Legislation

Many countries have strict rules that limit retail expansion, restrict a retailer's ability to terminate employees, and regulate hours of operation. Japan is often cited for its restrictive legislation. However, most European countries have laws that are just as restrictive as Japan's.

Governments often do not like retailing. There are several reasons for this. First, retailing does not improve a country's balance of trade. Countries like to export merchandise and the retailing business function does not do this. Second, many countries protect small retailers. They do this because small retailers are considered desirable to maintain the economic viability of downtown areas. Also retail businesses are often considered an employment sponge. They absorb unemployed workers.

A Japanese law called the *Daiten Ho* (Large-Scale Retail Store Law) once regulated the opening of stores of more than 1,000 square meters. When a new large store was proposed, small shops in the area determined whether they wanted the new business as a neighbor. As might be expected, these small businesses were usually not eager to have a large-scale competitor in their midst. As a result, it often took up to 10 years to open a new store. In response to intense pressure from the United States, Japan reduced the restrictiveness of this law. New measures have been put into place to reduce the time needed to get new store approval. New applications are supposed to take less than 2 years. Belgium has a similar set of laws called the Padlock Laws and France has the *Loi Royer*.

## Possession of a Unique Market Format

It is difficult for a retail store to protect new ideas. Retail innovations cannot be patented or copyrighted. Once a new retail format is introduced, competitors begin to imitate it. One of the best ways for retailers with a unique retail format to exploit the benefits of this format is to expand aggressively into foreign markets, knowing that if they do not expand themselves, imitators will replicate their unique format and enjoy the benefits of innovation.

Zara is a good example of this strategy. Zara has developed a very rapid inventory replenishment system. Turnover is very high, creating a feeling in consumers that if they do not buy the product right away, it will be gone.

Aldi is unique because of its development of the hard discount format. Because the size of the hard discount store is so small, it generally is not covered by the government's attempts to regulate large-scale retailers.

## Intense Competition at Home

Some markets are more competitive than others. Retailers in highly competitive markets such as Japan or the United States may decide to enter other markets with greater growth potential and less competition. Japanese department stores moved to Hong Kong in the 1990s. The first Japanese department stores to expand there were retailers that were less successful at home. They did well in Hong Kong until the more successful Japanese retailers expanded there; then competition was as severe as it was in their home market. Many Japanese department stores pulled out of the Hong Kong market because of stagnant or declining market share in Japan.

U.S. retailers who have moved into Mexico provide another example. In the United States, Kmart has been losing its battle with Wal-Mart for supremacy in the discount retailing arena. Rather than continuing to cannibalize its stores in the United States, Kmart decided to expand internationally in areas where it would not face direct competition from Wal-Mart. None of Kmart's international operations were successful.

## Economic Downturn at Home

Recessions hit retailers early and hard. During periods of poor economic growth in the home market, international expansion may appear very desirable. In the early 1990s, Japan's retail sales declined for 44 straight months before finally posting an increase in the third quarter of 1995. The People's Republic of China, by contrast, had double-digit retail sales increases for more than five years in this period.

Retailers have the additional advantage of being able to open new stores with little LEAD TIME. If the economic climate at home is less than optimal, they can quickly move into another location. After the Berlin Wall fell, West German retailers sent mobile stores to East German cities. Often, these mobile stores consisted of nothing more than semitrailer trucks filled with merchandise. The trucks would be driven to the center of an East German town or city and, presto, the West German retailer would be open for business. The smaller the retailer, the quicker such moves based on economic conditions can be made.

## First-Mover Advantages

Every city has a limited number of ideal retail sites. One of the oldest adages used to explain retail success is "location, location, location." The problem of finding a

## Retail International Expansion: Who Goes Where?

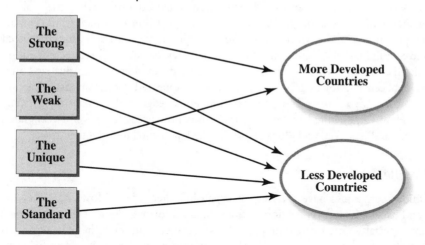

**Figure 1.2**
The profile of a retail company can be used to predict where the retailer will go. Strong and unique companies may expand to either more developed countries or less developed countries. The weak and standard companies will tend to expand to less developed countries, where their retail offering will face less competition.

good location is greater for large-scale stores such as department stores and mass merchandisers than it is for specialty stores.

Location is critical to retailer success. Being first in the market, when the premier sites are still available, is extremely important. Manufacturers have a far broader range of locational alternatives than retailers. Because manufacturers do not need direct access to consumers, they can build their factories on the periphery of cities, or in rural areas where land is less expensive. Good location is so important to retailers that it can be a deciding factor in a company decision to expand internationally.

### > WHAT TYPES OF RETAIL FIRMS EXPAND INTO INTERNATIONAL MARKETS?

All types of retailers contemplate international expansion. The strong, the weak, the unique, and the standard all aspire to expand. Where a retailer will go can be predicted based on its categorization as one of these four general types.

### The Strong

Strong companies seek international markets when worldwide distribution is their goal. Although McDonald's is the strongest competitor in the fast-food business, the company realized that if it did not take its retail format into international markets, imitators would replicate it, denying the company future international growth. Innovators of a new idea have the best chance of maintaining a dominant market share if they continue to expand (Figure 1.2).

Strong companies have their choice of where to expand. They also have a choice of whether to expand in their initial retail format or in a modification of that format. Ikea is an example of a strong company. In each market it has entered, the company has become a market share leader.

## The Weak

Weak companies are often forced into international expansion when they cannot maintain a market share in the home market. Their internationalization is an attempt to find a market with less cutthroat competition. Kmart entry into the Czech and Slovak market in 1993 exemplifies this strategy. No strong foreign competition existed in Prague, where domestic department stores were being privatized after having been state-owned for years. This market appeared to offer an ideal situation for a company unsure of retaining its competitive edge in the domestic U.S. market. However, as noted earlier, this move was not successful. Several years later, Kmart sold its Czech and Slovak stores to the UK-owned food retailer Tesco.

## The Unique

Unique companies have a variety of expansion alternatives. Most often, they expand using an exact replication of their standard format. These retailers generally use a specialty store format; they are lifestyle retailers. Although they can expand to both less developed and more developed countries, they may choose to focus on more developed countries, in which a distinctive global consumer is found. There are groups of consumers located in the major world cities that are very similar. A strategy of unique retailers is to appeal to this similar consumer without having to change the product. Zara, Mango, and H&M are clothing retailers that distinguish themselves from others with a unique line of PRIVATE LABEL merchandise.

## The Standard

Standard companies expand to international markets to capitalize on their large-scale format. These retailers focus on a type of vocational technical training, which teaches sales employees to provide high levels of service. Locating in areas where land and labor are inexpensive best serves these stores. They need to identify countries where consumers' disposable income is increasing. Generally the movement of a standard company is from a more developed country to a less developed country. The French hypermarkets' entry into Spain is an example of this type of movement.

## > SUMMARY

This chapter presents much of the foundation needed for understanding the theories presented in Chapter 2 and the rest of the book. Chapter 2 presents theories of international retailing. You might have heard it said that something is not practical, it is just theory. This saying could not be more incorrect. Good theory is our best guess at reality . . . before we have proof. Theory that is not grounded in reality needs to be revised until it matches reality. The basis for theory is a set of conditional relationships called propositions. Propositions present the relationship between two or more constructs or concepts. Let me give you an example. You have probably heard: "As price increases, quantity demanded decreases." Here we are stating the relationship between two constructs/concepts, price, and quantity demanded. It is what we call an indirect (negative) relationship. As one increases, the other decreases. If we change the statement a little to say, "As price increases, quantity supplied will increase," then we have another proposition showing a direct (positive) relation-ship. As one increases, the other also increases; likewise if one decreases, the other decreases. Propositions are the basis for theory, sort of like legs on a table. Propo-sitions help us to generalize. The propositions presented in Chapter 2 are my best guesses at reality. They haven't been proven, but I will explain why I think they are true.

## ❯ KEY TERMS

ADAPTATION

CULTURAL GEOGRAPHY

ECONOMIC GEOGRAPHY

EXPORT

FRANCHISING

INTERNATIONALIZATION

JOINT VENTURE

LEAD TIME

LICENSE

LICENSING

OVER-STORED

PRIVATE LABEL

STANDARDIZATION

WHOLLY OWNED SUBSIDIARY

## ❯ DISCUSSION QUESTIONS

1. Consider the macro-marketing environment (economic, competitive, techno-logical, social, and governmental/legal). How would each of these environments affect a manufacturer distributing to the country versus a retailer operating in a country?
2. Retailers and manufacturers have different international expansion options. Since retailers must have a geographic presence in the country, how does this limit their expansion alternatives?
3. How can weak companies be successful in internationalizing?

## ❯ ENDNOTES

1. Deloitte. (2005). *Global Powers of Retailing*. Chain Store Age Special Report.

## Chapter 1 Appendix › Top 200 Retailers Worldwide

| Rank | Company | Home Country | Primary Retail Sector | Net Sales (Millions USD) | Sales Growth 2003–2004 | Sales Growth Compound Annual Growth Rate 1999–2004 | Total Stores (incl. company-owned and networked) |
|---|---|---|---|---|---|---|---|
| 1 | Wal-Mart Stores, Inc. | United States | FDM | $285,222 | 11.3% | 11.8% | 5,309 |
| 2 | Carrefour Group | France | FDM | $101,235 | 3.2% | 9.4% | 11,080 |
| 3 | The Home Depot, Inc. | United States | Homegoods | $73,094 | 12.8% | 13.7% | 1,890 |
| 4 | Metro AG | Germany | FDM | $70,162 | 5.3% | 5.1% | 2,446 |
| 5 | Tesco PLC | United Kingdom | FDM | $62,274 | 10.5% | 14.6% | 2,365 |
| 6 | Ito-Yokado Co., Ltd | Japan | FDM | $56,812 | 2.8% | 4.2% | 29,015 |
| 7 | The Kroger Co. | United States | FDM | $56,434 | 4.9% | 4.5% | 3,763 |
| 8 | ITM Entreprises SA | France | FDM | $47,264 | 13.8% | 5.2% | 7,247 |
| 9 | Costco Companies, Inc. | United States | FDM | $47,146 | 13.1% | 11.8% | 417 |
| 10 | Royal Ahold | Netherlands | FDM | $45,864 | −8.6% | 3.5% | 7,289 |
| 11 | Target Corporation | United States | FDM | $45,582 | 11.5% | 6.5% | 1,308 |
| 12 | Schwarz Group | Germany | FDM | $44,777 | 11.0% | 20.3% | 6,080 |
| 13 | Aldi Group | Germany | FDM | $42,506 | −5.6% | 3.6% | 7,517 |

| Home Region | Level of Internation- alization | Number of Countries | % of Sales in Foreign Countries | Countries |
|---|---|---|---|---|
| North America | Global | 11 | 19.7% | N AMERICA: Canada, United States; LATIN AMERICA: Argentina, Brazil, Mexico, Puerto Rico; W EUROPE: Germany, United Kingdom; ASIA-PACIFIC: China, Japan, South Korea |
| W Europe | Global | 31 | 50.8% | LATIN AMERICA: Argentina, Brazil, Colombia, Mexico, Santo Domingo; W EUROPE: Belgium, France, Greece, Italy, Norway, Portugal, Spain, Switzerland; CE EUROPE: Czech Republic, Poland, Romania, Slovakia; ASIA-PACIFIC: China, Indonesia, Japan, Malaysia, Singapore, South Korea, Taiwan, Thailand; AFRICA-MIDDLE EAST: Egypt, Oman, Qatar, Tunisia, Turkey, United Arab Emirates |
| North America | Regional | 3 | 6.0% | N AMERICA: Canada, United States; LATIN AMERICA: Mexico |
| W Europe | Global | 29 | 48.9% | W EUROPE: Austria, Belgium, Denmark, France, Germany, Greece, Italy, Luxembourg, Netherlands, Portugal, Spain, Switzerland, United Kingdom; CE EUROPE: Bulgaria, Croatia, Czech Republic, Hungary, Moldova, Poland, Romania, Russia, Slovakia, Ukraine; ASIA-PACIFIC: China, India, Japan, Vietnam; AFRICA-MIDDLE EAST: Morocco, Turkey |
| W Europe | Global | 13 | 23.0% | W EUROPE: Ireland, United Kingdom; CE EUROPE: Czech Republic, Hungary, Poland, Slovakia; ASIA-PACIFIC: China, Japan, Malaysia, South Korea, Taiwan, Thailand; AFRICA-MIDDLE EAST: Turkey |
| Asia-Pacific | Global | 17 | 32.2% | N AMERICA: Canada, United States; LATIN AMERICA: Mexico; W EUROPE: Denmark, Norway, Sweden; ASIA-PACIFIC: Australia, China, Hong Kong, Japan, Malaysia, Philippines, Singapore, South Korea, Taiwan, Thailand; AFRICA-MIDDLE EAST: Turkey |
| North America | Single Country | 1 | 0.0% | N AMERICA: United States |
| W Europe | Regional | 9 | 29.0% | W EUROPE: Belgium, France, Germany, Portugal, Spain; CE EUROPE: Bosnia, Poland, Romania, Serbia |
| North America | Global | 7 | 18.0% | N AMERICA: Canada, United States; LATIN AMERICA: Mexico; W EUROPE: United Kingdom; ASIA-PACIFIC: Japan, South Korea, Taiwan |
| W Europe | Global | 18 | 84.3% | N AMERICA: United States; LATIN AMERICA: Argentina, Costa Rica, El Salvador, Guatemala, Honduras, Nicaragua; W EUROPE: Denmark, Netherlands, Norway, Portugal, Sweden; CE EUROPE: Czech Republic, Estonia, Latvia, Lithuania, Poland, Slovakia |
| North America | Single Country | 1 | 0.0% | N AMERICA: United States |
| W Europe | Regional | 19 | 50.0% | W EUROPE: Austria, Belgium, Finland, France, Germany, Greece, Ireland, Italy, Netherlands, Norway, Portugal, Spain, Sweden, Switzerland, United Kingdom; CE EUROPE: Czech Republic, Hungary, Poland, Slovakia |
| W Europe | Global | 13 | 35.6% | N AMERICA: United States; W EUROPE: Austria, Belgium, Denmark, France, Germany, Ireland, Luxembourg, Netherlands, Spain, Switzerland, United Kingdom; ASIA-PACIFIC: Australia |

*continued*

| Rank | Company | Home Country | Primary Retail Sector | Net Sales (Millions USD) | Sales Growth 2003–2004 | Sales Growth Compound Annual Growth Rate 1999–2004 | Total Stores (incl. company-owned and networked) |
|---|---|---|---|---|---|---|---|
| 14 | Rewe-Gruppe | Germany | FDM | $40,635 | 1.5% | 1.4% | 11,665 |
| 15 | Albertsons, Inc. | United States | FDM | $39,897 | 13.6% | 1.3% | 2,305 |
| 16 | Edeka-Gruppe | Germany | FDM | $38,993 | 1.0% | 1.4% | 14,000 |
| 17 | Walgreen Co. | United States | FDM | $37,508 | 15.4% | 16.0% | 4,579 |
| 18 | Auchan Groupe | France | FDM | $37,371 | 4.7% | 6.4% | 2,560 |
| 19 | Aeon Co., Ltd. | Japan | FDM | $36,477 | 20.0% | 10.9% | 6,792 |
| 20 | Lowe's Companies, Inc. | United States | Homegoods | $36,464 | 18.2% | 18.0% | 1,087 |
| 21 | Safeway Inc. | United States | FDM | $35,823 | 0.3% | 3.1% | 1,803 |
| 22 | Sears, Roebuck and Co. | United States | Homegoods | $35,718 | −1.8% | −0.6% | 2,418 |
| 23 | Tengelmann Waren-handelsgesellschaft | Germany | FDM | $35,203 | 5.6% | 2.7% | 7,362 |
| 24 | Centres E. Leclerc | France | FDM | $34,969 | 4.3% | 4.2% | 1,538 |
| 25 | CVS Corporation | United States | FDM | $30,594 | 15.1% | 11.1% | 5,375 |
| 26 | Rallye (i.e., Casino) | France | FDM | $29,630 | 0.9% | 8.5% | 9,417 |
| 27 | Best Buy Co., Inc. | United States | Homegoods | $27,433 | 12.0% | 17.0% | 832 |
| 28 | J Sainsbury PLC | United Kingdom | FDM | $27,337 | 4.9% | −1.4% | 727 |
| 29 | Coles Myer Ltd. | Australia | FDM | $23,764 | 19.4% | 7.5% | 2,534 |
| 30 | IGA Inc. (Independent Grocers Alliance) | United States | FDM | $23,625 | 12.5% | 3.8% | 4,500 |
| 31 | Woolworths Limited | Australia | FDM | $22,687 | 14.1% | 9.6% | 2,215 |

| Home Region | Level of Internation- alization | Number of Countries | % of Sales in Foreign Countries | Countries |
|---|---|---|---|---|
| W Europe | Regional | 14 | 28.0% | W EUROPE: Austria, France, Germany, Italy, Switzerland; CE EUROPE: Bulgaria, Croatia, Czech Republic, Hungary, Poland, Romania, Russia, Slovakia, Ukraine |
| North America | Single Country | 1 | 0.0% | N AMERICA: United States |
| W Europe | Regional | 5 | 5.2% | W EUROPE: Austria, Czech Republic, Denmark, Germany, Russia |
| North America | Single Country | 1 | 0.0% | N AMERICA: United States |
| W Europe | Global | 12 | 39.3% | LATIN AMERICA: Argentina; W EUROPE: France, Italy, Luxembourg, Portugal, Spain; CE EUROPE: Hungary, Poland, Russia; ASIA-PACIFIC: China, Taiwan; AFRICA-MIDDLE EAST: Morocco |
| Asia-Pacific | Global | 11 | 12.1% | N AMERICA: Canada, United States; W EUROPE: United Kingdom; ASIA-PACIFIC: China, Japan, Malaysia, Philippines, Singapore, South Korea, Taiwan, Thailand |
| North America | Single Country | 1 | 0.0% | N AMERICA: United States |
| North America | Regional | 3 | 10.0% | N AMERICA: Canada, United States; LATIN AMERICA: Mexico |
| North America | Regional | 2 | 12.6% | N AMERICA: Canada, United States |
| W Europe | Global | 15 | 52.1% | N AMERICA: Canada, United States; W EUROPE: Austria, Germany, Italy, Portugal, Spain, Switzerland; CE EUROPE: Bosnia-Herzegovina, Czech Republic, Hungary, Poland, Russia, Slovenia; ASIA-PACIFIC: China |
| W Europe | Regional | 6 | 5.3% | W EUROPE: France, Italy, Portugal, Spain; CE EUROPE: Poland, Slovenia |
| North America | Single Country | 1 | 0.0% | N AMERICA: United States |
| W Europe | Global | 17 | 19.4% | N AMERICA: United States; LATIN AMERICA: Argentina, Brazil, Colombia, Mexico, Venezuela; W EUROPE: Belgium, France, Netherlands; CE EUROPE: Poland; ASIA-PACIFIC: Taiwan, Thailand, Vietnam; AFRICA-MIDDLE EAST: Reunion, Madagascar, Mayotte, Mauritius |
| North America | Regional | 2 | 10.2% | N AMERICA: Canada, United States |
| W Europe | Single Country | 1 | 0.0% | W EUROPE: United Kingdom |
| Asia-Pacific | Regional | 2 | 0.5% | ASIA-PACIFIC: Australia, New Zealand |
| North America | Global | 45 | 70.0% | N AMERICA: Canada, United States; LATIN AMERICA: Anguilla, Antigua & Barbuda, Aruba, Barbados, Brazil, Cayman Islands, Dominica, Dominican Republic, Grenada, Jamaica, St. Kitts, Trinidad & Tobago, Turks & Caicos Islands; W EUROPE: Spain; CE EUROPE: Czech Republic, Poland; ASIA-PACIFIC: Australia, Cambodia, China, Indonesia, Japan, Malaysia, Papua New Guinea, Philippines, Singapore, South Korea, Thailand, Vietnam; AFRICA-MIDDLE EAST: Botswana, Kenya, Lesotho, Malawi, Mauritius, Mozambique, Namibia, South Africa, Swaziland, Zambia, Zimbabwe |
| Asia-Pacific | Regional | 2 | 0.3% | ASIA-PACIFIC: Australia, New Zealand |

*continued*

Chapter 1 Appendix › *Continued*

| Rank | Company | Home Country | Primary Retail Sector | Net Sales (Millions USD) | Sales Growth | | Total Stores (incl. company-owned and networked) |
|------|---------|--------------|----------------------|--------------------------|--------------|--------------|---------------------|
| | | | | | 2003–2004 | Compound Annual Growth Rate 1999–2004 | |
| 32 | Delhaize "Le Lion" Group | Belgium | FDM | $22,355 | −4.5% | 0.2% | 2,565 |
| 33 | Wm Morrison Supermarkets PLC | United Kingdom | FDM | $22,209 | 145.1% | 32.5% | 498 |
| 34 | Loblaw Companies Limited | Canada | FDM | $20,134 | 3.9% | 6.9% | 1,577 |
| 35 | Kmart Holding Corp. | United States | FDM | $19,701 | −15.3% | −11.3% | 1,480 |
| 36 | Pinault-Printemps-Redoute SA | France | Softgoods | $19,662 | 8.4% | 12.6% | 962 |
| 37 | Publix Super Markets, Inc. | United States | FDM | $18,554 | 10.7% | 7.3% | 886 |
| 38 | J.C. Penney Company, Inc. | United States | Softgoods | $18,424 | 3.6% | −0.6% | 1,079 |
| 39 | Système U | France | FDM | $18,266 | 6.5% | 9.7% | 849 |
| 40 | El Corte Ingles | Spain | Softgoods | $17,413 | 7.7% | 9.6% | 390 |
| 41 | Rite Aid Corporation | United States | FDM | $16,816 | 1.3% | 4.7% | 3,356 |
| 42 | Karstadt Quelle AG | Germany | Softgoods | $16,385 | −6.9% | −4.2% | 220 |
| 43 | Gap Inc. | United States | Softgoods | $16,267 | 2.6% | 6.9% | 2,994 |
| 44 | IKEA AB | Sweden | Homegoods | $15,921 | 13.0% | 10.8% | 201 |
| 45 | Federated Department Stores, Inc. | United States | Softgoods | $15,630 | 2.4% | −2.5% | 459 |
| 46 | The TJX Companies, Inc. | United States | Softgoods | $14,913 | 11.9% | 11.1% | 2,224 |
| 47 | Staples, Inc. | United States | Homegoods | $14,450 | 11.4% | 10.1% | 1,680 |
| 48 | The May Department Stores Company | United States | Softgoods | $14,441 | 8.2% | 0.8% | 1,190 |

| Home Region | Level of Internation- alization | Number of Countries | % of Sales in Foreign Countries | Countries |
|---|---|---|---|---|
| W Europe | Global | 9 | 79.6% | N AMERICA: United States; W EUROPE: Belgium, Czech Republic, Germany, Greece, Luxembourg, Slovakia, Romania; ASIA-PACIFIC: Indonesia |
| W Europe | Regional | 2 | 0.6% | W EUROPE: United Kingdom, Ireland |
| North America | Single Country | 1 | 0.0% | N AMERICA: Canada |
| North America | Single Country | 1 | 0.0% | N AMERICA: United States |
| W Europe | Global | 17 | 50.7% | N AMERICA: United States; LATIN AMERICA: Brazil; W EUROPE: Belgium, France, Italy, Luxembourg, Portugal, Spain, Switzerland, United Kingdom; CE EUROPE: Croatia; ASIA-PACIFIC: Taiwan |
| North America | Single Country | 1 | 0.0% | N AMERICA: United States |
| North America | Regional | 2 | 1.8% | N AMERICA: United States; LATIN AMERICA: Brazil |
| W Europe | Single Country | 1 | 0.0% | W EUROPE: France |
| W Europe | Regional | 2 | 1.7% | W EUROPE: Portugal, Spain |
| North America | Single Country | 1 | 0.0% | N AMERICA: United States |
| W Europe | Regional | 19 | 15.0% | W EUROPE: Austria, Belgium, France, Germany, Hungary, Italy, Netherlands, Portugal, Spain, Switzerland; CE EUROPE: Croatia, Czech Republic, Estonia, Latvia, Poland, Romania, Russia, Slovakia, Slovenia |
| North America | Global | 5 | 14.0% | N AMERICA: Canada, United States; W EUROPE: France, United Kingdom; ASIA-PACIFIC: Japan |
| W Europe | Global | 32 | 93.1% | N AMERICA: Canada, United States; W EUROPE: Austria, Belgium, Denmark, Finland, France, Germany, Greece, Iceland, Italy, Netherlands, Norway, Spain, Sweden, Switzerland, United Kingdom; CE EUROPE: Czech Republic, Hungary, Poland, Russia, Slovakia; ASIA-PACIFIC: Australia, China, Hong Kong, Malaysia, Singapore, Taiwan; AFRICA-MIDDLE EAST: Israel, Kuwait, Saudi Arabia, United Arab Emirates |
| North America | Regional | 1 | 0.0% | N AMERICA: United States |
| North America | Global | 4 | 17.4% | N AMERICA: Canada, United States; W EUROPE: Ireland, United Kingdom |
| North America | Global | 18 | 24.2% | N AMERICA: Canada, United States; W EUROPE: Austria, Belgium, France, Denmark, Germany, Italy, Luxembourg, Netherlands, Portugal, Spain, Sweden, Switzerland, United Kingdom; CE EUROPE: Czech Republic, Hungary, Poland |
| North America | Single Country | 1 | 0.0% | N AMERICA: United States |

*continued*

| Rank | Company | Home Country | Primary Retail Sector | Net Sales (Millions USD) | Sales Growth | | Total Stores (incl. company-owned and networked) |
|------|---------|--------------|------------------------|--------------------------|--------------|--|--------------------------------------------------|
| | | | | | 2003–2004 | Compound Annual Growth Rate 1999–2004 | |
| 49 | Marks & Spencer PLC | United Kingdom | Softgoods | $14,133 | −1.5% | −0.3% | 675 |
| 50 | Kingfisher PLC | United Kingdom | Homegoods | $14,022 | 8.7% | −6.8% | 599 |
| 51 | COOP Italia | Italy | FDM | $14,014 | 2.7% | 5.0% | 1,276 |
| 52 | The Daiei Inc. | Japan | FDM | $13,984 | −8.6% | −7.1% | 1,681 |
| 53 | Migros - Genos-senschaftsbund | Switzerland | FDM | $13,878 | 0.5% | 3.6% | 1,477 |
| 54 | Office Depot, Inc. | United States | Homegoods | $13,565 | 9.8% | 5.7% | 1,154 |
| 55 | Ace Hardware Corporation | United States | Homegoods | $13,410 | 2.4% | −0.9% | 5,321 |
| 56 | Dixons Group | United Kingdom | Homegoods | $12,800 | 7.6% | 12.8% | 1,450 |
| 57 | Meijer, Inc. | United States | FDM | $12,500 | 2.1% | 6.2% | 163 |
| 58 | Lotte Group | South Korea | FDM | $12,490 | 18.2% | | 2,171 |
| 59 | Lawson | Japan | FDM | $12,289 | 3.4% | 1.7% | 8,287 |
| 60 | True Value Co. | United States | Homegoods | $12,200 | 0.0% | N/A | 6,060 |
| 61 | Otto Versand Gmbh & Co | Germany | Softgoods | $11,847 | −3.0% | −7.1% | 361 |
| 62 | Kohl's Corporation | United States | Softgoods | $11,701 | 13.8% | 20.8% | 637 |

| Home Region | Level of Internation-alization | Number of Countries | % of Sales in Foreign Countries | Countries |
|---|---|---|---|---|
| W Europe | Global | 32 | 8.8% | N AMERICA: United States; LATIN AMERICA: Bermuda; W EUROPE: Gibraltar, Greece, Guernsey, Ireland, Jersey, Malta, United Kingdom; CE EUROPE: Croatia, Czech Republic, Hungary, Poland, Romania; ASIA-PACIFIC: Hong Kong, India, Indonesia, Malaysia, Philippines, Singapore, South Korea, Thailand; AFRICA-MIDDLE EAST: Bahrain, Cyprus, Gran Canaria, Kuwait, Oman, Qatar, Saudi Arabia, Tenerife, Turkey, United Arab Emirates |
| W Europe | Global | 9 | 43.6% | W EUROPE: France, Ireland, Italy, Spain, United Kingdom; CE EUROPE: Poland; ASIA-PACIFIC: China, Taiwan; AFRICA-MIDDLE EAST: Turkey |
| W Europe | Regional | 2 | 0.4% | W EUROPE: Italy; CE EUROPE: Croatia |
| Asia-Pacific | Global | 2 | 1.0% | N AMERICA: United States; ASIA-PACIFIC: Japan |
| W Europe | Regional | 3 | 1.4% | W EUROPE: France, Germany, Switzerland |
| North America | Global | 23 | 26.4% | N AMERICA: Canada, United States; LATIN AMERICA: Costa Rica, El Salvador, Guatemala, Mexico; W EUROPE: Austria, Belgium, France, Germany, Ireland, Italy, Luxembourg, Netherlands, Portugal, Spain, Switzerland, United Kingdom; CE EUROPE: Hungary, Poland; ASIA-PACIFIC: Japan, Thailand; AFRICA-MIDDLE EAST: Israel |
| North America | Global | 70 | 10.7% | N AMERICA: United States; LATIN AMERICA: Antigua, Aruba, Bahamas, Barbados, Belize, Bermuda, Bolivia, Brazil, Caico Islands, Cayman Islands, Chile, Colombia, Costa Rica, Dominican Republic, Ecuador, El Salvador, Granada, Guadeloupe, Guatemala, Honduras, Jamaica, Mexico, Nicaragua, Panama, Peru; W EUROPE: Finland, Iceland, Netherlands, Northern Ireland; CE EUROPE: Estonia, Russia; ASIA-PACIFIC: American Samoa, Guam, Indonesia, Japan, Malaysia, Marshall Islands, Micronesia, New Zealand, Palau, Philippines, Saipan Islands, South Korea, Tahiti, Taiwan, Thailand, Western Samoa; AFRICA-MIDDLE EAST: Eritrea, Israel, Kuwait, Saudi Arabia, Tunisia, United Arab Emirates |
| W Europe | Regional | 14 | 31.0% | W EUROPE: Denmark, Faroe Islands, Finland, France, Greece, Iceland, Ireland, Italy, Norway, Spain, Sweden, United Kingdom; CE EUROPE: Czech Republic, Hungary |
| North America | Single Country | 1 | 0.0% | N AMERICA: United States |
| Asia-Pacific | Regional | 2 | | ASIA-PACIFIC: China, South Korea |
| Asia-Pacific | Regional | 2 | 0.3% | ASIA-PACIFIC: Japan, China |
| North America | Global | 59 | | N/A |
| W Europe | Global | 19 | 44.0% | N AMERICA: United States; W EUROPE: Austria, Belgium, France, Germany, Italy, Netherlands, Portugal, Spain, Switzerland, United Kingdom; CE EUROPE: Czech Republic, Hungary, Poland, Romania; ASIA-PACIFIC: China, Japan, South Korea, Taiwan |
| North America | Single Country | 1 | 0.0% | N AMERICA: United States |

*continued*

| Rank | Company | Home Country | Primary Retail Sector | Net Sales (Millions USD) | Sales Growth | | Total Stores (incl. company-owned and networked) |
|---|---|---|---|---|---|---|---|
| | | | | | 2003–2004 | Compound Annual Growth Rate 1999–2004 | |
| 63 | Coop Norden AB | Sweden | FDM | $11,458 | 1.2% | | 2,434 |
| 64 | Dell Computer Corp. | United States | Homegoods | $11,355 | 16.7% | 15.1% | 0 |
| 65 | Cora Group/Louis Delhaize | France | FDM | $11,316 | 5.3% | 3.5% | 775 |
| 66 | Do It Best Corporation | United States | Homegoods | $11,300 | 5.6% | 7.7% | 4,100 |
| 67 | The Coop Group | Switzerland | FDM | $11,251 | −2.9% | 3.7% | 1,433 |
| 68 | Toys "R" Us, Inc. | United States | Homegoods | $11,100 | −1.9% | −1.3% | 1,499 |
| 69 | H. E. Butt Grocery Company | United States | FDM | $11,100 | 4.7% | 8.2% | 304 |
| 70 | GUS plc | United Kingdom | Homegoods | $10,913 | 7.9% | 5.9% | 1,444 |
| 71 | Mercadona | Spain | FDM | $10,908 | 21.5% | 31.7% | 862 |
| 72 | SuperValu Inc. | United States | FDM | $10,549 | 0.0% | 5.5% | 1,549 |
| 73 | Circuit City Stores, Inc. | United States | Homegoods | $10,475 | 6.2% | −0.2% | 1,564 |
| 74 | Yamada Denki Co. Ltd. | Japan | Homegoods | $10,193 | 17.4% | 27.1% | 258 |
| 75 | Winn-Dixie Stores, Inc. | United States | FDM | $10,000 | −6.0% | −6.1% | 913 |
| 76 | LVMH | France | Softgoods | $9,627 | 7.7% | −2.0% | 1,693 |
| 77 | Hutchison Whampoa Limited | Hong Kong | FDM | $9,558 | 16.4% | 25.6% | 4,797 |

| Home Region | Level of Internation- alization | Number of Countries | % of Sales in Foreign Countries | Countries |
|---|---|---|---|---|
| W Europe | Regional | 3 | 68.7% | W EUROPE: Denmark, Norway, Sweden |
| North America | Global | 43 | 33.1% | N/A |
| W Europe | Global | 7 | 29.0% | LATIN AMERICA: Antilles; W EUROPE: Belgium, France, Luxembourg, United Kingdom; CE EUROPE: Hungary, Romania |
| North America | Global | 40 | N/A | N AMERICA: United States; LATIN AMERICA: Antigua and Barbuda, Bahamas, Barbados, Belize, Bermuda, British Virgin Islands, British West Indies, Colombia, Costa Rica, Dominican Republic, Ecuador, El Salvador, Grenada, Guyana, Haiti, Honduras, Jamaica, Mexico, Netherlands Antilles, Puerto Rico, Re; W EUROPE: Ireland; ASIA-PACIFIC: American Samoa, French Polynesia, Guam, Marshall Islands, Micronesia, Northern Mariana Islands, Palau, Philippines, Thailand, Vanuatu; AFRICA-MIDDLE EAST: Bahrain |
| W Europe | Single Country | 1 | 0.0% | W EUROPE: Switzerland |
| North America | Global | 30 | 24.7% | N AMERICA: Canada, United States; W EUROPE: Austria, Denmark, France, Germany, Netherlands, Norway, Portugal, Spain, Sweden, Switzerland, United Kingdom; ASIA-PACIFIC: Australia, Hong Kong, Indonesia, Japan, Malaysia, Singapore, Taiwan; AFRICA-MIDDLE EAST: Bahrain, Egypt, Israel, Kuwait, Mauritius, Oman, Qatar, Saudi Arabia, South Africa, Turkey, United Arab Emirates |
| North America | Regional | 2 | 6.6% | N AMERICA: United States; LATIN AMERICA: Mexico |
| W Europe | Global | 4 | 7.3% | W EUROPE: Ireland, Netherlands, United Kingdom; AFRICA-MIDDLE EAST: South Africa |
| W Europe | Single Country | 1 | 0.0% | W EUROPE: Spain |
| North America | Single Country | 1 | 0.0% | N AMERICA: United States |
| North America | Regional | 2 | 4.3% | N AMERICA: Canada, United States |
| Asia-Pacific | Single Country | 1 | 0.0% | ASIA-PACIFIC: Japan |
| North America | Regional | 2 | N/A | N AMERICA: United States; LATIN AMERICA: Bahamas |
| W Europe | Global | 56 | 82.6% | N AMERICA: Canada, United States; LATIN AMERICA: Argentina, Bermuda, Brazil, Chile, Mexico, Puerto Rico, Uruguay, Venezuela; W EUROPE: Austria, Belgium, Denmark, Finland, France, Germany, Greece, Ireland, Italy, Luxembourg, Monaco, Netherlands, Norway, Portugal, Spain, Sweden, Switzerland, United Kingdom; CE EUROPE: Czech Republic, Poland, Russia; ASIA-PACIFIC: Australia, Cambodia, China, Guam, Hong Kong, India, Indonesia, Japan, Malaysia, Marianna Islands, Palau, Philippines, Singapore, South Korea, Taiwan, Thailand, Turkey, Vietnam; AFRICA-MIDDLE EAST: Israel, Kuwait, Lebanon, Morocco, Saudi Arabia, United Arab Emirates |
| Asia-Pacific | Global | 18 | 73.2% | W EUROPE: Belgium, Germany, Netherlands, United King- dom; CE EUROPE: Czech Republic, Hungary, Latvia, Lithuania, Poland; ASIA-PACIFIC: China, Hong Kong, Macau, Malaysia, Philippines, Singapore, South Korea, Taiwan, Thailand |

*continued*

| Rank | Company | Home Country | Primary Retail Sector | Net Sales (Millions USD) | Sales Growth 2003–2004 | Compound Annual Growth Rate 1999–2004 | Total Stores (incl. company-owned and networked) |
|---|---|---|---|---|---|---|---|
| 78 | The Seiyu, Ltd | Japan | FDM | $9,538 | −4.0% | 0.2% | 404 |
| 79 | Limited Brands, Inc. | United States | Softgoods | $9,408 | 5.3% | −0.7% | 3,779 |
| 80 | Kesko Ltd. | Finland | FDM | $9,377 | 5.4% | 9.3% | 1,684 |
| 81 | Empire Company Limited | Canada | FDM | $9,364 | 10.3% | 2.1% | 1,352 |
| 82 | UNY Co., Ltd | Japan | FDM | $9,268 | 2.0% | 0.0% | 7,387 |
| 83 | FamilyMart Co., Ltd. | Japan | FDM | $9,232 | 4.6% | 5.0% | 11,501 |
| 84 | Takashimaya Company, Limited | Japan | Softgoods | $8,911 | −3.1% | −3.1% | 24 |
| 85 | OfficeMax, Inc. | United States | Homegoods | $8,852 | 119.9% | 12.5% | 1,031 |
| 86 | CONAD | Italy | FDM | $8,814 | 10.9% | 4.0% | 3,144 |
| 87 | John Lewis Partnership PLC | United Kingdom | FDM | $8,720 | 5.7% | 7.1% | 192 |
| 88 | SPAR Austria Group | Austria | FDM | $8,714 | 6.8% | 21.0% | 2,357 |
| 89 | The Boots Company PLC | United Kingdom | FDM | $8,611 | 3.9% | 3.2% | 1,877 |
| 90 | Somerfield PLC | United Kingdom | FDM | $8,573 | 4.3% | −3.1% | 1,308 |
| 91 | Millennium Retailing | Japan | Softgoods | $8,477 | −5.6% | 0.0% | 29 |
| 92 | Wakefern Food Corporation | United States | FDM | $8,400 | 6.0% | 8.8% | 190 |
| 93 | ICA Sverige AB | Sweden | FDM | $8,311 | −0.9% | 4.1% | 2,711 |
| 94 | S Group | Finland | FDM | $8,278 | 12.6% | 11.4% | 1,019 |
| 95 | Anton Schlecker | Germany | FDM | $8,209 | 0.8% | 7.5% | 13,750 |
| 96 | Bailian Groups | China | FDM | $8,131 | N/A | N/A | 5,493 |
| 97 | Army and Air Force Exchange Service | United States | FDM | $7,951 | 5.0% | 3.5% | 3,100 |
| 98 | Mitsukoshi Ltd | Japan | Softgoods | $7,885 | −3.2% | −1.1% | 40 |
| 99 | Alimentation Couche-Tard | Canada | FDM | $7,848 | 74.0% | 45.4% | 9,020 |
| 100 | Dansk Supermarked A/S | Denmark | FDM | $7,798 | 5.6% | 4.2% | 1,011 |
| 101 | Dollar General Corporation | United States | FDM | $7,661 | 11.5% | 14.5% | 7,320 |
| 102 | Avon Products Inc. | United States | FDM | $7,656 | 13.0% | 7.7% | 6,300 |
| 103 | Dillard's, Inc. | United States | Softgoods | $7,529 | −0.9% | −2.8% | 329 |

| Home Region | Level of Internation- alization | Number of Countries | % of Sales in Foreign Countries | Countries |
|---|---|---|---|---|
| Asia-Pacific | Global | 4 | 1.2% | ASIA-PACIFIC: Japan, Hong Kong, Singapore, Vietnam |
| North America | Single Country | 1 | 0.0% | N AMERICA: United States |
| W Europe | Regional | 5 | 11.8% | W EUROPE: Finland, Sweden; CE EUROPE: Estonia, Latvia, Lithuania |
| North America | Single Country | 1 | 0.0% | N AMERICA: Canada |
| Asia-Pacific | Single Country | 1 | 0.0% | ASIA-PACIFIC: Japan |
| Asia-Pacific | Regional | 5 | 3.7% | ASIA-PACIFIC: China, Japan, South Korea, Taiwan, Thailand |
| Asia-Pacific | Global | 5 | N/A | N AMERICA: United States; W EUROPE: France; ASIA-PACIFIC: China, Japan, Singapore |
| North America | Global | 5 | 12.7% | N AMERICA: Canada, United States; LATIN AMERICA: Mexico; ASIA-PACIFIC: Australia, New Zealand |
| W Europe | Single Country | 1 | 0.0% | W EUROPE: Italy |
| W Europe | Single Country | 1 | 0.0% | W EUROPE: United Kingdom |
| W Europe | Regional | 5 | 37.4% | W EUROPE: Austria, Italy; CE EUROPE: Czech Republic, Hungary, Slovenia |
| W Europe | Global | 11 | N/A | W EUROPE: Switzerland, Netherlands, Finland, Ireland, Norway; ASIA-PACIFIC: Australia, Hong Kong, New Zealand, Taiwan, Thailand; AFRICA-MIDDLE EAST: South Africa |
| W Europe | Single Country | 1 | 0.0% | W EUROPE: United Kingdom |
| Asia-Pacific | Single Country | 1 | 0.0% | ASIA-PACIFIC: Japan |
| North America | Single Country | 1 | 0.0% | N AMERICA: United States |
| W Europe | Regional | 5 | 36.0% | W EUROPE: Norway, Sweden; CE EUROPE: Estonia, Latvia, Lithuania |
| W Europe | Regional | 2 | 0.9% | W EUROPE: Finland; CE EUROPE: Estonia |
| W Europe | Regional | 9 | 18.2% | W EUROPE: Austria, Belgium, Denmark, France, Germany, Italy, Netherlands, Spain; CE EUROPE: Poland |
| Asia-Pacific | Single Country | 1 | 0.0% | ASIA-PACIFIC: China |
| North America | Global | 30 | 37.3% | N/A |
| Asia-Pacific | Global | 9 | 20.8% | N AMERICA: United States; W EUROPE: France, Germany, Italy, Spain, United Kingdom; ASIA-PACIFIC: Hong Kong, Japan, Taiwan |
| North America | Global | 7 | 76.3% | N AMERICA: Canada, United States; LATIN AMERICA: Mexico; ASIA-PACIFIC: China, Indonesia, Japan, Taiwan |
| W Europe | Regional | 5 | 32.5% | W EUROPE: Denmark, Germany, Sweden, United Kingdom; CE EUROPE: Poland |
| North America | Single Country | 1 | 0.0% | N AMERICA: United States |
| North America | Global | 60 | 70.9% | N/A |
| North America | Single Country | 1 | 0.0% | N AMERICA: United States |

*continued*

| Rank | Company | Home Country | Primary Retail Sector | Net Sales (Millions USD) | Sales Growth | | Total Stores (incl. company-owned and networked) |
|------|---------|--------------|-----------------------|--------------------------|--------------|--|--------------------------------------------------|
| | | | | | 2003–2004 | Compound Annual Growth Rate 1999–2004 | |
| 104 | H & M Hennes & Mauritz AB | Sweden | Softgoods | $7,307 | 11.3% | 14.0% | 1,068 |
| 105 | C&A | Belgium | Softgoods | $7,282 | N/A | N/A | 943 |
| 106 | Kesa Electricals | United Kingdom | Homegoods | $7,257 | 5.0% | 4.4% | 800 |
| 107 | The Jean Coutu Group Inc. | Canada | FDM | $7,231 | 142.9% | 24.0% | 2,231 |
| 108 | BJ's Wholesale Club | United States | FDM | $7,220 | 10.2% | 11.9% | 157 |
| 109 | Nordstrom, Inc. | United States | Softgoods | $7,131 | 10.6% | 6.8% | 180 |
| 110 | INDITEX Group (i.e., Zara) | Spain | Softgoods | $7,053 | 23.6% | 22.7% | 2,244 |
| 111 | Amazon.com | United States | Homegoods | $6,921 | 31.5% | 33.4% | 0 |
| 112 | Leroy Merlin | France | Homegoods | $6,841 | 14.6% | 13.1% | 791 |
| 113 | Grupo Eroski | Spain | FDM | $6,641 | 6.1% | 6.8% | 1,582 |
| 114 | Saks Incorporated | United States | Softgoods | $6,437 | 6.3% | 0.0% | 384 |
| 115 | Daimaru Group | Japan | Softgoods | $6,349 | −2.7% | 0.6% | 81 |
| 116 | The Co-operative Group | United Kingdom | FDM | $6,326 | −1.1% | 15.6% | 2,178 |
| 117 | Norges Gruppen ASA | Norway | FDM | $6,128 | 3.3% | 7.7% | 2,713 |
| 118 | Menard, Inc. | United States | Homegoods | $6,100 | 8.9% | 6.3% | 195 |
| 119 | Alticor/Amway | United States | FDM | $6,100 | 26.5% | 4.1% | N/A |
| 120 | ISETAN Company Limited | Japan | Softgoods | $5,693 | 2.1% | 1.4% | 40 |

| Home Region | Level of Internation- alization | Number of Countries | % of Sales in Foreign Countries | Countries |
|---|---|---|---|---|
| W Europe | Global | 20 | 91.2% | N AMERICA: Canada, United States; W EUROPE: Austria, Belgium, Denmark, Finland, France, Germany, Italy, Luxembourg, Netherlands, Norway, Portugal, Spain, Sweden, Switzerland, United Kingdom; CE EUROPE: Czech Republic, Poland, Slovenia |
| W Europe | Global | 15 | 94.1% | LATIN AMERICA: Argentina, Brazil, Mexico; W EUROPE: Austria, Belgium, France, Germany, Luxembourg, Netherlands, Portugal, Spain, Switzerland; CE EUROPE: Czech Republic, Hungary, Poland |
| W Europe | Regional | 6 | 61.2% | W EUROPE: Belgium, France, Netherlands, United Kingdom; CE EUROPE: Czech Republic, Slovakia |
| North America | Regional | 2 | 82.3% | N AMERICA: Canada, United States |
| North America | Single Country | 1 | 0.0% | N AMERICA: United States |
| North America | Global | 15 | 1.3% | N AMERICA: United States; LATIN AMERICA: Aruba, Bahamas, Dominican Republic, Ecuador, Honduras, Panama, Venezuela; W EUROPE: Belgium, France, Portugal, Spain, Switzerland; ASIA-PACIFIC: Taiwan; AFRICA-MIDDLE EAST: Turkey |
| W Europe | Global | 57 | 54.5% | N AMERICA: Canada, United States; LATIN AMERICA: Argentina, Brazil, Chile, Dominican Republic, El Salvador, Mexico, Panama, Uruguay, Venezuela; W EUROPE: Andorra, Austria, Belgium, Cyprus, Denmark, Finland, France, Germany, Greece, Iceland, Ireland, Italy, Latvia, Lithuania, Luxembourg, Malta, Netherlands, Norway, Portugal, Spain, Sweden, Switzerland, United Kingdom; CE EUROPE: Czech Republic, Estonia, Hungary, Poland, Romania, Russia, Slovakia, Slovenia; ASIA-PACIFIC: Hong Kong, Japan, Malaysia, Singapore; AFRICA-MIDDLE EAST: Bahrain, Israel, Jordan, Kuwait, Lebanon, Morocco, Qatar, Saudi Arabia, United Arab Emirates, Turkey |
| North America | Global | 7 | 54.5% | N AMERICA: Canada, United States; W EUROPE: France, Germany, United Kingdom; ASIA-PACIFIC: China, Japan |
| W Europe | Global | 8 | 42.7% | LATIN AMERICA: Brazil; W EUROPE: France, Italy, Portugal, Spain; CE EUROPE: Poland, Russia; ASIA-PACIFIC: China |
| W Europe | Regional | 2 | | W EUROPE: France, Spain |
| North America | Single Country | 1 | 0.0% | N AMERICA: United States |
| Asia-Pacific | Single Country | 1 | 0.0% | ASIA-PACIFIC: Japan |
| W Europe | Single Country | 1 | 0.0% | W EUROPE: United Kingdom |
| W Europe | Single Country | 1 | 0.0% | W EUROPE: Norway |
| North America | Single Country | 1 | 0.0% | N AMERICA: United States |
| North America | Global | 80 | 83.6% | N/A |
| Asia-Pacific | Regional | 6 | 7.3% | ASIA-PACIFIC: China, Japan, Malaysia, Singapore, Thailand, Taiwan |

*continued*

| Rank | Company | Home Country | Primary Retail Sector | Net Sales (Millions USD) | Sales Growth 2003–2004 | Compound Annual Growth Rate 1999–2004 | Total Stores (incl. company-owned and networked) |
|------|---------|--------------|----------------------|--------------------------|--------------------------|----------------------------------------|---------------------------------------------------|
| 121 | Liberty Media Corp. (QVC) | United States | Homegoods | $5,687 | 16.3% | 14.8% | 8 |
| 122 | Shinsegae | South Korea | FDM | $5,686 | 12.2% | 23.5% | 86 |
| 123 | AutoZone, Inc. | United States | Homegoods | $5,637 | 3.3% | 6.5% | 3,483 |
| 124 | Hudson's Bay Company | Canada | FDM | $5,431 | –4.5% | –0.6% | 547 |
| 125 | Groep Colruyt | Belgium | FDM | $5,405 | 17.6% | 16.7% | 616 |
| 126 | Foot Locker Inc. | United States | Softgoods | $5,355 | 12.1% | 6.5% | 3,967 |
| 127 | Yodobashi Camera Co. Ltd. | Japan | Homegoods | $5,342 | 6.0% | 11.1% | 19 |
| 128 | Globus Holding GmbH & Co. | Germany | FDM | $5,320 | 4.3% | 10.0% | 111 |
| 129 | Family Dollar | United States | FDM | $5,282 | 11.2% | 13.9% | 5,466 |
| 130 | Defense Commissary Agency | United States | FDM | $5,235 | 3.9% | 1.1% | 273 |
| 131 | Giant Eagle Inc. | United States | FDM | $5,200 | 2.0% | 4.3% | 219 |
| 132 | Esselunga S.p.A. | Italy | FDM | $5,197 | 3.6% | 9.2% | 125 |
| 133 | Bed, Bath & Beyond Inc. | United States | Homegoods | $5,148 | 15.0% | 22.6% | 721 |
| 134 | Royal Vendex KBB N.V. | Netherlands | Homegoods | $5,100 | –0.5% | 2.5% | 1,700 |
| 135 | Canadian Tire Corp. Ltd. | Canada | Homegoods | $5,018 | 8.2% | 8.2% | 1,078 |
| 136 | Shoppers Drug Mart Corp. | Canada | FDM | $4,971 | 6.8% | 8.6% | 964 |
| 137 | Pick 'n Pay Stores Ltd. | South Africa | FDM | $4,951 | 8.9% | 18.6% | 642 |
| 138 | Groupe Galeries Lafayette | France | Softgoods | $4,931 | 1.0% | –0.5% | 520 |
| 139 | Bauhaus | Germany | Homegoods | $4,884 | 7.8% | 13.9% | 180 |
| 140 | Barnes & Noble, Inc. | United States | Homegoods | $4,874 | 11.5% | 6.9% | 820 |
| 141 | RadioShack Corporation | United States | Homegoods | $4,841 | 4.1% | 3.2% | 7,433 |
| 142 | NEXT PLC | United Kingdom | Softgoods | $4,749 | 22.5% | 4.1% | 428 |
| 143 | Shoprite Holdings Ltd. | South Africa | FDM | $4,633 | 12.0% | 10.3% | 1,005 |

| Home Region | Level of Internation-alization | Number of Countries | % of Sales in Foreign Countries | Countries |
|---|---|---|---|---|
| North America | Global | 4 | 27.2% | N AMERICA: United States; W EUROPE: Germany, United Kingdom; ASIA-PACIFIC: Japan |
| Asia-Pacific | Regional | 2 | 1.6% | ASIA-PACIFIC: China, South Korea |
| North America | Regional | 2 | 2.0% | N AMERICA: United States; LATIN AMERICA: Mexico |
| North America | Single Country | 1 | 0.0% | N AMERICA: Canada |
| W Europe | Regional | 2 | 8.5% | W EUROPE: Belgium, France |
| North America | Global | 19 | 25.6% | N AMERICA: Canada, United States; W EUROPE: Austria, Belgium, Denmark, France, Germany, Ireland, Italy, Luxembourg, Netherlands, Portugal, Spain, Sweden, United Kingdom; CE EUROPE: Hungary; ASIA-PACIFIC: Australia, New Zealand; AFRICA-MIDDLE EAST: Canary Islands |
| Asia-Pacific | Single Country | 1 | 0.0% | ASIA-PACIFIC: Japan |
| W Europe | Regional | 2 | 14.1% | W EUROPE: Germany; CE EUROPE: Czech Republic |
| North America | Single Country | 1 | 0.0% | N AMERICA: United States |
| North America | Global | 13 | N/A | N AMERICA: United States; W EUROPE: Azores, Belgium, Germany, Iceland, Italy, Netherlands, Spain, United Kingdom; ASIA-PACIFIC: Japan, South Korea; AFRICA-MIDDLE EAST: Egypt, Turkey |
| North America | Single Country | 1 | 0.0% | N AMERICA: United States |
| W Europe | Single Country | 1 | 0.0% | W EUROPE: Italy |
| North America | Single Country | 1 | 0.0% | N AMERICA: United States |
| W Europe | Regional | 7 | 20.0% | W EUROPE: Belgium, Denmark, France, Germany, Luxembourg, Netherlands, Spain |
| North America | Single Country | 1 | 0.0% | N AMERICA: Canada |
| North America | Single Country | 1 | 0.0% | N AMERICA: Canada |
| Africa-Middle East | Global | 6 | 12.2% | ASIA-PACIFIC: Australia; AFRICA-MIDDLE EAST: South Africa, Botswana, Namibia, Swaziland, Zimbabwe |
| W Europe | Regional | 2 | 0.0% | W EUROPE: France, Germany |
| W Europe | Regional | 10 | 32.0% | W EUROPE: Austria, Denmark, Finland, Germany, Spain, Sweden; CE EUROPE: Croatia, Czech Republic, Slovenia; AFRICA-MIDDLE EAST: Turkey |
| North America | Single Country | 1 | 0.0% | N AMERICA: United States |
| North America | Regional | 3 | 0.0% | N AMERICA: United States |
| W Europe | Global | 14 | 1.0% | W EUROPE: Iceland, Ireland, United Kingdom; ASIA-PACIFIC: Japan; AFRICA-MIDDLE EAST: N/A |
| Africa- Middle East | Regional | 16 | 9.8% | AFRICA-MIDDLE EAST: Angola, Botswana, Egypt, Ghana, Lesotho, Madagascar, Malawi, Mauritius, Mozambique, Namibia, South Africa, Swaziland, Tanzania, Uganda, Zambia, Zimbabwe |

*continued*

| Rank | Company | Home Country | Primary Retail Sector | Net Sales (Millions USD) | Sales Growth 2003–2004 | Compound Annual Growth Rate 1999–2004 | Total Stores (incl. company-owned and networked) |
|---|---|---|---|---|---|---|---|
| 144 | Longs Drug Stores Corp. | United States | FDM | $4,575 | 1.7% | 4.5% | 472 |
| 145 | Kojima Co. Ltd. | Japan | Homegoods | $4,531 | 3.1% | 2.8% | 229 |
| 146 | Modelo Continente SGPS (Sonae) | Portugal | FDM | $4,450 | 3.1% | 2.0% | 452 |
| 147 | Big Lots Inc. | United States | FDM | $4,375 | 4.8% | 8.3% | 1,502 |
| 148 | Laurus | Netherlands | FDM | $4,351 | -13.9% | -8.9% | 721 |
| 149 | Foodland Associates Ltd. | Australia | FDM | $4,337 | 2.6% | 11.6% | 450 |
| 150 | Companhia Brasileira de Distribuicao | Brazil | FDM | $4,294 | 16.3% | 16.7% | 551 |
| 151 | Ross Stores Inc. | United States | Softgoods | $4,240 | 8.1% | 11.4% | 649 |
| 152 | Hy-Vee, Inc. | United States | FDM | $4,230 | 6.4% | 5.2% | 221 |
| 153 | Bic Camera Co. | Japan | Homegoods | $4,222 | 7.3% | 16.7% | 17 |
| 154 | Foodstuffs Ltd. | New Zealand | FDM | $4,205 | 5.6% | | 652 |
| 155 | Woolworths Group plc | United Kingdom | FDM | $4,169 | -1.3% | 2.4% | 905 |
| 156 | ReitanGruppen | Norway | FDM | $4,145 | 2.5% | 14.8% | 1,885 |
| 157 | Edion Corp. | Japan | Homegoods | $4,050 | 0.9% | 14.4% | 786 |
| 158 | Marui Co. Ltd. | Japan | Softgoods | $4,014 | 0.1% | -1.6% | 31 |
| 159 | Jeronimo Martins | Portugal | FDM | $4,007 | 3.1% | 1.8% | 1,020 |
| 160 | Pathmark Stores, Inc. | United States | FDM | $3,979 | -0.3% | 1.5% | 143 |
| 161 | Sherwin-Williams Company | United States | Homegoods | $3,977 | 14.6% | 5.8% | 3,054 |
| 162 | Dairy Farm International Holdings Limited | Hong Kong | FDM | $3,957 | 14.5% | -7.7% | 2,902 |
| 163 | SHV Holdings N.V. (Makro) | Netherlands | FDM | $3,916 | 11.0% | -5.0% | 159 |
| 164 | Borders Group Inc. | United States | Homegoods | $3,880 | 4.9% | 5.3% | 1,288 |
| 165 | Whole Foods Market Inc. | United States | FDM | $3,865 | 22.8% | 19.8% | 163 |
| 166 | dm-drogerie markt GmbH & Co. KG | Germany | FDM | $3,828 | 7.5% | 11.4% | 1,498 |
| 167 | Izumi | Japan | FDM | $3,814 | 4.2% | 8.0% | 116 |
| 168 | Advance Auto Parts Inc. | United States | Homegoods | $3,770 | 7.9% | 11.3% | 2,652 |
| 169 | Organización Soriana, S.A. de C.V. | Mexico | FDM | $3,719 | 14.1% | 15.8% | 138 |
| 170 | Littlewoods Retail Ltd. | United Kingdom | Softgoods | $3,666 | 8.4% | 1.1% | 171 |
| 171 | Stater Bros. Holding Inc. | United States | FDM | $3,629 | 31.8% | 14.7% | 158 |
| 172 | Life Corp. | Japan | FDM | $3,576 | 2.8% | 0.2% | 189 |
| 173 | The Neiman Marcus Group | United States | Softgoods | $3,546 | 14.4% | 6.8% | 51 |

| Home Region | Level of Internation- alization | Number of Countries | % of Sales in Foreign Countries | Countries |
|---|---|---|---|---|
| North America | Single Country | 1 | 0.0% | N AMERICA: United States |
| Asia-Pacific | Single Country | 1 | 0.0% | ASIA-PACIFIC: Japan |
| W Europe | Global | 2 | 27.2% | N AMERICA: Brazil; W EUROPE: Portugal |
| North America | Single Country | 1 | 0.0% | N AMERICA: United States |
| W Europe | Regional | 2 | 0.7% | W EUROPE: Belgium, Netherlands |
| Asia-Pacific | Regional | 2 | 60.4% | ASIA-PACIFIC: Australia, New Zealand |
| Latin America | Single Country | 1 | 0.0% | LATIN AMERICA: Brazil |
| North America | Regional | 2 | 0.0% | N AMERICA: United States |
| North America | Single Country | 1 | 0.0% | N AMERICA: United States |
| Asia-Pacific | Single Country | 1 | 0.0% | ASIA-PACIFIC: Japan |
| Asia-Pacific | Single Country | 1 | 0.0% | ASIA-PACIFIC: New Zealand |
| W Europe | Single Country | 1 | 0.0% | W EUROPE: United Kingdom |
| W Europe | Regional | 5 | 25.4% | W EUROPE: Denmark, Norway, Sweden; CE EUROPE: Latvia, Slovakia |
| Asia-Pacific | Single Country | 1 | 0.0% | ASIA-PACIFIC: Japan |
| Asia-Pacific | Single Country | 1 | 0.0% | ASIA-PACIFIC: Japan |
| W Europe | Regional | 2 | 32.8% | W EUROPE: Portugal; CE EUROPE: Poland |
| North America | Single Country | 1 | 0.0% | N AMERICA: United States |
| North America | Regional | 7 | N/A | N AMERICA: Canada, United States; LATIN AMERICA: Argentina, Brazil, Chile, Mexico, Uruguay |
| Asia-Pacific | Regional | 8 | N/A | ASIA-PACIFIC: China, Hong Kong, India, Indonesia, Malaysia, Singapore, South Korea, Taiwan |
| Asia-Pacific | Global | 9 | 100.0% | LATIN AMERICA: Argentina, Brazil, Colombia, Venezuela; ASIA-PACIFIC: China, Indonesia, Malaysia, Philippines, Thailand |
| North America | Global | 6 | 13.2% | N AMERICA: United States; W EUROPE: United Kingdom; ASIA-PACIFIC: Australia, New Zealand, Singapore |
| North America | Global | 3 | 1.4% | N AMERICA: United States, Canada; W EUROPE: United Kingdom |
| W Europe | Regional | 9 | 27.9% | W EUROPE: Austria, Germany, Italy; CE EUROPE: Croatia, Czech Republic, Hungary, Serbia, Slovakia, Slovenia |
| Asia-Pacific | Single Country | 1 | 0.0% | ASIA-PACIFIC: Japan |
| North America | Single Country | 1 | 0.0% | N AMERICA: United States |
| Latin America | Single Country | 1 | 0.0% | LATIN AMERICA: Mexico |
| W Europe | Single Country | 1 | 0.0% | W EUROPE: United Kingdom |
| North America | Single Country | 1 | 0.0% | N AMERICA: United States |
| Asia-Pacific | Single Country | 1 | 0.0% | ASIA-PACIFIC: Japan |
| North America | Single Country | 1 | 0.0% | N AMERICA: United States |

*continued*

Chapter 1 Appendix › *Continued*

| Rank | Company | Home Country | Primary Retail Sector | Net Sales (Millions USD) | Sales Growth 2003–2004 | Sales Growth Compound Annual Growth Rate 1999–2004 | Total Stores (incl. company-owned and networked) |
|------|---------|--------------|------------------------|--------------------------|------------------------|---------------------------------------------------|--------------------------------------------------|
| 174 | Norma Lebensmit-telfilialbetrieb GmbH & Co. KG | Germany | FDM | $3,506 | 8.0% | 6.6% | 1,297 |
| 175 | The Pantry Inc. | United States | FDM | $3,493 | 27.0% | 15.8% | 1,361 |
| 176 | Caprabo | Spain | FDM | $3,490 | 20.2% | 17.9% | 622 |
| 177 | Debenhams plc | United Kingdom | Softgoods | $3,488 | 5.1% | 1.0% | 118 |
| 178 | RONA Inc. | Canada | Homegoods | $3,466 | 22.6% | 23.0% | 550 |
| 179 | Raley's | United States | FDM | $3,465 | 5.0% | 4.0% | 135 |
| 180 | HMV Group plc | United Kingdom | Homegoods | $3,456 | 5.1% | 6.3% | 588 |
| 181 | Wegmans Food Markets Inc. | United States | FDM | $3,400 | 3.0% | 4.7% | 68 |
| 182 | Michaels Stores Inc. | United States | Homegoods | $3,393 | 9.8% | 12.5% | 1,027 |
| 183 | Hankyu Department Stores | Japan | Softgoods | $3,385 | −0.3% | −1.2% | 12 |
| 184 | PETsMART Inc. | United States | FDM | $3,363 | 12.4% | 9.8% | 726 |
| 185 | Controladora Comercial Mexicana | Mexico | FDM | $3,329 | 2.2% | 4.0% | 239 |
| 186 | Axfood (Axel Johnson AB) | Sweden | FDM | $3,322 | 4.7% | −4.3% | 317 |
| 187 | Heiwado Co. Ltd. | Japan | FDM | $3,303 | 6.2% | 3.6% | 90 |
| 188 | Home Hardware Stores Ltd. | Canada | Homegoods | $3,227 | 10.5% | | 1,000 |
| 189 | Izumiya | Japan | FDM | $3,197 | −0.6% | −1.3% | 87 |
| 190 | Maruetsu Inc. | Japan | FDM | $3,195 | −3.5% | 1.2% | 276 |
| 191 | Gruppo PAM S.p.A. | Italy | FDM | $3,176 | 7.5% | 4.4% | 521 |
| 192 | Burlington Coat Factory Warehouse Corp. | United States | Softgoods | $3,171 | 11.9% | 7.6% | 362 |
| 193 | ShopKo Stores Inc. | United States | FDM | $3,167 | −0.5% | 0.8% | 363 |
| 194 | Fast Retailing | Japan | Softgoods | $3,144 | 9.8% | 25.1% | 644 |
| 195 | Dollar Tree Stores Inc. | United States | FDM | $3,126 | 11.6% | 21.1% | 2,735 |
| 196 | SPAR South Africa | South Africa | FDM | $3,047 | 18.4% | | 1,070 |
| 197 | Arcadia Group | United Kingdom | Softgoods | $3,038 | 0.5% | 2.0% | 2,250 |
| 198 | Roundy's Inc. | United States | FDM | $3,011 | 24.2% | 56.2% | 161 |
| 199 | Shimamura Co. Ltd. | Japan | Softgoods | $3,008 | 8.6% | 9.7% | 1,094 |
| 200 | CompUSA | United States | Homegoods | $3,006 | −5.1% | −12.6% | 300 |

| Home Region | Level of Internation-alization | Number of Countries | % of Sales in Foreign Countries | Countries |
|---|---|---|---|---|
| W Europe | Regional | 3 | 6.0% | W EUROPE: France, Germany; CE EUROPE: Czech Republic |
| North America | Single Country | 1 | 0.0% | N AMERICA: United States |
| W Europe | Single Country | 1 | 0.0% | W EUROPE: Spain |
| W Europe | Global | 12 | 0.0% | W EUROPE: Denmark, Iceland, Sweden, United Kingdom; CE EUROPE: Czech Republic; ASIA-PACIFIC: Malaysia; AFRICA-MIDDLE EAST: Bahrain, Cyprus, Kuwait, Qatar, Saudi Arabia, United Arab Emirates |
| North America | Single Country | 1 | 0.0% | N AMERICA: Canada |
| North America | Single Country | 1 | 0.0% | N AMERICA: United States |
| W Europe | Global | 7 | 27.1% | N AMERICA: Canada; W EUROPE: Ireland, United Kingdom; ASIA-PACIFIC: Australia, Hong Kong, Japan, Singapore |
| North America | Single Country | 1 | 0.0% | N AMERICA: United States |
| North America | Regional | 2 | 5.2% | N AMERICA: Canada, United States |
| Asia-Pacific | Single Country | 1 | 0.0% | ASIA-PACIFIC: Japan |
| North America | Regional | 2 | 2.6% | N AMERICA: United States, Canada |
| Latin America | Single Country | 1 | 0.0% | LATIN AMERICA: Mexico |
| W Europe | Regional | 2 | 21.2% | W EUROPE: Finland, Sweden |
| Asia-Pacific | Single Country | 1 | 0.0% | ASIA-PACIFIC: Japan |
| North America | Single Country | 1 | 0.0% | N AMERICA: Canada |
| Asia-Pacific | Single Country | 1 | 0.0% | ASIA-PACIFIC: Japan |
| Asia-Pacific | Single Country | 1 | 0.0% | ASIA-PACIFIC: Japan |
| W Europe | Single Country | 1 | 0.0% | W EUROPE: Italy |
| North America | Single Country | 1 | 0.0% | N AMERICA: United States |
| North America | Single Country | 1 | 0.0% | N AMERICA: United States |
| Asia-Pacific | Global | 3 | 0.8% | W EUROPE: United Kingdom; ASIA-PACIFIC: China, Japan |
| North America | Single Country | 1 | 0.0% | N AMERICA: United States |
| Africa-Middle East | Regional | 3 | 4.7% | AFRICA-MIDDLE EAST: Botswana, Namibia, South Africa |
| W Europe | Global | 31 | 7.0% | LATIN AMERICA: Chile; W EUROPE: Austria, Denmark, France, Germany, Gibraltar, Greece, Iceland, Malta, Netherlands, Portugal, Spain, Sweden, United Kingdom; CE EUROPE: Bosnia, Croatia, Hungary, Poland, Slovenia; ASIA-PACIFIC: Malaysia, Philippines, Singapore; AFRICA-MIDDLE EAST: Bahrain, Cyprus, Israel, Kuwait, Lebanon, Qatar, Saudi Arabia, United Arab Emirates, Turkey |
| North America | Single Country | 1 | 0.0% | N AMERICA: United States |
| Asia-Pacific | Single Country | 1 | 0.0% | ASIA-PACIFIC: Japan |
| North America | Single Country | 1 | 0.0% | N AMERICA: United States |

*Source:* Retail Foward, 2004.

# 2

# STRATEGIC INTERNATIONAL RETAIL EXPANSION EXTENDED MODEL AND PROPOSITIONS (SIRE$^2$)

## After reading this chapter, you should understand

> Concepts that make international retailing different from international marketing.

> Entry strategies available to international retailers and how these strategies affect a retailer's market exposure and long-term potential for internationalization.

> Why retailers engage in international expansion.

> The different expansion pattern for global versus multinational retailers.

> Why the macro-marketing environments affect a retailer's decision to enter foreign markets.

There has been very little theoretical development leading to an explanation of how, why, and where retailers internationalize. Most theories of internationalization begin with the assumption that the company has an export option, but retailers do not have an export option. Since the retail function is one that requires selling to an ultimate customer, a retailer must have a physical presence in the country. In the case of an Internet retailer, this presence might take the form of a website. Figure 2.1 shows a continuum of entry-mode alternatives available to retailers.

Even though recent studies within the retailing sector have focused on different aspects of retail internationalization, such as motivation and degree of involvement, and have provided case evidence on some firms and markets, research in ENTRY-MODE STRATEGY is still scanty.

Two major problems have limited the development of a comprehensive theory of retail internationalization. The first problem is that most researchers have assumed that all retailers' internationalization is the same. Salmon and Tordjman

**Figure 2.1**
Entry Modes

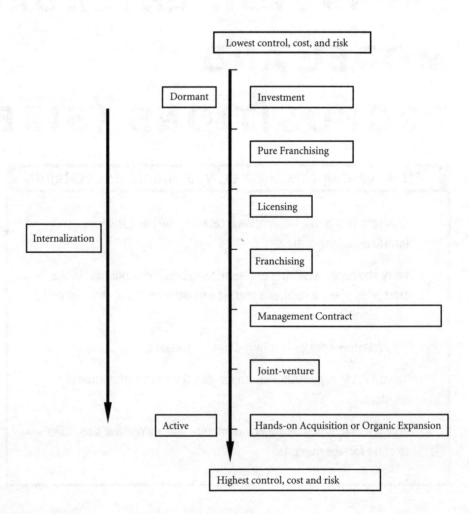

were the first to identify two different types of retailers that they termed global and multinational.[1]

However, other than Sternquist,[2] major researchers have not followed up with this designation; instead, all types of retailers are grouped together for analysis. Based on my experience, I have found at least four different types of retailer internationalization (investment, pure franchisor, global, and multinational), each with a different expansion pattern, partly because of the way the company is organized. Differentiation of retailer types helps to distinguish how different retailers internationalize.

The second major problem is that most researchers have observed only retailers' successful international moves without analyzing the actions that are not successful. It is essential to analyze the international failures in order to fully develop a model of successful retail internationalization. Companies are more likely to analyze failures rather than success, plus failures represent the definitive answer about whether an expansion pattern is correct. The ideas presented in this chapter are normative, rather than descriptive, meaning that they represent what could be interpreted as a correct pattern of internationalization. Movements that do not fit this pattern are expected to result in withdrawal over time.

## 〉 TYPES OF RETAIL INTERNATIONALIZATION

### Acquisition

ACQUISITION refers to purchasing an existing well-managed company and allowing management to continue operations. This is a DORMANT TYPE OF MANAGEMENT. This strategy was used by Delhaize, Ahold, and Sainsbury when they first entered the United States. Investment also appears to be the strategy used by Wal-Mart in their purchase of ASDA, a supermarket chain in the United Kingdom. Dave Ferguson, president and CEO of Wal-Mart Europe said, "We've got a company that we were smart enough not to try and change."[3]

Companies using investment strategy are looking for: 1) higher than domestic RETURN ON INVESTMENT, 2) a safe foreign international investment environment and/ or 3) access to RETAIL KNOW-HOW. The motivation for purchasing companies in other countries rather than the home market is to diversify the company's investment. Delhaize purchased Food Lion in the United States at the height of the cold war. They wanted the chance to put company resources in a more stable geopolitical environment.

Internationalization through investment leads to little knowledge transfer. Therefore, it does not necessarily lead to more active models of management. Investment is also an expensive internationalization strategy because the purchaser is buying a well-managed company, rather than a company in trouble, and will therefore pay top dollar. Return on the international investment will be difficult to recoup. Ahold sought the "gem" retailers in each country they entered. If they could not purchase the country gem, Ahold would not enter the market. We can see from the recent disposal of Ahold acquisitions in South America and Asia that the investment strategy is difficult to pull off.

```
┌─────────────────────────────────────────────────┐
│  Box 2.1                                          │
│  Acquisition-Hands Off Management                 │
│                                                   │
│   ›  Select well managed companies                │
│   ›  Look for fragmented markets                  │
│   ›  Stable government & economy                  │
│   ›  Developed market                             │
│   ›  Transfer of technology to purchasing firm    │
│   ›  Low returns due to high price paid for goodwill │
│   ›  Ex. Ahold's acquisition of US food retailers │
└─────────────────────────────────────────────────┘
```

Box 2.1 contains a summary of the requirements for acquisition form of management.

## Pure Franchisors

Another form of dormant management is a PURE FRANCHISOR. These companies use franchising exclusively in their international expansion. Pure franchisors typically focus on master franchising networks given to individuals on a countrywide basis. They regularly expand internationally for OPPORTUNISTIC reasons. Opportunistic means that someone comes to the company with the idea for a franchise, rather than the company developing an interest in the country for strategic purposes. For instance, the master franchise for McDonald's in Japan was given to an entrepreneurial handbag/shoe salesman with an account at Mitsukoshi. Even though McDonald's was not interested in opening company stores in Japan at that time, he convinced the corporation that their burgers and fries would be a hit. For master franchisors the identification of a skillful person to develop the network is more important that identifying the best country to enter. For this reason, when you view the expansion pattern of MASTER FRANCHISORS it is into a random variety of countries rather than a stages type of expansion where a company enters culturally similar countries sequentially.

Both investment and pure franchisor internationalization are based on dormant management. Because management is dormant there is little knowledge transfer. Also, neither method is a strategic retail decision. Both of these options are financial decisions that do not lead to further international expansion in a predictable way. Retailers using these approaches need to be excluded from modeling the internationalization of retailers not because they are strategic and rational but rather because they are opportunistic and random. Events that are random cannot be successfully modeled. In other words, you cannot take their experiences into consideration when developing propositions that will explain internationalization.

In this chapter, I will focus on the two types of retailers whose moves can be considered strategic. The terms global and multinational retailers, initiated by

---

**Box 2.2**
**Global Retailers**

> Standard retail format
> Centralized management
> Often vertically integrated backwards
> Extensive use of private label
> Generally small-medium size
> Ex. Zara

---

Salmon and Tordjman,[1] will be used. The names global and multinational do not indicate their degree of internationalization, instead it refers to the concept of STANDARDIZATION (global) versus ADAPTATION (multinational). Boxes 2.2 and 2.3 summarize the characteristics of these two types of retailers. There is controversy about these terms. In the marketing literature multinational firms are often referred to as multi-local. But this concept does not convey the idea that multinational retailers learn from each international movement; this knowledge is important in determining future international actions. Not every retailer can be classified as totally global or totally multinational; most retailers have some characteristics that cross over.

Pelligrini presents an important distinction to explain paths for growth.[4] He identifies the search for growth related to: 1) an attempt to extend the application of the firm's proprietary know-how to get the benefits of internationalization; this is called rents in the management literature, 2) an attempt to optimize the scale of operations (ECONOMIES OF SCALE), or 3) an attempt to expand the mix of operations (ECONOMIES OF SCOPE) to reduce costs and increase efficiency. In the next section the paths for growth for global and multinational retailers are considered.

---

**Box 2.3**
**Multinational Retailers**

> Decentralized
> Concentrate expansion within a geographic area
> Change retail offering based on customer and cultural differences
> Generally large sized retailers such as hypermarkets, cash and carry
> Ex. Carrefour, Wal-Mart

---

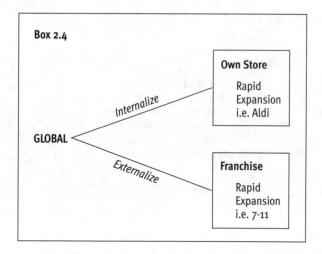

**Box 2.4**

Own Store

Rapid
Expansion
i.e. Aldi

GLOBAL

*Internalize*

*Externalize*

Franchise

Rapid
Expansion
i.e. 7-11

## Global

GLOBAL RETAILERS are CENTRALIZED, standardized, generally small-format retailers. These retailers are often VERTICALLY INTEGRATED, frequently focusing on PRIVATE LABEL or exclusive merchandise. Examples of global retailers are Zara, Mango, and Gap. When they enter foreign markets, they look for a universal, global market segment that will accept their retail offering without much change. Because these retailers are relatively small in scale and centralized, it is possible to develop business format franchises for the system. Because they have a standard format they can be replicated very rapidly in new locations. Box 2.4 summarizes this type of retailer.

Global retailers begin their internationalization not to countries, but to world-class cities where they expect to find a segment of consumers who are indistinguishable throughout the world. They do not need to change their offering because their consumer is fundamentally the same wherever they go.

Global retailers, particularly fast-food retailers, have been discussed as new forms of GLOBAL IMPERIALISM. Global imperialism means that the retailers alter material culture wherever they go. Authors such as Ronald Steel and Thomas Friedman argue that McDonald's and other manifestations of global culture serve the interests of middle classes that are emerging in autocratic, undemocratic societies.

Global retailers' motivation for international expansion is to exploit a unique concept before others have a chance to do this. Global retailers therefore may expand to other countries without saturating their home market. Their quest is not a simple quest for growth but the need to colonize their concept.

COLONIZING A CONCEPT means that you expand very rapidly before others can mimic your idea. Although all global retailers expand internationally more rapidly than multinational retailers, there is a group of exceptionally fast internationalizers. These companies expand internationally nearly from their inception. In the marketing literature, Knight and Cauvisgil term these companies BORN GLOBAL.[5] The Born Global literature focuses on learning in networks to explain the quick international expansion. The early movers in retailing do not depend on learning networks but instead focus on colonizing the concept. Being first with the idea gives significant first-mover advantages. Because these retailers are not changing their offering, there is no real need to learn about the international environment.

## Multinational

The second type, a MULTINATIONAL RETAILER, is DECENTRALIZED and adapts its product to the culture it is serving. It is usually a large-scale format, which would be difficult or impossible to develop into a business format franchise. If this type of retailer wishes to use a low-cost alternative for international expansion, there is not an option of franchising; licensing will have to be used instead. Wal-Mart's Supercenters, warehouse clubs such as PriceClub, and supermarkets such as Tesco are multinational retailers. These retailers adapt to the cultures they are entering. They generally source merchandise locally and try to hire and train management from the local area. Box 2.5 summarizes this type of retailer.

We can best understand multinational retailer's internationalization as a strategy for growth. These retailers generally do not internationalize before they have SATURATED THEIR HOME MARKET. This saturation may be because of natural market expansion or, as we more often find in Europe, government restriction on large-scale store expansion, which explains why European food retailers have been the most aggressive in cross-border expansion. Although the major global brands are often American, the European retailers sell them.

Some of the first multinational retailers to expand internationally were the Japanese department stores and General Merchandise Stores (GMS). These companies moved into Hong Kong and Taiwan to avoid the competitive environment of Japan where large-scale store laws prevented their expansion at home. These early international moves were defensive. The first Japanese department stores to internationalize, such as Yaohan, were weak in their home market. In the end, most of

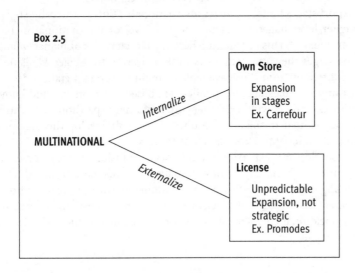

**Box 2.5**

MULTINATIONAL

*Internalize* →

**Own Store**

Expansion
in stages
Ex. Carrefour

*Externalize* →

**License**

Unpredictable
Expansion, not
strategic
Ex. Promodes

the early Japanese department store retailers' international expansion failed. A second wave of Japanese department stores expanded to Hong Kong and Taiwan with the intention of learning how to do business in the Chinese business environments. These companies, such as Isetan, were successful in using Hong Kong and Taiwan to launch operations in China.

Most large-scale European retailers that internationalized were food retailers.[6] They generally did not enter foreign countries until they had saturated the home market. Growth needs fueled their international expansion. In this case, unlike the Japanese early expander, international expansion was part of their strategic growth.

Because multinational retailers have a large-scale format they do not have a franchising option. FRANCHISING requires that the business format be standardized, essentially codifying the knowledge, which can then be transferred to foreign outlets. Multinational retailers who want to use a low-risk alternative must use licensing rather than franchising. LICENSING is a risky move for a company because it has little control over what the licensee will do with the name.

## > THEORETICAL EXPLANATIONS
## FOR INTERNATIONALIZATION

The propositions presented here have elements of earlier theories (for a model, see Figure 2.2). STAGES THEORY focuses on the pattern of internationalization. According to Stages Theory a company will initially expand to countries that are the most similar to their home market, then with experience they will expand to countries that are less similar. DUNNING'S ECLECTIC THEORY[7] focuses on Ownership, Location, and Internalization factors. INSTITUTIONAL THEORY explains the influences of macro-environment and micro-environment on a company's decision to internationalize. The final conceptual link is RISK THEORY. Retailers evaluate foreign markets according to their perceived level of risk. Much of a retailer's in-country investment is for inventory and physical facilities—an investment that is not liquid, and therefore not salvageable in the short run if a government determines that the company should not operate there anymore, or if it simply cannot survive.

The export stages literature views internationalization as a step-by-step process where higher-level stages represent a higher level of international involvement than lower stages.[8, 9] This paradigm relies on characteristics of management to delineate the stages they are ready to assume. However, the stages available for retailers are different from those available to manufacturers. Retailers do not have an export option. The stages for retailers are based more on risk and knowledge. Multinational retailers will begin their international expansion in countries that are culturally similar to the home country. They will develop this area or region and then make a JUMP TO ANOTHER GEOGRAPHIC AREA that is not culturally similar; there they develop area expertise through local expansion. As they gain experience in each country or region, they move into another area. Eroglu provides the basis for predicting which firms will seek international expansion because of organizational characteristics such as size, experience, and international orientation.[10] These organizational characteristics are directly related to the propensity for international expansion.

Retailers make mistakes in their internationalization efforts. A failure can be very valuable for a retailer's long-term success because failures are analyzed more than successes. Analysis leads to learning. Carrefour is a good example of a company that withdraws from markets in which it is not successful. Table 2.1 is a summary of Carrefour's international expansion and, what is more important, its international withdrawal. As a result of this trial learning the company has compiled a vast portfolio of information about how to do business in other countries. In 2000 Carrefour acquired GB, a Belgium firm. Belgium was the first country Carrefour entered, in 1969. They withdrew after their initial entry; however, after over thirty years of international experience, Carrefour is ready to re-enter through acquisition.

Researchers have developed most international business models from the manufacturing perspective. The two major international business research paradigms are the behavioral school and the export stages view. The behavioral school considers internationalization as an incremental process of strategic growth based on a firm's general and experiential market knowledge and resources. Increased market knowledge enables the firm to have higher international involvement. This view holds that knowledge and experience accumulates in firms' internationalization growth and allows the firm to control risks associated with internationalization. The behavioral internationalization paradigm has been used as a model for international retail involvement. Results confirm that strategic management characteristics, competitive advantage related to retail concept and LOGISTICS, and retailer's size are related to retail internationalization.[12]

The export stages view focuses on a market view of international expansion. Companies begin with the least resource commitment, i.e., exporting and then move into greater stages of international involvement leading finally to foreign direct investment.

Both these models assume that international activities are higher risk than domestic expansion, and that the internationalization process is sequential (lower involvement leading to higher involvement), and that internal firm factors influence international involvement rather than macro-environmental factors.

Retailing differs from manufacturing internationalization. Retailers often do not use sophisticated decision models before internationalizing. They are more likely to take an international move and then assess the impact of the move. Yip, Biscarri, and Monti observed this ad hoc approach when they studied the internationalization of small and medium sized firms.[13] Retailers also consider country economic characteristics more than manufacturers, because they must have a physical presence in the country. Therefore a theory to explain retailer's international expansion should include 1) the exits, as well as the entry, into foreign markets and 2) competitive, economic, and development factors within the country.

Dunning's Eclectic Theory focuses on Ownership (O), Location (L), and Internalization (I), (OLI) factors that influence a company's decision to internationalize.[7] Box 2.6 summarizes these factors. In addition, institutional theory helps explain how a retailer's macroenvironment—the host country and home country, and microenvironment—the retailer's past experience and competitors' move—affect the retailer's internationalization decision.

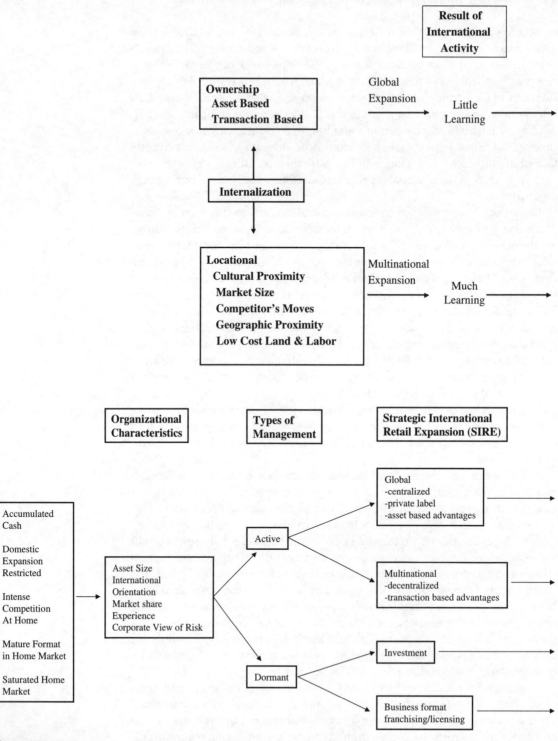

**Figure 2.2**
Model of Strategic
International Retail
Expansion (SIRE)

**Predicted Expansion Pattern**      **Low Risk Alternative**

**Own Store Rapid Expansion**
*Small Size Stores-Hard Discounters, Convenience*
*Operating Experience*
*International Orientation*
*Tolerance for Risk*
*Competitive Advantage- Asset Based (AB)*

**Franchising**
*Small Size*
*Limited Operating Experience*
*Limited International Orientation*
*Low Tolerance for Risk*
*Little Competitive Advantage*

**Own Store Expansion in Stages**
*Countries with attractive locational advantages*
*Large Size Stores - Hypermarkets*
*Cash and Carry*
*International Orientation*
*Tolerance for Risk*
*Competitive Advantage - Transaction Based (TB)*

**Licensing**
*Large Size Stores*
*Limited Operating Experience*
*Limited International Orientation*
*Low Tolerance for Risk*
*Little Competitive Advantage*

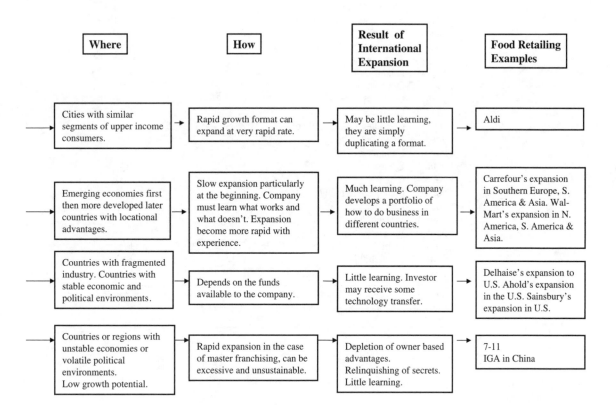

**Where** | **How** | **Result of International Expansion** | **Food Retailing Examples**

| Where | How | Result of International Expansion | Food Retailing Examples |
|---|---|---|---|
| Cities with similar segments of upper income consumers. | Rapid growth format can expand at very rapid rate. | May be little learning, they are simply duplicating a format. | Aldi |
| Emerging economies first then more developed later countries with locational advantages. | Slow expansion particularly at the beginning. Company must learn what works and what doesn't. Expansion become more rapid with experience. | Much learning. Company develops a portfolio of how to do business in different countries. | Carrefour's expansion in Southern Europe, S. America & Asia. Wal-Mart's expansion in N. America, S. America & Asia. |
| Countries with fragmented industry. Countries with stable economic and political environments. | Depends on the funds available to the company. | Little learning. Investor may receive some technology transfer. | Delhaise's expansion to U.S. Ahold's expansion in the U.S. Sainsbury's expansion in U.S. |
| Countries or regions with unstable economies or volatile political environments. Low growth potential. | Rapid expansion in the case of master franchising, can be excessive and unsustainable. | Depletion of owner based advantages. Relinquishing of secrets. Little learning. | 7-11 IGA in China |

**Table 2.1**
**Carrefour's Overseas Expansions**

| Entry time | Entry location | Entry mode | Total Stores by 09/2005 | Formats (Store No.) |
|---|---|---|---|---|
| 1969 | Belgium (out in 1978; reentered in 2000) | | 496 | H(56); S(265); C(175) |
| 1969 | United Kingdom (out in 1983) | | 0 | |
| 1972 | Italy (out in 1984; reentered in 1993) | | 1,500 | H(43); S(390); C(697); C&C(17) |
| 1973 | Spain | JV | 3030 | H(137); S(177); HD(2687); C&C(29) |
| 1975 | Brazil | JV | 414 | H(96); S(97); HD(221) |
| 1976 | Austria (out in 1979) | | 0 | |
| 1977 | Germany (out in 1979) | | 0 | |
| 1982 | Argentina | JV | 480 | H(28); S(114); HD(338) |
| 1988 | United States (out in 1993) | JV | 0 | |
| 1989 | Taiwan | JV | 36 | H(36) |
| 1991 | Greece | | 622 | H(19); S(142); HD(335); C(126) |
| 1992 | Portugal | JV | 379 | H(7); HD(372) |
| 1993 | Malaysia | JV | 8 | H(8) |
| 1993 | Turkey | JV | 434 | H(12); S(84); HD(338) |
| 1995 | Mexico (out in 2005) | JV | 0 | |
| 1995 | China | JV | 284 | H(64); S(8); HD(212) |
| 1995 | United Arab Emirates | F | 8 | H(8) |
| 1996 | South Korea (out in 2006) | WOS | 31 | H(31) |
| 1996 | Thailand | JV | 22 | H(22) |
| 1996 | Hong Kong (out in 2000) | WOS | 0 | |
| 1997 | Singapore | WOS | 2 | H(2) |
| 1997 | Poland | WOS | 102 | H(31); S(71) |
| 1998 | Indonesia | JV | 18 | H(18) |
| 1998 | Chile (out in 2004) | | 0 | |
| 1998 | Colombia | JV | 18 | H(18) |
| 1998 | Czech Republic (out in 2005) | WOS | 0 | |
| 2000 | Japan (out in 2005) | WOS | 0 | |
| 2000 | Slovakia (out in 2005) | | 0 | |
| 2000 | Qatar | F | 1 | H(1) |
| 2000 | Oman | F | 1 | H(1) |
| 2000 | Dominican Republic | F | 1 | H(1) |
| 2001 | Romania | F | 4 | H(4) |
| 2001 | Switzerland | JV | 12 | H(12) |
| 2001 | Tunisia | F | 2 | H(1); S(1) |
| 2002 | Egypt | F | 2 | H(2) |
| 2004 | Saudi Arabia | F | 1 | H(1) |
| 2004 | Norway | F | 5 | S(5) |

Note: JV—Joint Venture; F—Franchising; WOS—Wholly-owned Subsidiary; H—Hypermarket; S—Supermarket; C—Convenience Store; C&C—Cash & Carry; HD—Hard Discounter

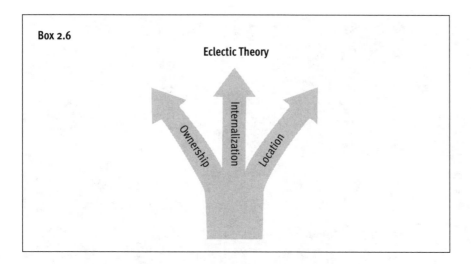

Box 2.6

Eclectic Theory

Ownership
Internalization
Location

> ECLECTIC THEORY

## Ownership Advantages (O)

OWNERSHIP ADVANTAGES include innovative or unique products or processes the company can use to obtain market power. Included in this grouping are asset-based advantages and transaction-based advantages. ASSET-BASED ADVANTAGES refer to tangible items such as patents or unique products. Global retailers generally have significant asset-based ownership advantages, since they often focus on private label merchandise. Private label can be considered an important ownership advantage; however, private label does not necessarily translate well when a company internationalizes. Retailers such as Zara (Figure 2.3) and Mango are defined by their private label concept. In this case the private label is an asset in international expansion. Also, because private label is easily expanded to international settings, it makes the asset transportable. In contrast, multinational retailers are generally mass merchandisers; for these retailers private labels do not transfer well in an international setting. A good example of this is Marks & Spencer, a UK company that focuses on general merchandise and food offerings. Although they had a very successful start at internationalization in selling their products in Hong Kong (a former British colony) and other communities where there was a strong affiliation to the Marks & Spencer concept, this success diminished when they had less of an expatriate clientele. As a result they have had to back out of many markets where they thought they would be successful. In their study of European food retailers, Gielens and Dekimpe found that private label was not related to sales and efficiency.[14] The bottom line is that very targeted retailers such as Mango and Zara are looking for a distinct segment of consumers who like their product throughout the world, but large-scale retailers have a difficult time using their private label effectively because the mass population are not familiar with—and do not accept private label merchandise from—a retailer they do not know.

TRANSACTION-BASED ADVANTAGES come about because of the way things are done. Customer service and centralized buying are examples of transaction-based advantages. Transaction-based knowledge is highly tacit; transferring it to others is difficult. Tacit knowledge is characterized through learning by doing (TACIT LEARNING).

**Figure 2.3**
Zara, a Spanish retailer, is a leader in Fast Fashion. It capitalizes on very high inventory turns, creating a feeling in customers that if they see something they like they better buy it right now . . . or it will be gone. *Courtesy of Condé Nast.*

Transaction-based ownership advantages are difficult to transfer to another country. This both protects this type of ownership advantage from being copied, but also makes it difficult to use franchising to transfer the knowledge.

Transaction-based advantages include knowledge about how to internationalize. Carrefour (France) opened 40 new stores in foreign countries in 2001.[15] This is up from 35 in 1997, 30 in 1996, and 23 in 1995 to 1997.[16] Carrefour and Makro (Dutch) are two food retailers with long-standing experience in emerging markets, which has given them ownership advantages in three major areas. The first is people. Carrefour's years of international experience have given them a pool of experienced managers. These managers can be used to open new stores throughout the world. Carrefour has decentralized stores, giving managers extensive decision-making experience. Recently, Carrefour has been moving toward greater centralization to gain economies of scale in purchasing. The second area advantage is the hypermarket concept. This concept is particularly well adapted to emerging markets, where consumer purchasing power is growing rapidly from low initial levels. Also large store formats benefit from being in areas where land is reasonable, available, and not heavily regulated by the government. The third area of ownership advantage is their negotiating position with suppliers. Recently Carrefour has lost some of its vigor.

Daniel Barnard, the CEO, resigned in February 2005 because of a downturn in performance. However, the company's international expansion is a textbook example of how a multinational retailer internationalizes. Carrefour's early international success came about because of their FIRST MOVER ADVANTAGE. Their first internationalization efforts were to Northern European countries; these movements were not successful and the company retreated. Over time the company began to expand to less developed countries such as Spain, where they had a great deal of cultural similarity. They then expanded to South America, where they were able to capitalize on their knowledge of doing business in Latin cultures. As other multinational food retailers entered the markets and competition increased they have begun to struggle.[15] In 2005, Carrefour withdrew from Mexico, forced out by Wal-Mart's initiated price wars.

In my interviews with retailers, I would hear them say over and over that they internationalized because they had this "wall of cash" that they had to do something with. They had been successful and now they had to reinvest their earnings. This "extra" is called SLACK. Several propositions focus on how various types of slack will influence the decision to internationalize. Also many retailers I talked with said that the investment community expected them to internationalize, and would look at their company unfavorably if they didn't move outside their home borders. This means that stock market analysts would not suggest investing in their company if they did not expand. So some international expansion is related to satisfying the investment community, a source of revenue for PUBLICLY HELD COMPANIES. Publicly held companies are those sold on the stock market.

Propositions Related to Ownership Advantages

P1:  The greater the ownership advantages for retailers, the less likely they will franchise or license.

Explanation:  Companies that have significant ownership advantages do not want to give away their secrets. They prefer to use wholly owned investment to allow them to contain their secrets.

P2:  The greater the available organizational slack the greater the likelihood of expanding internationally.

[Ratio of current assets to current liabilities (3-year average before their first international expansion)] (Rhee and Cheng)[17]

Explanation:  This is called the current ratio. The more excess liquid cash the company has, the more likely they are to feel that they need to invest this capital in themselves. Companies feel that their best investment is in themselves, so therefore they want to use this capital for expansion. If they have saturated the home market, the likely mode for expansion is in international markets.

P3:  The greater the recoverable slack, the greater the likelihood of expanding internationally.

[Ratio of general and administrative expenses to sales (3-year average before their first international expansion)]

Explanation: The greater the amount of money that a company can use in a broader range of operations, i.e., expanding their costs (general and administrative expenses) to a larger sales volume, the more likely that they will expand. In other words, some expenses become less with greater volume. If the company expands, this expense becomes a smaller percent of their overall sales.

P4: The greater the potential slack, the greater the likelihood of expanding internationally.

[Ratio of equity to capital (3-year average before their first international expansion)]

Explanation: The more the company has in ownership, (equity) to capital, the more attractive international expansion will be to them. It is investing on behalf of the people who own the company; this has a positive motivation for internationalization.

P5: Percent of private label is positively related to retail success for a global retailer's internationalization, but negatively related to multinational retailer's success.

Explanation: Earlier I talked about the effect of private label on a retailer's success in internationalization. Global retailers who have a very specific niche are the most likely to capitalize on a private label line. They are looking at a very specific segment of the population, essentially the same lifestyle group in major world cities. It is much harder for multinational retailers to do this. They are dealing with the mass market; they need to have a general offering that appeals to the people within the country.

## Locational Advantages (L)

LOCATIONAL ADVANTAGES relate to how suitable the host country is with respect to the firm's strategies. In other words, how well does the country provide a comfortable place for the retailer to reside? Pellegrini's 1991 work identifies issues relevant to retailing.

CULTURAL PROXIMITY    People in some countries share similar patterns of life. Midwesterners in the United States are more like Midwesterners in Canada than U.S. residents on either coast. Europe has three bands of culturally similar groups divided geographically by horizontal bands, rather than distinct country groupings. French hypermarkets dominate the Spanish market. German department stores have expanded rapidly into what had been East Germany. The third band is the Northern European groups. These are examples of retailers expanding into culturally similar environments. Cultural proximity is more important for MULTINATIONAL RETAILERS, and becomes insignificant when retail concepts involve narrowly defined consumer markets, GLOBAL RETAILERS.

Evans and Mavondo considered the relationship between psychic distance and organizational performance.[18] PSYCHIC DISTANCE is conceptually the opposite of cultural proximity. They found that psychic distance has a positive effect on organizational performance. Retailers who perceive a difference in culture between the home and the host country will make adaptations while those who perceive no distance will not make adaptations. This finding is an example of where the type of retailer is likely confounding the results. If these authors had separated retailers into GLOBAL versus MULTINATIONAL they would likely find that psychic distance is not important to global retailers because they are selling to essentially the same customers throughout the world. Global retailers will enter world cities, selling essentially the same thing they sell at home. Multinational retailers will initially enter countries that have the smallest cultural distance to the home market, but over time they will expand to countries that are culturally distant.

**MARKET SIZE**    There are both push and pull factors related to market size. **PUSH FACTORS** mean that the retailer's growth in the home market is limited and they need to seek other environments. Saturation in the home country is an impetus for foreign direct investment by multinational retailers. Ample space for expansion must be available, particularly if the firm needs to reach a certain size to exploit economies of scale. Legal restrictions governing growth in the home country can be considered a motive for companies moving to foreign locations. France, Belgium, Germany, and Spain have stringent requirements that limit large scale retailers' growth, pushing retailers to expand outside national borders.

The French government passed a law in 1996 that set much more restrictive limits on new store openings. The law has essentially put an end to new hypermarket openings. Hard discount retailing, the small-scale version of warehouse clubs, will also be affected by the law. Hard discount stores are typically 900 square meters. The new legislation lowers the minimum store size requiring authorization to 300 square meters. This limits further growth even for hard discounters.

Market **PULL FACTORS** are those that make a foreign market look attractive. Multinational retailers will seek countries that are less developed than their home market. Markets with high growth in income can provide retailers with double digit growth. Global retailers are not affected by the level of economic development in the country. They seek world capitals where a homogeneous consumer resides.

Multinational retailers who enter less developed countries are also expected to alter their product offering so that food becomes a larger percent of sales. Consumers in less developed countries spend a higher percentage of their total disposable income on food. Wal-Mart sold very little food in its stores until they entered Mexico. In Mexico their joint venture partner, CIFRA, was the country's major food retailer. Their joint venture businesses had a heavy focus on food. This joint venture has subsequently terminated.

**COMPETITORS' MOVES**    A first-mover advantage may be lost if competitors enter a foreign market. Competitors may secure prime retail locations and block out other firms. Within any major city, there are only so many prime retail sites. The larger the retailer considering international expansion, the more crucial it is to be an early mover. Like a strategic game of chess, the early moves of a large retailer set the stage for a long-term competitive advantage. Competitor's moves have little impact on global retailers.

**GEOGRAPHIC PROXIMITY**    Expanding closer to home reduces costs related to transportation and corporate communication. **GEOGRAPHIC PROXIMITY** is important for retailers selling private labels produced in a central location. Geographic proximity is less important for decentralized companies because they are allowed to operate as independent units, generally sourcing from within the country. Even before the peso devaluation, Wal-Mart Mexico purchased 80–90 percent of their products from Mexican sources.

**LOW COST LAND AND LABOR**    Carrefour makes a policy of owning their stores. When Carrefour opens in a new commercial zone, it attracts the best tenants to the hypermarket complex. Tenants are given a strong economic justification to own their own outlets, and the whole shopping center if possible. Only in countries where the cost of commercial land is exorbitantly high, or where, for legal reasons, they cannot obtain title, does Carrefour agree to be a tenant. This was the case in Taiwan until 1996, when the government reduced restrictions on foreign ownership of land. Even in China, where land cannot actually be owned, only obtained through a long-term lease, Wal-Mart builds its own stores.

Propositions for Locational Advantages

Multinational Companies (High Adaptive-Decentralized)
P6:  Multinational retailers will move to countries with lower disposable income than their home country.
P7: Multinational retailers will move to countries that have a high positive change in GDP. GDP is GROSS DISPOSABLE PRODUCT. It is an indicator of wealth.

$$\frac{(\text{GDP 5 years before expansion—GDP at the time of expansion})}{\text{GDP R5 years before expansion}}$$

P8:  Multinational retailers will move to countries that have a high positive change in service-value added as percentage of GDP, which refers to what part of the national wealth is spent on services as compared to production of goods. Services include hiring cleaning ladies, lawn care specialists, and painters. As people become wealthy there is a tendency to hire others to take care of tasks.

$$\frac{(\text{Service percentage of GDP 5 years before expansion—}\text{Service percentage of GDP at the time of expansion})}{\text{Service percentage of GDP 5 years before expansion}}$$

P9:  Multinational retailers will first move to countries that are culturally the most similar to their home country. (Hofstede's indicators Home country-Host country for four factors, MvsFHuvsLU; IndvsCol; HPDvsLPD)
Explanation: Since multinational retailers will alter their offering in different countries, it is important for them to understand a country's culture. The closer the two cultures, the more likely the company is to understand the second culture. A retailer must be careful, though, not to fall into the cultural distance paradox, when companies believe that because two countries are similar, there is no need for adaptation. Their view of cultural similarity prevents them from dealing with cultural differences.
P10:  Multinational retailers will expand within the country and then will expand regionally within that area (for example, expanding to Brazil and then Argentina and Chile).
Explanation: Once a multinational retailer has moved into a country they will expand there before entering another country. They need to set up a company

infrastructure that will support their logistics and warehouse system. Also, they are in the process of learning the culture of the new country so continuing to expand within this environment is helpful. They expand within the region for the same reason; they are likely to better understand the culture of the region as they have more experience.

P11: Periodically the multinational retailers will "jump" to a new geographic area and begin the stages form of expansion.

Explanation: When a multinational retailer has expanded within a region and is ready for further expansion, it will target a new geographic area and take leap to expand there. For instance Wal-Mart started opening stores in Mexico, then South America. Before the retailer had saturated South America, it jumped to Asia, opening a store in Hong Kong, then going into China. The Hong Kong operation was very short lived, mainly geared as a site to learn about the China market.

P12: Multinational retailers will move to countries that are geographically close to the home country initially, and then expand to more distant countries. (Miles from Home Country to Host country)

P13: Multinational retailers will move to countries with large population bases.

Global Companies (Standard format-centralized)

P14: Global companies will move to the largest (capital) cities in a country.

P15: Global companies will not be attracted by population size, income, cultural proximity, or geographical proximity.

## Internalization (I)

The greater a company's ownership assets, the more important it is to protect these assets by guarding company secrets. INTERNALIZATION means keeping the information within the company. In retail franchising, the company sells or leases ownership assets to other firms. Therefore, franchising is a particularly dangerous idea for retailers with strong transaction-based ownership advantages. Retailing innovations are difficult to defend from imitators. Competitors can freely copy innovations because there are no patents on retail know-how; therefore, to maintain a competitive advantage, the retail company needs to internalize its innovations. The only way for a retail company to protect its operating secrets is to open WHOLLY OWNED SUBSIDIARIES in various countries. This is too expensive for many companies. They are forced to franchise their retail innovations to expand rapidly. However, over time they may regret this decision because they will have lost organic growth opportunities in that area. There is one instance where franchising is actually a smart strategic move—if you know that your retail format will be copied rapidly and you must franchise to be able to move quickly enough.

A primary attraction for the use of franchising in overseas markets might be rapid expansion. For some companies, foreign markets may be viewed as providing favorable opportunities for growth, regardless of the level of development of the domestic market. Many retailers, for example, The Body Shop, Benetton, Marks & Spencer, Mango, and Next have increasingly adopted franchising as an expansion method. This tendency is consistent with the premise that the global retailer with

| Table 2.2 Next's Overseas Expansions | |
|---|---|
| **Entry Location** | **Entry Mode** |
| Rep. of Ireland | Wholly-owned |
| France (out in 1998) | Wholly-owned |
| Belgium (out in 1998) | Wholly-owned |
| USA (out in 1998) | Joint venture |
| Malta | Franchising |
| Saudi Arabia | Franchising |
| United Arab Emirates | Franchising |
| Kuwait | Franchising |
| Oman | Franchising |
| Qatar | Franchising |
| Cyprus | Franchising |
| Czech Republic | Franchising |
| Bahrain | Franchising |
| Lebanon | Franchising |
| Indonesia | Franchising |
| Japan | Franchising |
| Iceland | Franchising |
| Denmark | Franchising |

an innovative concept expands rapidly to fully exploit the ownership asset. Many retail firms use other strategies to achieve rapid growth objectives. With a highly innovative retail and brand concept, and a primary growth method through wholly owned subsidiaries, *Zara* almost instantly expanded into 30 countries, adding nearly 250 stores from 2001 to 2003. Also, with well-defined concepts, Gap has used direct investment, rather than franchising, and achieved rapid expansion. Given the existence of global retailers using the wholly owned entry mode to expand rapidly, there may be some intervening factor that influences a global retailer's mode choice of entry with regard to rapid expansion. Table 2.2 summarizes Next's overseas expansion by entry mode.

There are two theoretical explanations for franchising: AGENCY THEORY and RESOURCE-BASED THEORY. Agency theory suggests that companies franchise because monitoring the foreign subsidiary is very difficult. Making the foreign entity an owner-manager will reduce the tendency to cheat. Resource-based theory suggests that firms franchise because they cannot afford to expand on their own. Although we cannot tell which theory explains a firm's decision to franchise when they begin the internationalization experience, over time we can have an idea of the true explanation. When the company begins to amass resources if they reacquire their franchise outlets, this would lend support to the resource-based theory. In other words, if they find themselves with money and they use this money to buy back franchisees, then we know resource-based theory is in play.

JOINT VENTURES occur when two companies join together to create a new entity. For instance, when Wal-Mart went to Mexico, they entered into a joint venture with Cifra to open supercenters called Bogata. In a joint venture partners share information and knowledge, which means that this involvement offers less protection of secrets than a wholly owned subsidiary. Sometimes joint ventures are needed when entering a different cultural environment, or because of government regulations. Many developing countries requiring domestic ownership have controlling interest of multinational companies. International retail joint ventures nearly always involve a multinational retailer. Generally the FOREIGN RETAIL JOINT VENTURES involve a foreign company that needs to learn the culture and business practices in a new country. They select a joint venture partner in the country that will provide them with this type of information. However, once the foreign retailer learns how to do business in the foreign country, they are likely to acquire the newly formed enterprise. Therefore retail foreign joint ventures are posited to be temporary in duration. That foreign joint ventures are useful only until the foreign company has learned the culture is interesting.

P16: The greater the asset-based (100% private-label line) ownership advantages of a global retailer, the more likely they are to franchise.

Explanation: If a global retailer's major ownership advantage is 100 percent private-label line, and particularly if this retailer produces and sells with very quick inventory turns, it is difficult if not impossible for others to copy them. The concept of fast retailers comes to mind here. For fast retailers it probably would not be a problem to franchise because the inventory turnover is so fast.

P17: The greater the transaction-based ownership advantages of a global retailer, the less likely they are to franchise.

P18: The greater the available organizational slack, the greater the likelihood that global retailers will reacquire international franchisees.
[Ratio of current assets to current liabilities (3-year average before they begin reacquisition)]

P19: The greater the recoverable slack, the greater the likelihood that global retailers will reacquire international franchisees.
[Ratio of general and administrative expenses to sales (3-year average before they begin reacquisition)]

P20: The greater the potential slack, the greater the likelihood that global retailers will reacquire international franchisees.
[Ratio of equity to capital (3-year average before they begin reacquisition)]

P21: Foreign retail joint ventures are temporary and will be acquired by the foreign partner once the local culture and customs are assimilated by the foreign enterprise.

## > OTHER THEORETICAL EXPLANATIONS
### FOR INTERNATIONALIZATION

The propositions presented as part of the SIRE2 Model have elements of earlier theories. STAGES THEORY focuses on the pattern of internationalization. DUNNING'S ECLECTIC THEORY focuses on Ownership, Location, and Internalization (OLI) factors.[7] INSTITUTIONAL THEORY explains the influences of macro-environment and micro-environment.

> **Table 2.3**
> **The Characteristics of Different Entry Modes**
>
> | Entry mode control | Ownership commitment | Resource |
> | --- | --- | --- |
> | Wholly owned subsidiary | High | High |
> | Joint venture | Medium | Medium |
> | Franchising or licensing | Low | Low |
>
> Source: adapted from Hill, Hwang & Kim (1990)[21]

## Institutional Theory

Institutional theory emphasizes that a retailer's INSTITUTIONAL ENVIRONMENT influences its decisions and behaviors. Here the institutional environment consists not only of REGULATORY STRUCTURES, LAWS, RULES, CULTURAL BELIEFS, NORMS, and HABITS, but also of customers, suppliers, and retailer itself. Retailers' international expansion leads to the transfer of RETAIL MANAGEMENT TECHNOLOGY across boundaries. External environment factors such as different cultural, legal, political, social, and economic issues affect retailers before making the decisions as to where, when, and how to expand into another country. Half of the top 50 companies in the Standard & Poor's 500 were established within the past 20 years, yet they began to internationalize only within the past 10 years. These companies include retailers such as Home Depot and Best Buy. As retailers increasingly consider international expansion as a viable growth option, ENTRY LOCATION, ENTRY TIMING, and ENTRY MODE remain as the cornerstones of retailers' market entry strategy. For retailers, franchising (or licensing), entering into a joint venture, and setting up a wholly owned subsidiary are the most distinct modes of entry into a foreign market. Different entry modes represent different levels of RESOURCE COMMITMENT, and control over the foreign operation. Table 2.3 show the characteristics of different entry modes.

Scott classified three dimensions of institutional systems—REGULATIVE, NORMATIVE, and COGNITIVE—representing legal, social, and psychological elements. We will focus on the influences of these three dimensions on retailers' decision making and behaviors of international expansion.[19]

## Regulative Dimension

Institutional theory emphasizes legal and political factors specific to a country. The home and the host country's legal regulations represent the strongest environmental pressures faced by retailers. For example, the Large-Scale Retail Store Law (LSRS) in Japan not only significantly impeded the expansion of foreign retailers such as Toys "Я" Us,[18] but also pushed Japanese retailers such as Isetan to expand internationally.

A country with a strong RULE OF LAW is defined as one having sound political institutions, a strong court system, and provisions for orderly succession of power. A strong rule of law represents freedom of transacting, security of property rights, and transparency of government and legal process. The rule of law is a double-edged sword. On the one hand, rules establish a stable structure to reduce uncertainty about what protection retailers can expect from the legal system of the host country. On the other hand, foreign operation restrictions can be barriers to retail firms.

Countries with a weak governance infrastructure have to improve to be able to attract foreign investment. Researchers have found that the improved legal environment is a significant determinant of the timing of entry. Retailers are more likely to establish wholly owned subsidiaries in transitional economies that have progressed furthest in institutional reform. However, if the rule of law gets more and more restrictive, such as Japan's LSRS law, retailers may lose interest in expanding or prefer entering using franchising or licensing.

## Normative Dimension

The normative dimension of the institutional theory gives priority to norms and cultural influence. For a retailer who sells consumer goods overseas, the cultural difference between consumers from the home and the host country will probably be one of the most important factors to be taken into consideration when determining the form of market entry. Toys "Я" Us expands with some adaptation to different markets. Though the overseas stores are formatted similarly to those in the United States, its merchandising selections are different. Twenty percent of its merchandising assortment is chosen for local consumer interests. For example, the Japanese market prefers porcelain dolls whereas Germans prefer wooden toys.

The cultural distance between the retailer's home country and the host country affects the choice of foreign expansion form. Many researchers support that greater cultural distance results in low control entry modes such as franchising and licensing. In the case of high cultural distance, retailers may perceive high risk of entering a foreign market and feel pressure from serving different customers. Accordingly, they may prefer not to enter the country or delay the entry. However, if the benefits to be reaped in the foreign market are high enough, retailers may still wish to enter into the country. In order to fit into the new environment, retailers may choose adaptation. Wal-Mart did not initially adapt its retail format in Argentina to the local culture. However, the retailer learned valuable lessons there to help its subsequent operations in similar situations.

Adaptation is a long-term and accumulative process. Retailers may seek local partners to accelerate the process. On the contrary, retailers are more likely to enter countries with cultures that are similar to the home market before entering countries with less similar cultures. In this case, retailers may choose wholly owned subsidiary because a high level of understanding of norms and values has already been shared; therefore, local partners are less needed.

## Cognitive Dimension

The cognitive dimension of the institutional theory explains why a global retailer such as The Body Shop always uses the same entry mode during international expansion. From a cognitive perspective, organizations possess habits and INERTIA. As

Porter notes: "Firms would rather not change. . . . Past approaches become institutionalized in procedures and management controls. . . ."[20] Retailers tend to use entry modes consistently especially when the situations are similar to the past. The primary form that the internal institutional environment can influence entry mode choice is through habit, which means that once a practice or decision has been chosen and implemented, the likelihood of alternatives being considered and used in future decisions will be reduced. Habits and inertia preclude rational changes.

Further, retailers can learn not only from their own experience but also from the experience of others, such as competitors. Strategic choice theories suggest that IMITATION can be a strategic response to competitor activities, whereby SECOND MOVERS take advantage of the fact that the risk associated with a new situation has been absorbed by the first movers. In other words, copycats can be successful too. A retailer could decide which country to enter by following other retailers. For example, China has been one of the most popular investment destinations in the world. For several years in the 1990s, China was the second-largest recipient of Foreign Direct Investment (FDI) worldwide. One motivation for foreign firms investing in China is to meet their competitors' move to China and/or forestall or reduce competition from other firms' earning markets in the same geographical area. When considering a totally unknown foreign area in which little similarity can be found in terms of previous practices, retailers will naturally avoid or try to postpone the consideration. Nevertheless, if the retailer decides to expand into this new area and has no past experience upon which to rely, the retailer may resort to other retailers' experience, that is, to mimic others' expansion behaviors.

## Risk Theory

The final theory is related to risk. Retailers will begin their international expansion in countries that are culturally similar to the home country. As they gain experience in each country or region, they move into another area. In Eroglu's conceptual model, she provides the basis for predicting which firms will seek international expansion because of organizational characteristics such as size, experience, and international orientation.[21] These characteristics reduce risk or increase knowledge which is needed to handle risk.

Risk theory also relates to how much investment a company puts into international expansion. Global retailers who seek a less risky alternative can choose to franchise. Multinational retailers who seek a less risky alternative will have to license. Franchising and licensing both require the relinquishing of company assets.

### > SUMMARY AND CONCLUSIONS

Research propositions are meant to be the beginning of a critical discussion. The ideas presented here are meant to be open for discussion and debate. This is the only way that theory can be refined and improved.

This chapter provides the conceptual overview for understanding international retailing. The study of international retailing and retail internationalization is very different from the study of international marketing and market internationalization. Retailing is geographically based. Laws regulating international trade do not

## Retail Internationalization Decision Scheme

Figure 2.4
Deciding how to internationalize takes into consideration ownership advantages and the need to internalize company information. Deciding where to go takes into consideration locational advantages.

affect international retailing, as the retailers can source in each domestic market. Instead, retailers need to be aware of intra-country business laws and regulations.

Retailers must assess their company's strengths and the relative attractiveness of continued domestic growth or international growth. They must determine whether it is important to keep company knowledge to themselves and use it for their continued international expansion.

Retailers use the macro-environment—economic, competitive, technological, social, and governmental—and the micro-environment—competitors, past experience—to make decisions about their retail offering. This decision is twofold: First, should they enter the foreign market? If they decide to enter the market, should they use a standard retail format (global), or should they adapt their retail offering (multinational)? The issues are who should go, where to go, and how to go. Such issues are also related to the decision to rely on centrally versus decentrally managed operations.

This decision framework is summarized in Figure 2.4. The macro-environment influences a country's locational advantage. A company's ownership advantages will influence whether it will internalize its secrets. This decision will, in turn, influence whether the company uses a standard format or a format that is individualized for each country.

> **KEY TERMS**

ADAPTATION

AGENCY THEORY

ASSET-BASED ADVANTAGES
BORN GLOBAL
CENTRALIZED
COGNITIVE
COLONIZING A CONCEPT
CULTURAL BELIEFS
DECENTRALIZED
DORMANT TYPE OF MANAGEMENT
DUNNING'S ECLECTIC THEORY
ECONOMIES OF SCALE
ECONOMIES OF SCOPE
ENTRY LOCATION
ENTRY MODE
ENTRY-MODE STRATEGY
ENTRY TIMING
FIRST MOVER ADVANTAGE
FOREIGN RETAIL JOINT VENTURES
FRANCHISING
GEOGRAPHIC PROXIMITY
GLOBAL IMPERIALISM
GLOBAL RETAILERS
GROSS DISPOSABLE PRODUCT (GDP)
HABITS
IMITATION
INERTIA
INTERNALIZATION
INSTITUTIONAL ENVIRONMENT
INSTITUTIONAL THEORY
JOINT VENTURE
JUMP TO ANOTHER GEOGRAPHIC AREA
LAWS
LICENSE
LICENSING
LOCATIONAL ADVANTAGES
LOGISTICS
MASTER FRANCHISORS
MULTINATIONAL RETAILER
NORMATIVE
NORMS
OPPORTUNISTIC
OWNERSHIP ADVANTAGES
PRIVATE LABEL
PSYCHIC DISTANCE
PSYCHIC DISTANCE PARADOX
PUBLICLY HELD COMPANIES
PULL FACTORS
PURE FRANCHISOR
PUSH FACTORS

REGULATIVE

REGULATORY STRUCTURES

RESOURCE COMMITMENT

RESOURCE-BASED THEORY

RETAIL KNOW-HOW

RETAIL MANAGEMENT TECHNOLOGY

RETURN ON INVESTMENT

RISK THEORY

RULE OF LAW

RULES

SATURATED THEIR HOME MARKET

SECOND MOVERS

SLACK

STAGES THEORY

STANDARDIZATION

TACIT LEARNING

TRANSACTION-BASED ADVANTAGES

VERTICALLY INTEGRATED

WHOLLY OWNED SUBSIDIARY

## > DISCUSSION QUESTIONS

1. Some theories discuss retail internationalization in terms of push and pull factors. Push factors nudge retailers out of their home markets. Pull factors attract retailers into new markets. Can you explain how each of the following reasons for internationalization could be considered push or pull factors?
   (a) mature home market-low growth potential,
   (b) need to diversify investment,
   (c) expansion at home blocked due to legislature,
   (d) possession of a unique market format,
   (e) intense competition at home,
   (f) economic downturn at home, and
   (g) first mover advantages.
2. What is the relationship between Dunning's theory of the eclectic firm and Salmon and Tordjman's theory of internationalization through global versus multinational retailers?
3. What is the relationship between locational advantage and the regulative dimension of the institutional theory?
4. Theories of retail internationalization explain retailers' expansion in terms of external and internal factors facing retailers. Analyze Dunning's theory of the eclectic firm and institutional theory; which aspects are external factors and which ones are internal factors?

## > ENDNOTES

1. Salmon, W. and A. Tordjman (1989). "The Internationalization of Retailing." *International Journal of Retailing*, 4(2): 3–16.

2. Sternquist, B. (1997a). "A Conceptual Model of Strategic International Retail Expansion." *International Journal of Retail & Distribution Management,* (25) 8, 262–268.

3. "ASDA, A Model Acquisition." (June 2001). *Chain Store Age Executive,* 77 (6) 58.

4. Pellegrini, L. (1994). "Alternatives for Growth and Internationalization in Retailing." *The International Review of Retail, Distribution and Consumer Research,* 4(2):121–148.

5. Knight, G. and T. Cauvisgil (1996). "The Born Global Firm: A Challenge to Traditional Internationalization Theory." *Advances in International Marketing,* 8, 11–26.

6. Sternquist, B. (1997b). "Internationalization of Japanese Department Stores." *International Journal of Commerce and Management,* Special Issue on Global Retailing. (7) 1, 57–73. Sternquist, B. (1998) *International Retailing.* New York: Fairchild Press.

7. Dunning, J.H. (1981). *International Production and the Multinational Enterprise.* London: Allen & Unwin.

8. Cavusgil, T.S. (1982). "Some Observations on the Relevance of Critical Variables for Internationalization Stages." *Export Management: An International Context,* M.R. Czinkota & G. Tesar, eds. New York: Praeger, 55–62.

9. Cavusgil, T.S. (1984). "Organizational Characteristics Associated with Export Activity." *Journal of Management Studies,* 21(1):3–50.

10. Eroglu, S. (1992). "The Internationalisation Process of Franchise Systems: A Conceptual Model." *International Marketing Review,* 9(5):11–39.

11. "Global Powers of Retailing" (2005). *Stores.* January, Section 2. Guy, C. (2001). "Internationalisation of Large-Format Retailers and Leisure Providers in Western Europe: Planning and Property Impacts." *International Journal of Retail & Distribution Management* 29(10): 452–461.

12. Vida, I., J. Reardon, and A. Fairhurst (2000). Determinants of International Retail Involvement: The Case of Large U.S. Retail Chains. *Journal of International Marketing,* 8(4): 37–60. Watson, J. "China's Big Mac Attack." *Foreign Affairs.* May/June, 120–134.

13. Yip, G.S., G. Biscarri, and J.A. Monti (2000). The Role of the Internationalization Process in the Performance of Newly Internationalizing Firms. *Journal of International Marketing,* 8(3):10–35.

14. Gielens, K. and M. Dekimpe (2001). "Do International Entry Decisions of Retail Chains Matter in the Long Run?" *International Journal of Research in Marketing* 18, 235–259.

15. "French Food Retailing: Strategic Threats to Hypermarkets." (January 23, 2001). Schroder Salomon Smith Barney, in *Investext Plus.*

16. ABN AMRO HOARE GOVETT-MFK (May 20, 1997). *Carrefour-Company Report in Investext Plus.*

17. Rhee, J. and L.C. Cheng (2002). "Foreign Market Uncertainty and Incremental International Expansion: The Moderating Effect of Firm Industry and Host Country Factors." *Management International Review,* 42, 419–439.

18. Evans, J. and F. Mavondo (2002). "Psychic Distance and Organizational Performance: An Empirical Examination of International Retailing Operations." *Journal of International Business Studies,* 33, 3, 515–532.

19. Scott, W. R. and S. Christensen, eds. (1995). *The Institutional Construction of Organizations.* Thousand Oaks, CA: Sage.
20. Porter, M.E. (1990). *Competitive Advantage of Nations.* NY: The Free Press.
21. Hill, C.W., P. Hwang, and W.C. Kim (1990). "An eclectic theory of the choice of international entry mode." *Strategic Management Journal,* 11, 117–128.

# 3

# LOCATION FACTORS

## After reading this chapter, you should understand

> Five macro-environment elements and why the macro-marketing environments affect a retailer's decision to enter foreign markets.

> Four major types of competitive environment.

> Four major types of legal systems.

> Four factors of production.

> How the four factors of production help to explain the theory of comparative advantage and how the concepts of absolute and relative advantages relate to international trade.

## › MACRO-MARKETING DECISION-MAKING FRAMEWORK

A retail company does not have control over every element that affects its business. The environmental elements the company cannot control are called the macro-environment. The macro-environment consists of five sub-environments: economic, competitive, technological, social, and governmental. To gain a competitive edge, a company should monitor these environments and use the information to change the elements of the environment that *are* controllable, the micro-environment. The micro-environment consists of price, product, promotion, distribution, and management. The macro-environment is different for each country a company may consider entering. It is very important that multinational companies monitor this environment carefully.

The economic environment is an important consideration for retailers. Some countries do not allow foreign firms of any kind to operate within them. China did not open its door to foreign joint ventures until 1992. A **FOREIGN JOINT VENTURE** is a partnership between a foreign company and a local company. India still does not allow retail foreign joint ventures. The only exception is if a retailer sells only their own brand, then they can operate in India. Yaohan, a Japanese retailer, had to enter into an agreement with a Chinese retailer in order to enter China. Yaohan chose Number One Department Store, the largest retailer in Shanghai. Wal-Mart entered a joint venture with CIFRA, the largest retailer in Mexico, as a preliminary step in its planned move into that country.

### Economic Environment

The biggest consideration for a company entering a foreign market is the basis of the economic system. In a centrally planned economy, there will be little opportunity for foreign retailers to enter the market. Under this system, the government determines what merchandise will be produced and where it will be distributed. North Korea is one of the few remaining centrally planned systems. Countries such as the People's Republic of China (PRC) actually have a mixed system. The PRC is today privatizing stores that were once government owned and allowing free market retailers to operate. Russia and most parts of the former Soviet Union are undergoing similar transformations. There is a wide continuum of economic systems between socialist and capitalist countries. Most European countries and Mexico are more socialistic than the United States. In these countries, businesses must provide a high level of social welfare programs including unemployment compensation, health care, and child care. Countries such as the United States and Hong Kong are capitalistic. They give companies a free hand in conducting business within their borders.

The economic environment includes the current economic health of the area. Inflation, unemployment rates, disposable income, and savings rates have an influence on retail health and viability. Retail sales are a barometer for economic change. Consumers can postpone expenditures for nonessential purchases. Thus, when sales for nonessentials increase, it is an indicator of overall economic health.

The economic environment is important in helping a retailer assess whether a country is an attractive destination. But even if a country is identified as attractive, it may still be a difficult area to enter. Japan is a good example of a country that, before the economic bubble burst, was viewed as a very desirable destination for foreign retailers. However, the competitive environment in Japan is very intense,

## Types of Competition

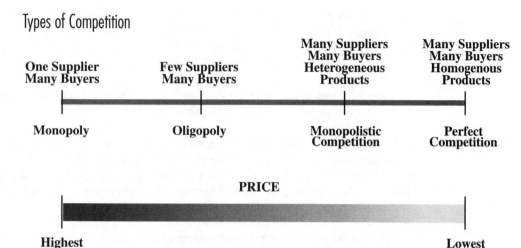

Figure 3.1

and most of the best locations are taken. In short, the economic environment said "go," but the competitive environment said "no."

## Competitive Environment

There are four major types of competitive environments: monopoly, oligopoly, monopolistic competition, and perfect competition. These types define competitive environments in terms of number of producers and number of consumers. Each competitive situation has a set of subcharacteristics related to price. The categorization is based on the number of suppliers, number of buyers, and whether the product is homogeneous or differentiated (Figure 3.1).

MONOPOLY    The first type of competitive environment is a MONOPOLY. There is one supplier and many buyers. Monopolies exist in the United States when an individual or company is awarded a patent or copyright, or when the government deems that a particular service is vital to the country. Monopolies that provide an essential service are utility companies and transportation providers, such as Amtrak, the U.S. national rail service. The United States used to have more service providers that were considered essential, such as the long-distance telephone companies.

Overall, competition reduces the price consumers pay. Monopolies will tend to charge the highest possible price because there is no competition. Monopolies that do not charge high prices are usually distinguished by their lack of service. Before market reforms in China and Russia, the state owned all the stores. The prices were set very low, particularly for necessities. However, selection and service were terrible.

OLIGOPOLY    An OLIGOPOLY is the next type of competition. In this market situation, a few companies control the market. Generally, an industry is considered an oligopoly if it has a 4/50 concentration. This means that the top four companies provide 50 percent of the market. Oligopolies do not compete on price, but, rather, on service. There is a simple explanation for this. Because there are only a few

Figure 3.1
Competition is defined by the number of suppliers and the number of buyers operating in the market. Price will be highest when there is only one producer, because there is no competition to challenge the producer on price. Monopolistic competition and pure competition have many suppliers and many buyers. The difference between these two types of competition is the product. If consumers view the products of all the suppliers as the same, it is pure competition. This type of competition will result in the lowest price possible.

competitors, comparing various offerings is very easy for consumers. If the price of one company is lower, consumers will select that alternative. Price competition will lead to price wars, which hurts the entire industry. The company with the largest market share is usually the price leader. The automobile industry and the airline industry are examples of oligopolies. Oligopolies occur most often where the industry is capital intensive and there are significant barriers to entry. BARRIERS TO ENTRY means that entering the market is difficult for new firms.

MONOPOLISTIC COMPETITION    In MONOPOLISTIC COMPETITION, many suppliers and many sellers are in the market. The products provided by suppliers are considered different from each other by buyers. By providing a HETEROGENEOUS PRODUCT—that is, one that consumers view as different from their competitors'—the companies can charge a higher price.

PERFECT (PURE) COMPETITION    PERFECT COMPETITION also has many suppliers and buyers; however, consumers view the products as identical. Agricultural products are a good example of this type of competitive environment. When we go into a grocery store, we generally do not specify that we want to buy Farmer Brown's milk. Milk is just milk. In perfect competition, price will be a perfect interplay of supply and demand. The lowest price will be found in this competitive environment.

The differences between monopolistic and perfect competition most often confuse people. Consider the purchase of bananas. Usually when we go to a grocery store to buy bananas, we just find an attractive bunch and purchase it. However, one consumer might notice a little sticker on a bunch that says "Chiquita Bananas." The well-known advertising jingle runs through that person's mind. "I'm Chiquita Banana and I'm here to say. . . ." If this consumer buys the Chiquita bananas, he or she has moved from a situation of perfect competition to one of monopolistic competition. By considering Chiquita bananas superior, or at least more desirable, the consumer may be willing to pay a higher price. The product—bananas—is no longer perceived as identical, but as heterogeneous.

## Technological Environment

The technological environment consists of equipment and infrastructures that make retailing more efficient and profitable. This will greatly aid the development of sophisticated retailing information systems (RIS).

In 1992, I visited one of the first government-owned supermarkets in Shanghai. The PRC had a problem with power failures. This does not bode well for industries that depend on refrigeration units or computer usage. When supermarkets first opened, they sold primarily staples, packaged merchandise, not refrigerated or frozen food. Shortly after this pioneering supermarket opened in Shanghai, it installed a large chest freezer for frozen meat. I asked the store owner about this, knowing that most Chinese did not have freezer space in their homes. The manager said the frozen meat was considered a novelty. People bought the frozen meat, took it home, thawed it out, and cooked it. The supermarket also had computers at the checkout lanes, with scanning capability. However, the scanning devices were not hooked up. The computers were used like old-fashioned cash registers, and as a place to store the money. Although these checkout clerks used the computers to add up the bill,

**Photo 3.1**
These small shops in Damascus, Syria, are located in permanent store locations, overflowing into the street. The shops are barely large enough for one customer; the owner parks himself outside. *Courtesy of the United Nations.*

sales clerks in department stores generally still use an abacus. They can add as quickly with an abacus as they can with a calculator.

Sometimes governments help promote technological adaptations. The Chinese government played a role in increased computer use. They invested large sums of money to promote the installation of broadband wire. One of the most important technological advances required for modern retailing systems is an up-to-date packaging system. As a country begins to develop economically, retailers begin to use more self-service-oriented displays. Packaging protects products from consumers unaccustomed to self-service. At later stages of economic development, packaging plays a role in making the product more attractive and less perishable.

## Social Environment

The social environment for retailing is very important. In some cultures, shopping is a woman's major activity. Days filled with selecting food and other items for the family's needs legitimize a wife's position outside the home. Family life in Ecuador follows this pattern. A homemaker spends her day selecting ingredients for the evening meal. As she goes about her shopping, she exchanges news and information with the shopowners and other shoppers. The marketplace thus serves a variety of important functions; it is not simply a place to obtain products.

There was a time when women in the United States loved to shop. Shopping was considered a pleasurable way to spend leisure time. I do not know of any professional woman who still feels this way. Today's working women and mothers look for places where they can get in and out quickly and conveniently. Women want to reduce the time they spend shopping so they can maximize their time with family and friends. Retailers are now struggling to come up with ideas that will make shopping fun again.

Even teenagers, once called "mall rats," are turning up their noses at mall environments. Malls are becoming "uncool." Tower Records company, for one, has adopted a strategy of avoiding mall locations, focusing instead on freestanding locations in shopping neighborhoods. Tower is anticipating that its target market, teenagers and young adults, are looking for a less sanitized shopping environment than the typical mall.

## Governmental Environment

The last type of macro-environment is the governmental and legal system. A legal system applies only within a specific country. No country has the authority to dictate to another country what is legal and what is illegal. No supreme judicial body solves the legal problems of the world. Although the World Court considers grievances of its member countries, the court has no authority or ability to intervene.

There are four major types of legal systems: code law, common law, Islamic law, and Marxist law. Most countries allowing foreign ownership of retailing are either code law or common law countries. Countries with Islamic law and Marxist law systems discourage exposure to outside influences.

CODE LAW countries require that every action fit within a preexisting law. France and Italy are examples of code law countries, in which registration determines ownership. Tradition, past practices, and legal precedence influences a COMMON LAW country's decisions. Common law changes as society changes. Countries that were once under the British legal system are likely to be common law countries. The United States, Great Britain, Canada, and Australia are common law countries. In a code law country, a man and a woman would need to be formally married to be protected by joint property rights. The marriage certificate is their registration of the relationship. In common law countries, if a man and a woman live together for a period, functioning as husband and wife but never formally marrying, they can be considered married. If they separate, both parties can sue for ownership of property. This is where we get the term "common law wife." Common law is also the basis for palimony suits.

Have you ever heard the saying, "Possession is nine tenths of the law"? This phrase also has its basis in common law. Suppose my neighbor put up a fence between our two properties. If the fence were two feet onto my property but I did not say anything about it for several years, I could lose my ownership rights to that land. My neighbor could make the claim that I knowingly allowed him to claim those two extra feet of property. Prior use establishes ownership under common law.

In a code law country, patents and copyrights are determined by registration. In a common law country, patents and copyrights are determined by the party that can prove it had the idea first. "Red-Tape Traumas" (Box 3.1) illustrates how governmental regulations affect business in the "Big Three" countries: the United States, Japan, and Germany.

ISLAMIC LAW is based on interpretation of the Koran. This type of legal system is found in Pakistan, Iran, and other Islamic countries. Islamic law prescribes a total

**Box 3.1**
**Red-Tape Traumas**
*By Bob Davis, Peter Gumbel, and David P. Hamilton.*

You think the government's on your back? Just look at Big Government through the eyes of discount retailers in the world's Big Three economies.

In Recklinghausen, in Germany's industrial Ruhr, Allkauf SB-Warenhaus GmbH has struggled to build a store for 15 years. The discounter owns the land, but that doesn't matter much. Local authorities can—and do—bar new stores if they believe existing ones will suffer. Even at best, it takes about five years to get authorization. And if a community opposes a store, Allkauf Chairman Eugen Viehof says, "there's no use even trying."

In the city of Saga on Japan's southernmost island of Kyushu, Mr Max Corp. has spent three years persuading more than 20 farmers to sell their land and petition the government to rezone it for commercial use. Next come at least 18 months of haggling with local merchants who legally can demand concessions when new stores open nearby. Mr Max expects to open its new outlet by early 1997, but to placate opposition will almost certainly have to shrink the store's planned size at least 20% and pay inflated membership fees to a local trade association.

In Abilene, Kan., Duckwall-Alco Stores Inc. can act quickly. It sneaks into small Midwestern towns and quietly takes options on property. only then is the local mayor contacted. "I say, 'We're a discounter and want to move into your town,'" says John Hedeen, Alco's vice president for real estate. "There's silence on the line. They think, 'My God, this will ruin the town.'" But if the property is already zoned commercial the town can do little. (Eventually, most towns wind up welcoming the stores and the new jobs.)

**The American Advantage**

Most businesses around the world complain about red tape, often with good reason. But a comparison of regulatory burdens in the U.S., Japan and Germany shows that while many American businesses have valid complaints, they generally have it much easier than their foreign counterparts. "If you look at the details of the system, few people in the U.S. would substitute the Japanese or German economies for their own," says Edward Hudgins, director of regulatory studies for the libertarian Cato Institute in Washington.

Each nation's regulations reflect and reinforce its brand of capitalism—predatory in the U.S., paternal in Germany and protected in Japan—and its social values. It's easier to open a business in the U.S. than in Germany because Germans value social consensus above risk-taking, but it's harder to hire people because Americans worry more about discrimination lawsuits. It's easier to import children's clothes in the U.S. than Japan because Japanese bureaucrats defend a jumble of import restrictions, but it's harder to open bank branches across the U.S. because Americans strongly defend state prerogatives.

Although global competition makes many industries around the world resemble their rivals, business conditions on their home turfs vary strikingly. Government rules in the Big Three economies affect managers, workers and customers of discount chains, for example, very differently, with Germany's many regulations pushing prices of most goods much higher than in the U.S. and even Japan.

**A Hovering Presence**

Retailing has yet to become a global business like the auto industry, even though the three retailers sell generally similar merchandise. One big influence on each of these chains isn't a government agency at all but the world's largest retailer: Wal-Mart Stores Inc. Alco's strategy is run-and-hide, opening stores—typically with 18,000 square feet—in towns with fewer than 5,000 people. It figures Wal-Mart won't bother with such small markets, and it feels safe so long as no Wal-Mart is within about 30 miles.

In Germany and Japan, where retail consolidation lags behind that in the U.S., Allkauf and Mr Max dream of becoming the next Wal-Mart. Allkauf wants to emulate Wal-Mart's electronic

*continued*

**Box 3.1** *Continued*

scanners and computerized inventory controls to cut costs. Its stores usually have at least 50,000 square feet. Mr Max wants to copy Wal-Mart's mega-size, opening 100,000-square-foot stores in a format it calls "Hyper Mall Merx"—a U.S.-style shopping center anchored by a Mr Max and a supermarket and including a dozen small retailers.

Of the three discount chains, Moenchengladbach-based Allkauf is by far the largest, with sales of $2.55 billion in its latest fiscal year and 9,000 employees. Fukuoka-based Mr Max's sales totaled $588.3 million; it has 518 permanent employees and more than 500 part-timers. Alco, of Abilene, rang up sales of $242.1 million and has 3,500 employees. Allkauf, which is closely held, doesn't report net income; Mr Max earned $11.7 million and Alco $4.1 million in their latest years.

In a store's day-to-day operations, the hand of government is nearly invisible in the U.S. Alco stores open every day except Thanksgiving, Christmas and Easter and stay open as late as they choose, though 8 p.m. is usually late enough for customers on the prairie. Each season, the stores feature a sale in the center aisle—of Halloween candy, of Christmas ornaments, of lawn furnishings in spring.

Germany, though, has a welter of rules, some dating to the Kaiser's era, limiting store hours and competition. That gives store clerks regular hours and helps Allkauf's smaller rivals but inconveniences customers. Allkauf stores can be open only $68\frac{1}{2}$ hours a week and must close at 6:30 p.m. on weekdays and at 2 p.m. on Saturdays. Sunday shopping is forbidden. At Allkauf's Moenchengladbach store, the crush of shoppers is unbearable on Friday evenings and Saturday mornings; the rest of the week, the store is fairly quiet.

Meanwhile, under a Hitler-era "rebate law," German stores can hold full-scale "sales" only twice a year, usually in January and late July. Even then, they can't discount food. The rules are enforced by regulatory cops from the industry-run Central Institute for the Combating of Unfair Competition, which fielded 20,000 complaints about violations in 1994. There's talk in parliament of easing the restrictions, but so far nothing has changed. "Every structure must have rules ensuring order so as not to hurt the rights of others," says Reiner Muenker, the institute's deputy director.

### Forced 'Holidays'

At first glance, Japan seems a shoppers' paradise by comparison. Mr Max usually can stay open until 8 p.m. But to placate smaller retailers, Japanese law requires it to take 24 days of "holiday" a year, closing its stores twice a month for no other reason.

And Mr Max faces restrictions that would appall a U.S. retailer. It can't give discount coupons, for fear of violating laws designed to protect consumers from "confusion." Moreover, the government's antitrust watchdog, the Fair Trade Commission, forbids it to discount such copyrighted products as compact disks, books and magazines. (Mr Max offers a 10% break on CD purchases anyway but doesn't advertise it so as not to draw fire.)

Mr Max faces one of its toughest government burdens when importing goods, which it needs to do to keep prices low. Motioning toward the kitchenware in a store near corporate headquarters in Fukuoka, Yoshiaki Hirano, Mr Max's 37-year-old president, sounds as frustrated as U.S. trade negotiators describing Japan's barriers.

Japanese customs officials once decreed that each carton of Thai-made plastic food containers must be tested six times, once for each of three different-size containers and their lids. So Mr Max decided to buy from a domestic wholesaler and now charges about $3.45 a container. "If we could have imported, we could sell for maybe one-third or one-fourth what the Japanese consumer pays now," Mr. Hirano says.

Another time, Japan's health authorities held up a shipment of American-made baby-size T-shirts because they contained too much Formalin, a chemical the ministry claims causes skin disease. Mr Max eventually gave up on that issue, too. "We're just asking them, 'If it's good enough for a U.S. child, why can't we sell it here?'" says Toshio Yamamoto, Mr Max's merchandising manager.

Other rules rankle, too. Japanese fire codes were designed for cramped, multi-story buildings. So, Mr Max must install fire shutters that lower automatically to contain a fire, even though fires wouldn't spread vertically in its big single-story stores. The codes also require an exit at the end of each aisle. Mr Max builds the doors but then, despite the local inspectors, puts shelves and products in front of them. In all, Mr Max calculates that the requirements add 30% to construction costs.

In the U.S., Alco wrestles with liability laws. Alco won't sell exercise equipment or child carseats unless the supplier carries as much as $5 million in liability insurance. And the retailer won't buy property unless the owner certifies that any environmental mess has been cleaned up. That's necessary, Alco executives say, because under U.S. law retailers can be sued for problems arising from the goods they sell or the property they buy even if they didn't create the problems.

Alco also faces tough antidiscrimination laws—and U.S. commitments to a multiethnic society that are lacking in Germany and Japan. Alco gives store managers a list of questions they can't ask job applicants: Don't ask a woman if she wants to be called Miss, Mrs. or Ms., don't talk about "mother tongue," and don't ask where an applicant was born. Such questions, Alco worries, could be used in a lawsuit by someone rejected for a job.

In the U.S., of course, an employer would be especially leery about asking a job applicant about religious preferences, even if the question might seem appropriate. But in Germany, employers don't have a problem: A person's religion is listed on work papers because, by law, German churches get a slice of income-tax revenue, and the tax authorities need to know which denomination should receive the money.

### Minimum Wages

Even more critical for Alco are minimum-wage levels. Its clerks and cashiers make the federal minimum of $4.25 an hour. Department supervisors earn $6 an hour. None get health insurance. Yet in rural Kansas, where four-bedroom houses sell for $50,000 and jobs are scarce, Alco often has five applicants for every opening. The stores frequently hire mothers who work part time while their children are in school. Alco worries that the government will raise the minimum wage by 25 cents an hour, which, the company calculates, would have reduced last year's $6.7 million pretax earnings by $912,000—about 15%.

Alco's mix of cheap wages, cheap land and cookie-cutter buildings helps it keep prices low by international standards. A gallon of Alco paint, for instance, costs about $12; Allkauf's and Mr Max's equivalents cost about $60. A 25-inch Magnavox color television set goes for $399 at Alco, compared with the $570 Allkauf charges for a 25-inch Condor and the $468 Mr Max charges for a 25-inch Sharp. Alco isn't always the cheapest, though. The Japanese chain sells Ma Montre brand jeans for $14.88, Alco sells Rustler jeans for $14.99, and Allkauf sells Red Baron jeans for $36.

Germany's regulatory system is designed to keep peace between labor and management even if consumers pay more. Through its collective-bargaining system, clerks at Allkauf and throughout German retailing earn the equivalent of $16 an hour and get six weeks of vacation. Forget about firing them. Unions have a major say in setting severance pay. When Allkauf closed a Hanover store, it ended up paying just over $20,000 to each of its 100 employees there. When Alco closes a Midwest store, by contrast, it pays no severance. Alco helps workers fill out unemployment-compensation forms, gives them a letter of thanks and asks whether they are willing to move to another location.

The Japanese minimum wage isn't a problem for Mr Max, which pays part-time employees about $6.60 an hour, some 10% above the local minimum wage. After adjusting for Japan's steep cost of living, which is almost twice that of the U.S., the part-timers earn less than Alco wages. Mr Max's career (or "lifetime") employees, all university graduates, start at about $32,000 a year, roughly as much as a veteran Alco store manager. Japanese workers benefit from a national social-security system that provides health care and a small pension, although they must make income-based contributions; career employees get more generous company-sponsored health and pension plans, plus a chance at rapid advancement.

No rules prevent Mr Max from laying off career workers, but Mr. Hirano says he wouldn't do so for fear of damaging the company's reputation among college seniors. In addition, the

*continued*

**Box 3.1** *Continued*

Labor Ministry scrutinizes all firings for cause and weighs in when its investigators think that a company acted unjustly. The ministry is known for leaning quietly on employers to prevent layoffs.

While the German regulatory system is virtually immovable, Japan is slowly loosening its rules. For years, Japan's Large-Scale Retail Store law made opening new stores nightmarish. Now, Mr Max owes its growth to 1990 changes that facilitated expansion. Local retailers can't stop big stores from opening, though they can still insist on restrictions.

Mr Max usually has to scale back the size of planned stores to win their approval, sometimes as much as 70%. Once, in Saga, merchants even made it promise *not* to close one of its older consumer-electronics stores in a nearby shopping center. They feared for their own businesses if it pulled out.

Now Mr Max can co-opt some opposition by opening mallsize retailing centers. "We're in a position to ask [local retailers] to join us," says Mr. Hirano, who once worked as a New York investment banker. With greater leverage, Mr Max can open stores faster. It started budding its latest Hyper Mall Merx only two years after buying the property—slow by U.S. standards but fast compared with the nearly eight years Mr Max needed to get approval in the town of Kasuga, near Fukuoka.

For Allkauf, German unification was a breakthrough that allowed it to expand in ways impossible in West Germany. Federal authorities were so eager to provide goods for people to buy that they waived most store-opening rules in East Germany. And East Germans were so starved of goods that, for several years, they bought like crazy, often on credit. Allkauf's revenues grew 25% during those years.

Neither Japan nor Germany, though, is likely to match one advantage of the U.S. regulatory system: A company can start over. In 1989, crushed by debt and too much competition from Wal-Mart and Kmart Corp., Alco filed for bankruptcy protection. All three nations have bankruptcy laws, but they are used more extensively in the U.S., where business failure isn't considered a moral disgrace.

Over the next two years, Alco negotiated to repay its unsecured creditors, settling for nine cents on the dollar, and devised a new retail strategy. By 1991, it was out of bankruptcy proceedings. Three years later, it raised $13 million in a public stock offering. Hardly any company likes government rules, but in this case they gave Alco a second chance.

Source: *The Wall Street Journal,* (1997). December 14.

---

pattern of life for its followers. It includes issues such as property rights, economic decision-making, and types of economic freedoms. Charging interest is illegal under Islamic law. As you might expect, this makes business capitalization very difficult. Islamic banks have developed a solution. Instead of providing interest-bearing loans, a bank will purchase company stock, then sell it back to the company later for a greater amount. The difference between the purchase and resale price equals the additional charge paid as interest in non-Islamic countries.

MARXIST LAW is based on a code law system. The basic premise of Marxist law is that of socialist ownership. North Korea still uses Marxist law. The state owns all the factories, retail stores, and educational institutions. China is now operating under a mixed system, is privatizing most of what the state owned. In 1992, China changed its system to allow foreign retail joint ventures; however, no laws were written to cover these ventures. The first foreign retailers to begin moving into China were Japanese. These retailers entered China before rules were written, and some retailers have since learned that operating under Marxist law can be fraught with uncertainty. After building Yaohan, the biggest retail store in China, the first Japanese retailer to enter a joint venture in China found out that the government expected them to build a housing project for residents of the area who had been displaced by the store. From a Marxist viewpoint this expectation makes a great deal of sense, but not so to the capitalist retailers.

## Government Influences on Ownership

Governments have a major impact on retailing in areas other than the legal system. As we saw in Chapter 1, each country has laws that regulate where new stores can be opened, what hours they can operate, and what kinds of products they can sell. Recall that in Japan, the Daiten Ho (Large-Scale Retail Store Law) once made the approval process for new stores very difficult. Obtaining permission to open a store sometimes took 10 years or more. Japan has since altered this law to make the process less time consuming. The law was deregulated and finally abolished in 2000. After deregulation, foreign retailers began moving into Japan.

Governments can also force retailers operating within their country to relinquish ownership. There are four types of governmental interference with ownership: confiscation, expropriation, domestication, and nationalization.

With CONFISCATION, the government simply takes over a company, making no payment to the owners. Generally, a country confiscates property only during times of political strife. In the 1950s, the communist government took over private property in China. Several large foreign retailers, such as Wing On and Sincere, lost their retail stores in Shanghai. After property is confiscated, a government may sell the assets and then close the business. The result of confiscation is that the government gains the company assets.

EXPROPRIATION occurs when the government takes over a company but compensates the owners in some nominal way. For instance, a government that gives business owners $1 for each $100 in property value is using expropriation. The key point is that the owner does not have a choice in selling the property. By giving some token payment, however, the government can justify its actions more readily. As with confiscation, the government may dispose of the assets and then close the business. Again, the government gains the company assets.

DOMESTICATION refers to the situation in which a government forces a company to transfer ownership in the company to NATIONALS (the people who live in the country). Domestication often occurs when strong nationalistic sentiments arise over foreign ownership of a country's property. Suppose Mexico were to pass a foreign ownership law, restricting the percentage of ownership allowed by foreigners. If a company wanted to continue to operate in Mexico, it would need to sell part of its company to Mexicans. When Sears first entered the Mexican market, the company set the stage for becoming an important addition to the Mexican business environment by using a process called PREDETERMINED DOMESTICATION. That is, the company undertook domestication as part of a long-term market strategy. Predetermined domestication includes four dimensions: (1) selling equity in the company at a fair market price; (2) including nationals in middle and upper management positions, not just in low level positions; (3) purchasing merchandise from the host country; and (4) including host country suppliers in the company's global operations. By undertaking predetermined domestication, a company is insuring itself against government-forced domestication. If domestication occurs gradually, it can be beneficial to the company.

NATIONALIZATION occurs when the government takes over the ownership of a business and operates it as a government institution. Generally, nationalization occurs throughout an industry, not just on a company-by-company basis. Governments nationalize industries under the guise of protecting the national welfare of the country. The Canadian government nationalized the railroads in Canada in 1881 to bring all ownership under one domain. In the 1950s, as mentioned earlier, the Chinese government nationalized all industry, bringing all property and business ownership under the domain of the People's Republic of China.

The international macro-marketing environment includes economic, competitive, technological, social, and government environments. This environment cannot be controlled by the retail company, but the company can monitor this environment and use it for decision-making.

## › FACTORS OF PRODUCTION

Theories of international trade focus on explaining trade flows. The basic determinants of what a country will make are called factors of production. There are four factors of production: land, labor, capital, and entrepreneurship. In effect, these factors are for countries what personal assets are for people. One person may be very intelligent, another very athletic. These assets determine what types of jobs a person will be good at performing. In the same way, if we know how a country is endowed with respect to land, labor, capital, and entrepreneurship, we can predict what it will efficiently produce. Understanding the four factors of production will also help us to understand the theories of internationalization discussed later in this chapter and the motivations for countries to form multinational markets, discussed in Chapter 7.

## Land

The land factor refers to natural resources. Agricultural areas, forests, rivers, and oil reserves are all considered part of the land factor. Canada, Russia, China, and the United States are examples of countries that have an abundant supply of land resources. Japan, which has heavily populated and untillable areas, illustrates a weak supply of land.

Countries with a strong factor of production in land tend to be self-sufficient. Their economic base derives historically from agriculture. Without a strong agricultural base, a country is forced to engage in international trade to obtain the resources needed for production. Countries with a strong land factor of production can adopt isolationist views; those without land cannot.

Countries with a weak land factor will try to protect land from development. Germany is a good example of a country that has enacted restrictive retail development laws to retain its green spaces. Large-scale stores are restricted to urban areas. This limits the introduction of certain retail formats, such as warehouse clubs, that require a vast expanse of land.

## Labor

Labor as a factor of production does not refer to the skilled labor force, but rather to unskilled and semiskilled workers. Countries with a low minimum wage are considered strong in this factor. Less-developed countries generally have a stronger supply of labor because their minimum wage is low. However, they sometimes camouflage the true labor rate because of high social welfare costs associated with doing business in their country. In Mexico, for instance, the minimum wage is about $0.70 per hour. However, government-mandated worker benefits nearly triple the actual wage.

Countries with a strong labor factor will attract labor-intensive industries such as apparel manufacturing. The production of apparel moves from one geographical region to another as the costs of labor increase with economic development.

Countries can attract some retailers such as large department stores with lower cost labor. In Hong Kong, department stores imported workers from mainland China because they could pay them lower wages. Service industries flourish where there is a large disparity between the rich and the poor. The rich can afford to hire; the poor are needed as the service providers. Fast-food retailers have typically hired teenagers to work in their operations. A few years ago, companies like McDonald's and Burger King had difficulty finding teenage employees in wealthy U.S. communities, where teenagers viewed their time as more valuable than the wage paid by the fast-food retailers. The companies solved the problem by recruiting retired workers who wanted only a supplementary income.

## Capital

Capital refers to money, machinery, and infrastructure. Countries with these resources are considered strong in this factor. The United States and Germany are examples of countries that have a strong factor for capital. Because both are considered safe countries in which to invest, they have more resources to lend to entrepreneurs. The capital resource is generally stronger in more developed countries.

United States and Germany are considered "safe" because they have stable political systems and currencies that do not fluctuate wildly. For many years, Brazil was known as a country with an unstable economic environment. Inflation was so high that prices had to be changed daily in stores. Investors did not see the Brazilian economy as a stable place to put their capital.

## Entrepreneurship

Entrepreneurship refers to creative management and ideas; that is, how people solve problems and look for opportunities. Entrepreneurship as a factor of production does not simply refer to small business management, as we often use the term. Small business management is a part of this factor, but not the whole factor. One of the major exports of the United States is management, reflecting the country's strong factor in this area. Germany is another country with strong abilities in entrepreneurship. Particularly in retail innovations, France has also shown strong entrepreneurship. The French were the first to develop hypermarkets, a retail format that they have transferred successfully to other countries.

Industries are often described as being labor intensive or capital intensive. The apparel industry is an example of a labor-intensive industry. The basic unit of production is the sewing machine. Increasing output means adding more workers. Labor-intensive industries generally have diseconomies of scale. With ECONOMIES OF SCALE, as an organization gets bigger, it produces things more efficiently, reducing costs. With DISECONOMIES OF SCALE, the opposite occurs. As the organization grows, it produces things less efficiently, increasing costs. Have you ever worked on a group project with many people? You may have found that the effort to get everyone working as a team was more time consuming than just doing the work yourself or with a smaller group. Often, we assume that having more people working on something will reduce the effort of everyone, but this rarely happens. Whether you have a group of four or fourteen people, it is likely that three or four people will do 90 percent of the work.

The chemical industry is capital intensive, meaning that machines, not people determine output. Capital-intensive industries generally have economies of scale. The more they produce, the lower the per unit cost.

Industries are not 100 percent labor intensive or 100 percent capital intensive. Nevertheless, it helps to have some idea about how an industry is classified. The important point is that labor-intensive industries will naturally gravitate to those countries that have a strong labor factor of production (i.e., a low minimum wage). Capital-intensive industries will gravitate to those countries that have a strong capital factor of production (i.e., money, high-technology machinery, and the infrastructure needed to support it).

These factors will help you to understand the theory of comparative advantage, the building block for other theories discussed in this book.

## > THEORY OF COMPARATIVE ADVANTAGE

International trade theory is based on the idea of comparative advantage. Understanding this idea is important in determining which countries will initiate and welcome contact with the world. Some countries choose to remain isolated from other countries. For many years, China, one of the greatest civilizations in the world, rejected trade with other countries. Japan kept its doors closed until forced, literally at gunpoint, to accept trade with outsiders. Today, North Korea has little interaction with the rest of the world.

The ideas of absolute and relative advantage help to explain how and when we expect international trade to develop.

### Absolute and Relative Advantage

Suppose you know a surgeon who also loves to do woodworking. If he spent his day doing surgery, he could make $4,000 a day. If he concentrated on making cabinets, he could make $1,000 a day. Even if both of those figures are greater than what other surgeons or other woodworkers could make, it is still in his best interests to focus on what will give him the greatest economic return—surgery—and have someone else do the cabinetmaking. The fact that this person can make more than others in either category means he has an absolute advantage.

**Table 3.1**
**Comparison of Country X and Country Y Production of Textiles and Wine**

| | Production Per Day | |
| --- | --- | --- |
| | **Cotton Textiles** | **Wine** |
| Country X | 5,000 yds (in millions) | 4,000 bottles (in thousands) |
| Country Y | 3,000 yds (in millions) | 1,000 bottles (in thousands) |

In international trade, a country that can produce things more efficiently than its trading partners has an ABSOLUTE ADVANTAGE. In the example provided in Table 3.1, the United States can be seen to produce both beef and wine more efficiently than China. It has the absolute advantage over China. For the most efficient trade, the country with the absolute advantage should produce what it is more difficult for its trading partner to produce. In this example, the United States should produce wine and China should produce beef. This is called RELATIVE ADVANTAGE. The idea of relative advantage applies when a country produces what it can make the most money selling, and trades with other countries for other goods. In effect, the country is focusing its production efforts on what will give it the greatest overall gains.

Let's expand on the preceding example. Suppose China is considering trade alternatives with Mexico. Both countries can produce footwear and cotton textiles. If China devotes all of its resources to producing footwear, it can produce six million pairs of shoes a year. If it devotes all of its resources to producing cotton textiles, it can produce 10 million yards of cotton textiles. If Mexico concentrates its resources in the same way, it can produce three million pairs of shoes or eight million yards of cotton textiles. In this situation, China has the absolute advantage. It can produce both shoes and cotton textiles more efficiently than Mexico. However, it can still be in China's best interests to focus its production efforts on the product that is harder for Mexico to produce—in this case, shoes.

Relative advantage depends on one's strengths and the strengths of one's trading partners. Some countries do everything well. Maybe they have large amounts of each factor of production and can choose to produce whatever they want. Even in this situation, there is good reason for countries to specialize, producing the products that are more difficult for other countries to produce and then trading for other products. This idea is referred to as the SPECIALIZATION OF LABOR.

## ❯ OTHER FACTORS INFLUENCING INTERNATIONAL TRADE

The theory of comparative advantage explains how countries choose what they will produce. We can relate this theory to the ideas about factors of production discussed earlier, the elements of land, labor, capital, and entrepreneurship that each country possesses in different degrees. Each type of industry has different requirements for production efficiency. As previously mentioned, apparel manufacturing requires labor as a factor of production; as a result, the apparel manufacturing industry has moved, over the years, to countries that have low-cost labor. Once the United States had a healthy apparel manufacturing industry. However, as wages increased in the United States, other low-wage countries became more attractive locations for apparel production. First, production moved to Japan. Then, as wages increased in Japan, production moved to Korea. As wages increased in Korea, production moved to the People's Republic of China. Now the apparel industry is located in areas with lower labor costs than China—Sri Lanka, for instance. Each geographical move is prompted by the need to find low-cost labor, the basic factor of apparel production.

Of course, government officials did not one day suddenly suggest, "Well, it's time to switch from apparel manufacturing, which is labor intensive, to computer software production, which is entrepreneurship intensive." Instead, a natural trend became apparent in the country's trade relations. When an industry begins to gather trade deficits, analysts know the industry is no longer competitive. Countries facing this situation have two options: they either allow the natural flow of trade to continue, or they attempt to build trade barriers to reduce the natural trade flow.

Countries restrict natural trade flows by imposing tariffs. A TARIFF is a tax placed on imported goods. This tax is added to the cost of these goods, making them more expensive. When a country puts tariffs on imported merchandise, it makes the people who buy that merchandise pay higher prices. Essentially, these people pay to support the domestic industry.

There are three types of tariffs: specific, ad valorem, and combination. A SPECIFIC TARIFF is a certain dollar amount added to each product. For instance, if shoes have a $2 specific tariff, $2 is added to the cost of each imported pair of shoes. Specific tariffs encourage importers to ship more expensive merchandise. A $2 tariff is 20 percent of a $10 pair of shoes, but only 10 percent of a $200 pair of shoes. An AD VALOREM TARIFF is a percent of the value of the imported goods. A 10 percent ad valorem tariff on a $10 pair of shoes would be $1. A 10 percent ad valorem tariff on a $30 pair of shoes would be $3. A COMBINATION TARIFF adds together a specific and an ad valorem tariff. You might have a combination tariff of $2 plus a 10 percent ad valorem tariff. For a $40 pair of shoes that would be $2 + $40(.10) = $6.

QUOTAS are a numerical restriction on the amount of merchandise that can enter a country. Countries allocate quotas to other countries as part of negotiated trade agreements. For instance, the United States might tell Equador that it can ship 500,000 pairs of shoes to this country. After that level is reached, any additional shoes shipped to the United States must be held in storage until the next quota period. Quotas increase the price of products because they restrict supply. The smaller the supply, the higher the price.

Both tariffs and quotas are regressive. By this we mean they hurt lower-income people proportionately more than higher-income people. Particularly with products such as apparel, low-income people buy more low-cost import products. For many years, the U.S. government protected the apparel industry because that industry employed many people. Only in the past 15 years has the government phased out its protection program. Similarly, France and Japan have a long history of restricting agricultural imports. They do this to protect their farmers from competition that might put them out of business. The purpose of the new worldwide governing policy for trade, the World Trade Organization, is to reduce trade restrictions. When countries join this organization they make a commitment to keep their doors open to trade.

Governments also use currency exchange to reduce imports. CURRENCY EXCHANGE is the rate at which one country buys and sells another country's currency. Each day in *The Wall Street Journal,* you can find a chart that tells what the currencies from around the world are worth. Traders from around the world buy and sell currencies every day. However, countries also maintain an official currency exchange for the exchange of goods and services between countries. Governments can keep this official currency rate artificially low to discourage imports. If the dollar exchange rate is low, consumers will need more dollars to purchase foreign merchandise. Let me give you an example. When I first started going to Japan in 1985, $1 purchased nearly 200 yen. Today, the dollar purchases only 112 yen. The same is true when products are exported from Japan to the United States. If the dollar is low, it costs more dollars to buy Japanese products. This makes them seem expensive relative to other domestic products.

Governments always want to show a FAVORABLE BALANCE OF TRADE, which means that one exports more than one imports. As we just saw, by keeping the official value of the dollar low, the United States can discourage imports by making those imports more expensive. Keep in mind that the value of the dollar is different for each currency in the world. You can use the accompanying chart from *The Wall Street Journal* to determine the value of the U.S. dollar in comparison to other world currencies. Currency exchange is a relative economic indicator, though. The number of dollars needed to buy yen has no bearing on the number of dollars needed to buy British pounds.

## > WORLD TRADE ORGANIZATION

Tariffs and quotas will probably never go away, but the WORLD TRADE ORGANIZATION (WTO) is setting the stage for removing these obstacles to trade. The WTO deals with the rules of trade between nations at a global level. It is an organization whose primary purpose is to liberalize trade. It is a forum for governments to settle trade disputes. It operates a system of trade rules.

The WTO originated out of a set of negotiations associated with the 1986–94 trade negotiations called the Uruguay Round, and under earlier negotiations under the General Agreement on Tariffs and Trade (GATT). The WTO began officially on January 1, 1995. The WTO is currently conducting new negotiations under the "Doha Development Agenda" launched in 2001 . . . but continuing.

The agreements provide the ground rules for international commerce. They are contracts, binding governments to keep their trade policies within agreed limits. The goal is to provide a secure environment, without unexpected changes, for producers of goods and services, exporters, and imports to conduct business.

A basic premise of WTO is trade without discrimination. All trading partners are treated equally, that means that if France negotiates a more favorable treatment of retailing in China, than the United States did, the United States gets equal access to this more favorable agreement. I had a personal example of this. When I was meeting with a high ranking Chinese official, we were discussing China's coming opening of the retail sector, he said, "The United States was not nearly as demanding in the retail sector as France. The United States didn't seem to be concerned with Wal-Mart's ability to open more stores in China, but France was certainly concerned with enabling Carrefour to open more stores." Of course, as I already said, the best deal negotiated by any WTO member applies to all WTO members, and we call this a MULTILATERAL AGREEMENT.

Another stipulation of WTO is that foreigners and locals are treated equally. This principle of NATIONAL TREATMENT is important because governments tend to give preference to local companies. WTO bans this system. Imported and locally produced goods should be treated the same. This also extends to foreign and domestic services and to foreign and local trademarks, copyrights, and patents.

## › KEY TERMS

ABSOLUTE ADVANTAGE

AD VALOREM TARIFF

BARRIERS TO ENTRY

CODE LAW

COMBINATION TARIFF

COMMON LAW

CONFISCATION

CURRENCY EXCHANGE

DISECONOMIES OF SCALE

DOMESTICATION

ECONOMIES OF SCALE

EXPROPRIATION

FAVORABLE BALANCE OF TRADE

FOREIGN JOINT VENTURE

HETEROGENEOUS PRODUCT

ISLAMIC LAW

MARXIST LAW

MONOPOLY

MONOPOLISTIC COMPETITION

MULTILATERAL AGREEMENT

NATIONALS

NATIONAL TREATMENT

NATIONALIZATION

OLIGOPOLY

PERFECT COMPETITION

PREDETERMINED DOMESTICATION

QUOTA

RELATIVE ADVANTAGE

SPECIALIZATION OF LABOR

SPECIFIC TARIFF

TARIFF

WORLD TRADE ORGANIZATION (WTO)

## › DISCUSSION QUESTIONS

1. Give an example for each competitive situation—monopoly, oligopoly, monopolistic competition, and perfect competition.

2. We discussed Dunning's eclectic theory in Chapter 2. Explain the four factors of production and how they help apply Dunning's eclectic theory to retail internationalization.

3. Explain the five macro-environment elements. Use institutional theory to explain retail entry strategies when facing different environment situations.

4. Pick any two countries you are familiar with and practice how the absolute and relative advantages help explain the trade between them.

5. What are the elements of predetermined domestication? When would a country use this strategy?

# 4

# INTERNATIONAL CULTURE AND HUMAN BEHAVIOR

## After reading this chapter, you should understand

> Why culture affects international retailing.

> How high context and low context cultures differ in their use/ understanding of material possessions, friendship patterns, agreements across cultures and time.

> The methods by which societies teach their members to belong to their own cultural group.

> How Hofstede's cultural dimensions model helps to categorize groups of nations on four major dimensions. These theoretical dimensions of difference can be used to strategically position international retailers' offerings.

The focus of international retailing is on the marketing link that directly touches consumers. It is impossible to understand the retail system within a country without understanding the culture of that country. Culture influences what people purchase and how those items are used. Artifacts that may look the same in different countries may serve very different purposes. For instance, on my first trip to Japan, I was touring a department store in Tokyo. We were in the housewares division and I saw a big display of what looked to me like trays that Americans would use to serve breakfast in bed. The quantity of breakfast in bed trays was very large. This led me to comment to my Japanese host, "The Japanese must be very romantic, with such an emphasis on serving breakfast in bed." My host looked a little puzzled, but then explained that what I had called breakfast trays were, in fact, short-legged tables. Japanese families sit around this table with their feet down in a sunken floor unit outfitted with electrical heating. The table has a quilt over it to preserve the heat and keep everyone warm. It was not quite the use I had envisioned.

This chapter explores the ways in which culture alters our view of the world. Retailing is greatly affected by culture. In fact, most retail failures in international markets can be attributed to cultural factors.

## › DEFINING CULTURE

PRIMARY SOCIALIZATION is the term social theorists use to describe the process by which people in a society learn symbols and their meanings within that society. We use this process to classify the world around us.[1] Culture provides the kind of shared understanding among people in a society that allows them to predict and coordinate social activity. Although we "learn" culture, it is not homogeneous

**Photo 4.1**
The Japanese *kotatsu* is a low dining table. Family members sit on the floor while dining or drinking tea. When I first saw one in a department store I thought it was a breakfast-in-bed tray.

throughout society. Differences in gender, ethnicity, region, social class, and religion all influence the way in which an individual is socialized to his or her culture.

We view culture through learned behavior. The functions of what a social group does are very much the same. Food, housing, and emotional ties to others are basic requirements for all individuals; however, the way that society meets these requirements may differ significantly.

Some countries are considered MULTICULTURAL, meaning that they have several or many cultures within their borders. India, China, the United States, Canada, and South Africa are examples of multicultural countries. Other countries such as those in Scandinavia (Denmark, Norway, and Sweden) are generally considered to comprise one cultural group. This is, of course, a generalization. In the rural Swedish community of South Dakota where I grew up, one of the favorite topics of jokes and conversations was the differences between Swedes and Norwegians. The Latin American countries of Venezuela, Columbia, and Ecuador are also considered to be one cultural group.[2]

One of the simplest ways to explain group differences is through the designation high context and low context cultures. Being able to categorize countries on this dimension will help you to make many retail generalizations.

## 〉 HIGH CONTEXT AND LOW CONTEXT CULTURES

Edward Hall,[3] a noted sociologist, was the first to identify these two theoretical dimensions of culture. Hall made the distinction between cultures where meaning of individual behavior depends on the situation—HIGH CONTEXT—and those where meaning is based on the words—LOW CONTEXT. Without exchanging words, people in high context cultures can communicate quite effectively. Nonverbal exchanges occur in low context cultures too; however, the meaning is generally unintentional. Words convey most of the important meanings.

**Photo 4.2**
Restaurants in Saudi Arabia have two entrances; women, children, and families eat on one side, single men on the other side. The wall to the left of the male customer in this photo separates the two sides. The Muslim religion calls for this type of separation. *Courtesy of Amal Aswailem.*

## Contextual Background of Various Countries

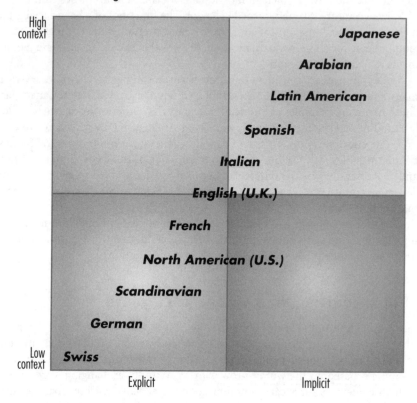

**Figure 4.1**
In high context countries, such as Japan and Saudi Arabia, the cultural context is as important as what is actually said; the speaker and the listener use a common understanding of the context. Low context countries, such as Germany and Switzerland, communicate information explicitly, with words.

Source: Cateora, P. R. (1996). *International Marketing*, Burr Ridge, IL: Irwin, p.137.

Nonverbal messages have important and intended meanings in high context cultures. To read these nonverbal messages requires a similarity of background. High context cultures teach children this communication in the family from an early age. Other social institutions such as school, religious organizations, and work continue the process. If a country has one religion, one language, and a highly coordinated educational system, this type of acculturation process is more likely.

Saudi Arabia and Japan are two of the countries rated high context. Figure 4.1 gives a distribution of selected countries on the high versus low context continuum.

In low context cultures, intentions and feelings are expressed verbally. Situations do not change the meaning of words and behavior. What you say is what you mean. This type of communication system occurs most often in countries that are multicultural and where people have different value systems. The United States, India, China, Australia, and New Zealand are countries with low context cultures.

The difference between high context and low context cultures is illustrated through what Hall called the silent languages. These languages include: space, material possessions, friendship patterns, agreements across cultures, and time. In the following discussion, AE stands for American-European cultures.

## Space

Space refers to the distance between two people having a conversation. For example, Middle Eastern men stand very close to each other when they have a conversation. This closeness would make most Americans feel uncomfortable. A visitor to shops in Middle Eastern countries will notice that they are very crowded. Merchandise is crammed into every area, and people can hardly move without bumping into each other. A Middle Eastern shop is a busy, crowded place, that would give Americans claustrophobia.

AE cultures like an organized, uncluttered look for stores. Research has shown that consumers in these cultures psychologically associate merchandise that is crammed into a store with sales. Similarly, if stores lay out sale merchandise too neatly, people are distrustful.

AE cultures like private spaces. The most prestigious offices are those that are large, spacious, and private. It is preferable to have a secretary or two who screen entrants. In contrast, in Japan, a high context culture, a person who has a private office, away from the action, is considered no longer important to the company. That person has been "put out to pasture." An important Japanese executive has his desk in the center of a large office that includes his whole department. Assistants have desks around the room. Everyone is within shouting distance. An interoffice memo is unheard of in a Japanese office system. If you want to tell someone something, you shout at him, or get up and go over to talk with him.

## Material Possessions

MATERIAL CULTURE is a term that describes the learned social meaning of possessions. Retailing is about the diffusion of material culture. Countries often limit the opening of foreign retailers because they are uncomfortable with the distribution of that culture's material objects.

Designer brand names express social status. Before the economic bubble burst in Japan, consumption of designer brands was very high. Although this trend has slowed, conspicuous consumption is still evident among the Japanese. CONSPICUOUS CONSUMPTION means that people purchase possessions to express their wealth and status.

McCracken[3] has observed that new objects have only recently taken on great value to consumers worldwide. In Europe, it was once the PATINA, or appearance of age, that made objects desirable. Silver and furniture passed down through generations held greater value than products bought new. Old wealth was seen as more desirable than new wealth. We would expect such high context cultures to place greater value on objects with family history; the family history is the object's context.

When a high context culture's material culture is threatened by a low culture's crassness, concerns about the social order become evident. Youth in developing countries who drink Coke and wear Nike shoes and Levi jeans pose a threat to the older cultural norms. This new material culture is visible for all to see, and difficult for the older generation to ignore. The increased visibility of changing consumption patterns may be one reason that foreign retailers are often barred from doing business in countries with less developed or planned economies.

## Friendship Patterns

The way that people relate to one another illustrates cultural patterns. Friendships and even marriages in the United States tend to be temporary, rather than permanent. In addition, Americans often develop immediate friendships with people. Within hours of making a new friend, Americans may reveal intimate information—the type of information that other cultures would take decades to reveal, if it were revealed at all. For this reason, people from other cultures sometimes view Americans as friendly but shallow. Many foreigners feel that Americans ask "How are you doing?" but do not really care about your answers.

Such informality is also found in the way retail salespersons address customers in the United States. Salesclerk and waitresses are quick to adopt a person's first name or refer to the person with familiar terms such as "dear" or "honey." Salespeople believe they are being helpful by giving customers advice.

Interpersonal communications in other cultures may be very different from the informal American norm. In the seventies and eighties, salespeople in China usually called a customer "comrade." In the 90s, they usually called a customer "Miss" or "Mister." They usually do not call customers by their first names. Even the patterns and methods of giving gifts differ across cultures (Box 4.1).

## Agreements Across Cultures

Low context cultures rely on contracts that list the specifics of an agreement. They expect partners to keep the specific terms of the contract. Americans have a phrase for this—"adhering to the letter of the law." High context cultures rely more on general agreement with the basic intent of the partners.

Doing business in Japan can be very frustrating for foreigners who do not understand this concept. They may spend long periods negotiating the specific details of

---

**Box 4.1**
**It's Not the Gift that Counts, but How You Present It**

Giving a gift in another country requires careful attention to culturally appropriate behavior. Here are a few suggestions:

**Japan:**
> Do not open a gift in front of a Japanese counterpart unless asked and do not expect the Japanese person to open your gift.
> Avoid ribbons and bows as part of gift wrapping. Bows as we know them are considered unattractive and ribbon colors can have different meanings.
> Do not offer a gift depicting a fox or badger. The fox is the symbol of fertility; the badger, cunning.

**Europe:**
> Avoid red roses and white flowers, even numbers, and the number 13. Do not wrap flowers in paper.
> Do not risk the impression of bribery by spending too much on a gift.

**Arab Countries:**
> Do not give a gift when you first meet someone. It may be interpreted as a bribe.
> Do not present the gift when alone with the recipient unless you know the person well. Gifts should be given in front of others in less personal relationships.

**Latin America:**
> Do not give a gift until after a somewhat personal relationship has developed unless it is given to express appreciation for hospitality.
> Gifts should be given during social encounters, not in the course of business.
> Avoid the colors black and purple; both are associated with the Catholic Lenten season.

**China:**
> Never make an issue of a gift presentation—publicly or privately.
> Gifts should be presented privately, with the exception of collective ceremonial gifts at banquets.

Source: Cateora, P. R. (1996). *International Marketing*. Chicago: Irwin, p. 109.

---

a contract only to have their Japanese partners ignore the contract once it has been signed. In Chapter 15, I discuss some specific cultural terms related to this behavior.

The Japanese use time to their advantage in contract signing. They know that Americans are impatient to get things done. Thus, the Japanese will often delay meetings until they gain favorable concessions.

## Time

In Germany, grocery stores generally close at 6:00 P.M. German salesclerks understood this to mean that no checkouts are done after that time. Although German customers line up by 5:45 to check out their groceries, at 6:00 P.M., half-filled carts will be left in the aisles or at the registers. In the United States, in contrast, although a closing time might be 10:00, it is expected that anyone who is in the checkout line by 10:00 will be served. Under a 1956 German LAW, stores had to close by 6:30 P.M.

on all weekdays but Thursday and at 2:00 P.M. on Saturday. The federal law in the mid-1990s allowed stores to remain open until 8:00 P.M. on weekdays and 4:00 P.M. on Saturdays. The law requires shops to close at 8:00 P.M. every day, while trading on Sundays is prohibited. In 2004, the upper house of the German parliament, which represents the country's states, voted to end restrictions on shopping hours. States now have the power to determine their own opening times, although it has been reported that half still plan to keep stores closed on Sundays. During the 2006 World Cup stores got a temporary ordinance ("city law") allowing shops to stay open until 10:00 P.M.

Hall has identified two types of time systems, which he calls monochronic and polychronic time. Monochronic time is based on the northern European model, in which one thing is scheduled at a time. Polychronic time is based on the Mediterranean model, which entails involvement in several things at once. The two systems are logically and empirically very distinct, and difficult to mix.[4] Polychronic time focuses on people and completion of transactions rather than adherence to preset schedules. Appointments are not considered important and are broken frequently. For polychronic people, time is less tangible; they generally do not think of time as wasted or saved.

The polychronic environment in the markets, stores, and souks of Mediterranean and Arab countries can be very frustrating for northern Europeans or Americans. The shopping atmosphere seems chaotic. Customers all compete for the attention of one clerk who is trying to wait on everyone at once. There is no apparent order, no line or number to suggest who has been waiting the longest.[4]

The same patterns can be seen at the office of an important government official in a Mediterranean country. The private office has a large reception area. Small groups of people wait here and are visited by the minister or his aides. They conduct most of the actual business outside the formal office in the semipublic setting. The official will move from group to group conferring with each in turn. For those whose problems are more difficult to solve, the minister will return again and again until a solution has been found. The minister, like the clerk in the store, is waiting on several groups at once, the essence of polychronic time.

Hall makes the point that we can relate polychromatic time to feminine lives. Think of the way a mother takes care of her family. She does not rigidly set a certain amount of time for each family member; instead, she spends a few minutes supervising one child, then moves to another child while folding the clothes and making dinner. Polychronic cultures put the emphasis on human relationships, not on schedules. Although a society may be more oriented to polychronic time or monochronic time, it may also successfully combine the two. Japan is a society that is polychronic time oriented when dealing with other Japanese, but monochronic time oriented when dealing with outsiders. The Japanese ability to combine the best of both orientations can be seen in their success in international markets.

Monochronic time is not better than polychronic time. It is just a different way of viewing the world. Societies that rely on monochronic time feel that time is theirs to be managed and controlled. Time does not have such a designation for societies that are polychronic time oriented.

The next part of this chapter focuses on the building blocks of culture. Societies build culture through product use, people's interactions with each other, art, and language. Retailing affects and is affected by each of these.

## 〉 DIMENSIONS OF CULTURE

Societies may be very different from one another. However, the basic tools a society needs to make its members a part of it are quite similar. We call these tools CULTURAL UNIVERSALS. Cultural universals include material elements, social institutions, belief systems, aesthetics, and language.

## Material Elements

Material elements are dependent on a country's infrastructure. The basic economic and technological systems available in a country affect the products that can be sold. Technological advancements are also a leading cause of cultural change.

Economics is the manner in which a society uses its capabilities and benefits from these capabilities. This includes the production of goods and services, their distribution and consumption, means of exchange, and the income derived from the creation of utilities. Material culture affects the amount demanded, the quality of products demanded, and the functions of the products.[5]

Less developed countries may not have the idea of preventive maintenance. Owning an expensive automobile that requires dealer servicing may not be an option for a person living in such a country. Owning a car that can be worked on by oneself is probably a better option.

When Russia and China used strict government planning systems, few luxury consumer goods were available to the average person. The government supported only purchases of goods that would help industrial production, not goods that would enrich consumers' lives. Under a planned economy, retailing is viewed with a disdainful eye. It is seen as a negative influence that corrupts people by creating desires for non-necessities. The value put on what others think about a person's purchase is the basis for the next section.

## Social Institutions

REFERENCE GROUPS are an important part of consumers' socialization process; they provide values and attitudes that influence and shape purchasing behavior. The family is an important reference group when children are young. Adolescents are more likely to respond to the influence of peers.

The concept of family differs throughout the world. In the United States, a family may be several unrelated single people living together. Asians are likely to consider a married couple's parents and grandparents part of their intimate family.

Three other groups of people that have an impact on consumers' decisions include change agents, opinion leaders, and gatekeepers. CHANGE AGENTS influence consumption decisions, but they are outside the person's reference group. Change agents are people with great visibility, such as politicians and actors. When a change agent uses a product, there may be a mad rush of others imitating this behavior.

OPINION LEADERS are people within a consumer's reference group who influence purchases. Opinion leaders are tastemakers at a local level. Their influence is greater than change agents.

GATEKEEPERS are individuals who have the authority to decide what consumers will purchase. Parents are gatekeepers for their younger children. They control the money and can decide what is a reasonable purchase. Retail buyers are gatekeepers.

They select the merchandise a retail store will offer. If a buyer has not selected a certain product for the store, the consumer will not have that product as a purchase alternative.

For example, after each Academy Awards ceremony, the designer clothing worn by movie stars or celebrities will be altered by some manufacturers into affordable fashions and sold in retail stores. In these cases, the movie star or celebrity is the change agent. The first people who buy and wear the fashion are the opinion leaders.

In the next section, we will consider how people are influenced by nonhuman cultural dimensions. These groups of cultural influences include religion, belief systems, superstitions, and other related world views.

## Belief Systems

*Feng Shui* is an important element in Chinese culture. It is the belief that constructed environments like buildings and homes must be positioned in harmony with the spirits. The Chinese will call in a Feng Shui expert before they begin construction on a new building. In fact, the Regent Hotel in Hong Kong altered its construction plans to improve its connections with the spirits. The Chinese also believe that man should live in harmony with and not attempt to control nature. In this culture, much of what occurs is viewed as fate. If products do not perform as they should, Chinese consumers believe it is their fault for selecting inferior products rather than the fault of the manufacturer.

Retailers need to consider such culturally linked beliefs when internationalizing. For instance, McDonald's fast-food restaurant has had to alter its standard menu to do business in India. The reason is that most Indians are Hindu, a religious group that considers cows sacred. McDonald's Indian menus now consist exclusively of non-meat items.

ETHNOCENTRISM is the tendency to consider one's own culture as superior to others. Many Americans are surprised to find that their culture is not the envy of the world. A colleague from Great Britain told me his students often remark, "Americans are so stupid." His reply was, "If they are so stupid, why are they so rich?" A Swedish colleague told me she could never live in the United States. She said, "America is such a hard society. You do not take care of your poor and elderly." Most international marketing mistakes are made because people do not put aside their SELF-REFERENCE CRITERION, the unconscious reference to one's own cultural values.

## Aesthetics

A culture's aesthetic values affect what people buy. Standards of beauty, appreciation, and meaning and various methods of artistic expression affect consumers' purchases. Objects of art also differ from society to society. As an example, Tokyo has many wonderful art galleries and I often visit museums on Sundays when I'm there. During one visit in the Ginza area, I noticed a sign for an art museum and I made a special trip, paid my admission fee, and entered the gallery. The entire museum was devoted to calligraphy scrolls, wall after wall of Japanese writing that I could not read or really appreciate. I sat on a bench for a while so my departure would not be so rapid as to be embarrassing.

Until about 75 years ago, the Chinese bound girls' feet, beginning in infancy. Small feet were considered a source of beauty. The foot-binding process is not pretty.

The toes are broken and bent under the foot. Walking becomes very difficult. Tiny bound feet gained an erotic dimension. Catching a glimpse of the space between the toes had much the same arousal factor as a glimpse of breast cleavage for today's men.

## Language

A Japanese colleague once asked me, "What is the meaning of 'Speak Lark'?" I looked at her with a puzzled expression. She pointed to a huge billboard with a picture of a blond woman enjoying a Lark brand of cigarette. The billboard's text was "Speak Lark." I told her that it did not have a real meaning. Differences in language have caused many mistakes in international marketing. Literal translations of company names and advertising themes rarely work. It is more important to translate to an equivalent idea.

Japanese has three different writing systems: hiragana, katakona, and kanji. The kanji is based on a pictorial representation of the object. The word for one tree looks like a single tree. The word for a forest is a combination of three symbols for a tree. This is quite a simple example for a very complex writing system.

Japanese advertising often features English words that have little meaning to the message being presented. The English words are included because they look attractive, or convey a Western flavor or attitude. This may seem really bizarre until you consider that American advertising often includes Japanese symbols just for decoration. When Americans see Japanese letters, they see an illustration—a symbol of another culture—not a word that has meaning.

## › HOFSTEDE'S CULTURAL DIMENSIONS MODEL

The distinction between high context and low context culture provides a means for broadly classifying cultural groups. These building blocks of culture, in turn, determine an individual's pattern of daily life. Another useful model for describing cultural groups is Hofstede's dimensions of difference. These four major dimensions can also be generalized to retail situations.

Geert Hofstede, a researcher from the Netherlands, has developed one of the most frequently used theories of cultural differences. He developed a paradigm to study the impact of national culture on individual behavior. What makes his work so unique is that he developed the model after examining the values and beliefs of 116,000 IBM employees in forty countries throughout the world. Later he expanded this study to ten other countries. Hofstede developed a typology consisting of four national, cultural dimensions through which society can be classified. These four dimensions are INDIVIDUALISM, UNCERTAINTY AVOIDANCE, POWER DISTANCE, and MASCULINITY. This typology is often used in international management. However, there are important, distinct implications for international retailing.

## Individualism

Table 4.1 summarizes the essential elements of the dichotomy between individualism and collectivism. The foundation of this dimension is I (individualism) versus we (collectivism). Hofstede did not make the transfer from these cultural dimensions

**Table 4.1**
**Hofstede's Dimension of Individualism**

| Collectivist | Individualist | Applications to Retailing and Consumer Behavior |
|---|---|---|
| In society, people are born into extended families or clans who protect them in exchange for loyalty. | In society, everybody is supposed to take care of himself or herself and his or her immediate family. | Government support for small businesses versus no government involvement. |
| "We" consciousness holds sway. | "I" consciousness holds sway. | Government control of retail sector and state ownership of stores versus individual entrepreneurs. |
| Identity is based in the social system. | Identity is based in the individual. | Status comes from employment with large, old companies versus status is given to the entrepreneur and self-owner. |
| The emphasis is on belonging to organizations; membership is the ideal. | The emphasis is on individual initiative and achievement; leadership is the ideal. | Teamwork and group achievement versus individual initiative and leadership. |
| Private life is invaded by organizations and clans to which one belongs; opinions are predetermined. | Everybody has a right to a private life and opinion. | Company has the right to know about employee's life versus separation of work and private life. |
| Value standards differ for in-groups and out-groups (particularism). | Value standards should apply to all (universalism). | Group member gives purchase rights versus all consumers have the right to purchase any products they chose. |

Source: Adapted with the author's permission from Hofstede, G. (1992). "Motivation, Leadership, and Organization: Do American Theories Apply Abroad?" In H. Lane and J. DiStefano, eds., *International Management Behavior,* 2nd Edition. Boston: PWS-Kent, pp. 98–122. Reprinted from *Organizational Dynamics,* Summer 1980. All rights reserved, Geert Hofstede.

to retailing. However, we might predict certain things about societies that are at the extremes of these two dimensions.

We would expect small businesses and entrepreneurism to flourish in individualistic societies. Greater product variety and consumption with the purpose of differentiating the purchaser from others are also predictable.

In collectivist societies, we could predict that consumers would use products to convey the status of group membership. Brand names are likely to be dominant in collectivist cultures.

## Uncertainty Avoidance

The dimension of uncertainty avoidance focuses on a society's willingness to take risks. Societies in which people avoid risks are viewed by Hofstede as high in uncertainty avoidance. Societies in which people believe in taking risks are low in uncertainty avoidance. The major dimensions of uncertainty avoidance are summarized in Table 4.2.

The Japanese place great importance on gift giving and carefully choose the type of store where they purchase a gift. The prestige of the store reduces the risk of pur-

**Table 4.2**
**Hofstede's Dimension of Uncertainty Avoidance**

| High Uncertainty Avoidance | Low Uncertainty Avoidance | Applications to Retailing and Consumer Behavior |
|---|---|---|
| Ease and lower stress are experienced. | Higher anxiety and stress are experienced. | Shopping is an enjoyable, family experience versus stressful and to be minimized. |
| Time is free. | Time is money. | Full service versus self-service as ideal. |
| Aggressive behavior is frowned upon. | Aggressive behavior of self and others is accepted. | Low-key sales approach versus hard sell. |
| A strong need for consensus is involved. | More acceptance of dissent is entailed. | Products purchased to show affiliation to the group versus products that maintain individualism. |
| Deviant persons and ideas are dangerous; intolerance holds sway. | Deviation is not considered threatening; greater tolerance is shown. | Deviance is demonstrated through thoughts and secret acts versus visible products such as clothes. |
| Younger people are suspect. | More positive feelings toward younger people are seen. | Youth as troublemakers to be monitored versus youth as important target group. |
| If rules cannot be kept, we are sinners and should repent. | If rules cannot be kept, we should change them. | Prescribed application of law versus common law applied to commercial activities. |
| Belief is placed in experts and their knowledge. | Belief is placed in generalists and common sense. | Innovations come from powerful and wealthy people versus innovations come from the common person. |

Source: Adapted with the author's permission from Hofstede, G. (1992). "Motivation, Leadership, and Organization: Do American Theories Apply Abroad?" In H. Lane and J. DiStefano, eds., *International Management Behavior,* 2nd Edition. Boston: PWS-Kent, pp. 98–122. Reprinted from *Organizational Dynamics,* Summer 1980. All rights reserved, Geert Hofstede.

chasing the gift. In Japan, a society high in uncertainty avoidance, large retailers with a long history provide the lowest levels of risk associated with a purchase. A purchase from a small retailer carries greater risk.

## Power Distance

This dimension refers to how well a society tolerates inequality. Small power distance societies believe that they should reduce inequality. Large power distance societies believe there should be an ordered inequality in the world. In this view, everyone has a rightful place, high and low, and the order protects this rightful place. The major elements of the power distance concept are presented in Table 4.3.

Malaysia, Guatemala, Panama, and the Philippines have the largest power distance; Denmark, Norway, and Sweden the smallest. In large power distance societies, power holders are entitled to privileges. Those in power are expected to look and act powerful.

**Table 4.3**
**Hofstede's Dimension of Power Distance**

| Small Power Distance | Large Power Distance | Applications to Retailing and Consumer Behavior |
|---|---|---|
| Inequality in society should be minimized. | There should be an order of inequality in this world in which everybody has a rightful place; high and low are protected by this source. | Purchases avoid the illusion of wealth and power versus conspicuous consumption and flaunting of wealth. |
| Hierarchy means an inequality of roles, established for convenience. | Hierarchy means existential inequality. | Salespeople are empowered to handle customer problems versus only upper managers can address problems. |
| Superiors are accessible. | Superiors are inaccessible. | Success of small retailers who interact with customers versus large companies in which chief executive officers are distant from consumers. |
| All should have equal rights. | Power holders are entitled to privileges. | Everyone waits in the same line to be serviced versus the powerful go to the front of the line. |
| People at various power levels feel less threatened and are more prepared to trust people. | Other people are a potential threat to one's power and can rarely be trusted. | General supervision, flexible work time versus highly rigid work schedules. |

Source: Adapted with the author's permission from Hofstede, G. (1992). "Motivation, Leadership, and Organization: Do American Theories Apply Abroad?" In H. Lane and J. DiStefano, eds., *International Management Behavior,* 2nd Edition. Boston: PWS-Kent, pp. 98–122. Reprinted from *Organizational Dynamics,* Summer 1980. All rights reserved, Geert Hofstede.

## Masculinity/Femininity

This dimension looks at how distinctly roles in society are defined. The contrast is between masculine and feminine orientations. This dimension does not relate to which of the sexes has power within the society. Rather, it is used to describe how people live their lives and what is important to them. Societies with a masculine orientation focus on assertiveness, domination, and high performance. In this orientation, money and things are important; big and fast are considered beautiful; independence is the ideal. Societies with a feminine orientation believe that there should be equality between the sexes. Quality of life is important, and interdependence is the ideal. Small and slow are considered beautiful. People in masculine societies "live to work." People in feminine societies "work to live." The major elements of these dimensions are outlined in Table 4.4.

## Combining Dimensions

A more complete profile of the dimensions of difference between nations becomes evident when two dimensions are viewed together. Figure 4.2 combines the individualism with power distance measures on a grid. It groups similar countries together in a shaded area. Most Asian and Central and South American countries cluster together in a group that embodies large power distance and low individual-

**Table 4.4**
**Hofstede's Dimension of Masculinity/Femininity**

| Feminine | Masculine | Applications to Retailing and Consumer Behavior |
|---|---|---|
| Men needn't be assertive, but can also assume nurturing roles. | Men should be assertive. Women should be nurturing. | Sex neutral products versus sex-specific products. |
| Sex roles in society are more fluid. | Sex roles in society are clearly differentiated. | Same as above. |
| Quality of life is important. | Performance is what counts. | Environmentally friendly companies versus high profit at all cost companies. |
| You work in order to live. | You live in order to work. | Retailers close during evenings and weekends versus importance of 24-hour shopping. |
| People and environment are important. | Money and things are important. | Green products versus large market share products. |
| Interdependence is the ideal. | Independence is the ideal. | Cooperatives versus corporate retailers. |
| Service provides the motivation. | Ambition provides the drive. | Long-term sustainable customer service versus high growth, short lived products. |
| One sympathizes with the unfortunate. | One admires the successful achiever. | Corporate sponsorship of community events versus separation of corporate and community goals. |
| Small and slow are beautiful. | Big and fast are beautiful. | Unique and independent businesses versus large corporations. |

Source: Adapted with the author's permission from Hofstede, G. (1992). "Motivation, Leadership, and Organization: Do American Theories Apply Abroad?" In H. Lane and J. DiStefano, eds., *International Management Behavior,* 2nd Edition. Boston: PWS-Kent, pp. 98–122. Reprinted from *Organizational Dynamics,* Summer 1980. All rights reserved, Geert Hofstede.

ism. The United States falls within a group that displays small power distance and high individualism. Australia, Germany, the Netherlands, Canada, and New Zealand are part of the U.S. group.

Masculinity and uncertainty avoidance are profiled together in Figure 4.3. The United States falls within a group in the weak uncertainty avoidance and high masculine orientation quadrant. Ireland, Germany, India, the Philippines, New Zealand, South Africa, Canada, and Australia are other countries in this group. We could predict that individuals in this group believe taking risks is important for success. They judge success by performance, power, money, and things. They live to work.

The Scandinavian countries cluster together in the weak uncertainty avoidance and high feminine orientation quadrant. We could predict that individuals in this group believe in taking risks as well. However, they judge success in terms of quality of life. People and the environment are important. They work to live, rather than letting work consume their lives.

In the next section, some of these cultural elements are put together into a model to help describe the cross-cultural process.

## Individualism and Power Distance

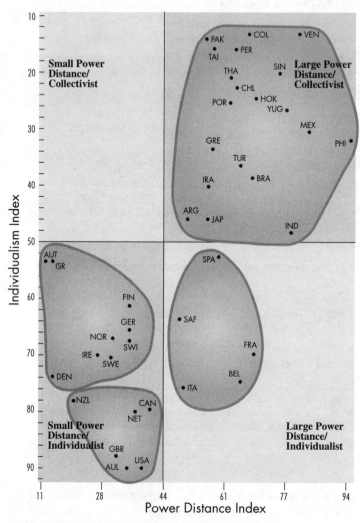

**Figure 4.2**
Hofstede's four dimensions of difference help us to understand people from various cultures. This figure indexes the power distance and the individualism dimensions. The United States, Great Britain, New Zealand, the Netherlands, Canada, and Australia fall in the small power distance/individualist quadrant. *Small power distance* refers to the belief that people are equal. *Individualist* refers to the importance of individual rather than group, or collectivist, efforts.

| | | | | | |
|---|---|---|---|---|---|
| ARG | Argentina | HOK | Hong Kong | POR | Portugal |
| AUL | Australia | IND | Indonesia | SAF | South Africa |
| AUT | Austria | IRA | Iran | SIN | Singapore |
| BEL | Belgium | IRE | Ireland | SPA | Spain |
| BRA | Brazil | ISR | Israel | SWE | Sweden |
| CAN | Canada | ITA | Italy | SWI | Switzerland |
| CHL | Chile | JAP | Japan | TAI | Taiwan |
| COL | Columbia | MEX | Mexico | THA | Thailand |
| DEN | Denmark | NET | Netherlands | TUR | Turkey |
| FIN | Finland | NOR | Norway | USA | United States of America |
| FRA | France | NZL | New Zealand | | |
| GBR | Great Britain | PAK | Pakistan | VEN | Venezuela |
| GER | Germany | PER | Peru | YUG | Yugoslavia |
| GRE | Greece | PHI | Philippines | | |

## Masculinity/Femininity and Uncertainty Avoidance

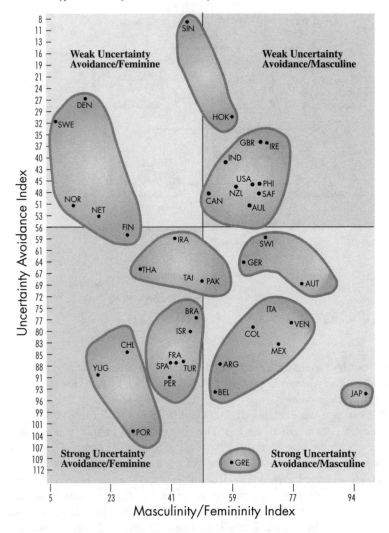

**Figure 4.3**
This figure indexes the uncertainty avoidance and masculinity dimensions of Hofstede's four dimensions of difference. Uncertainty avoidance refers to how people view risk: those who are high on uncertainty avoidance do not take risks; those who are low on uncertainty avoidance view risk taking as a part of life and believe you must gamble to gain. Masculinity/femininity refers to how well-defined male and female roles are in society. Societies that are high on the masculinity dimension have a "live to work" attitude, valuing things that are big, fast, and beautiful. Societies that are high on femininity have a "work to live" attitude: they value relationships, and men and women share in child-rearing. Countries that are low on uncertainty avoidance and high on the femininity dimension are Denmark, Sweden, Norway, the Netherlands, and Finland.

Source: Hofstede, G. (1980). *Culture's Consequences: International Differences in Work-Related Values.* London: Sage Publications.

## > MODEL OF CROSS-CULTURAL BEHAVIOR

Retail success can change consumer behavior. The introduction of McDonald's set the stage for a variety of fast-food formats in the United States. This cultural change has also occurred in many of the countries McDonald's entered following its success in its home market. McDonald's did not originate the fast-food idea. However, the company's aggressive franchising efforts made it the a worldwide symbol of Americana.

A model for analyzing cross-cultural buying behavior is presented in Figure 4.4. This model could be used to analyze the spread of new retail formats throughout a

## A Model of Cross-Cultural Behavior

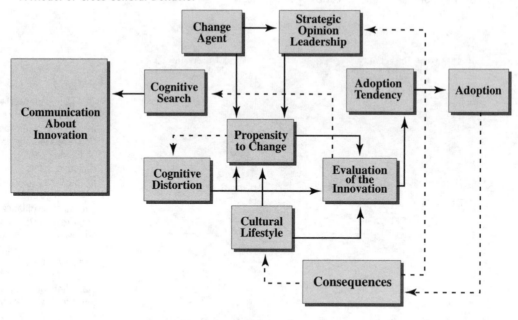

Source: Czinkota, Rivoli, and Ronkainen. (1992). *International Business*, 2nd ed., p. 217. Fort Worth: Dryden Press.[6]

**Figure 4.4**
New ideas are communicated across cultures through a complex process, which could be diagrammed as shown above. Strategic opinion leaders and change agents influence whether average consumers will adopt an innovation. Cultural norms can influence the consequences of adopting an innovation.

large country, where different regions represent different cultural groups. It is used more frequently, however, to study how new products or retail formats are adopted from country to country.

We can use the example of McDonald's introduction into Japan to explore the model. Let's begin at the top. The change agent, in this instance, is the first McDonald's franchise operator, a Japanese entrepreneur named Den Fujita. Fujita started an import business at the age of 25, importing golf clubs and Florsheim shoes. He switched to women's accessories shortly after, correctly deciding that women were more likely to purchase imported designer products. Fujita found out through his trading company representative in Chicago that McDonald's was interested in internationalizing. Typically McDonald's approved single franchises only to individuals. Fujita, however, first convinced the company that it should approve the opening of several restaurants throughout Japan, and second, that he should be given a free hand in running the restaurants.

He ignored the advice of McDonald's analysts who recommended finding a suburban location like those that are successful in the United States. He wanted to open the first McDonald's in Ginza, the most famous and the busiest shopping area in Tokyo. Mitsukoshi, a prestigious department store in Ginza, had long been one of his customers for women's accessories. Through his contacts there, he arranged to open a McDonald's restaurant in a space only one-fifth the size of a normal McDonald's, the same space he used to sell designer handbags. Fujita designed a compact kitchen and substituted stand-up customer counters instead of seats. There was one catch. The department store did not want construction at the location to inconvenience its regular shoppers. Mitsukoshi is closed on Mondays. Fujita thus had from 6:00 P.M. Sunday to 9:00 A.M. Tuesday to construct his tiny restaurant. That is 39 hours to assemble a store that normally takes 3 months.

Fujita accepted the terms. He rented a warehouse on the outskirts of Tokyo, where his construction crews practiced assembling a McDonald's unit in the allocated 39 hours. They went through trial runs, constructing the store and tearing it down until they got the time down. Fujita telexed Chicago that the grand opening would be July 20, 1971. Ray Kroc, the grand man of McDonald's, and other company officials arrived in Tokyo on Saturday, July 17, to attend the opening. When they asked to see the store, Fujita took them to the Mitsukoshi window where the store would be and said, "Here's where it goes." McDonald's officials could not believe Fujita's story. They were frantic about the scheduled grand opening.

The construction crew performed their well-rehearsed movements, however, and when the officials showed up for the grand opening, the store was ready. Three days after the first store opened, Fujita opened another store in Shinjuku, one of the busiest commuter train terminals in Tokyo. A day later, a third unit opened. All were successful. After 18 months Fujita had 19 McDonald's restaurants throughout Japan.[7]

In the model, STRATEGIC OPINION LEADERSHIP refers to the actions by which a change agent appeals to influencers within a cultural group. Convinced that Japan's youth would be the ones most likely to accept the fast-food concept, Fujita aimed his advertising at children and young families. This group of Japanese were those with the greatest PROPENSITY TO CHANGE. Fujita said, "The eating habits of older Japanese are very conservative, but we could teach the children that the hamburger was something good." Fujita went so far as to make advertising claims that hamburgers would improve the health of Japanese children, making them grow bigger and stronger. Much to the chagrin of McDonald's officials, he even claimed that hamburgers would lighten Japanese skin.

Fujita made marketing modifications in order to succeed in Japan. He clarified that McDonald's Japan was run by Japanese, not Americans. This reduced the COGNITIVE DISTORTION and increased the EVALUATION OF THE INNOVATION. He advertised on television, making sure the spots had a Japanese flavor (COMMUNICATION ABOUT INNOVATION). He changed the pronunciation of the McDonald's name to Makudonaldo because the name was difficult for Japanese to pronounce. For the same reason, Ronald McDonald became Donald McDonald. This improved the ADOPTION TENDENCY and, ultimately, the consumer's ADOPTION of McDonald's restaurants. As the popularity of McDonald's restaurants increased, the CONSEQUENCES of adoption became clearer. Youthful consumers who might have purchased a traditional Japanese boxed lunch were now opting for fast foods. Just like families in the United States, Japanese families' CULTURAL LIFESTYLES have changed. Fast-food outlets are expanding throughout the country. Each year fewer families sit down to a traditional family meal for breakfast, lunch, or dinner.

Not all internationalization of retail innovations alters culture. Most of international retailing goes unnoticed by consumers within a country. Few people know or care that a retail concept is of foreign origin. Each year, many retailers expand internationally, only to retreat shortly afterward. Retail innovations have a life cycle, like a product life cycle, that can be used to predict success.

## › SUMMARY

Culture influences retailing in many ways, but retailing can also influence culture. Over time, the products we purchase and how we purchase them influences culture. Culture is a learned pattern of life. We are socialized into our culture as children and continue to learn about it until we die. In this chapter, I have presented some theoretical concepts that can help you generalize about and predict behavior of people from other cultures.

Understanding whether groups have a polychronic or monochronic time orientation helps us to be patient if we are monochronic time oriented, or tolerant of rushing if we are polychronic time oriented. Knowing that a group of people are high context communicators helps us realize that we probably will not understand all of what is being communicated unless we are a part of that culture. Low context cultures can communicate quite adequately with each other because they put everything into words. However, low context cultures will never have the depth of silent communication present in high context interactions.

Hofstede's cultural dimensions provide another mechanism for generalizing about cultural groups. Some of his dimensions, such as individualism versus collectivism, can be related to monochronic time and polychronic time and high context versus low context. Countries that are classified as being individualist are also monochronic time oriented and low context.

In this chapter, we have seen how retailing can affect cultural change. Retailing both affects and is affected by economic change. In the next chapter, we will consider the evolution of retailing with increased economic development.

## › KEY TERMS

ADOPTION
ADOPTION TENDENCY
CHANGE AGENTS
COGNITIVE DISTORTION
COMMUNICATION ABOUT INNOVATION
CONSEQUENCES
CONSPICUOUS CONSUMPTION
CULTURAL LIFESTYLES
ETHNOCENTRISM
EVALUATION OF THE INNOVATION
GATEKEEPERS
HIGH CONTEXT
INDIVIDUALISM
LAW
LOW CONTEXT
MASCULINITY
MATERIAL CULTURE
MULTICULTURAL
OPINION LABORS
PATINA
POWER DISTANCE

PRIMARY SOCIALIZATION
PROPENSITY TO CHANGE
REFERENCE GROUPS
SELF-REFERENCE CRITERION
STRATEGIC OPINION LEADERSHIP
UNCERTAINTY AVOIDANCE

## › DISCUSSION QUESTIONS

1. It is often said that culture is learned behavior. Give three examples of learned behaviors that affect international retailing.
2. Provide three examples of high context cultures and three examples of low context cultures. How would you expect these cultures to feel about the following elements: a. material possessions, b. friendship patterns, c. agreements across cultures, and d. time.
3. Societies teach their members to belong to their cultural group through material elements, social institutions, belief systems, aesthetics, and language. What people and institutions have provided you with your cultural perspective in these areas?
4. Use Hofstede's cultural dimensions model to make some strategic decisions about a specific retail activity. Suppose you are interested in opening a toy store in Japan. Japan is considered low on individualism, high on power distance, high on masculinity, and low on risk tolerance. How would your decisions reflect these dimensions?
5. No doubt you have heard people say, "English is the international language of business. If you want to do business with me, you'd better speak my language." What is the term for this view and what are the repercussions for international retailers?

## › ENDNOTES

1. Terpstra, V. and K. David (1985). *The Cultural Environment of International Business.* Cincinnati: South-Western Publishing Company.
2. Johansson, J. (1997). *Global Marketing: Foreign Entry, Local Marketing and Global Management.* Chicago: Irwin.
3. McCraken, G. (1988). *Culture and Consumption: New Approaches to the Symbolic Character of Consumer Goods and Activities.* Bloomington: Indiana Press.
4. Hall, E. (1983). *The Dance of Life.* New York: Anchor Books-Doubleday.
5. Hall, E. (1983).
6. Cateora, P. (1993). *International Marketing.* 8th ed. Irwin.
7. Love, J. (1995). *McDonald's: Behind the Arches.* New York: Bantam Books.

# 5

# RETAILING IN DEVELOPING COUNTRIES

## After reading this chapter, you should understand

> Characteristics of traditional retailers and how economic development affects these characteristics.

> How the role of retail buyer as gatekeeper of products is an important transition.

> Characteristics of buyer's and seller's markets and how these characteristics affect power within the distribution system.

> Why prices need to be fixed for modern retail systems to function.

> How female employment is related to self-service retailing.

## › DEFINING DEVELOPING COUNTRIES

Economists generally classify a country's level of development by its GROSS DO-MESTIC PRODUCT (GDP); that is the total value of goods and services produced during the year by people in that country. The World Bank compiles an index that lists countries according to their rank, from least developed to most developed. The index number is precise and simple and handy to use. Unfortunately, it really tells us little about how retailing operates within that country. As a student of retailing, you might consult these figures and have little idea about the way people actually live there.

I find that more tangible elements help me to understand how people live their lives. Nevertheless, what I find really interesting is the percent of households that have what we might consider everyday necessities. These necessities are piped water, flush toilets, and electrical lighting.

To me, toilets provide a good indicator of everyday living standards. Consider the following example. I work with colleagues at two universities in China. Both institutions are highly respected, but their toilets are, by Western standards, something from the dark ages. I have never visited the toilet at one institution, although I have spent several days in a row there. Once when I mentioned using the toilet to a female colleague, she arranged for a car to take me to a hotel. She never would let me see the toilet, saying, "It was better this way." This institute is centrally located in the largest city in China. Yet its toilet is outdoors and has no plumbing.

Use of toilet paper is, of course, a culturally prescribed behavior. Only one out of five high-income consumers in India uses toilet paper. An Indian native, educated at the London Business School, is quoted as saying, "I'd be willing to bet that no minister in the entire Indian cabinet uses toilet paper."[1] *The Wall Street Journal* article in Box 5.1 contains some interesting comparisons of the difficulties in marketing Western products to consumers in India and China.

## › STAGES OF DEVELOPMENT

There are measures of economic development other than the availability of toilets and toilet paper. Rostow, for instance, classified countries according to production and consumption capability. Farmer classified societies based on how they view trash.

Rostow became well known for presenting a model that classifies countries by five stages of development: (1) the traditional society, (2) the preconditions for takeoff, (3) the takeoff, (4) the drive to maturity, and (5) the age of high mass consumption (see Figure 5.1). Countries in the first three stages are considered underdeveloped. Those in stages 4 and 5 are considered developed. A country's stage of development in this model can be tied to specific retailing strategies as the following discussion illustrates.

### Stage 1: The Traditional Society

Countries in this stage lack the capability of significantly increasing their level of productivity. There is a marked absence of systematic application of the methods of modern science and technology. Literacy is low.

**Box 5.1**
**Marketing Gurus Say: In India, Think Cheap, Lose the Cold Cereal**
*By Miriam Jordan*

Bombay, India—How do you pitch spaghetti in a country where people eat with a bare hand? Or disposable lighters to consumers so frugal, they refill them?

Such are the marketing riddles that confound Western multinational companies in India. Furnishing answers is the business of marketing guru K. M. S. Ahluwalia.

When Avon Products Inc. came calling, Titoo—as Mr. Ahluwalia is nicknamed—advised the cosmetics giant not to go ringing doorbells in India, where only bric-a-brac salesmen sell door-to-door. Since founding India's largest market-research firm, ORG-MARG, Titoo has served as a guide to multinationals like Coca-Cola Co., Gillette Co., and Unilever PLC that are wooing India's seemingly Western-oriented consumers.

"Repeat after me," he says in an interview, reciting his mantra for Western clients: "India is different, India is different, India is different."

This reality check is in order. Many Western companies see vast riches in this market of 950 million consumers. Most of India's people are poor, but the middle class is estimated to equal in number the entire U.S. population, though it isn't nearly as well off. Free-market reforms launched five years ago have given more Indians a taste of prosperity. They now have a wider choice of products and greater exposure to Western lifestyles: MTV and "Baywatch" are beamed into many living rooms via satellite television.

But Western consumer marvels are colliding with a force that belies appearances and can't be swept aside as quickly as India's formerly socialist economy: its 4,000-year-old culture.

"I'd be willing to bet that no minister in the entire Indian cabinet uses toilet paper," declares Titoo, a 50-year-old London Business School graduate and former advertising man, who counts himself among those in favor of traditional Indian cleansing. Though he hasn't surveyed the politicians, he has polled consumers, and found that only one out of five high-income earners use toilet paper.

The outlook isn't any better for antiperspirants in this sweltering country, as Gillette discovered. Indians typically bathe twice a day—it's a mammoth market for soap—but deodorant penetration is just 2% among urban dwellers.

India's outward modernity can be deceptive. "Indians are capable of living in several centuries at once," says Daraius Ardeshir, managing director of Nestle India Ltd., the local unit of the Swiss food company. "When I visit my father's house, I still kiss his feet," he says.

Indians who study in the U.S. and Britain often return home to arranged marriages. Even many people who have chosen their own spouses opt to move in with their extended families. Such traditional family bonds inhibit Western marketers' access: Yuppies, deferring to their elders, don't make household-purchasing decisions.

The response to consumer products launched in India over the past three years has disappointed many multinational companies hoping for quick success. When Titoo's team recently surveyed marketing managers in India, only 27% of food-company marketers said their expectations had been met; among those selling consumer items, the figure was 33%.

A sweeping new Gallup poll of consumer attitudes confirms what tough customers Indians can be. In India, where urban temperatures top 110 degrees in the summer, just 1% of households have an air conditioner, Gallup found—and only 1% plan to buy one within the next two years.

Marketing problems include nightmarish distribution hassles and a diverse population with dozens of regional groups—each with its own language. A more fundamental challenge is to strike the right cultural chord.

Lesson one: Indians are champion recyclers. Even as they prosper, they remain frugal. For many middle-class smokers, for example, it would be inconceivable to throw away a disposable cigarette lighter when it can be refilled cheaply.

A similar challenge frustrates sanitary napkin marketers. "You'd think that in a country with a huge population, you'd make a fortune selling sanitary napkins," says P. H. Lele,

*continued*

**Box 5.1** *Continued*

executive vice president of Johnson & Johnson Ltd., a unit of the U.S. personal-care-products giant.

Not yet. Indian women recycle old cotton saris or sheets instead. Fewer than 2% of all Indian women and just 23% of adult urban women use sanitary napkins.

India's men are a hard sell, too. India is the world's largest market for razor blades—but not for disposable shavers. Less than 1% of blades bought in cities are attached to a plastic handle. People can't stand to toss them away. Still, Gillette believes the market will come around. "India has the size as well as the fuzz," says Pradeep Pant, managing director of Indian Shaving Products Ltd., a Gillette-controlled joint venture.

Cultural psychologist Sudhir Kakar says frugality has deep historical roots in India. Mohandas K. Gandhi, who led India's fight for independence from Britain, tapped this value when he urged countrymen to spin their own cloth for clothing instead of buying British imports.

And Indians have never had a social-security system to fall back on. Though median household income is only $480, the private savings rate is an impressive 24%. "Unconsciously," says Dr. Kakar, the psychologist, "even the richest man fears sinking into the sea of poverty that surrounds him."

This mindset drives Indian consumers—wealthy or not—to spend a little money at a time, even though that may not be the cheapest way to buy a product. And so marketers don't recommend selling family-sized packages of detergents, shampoos or tea leaves.

To trim costs, Indians often ignore manufacturers' instructions. If a drink mix calls for a heaping teaspoon, they'll plop in a level teaspoon. "Culturally, we are underdosers," says Rama Bijapurkar, a McKinsey & Co. consultant. "We underconsume to be economical."

But frugality isn't the main cultural hurdle for multinationals. Of all areas, food is the most treacherous, since many Indians believe food shapes personality, mood and the mind.

Tang orange drink may have succeeded in outer space, but it burned on entry in India, where people believe that citrus and milk are bad for the stomach—and sour your mood—when consumed at the same time. Kraft Foods International, a unit of Philip Morris Cos., positioned Tang as a drink for breakfast, when tea with milk is customary. Kraft, which also marketed Maxwell House coffee in India, quit the country in the early 1990s. In China, Tang's futuristic image has made it such a hit that Kraft has just opened a $20 million plant outside the city of Tianjin.

Kellogg Co. is getting a cold shoulder from Indians, who prefer hot food for breakfast because they feel it infuses them with energy. Consumers indulged their curiosity when Kellogg's Corn Flakes arrived two years ago. Recently, though, sales have plummeted, people close to the company say, as Indians returned to their breakfast of flat bread with eggs or cooked vegetables. Indians are willing to try new foods, marketers have concluded, but usually return to traditional fare.

To be sure, the popularity of Western restaurants such as Kentucky Fried Chicken and Pizza Hut demonstrates Indians' appetite for new cuisines. But that change hasn't entered the home. At least not when a Western food, such as cold cereal, is pitched as a replacement for a main meal. "As long as it's a food for casual eating, you have a good chance of succeeding," says Sunil Alagh, managing director of Indian biscuit maker Britannia Industries Ltd. "When you try to get into the main meal, that's where you flop."

Nestle SA has learned that the snack is where it's at for Western food companies. In 1983, Nestle launched its Maggi brand of instant noodles. Unlike competitor Unilever, which tried to convert Indians to eating pasta meals, Nestle has recently found success by pitching Maggi noodles as a snack between meals. Its advertisements showed children playfully shoving the noodles into their mouths. Most Indians eat with their fingers.

Nestle is setting an example for other food companies in India by working the margins of the market, localizing its products and appeasing price-conscious housewives, who typically control half of the family budget. Between 1991 and 1995, Nestle India more than doubled its sales to 10 billion rupees ($280 million) and increased net profit 50% to 532 million rupees.

In the process, the company adapted to the Indian reality "rather than saying, 'This is good for you, eat it,'" says Mr. Ardeshir, the managing director. "If you want to be big in India, you have to get in with local foods."

Nestle has created an Indian instant coffee, Sunrise, which is blended with chicory to give a strong and familiar flavor. Sunrise outsells the world-famous Nescafe in India. The company also markets mixes for traditional desserts, as well as a mint that's flavored with betel nut, a popular mild stimulant. It has commissioned local pickle maker Chordia Foods Ltd. to manufacture Indian chutneys under the Nestle name.

But the right product needs the right price, even among Nestle's elite target market of India's 20 million wealthiest households. More than half of 119 Nestle products sold in India cost less than 25 rupees (70 cents). Sales of Maggi noodles have tripled since January 1994, when the price was cut to about 14 cents from 19 cents a package. "It took us 10 years to realize we can have a mass market," says Mr. Ardeshir, who concedes that Nestle stumbled after entering India in 1962.

Despite the dramatic economic changes in India in the past five years, the most successful consumer-product multinationals are those that have been in India for decades—though success is relative. After 35 years in India, Johnson & Johnson's turnover of $50 million is roughly equal to its sales in Malaysia, home to just 19 million people.

While newer entrants must sit tight through years of losses, at least one marketing executive is prospering: Titoo. His company's turnover has surged 56% a year on average since 1991, as multinationals troop into his office. This year he will sell a stake in his firm to a Dutch publishing and information company, one of several suitors. "I'm getting rich," he says, "but I'm losing my hair."

Source: *The Wall Street Journal,* October 11, 1996.

**Figure 5.1**
Stages of Development

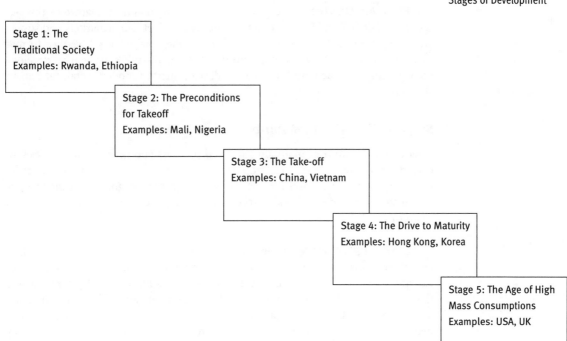

**RETAIL APPLICATION**    Countries such as Rwanda, Mozambique, Ethiopia, Tanzania, and Burundi could fit under this classification. Vendors moving from village to village with a bag of assorted merchandise dominate retailing in these countries. Stores in permanent locations also have very scrambled merchandise. SCRAMBLED MERCHANDISE means that they sell an unrelated grouping of goods. A vendor might have clothes, food, magazines, and soft drinks as part of the merchandise assortment.

## Stage 2: The Preconditions for Take-Off

This second stage includes those societies that are in the process of transition to the take-off stage. During this period, the advances of modern science are beginning to be applied in agriculture and production. The development of transportation, communications, power, education, health, and other public undertakings are begun in a small but important way.

**RETAIL APPLICATION**    Countries such as Mali and Nigeria probably fit this classification. Retailers are mainly situated in permanent structures, although their merchandise is still very scrambled. If retail businesses are not government owned, they are single-family, single-unit operations.

## Stage 3: The Take-Off

At this stage, countries achieve a growth pattern that becomes a normal condition. People and social overhead have been developed to sustain steady development. Agricultural and industrial modernizations lead to rapid expansion in these areas.

**RETAIL APPLICATION**    Countries such as Vietnam and Zimbabwe fit this description. Foreign retailers are eager to enter the market. Supermarkets and superettes are emerging. Superettes are small-scale supermarkets, a self-service format that is introduced into developing countries before full-scale supermarket development. Commercial activities include the development of modern retail formats in shopping centers.

## Stage 4: The Drive to Maturity

After take-off, countries maintain sustained progress and their economies seek to extend modern technology to all fronts of economic activity. The economy takes on international involvement. In this stage, an economy shows that it has the technological and entrepreneurial skills to produce anything, but not everything, it chooses to produce.

**RETAIL APPLICATION**    China would be included in this stage. Supermarkets and other forms of modern retailing are well established, although they may coexist with traditional wet markets. Wet markets are traditional food markets where fresh foods are sold in a nonrefrigerated environment, sort of like the American farmer's market. Until supermarkets become the dominant form of retailing most people purchase their fresh produce in wet markets. Fish are sold live. Meats may

**Photo 5.1**
One of the most basic forms of retailing is an itinerant trader selling merchandise out of a bag. This Liberian merchant travels from village to village selling his wares. *Courtesy of the United Nations/B. Wolff.*

still be steaming. Vegetables are fresh from the farmer. Shopping centers may have been overbuilt during the take-off phase and are currently experiencing decline.

## Stage 5: The Age of High Mass Consumption

The age of high mass consumption leads to shifts in a country's leading economic sectors toward durable consumer goods and services. Real income per capita rises to the point where a very large number of people have significant amounts of discretionary income.[2]

RETAIL APPLICATION    This stage would include most countries listed under high-income economies. Their retail offerings are very specialized. Logistics is an important part of improving distribution efficiencies. Retailers are integrated both vertically and horizontally.

Although these indicators of development are important, conditions are less predictable now than they were in the past. In the last decade, several countries have experienced an explosion in economic development. The trend began with the Four Tigers—and the speed of their economic growth has been amazing. In these countries and other highly developed countries, traditional retail systems coexist with modern forms of retailing. Knowing how such traditional retail systems operate is the basis for understanding the impact of modern retail systems. The next section will explore this subject.

Developing countries use many ways to promote economic growth. One of those is through attracting FDI (FOREIGN DIRECT INVESTMENT). Researchers have provided evidences that FDI helps advancing economic growth and stimulating domestic investment as well.[3]

## ⟩ TRADITIONAL RETAIL SYSTEMS

Traditional retail systems are made up of small and independent stores. Shop-keepers in these systems generally know their customers. Shopping is a daily activity, time consuming but pleasant, which is usually carried out by women. In such a system the female head of household would likely spend some time chatting with each of the shopkeepers whom she encounters each day. Daily shopping in this environment is thus a social and cultural exchange, as well as an economic activity.

I once worked with a graduate student from Ecuador. He came from an affluent family in Quito and he was married to a very talented interior designer who was just finishing her undergraduate degree at Michigan State University. After graduation, they returned to Ecuador. He explained that when they returned home, his wife would not work because although they had a live-in cook, it would take his wife, as female head of the household, most of the day to do the shopping for the family meal. I visited them a few years ago. His wife was working, part-time, but she still had the responsibility of selecting the family food. The live-in maid did the cooking.

In many countries with traditional retail systems, the female head of household does the shopping. This is not the case in Saudi Arabia, where cultural restrictions prohibit women from driving and discourage them from going out of the house. A Saudi woman typically makes up the shopping list, but a male member of the household does the shopping.[4]

There is a relationship between women seeking employment outside the home and the emergence of modern self-service supermarkets. It is not clear, however, which came first. Are self-service supermarkets introduced because women are entering the professional workforce and have less time to do the family shopping? Or does it follow that when self-service supermarkets enter the retail system, the time women need to spend shopping is reduced and therefore they have time to

**Photo 5.2**
These small shops in Damascus, Syria, are located in permanent store locations, overflowing into the street. The shops are barely large enough for one customer; the owner parks himself outside. *Courtesy of the United Nations.*

seek employment outside the home? Probably neither scenario is totally correct. The two situations are complementary to each other.

When I was growing up on a farm in South Dakota, traditional grocery stores were located 1 mile from our home in one direction and 1/4 mile in the other. Each of these grocery stores relied on business from a 5-mile radius of farm families. Before I had graduated from the eighth grade, both of the grocery stores had closed. I include this example because students are often tempted to think that these types of traditional retailers disappeared from American society after the early 1900s. In fact, ethnic areas in large cities such as New York and Los Angeles still have a traditional retail sector. Most European and Asian cities also have traditional retail sectors, coexisting with modern supermarkets.

Traditional retail systems, as we will see next, are characterized by fragmented markets, long channels, atomistic competition, limited product variety, flexible prices with bargaining, and informal credit.

## Fragmented Markets

In **FRAGMENTED MARKETS,** the decision-making unit is the individual shop. Each shop operates independently of others. There are no chains of stores. Stores have little power within the distribution system. As a country becomes more developed, the role of coordinated chains becomes more prevalent. Stores join together to obtain economies of scale in purchasing and possibly promotion. With greater economic development, markets become more integrated.

## Long Channels

A channel is the path products take from producer to retailer. The length of a channel is related to the economic development within a country. In very traditional retail settings the channel is quite long, often encompassing several different stages of distribution. Let's look at a specific example. Although Japan is a highly developed country, it has retained a large traditional retail sector that operates alongside the modern retail sector. A Japanese homemaker will generally visit several small mom-and-pop stores daily or every other day to select food. Japanese homes are small, making storage a problem. In addition, the Japanese like very fresh fish and food products; shopping on a daily basis ensures the freshest fish and produce available. The mom-and-pop stores in Japan are also very small; they rely on frequent deliveries to alleviate storage problems. Mom-and-pop stores in less urban areas of Japan may purchase from a third-level wholesaler. The fish may pass through even more wholesalers before reaching the small store.

An important activity for wholesalers is to break bulk cartons and distribute a smaller amount of a product to retailers. A wholesaler may order a case containing 100 dozen eggs. These are then divided among say, 20 retailers, with each receiving 5 dozen eggs to sell each day. In a traditional retail system, where stores are small, retailers purchase a small amount at a time, making the role of wholesalers very important. *The smaller the order placed, the longer the channel.*

Product characteristics influence channel length. If a product is not perishable, a larger amount can be purchased at one time and stored. *But the more perishable the product, the longer the channel.* When I tell this to students in my class, they do not think it makes sense. It would seem that a shorter channel would get perishable products to customers faster. Nevertheless, longer channels are really a speed track. Perhaps you have seen a depiction of the method old-fashioned firefighters used to put out fires. Each firefighter did not carry his bucket to the fire and pour it on. Instead, one person filled the buckets, which were then passed from person to person in a "bucket brigade." Product distribution is like that bucket brigade. If you have watched people building a wall of sand bags to keep a river within its banks, you have seen that same type of bucket brigade. This time, the buckets were sand bags being passed from one link to the next. Passing the bucket or the sand bag to the next person in line is like passing the product to another intermediary.

The distribution of fresh fish is one of the longest channels in food sales. Fish must be absolutely fresh. Daily, if not twice-a-day delivery is required to maintain quality.

## Atomistic Competition

Traditional retail systems feature geographical competition and, eventually, geographical concentration and customer draw. Because each individual unit does not have much competitive pull, the retailers benefit by creating a central place to attract customers. A central place means that consumers will be drawn to the location because of the greater variety offered there. Additional competitors are advantageous because they add to the attraction of the location as a central place. This concept is the basis for CENTRAL PLACE THEORY.[5]

In Chapter 9, which focuses on Mexico, I talk about informal markets. These markets focus their offerings to create a draw for customers. Dozens of vendors locate in the same area, creating an additional draw for customers. According to central place theory the maximum distance customers will travel for convenience goods is much smaller than the distance they will travel for specialized goods. Fig-

**Photo 5.3**
Consumers haggling with Mexican street vendors. Nearly every church courtyard in Mexico contains street vendors. *Courtesy of the author.*

## Central Place Theory: Hypothetical Demand Cones

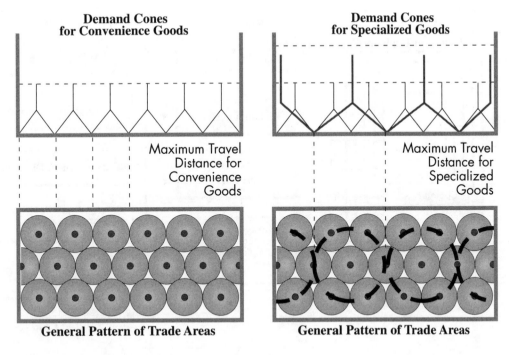

**Demand Cones for Convenience Goods**

Maximum Travel Distance for Convenience Goods

**General Pattern of Trade Areas**

**Demand Cones for Specialized Goods**

Maximum Travel Distance for Specialized Goods

**General Pattern of Trade Areas**

Source: Brown, S. (1995). "Christaller Knew My Father: Recycling Central Place Theory." *Journal of Macro Marketing*, Spring, p. 62.

**Figure 5.2**
Convenience goods are goods that you purchase frequently. You shop at the most convenient location for the product; you do not travel much distance to make the purchase. Specialized goods benefit from a central place where people can comparison shop. The maximum travel distance for specialized goods is much greater than for convenience goods. In this illustration the demand cone, or shopping area, is twice as large for specialized goods than for convenience goods.

ure 5.1 represents this graphically.[6] If you are going to purchase only a carton of milk, you will go to the closest convenience store, purchase the milk, and leave. If you are shopping for a pair of shoes, you will travel to an area that has a wide selection of shoes. You will probably pass by individual stores that sell shoes on your way to the geographically concentrated shoe-selling area. This might be a mall, or a central business district. When you are at the location, you will visit all the shoe stores that could possibly have shoes in your price and quality range. As Figure 5.2 illustrates, shopping for specialized goods has a different shopping pattern than shopping for convenience goods. This is represented by the wider demand cones (greater distance you are willing to travel) and the circular flow in the general pattern of trade area (visiting each shoe store that might have shoes you are interested in purchasing).

Beach vendors understand central place theory. Rather than spreading themselves out, they concentrate their sales in one area. Several vendors selling hot dogs, together with others selling ice cream, become a beach fast-food outlet. Instead of being competition for each other, each vendor is an attraction, a contribution to the central place. Suppose you are on the beach. Suddenly you have the desire for a cold drink. You look up and see a vendor one block from you; his sign says Coca-Cola. You also know that three blocks away, a cluster of vendors are selling all types of food and cold drinks. If a Coca-Cola is what you want you go to the closest vendor, buy your drink, and leave. The Coke is a convenience good in this instance. You

## Berry's Typology of Urban Retailing

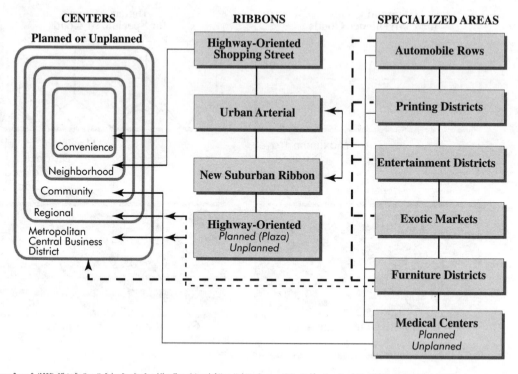

Source: Brown, S. (1995). "Christaller Knew My Father: Recycling Central Place Theory." *Journal of Macro Marketing,* Spring, p. 67. Reprinted from Berry, B. and J. Parr. (1988). *Market Centers and Retail Location.* Upper Saddle River, N.J.: Prentice-Hall, p. 39.

**Figure 5.3**

According to Berry, specialized shopping areas are connected to shopping centers by ribbons of shopping. Convenience and neighborhood centers are connected by traditional shopping highway-oriented streets. Community, regional, and metropolitan central business districts are linked to specialized areas by urban arterial, new suburban ribbon, and highway-oriented roads.

know you are going to buy this product, so you go to the closest market offering it. Now consider what you would do if you are not quite sure what you want to drink. You might be interested in iced tea or bottled water instead of a Coke. In this case, you would be inclined to travel the greater distance and visit several vendors before deciding what you want to drink.

Berry extended the central place concept to present a three-category typology of urban retailing (Figure 5.3) focusing on *centers* and *specialized areas.*[7] Centers include the central business district or other planned or unplanned shopping centers. Specialized areas are groupings of retailers who have gathered. These clustering retailers create automobile rows, printing districts, entertainment districts, exotic markets, and furniture districts. *Ribbons* are linear shopping areas that stretch along the major transportation routes, joining the centers and the specialized areas. Such ribbons include traditional shopping streets and highway-oriented shopping areas.

I have seen some evidence that these three categories may exist in informal markets. In Mexico City, informal markets are a part of every cathedral square. The cathedral and the market in a square could be considered the center in Berry's typology. On side streets from the square, ribbons of informal vendors line the narrow linear street. At the end of the street, an opening is found; it is the home of a specialized group, such as handbag retailers. These retailers gather together to create a draw for consumers. The stores are independently operated, but they recognize that by gathering, they gain the advantages of a central place.

## Limited Product Variety

In Mexico, I visited many small shops. Nearly every store would have the same selection. Even in the informal shopping sectors in Cancun, where there are lots of tourist dollars, the stores selling belts would all display nearly identical belts. The stores selling lace dresses would have virtually the same dresses. The vendors of chessboards would have the same three or four chess sets. The same scenario holds true in traditional markets throughout the world. Why would these small retailers sell the same merchandise? Are they not aware that they could increase their sales by selling a unique product?

The answer to these questions is found in the limited number of suppliers who will do business with these retailers. Because they are so small, the retailers need to find suppliers who will give them a constant source of products. The few suppliers, for their part, feel little motivation to provide good service to their small retailers, and the selection they offer is limited. As Mexico or another country becomes more developed, however, we would expect to see more suppliers. This competition would force all of the suppliers to provide service to their retailers and to provide a wider product choice.

As this process continued, manufacturers might begin to differentiate themselves from other manufacturers by developing brand names. When a manufacturer develops a brand name, it is giving consumers a guarantee about the product. It guarantees that the product will meet certain standards whenever it is purchased. For canned vegetables, the guarantee may be one of food safety and product quality. In clothing, the guarantee may be expectations related to fit and product durability. A manufacturer that develops a brand name can charge a premium for the product to offset the price of enforcing its product guarantee.

Manufacturers can promote their products in two ways. They can promote to the retailer, convincing the retailer that they have the best product selection for the price; this is done with trade promotion. An alternative is to promote the product to the consumer by establishing a brand name. The expense of reaching a consumer audience is much greater, but it gives the manufacturer greater protection from competition.

In many developing countries, foreign brands carry the highest prestige. In the People's Republic of China, however, foreign companies were not allowed to advertise or sell their products for more than 30 years. During China's planned economy, local manufacturers could not use brand names and could not even promote their own products. The central government would tell the manufacturers what to produce and which large government wholesaler to ship it to. Even with this attempt to depersonalize production, however, consumers began to recognize that products from some manufacturers were superior to others. Consumers would line up to buy bicycles from Number One Bicycle Manufacturer because this manufacturing facility gained a word-of-mouth reputation as being superior to other bicycle manufacturers.

**Photo 5.4**
Wooden kitchen utensils
for sale in Souk El
Hammadeya in Damascus,
Syria. *Courtesy of the
United Nations.*

## Flexible Prices and Bargaining

It takes time to shop in a less-developed country. Small shops generally do not have prices marked, and even when it is marked, the price is negotiable. In small shops, an item's selling price is at the owner's discretion. For nonfood items, the initial asking price is much greater than what the retailer will accept. A shopper asks the owner the price of an item. The owner quotes a price. The shopper may then offer half of what the owner is asking, and the bargaining begins. There is an unwritten rule about bargaining in good faith. Bargaining without the intent to buy is a bit like being labeled a tease. If the shopper begins negotiations with a vendor and is given a good price, the shopper should be prepared to make a purchase. Shops with flexible prices do not accept merchandise returns.

The shopkeeper might settle on a lower price for the first sale of the day, or the final sale of the day, to bring good luck. When retailers change their format from independent to chain, they generally move away from flexible pricing. One reason is that store managers cannot be trusted to make the same decision an owner or operator would make. This is an example of the agency theory. A shop owner can trust relatives to negotiate in good faith and the business' best interest, but when hired employees are added, prices need to be fixed.

Department stores are often the first fixed-price merchants to appear as a country develops economically. With so many salespeople in a department store, the pricing decisions need to be centrally made and communicated through fixed prices.

## Informal Credit

Small retailers frequently extend credit to their customers. This informal credit is used to stimulate sales and to develop a long-term partnership between the retailer and the consumer. Consumers may buy from a particular retailer because they can receive credit rather than because the retailer has the most attractive products and pricing.

The introduction of formal credit is an important step as a country becomes more economically developed. Formal credit is based on a person's ability to repay, not like informal credit which is based on familiarity or geographic location. Formal credit can be taken by a consumer from one location to another. Some companies gain their market presence through attractive credit policies. Sears lenient credit requirements enable young families or people with few credit alternatives to buy their first appliances. Credit is an important aspect in consumer freedom. It allows consumers to buy good quality products, perhaps not at the lowest possible price, but at a price they can afford over a specified period. In Mexico, a company called Eurika has also used this type of easy credit policy. In Eurika's case, a unique sales promotional program was also developed whereby relatives in the United States can purchase electrical appliances for relatives or friends in Mexico. The use of formal credit allows consumers to make more rational purchase decisions for large-ticket items.

Several of the macro-environmental factors described in Chapter 1 affect retailing in less developed countries. In such countries, it is likely that the government uses regulation to control distribution channels. Price controls are quite prevalent, products are subsidized, and rationing contributes to the black market. Consumers use forward buying when inflation is expected to cause prices to increase. In less developed countries, it is likely that the government owns distribution or cooperatives. Forward buying means that people purchase more than they immediately need. It is a type of whording. Greece is an example of a country in which the government once controlled distribution of consumer products.

In less developed countries, retailers depend on suppliers to extend supplier credit. This ultimately causes retailers to become dependent on suppliers. Just as consumers become tied to retailers through the credit they owe, retailers become tied to the suppliers they owe. In some areas such as the Overseas Chinese, the Chinese business group extends credit to the persons who are a part of their group. This family funding replaces the venture capital available in other markets.

## > RETAIL EVOLUTION

### Seller's Market to Buyer's Market

A SELLER'S MARKET exists when consumers want to buy more products than sellers can provide. Sellers have the power in this type of market, and consumers must settle for what is available. Tickets to Red Wings hockey games in Detroit are generally sold out. More people want to buy hockey tickets than the current supply provides. Most subscribers have bought tickets for years. In this instance, the ticketholders can sell their tickets for more than face value, a practice known as scalping.

Scalping occurs in retailing also. In seller's markets, the sellers hold products that are in great demand. They can charge higher prices for these products. Seller's markets for most products exist in developing countries. Retailers in many developing countries face the out-of-stock problem on account of insufficient distribution systems and technology.[8] In seller's markets, the sellers usually do not care much about the problem because consumers will have to come back for the products and they expect this kind of situation to happen. In buyer's markets, sellers have to work hard to reduce the out-of-stock cost and win consumers back by developing store loyalty and/or brand loyalty.[9]

A BUYER'S MARKET exists when sellers have more products available than consumers want. Here sellers compete to gain sales, and buyers have the market strength. This system occurs in most developed countries. The competition for consumers' dollars reduces prices, benefitting consumers.

Instead of scalping, a buyer's market is characterized by discounting. Suppliers reduce their price to gain consumers' purchases. If the Michigan State hockey team did not do well for years, ticketholders might begin to sell their season tickets. In fact, this has happened with Michigan State's football tickets. At most home games, $20 tickets can be purchased at the door for $5. Football tickets have become a buyer's market.

The relationship between buyers and sellers is altered depending on whether the situation is a buyer's or a seller's market. Excellent research exploring this phenomenon is available. Kale developed several research propositions that highlight the differences between buyer's and seller's markets. His research focused on manufacturer and supplier relationships, but with some altering of terms, Kale's findings have great relevance to understanding the roles of retailers (buyers) and their suppliers (sellers). His generalizations also make a meaningful contribution to understanding the relationship between consumers (buyers) and retailers (sellers).

Kale presents his theory of relationships in three stages: initiation, implementation, and review (Table 5.1). I will discuss each of these stages separately to clarify how they relate to buyer's and seller's markets.

INITIATION    This is the introductory stage of a buyer-seller relationship. In a buyers' market, the retailer will evaluate suppliers in an objective manner. Does this supplier have the quality of merchandise the retailer wants to sell in the store? Can this supplier provide good delivery and service? Does this supplier sell the same products to competitors? In a seller's market the retailer does not have many choices of suppliers. Suppliers have the power. In a seller's market, the initiation process will be informal and the decision of whom to sell to will be based on subjective and personal criteria.

IMPLEMENTATION    This is the performance part of the relationship. In a buyers' market, a supplier's performance will determine market power. If a supplier is providing a product that sells successfully and this product is consistently made available to the retailer, the supplier will have power. In a seller's market, there are few alternatives for the retailer, so performance of the supplier is not what conveys power. Power comes by virtue of the lack of alternative suppliers. Even if a supplier is not performing adequately, the retailer will continue to deal with the supplier because there are no alternatives. Because performance will not affect power, the supplier is inclined to provide poorer and poorer service.

In a buyer's market, more powerful suppliers use unpressurized influence strategies, while less powerful suppliers use pressurized influence strategies. The more dependent the retailer is on the supplier, the less the retailer will acknowledge this dependence. In a seller's market, powerful suppliers use pressurized influence strategies and the less powerful use unpressurized influence strategies. The more dependent the retailer is on the supplier, the more power the retailer attributes to the supplier.

**Table 5.1**
**Differences in the Supplier-Retailer Relationship in a Buyer's versus a Seller's Market**

| Relationship Stage | Buyer's Market | Seller's Market |
|---|---|---|
| Initiation | > Formal, well thought out<br>> Supplier chooses retailer based on objective criteria | > Relatively less well thought out<br>> Supplier chooses retailer based on relatively subjective and personal criteria<br>> Supplier has many choices of retailers, whereas retailer's choices are few |
| Implementation | Channel Power<br>> Supplier's role performance determines retailer's dependence and supplier's power<br><br>Supplier's Power and Influence Strategies (to alter retailer's decision-making)<br>> Powerful supplier → unpressurized influence strategies<br>> Less powerful supplier → relatively pressurized influence strategies | Channel Power<br>> The lack of alternative channel participation opportunities determines retailer's dependence and supplier's power<br><br>Supplier's Power and Influence Strategies (to alter retailer's decision-making)<br>> Powerful supplier → relatively pressurized influence strategies<br>> Less powerful supplier → unpressurized influence strategies |
| Review | Retailer's Dependence and Attributed Supplier<br>> Negatively correlated to supplier<br>> Supplier attributes credit to his retailer<br>> If losing, supplier blames self, retailer, or the situation; the supplier-retailer dependence varies accordingly<br>> Retailer is concerned more about equity in a channel relationship | Retailer's Dependence and Attributed Supplier<br>> Positively correlated to his supplier<br>> Supplier attributes credit to himself<br>> If loosing, supplier and retailer blame one another; resulting in channel conflict<br><br>> Retailer grudgingly maintains the channel relationship; motivational investment reduced; searches for other supplier, which is very time-consuming and may not materialize |

Source: Kale, S. H. (1989). "Impact of Market Characteristics on Producer-Distributor Relationships." L., Pellegrini , S. K. Reddy, eds., *Retail and Marketing Channel,* New York: Routledge, pp. 100–114.

**REVIEW PROCESS**    In a buyer's market, if the relationship is successful the supplier will credit the retailer. Suppliers are concerned with equity in a channel relationship. This sets the stage for relationship marketing. In a seller's market, if a supplier is doing well, it credits itself. If the dyad is not doing well, they blame each other, creating channel conflict. In a seller's market, the retailer grudgingly continues the relationship, constantly looking for a new supplier. This search is time consuming and detracts from current performance.

The role of retailers changes with economic development. In less developed countries, retailers sell whatever they can get. This situation is one of opportunistic sourcing. As retailers acquire more choices of suppliers, they take on a new role: retailers become merchandise assemblers.

## The Importance of Retailer as Assembler of Goods

I believe that the role of retailer as assembler of goods is an important mark of a retailing maturity as a country moves from a less developed to a more developed status.

In less developed countries, retailers sell what they have access to. They do not search the market to find products that fit the needs of their clientele. As a country develops and competition increases, retailers need to differentiate themselves, focusing on products their customers really want and need. At this stage, retailers take on a different role. Rather than serving as warehouses of what is available, they become interpreters of their customer's tastes: gatekeepers to the desired products. They search the market looking for merchandise that distinguishes them as retailers. The assumption of the role of gatekeeper is important. Before this transition occurs, consumers wander from one retailer to another. When the gatekeeper role emerges, retailers become the assemblers of goods for consumers. This eases the burden of shopping for consumers as retailers strive to offer consumers the best products for their money.

## › THEORY OF ECONOMIC DEVELOPMENT AND RETAIL CHANGE

Samiee provides a summary of research propositions that can serve as the foundations of a theory of economic development and retail change.[10] Although these propositions are an excellent contribution to international retailing research, I think several are incorrect or in need of modification. Table 5.2 provides examples of instances in which Samiee's explanation of the relationship does not seem accurate.

Samiee organizes the propositions under seven categories: environment, consumer characteristics, channel characteristics, retail and wholesaling practices, channel communication, market research, and channel performance.

### Environment

Channels in less developed countries are longer; however, channel length does not mean that the channel is inefficient. Long channels could mean that retailers are holding smaller inventory, or that they are selling very perishable products. The concept that channel length indicates inefficiency is simply inaccurate. For years, a popular argument held that Japan's distribution system is inefficient, because the Japanese have longer channels. But if one controls the perishability of the product, there is no difference between channel length in the United States and Japan.

Governments do play a much greater role in less developed countries. Price controls, rules excluding foreign ownership, and state-owned distributors are some problems in this environment. Most developing countries have some laws that limit foreign ownership of retail activities.

### Consumer Characteristics

I think the propositions outlined by Samiee are accurate. Retailers need packaging to protect merchandise through the transportation and selling phase. In less developed countries, packaging is protective, not provocative. Shopping is an enjoyable activity, an important level of social interaction.

### Channel Characteristics

Earlier, I used the term scrambled merchandise. Samiee uses the term retail generalists. We are observing the same phenomena. Retailers in less developed countries

**Table 5.2**
**Analysis of Samiee's (1993) Research Propositions: Economic Development and Retail Change**

| Channel/Retailing Element | Proposition | Sternquist's Observations |
|---|---|---|
| Environment | The level of economic development significantly influences the structure of the distribution channels in less developed countries such that: | |
| | › Channels are longer and less efficient | › Longer yes, but this has nothing to do with efficiency |
| | › Channels are a major source of employment | › Not necessarily |
| | › Major segments of the population are self-sufficient (e.g., food and apparel) | › Not necessarily |
| | › There is a seller's market in many product categories | › Yes, most sectors are seller's markets |
| | Government regulations and controls influence the distribution channels through: | |
| | › Frequent or ongoing price controls, subsidized products, and rationing leading to the presence of black markets | › Yes |
| | › Consumers practice forward-buying in hyper-inflationary environments | › Yes |
| | › Government-supported or -owned distributors and cooperatives | › Yes |
| | Buyers and sellers in the channel know each other well and channel operations are influenced by high-context cultures that impact various aspects of business communications and negotiations. | Yes, high-context relationships are evident in the social dimensions of shopping |
| Consumer Characteristics | Consumer characteristics in less developed countries lead to retailers' need for smaller but more frequent purchases from their suppliers, which, in turn, may lead to product and package modification by manufacturers. Typically, the following are expected: | |
| | › Smaller packages of products | › Yes |
| | › Smaller cases containing a larger variety of products | › Yes |
| | › Product modifications to ensure longer shelf-life | › Yes |
| | › Package modifications to ensure safe delivery | › Yes |
| | › Retailers offer credit to their regular clientele on an informal basis | › Yes |
| | › Shopping is a more important form of social interaction as compared with developed nations | › Yes |
| Channel Characteristics | Channel structures are fragmented and the networks are uncoordinated. The channel is further characterized by: | › Yes |
| | › Relatively small institutions | › Yes |

*continued*

**Table 5.2** *Continued*

| Channel/Retailing Element | Proposition | Sternquist's Observations |
|---|---|---|
| | › Channel members are generalists and their functions become more specialized (i.e., separated) with economic development | › Yes, scrambled merchandise |
| | › Retail establishments vary in form and functions performed and may cater to a different class of customers as compared with developed nations | › Yes |
| | › Limited financial and managerial resources | › Yes |
| | › Adoption and popularity of self-service retailing are dependent on the availability of packaged goods and on a shortage of labor | › No, packaging follows the self-service industry; shortage of labor is not related to self-service, the origins of self-service are not related to cost reduction but instead to consumer exposure to products and prestige of the retail innovation. Self-service stores first locate in wealthiest sections of the city. |
| | › Limited presence of vertical marketing systems | › Yes |
| Retail and Wholesaling Practice | As compared with developed nations, less developed countries' retailing practices are characterized by: | |
| | › Limited working capital of channel members, particularly retailers | › Yes, capital if available comes from family members |
| | › Intermediaries typically obtain financing for purchases with no or low interest or carrying charges from suppliers | › Yes |
| | › Dominance of family-owned and -operated firms | › Yes |
| | › Sporadic or routine importing by various channel members | › Yes |
| | › Limited vendor loyalty | › Yes, this is elaborated and supported by Kale (see earlier discussion in this chapter) |
| | › More emphasis on carrying and dispensing bulk or staple products | › Yes |
| Channel Communication | Channel communication is characterized by the limited availability and use of print media and various forms of intra-channel promotion. | › No, informal means of communication are available; extensive print and radio communication are found in all but the most undeveloped countries |
| | Numerous brokers and agents are instrumental in the communications process as they expedite transactions, such that: | |
| | › They assist in providing total market coverage | › No |
| | › The are specialized by customer/channel member, region, or product | › No |

**Table 5.2** *Continued*

| Channel/Retailing Element | Proposition | Sternquist's Observations |
|---|---|---|
| Market Research | The following patterns are generally expected: | |
| | › Little use of formal market information is made by less developed countries' channel members; use of market research increases with greater economic development and the size of the channel member; in less developed countries, retailers typically do not have market research departments and seldom use outside suppliers | › No, the difference is probably related to size, not economic development |
| | › Informal and underground distribution channels play major roles in LDCs and this activity is not reflected in official statistics | › Yes, and this informal activity can be highly effective |
| Channel Performance | Retail performance is lower than in the developed markets and characterized by: | |
| | › Flexible, but generally low, channel mark-ups | › No; it is different for product groups but markups are higher with less competition and become lower with greater competition |
| | › The practice of one-price policy increases with increased foreign participation in the distribution sector | › No; fixed price comes with larger stores, or chain operations; it is not related to foreign retailers' market participation |
| | › Prices, terms of sales, and payment arrangement are negotiable; low net profit margins | › No. |

Source: Samiee, Saeed (1993). Retailing and channel considerations in developing countries: a review and research propositions, *Journal of Business Research*, 27, pp. 103–130.

do not narrowly define their product offerings. They carry whatever products they think they can sell. Recently, my colleagues who conduct research in Russia noticed that the kiosks in Moscow had begun to define and focus their product line. Previously a kiosk might have sold razors, magazines, shirts, and gum. Now it might offer only magazines.

Samiee makes a statement in this section regarding self-service retailing, claiming its dependency on the availability of packaged goods and on a shortage of labor. I believe he has the relationships reversed, and this is a serious error. Self-service enters less developed countries in a predictable pattern. The first self-service stores are supermarkets or superettes. Developers put these self-service stores in the wealthiest sections of the city. Prices in these first supermarkets are very high. The stores gain a successful niche with wealthy local residents and expatriates (foreigners) living in the area. Customers pay the high prices because the supermarket is considered a prestigious place to buy food and carries some imported products. The packaging industry to support this initial supermarket offering is developed by the supermarket itself. Supermarkets have their own shrink wrap and disposable trays. It is only later that an independent packaging industry emerges to provide service to the supermarkets. Also, self-service does not emerge to save labor costs. It originates

**Photo 5.5**
These small shops in Mexico carry very mixed merchandise. The store at center right is closed; the sliding corrugated door pulls down and locks for security. When all of these shops are similarly closed, it is nearly impossible to tell that this is a shopping street. There is no window shopping in this neighborhood. *Courtesy of the author.*

to give consumers more control over their exposure to products, allowing them to handle and examine the product.

### Retail and Wholesaling Practice

Samiee's propositions in this section parallel my findings. In less developed countries, the businesses are small and family owned. Working capital, if it is available at all, comes from other family members. Commercial credit is not available to these businesses.

There is limited vendor loyalty. Kale's work reinforces the point that in seller's markets the buyer is constantly looking for a better provider. How well a supplier performs its role does not define the retailer-supplier; instead, the relationship continues because there are few alternatives.

### Channel Communications

Channel communication in less developed countries can be very good, but it is informal communication. Word-of-mouth advertising is an important element in less developed country channel communications.

Except in the least developed countries, there is communication media. Print media actually flourishes in less developed countries. China in the 1930s had many newspapers, radio stations, and television stations.

### Market Research

Samiee considers the absence of formal market research a phenomenon of less developed countries. I do not agree. Few retailers in the United States conduct formal market research. Those that do are very large. If the size variable is removed, there is probably no difference between the use of market research in less developed and more developed countries. For example, most research conducted in Japan is grass-roots research. Manufacturers hire employees to sell merchandise in retail stores. By having their employees, not the retailers, talk with customers, the manufacturers get direct feedback about their product lines.

## Channel Performance

Samiee indicates that markups and net profit margins are lower in a less developed country and increase with greater development. I think the relationship is more complex than this. This proposition is also not compatible with one of Samiee's previous propositions stating that less developed countries are typically seller's markets. In seller's markets, there is little competition, and without competition, price is higher. Profit margins are also probably different for different types of merchandise. In food retailing, the lowest profit margins are found in the most developed countries. It may be that margins in certain types of merchandise have a curvilinear relationship. At lower levels of development, margins are the lowest, then they increase with market development, and finally fall when competition becomes intense.

Samiee also offers a proposition to the effect that use of a one-price policy increases with increased foreign participation. I do not think a one-price policy has anything to do with foreign participation. It depends, instead, on store size and whether a store is operated by nonowners or family members. When larger stores, such as department stores, enter a market area, fixed pricing is adopted. These large stores can be foreign or local; the effect will be the same. Historical development of retailing in Japan, China, and Mexico supports this idea. The change agent that moves a society toward fixed price rather than bargaining is the size of the retailer and the need to give agency power to the salesperson to continue flexible pricing. AGENCY POWER means giving someone else the authority to act on your behalf. In a

**Photo 5.6**
Fresh fruit is displayed at this stall in a Lebanese market. Such markets do not have refrigeration. *Courtesy of the United Nations.*

large store with many salespersons, an owner who did not adopt fixed pricing would have to entrust each employee with agency power to negotiate the sales price.

## ❯ SUMMARY

Traditional retail systems have a number of characteristics. They are fragmented, with retailers operating as single units. This gives them limited negotiating power with suppliers. Markets in less developed countries are typically supplier's markets. There is a greater demand for products than there is a supply. Suppliers can dictate terms to buyers and have little motivation to provide good service.

Long channels correspond to small purchases. Consumers purchase little each time they shop. Retailers carry little inventory. Each level of the channel depends on the next level to warehouse products.

Product variety is limited in less developed markets. There are few brand names and little competition other than price competition. Prices are flexible with informal bargaining and informal credit. This informal credit applies both to consumers and to interim channel credit.

## ❯ KEY TERMS

AGENCY POWER
BUYER'S MARKET
CENTRAL PLACE THEORY
FOREIGN DIRECT INVESTMENT (FDI)
FRAGMENTED MARKETS
GROSS DOMESTIC PRODUCT (GDP)
INFORMAL CREDIT
SCRAMBLED MERCHANDISE
SELLER'S MARKET

## ❯ DISCUSSION QUESTIONS

1. How does female labor participation affect retailing? How do modern forms of retailing facilitate female labor participation?
2. Why do prices need to become fixed in a modern retail format?
3. Discuss the role of retail buyer as gatekeeper. How does this change the importance of retailing to the marketing system?
4. What is a fragmented retail system? Why would a retailer remain in a fragmented system when an integrated system would offer economies of scale?
5. How do the roles of retailer and supplier change when one is dealing with a seller's market versus a buyer's market?

## ❯ ENDNOTES

1. Jordon, M. (1996). "Marketing Gurus Say: In India, Think Cheap, Lose the Cold Cereal." *Wall Street Journal*, October 11, p. A9.

2. Cateora, P. R. (1996). *International Marketing.* 5th ed. Homewood, IL: Irwin, p. 316.

3. Makki, S. and A. Somwaru (2004). "Impact of Foreign Direct Investment and Trade on Economic Growth: Evidence from Developing Countries." *American Journal of Agricultural Economics,* Vol. 83 (3), pp. 795–801.

4. Alawi, H. (1986). "Saudi Arabia: Making Sense of Self-Service." *International Marketing Review,* Spring, p. 21–38.

5. Christaller, W. (1963). (C. Baskin, trans.). *Central Places in Southern Germany.* Englewood Cliffs, NJ: Prentice-Hall.

6. Berry, B. (1967). *Geography of Market Centres and Retail Distribution.* Englewood Cliffs, NJ: Prentice-Hall.

7. Berry, B. (1963). *Commercial Structure and Commercial Blight; Retail Patterns and Processes in the City of Chicago.* Research Paper No. 85. Chicago: University of Chicago, Department of Geography.

8. Kucuk, S. (2004). "Reducing the Out-of-Stock Costs in a Developing Retailing Sector." *Journal of International Consumer Marketing,* Vol. 16(3), pp. 75–104.

9. Kucuk, S. (2004).

10. Samiee, S. (1993). "Retailing and Channel Considerations in Developing Countries: Review and Research Propositions," *Journal of Business Research,* Vol. 27, pp.103–130.

# 6

# LICENSING, FRANCHISING, AND STRATEGIC ALLIANCES

## After reading this chapter, you should understand

> Why retailers would license or franchise their businesses.

> The theoretical basis for franchising and international franchising.

> The role of strategic international alliances for retailers and the criteria for selecting partners.

> How retailers can develop partnership alternatives that help them to sustain important competitive advantages.

As we saw in Chapter 1, retailers expanding internationally do not have all the options available to manufacturing companies. Manufacturers can produce at home and then simply sell their products overseas. International retailers must have a presence in the market. The levels of international involvement for retailers are licensing, franchising, joint venture, and wholly owned subsidiary. Of these, licensing offers the least control; wholly owned subsidiary, the most. On a continuum it would look something like this:

**Licensing**    → **Franchising** → **Joint Venture** → **Wholly Owned Subsidiary**
*Least Control*                                                    *Most Control*

In this chapter, I first explore the reasons why retailers would choose to license or franchise their businesses. Next, I present a theory of franchising that differentiates among four types of franchisors. A discussion of strategic alliances follows, in which two types of strategic alliances are contrasted. The chapter concludes with a consideration of the ways in which companies can use strategic alliances to their greatest benefit when expanding into international markets.

## > LICENSING

Licensing refers to the offering of a company's know-how or other intangible assets to another company for a fee, royalty, or other type of payment. The licensee obtains the use of the licensor's proprietary knowledge. The licensor receives financial gain and the opportunity to have greater visibility for its retail concept. The drawback is that the licensee partner may eventually become a competitor, gaining market momentum with the specific knowledge gained from the licensor. An example of licensing could be Michigan State University licensing its name to Steve & Barry's University Sportswear Co. Obviously Michigan State University is not in the business of making apparel, but it can license the name so that apparel will carry its name.

A retail company that allows a foreign retailer to use its company name has often entered into a licensing arrangement. There are great risks in licensing. The most important risk is that the company is giving up one of its most important assets, its company name. If the licensee runs the company in a sloppy manner, it reflects poorly on the licensor. Furthermore, licensing agreements may offer little protection to the licensor. Table 6.1 provides an overview of important considerations that should be included in a licensing agreement. Generally a licensor receives 5 percent of sales royalty. However, this number can vary. Disney World Corporation receives 7 percent royalties from its Japanese licensee. When it decided to open a theme park in Europe, the corporation had opted to change from a licensee arrangement to a joint venture arrangement that would give it more control.

Manufacturers are more likely than retailers to use licensing. A manufacturer may license a manufacturer or retailer in a foreign country to produce products under its name. The products are generally meant to be sold in that foreign country. The products produced under the licensing arrangement might be the same quality as those produced in the manufacturer's other factories, or they may not.

Retailing is a way of doing business, a learning-by-doing or tacit learning type of education. Large-scale retailers are more likely to license than to franchise because

**Table 6.1**
**Elements of a Licensing Contract**

**Technology package**
> Definition/description of the licensed industrial property (patents, trademarks, know-how)
> Know-how to be supplied and its method of transfer
> Supply of raw materials, equipment, and intermediate goods

**Use conditions**
> Field of use of licensed technology
> Territorial rights for manufacture and sale
> Sublicensing rights
> Safeguarding trade secrets
> Responsibility for defense/infringement action on patents and trademarks
> Exclusion of competitive products
> Exclusion of competitive technology
> Maintenance of product standards
> Performance requirements
> Rights of licensee to new products and technology
> Reporting requirements
> Auditing/inspection rights of licensor
> Reporting requirements of licensee

**Compensation**
> Currency of payment
> Responsibilities for payment of local taxes
> Disclosure fee
> Running royalties
> Minimum royalties
> Lump-sum royalties
> Technical assistance fees
> Sales to and/or purchases from licensee
> Fees for additional new products
> Grantback of product improvements by licensee
> Other compensation

**Other provisions**
> Contract law to be followed
> Duration and renewal of contract
> Cancellation/termination provisions
> Procedures for the settlement of disputes
> Responsibility for government approval of the license agreement

Source: Adapted from Johansson, J. K. (1997). *Global Marketing*. New York: Times Mirror Books, p. 196.

it is very difficult to codify all the operations needed to run a large scale store. Specialty stores are more likely to offer a franchise arrangement. The designations used in Chapter 2—multinational versus global retailers—are helpful here. International expansion using a multinational format means the retailer uses decentralized management and adjusts the store to cultural differences. This format is more compatible with licensing rather than franchising. International expansion using a global format means the retailer uses centralized management, a standard retail offering throughout the world, and often private label merchandise. This format is more characteristic of franchising.

## › FRANCHISING

Franchising is a type of licensing arrangement that provides the seller with greater control over the retail format. A FRANCHISE is the right to operate a business under a company's name. The FRANCHISOR is selling the right to a proven way of doing business. The FRANCHISEE is buying this right. McDonald's Corporation is a worldwide franchisor. It sells the right to use the McDonald's name and method of operation. If you decide to open a McDonald's restaurant, you would be a franchisee. In the most tightly controlled franchise operations, a company provides a complete retail operation. The companies with the most successful international franchisors are those that have developed a strong franchise network in their home market before internationalizing.

Franchisees may receive a total system for conducting business, including how to recruit and train employees. The local franchisee raises the necessary capital and manages the franchise, paying an initial fee and a royalty percentage on total sales to the franchisor. Table 6.2 provides examples of several major international franchisors and summarizes their requirements for opening one of their franchises.

In some countries people use the term "franchise" quite loosely, and use it interchangeably with the term "license." When we use franchise in the United States, we mean a business format franchise.

Under U.S. law, the basic elements of a franchise include:

> A contract (but it need not be in writing to be covered by the U.S. statutes).
> A system.
> A branding, i.e., trademark, service mark, trade name, etc.
> A granting of rights.
> Payment of money.

There are two general types of franchises, direct and master. A DIRECT FRANCHISE is given to an individual store owner. Each application is considered separately. One individual might obtain multiple franchises, but each one must be applied for individually. The advantage of this type of franchise is that it is more likely to consist of owner-operators who will run the store with more care than hired managers.

A MASTER FRANCHISE is given to an individual who is then given the right to develop a particular state, country, or region. The holder of a master franchise is generally given the right to sublease franchise agreements throughout the region. A master franchise holder becomes an intermediary between the corporate franchisor and the individual franchisees. This type of franchise is the newest form of retail expansion. Athlete's Foot has used this method to expand internationally, awarding a master franchise for each country. The man who developed the master franchise in Australia is now one of Athlete's Foot's highest corporate officers. Mr. Fujita, who introduced the first McDonald's into Japan, (Chapter 2), became the master franchisor of McDonald's for his country.

### Plural Forms

Some companies use PLURAL FORMS, a combination of company-owned stores and franchised outlets. By having some of their own stores, they can benchmark the productivity of the franchise outlets. BENCHMARKING means that they use the outlets as a basis for comparison. If, for instance, they find that their company-owned stores are significantly more successful than the franchised units, they may have reason to believe that the franchisee is under-reporting sales, or is not managing the outlets properly. An example of a company using plural forms is Baskin Robbins. While there are 3,456 franchises in the United States and in 44 countries, they still obtain four company-owned units. There are advantages and disadvantages to both company-owned franchises and plural forms. These are further explained in the tables.

## Theory of Franchising

There are three perspectives that can explain why a firm would decide to franchise: (1) to extend limited resources, (2) to improve administrative efficiency, and (3) to provide risk management. In Chapter 2 I discussed the three theoretical explanations for franchising. You'll recall that when discussing the SIRE model, I said that when companies license or franchise they give away one of their most important ownership advantages, their secrets. Why, then, would any company franchise? There are three theories that explain franchising. They are resource-based theory, agency theory, and risk theory. The first perspective suggests that firms franchise to extend their scarce corporate resources. Because the franchisee puts up an initial fee and much of the initial capital investment, franchisors can expand their markets without having to generate capital themselves. This may be particularly relevant to fast-food franchises, for whom many units are needed to achieve brand name recognition and market share.

The administrative efficiency perspective derives from **AGENCY THEORY,** which predicts that individuals who own their own stores will be more likely to perform at a high level than hired managers. Owners of franchised units earn salary in relation to performance and are likely to need monitoring. Hired managers can be monitored, but at a great cost to the company. For instance, when Taco Bell uses hired managers, the company relies on a variety of incentives to enhance the managers' performance. It pays higher-than-industry average salaries, and gives managers more decision-making and unit performance bonuses.

The final perspective for explaining the decision to franchise is risk management. This view suggests that franchisors will reduce risk by owning their own stores only in areas that are more reliable and will franchise in locations that may have higher risk. Higher risk may be due to geographical distance and cultural differences.[1] For instance, even if Baskin Robbins thinks that Iran is a risky business environment, they might franchise there because someone else will be taking the risk.

It is not always initially apparent which of these theories explains why a particular company franchises. For instance, if a company begins to reacquire franchise outlets after they have more money, or if they stop franchising and open their own stores only after they have more money, then this would point toward resource-based explanations. If they franchise for agency-based reasons, there would be no reason to expect them to stop doing this just because they could afford their own stores. Risk theory can be identified if a company uses franchising in high risk countries, but then later after they have either more experience or the country becomes less risky, they enter the country with their own stores.

When I travel to China different groups often ask me to give presentations. In 2002 the China Chain Store and Franchising Association asked me to speak to a group

**Table 6.2**
**Selected International Retail Franchisors**

| Name and Address of Business | Product or Service Offering | International Locations | Franchising Fee | Capital Requirements | Training and Support Available |
|---|---|---|---|---|---|
| **The Athlete's Foot** 1950 Vaughn Rd. Kennesaw, GA 30144 (800) 524-6444 | Athletic footwear | Located in over 40 countries | $25,000 | $175,000–$325,000 | **Yes:** two-week training program and on-going support provided |
| **Baskin-Robbins** 130 Royall St. Canton, MA 02021 (781) 737-3000 | Food: ice cream and yogurt | Located in 44 countries, including India | $30,000 | $600 K liquid assets; 1.2 mil net worth | **Yes:** not specified |
| **Coffee Beanery, Ltd.** 3429 Pierson Pl. Flushing, MI 48433 (810) 733-1020 | Specialty coffees and teas from around the world | Located in 8 countries | $27,500 | $338,500–$501,500 | **Yes:** Comprehensive 21 day training at Corporate HQ |
| **Furla** 389 Fifth Ave., Ste 700 New York, NY 10016 (212) 213-1177 x15 | Women's handbags, shoes, belts, small leather goods, watches and accessories | Located in 5 countires | $25,000 | $284,400–$408,000 | **Yes:** Week-long training program in NYC office and in corporate stores |
| **General Nutrition Companies, Inc. (GNC)** 300 Sixth Ave. Pittsburgh, PA 15222 (800) 766-7099 | Specialty retailer of vitamins, minerals, herbs, and sports nutrition supplements | Located in 38 countries | $40,000 | $132,681–$182,031 | **Yes:** new franchisees receive three weeks of initial training, including an intensive one-week training class at corporate headquarters |
| **Gymboree Play and Music** 500 Howard St. San Francisco, CA 94105 (800) 520-7529 | Interactive parent-child play and music program | Located in 26 countries | $45,000 | Minimal intital investment is an average of $141,400–$286,765 | **Yes:** In addition to the mandatory initial franchise training, franchisees also receive regional trainings |
| **Little Caesars Pizza** 2211 Woodward Ave. Detroit, MI 48201-3400 (800) 553-5776 | Food: pizza, breads, sandwiches, and salads | Located in 20 countries | $20,000 | $50,000 liquid and $150,000 total net worth | **Yes:** 6-week training class is available with support from Architectre to strategic market development support provided |

| Franchise | Product/Service | Locations | Franchise Fee | Total Investment | Training |
|---|---|---|---|---|---|
| **Mango**<br>P.O Box 280<br>08184 Palau de Plegamans<br>Barcelona, Spain<br>(34-3) 864-44 44 | Fashionable woman's apparel | Located in various countries around Europe including Spain, France, Greece, and Portugal | $24,950 | $97,430–$145,650 (total investment) | **Yes:** two-week training course, one week in-store and ongoing |
| **Marble Slab Creamery**<br>3100 S. Cessner, Ste. 305<br>Houston, TX 77063<br>(713) 780-3601 | Food: ice cream made fresh daily | Located in 11 countries | $28,000 | $275,000 net worth, $70,000 liquid | **Yes:** Ten-day training program in Houston, Texas, store opening assistance, continued field supervision, and advertising/public relations assistance |
| **Novus Auto Glass Repair & Replacement**<br>12800 Highway 13 S., 500<br>Savage, MN 55378<br>(952) 946-0447 | Variety of auto glass and replacement products and services | Located in 42 countries | $7,500 | $410,500–$185,099 | **Yes:** 3 weeks |
| **PostNet**<br>1819 Wazee<br>St. Denver, CO 80202<br>(800) 338-7401 | Postal delivery and services | | $29,900 | $174,325–$195,800 | **Yes:** In-depth training, based on detailed operations manual, includes customer service, merchandising, marketing, administration and daily operations |
| **Subway**<br>325 Bic Drive<br>Milford, CT 06460<br>(203) 877-4281 | Food: submarine sandwiches and salads | Located in 55 countries | $12,500 | $87,300–$218,800 | **Yes:** two-week training program and follow-up support |

**References for franchise chart:**

The Athlete's Foot: www.theathletesfoot.com
Baskin-Robbins: www.thefranchisehandbook.com Also used: www.franchise.com
Coffee Beanery Ltd.: www.thefranchisehandbook.com Also used: www.franchise.com
Furla: www.thefranchisehandbook.com Also used: www.furla.com
GNC: www.thefranchisehandbook.com Also used: www.gnc.com
Gymboree Play and Music: www.thefranchisehandbook.com
Little Caesar's Pizza: www.thefranchisehandbook.com
Mango: www.mango.com
Marble Slab Creamery: www.thefranchisehandbook.com
Novus Auto Repair & Replacement: www.thefranchisehandbook.com
PostNet: www.thefranchisehandbook.com Also used: www.franchise.com
Subway: www.franchise.com

**Table 6.3**
**Advantages and Disadvantages of Franchise Forms**

| Advantages of predominantly franchise systems chains (for operator) | Disadvantages of predominantly franchise systems chains (for operator) |
|---|---|
| *From a financial perspective:*<br>Low initial investments for franchisor | *From a financial perspective:*<br>Limited individual financing capability, thus second-string position lower margin, even if manufacturers make up for it through retail sales margin |
| *From an economic perspective:*<br>Possibility of moving merchandise (economies of scale) | |
| *From a strategic perspective:*<br>Rapid chain development | *From a strategic perspective:*<br>Risk of former franchisees copying concept and creating a competitive chain |
| *From a managerial perspective:*<br>Franchisee is an entrepreneur, i.e., more dynamic than an employee<br>Generally franchise systems are more dynamic and less bureaucratic<br>Less administrative control | *From a managerial perspective:*<br>Risk of former franchisees copying concept and creating a competitive chain |
| | *From a managerial perspective:*<br>Presence of different franchisees in the same city leads to structural problems<br>Pure franchise chains are difficult to renovate<br>Incomplete information available on performances<br>Difficult to control recruitment standards for franchisee employees<br>Higher transaction costs |
| *From a marketing perspective:*<br>Better knowledge of local markets | *From a marketing perspective:*<br>Risk of losing concept control and trademark integrity |

| Advantages of predominantly company-owned chains (for operator) | Disadvantages of predominantly company-owned chains (for operator) |
|---|---|
| *From a financial perspective:*<br>Better profitability mentioned by service-oriented advocates<br>Financial benefits are not shared with franchisees | *From a financial perspective:*<br>High development costs<br>Lower profits for product manufacturers as company-owned stores play a role not offered to franchisees |
| *From a managerial perspective:*<br>Easier to locate at the best sites<br>Greater chance of being bought up by a larger group | *From a strategic perspective:*<br>Slower development |
| *From a managerial perspective:*<br>No organizational problems due to the strong hierarchic relationship<br>Compensates for the lack of good franchise candidates<br>Easier to control training sessions | *From a managerial perspective:*<br>Lack of flexibility<br>Standard problems of agency relationships between operator and salaried directors |
| *From a marketing perspective:*<br>Total concept control<br>Higher trademark integrity | *From a marketing perspective:*<br>Difficulties in adapting concept locally<br>Less innovation |

| Table 6.3 *Continued* | |
|---|---|
| **Advantages of plural-form chains (for operator)** | **Disadvantages of plural form chains (for operator)** |
| *Solves problem of location speed/concept control (adding units/uniformity):* Rapid development and territory coverage through complementary (franchises and company-owned outlets can play complementary roles in different chains) Rapidly cross over critical threshold Consolidation concept control using company-owned outlets Association of flagship stores with standardized franchise stores | *Difficulty in reconciling two different management modes: franchises or company-owned stores:* Need for dual organizational structure as relationships between franchisor and franchisees or between franchisor and company-owned outlets are not the same: alternate authority/persuasion |
| *Greater organizational flexibility (adaptation):* Demonstration of franchisor know-how (rather than concept because of the service dimension) through pilot stores located near franchises for training and simulation (showcase effect) Company stores are used and test laboratories for concept development: few company-owned stores are required (10%) Combining franchises and company-owned stores provides complementarities | *Risks of demotivating and creating anxiety among franchisees due to presence of company-owners:* Locally, when company-owned stores are located nearby System-wide, when proportion of company-owned stores is too high |
| *Greater economic efficiency:* Lower financial investments due to franchises Increased investment capacity due to partners' external financial input | |

Source: Cliquet, Gerard and Croizean, Jean-Philippe (2002). "Towards Plural Forms, Franchising/Company-Owned Systems, in the French Cosmetics Retail Industry." *International Journal of Retail & Distribution Management.* 30 (5), pp.136–137.

about franchising. I told them that franchising is not my real area of expertise, but they wanted me to cover this topic anyway. Every time I go to China I conduct interviews with business executives and government officials. I decided to ask the government officials some questions about franchising, for example, did they have a specific franchising law and could companies EXPATRIATE PROFITS? Expatriation of profits means that the franchiser can take the money out of the country. No one I asked seemed to have an answer to either of those two questions until I got to a high level government official who told me that China did not have a franchising law— and profits could not be expatriated. Finally the day came for my presentation on franchising. My hosts picked me up and took me to the event. Imagine my surprise when I learned that I was a featured speaker at the China Convention on Franchising! I gave my presentation and later strolled around the convention talking with some of the hopeful franchisors. I asked them the questions that I had asked the government officials. Most of the companies I talked with thought that yes, of course there were franchising laws and of course they could take their profits home. As I mentioned earlier, in reality at that time, there was no law covering franchising and

**Photo 6.1**
A mother and child are leaving a 7-Eleven store in Japan. These convenience stores offer non-product services, such as fax facilities and payment centers for purchasing from catalogs or paying utility bills. *Courtesy of AP/Wide World Photos.*

no guarantee that profits could be expatriated. China did not pass a franchising law until 2005.

China is a country where the commercial interest and activity have developed more rapidly than its laws. The RULE OF LAW concept means that a country has codified its laws so that all market participants know what is legal and what is illegal. Before laws are written down there is much greater risk to companies doing business in the country. The current China Franchising Law does make it possible for franchisors to repatriate profits; however, a business will not be able to enter China as a pure franchisor. The law requires that a company operate two stores of their own in China before they can be given the go-ahead to start franchising.

The reason businesses franchise internationally seems to be different from the general reasons for entering into a franchising arrangement. The primary reasons companies give for not expanding internationally are sufficient opportunities at home and lack of international knowledge and competencies.[2] Experience and size are important factors that help determine whether a company will pursue international franchising.[3]

As we will see in the next section, a theory of international franchising depends on maximizing both managerial abilities and risk management.

## Theory of International Franchising

In an article on international franchising, Fladmoe-Lindquist identifies a typology for understanding international franchise types. The typology utilizes resource-based theory. According to this theory, know-how-based resources or routines for operating provide competitive advantage to firms. In addition, some companies are simply better than others at generating ideas and new ways to do things. Resource-based theory emphasizes the importance of not just possessing resources, but of

**Table 6.4**
**International Franchising Capabilities and Capacity for Development**

| Capacity for Developing International Capabilities | Existing International Franchising Capabilities | |
|---|---|---|
| | **Low** | **High** |
| **High** | *Integrating franchisors*<br>› Pursues cautious growth<br>› Uses multiple forms of franchising<br>› Proactive evaluation | *Worldwide franchisors*<br>› Focus on global markets<br>› Use multiple forms of franchising<br>› Both proactive and reactive |
| **Low** | *Constrained franchisors*<br>› Locally international<br>› Limited involvement in international markets<br>› Reactive evaluation | *Conventional franchisors*<br>› Focus on several foreign markets<br>› Use fewer forms of franchising<br>› Often reactive with some proactive efforts |

continual organization learning. Growth of a firm involves combining existing resources and capabilities with the ability to develop new resources and capabilities. Effective learning requires that the franchisor acquire and process information, thus creating knowledge. This is the basis for new franchise strategies for international franchisors as they learn about the international competitive environment.[4]

Table 6.4 is a summary of Fladmoe-Lindquist's typology. She identifies four types of international franchisors: constrained franchisors, integrating franchisors, conventional franchisors, and worldwide franchisors. An important point made by Fladmoe-Lindquist is that learning and capabilities are not constant over time. Abilities of companies to learn and integrate knowledge is stronger at some points in time than at others. This helps to explain why franchisors expand at some times, retreat at others, and sit idol for periods of times.

CONSTRAINED FRANCHISORS have limited international management capabilities and little capacity for learning. A company in this category is not likely to pursue significant international franchise development. Such "locally international" franchisors will limit their international expansion to the country closest to them, geographically or culturally. Many American companies have extended their franchise operations to Canada but have little interest in going elsewhere. Bruegger's Bagels is an example of a constrained franchisor. Bruegger's opened its first bagel shop in 1983 but did not begin franchising until 1991. The company's international growth interest is limited to Canada.[5]

INTEGRATING FRANCHISORS have limited international franchising capabilities but considerable capacity for learning from experience and integrating experiences into operations. These firms are more likely to initiate international expansion early in their life cycle. The British franchisor Tie Rack fits this typology. Tie Rack expanded within Great Britain before considering international expansion. The company enters each market using an approach that reflects an awareness of different national tastes, regulations, and franchise partners. The French market was entered using a master license with a joint venture partner. In Norway, a direct license for a single shop with an independent franchisee was used instead. Tie Rack entered the U.S. market with a wholly owned subsidiary of the franchisor.[6]

CONVENTIONAL FRANCHISORS have some of the capabilities needed for international expansion but do not have a great ability to develop what is needed to succeed in a broader global setting. If they expand internationally, retailers in this group typically find themselves in a less than ideal location. They are likely to enter a market and then withdraw. These franchisors are also likely to expand into international franchising through foreign solicitations by prospective franchisees. A businessperson from South Africa who approaches the Gap, a retailer of casual clothing, about opening a Gap franchise in Cape Town is an example of a foreign solicitation by a prospective franchisee. Gap has not selected South Africa as a strategic area where it should expand its offerings. It is simply responding to an offer from an outside businessperson.

This is similar to what happens to many manufacturing firms, who begin their international involvement responding to unsolicited orders from foreign countries. An order is placed by a company in a foreign country, and the manufacturer responds by exporting the product to them. It is a first step in internationalization, but it is an opportunistic, not a strategic decision. The British franchisor Fastframe fits this profile. The firm had been successful in Britain, but it was not really ready for international expansion. An American convinced Fastframe to expand to California. Although the firm has been moderately successful, management will tell you they made many mistakes in the initial effort. This includes poor research regarding project viability, poor site selection, and short-sighted contract provisions that constrained the franchisor.[7]

WORLDWIDE FRANCHISORS are generally larger retailers with a greater amount of experience and greater capabilities in both administrative efficiency and host country risk management. These franchisors operate in many countries. They use a variety of ownership and franchise agreement configurations. They have operated internationally for a long period of time, gathering additional knowledge in a variety of markets. McDonald's fits into this group. These companies make mistakes during their early international expansion efforts, but they integrate these experiences into their international franchising routines and capabilities and go on to hold successful worldwide positions.

A retailer may start as one type of franchise developer and shift to another typology. A traditional method of movement is for a constrained franchisor to become a conventional franchisor. In this scenario, a domestic or "locally international" franchisor moves to a broader international position without having internalized or integrated any new knowledge into the franchise operations. The company is able to follow this path because it has been relatively successful at home and in neighboring markets. It believes it is time to attempt a more extensive international position. However, this can be a risky move. Success in home and neighboring markets combined with a lower level of "international awareness" can result in expansion to foreign markets before the company develops an understanding of host country risk. Actually, success is a very poor teacher, because when you succeed, you rarely go back and examine why you succeeded. Greater learning comes from failure, or at least problems that need to be attended to. Midas's entry into the British market using home-based corporate employees on temporary assignments is an example of a company moving from constrained to conventional franchisor. Most of the franchise units failed.

Companies may also move from constrained to integrating franchisors. This move occurs primarily among domestic franchisors who increase their set of capabilities before attempting to broaden their international operations. This is a proactive pattern of internationalization. Tie Rack's expansion into France, Scandinavia, and the United States reflects this type of analytical capabilities development.[8]

A franchisor that maintains the learning capacity developed as an integrating franchisor may develop into a worldwide franchisor. The path generally begins with a retailer moving from a constrained to an integrating and then to a worldwide franchisor. Subway's ability to keep entrepreneurial[9] and Midas's successful expansion to other countries after its initial failure in Great Britain are good examples of this route.[10]

Some companies make the change from conventional franchisor to worldwide franchisor. This change requires that the company put great energy into finding new ideas and products for foreign markets. This type of franchisor usually finds itself operating in several international markets as a series of reactive responses to foreign franchisees. During the early days of Dairy Queen's international expansion, the company found itself in less obscure markets because potential franchisees solicited it. Dairy Queen was smart enough to recognize that additional skills and capabilities were needed to continue successful operations.

The last type of movement occurs among franchisors with high capabilities from the start. These companies move from integrating franchisors to worldwide franchisors. They begin operations already in a learning mode and continue to integrate new information while gaining resources and capabilities along the way. If the capacity for learning and integration does not diminish, such firms are likely to expand worldwide more quickly than any other type of franchisor. As Fladmore-Lindquist's international franchisor typology emphasizes, a company's capabilities (ownership advantages) and willingness and ability to learn from previous actions will determine its ability to take advantage of international franchising opportunities.

## Regulation of Franchising

Most countries do not have laws that deal specifically with franchising. Although the leader in franchise development, the United States has specific franchising laws, in Europe, only France and Spain have such laws. Franchising thrives in Japan, yet there is no specific law that relates to this business activity.

Central and South America, including Mexico, have experienced a great increase in franchise development. There are more than 800 members in the Latin American franchise associations. In 1994, Mexico introduced a set of disclosure requirements that are similar to the franchise laws in the United States and France. Brazil enacted its own franchising law about the same time as Mexico. Both Mexico and Brazil's laws include a stipulation that the franchisee has 10 days to review the information and make a decision regarding the franchise purchase. Spain's law requires that franchisors register their companies with a government registry and deliver key investment information to prospective franchisees at least 20 days before the franchisee signs the purchase contract or pays any money. Russia has a franchise law that relies less on the delivery of investment information and more on registration and requirements of the franchise relationship.

Running a successful international franchising empire requires careful and continuous quality control. McDonald's restaurants are an example of a tightly run and successful franchising system considered to be one of the most successful in the world. McDonald's has a reputation for solid franchisor-franchisee relationships, and is built on the idea that the corporation should make money only from its franchisees' food sales. McDonald's headquarters does not sell equipment, food, or packaging to its franchisees. All of their equipment and supplies are purchased from company-approved third-party suppliers. When this philosophy was originated, it was unique. Until that time, franchise operations made much of their money by selling equipment.

When a franchise in Paris failed to keep its restaurant clean, McDonald's terminated the relationship. The franchisee took McDonald's to court but lost and received a scolding from the French judge for letting down a great organization like McDonald's.

Recently, franchisors have begun teaming business concepts together. The idea of dual branding or co-branding is changing the look of franchising by combining two or more concepts under one roof. Ideally, co-branding creates synergy between concepts. Baskin-Robbins and Dunkin' Donuts offer this type of synergy. Traffic is highest for Dunkin' Donuts in the morning and highest for Baskin-Robbins in the afternoon.

As previously noted, the major problem with franchising is that the founding company relinquishes its company secrets to the franchisee. The company gains quick growth and immediate returns but loses control of its company secrets and the information that has made it unique. Strategic alliances, which will be discussed next, are another method for joint expansion activities.

## > INTERNATIONAL STRATEGIC ALLIANCES

STRATEGIC ALLIANCES are business relationships established by two or more companies who cooperate out of mutual need and to share risk in achieving a common objective. This means that the companies involved determine that:

> Common objectives exist.
> One partner's weakness is offset by the other's strength.
> Reaching the objectives alone is too costly, takes too much time, or will be too risky.
> Together their respective strengths make possible what otherwise would be unattainable.

To be considered a strategic alliance, three characteristics need to be present. The alliances must be horizontal, collaborative, and mutually beneficial to all parties. Companies form strategic alliances to fill the gaps in skills. Good alliances operate like good marriages; poor alliances, in turn, are very similar to bad marriages.

To be characterized as HORIZONTAL, partners in the alliance must be at the same channel level. A retailer-to-retailer alliance would be horizontal. A retailer-to-manufacturer alliance would be vertical. Strategic alliances would include only the retailer-to-retailer agreements.

An alliance based on mutually defined objectives is COLLABORATIVE. Strategic alliances are not dictated from a stronger channel member to a weaker member.

In a MUTUALLY BENEFICIAL arrangement, as one would expect, benefits occur for all of the participants. In the period from the 1950s through the 1970s, many international retail alliances were formed. However, most of these alliances were formed to limit political risk or meet legal requirements in a specific country. For instance, until 2005 a foreign company could not invest in China without a Chinese partner, who had to own 51 percent of the enterprise. These business alliances were generally not strategic, that is, formed to be collaborative, horizontal, and mutually beneficial. Rather, they were legislated alliances.

Today, the purpose of strategic international alliances is to be competitive in global markets by meeting or exceeding new standards for products and technology use. Most successful alliances are between partners of equal strength in their home markets. The strategic international alliance between Wal-Mart and CIFRA, the Mexican retailer, is a good example of this new breed of business cooperation. CIFRA has long held the position of the dominant retailer in Mexico. It has a variety of retail formats, a long history in Mexico, and strong partnerships with local suppliers. In turn, Wal-Mart brought to the alliance with CIFRA one of the most sophisticated logistics and purchasing systems in the world.

There are three major reasons why a retailer would form an alliance:

1. To create new retail companies in another country with a local retailer as partner.
2. To enhance purchasing power.
3. To facilitate exchange of knowledge or know-how.

These reasons are not mutually exclusive. In the Wal-Mart-CIFRA alliance, all three of these reasons were a motivation for the parties involved. However in the end Wal-Mart acquired CIFRA. This lends support for the concept that retail joint ventures are by nature short term, lasting generally until the foreign firm learns the culture of the new country. Some joint ventures are strategic alliances, others are not. It depends on if the three requirements for a strategic alliance are met.

## Alliance Types

There are two types of alliances. EQUITY ALLIANCES include a cross shareholding between members. NONEQUITY ALLIANCES involve collaboration in business activities that can be mutually beneficial, such as cooperative buying groups, branding, expertise exchange, and product marketing.[11] Nonequity groups generally have a central office to administer the work of the alliance. They often refer to these offices as alliances with central secretariats. Such alliances are more fluid than the equity alliances, with members entering and leaving.

## Joint Ventures

JOINT VENTURES are formed when two or more retailers come together to create a new enterprise. The key term here is NEW ENTITY—it is not just one company taking over another company, but two companies coming together to produce something new. The new enterprise may be considered a joint venture if it has the three characteristics of a strategic alliance. Earlier, I mentioned that many of the international retail alliances of the 1950s through the 1970s were formed to meet host government regulations related to local ownership. In such cases, the joint venture would not be considered a strategic alliance because there is no evidence that it meets the requirement of being collaborative and mutually beneficial. The joint ventures created by governments that require a certain level of local ownership might be compared to a shotgun wedding. The two parties are legally joined, but they are not necessarily happy about the situation. In contrast, a strategic alliance is like a marriage based on love and respect. Each partner gains from the joining (mutually beneficial), they share a similar objective (a wonderful life together), and the partnership is between two equals (horizontal).

## › SUMMARY

Licensing, franchising, and strategic alliances involve sharing company secrets. The problems for retailers involved in these types of arrangements can be significant. Of these methods of cooperation, strategic alliances provide retailers with the greatest potential to gain market presence over the long run.

Companies originally used joint ventures in foreign markets because they were mandated by the host country. Today, in order to protect their local investment interests, many countries will not allow wholly owned foreign retailers to operate within their borders. Some of the most successful international expansion involves strategic alliances. Strategic alliances are characterized by being horizontal, collaborative, and mutually beneficial to all parties. When used in good faith, the strengths gained in a strategic alliance are powerful. When the partners do not operate as faithful partners, the outcome is trouble.

## › KEY TERMS

AGENCY THEORY

BENCHMARKING

COLLABORATIVE

CONSTRAINED FRANCHISORS

CONVENTIONAL FRANCHISORS

DIRECT FRANCHISE

EQUITY ALLIANCE

EXPATRIATE PROFITS

FRANCHISE

FRANCHISEE

FRANCHISOR

HORIZONTAL

INTEGRATING FRANCHISORS

JOINT VENTURES

MASTER FRANCHISE

MUTUALLY BENEFICIAL

NEW ENTITY

NONEQUITY ALLIANCE

PLURAL FORMS

RULE OF LAW

STRATEGIC ALLIANCES

WORLDWIDE FRANCHISORS

## › DISCUSSION QUESTIONS

1. What are the advantages and disadvantages of licensing and franchising for the companies described below?

a. **Photoark** is a company that has just developed a unique method of developing film at home. Consumers purchase the film and chemicals from a Photoark store, then take them home to shoot and develop. To keep the photo quality high it is very important that while the chemicals are held in the store, they be maintained at a constant temperature and that inventory be no more than 5 days old. Photoark wants to expand internationally, but the company knows that its technology will be copied by other retailers in a few years and it wants to gain market presence rapidly.

b. **Treetops** is a book retailer that focuses on selling innovative books. Its selection is vast; it has the largest store in the area in whatever market it enters. Treetops could be considered a category killer. Its most important business asset is an excellent logistics system, which the company uses in moving merchandise from one store to another to take advantage of regional preferences in books.

2. Why would the Disney World Corporation choose to use a licensing arrangement in Japan but a joint venture in France? Knowing what you do about this corporation, what mode of international expansion would you suggest?

3. Conventional franchisors often expand because of a solicitation from a businessperson in a foreign country. What is wrong with responding to these invitations to franchise?

4. Identify areas in which international strategic alliances would be a superior expansion route. What factors make the decision different for retailers as compared to manufacturers?

5. How can you determine if a joint venture is a strategic alliance? Are all strategic alliances joint ventures? Explain your answer.

## ❯ ENDNOTES

1. Fladmoe-Lindquist, K. (1996). "International Franchising: Capabilities and Development." *Journal of Business Venturing*, Vol. 11, pp. 419–438.

2. Aydin, N. and M. Kacker (1990). "International Outlook of U.S. Based Franchisers." *International Marketing Review*, Vol. 7, No. 2, pp. 43–53.

3. Huszagh, S. M., F. W. Huszagh, and F. McIntyre (1992). "International Franchising in the Context of Competitive Strategy and the Theory of the Firm." *International Marketing Review*, Vol. 9, No. 5, pp. 5–18.

4. Fladmoe-Lindquist, K. (1996).

5. Entrepreneur (1996). Seventeenth Annual Franchise 500. January, pp. 211–311.

6. Delnevo, R. (1990). "Tie Rack, plc. Case Study." In M. Abell, ed., *The International Franchise Option*. London: Waterlow Publishers, pp. 339–347.

7. Fladmoe-Lindquist, K. (1996).

8. Delnevo (1990).

9. Entrepreneur (1996).

10. Shook, C., and R. Shook (1993). *Franchising: The Business Strategy That Changed the World*. Englewood Cliffs, NJ: Prentice-Hall.

11. Robinson, T. M. and C. M. Clarke-Hill (1994). "Competitive Advantage Through Strategic Retail Alliances: A European Perspective," presented at Recent Advances in Retailing and Service Science Conference, University of Alberta, Canada, May 1994.

# 7

# RETAILING IN MULTINATIONAL MARKETS

## After reading this chapter, you should understand

> Some of the benefits and drawbacks of multinational cooperation.

> How factors of production influence the success of multinational groups and whether multinational cooperative agreements will be beneficial to consumers.

> The hierarchical structure of multinational markets.

> The antecedents to further levels of multinational cooperation.

> The effect different levels of cooperation have on domestic retailers and international retailers.

Along with the view of the world as a market comes the idea of multinational markets that link countries for trade. The European Union began with six founding member states in 1952. In 2004 they had 25 members; further enlargement is scheduled for 2007 with the addition of two states. It is estimated that eventually the EU will include 30 states. Some states are reluctant to surrender sovereignty to a supranational entity. The Scandinavian countries are part of this group. Some Eastern European countries like Belarus, Moldova, Kazakhstan, and Ukraine remain outside the EU. They all belong to the CIS and plan to have a further integrated model, like the EU, but for countries that were formerly linked to Russia. The United States, Canada, and Mexico have joined to form the North American Free Trade Association (NAFTA). Later in this chapter, we will identify which countries are part of the EU. Latin American countries have formed a multitude of multinational trade associations, some with more success than others. Asian countries have tremendous potential for creating multinational markets, and have joined together in a series of cooperative agreements. African countries have been the least successful in forging multinational arrangements because of the instability in that region.

Multinational agreements are most successful when member nations have dissimilar production capabilities. Production capabilities are directly related to a country's factors of production, discussed in Chapter 3. Multinational agreements between countries having different strengths offer the greatest long-term gains. A low-wage country that joins a country with strong capital and entrepreneurship creates a self-sufficient market relationship. The best combination of countries into a multinational market are those that have different factors of production, distinct strengths in what they can produce. It is this diversity that gives rise to a self-sufficient trading relationship.

Multinational cooperation offers some benefits and some drawbacks to member nations. Multinational markets also display a pattern of development ranging from the least formal to the most formal. The least formal level of agreement is a REGIONAL COOPERATIVE GROUP, an agreement between countries to jointly participate and to develop certain industries or infrastructures beneficial to the economies of member countries. The next level is a FREE TRADE ASSOCIATION; internal barriers to trade between member nations are eliminated at this level. The third level is a FULL CUSTOMS UNION, in which internal barriers are eliminated and common external barriers are established with external trading partners. The fourth level is a COMMON MARKET; this agreement eliminates internal barriers to trade, establishes common external barriers, and adds the free flow of capital and labor. The highest multinational level is a POLITICAL UNION, which includes the removal of internal barriers of trade, establishes common external barriers to trade, allows for the free flow of capital and labor, and adds the establishment of a unifying economic logic. I will discuss each of these levels of agreement in more detail later in the chapter, but first let's talk about the benefits and drawbacks of multinational integration.

## › BENEFITS OF MULTINATIONAL MARKETS

The four major benefits of multinational markets can be summarized as follows: (1) large mass markets are attractive to mass merchandisers, (2) improved channels of distribution provide a benefit to all types of retailers operating outside a local community, (3) increased trade with member nations can be an advantage to the participating members but a disadvantage to those outside the trade block, and (4) consumers benefit from lower costs if the multinational market includes countries with diverse factors of production.

## Large Mass Market

When countries remove rules and regulations that impede the free flow of merchandise between borders, they increase the sales area and the potential customer base. Large mass markets benefit retailers because they can take advantage of economies of scale in purchasing merchandise. The United States, with one of the largest mass markets in the world, has encouraged the growth of national chains. The most important retail innovations worldwide have occurred in the United States. Greater volume sets the stage for technological innovations and the profitable use of private label sourcing. There is a flip side to this benefit, though. Because U.S. retailers have had such a large mass market, they have not expanded internationally. Unlike European or Japanese retailers, who needed to expand because of national saturation, U.S. retailers have not developed the skills and abilities needed to become world retailers. They often view international expansion from a self-reference criterion, meaning anything that works well in the United States should work well in foreign markets. This attitude is not conducive to effective world retailing.

Large mass markets are more important to particular types of retailers. Mass merchandisers and discount operations benefit most from multinational markets. It is probably not a surprise that the early U.S. international retailers were mass merchandisers such as Sears and discounters such as Wal-Mart and Kmart. A second advantage of multinational markets derives from the ease of moving from one country to another. The ease of movement relates to products, people, and promotions.

## Improved Channels of Distribution, Advertising, and Transportation

If you traveled through Europe before 1992, customs officials interrogated you at the boundary of each country. At these checkpoints, you were required to show your passport and answer questions about your travel purpose. Now, when you move from France to Germany, for example, you may not realize that you have entered another country. The experience is similar to going from Michigan to Indiana. The only indication that you have entered another state is a sign—"Welcome to Indiana." The same situation occurs for merchandise moving from one EC country to another. Before 1992, transportation trucks were required to stop at customs, complete documentation forms, pay a tariff, and answer questions about the merchandise destination. All of these steps add to the cost of distribution. Likewise, removing these requirements reduces the cost of distribution.

Less regulation and supervision of cargo reduce transportation costs in multinational markets. Standard regulations related to freight cargo containers reduce the need to repack containers to meet national regulations.

Retailers can also economize advertising through a mass market. Although countries are still free to decide advertising standards, the regulations are straightforward. In Germany, using comparative advertising is not legal. However, adhering to these legal regulations is not too difficult.

Improved access to consumers and the attraction of a larger mass market lead to greater trade flows within the multinational market.

## Increased Trade with Member Nations

We know that the greatest benefits of multinational markets occur when member nations have complementary, not competitive, resources and factors of production. Mexico, for instance, has a lower labor cost than either the United States or Canada. Under the NAFTA between these countries, this lower cost would encourage production of more labor-intensive products south of the border. Opponents of NAFTA maintain that having a country with a low labor cost as a part of the multinational market is disastrous, leading to the loss of jobs at home. However, this is exactly what an agreement such as NAFTA should do. With its abundant supply of labor and low minimum wages, Mexico *should* produce labor-intensive products, leaving the United States and Canada with higher-paying jobs based in technology. When the EC added Spain to its multinational market, the same concern was expressed. Many Europeans believed that jobs would be lost elsewhere in Europe. When a country's factors of production are viewed as complementary resources rather than competitors, the arrangement is much more likely to be successful.

Agricultural products are often the most contested area of trade because each country views the maintenance of an agricultural industry as important to its national well being. Also, agriculture production is often duplicated among member countries. Continental Europe banned British beef exports when mad cow disease erupted in Britain. This ban was probably related more to market protection than to health interests. Earlier, Britain had banned French poultry exports, supposedly to protect British citizens from a poultry virus. At different times, France has banned Italian wine and the Irish have banned all poultry and eggs from other member countries. The reasons given were always related to health; however, the evidence points to market protection. The European Commission is a regulatory group that settles the European Common Market trade disputes. In each of these instances, the commission charged the countries with violations of EU regulations.

## Benefit to Consumers of Lower Internal Tariff Barriers

Tariffs are taxes on imported products. Reducing tariffs makes these products less expensive, which affects consumption, allowing consumers to purchase more of these and other goods and increasing the standard of living. When consumers purchase products produced within their multinational trading group, the cost to consumers should be lower.

The more diverse the production capabilities of these member countries, the greater the cost savings for consumers. As we saw earlier, adding Mexico to NAFTA provided a low-wage producer to this multinational market. This created initial panic from special interest groups representing U.S. labor. Presidential candidate Ross Perot commented at the time that NAFTA had created a great big sucking sound—the sound of U.S. jobs going south. In fact, this has not happened. Low-wage jobs lost to Mexico have been replaced with new jobs in other sectors of the economy.

**Photo 7.1**
The Euro currency which
is used by the countries
in the European Union.
*Courtesy of Condé Nast.*

## › DRAWBACKS OF MULTINATIONAL MARKETS

At this point in the discussion, you may believe that there are only minor drawbacks to multinational markets. Of course, that is not true. Although the benefits outweigh the drawbacks, there are some inherent winners and losers among countries engaging in multinational cooperation. For one thing, the more similar the production capabilities of the member countries, the less the economic gain. Competition also increases within the multinational block. This can be advantageous for consumers, who will likely benefit from lower prices. However, it will probably cause a consolidation of market players. Weak firms will go out of business and marginal firms will consolidate.

Another drawback is that the market, at first appearance, seems like a single market. This can lead retailers to misunderstand the need to be adaptive to cultural differences. Furthermore, inflation can be a problem if there is insufficient competition within the market to keep prices low. Finally, the increased layer of government involvement can contribute to inflation as well as to an overall problem with excessive red tape. Let's look at each of these, in turn.

### Increased Competition

After tariffs are eliminated, competition becomes much more intense. To understand why, consider the following examples of different schools' athletic teams. Suppose you attend a small high school of only 40 students. Your school needs 11 members to make a soccer team. As one of the 40 students, you have a very good chance of making the team. Now suppose your school is consolidated with another high school of 300 students. The chance that you will make the football team as one of 340 students competing is much less. However, the greater pool of potential players probably ensures that your school will have a much more competitive team.

In a multinational market, this increased competition will mean lower costs to consumers and a natural consolidation of companies. Companies that are capital intensive will benefit from consolidation; companies that are labor intensive may experience little change.

## Looks Like a Single Market, But It Is Not

Careless assessment of the remaining cultural complexity of multinational markets poses the next disadvantage. It is tempting to view multinational markets as one mass market, but that is a dangerous assumption (Table 7.1).

Are the United States and Mexico really any more similar after NAFTA than they were before? Probably not. Evidence even points toward the opposite effect. Similarly, there are signs that individual country identities are even more important after Europe's unification than they were before. When the European countries became joined at the hip economically, they cried out for a national identity in other ways. For instance, France has since passed a very restrictive law requiring that when a French word exists for a product being described in advertising or another form of communication, the French word must be used.

Even without the consideration of national pride and preservation of a national identity, there exists the problem of considering a heterogeneous group of people as homogeneous. If you have moved from one part of the United States to another

**Table 7.1**
**2005 Major Economic Data for 21 APEC Members**

| Country | Population (millions) | Land Area (1,000 sq. km) | GDP ($ billions) | Per Capita GDP ($) | GDP ($) Growth Rate[1] (%) 2005 | GDP Exports ($ billions) | Imports ($ billions) |
|---|---|---|---|---|---|---|---|
| 1. Australia | 20.2 | 7,692 | 692.4 | 33,629 | 2.5 | 86,551 | 103,863 |
| 2. Brunei Darussalam | 0.4 | 6 | 5.7 | 15,764 | 0.4 | 4,713 | 1,638 |
| 3. Canada | 32.0 | 9,971 | 1,084.1 | 33,648 | 2.9 | 315,858 | 271,869 |
| 4. Chile | 15.4 | 757 | 105.8 | 6,807 | 6.3 | 32,548 | 24,769 |
| 5. China | 1,299.8 | 9,561 | 1,851.2 | 1,416 | 10.2 | 593,647 | 560,811 |
| 6. Hong Kong | 6.9 | 1 | 174.0 | 25,006 | 7.3 | 265,763 | 273,361 |
| 7. Indonesia | 223.8 | 1,905 | 280.9 | 1,237 | 5.6 | 71,585 | 46,525 |
| 8. Japan | 127.3 | 378 | 4,694.3 | 36,841 | 2.6 | 566,191 | 455,661 |
| 9. Korea | 48.2 | 99 | 819.2 | 16,897 | 4 | 253,845 | 224,463 |
| 10. Malaysia | 25.5 | 330 | 129.4 | 4,989 | 5.2 | 125,857 | 105,297 |
| 11. Mexico | 105.0 | 1,958 | 734.9 | 6,920 | 3 | 177,095 | 171,714 |
| 12. New Zealand | 4.1 | 271 | 108.7 | 26,373 | 2.3 | 20,334 | 21,716 |
| 13. Papua New Guinea | 5.9 | 463 | 3.5 | 585 | 3.1 | 4,321 | 1,463 |
| 14. Peru | 27.5 | 1,285 | 78.2 | 2,798 | 6.4 | 12,111 | 8,872 |
| 15. Philippines | 86.2 | 300 | 95.6 | 1,088 | 5 | 39,588 | 40,297 |
| 16. Russia | 144.0 | 17,075 | 719.2 | 5,015 | 6.4 | 171,431 | 86,593 |
| 17. Singapore | 4.2 | 1 | 116.3 | 27,180 | 6.4 | 179,755 | 163,982 |
| 18. Chinese Taipei | 22.5 | 36 | 335.2 | 14,857 | 4.1 | 174,350 | 168,715 |
| 19. Thailand | 64.6 | 513 | 178.1 | 2,736 | 4.5 | 97,098 | 95,197 |
| 20. United States | 239.0 | 9,364 | 12,365.9 | 41,815 | 3.2 | 818,775 | 1,469,704 |
| 21. Viet Nam | 82.6 | 332 | 51.0 | 610 | 8.4 | 26,061 | 32,734 |

[1]Read GDP growth: Euromonitor International from International Monetary Fund (IMF), International Financial Statistics and World Economic Outlook/UN/national statistics

part, you have probably experienced different cultures. The life style of Los Angelinos is very different from that of New Yorkers, or even Michiganders. Treating an entire country or multinational market as one large mass market is generally a mistake.

## Inflation

Competition within a multinational market increases, as we have seen, but competition from countries outside the market decreases. Decreased competitive pressures, in turn, lead to increased prices for consumers.

Why would inflation be a problem in a multinational market? The answer depends on the partners taking place in the integration. If integration leads to oligopoly, the competitive structure in which a few companies control the market, the providers are likely to engage in nonprice competition. Without price competition, built-in (structural) price increases occur. If you review the characteristics of price and competition in an oligopoly (discussed in Chapter 3), you can predict what will happen.

We know that inflation within a multinational market increases when trade with countries outside the multinational membership is reduced. In multinational markets, tariffs decrease among member nations; however, tariffs placed on countries outside the membership may increase. Before European unification, there was much speculation that unification would result in a so-called FORTRESS EUROPE—a market that would be less friendly to nonmember countries. The concern was that if companies did not establish a presence in Europe before 1992, entrance to the market would be much more difficult thereafter. There is some evidence that this has come to pass. Foreign companies entering the European market need to comply not only with individual country requirements, but also with a separate level of governmental regulation.

## Additional Layer of Government Complexity

Government involvement with business is rarely viewed as productive. In a multinational market, there is an additional level of governmental considerations. Let's look at Europe. The European Commission is the executive body of the European Union. It is headquartered in Brussels. There are 25 commissioners, one representative from each of the member states; this was determined by the Treaty of Nice in 2000. By 2014 the composition of the European Commission is scheduled to be reduced to two-thirds of the member states. In the beginning the European Commission had 17 members, composed of two members from the most populated states and one member for each of the others; however, when the EU was expanded, each member got one seat (Table 5.2).

The ISO 9000 regulations, developed by the International Organization for Standardization, were designed to set minimum standards for European products. The 1992 regulations for the common market require that member states set minimum common standards, called downward harmonization. The minimum standards are those required for sale throughout the EU. DOWNWARD HARMONIZATION means that countries cannot prohibit the sale of products that do not meet their previous regulations.[2]

You now have a better idea about some of the benefits and drawbacks involved with multinational markets. These markets develop in a hierarchy from the least

**Table 7.2**

**Commercial Legislation in EU Regarding Retail Hours of Operation**

| Country | Weekdays | Sundays |
|---|---|---|
| Germany | Tues.–Fri.: 6 AM to 8 PM; Saturday until 4:00; can be open until 6:00 PM for Christmas Shopping | Closed |
| Austria | Mon.–Fri.: 6:30 AM to 7:30 PM Sat.: 6:30 AM to 5 PM; Can be open two nights per week until 9:00 PM maximum total of 66 hours | Closed and also closed on public holidays |
| Belgium | Can be open for a maximum of 91 hours per week but are free to be open at any time of day or night | |
| Netherlands | Recently liberalized, each district sets their own rules | |
| UK | No restrictions | Varies by area |
| Spain | Local authorities set limits but can not be restricted to less than 72 hours | By region: 12 per year maximum 8 minimum |
| Portugal | Varies by region | Law passed in 2001 limits Sunday opening hours of large supermarkets and hypermarkets |
| Italy | Retailers can decide their own opening hours between 7:00 AM and 10:00 PM but can not stay open more than 13 hours per day and has to choose its opening hours according to local government restrictions Retailers should close on Sunday and $\frac{1}{2}$ day during the week (by region) | Varies by region |
| Greece | Liberalized in 2005, all shops are able to open and close as they please up to a maximum of 12 hours per day. | |

Source: *GMID Country Reports 2006.*

integrated to the most integrated. At each level, an additional element of integration is added. These elements deal with (1) internal trade barriers, (2) external trade barriers, (3) free flow of capital and labor, and (4) unifying political and economic systems, as we will see next.

## › LEVELS OF MULTINATIONAL COOPERATION

### Regional Cooperative Group

The lowest level of integration is a REGIONAL COOPERATIVE GROUP. This is an agreement between countries to jointly participate and to develop certain industries or infrastructures beneficial to the economy. With this level of involvement, there is no elimination or lowering of internal tariffs or any other agreements regarding trade with other countries. This level of agreement generally leads to a higher level of participation.

## Free Trade Area

This level of involvement is the first to have any direct effect on retailing. If countries establish a **FREE TRADE AREA**, they eliminate or reduce internal barriers between member nations. They install no common external barriers and there is no free flow of capital and labor. NAFTA is an example of this type of agreement. Canada, Mexico, and the United States have agreed to reduce tariffs among the three countries, eventually having no tariffs. This type of agreement is an important step toward becoming a multinational market, but it is inherently unstable because external trade relationships are not similar.

Since the member countries have separate agreements with external trading partners, there is a weak link in this type of trade agreement. For example, if the United States charges 16 percent tariffs on merchandise coming from France, and Canada charges 13 percent tariffs on merchandise coming from France, products will flow through Canada to their destination in the United States. Until the United States and Canada establish similar external agreements with trading partners, there will always be a weak link. In the case of NAFTA, the United States has tried to reduce this problem by passing domestic content laws.

As we will see in the next section, a full customs union is a more stable level of multinational agreement than a free trade area because it gets rid of the weak link—different external trade agreements. If NAFTA is successful, it is likely that the three countries will move to a higher level of involvement.

Retailers in a free trade area may move to other countries within the member nations to take advantage of lower costs for land and labor. If a company depends on a high degree of service, it may benefit from relocating to the lower-wage developing country. Companies with mature retail formats may find that the less developed country in the group offers locational advantages. Consumers in less developed countries may view retail format as more innovative than consumers who live in more developed countries. Kmart's expansion to Mexico is one instance where this has occurred.

## Full Customs Union

A full customs union eliminates or reduces internal trade barriers; in addition, it establishes the same external barriers to trade. There is no free flow of capital or labor. This level of multinational trade is stable because the external barriers have been harmonized. Retailers benefit from this level of involvement because they have similar sources and costs of supply.

Most countries moving from a free trade area to a common market pass through this stage. The EC was a customs union before becoming a common market. Customs unions exist between France and Monaco, Italy and San Marino, and Switzerland and Liechtenstein.[2]

## Common Market

Common markets eliminate the internal barriers, establish the same external barriers, and allow the free flow of capital and labor. The EC is an example of this type of agreement. Retailers operating in a common market benefit from the lower cost of products, which are the result of the elimination of internal barriers. They also have the advantage of similar external barriers, making a stable and equalized trading situation. Labor-intensive retailers such as department stores benefit because they can recruit employees from lower wage countries to work in the domestic market. Banking institutions benefit because they can extend financing to less developed countries. Consumers benefit from this level of cooperation due to the increased competition. However, if the EU is a good indicator, the laws governing retail trade remain the domain of domestic concerns.

There are three common markets in Latin America: the Andean Common Market (ACM), the Central American Common Market (CACM), and the Southern Cone Common Market (Mercosur). Table 7.3 shows which European countries belong to the EU, as well as listing similar multi-national market groups in Latin America. Mercosur includes the Latin American powerhouse countries—Argentina, Brazil, Paraguay, and Uruguay. It is Latin America's largest common market with a population of 185 million people. A bilateral agreement with the United States was negotiated with Mercosur under the American Initiative Enterprise. The CACM union was the first to take the concept of a common market a step further. This union has implemented SECTORAL DEVELOPMENT, a process by which the union's governing body allocates production responsibility for certain manufactured products to particular countries. In this way, countries within the union do not duplicate production and the group is guaranteed the total CACM market for a product. CACM includes Guatemala, El Salvador, Costa Rice, Nicaragua, and Honduras. Earlier, I mentioned that multinational markets are most successful if they have different strengths in factors of production. This group of five countries has very similar factor endowments. Using the concept of sectoral development allows them to concentrate production and suppliers in a particular area. The total population for the group is around 25 million people.

Sectoral development can have negative effects on retailers. Transportation costs would increase for all products not allocated to the home country. Retailers would not be able to develop their own private sources to manufacture products unless the production capability for those products had been allocated to their country. Also, prices would likely increase for consumers because competition would be reduced. Sectoral development is the bi-product of multinational markets that do not have different factors of production. It is rarely ever successful.

## Political Union

The highest level of multinational cooperation is a political union. It has all the elements of a common market—a lowering or elimination of internal barriers of trade, the establishment of common external barriers of trade, and the free flow of capital and labor—plus a unifying economic logic. The United States is a type of political union. There are no tariffs between states. States do not enter into individual agreements with external trading partners; rather, the U.S. government ne-

**Table 7.3**
**Multinational Market Groups in Europe and Latin America**

| Association | Members |
|---|---|
| European Union (EU) | |
| *From 1952 (original ECSC membership):* | Belgium<br>Germany (former East Germany, joined in 1991)<br>France<br>Italy<br>Luxembourg<br>The Netherlands |
| *From 1973 (first enlargement):* | Denmark<br>Republic of Ireland<br>United Kingdom |
| *From 1981 (second enlargement):* | Greece |
| *From 1986 (third enlargement):* | Portugal<br>Spain |
| *From 1995 (fourth enlargement):* | Austria<br>Finland<br>Sweden |
| *From 2004 (fifth enlargement, part I):* | Cyprus<br>Czech Republic<br>Estonia<br>Hungary<br>Latvia<br>Lithuania<br>Malta<br>Poland<br>Slovakia<br>Slovenia |
| Andean Common Market (ANCOM) | Bolivia<br>Columbia<br>Ecuador<br>Peru<br>Venezuela<br>Panama (Associate) |
| Central American Common Market (CACM) | Guatemala<br>El Salvador<br>Costa Rica<br>Nicaragua<br>Honduras |
| Caribbean Community and Common Market (CARICOM) | Antigua and Barbuda<br>Anguilla (Associate)<br>Aruba (Observer)<br>Bahamas<br>Barbados<br>Belize<br>Bermuda (Associate)<br>British Virgin Islands (Associate)<br>Cayman Islands (Associate)<br>Columbia (Observer) |

| Table 7.3 *Continued* | |
|---|---|
| | Dominica |
| | Dominican Republic (Observer) |
| | Grenada |
| | Guyana |
| | Haiti |
| | Jamaica |
| | Mexico (Observer) |
| | Montserrat |
| | Netherlands Antilles (Observer) |
| | Puerto Rico (Observer) |
| | St. Kitts-Nevis |
| | St. Lucia |
| | St. Vincent-the Grenadines |
| | Trinidad-Tobago |
| | Turks-Caicos Islands (Associate) |
| | Venezuela (Observer) |
| Latin American Integration Association (LAIA) | Argentina |
| | Bolivia |
| | Brazil |
| | Cuba |
| | Chile |
| | Colombia |
| | Ecuador |
| | Mexico |
| | Paraguay |
| | Peru |
| | Uruguay |
| | Venezuela |

gotiates these agreements as a unified block. People can move from one state to another to take jobs. And the United States is unified under the economic ideology of capitalism.

The British Commonwealth is an example of a voluntary political union. The Council for Mutual Economic Assistance (COMECON) was an example of involuntary unification. COMECON was a centrally controlled group of countries organized by then-Soviet leader Joseph Stalin as a way to rebuild the Eastern European countries after World War II. Since 1989, when Eastern European countries began declaring their independence from the former USSR, COMECON began to falter. COMECON was dissolved in 1991. Most of the countries that had been a part of COMECON have joined or are preparing to join the EU.

Although a political union is the highest form of multinational cooperation, there are several major problems with this type of agreement. The economic logic of the member countries may be similar, but not their economic levels. In addition, language barriers and cultural barriers exist among members. There is also a tendency to consider these markets as difficult to penetrate.

The Treaty of Maastricht established the requirements for the European Community to become a political union; corresponding to this change, the name of the

## Stages in Multinational Cooperation

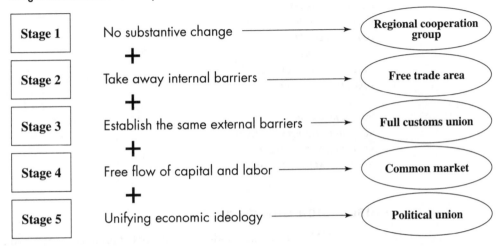

| | | |
|---|---|---|
| **Stage 1** | No substantive change ⟶ | Regional cooperation group |
| | **+** | |
| **Stage 2** | Take away internal barriers ⟶ | Free trade area |
| | **+** | |
| **Stage 3** | Establish the same external barriers ⟶ | Full customs union |
| | **+** | |
| **Stage 4** | Free flow of capital and labor ⟶ | Common market |
| | **+** | |
| **Stage 5** | Unifying economic ideology ⟶ | Political union |

**Figure 7.1**
Regional cooperation group is the first level of multinational cooperation. At each step, an additional type of unification is added. The highest level is a political union. At this level, there are no internal barriers to trade, the countries have the same external barriers, capital and labor flow freely, and there is a unifying economic ideology.

European Community was changed to European Union. In 1993 the Copenhagen European Council established three criteria that candidates for inclusion in the expanded EU must meet. These countries must have achieved:

> Stability of institutions guaranteeing democracy, the rule of law, human rights, and respect for and protection of minorities.
> The existence of a functioning market economy as well as the capacity to cope with competitive pressure and market forces within the Union.
> The ability to take on the obligations of membership including adherence to the aims of political, economic, and monetary unions.

The largest expansion of the EU occurred in 2004 (Fifth Enlargement), admitting 10 countries—Cyprus, the Czech Republic, Estonia, Hungary, Latvia, Lithuania, Malta, Poland, Slovakia, and Slovenia.

A summary of the stages of multinational cooperation is presented in Figure 7.1.

## > SUMMARY

The countries of the world are pairing off into economic units as never before. This multinational cooperation will only accelerate in the twenty-first century. Countries that do not belong to a strong, diverse trade group will be left behind. The history of multinational cooperation is not long.

The world will be watching the EU over the coming years. This association of countries represents the highest level of a true multinational market group available for study. If the EU's success continues, we can anticipate that the NAFTA group will increase its membership and move to a higher level of integration, such as a full customs union or common market.

## › KEY TERMS

COMMON MARKET
DOWNWARD HARMONIZATION
FORTRESS EUROPE
FREE TRADE AREA
FREE TRADE ASSOCIATION
FULL CUSTOMS UNION
ISO 9000
POLITICAL UNION
REGIONAL COOPERATIVE GROUP
SECTORAL DEVELOPMENT
UPWARD HARMONIZATION

## › DISCUSSION QUESTIONS

1. Analyze NAFTA from the standpoint of factors of production. Since you know that multinational groups are more successful if there is a diverse base of factor endowments, predict the future of NAFTA. What countries do you believe will be added? What is the ideal level for NAFTA within the multinational hierarchy?
2. What are the antecedents of each level of multinational cooperation? Are these steps essential or could a group jump from a free trade area to a political union?
3. How does access to a multinational market affect domestic retailers? What about international retailers from within the block? Or international retailers from outside the block?
4. Europe has used a system of downward harmonization for product standards. What would be the effect of changing this system and using upward harmonization?

## › ENDNOTES

1. Wolfe, A. (1991). "Single European Market: National or Euro-Brands." *International Journal of Advertising*, pp. 49–58.
2. Cateora, P. R. (1996). *International Marketing*. 9th ed. Chicago: Irwin.

# COMPANY FOCUS I.1

## 7-ELEVEN INTERNATIONAL EXPANSION

7-Eleven has made its mark in the convenience store industry by encompassing its transaction based assets and demanding success from all sides of the company. It is evident that they are in fact the world leader in convenience store service and continue to make innovative decisions that keep them current and fresh in the industry. Research done through online databases, the company website, and a personal interview with a member of the management team has made it apparent that the success of this company is based on its service, location, selection, and value of products offered on a 24-hour basis.

7-Eleven prides itself on its innovative inventory management databases and other technological advances that have catapulted the company into a strong international market. President and CEO James W. Keyes credits the success of the business to the commitment and involvement of their hard-working employees, franchisees, and licensees. Independent business owners of 7-Eleven stores see the mutual benefits of the company's strategy and continue to embrace and implement 7-Eleven's initiatives. They are a global company that plans to continue its expansion throughout the countries they have already entered as well as new countries in the future."[1,2]

Amanda Crane, Jennifer Koterba, Shanen McCourt,

Melissa Mina, Megan Radermacher

## History

7-Eleven began as Southland Ice Co., a Dallas-based company, in 1927. An employee became the innovator of the convenience store idea in the United States when he began selling milk, bread, and eggs from one of its docks. The company's initial convenience stores were titled Tote'm due to the nature the consumers took their purchases home. The name "7-Eleven" was inducted in 1946 (however, the corporate name of The Southland Corporation was not changed to 7-Eleven, Inc. until 1999), when the store hours were 7 A.M. until 11 P.M., considered extended hours in the mid 1900s. Competitors began to emulate 7-Eleven and set the same store hours. However, with the changing demographics and lifestyles in the 1960s, 7-Eleven realized that the average population was younger, busier, and needed products/services at all hours. In 1962 that 7-Eleven became a 24-hour convenience store open 7 days a week.

The change to 24-hour service was merely a mistake. A store in Austin, Texas, located near a college campus, was so busy with customers that they never closed one night. The manager then decided to be open around the clock, resulting in an even more lucrative business. This idea of nonstop service jumped to stores in Dallas, Fort Worth, and Las Vegas, then was adopted companywide. Now the majority of 7-Eleven stores worldwide are open 24 hours a day. Competitors and various other retail formats have taken 7-Eleven's lead and extended their establishment's hours to 24 hours a day.

Today 5,800 7-Eleven and other convenience stores throughout the United States and Canada are both operated and franchised, and serve 6 million customers. Of the 5,800 store in North America, 3,300 are operated by franchisees, 430 are operated by licensees, and the rest are company owned. In addition to North America there are approximately 18,000 licensees and affiliate convenience stores operated throughout the rest of the world.[3,4,5]

## Industry and Competition

7-Eleven is in a continually growing market. With 6,000 stores in North America under direct ownership

# 7-Eleven International Expansion

|  |  |
|------|-------|
| 2004 | First Store Opened in Beijing, PCR-Locations: 20 |
| 1996 | First Store Opened in Guangzhou, China |
| 1993 | First Store Opened in Denmark-Locations: 51 |
| 1992 | First Store opened in Shenzhen, China |
| 1989 | First Store Opened in S. Korea-Locations: 1,180<br>First Store Opened in Thailand-Locations: 3,095<br>First Store Opened in Turkey-Locations: 74 |
| 1987 | First Store Opened in Guam-Locations: 8 |
| 1986 | First Store Opened in Norway-Locations: 83<br>First Store Opened in Puerto Rico-Locations: 14 |
| 1984 | First Store Opened in Phillipines-Locations: 254<br>First Store Opened in Malaysia-Locations: 530 |
| 1983 | First Store Opened in Singapore-Locations: 277 |
| 1981 | First Store Opened in Hong Kong, China-Locations within China: 851 |
| 1980 | First Store Opened in Taiwan-Locations: 3,894 |
| 1978 | First Store Opened in Sweden-Locations: 73 |
| 1977 | First Store Opened in Australia-Locations: 359 |
| 1971 | First Store Opened in Mexico-Locations: 546<br>First Store Opened in Japan-Locations: 10,868 |
| 1969 | First Store Opened in Canada-Locations: 489 |
| 1927 | 7-Eleven, Inc. founded in Dallas, TX |

Source: International Licensing, 7-Eleven

or franchise agreement, and a worldwide existence of 20,000 additional units through license agreements, 7-Eleven dominates the convenience store sector.[6] Although 7-Eleven holds such an immense sector in its market, the company is still continually expanding. From 2000 through the end of first quarter of 2005, 7-Eleven has averaged 4.6 percent same store sales growth.[7]

Research analysts Robert Summers and Westcott Rochette of Bear Stearns see 7-Eleven as an innovative operator who increasingly leverages its refined retail technology to advance overall merchandising efforts and continue to impel sales. 7-Eleven has been able to maintain its concepts appeal,[8] helped them strengthen their core, with an end result of larger market share. They have done this by investing a great deal of time into product research so they can put more emphasis on the products most in demand, and eliminate those not selling well.[9] These tactics will help 7-Eleven continue to see growth in the coming years.

Exceptional management of 7-Eleven, both at the corporate and regional levels, has attributed to their continued growth. Management has adopted a "consumer centric approach and in general facilitates a pull system,"[10] making it possible for 7-Eleven to quickly adapt to changes within the industry. Some of these changes might be consumer demand, but they are also responses to what the competition is doing. The managers are making every effort to be on the top of their game to further 7-Eleven's growth.

Technology has also played an important role in 7-Eleven's growth. The company's strong technological platform has been a foundation for its past success and will prove vital to its future success.[11] In the past year, 7-Eleven has invested roughly $93 million in technology development,[12] mainly to further develop their RIS, retail information system.[13] This system allows managers to see how many items are selling, hour-to-hour, essentially driving revenue. IT, the technological system, furthers the productivity of convenience stores. Japan, the first 7-Eleven to use IT, sells high-quality sushi as IT scans the data, converts it into a friendlier format, and sends it back to the store managers.[14, 15] The buying decisions are still made by the managers because no one can replicate all the tasks of a human; however, technological advances are particularly effective in 7-Eleven's growth.

7-Eleven has been implementing several programs to help increase their growth. One is expanding their proprietary fresh food, beverages, and their service contributions.[16] Another program 7-Eleven participated in this year, during third quarter, was a campaign to promote fresh foods, specifically sandwiches.[17] Because 7-Eleven, and convenience stores in general, are not thought of as high quality fresh food suppliers, they need to take extra steps in order for this program to be a success. Customer perception and awareness must be addressed to make this program work.[18] People must come to believe these fresh items offered by 7-Eleven are of equal quality to those offered by other fresh-food providers. 7-Eleven has seen double-digit sales growth with fresh foods over the past five quarters.[19] President and Chief Executive Officer of 7-Eleven, James W. Keyes, attributes the improvement of their performance with their obsession with freshness. 7-Eleven has strong fundamentals which will benefit the company's growth and give them a higher return in the industry.[20]

7-Eleven's market structure is unique for the convenience store sector. After 7-Eleven's owner, Southland Corps, filed for bankruptcy in the early 1990s it was clear that in order for 7-Eleven to survive, it was going to have to be reinvented. The new program unveiled after their financial troubles focused on pricing strategy, business concept, interior/exterior remodeling, and internal ordering and distribution systems.[21] With this shift in structure, 7-Eleven implemented many new strategic initiatives. These strategies were aimed mainly at streamlining operations.[22] Their target customer from this point on was not just the blue collar male. 7-Eleven is a convenience store targeting the population on a whole with affordable convenience. 7-Eleven has established model markets in order to teach the principles and benefits of retailer initiative to its employees worldwide.[23] To date, there are nine model markets representing roughly 600 stores. These programs focus on advanced training, use of labor-saving equipment, and help to practice more effective merchandising techniques and skills. These training programs have led to double-digit growth as well as making 7-Eleven a competitive tool in the convenient store sector.

The market models being established have given 7-Eleven great leverage on the competition. 7-Eleven currently is the largest convenience store operator;

however, they generate just 3–4 percent of the industry sales.[24] There are still several ways 7-Eleven can capitalize on growth opportunities that will widen their competitive edge within the extremely fragmented market of convenience stores.

7-Eleven's advanced technology has helped increase their sales but more important, it has given them a competitive edge in their market. The technology platform 7-Eleven has developed drives both innovation and efficiency.[25] Summers and Rochette see scale and innovation as the primary variables for future success in the convenience store industry. Comparing 7-Eleven to other convenience stores using these factors, 7-Eleven wins,[26] giving the company the upper hand to drive more share gains and in turn produce more rapid growth. RIS and IT technology, both key factors in 7-Eleven's growth, are technological advances furthering the gap between 7-Eleven and other convenience stores.

The newest form of technology used to combat competition was introduced in June 2005. Radio frequency (RF) technology is a contactless payment system started at the 7-Eleven stores in the United States.[27] For purchases under $25, the customer can simply pass a card embedded with a radio-frequency identification chip within inches of a specialized scanner and then receive a confirmation signal that payment has been credited to their account.[28] For purchases over $25, the customer's signature is required. Technology is a huge factor in making 7-Eleven the leading convenience store.

The convenience store sector in general has been under attack by competitors. Recently, expanding hypermarket gas outlets have been putting pressure on convenience stores such as 7-Eleven to match their low margins,[29] creating a combination of "volume pressure and eroding overall margins for the industry."[30] Because 7-Eleven, with their extensive estate portfolio, is more insulated from hypermarket competition than many others in the industry, their strong market presence holds and their continued increase in gross margins should be enough for them to overcome the hypermarket competition.[31]

## Business Strategy

7-Eleven's mission consists of being forward-thinking, using technology that is proficient and quick to offer its customers the freshest convenience shopping whereever they may be. They maintain the power of a global retailer as a convenience store industry leader and focus on a store level of acting as an entrepreneur.[32]

One technological tool that 7-Eleven uses effectively is their retail information system, which provides their stores with historical sales data and key indicators of sales for any item. This system helps 7-Eleven know what to replenish along with customer requests, seasonal trends, and demographic preferences. Another technological tool 7-Eleven uses is their retailer initiation, which allows them to try new products. They can stock a new item one day, study how it sells with their technology along with customer responses, and take it off the shelf the next day if the product does not meet their satisfaction.[33]

Distribution of products to their stores is also vital for 7-Eleven's mission of freshness. Fresh items must be delivered daily and dry items twice a week. 7-Eleven stays above the competition by being able to replenish their stores in hours rather than days, not to mention lower distribution costs. 7-Eleven is constantly improving distribution by experimenting with twice-a-day deliveries of fresh items in some locations and also experimenting with suppliers to deliver more often.[34]

Understanding their target market is another key element of 7-Eleven's business strategy. This market consists of a wide range of ethnic, demographic, and socioeconomic backgrounds. Most of their customers walk to the store, considering their homes in high-density areas. 7-Eleven wants their customers to know they can run in and run out with exactly what they want. The company realizes that their customers who drive want something to be used easily while driving. They work with companies to create better packaging ideas for their customers' convenience, for example, snacks that fit into cup holders in vehicles. Recently 7-Eleven has noticed their target market is becoming healthier snackers, which has effected some changes in 7-Eleven products. The company started offering low-calorie, low-carbohydrate, high-nutrition products to meet customer demand.[35]

7-Eleven is offering something new to meet their customers' demand for financial services: Vcom (virtual commerce), a kiosk with 24-hour convenience, including ATM, check cashing, money order purchases, money transfers, and some telephone services for Verizon. Vcom is recently new but 7-Eleven already wants to improve it by adding bill payment, phone cards, store value cards, and lottery tickets.[36]

The staff of each 7-Eleven store learns merchandising techniques from the company's intense 12-week certification program. Staff can also continually learn while in the store with web-enabled, computer-based training. In addition, 7-Eleven offers a two-day advanced classroom training module on ordering techniques. 7-Eleven has proof that all these training programs have implemented their retailer initiative strategy to the highest degree by helping their staffs specialize in assortment, quality, value, cleanliness, and service.[37]

## Retail Culture

7-Eleven has a vast assortment of merchandise available for customers throughout every store nationwide. The stores carry anywhere from 2,300 to 2,800 retail items, which fall into 9 broad product categories.

> Tobacco: pipe tobacco, cigarettes, chewing tobacco, and cigars.
> Beverages: fountain drinks, prepackaged soft drinks, juices, noncarbonated beverages, bottled water, sport and energy drinks, frozen carbonated beverage (Slurpee), frozen noncarbonated beverages, coffee, tea, and hot chocolate.
> Beer/Wine/Liquor: Beer (domestic/premium/import, bottles/cans, multi-pack/single-serve), wine, wine coolers, malt beverages, and liquor.
> Candy/Snacks: gum, candy, mints, chips, pretzels, crackers, prepackaged bakery items, prepackaged meat snacks, and other prepackaged food items.
> Non-Food items: newspapers, magazines, health care, beauty supplies, personal hygiene, collectibles, batteries, film electronics, cards/stationery, school/office supplies, apparel/accessories, soap, and cleaning supplies.
> Fresh Foods: fresh bakery (donuts, cookies, muffins, pastries), hot dogs, sausages, Taquitos, hot sandwiches, cold sandwiches, deli wraps, salads, and fruit (whole/ prepared).
> Dairy: milk (variety of sizes, flavors and fat content), butter, cheese, sour cream, eggs, and ice cream.
> Services: ATM, check cashing, money orders, postage, lottery, pre-paid cellular, and payphone.
> Other: bread, packaged groceries, frozen groceries, and ice.[38]

All of these products are distributed to 7-Eleven by a large number of vendors on a weekly, and in some cases, daily, basis. 7-Eleven uses two main distribution methods. The first is referred to as DSD, which is Direct Store Delivery, while the other method is wholesale warehouse distribution. Products received through DSD are for the most part national or regional brands where the manufacturer has set up their own distribution networks to deliver their products to retailers. Some DSD suppliers are:

> Frito-Lay (salty snacks)
> Anheuser-Busch (alcohol)
> Miller Brewery (alcohol)
> Bread companies
> Coca-Cola
> 7-Up
> Pepsi
> Packaged cake (Interstate Brands: Hostess, Dolly Madison)
> Milk products
> Magazines (one supplier usually distributes all titles)
> Ice cream[39]

With beer and wine products, the manufacturer decides which independent distributor will supply each store. This is regulated by the state and each state has different rules. Products received through the warehouse distribution system can be national, regional, or private labels. Independent warehouses will supply 7-Eleven with anything and everything not covered by the DSD network. Warehouse programs can include salty snacks, bread, and soft drinks; however, they are not usually the national brand products. Almost everything in a supermarket with the exception of the above DSD items comes via the warehouse distribution system. Retailers can either distribute products themselves by setting up a warehouse distribution system (most supermarket chains do this) or contract with a wholesale supplier, which is what 7-Eleven elects to do.

7-Eleven also works with their retailers and distributors on a regular basis to insure the lowest cost of delivery, and to shift deliveries to off-peak hours. Vendors include independently owned and operated bakeries and commissaries that offer daily deliveries of fresh foods such as sandwiches, salads, and baked goods. It's important for the stores to find the lowest prices in merchandise in order to maximize on their profits.[40]

In 2003 7-Eleven upgraded their systems to the Oracle E-Business Suite so that they could incorporate the system and provide collaboration opportunities amongst vendors all over the United States and Canada. Oracle has helped them improve their supplier relationships and manage the customers' daily transactions. The Oracle Procurement Suite enables them to fill purchases and request quotes to make certain that 7-Eleven is getting the best prices from their vendors. The system has helped them decrease operating costs and increase productivity because of the powerful search engines and workflow-based support functions built into the program. 7-Eleven hopes that this system will make them more technologically advanced and generate a more productive situation for their stores.[41]

7-Eleven's business model is to give their customers "what they want when and where they want it." The typical convenience/gas stores cater to a core user, who are usually males in the age range of 18 to 34. 7-Eleven's strategy is to capture the core customers, plus children and the heads of household, who are usually females. Let's take a look at which products are marketed toward each of these consumer classes.[42]

Typical core customers buy cigarettes, beer, energy drinks, single serve snacks, fast food, fountain drinks, single cold beverages, newspapers, candy, gum and mints, coffee, and Slurpees. Typical child customers choose candy, gum, Slurpees, snacks, single serve soft drinks, and novelty toys. Typical heads of household select take-home soft drinks, multipack beer, milk and other dairy products, bread, grocery products, health and beauty care products, candy, coffee/cappuccino, ice cream, take-home salty snacks, and nutritional products.[43]

7-Eleven's philosophy on attracting children is that they need to be female friendly. In order to do this they limit the use of beer and cigarette banners to promote these items. They also feel that it's important to have a large selection of grocery items to meet the needs of the fill-in shoppers. They take pride in that they are more than a place to buy cheap beer, cigarettes, and adult magazines.

A well-trained, friendly staff may be their best form of advertising and promoting. 7-Eleven's staff is trained to greet customers on their way in and out of the store in an effort to make shoppers aware of the welcoming and accommodating shopping atmosphere they have entered. The staff is also educated on the importance of reciting new and discounted merchandise for the customers. 7-Eleven likes to consider their stores as customer service centers. They want to know how they can help their customers, and what kinds of products they can supply in order to best serve each and every consumer. On their website, (http://www.7-Eleven.com/default.asp), they designate a section to customer requests and responses. If customers would like to see a certain type of product in their local 7-Eleven store, or are irritated about the discontinuation of a product, they can request the item to be stocked for their convenience.[44]

7-Eleven feels that convenience and value is usually more important to their customers than price, but they are sensitive to the fact that their prices need to be competitive in the market place. They do state though that they are not out to attract the shopper who is looking only for price. Price marketing is a dead end as far as 7-Eleven is concerned. Location, service, selection, and value are what they market. When it comes to their strategy, they offer national brands at the sizes most often purchased at the supermarket at prices not much higher than what the supermarket charges. For example, a box of cereal in 7-Eleven stores is typically priced every day at about $.20 to $.30 above a supermarket, while a gallon of milk is usually the same price. It is also important for them to offer regular promotions to their customers that in most cases end up being the best price in the market. This month they have cereal priced at 2/$4.00 and a gallon of milk at $1.99. Both of these items are probably the lowest promoted prices you'll find anyplace.[45]

7-Eleven is implementing single-store marketing and expects each store to have its own uniqueness in configuration. Advertising is done from a corporate and a local level. Each store is allowed to advertise for itself, but each also benefits from a corporate advertising system that encompasses entire regions. Even though they use radio, television, and print to advertise to the market, 7-Eleven feels their main focus is with their storefront banners, window signs, and store point of purchase. They also use sales incentives with their store clerks to help get their promotional message out to their customers.[46]

The 7-Eleven convenience card was introduced in 2003 and serves not only as an easy way for shoppers to pay for their goods, but also as an inventory management device. It helps the company distinguish even the tiniest shifts in buying patterns, allowing the stores to provide for a varied consumer base. 7-Eleven store managers and franchisees are equipped with the most up-to-date and relevant information and make decisions far more enhanced than any individual supplier.[47]

Maintaining good vendor/supplier relations is very important to 7-Eleven. Both they and their suppliers need to make a profit. 7-Eleven has three marketing meetings every year, and they encourage their franchisees, store managers, and vendors to participate. They outline their marketing strategies and advertising focus for the upcoming months so everyone involved in 7-Eleven's business stays informed. They usually invite vendors to speak at these functions as a way of keeping their stores informed regarding the categories they represent. They also conduct seminars during these conferences as a way of educating and training their people. They feel that well-informed individuals are more capable of taking 7-Eleven's message back to their employees and ultimately their customers.[48]

## International Expansion

The largest operator, franchisor, and licensor of convenience stores in the world, 7-Eleven embarked upon franchising in 1964. Its first United States franchising agreement was signed in 1968. The first international agreement, with Mexico, was contracted in 1971. Internationally, countries such as Australia, Hong Kong, Sweden, Taiwan, and Thailand offer individual franchise prospects. In Mexico, designated applicants are able to sublicense in predetermined geographical areas. 7-Eleven convenience stores endeavor to cater to the diverse needs while utilizing technological advances and high-quality products to enable convenience and ease within consumers' everyday lives.

**Canada:**
    First Store Opened: 1969
    Number of Locations: 489

7-Eleven's goal since its opening in 1969 has remained "to provide you with the products and services that you want, when you want them, in a clean, safe, and friendly environment." Its original location on 17th Avenue SE in Calgary, Alberta, was the first retailer to remain open 24 hours a day, 7 days a week. In 7-Eleven's Canadian Manitoba province, they have earned the title, "Slurpee Capital," selling an average of 8,300 drinks per store each month, leading in Slurpee sales.

To ensure they maintain satisfied customers, 7-Eleven Canada has implemented a 24-hour toll-free customer service inquiry line. This enables the individual to receive appropriate attention within 48 hours of their inquiry.[49]

**Mexico:**
    First Store Opened: 1971
    Number of Locations: 546

Founded in Monterrey, Nuevo Leon, Mexico, a joint venture was formed between Grupo Chapa SA de CV, a dominant force in the grocery market, and 7-Eleven, Inc. of Dallas. With nearly 350 Mexican locations, as of January 1, 2003, 7-Eleven Mexico was the first retailer to offer 24-hour service, 365 days a year in Mexico. While it took nearly twelve years to open its first 100 stores in the Monterrey region, it quickly expanded within the last year, matching that amount. The convenience store is quickly replacing mom-and-pop stores, as residents accept the American lifestyle with great possibilities and increasing per-capita income. They forecast expanding their business to create 100 stores each year in the future.

Exclusive and propriety-branded Café Select hot beverages, Big Bite grill products, and Slurpee frozen beverages are among the selections of convenience goods offered within 7-Eleven Mexico. In addition, a management contract was established with Pemex franchise, Productos Seleccionados SA de CV, offering full-service petroleum products under the name PETRO-7 in among 30 locations.[50]

### Japan:
    First Store Opened: 1971
    Number of Locations: 10,868

Since the opening of its first location in Toyosu, Koto-ku, Tokyo, Seven-Eleven Japan has maintained its corporate philosophy to "modernize and revitalize small and medium-sized retail stores," and to achieve "coexistence and co-prosperity with our franchise." In the midst of economic growth, the company strives to provide its consumers with convenience through high-quality products and services. The convenience store sector is 51-percent owned by a Japanese retailer and Denny's franchisee, Ito-Yokado, who transferred its stake in 7-Eleven to Seven-Eleven Japan earlier in the year. The retailer formed a partnership with the Nihon Delica Foods association in 1979 in an effort to provide its customers with improved quality control and address increasing safety concerns. After an epidemic of E. coli in 1996, more strict standards and quality measures are taken to ensure all products distributed and sold within the store are safe.

In addition to its convenience products, Seven-Eleven Japan offers video games, music CDs, and DVDs. However, they do not sell Slurpee and Big Gulp drinks. They offer Japanese foods such as udon, odon, sandwiches without crusts, and bento. Rice balls are a large market item in Seven-Eleven Japan; 1,000,000 rice balls were sold in 2003.[51]

### Australia:
    First Store Opened: 1977
    Number of Locations: 359

The first location established in Oakleigh Victoria, 7-Eleven is among 283 additional outlets, a part of 7-Eleven Stores Pty. Ltd, developed in the metropolitan and provincial cities of Victoria, New South Wales, and Queensland.[52]

In April 2005, the 7-Eleven Proprietary Ltd entered an AU $200M ($155 M USD) supply contract with a grocery wholesaler, Metcash Ltd, that will provide strength and continued opportunities within the convenience stores. Currently, each 7-Eleven location receives direct shipment from manufacturers totaling nearly 80 monthly deliveries. However, the contract will decrease deliveries to 10 per month.[53]

### Sweden:
    First Store Opened: 1978
    Number of Locations: 73

Although 7-Eleven entered the market in 1978, it was acquired in 1992 by Small Shops Holding, who closed the existing stores and developed new, modern facilities settled in the most convenient locations. In 1997, Small Shops Holding was acquired by AB Svenska Pressabyran, who was later in the year sold to a Norwegian company, Narvesen.

Employing nearly 600 employees, most 7-Eleven locations are found in central Stockholm, central Gothenburg, and the south of Sweden. Only about 20 stores offer 24-hour service, while the rest operate under specified hours.[54]

### Taiwan:
    First Store Opened: 1980
    Number of Locations: 3,894

In February 1980, the first 7-Eleven store in Taiwan was opened in Taipei under the cooperation of President Enterprises Corp and Southland Corporation.

Operating a 7-Eleven under the Taiwan franchising system is referred to as one's "life entity," focusing on the gains and risks involved in such a venture. Most recently, President Enterprise Corp is integrating e-century life within its convenience stores to better improve customer service and work productivity.[55]

### China:
    First Store Opened: 1981
    Number of Chinese Locations: 851

7-Eleven convenience stores are among other foreign retailers aggressively moving into the Chinese market. The entrance of the Chinese into the World Trade Organization has opened the doors to foreign retailers to embark upon a growing economy. Although change and improvements are evident, research has shown that modifications must accommodate Chinese characteristics. They still hold close to their Chinese mom-and-pop stores and are accustomed to their usual ways and habits.[56]

## Singapore:
First Store Opened: 1983
Number of Locations: 277

While 206 7-Eleven stores operate here under a licensing agreement with 7-Eleven, Inc. of the United States, the remaining locations were licensed under the Jargine Matheson Group in 1983, and later acquired by Cold Storage Singapore Pte Ltd, a subsidiary of Diary Farm.

All 7-Eleven convenience stores offer 24-hour service, 7 days a week, with the exception of hospital establishments. The main proprietary brands include Big Gulp, Slurpee, Mr. Softee soft serve ice cream, and Quick Bites. In addition, 7-Eleven Singapore convenience stores offer cash and phone cards, parking coupons, UPS courier service, phone and utility payment services, and computer peripherals.[57]

## Philippines:
First Store Opened: 1984
Number of Locations: 254

Philippines Seven Corp. acquired a licensing agreement from Southland Corporation, Dallas, in 1982 to utilize the convenience store system within the Philippines. They aimed to introduce a new form of retailing—24-hour convenience to its local consumers. The first store opened its doors in February 1984 in Kamuning, Quezon City, and its second location opened in April 1984 at President Avenue, adjacent to an upscale subdivision. The two locations were used to target market consumers, determining them to be salaried, busy employees that stop in for a quick purchase on their way to the office or home.

Although Philippines Seven Corp. continues to make adjustments and tweak their methods of introducing new stores, they maintain clean, relaxed, and inviting stores to serve their local customers.

Some characteristics differentiate this 7-Eleven from its competing convenience stores: global brand recognition (Slurpees, Gulp, Hot Cups, and Quick Bites); and partnership with suppliers. 7-Eleven maintains a worldwide brand awareness enabling its adherence to standards to attract loyal customers. The exclusive 7-Eleven products grant the retailer a competitive edge in the market. The 7-Eleven company has developed relationships with various suppliers that have assisted the convenience store in driving its businesses.[58]

## Malaysia:
First Store Opened: 1984
Number of Locations: 530

Incorporated as Convenience Shopping Sdn. Bhd in 1984, it is the first of convenience stores to operate on a 24-hour basis daily. With its initial store opening in Jalan Bukit Bintang, Kuala Lumper, it remains home to nearly 128 convenience store locations, while Selangor houses 158 stores.[59]

## Puerto Rico:
First Store Opened: 1987
Number of Locations: 14

In June 2005, a stock purchase agreement was issued between Puerto Rico-7, owner and exclusive licensee of 7-Eleven stores within all Puerto Rico, and Prime Time Group, Inc., operator of Missouri convenience stores. The new owner and operator of 7-Eleven convenience stores intends to execute success, quality, and customer satisfaction. The growing economy sets the foundation for continued expansion of the convenience stores. Prime Time Group anticipates a strong marketing campaign to promote company awareness, in addition to developing a central distribution center to eliminate costs and increase profits.[60]

## Guam:
First Store Opened: 1987
Number of Locations: 8

Micronesia Seven, Inc. 7-Eleven is located on the island, Guam, a United States territory 1,550 miles southeast of Japan. Although the people of Guam speak English, they have a native language, Chamorro.

Guam's first location opened in Barrigada, while eight locations surround the 212-square-mile island.

Micronesia Seven, Inc. convenience stores operate 24 hours, 7 days a week, and close only during severe weather. In three of the eight locations, gasoline is sold. Eighty-five employees work at the total convenience stores in Guam.[61]

### South Korea:
First Store Opened: 1989
Number of Locations: 1,180

In September 2004, Korea 7-Eleven implemented the newest level of modernization to 600 of its locations. After completion of a profitable test in ten of its Seoul locations, an international express delivery service will be offered to consumers. 7-Eleven has formed ties with U.S. based global delivery service DHL International Ltd to provide immediate delivery of international mail and packages at a discounted rate.[62]

### Thailand:
First Store Opened: 1989
Number of Locations: 3,095

As the largest convenience store in Thailand, it serves millions of customers per day in its 3,000 locations. This chain has grown to the fourth-largest 7-Eleven chain in the world, earning 30 billion Thai Baht in the first half of 2003, and a profit of 750 million Thai Baht. The chain stands behind Japan, the United States, and Taiwan.[63]

### Beijing, PRC:
First Store Opened: 1994
Number of Locations: 20

After a long waiting period, the Chinese central government approved the joint venture of 7-Eleven between Seven-Eleven Japan and China National Sugar and Alcohol Corporation and Beijing Shoulian (Capital Allied) Commercial Group Co. This is the first convenience store to enter the Beijing area, and plans are being made for continual expansion to the area. New retail trends are entering the Beijing market, and chain selling is one of them.

By the end of the year, 150 locations are expected to be built, with 500 anticipated in the next five years. The company hopes to gain loyal customers among the wealthy consumers through adaptation to their lifestyle, including altering the hours from 1 A.M.–11 P.M. 7-Eleven aims to reach an annual sales figure of 2.8 billion yuan (337 million U.S. dollars).[64]

Based on the availability of international sources and language barriers, information could not be obtained for Norway, Turkey, and Denmark. However, Norway's first store opened in 1986 with 83 locations; Turkey began licensing in 1989 and has expanded to 74 locations; and Denmark opened its first store in 1993 and has grown to 51 convenience stores.[65]

As of October 25, 2005, 7-Eleven estimated its global store count to have reached 29,000 convenience locations. In 2004 alone, the global markets produced $41 million in sales for the convenience store chain. 7-Eleven continues to successfully equip convenience stores with innovative technology and high-quality products, enabling it to remain a leader in convenience.

The dynamics of 7-Eleven are continually changing. It was released within the last week that 7-Eleven Japan Co. Ltd. secured 95.4 percent of the 7-Eleven based from Dallas, Texas. 7-Eleven Japan Co. Ltd. bought into the company during their hardships in 1991 and in September 2005 7-Eleven Inc was offered a price of $32.50 per share; however, until the Japanese increased their offer to $37.50 per share, there was no deal. Once owner of 73 percent of 7-Eleven, they are now a wholly owned subsidiary of their Japanese counterpoint and no longer publicly traded on the New York Stock Exchange. With this new information we look forward to the future of 7-Eleven.[66]

## Discussion Questions

1. Is the retailer classified as a global retailer or a multinational retailer? Explain its pattern of expansion. What expansion strategy did/is the retailer use/using?
2. Based on Dunning's Eclectic Theory, how do ownership, locational, and internalization factors play in your retailer's international expansion?
3. What role do cultural proximity and geographical proximity play in the retailer's international moves?
4. Can you predict the retailer's future international expansion?

## Endnotes

1. Personal Interview (2005) Larry Hauck, 7-Eleven Marketing Director November 7.
2. 7-Eleven, Inc. 2003 Annual Report, http://www.7-Eleven.com/
3. *About 7-Eleven: History*. Retrieved October 3, 2005, from http://www.7-Eleven.com/about/history.asp
4. *News Room: Open Around the Clock*. Retrieved October 3, 2005, from http://www.7-Eleven.com/newsroom/houroperation.asp
5. "Bear, Sterns & Co., Inc Equity Research." (July 25, 2005). Investext Plus [Online Database]. Michigan State University: Information Access
6. Morgan Keegan June (2005).
7. Summers & Rochette (July 2005). "Bear, Sterns & Co., Inc Equity Research." (July 25, 2005). Investext Plus [Online Database]. Michigan State University: Information Access
8. Summers & Rochette (2005).
9. Summers & Rochette (2005).
10. Summers & Rochette (2005).
11. Summers & Rochette (2005).
12. Reda, Susan (2005, May). "7-Eleven Serves Convenience with a Big Gulp of Technology." *Stores*, Vol. 87, No. 5, 38.
13. Reda (2005).
14. Koch, Christopher (2005, May 15). "In the First of a Series of 'View from the Top' Interviews, 7-Eleven President and CEO James Keyes Says the Role of IT is to Help the Company Sell More Stuff by Creatively Using Point-of-Sale Data." *CIO*, Vol. 18, No. 15, 1.
15. Koch (2005).
16. Morgan Keegan (June 2005).
17. Coleman, John (2005). "Marketing Issues in Western Europe: Changes and Developments." *European Business Review*, Vol. 17, No. 6, 604.
18. Summers & Rochette (2005).
19. Summers & Rochette (2005).
20. Coleman (2005).
21. Heller (1998).
22. Heller (1998).
23. 7-Eleven Annual Report (2005).

24. Summers & Rochette (2005).
25. Summers & Rochette (2005).
26. Summers & Rochette (2005).
27. Morrow, Keith (2005, August). "King of Convenience." *Optimize*, Vol. 4, No. 8, 18.
28. Morrow, Keith (2005).
29. Summers & Rochette (2005).
30. Summers & Rochette (2005).
31. Summers & Rochette (2005).
32. O'Hanlon, John. (2000, November 6-12). Operates, franchises and licenses. *The Wall Street Corporate Reporter, Inc, 5* (40).
33. 7-Eleven Annual Report (2003).
34. Annual Report (2003).
35. O'Hanlon, John. (2000).
36. Annual Report (2003).
37. Annual Report (2003).
38. "7-Eleven, Inc. Company Report." (April 2, 2005). MarketLine Business Information Center [Library Database]. Michigan State University: Information Access. "7-Eleven, Inc Company Report." (October 3, 2005). Mergent Online [Online Database]. Michigan State University: Information Access.
39. Personal Interview (2005) Larry Hauck.
40. Personal Interview (2005) Larry Hauck.
41. 7-Eleven Upgrades to Oracle E-Business Suite. (2003, January 22). CRM Today Online Magazine.
42. "7-Eleven, Inc. Company Report." (April 2, 2005).
43. Personal Interview (2005) Larry Hauck.
44. "7-Eleven, Inc. Company Report." (April 2, 2005).
45. Personal Interview (2005) Larry Hauck.
46. Personal Interview (2005) Larry Hauck.
47. 7-Eleven Upgrades to Oracle E-Business Suite. (2003, January 22).
48. 7-Eleven Upgrades to Oracle E-Business Suite. (2003, January 22).
49. International License Profile-Canada.
50. International License Profile, Mexico.
51. Seven-Eleven Japan Co. Ltd. Website, Merchandise Report. Retrieved October 27, 2005 at www.sej.co.jp/english
52. International License-Australia.
53. Just.food.com, April 2005.
54. International License Profile-Sweden.
55. 7-Eleven Taiwan-English website
56. Chain Store Age, April 2003.
57. International License Profile-Singapore.
58. 7-Eleven Philippine website
59. International License Profile-Malaysia.
60. PrimeZone Media Network, Inc. (2005, June 1). Prime Time Group, Inc. to Purchase 7-Elevens in Puerto Rico. PrimeZone Media Network, Mergers and Acquisitions. Retrieved on November 12, 2005 from LexisNexis Academic.
61. International License Profile-Guam.

62. Asia Pulse Ptd Limited. (2004, September 21). Korea Seven-Eleven To Offer International Delivery Service. *Asia Pulse,* Northern Territory Regional. Retrieved November 12, 2005 from LexisNexis Academic.
63. Comtex. (2003, October 15). 7-Eleven Casts Eyes on China, *General BusinessFile ASAP.* (Alestron, Inc. News by Comtex). Retrieved on November 12, 2005 from MSU Libraries, General Business File ASAP.
64. International Licensing, 7-Eleven.
65. *News Room: Open Around the Clock.* Retrieved October 3, 2005.
66. Board, 2005; Yung 2005.

# PART II

# Retailing in North and South America

Part II of this text concerns retailing in the Americas. The North American countries discussed in this section—the United States, Mexico, and Canada—have quite different retail environments. In the chapter on the United States, I describe several characteristics that differentiate the U.S. retail market from many other markets. It is not my intent to say that no other country has these characteristics. The United Kingdom has been more aggressive in developing private label than the United States. Hong Kong's retail industry has developed under less governmental regulation than exists in the United States. Nevertheless, these characteristics will provide a set of benchmarks that you can use intellectually to summarize and compare the retailing environment of countries throughout the world.

Mexico is a developing country with a mixed retail system. Modern retailers exist side by side with informal street markets, which are very profitable in Mexico. They have low overhead as there is no building rent and employees are generally family members. In recent years, such markets have become sophisticated, emulating some aspects of product layout used in modern supermarkets.

U.S. retailers, using knowledge gained from expansion within the country, have been successfully moving into Canadian locations. Most of the major U.S. national chains now have representation in Canada. Such cross-border expansion does not seem to work both ways; few Canadian companies are successful in the United States. The intense market competitiveness in the United States may be the deterrent to Canadian expansion.

The final chapter in Part II discusses retailing in South America, a country with an unstable economic environment. Here we will see how retailing is different in environments with rapidly changing prices.

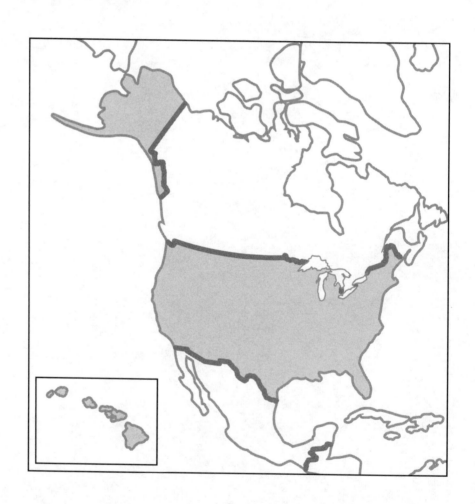

# 8

# RETAILING IN THE UNITED STATES

## After reading this chapter, you should understand

> How the role of retailing changes when retailers become assemblers of merchandise.

> Why buyers are considered profit centers in the United States and how this designation makes U.S. retailing different from retailing in other parts of the world.

> The importance of retailers providing definitive retail options for consumers.

> The role of distribution in a free market system and how we organize the concepts of sorting, spatial closure, and temporal closure in a formal logistics system.

The U.S. retail system possesses several characteristics that set it apart from many other retail systems in the world. In this chapter, I will discuss these characteristics and contrast them to the retailing environment in other countries. Preceding this discussion, a short overview outlines the evolution of retailing in the United States, tying the changing retail environment to key events in the nation's history. The chapter concludes with a segment focusing on a theory of distribution in a free market system. Three problems affecting distribution in this type of system are explored, and retailing responses to these problems are described.

## › COUNTRY BACKGROUND

Industrial growth began in the United States in the early 1800s and continued until the Civil War. In the years before the war, businesses were still small. Production capacity of industry was limited because hand labor was the unit of production. Most businesses served a small local market. The Civil War changed America dramatically. Machines replaced hand labor. More important, a new nationwide network of railroads allowed businesses to distribute goods throughout a broader area. Inventors developed new products, and businesses made the products in large quantities. Investors and bankers provided large amounts of capital. The country had a vast array of natural resources. Big businesses grew and helped complementary businesses prosper.

This industrial growth affected American life. The new business activity centered in the cities, bringing people from rural areas to urban areas in large numbers. Between 1870 and 1916, the country's population exploded. More than 25 million immigrants entered the United States. Immigration and natural population growth more than doubled the U.S. population, from 40 million to 100 million inhabitants. This population boom helped the country by providing a large market for products and by providing workers for the factories.

In the late 1800s, the railroad system bridged the continent. Train service increased from 9,000 miles in 1850 to 200,000 miles in 1900. Within the cities, trains helped to bring consumers to the city centers. Huge department stores emerged in growing cities. Marshall Field of Chicago, R. H. Macy of New York, and John Wanamaker of Philadelphia led the inner city department store growth. Montgomery Ward and Richard Sears began mail-order companies to serve people who lived far away from stores.

Mass production of the automobile in the early twentieth century brought another significant change. With personal transportation, families began to populate the suburbs. Retailing followed this population shift by inventing the suburban shopping mall. Today, few countries in the world have a higher use of individual automobiles than the United States. The U.S. retail environment is focused more than ever on the importance of location as a retail growth factor. Tables 8.1 and 8.2 summarize the major domestic and foreign retailers in the United States.

## › DEVELOPMENT OF SET PRICES AND LARGE STORE FORMATS

In the early days of retailing in the United States, as well as everywhere else in the world, prices were not fixed. People haggled over the price they would pay for a

**Table 8.1**
**United States—Leading Domestic Retailers, 2004**

| Company | Total Sales and Stores | | | | Global Rank and Penetration | | | Domestic Market | |
|---|---|---|---|---|---|---|---|---|---|
| | Primary Line of Trade | Net Sales ($US Mil) | % Chg Sales | Total Stores | 2004 Rank, Top 200 Retailers Worldwide | Single-country, Regional or Global? | Number of countries | Share of total sales | Share of total stores |
| 1 Wal-Mart Stores, Inc. | Hypermarkets/Supercenters | 285,222 | 11.3% | 5,309 | 1 | Global | 11 | 80% | 70% |
| 2 The Home Depot, Inc. | DIY/Home Improvement Stores | 73,094 | 12.8% | 1,890 | 3 | Regional | 3 | 94% | 88% |
| 3 The Kroger Co. | Supermarkets/Grocery Stores | 56,434 | 4.9% | 3,763 | 7 | Single Country | 1 | 100% | 100% |
| 4 Costco Companies, Inc. | Cash & Carries/Warehouse Clubs | 47,146 | 13.1% | 447 | 9 | Global | 7 | 82% | 78% |
| 5 Target Corporation | Discount Department Stores | 45,582 | 11.5% | 1,308 | 11 | Single Country | 1 | 100% | 100% |
| 6 Albertsons, Inc. | Supermarkets/Grocery Stores | 39,897 | 13.6% | 2,503 | 15 | Single Country | 1 | 100% | 100% |
| 7 Walgreen Co. | Drug Stores | 37,508 | 15.4% | 4,579 | 17 | Single Country | 1 | 100% | 100% |
| 8 Lowe's Companies, Inc. | DIY/Home Improvement Stores | 36,464 | 18.2% | 1,087 | 20 | Single Country | 1 | 100% | 100% |
| 9 Safeway Inc. | Supermarkets/Grocery Stores | 35,823 | 0.3% | 1,803 | 21 | Regional | 3 | 90% | 88% |
| 10 Sears, Roebuck and Co. | Department Stores | 35,718 | -1.8% | 2,418 | 22 | Regional | 2 | 87% | 82% |
| 11 CVS Corp. | Drug Stores | 30,594 | 15.1% | 5,375 | 25 | Single Country | 1 | 100% | 100% |
| 12 Best Buy Co., Inc. | Consumer Electronics & Appliances | 27,433 | 12.0% | 832 | 27 | Regional | 2 | 90% | 83% |
| 13 IGA Inc. | Supermarkets/Grocery Stores | 23,625 | 12.5% | 4,500 | 30 | Global | 45 | 30% | N/A |
| 14 Kmart Holding Corp. | Discount Department Stores | 19,701 | -15.3% | 1,480 | 35 | Single Country | 1 | 100.0% | 100.0% |
| 15 Publix Super Markets, Inc. | Supermarkets/Grocery Stores | 18,554 | 10.7% | 886 | 37 | Single Country | 1 | 100% | 100% |

Sources: Retail Forward, company annual reports and published reports

**Table 8.2**
**United States—Key Foreign Retailers, 2004**

| Company | Headquarters | Retail Sector | Primary Line of Trade | 2004 Rank, Top 200 Retailers Worldwide | Single-country, Regional or Global? | Number of countries |
|---|---|---|---|---|---|---|
| Aeon Co., Ltd. | Japan | Softgoods | General Merchandise Stores | 19 | Global | 11 |
| Aldi Group | Germany | FDM | Discount Food Stores | 13 | Global | 13 |
| Alimentation Couche-Tard | Canada | FDM | Convenience Stores | 99 | Global | 7 |
| Bertelsmann AG | Germany | Homegoods | Non-Store | – | Global | 22 |
| The Daiei Inc. | Japan | FDM | General Merchandise Stores | 52 | Global | 2 |
| Delhaize "Le Lion" Group | Belgium | FDM | Supermarkets/Grocery Stores | 32 | Global | 9 |
| Grupo Gigante, S.A. de C.V. | Mexico | FDM | Supermarkets/Grocery Stores | – | Regional | 5 |
| IKEA AB | Sweden | Homegoods | Furniture & Home Furnishings | 44 | Global | 32 |
| INDITEX Group (i.e., Zara) | Spain | Softgoods | Apparel Stores | 110 | Global | 56 |
| Ito-Yokado Co., Ltd | Japan | FDM | Convenience Stores | 6 | Global | 17 |
| The Jean Coutu Group Inc. | Canada | FDM | Drug Stores | 107 | Regional | 2 |
| La Senza Corp. | Canada | Softgoods | Other Apparel Specialty Stores | – | Global | 18 |
| LVMH | France | Softgoods | Other Apparel Specialty Stores | 76 | Global | 56 |
| Marks & Spencer PLC | United Kingdom | FDM | Department Stores | 49 | Global | 32 |
| Mitsukoshi Ltd | Japan | Softgoods | Department Stores | 98 | Global | 9 |
| North West Company | Canada | FDM | General Merchandise Stores | – | Regional | 2 |
| Otto Group | Germany | Homegoods | Non-Store | 61 | Global | 19 |
| Pinault-Printemps-Redoute SA | France | Softgoods | Non-Store | 36 | Global | 17 |
| Rallye (i.e., Casino) | France | FDM | Supermarkets/Grocery Stores | 26 | Global | 17 |
| Royal Ahold | Netherlands | FDM | Supermarkets/Grocery Stores | 10 | Global | 18 |
| Takashimaya Company, Ltd. | Japan | Softgoods | Department Stores | 84 | Global | 5 |
| Tengelmann Warenhandelsgesellschaft | Germany | FDM | Supermarkets/Grocery Stores | 23 | Global | 15 |

Source: Retail Forward, company annual reports, and published reports

product. This works all right as long as you have someone you can trust to negotiate the price for you. In small mom-and-pop stores the employees are almost always family members who have an interest in the business's well being. We can use AGENCY THEORY to explain this. You trust your relatives to negotiate in your absence. However, when a store becomes larger it is more likely that you will have employees that are not family members. Then you need a mechanism for establishing price.

Historic events made the development of the first large-scale stores—department stores—possible. The Industrial Revolution was important in the development of department stores. Until the production process was standardized it was not easy to carry a large product line where products could be purchased by a model number. When products are made by hand there is great variability in quality, based on the skill of the worker who constructed the product. With mass production the products become standard, the same, and it is possible to set hard prices. In conjunction with the Industrial Revolution, there came major world's fairs, designed to show off the products of this revolution. One of the major fairs was held in Paris. Seeing so many products drawn together gave an entrepreneur an idea to open the first department store, the Bon Marché in Paris.

Before the advent of department stores, women really did not go shopping by themselves. It was considered unseemly for a woman to stroll the streets alone. The first department stores were designed to be refuges for women, places where they could spend the day, including having lunch in the dining room. This concept gave rise to the idea of a shopping society where people bought products that they desired, not just necessities that they needed to replenish.

## > THE DYNAMIC RETAIL ENVIRONMENT

The retail industry in the United States is very diverse. Nearly every geographical area has a variety of retail formats that have value and meaning for consumers. Take, for instance, discount stores. Most American consumers believe that they can purchase merchandise at a lower price through discount outlets. They believe that this merchandise is identical to the full price merchandise in department stores. In this instance, the discount store has meaning and value to consumers.

When discount stores first enter a country, consumers are understandably wary about buying merchandise from these retailers, believing that only inferior products could possibly be sold in such a store. As consumers become more comfortable and experienced with buying from discount stores, their attitudes change, from disbelief that anyone would buy merchandise from a discount store to disbelief that anyone would buy certain types of merchandise anywhere other than a discount store. Think about the last time you bought an electrical appliance. If you are a U.S. consumer, you probably bought this product from a discount store such as Best Buy. You probably compared prices at only one or two stores, because these retailers guarantee their prices as being the lowest available. This means if you find the same product for a lower price someplace else, they will refund the difference. In this way, these stores eliminate price as a risk factor.

You probably have a clearcut idea of what products you would purchase at a discount store. You might not consider buying clothes at a mass merchandiser, like Kmart, but you are likely to buy household supplies there. A department store may

**Photo 8.1**
Sears, Roebuck and Company advertised itself as the cheapest supply house on earth. This 1897 Sears catalog provided an important retail link to rural Americans.

seem like the only appropriate place to buy a wedding gift. If you were buying the same product for yourself, you might buy it at a discount store.

## › SELF-SERVICE

The concept of self-service originated in the United States, in the supermarket industry. Several COMPLEMENTARIES are needed for effective self-service. The first is packaging. When customers are waited on, and products are handed to consumers, there is no need for PACKAGING. However, when customers start to handle merchandise themselves, packaging is needed to protect the products. The early foreign supermarkets in China brought their own shrink-wrap machines so they could package fresh fruits and vegetables before letting customers handle them. The second complementary is SHOPPING CARTS. Before the introduction of shopping carts, people carried wire or wicker baskets. They didn't buy any more than what they could carry. A third complementary of supermarkets is the AUTOMOBILE. Although there are supermarkets in countries where automobiles are not prevalent, their presence makes the transition from neighborhood mom-and-pop stores to supermarkets much easier.

Self-service is another important characteristic of distinctive types of retail formats. In more developed countries, self-service is considered part of a low cost, discount strategy. In less developed countries, the introduction of self-service has nothing to do with a discount image. It reflects consumers' freedom to hold and examine products without relying on salespersons. When self-service is first introduced to a less developed country, packaging is needed to protect the products from consumers. In developed countries, packaging is used to entice consumers to hold products.

I was talking to a class of business students at Shanghai University—International Business School in the 1990s. Self-service food stores were just being introduced to the People's Republic of China (PRC). I asked the group how they felt about these stores. A young woman volunteered, "When I go into a self-service store, I feel free as a bird. Free to hold merchandise and select those things that are right for me as a consumer." I was very surprised that self-service was such an emotional experience for this young woman. A few months later, I happened to be talking with my mother. Somehow we began to talk about the introduction of self-service stores

**Photo 8.2**
Warehouse stores feature products sold out of open boxes on warehouse pallets. Products are often packaged together or sold in commercial-size containers. Many shoppers, like the one in this picture, are overwhelmed by the volume. *Courtesy of SN.*

into the United States. To my surprise, my mother's first experience in a self-service store in the early 1960s was very similar to that of the young Chinese student. She used some of the same words, saying that she had felt free to compare products and really evaluate them.

Thirty years separate these two phenomena. During most of that time, China was closed to outside influences—a period corresponding to the cultural revolution and central government ownership of all businesses. Self-service stores were not introduced into Communist China until economic reforms were introduced. A planned economy does not endeavor to make shopping more efficient or enjoyable.

The retail industry in the United States uses a variety of formats that have meaning and value to consumers. But this alone does not fully explain the dynamic environment of U.S. retailing. After studying retailing in other countries, I began to identify several characteristics that set U.S. retailing apart. It is important to consider these characteristics before exploring retailing in other parts of the world. In Chapter 3, I talked about the self-reference criterion. This is the assumption that every other part of the world does or should do things as we do. It is also important to keep this assumption in mind as you compare U.S. retailing to retailing elsewhere in the world. You will find that retailing in the United States is quite different from retailing in other parts of the world. When I first studied retailing in Japan, I thought that Japan was the anomaly. But the more I know about retailing in other countries the more convinced I am that most countries are closer to Japan than to the United States.

## › WHAT SETS THE U.S. RETAIL INDUSTRY APART FROM OTHER COUNTRIES?

There are many characteristics that differentiate retailing in the United States from retailing in other countries. However, the following features stand out in my mind as being uniquely definitive of the U.S. system.

### Little Government Regulation

The United States has the most lenient government attitude toward the regulation of retailing of any country in the world. The governments in some countries regulate the hours that a store can be open. Opening new large-scale retail stores is very difficult in Belgium, France, and Japan. Terminating unneeded employees is very difficult in Europe. None of these areas are regulated by government in the United States.

In the United States there are no education or knowledge requirements for store owners. In Italy, every store operator has to attend a school to learn how to run his or her particular type of business. The Italian government determines where retail stores will be located. For instance, if you want to open a toy store, you would have to wait until a toy store location became available. In the United States, as long as an area is zoned for commercial development, most types of retail stores can be opened. The exception to this is liquor stores, which require a special license.

Retail researchers from Europe and Japan generally hold one big misconception about retailing in the United States. They believe that the Robinson-Patman Act plays a major role in U.S. pricing. In fact, many retailers and manufacturers have never heard of this act, and it has little influence on their business. The Robinson-Patman Act is an effort to specify illegal price discrimination. According to the act, illegal price discrimination exists when different prices are charged for goods of "like grade and quality . . . where the effect of such discrimination may be substantially to lessen competition or tend to create a monopoly in any line of commerce, or to insure, destroy, or prevent competition with any person who knowingly receives the benefit of such discrimination or with customers of either of them." Price discrimination is permissible when (1) there is a cost-savings (economies of scale) in the size of order; (2) the goods are subject to deterioration, obsolescence, or seasonal changes; and (3) there is no injury to competition. The general rule of thumb is that if a volume discount is offered to all customers who can order in the bulk specified, there is no price discrimination.

## Importance of Chains

Few other countries have the extensive network of retail chains that characterizes the United States. These chains include mass merchandisers, convenience stores, warehouse clubs, supermarkets, and specialty stores. Although department stores are less likely to have a national presence, they have strong regional presence. The degree of mergers and acquisitions in the retail industry makes it difficult to remember who owns whom. These national chains are the result of the large U.S. mass market.

Malls prefer national chains because their chance of failure is less than that of smaller chains or independents. Malls do not like to have empty spaces. The purchasing power of national chains allows them to have great power in the distribution channel. Many national chains sell their own private label exclusively. This removes them from competition with the national brand name discounters. However, finding the same stores in every major mall creates a degree of shopping boredom among consumers.

## Sophisticated Logistics

In retailing, logistics is the act of moving merchandise from a manufacturer to a store. Merchandise might go from the manufacturer to a distribution center and then to a store, or directly from a manufacturer to the retail store. Sometimes the merchandise goes from a manufacturer to a wholesaler and then to a retailer. When I owned a retail store, we would frequently buy jeans from a cash-and-carry wholesaler. We would buy ten pairs of jeans and when those sold, we would buy ten more pairs.

The discount mass merchandisers were the first to introduce technologically sophisticated logistics systems. Retailer-operated distribution centers emerged wherever national chains had enough stores to justify their existence. These sophisticated distribution centers made the chains more autonomous by ensuring that they had the merchandise available when their stores needed it. The Limited, for instance, has a completely computerized distribution center. Humans do not handle merchandise. Computers PICK (select) the merchandise based on orders from the individual stores. The merchandise comes from the manufacturer on hangers. The computer system selects the merchandise, hangs it in a box, and affixes a mailing label for the ordering stores.

Sophisticated distribution systems use CROSS DOCKING whenever possible. Merchandise comes by truck from the manufacturers. The trucks back into the warehouse and mini loaders transport merchandise to the distribution trucks heading for the store. This eliminates unloading the merchandise and having it sit on the floor.

Nearly all the national and regional chains have computerized retail inventory systems (RIS) to provide instantaneous information about inventory. Before these systems were introduced, retailers knew what merchandise they received but not how much merchandise they had sold until they did an actual physical count at the end of the year. Even small retailers can now know how much inventory they have at any instant.

Radio Frequency Identification (RFID) was developed during WWII to differentiate friendly aircraft from enemies. This technology, unlike bar codes, has several important advantages. First, a much larger amount of information can be stored on an RFID tag. Second, the RFID identifies individual items, not simply a category of merchandise. Third, the RFID tag can be read from a distance, or within a group of merchandise. Finally, the RFID tag can have additional information added to it, to provide enhanced value to the retailer, or to the consumer once it is in the home. In 2003 Wal-Mart announced that the company's top 100 suppliers would need to use RFID tags on pallets and cases beginning in 2005.[1]

## Strong Manufacturers—National Brand Names

Discount retailers cannot develop without strong national brand names. Let me explain that concept. In order to convince consumers that a discounter is really a discounter, consumers have to be able to make same merchandise comparisons. Only branded merchandise gives the consumer a comparable measure. The United States has well-known national brands in most merchandising categories. In some countries, the manufacturers are very small, and they never establish national or international recognition. Discount retailers receive recognition when consumers can determine that they are buying the same product for less in a discount store. Japan's discount industry has faltered because although the industry introduced low-cost stores, these stores did not have wide access to national brand names. If consumers cannot compare a discount store's products with products sold in traditional retailers, they will not perceive the discount offering as having value.

## Discount Format Well Established

As I said before, consumers do not believe that a discounter is really giving them value until they can see that the discounter is selling the same products as full-priced retailers, but at a lower price.

**Photo 8.3**
Gap stores in Paris sell
100% private label
merchandise, like Gap
stores in the United States.
Many retail stores are
investing large amounts of
money on design teams to
create unique product
offerings. *Courtesy of WWD.*

## Strong Private Labels

Private labels began in the United States as a low-cost alternative to nationally known brand names. Grocery stores introduced the first generic brands to cut costs. Store brands rapidly followed. The cost of store brands was positioned between that of the generic and the national brand names. In the United Kingdom, store brand foods were introduced at the higher priced points, intending to compete with the best-known national brands in quality and value for price.

Department stores introduced private labels to provide a hedge for themselves against brand name discounting. High status retailers found that they could gain great margins on merchandise that carried their store's name. Mass merchandisers entered the private label program to give them a greater merchandising coordination and enhanced margin. Specialty stores such as the Gap and Limited established their market presence by selling only private label products. Consumers identified with being a Limited customer, or a Gap customer.

## Retailers Can Terminate Employees

Retailing is very labor intensive and labor is one of a retailer's most important expenses. In the United States, retailers can hire and fire employees based on their sales needs. This is not so in most European countries. In Italy, retailers will close their doors for a month in the summer to allow employees to take a vacation. It is not that the retailers are so socially concerned. Rather, they are required by law to do this, as they cannot hire part-time employees while the vacationing employees are away.

## Retailers Hire College Graduates

Most U.S. retailers hire management trainees with college degrees. Retail buyers and managers in major U.S. retail companies are among the most educated in the world. They are also given much responsibility early in their career. After graduating from a university and completing a training program, a new employee is put into an assistant buyer or assistant manager position. If the person does well, after 3 to 5 years she or he could expect to be a buyer or a department manager. In Japan, by contrast, new workers might stay on the sales floor for 10 years before being promoted to management. Even then, horizontal moves within the organization would be more common than vertical (upward) moves.

German retailers hire high school graduates and offer an educational program as part of their company advancement plan. The educational program is not like the 6-to-8-week training program offered by U.S. retailers; it is a multiyear program.

## Short Channels

Retailers in the United States generally buy directly from the manufacturer. This is the shortest channel possible. The prevalence of large national chains also reduces the number of steps in the channel. However, short channels have more to do with the type of merchandise purchased than they have to do with efficiencies.

Greater volume → Shorter channel
More perishable → Longer channels

Permanent merchandise markets make it possible for small retailers to purchase directly from manufacturers. However, a manufacturer may require that a retailer place a minimum order of a dozen items of each product or a minimum order of $5,000. In this case, the retailer can go to a wholesaler and buy smaller amounts of the merchandise for a slightly higher fee. Wholesalers play an important role in breaking down bulk quantities and shipping in smaller lots.

Compared with food consumers in other developed countries such as Europe and Japan, U.S. consumers purchase less perishable merchandise. In many parts of Europe and in Japan, the family cook will shop on a daily basis for fresh produce to use in cooking.

## Characteristics for Soft Goods Retailing

Soft goods retailers are predominately department stores, specialty stores, and mass merchandisers. As in most other developed parts of the world, department stores in the United States have had stagnated growth. Department stores suffered from the "sameness problem"; they all carried the same brands and did not do a good job of differentiating themselves from other department stores and, more seriously, from specialty stores. Specialty stores in the United States have proven very adept at developing private label lines that differentiate their offering from that of competitors. Slow to do this, department stores have suffered in the process. As department stores redefine their target consumers and offer private label lines promoting their distinct offerings, they are likely to prosper. Department stores also suffered from the problem of selling brand name merchandise that became available in discount stores, a recipe for failure. But it is also the requirement for the establishment of discount stores. To establish the concept of discounting consumers need to see identical merchandise in full price stores. Consumers need to be able to make this direct price comparison.

## Production Is Based on Orders

Manufacturers produce a product line, have samples made, show these samples to retail buyers, then collect orders. They produce only those products for which sufficient orders are received; those products with insufficient orders are canceled. Generally, a manufacturer produces only a limited supply of extra products. Thus, merchandise gets into the store and sells very well, there is usually no chance to reorder. The more basic the merchandise, the more likely it is that manufacturers will produce more than ordered and retailers will have access to reorders.

If merchandise does not sell, the retailer continues to lower the price until someone finally buys it. Large dominant retailers may pressure their suppliers for markdown money sharing with profit loss due to slow-selling merchandise, but this is a recent trend. In general, retail stores carry the product risk in the United States.

Some categories of merchandise, such as cosmetics and books, are sold under the consignment system in U.S. stores. In these cases, manufacturers carry the product risk for this merchandise. They also decide when they will take markdowns.

## Healthy Independent Retailers

The United States has the healthiest small retailer sector of any country in the world. Government subsidies or entitlements do not protect small retailers. Therefore, they have to be competitive based on their own strengths, flexibility, and uniqueness. Small retailers in the United States have a high failure rate, but the result is a very healthy segment of successful independent retailers.

Located outside the mall area, independent retailers provide the variety that makes retailing interesting. Some major retailers such as Tower Records are beginning to avoid mall locations, believing that teenagers are tired of the artificiality of the mall.

## Retailers Are Assemblers of Lines of Goods

Each retail store or chains of stores have individuals whose major responsibility is to select merchandise for the store. These retail buyers serve an important function. Based on their view of their store's customers, they filter thousands of merchandise offerings, selecting merchandise that they view as the best value for the price in styles that will appeal to their customers. In other words, the buyers assemble products from which their consumers choose.

In many countries, manufacturers determine merchandise offerings in the retail stores. The manufacturers provide the merchandise and provide their own salespersons, and accept the return of unsold merchandise. The manufacturers take the product risk, and likewise claim the largest share of the profit margin.

## Retail Buyers Are Considered Profit Centers

Retail buyers have a very important role in U.S. stores. Companies evaluate buyers on their performance, sales, maintained markup, and turnover on a year-to-date basis. They reward buyers who have outstanding figures; they terminate those who fail to perform. In most companies, the buying role is totally separate from the selling role. Buyers may visit the departments they buy for, but their visits are to obtain information, not to sell merchandise. The degree of separation, buying from selling, is unique to U.S. stores. Retailers in some other countries have professional buyers, but they generally do not have the autonomy of buyers in the United States.

U.S. buyers make decisions in the same way as an individual consumer. In most cases, they individually select merchandise, examining the items in a vendor's line and making a "yes" or "no" decision about each item. Buyers in most other countries select a vendor but do not individually select each item. Furthermore, buyers in other countries generally must consult other executives or managers before making a purchase decision. This team decision making is more similar to industrial buying in the United States.

In the United States, centralized buying is a common practice. Buyers in this case make selections for stores located throughout the country. What is lost in not customizing the product line for various geographical locations is replaced by economies of scale that make possible an increase in volume and discount pricing.

Some companies use a system of buyers and allocators. The buyers select the merchandise for a wide variety of stores and the allocators determine the actual number of units that each store receives. These figures are based on past sales figures. They may transfer merchandise that is not selling at one store to another geographical location. However, this process is expensive.

## Permanent Merchandise Markets

Throughout the United States, there are large markets where retailers can go to buy merchandise. These markets allow small retailers to have the same access as large retailers to hundreds of manufacturers. The permanent merchandise markets provide an affordable way for retailers to find unique merchandise. Most other countries do not have such permanent merchandise markets. Instead, retailers buy from manufacturers with whom they have long-term relationships.

Permanent merchandise markets also give retailers information about market trends. Markets have special promotions called a market week. During this time additional vendors come to the market to display their products and show retailers market trends. Permanent markets enable smaller retailers to have access to many suppliers. Without a central market small business owners must spend additional time and money visiting suppliers. A list of permanent markets are included in Figure 8.1.

## › CHARACTERISTICS OF FOOD RETAILING

## Food Formats

Food is sold in a variety of retail formats in the United States. Although most food is purchased in supermarkets, there are a variety of formats that sell food. These

## Permanent Markets

**Figure 8.1**
Permanent merchandise markets are found throughout the United States, one of the few countries in the world with this extensive system. Retail buyers visit these markets to select merchandise for their stores. Having many manufacturers together in one location makes finding new suppliers much easier.

formats include HYPERMARKETS, WAREHOUSE CLUBS, SUPERMARKETS, HARD DISCOUNT STORES, SPECIALTY STORES, and CONVENIENCE STORES.

HYPERMARKETS are large scale stores selling both food and non-food items. They stock most of their merchandise on the floor. Meyers and Wal-Mart's superstores are hypermarkets. WAREHOUSE CLUBS are a bare-bones type of retailer. Merchandise is generally displayed on open pallets, with boxes cut open for display. Customers must buy memberships in order to shop in a warehouse club. Wal-Mart's Sam's Club, Costco, and BJs are examples of warehouse clubs. These three companies made up 93 percent of warehouse club sales in 2003.[2] Warehouse clubs are on the decline in the United States. Although their prices are very low, most of their revenue comes from sale of memberships. SUPERMARKETS sell a variety of food and non-food items and are the major place that Americans buy food. HARD DISCOUNT STORES have the atmosphere of a warehouse club but are the size of a convenience store. They are particularly good at providing low costs in an urban location. SPECIALTY STORES focus on either a particular product, like baked goods, or a particular lifestyle, like urban chic. Examples are Whole Foods or Trader Joe's. CONVENIENCE STORES focus on offering products at a location that is quick and easy to access. Their prices are higher than other formats, and in the United States they focus on staple merchandise. In other parts of the world convenience stores offer fresh produce and other services.

**NO NATIONAL CHAINS**    There are two regional U.S. supermarket chains, Safeway and Krogers, but there is not a national chain of retailers. A third company, Albertsons, is in the process of being broken up and sold off. There have been extensive mergers and acquisitions in the food industry, but none of these have resulted in a national chain. Since Wal-Mart has begun converting their discount stores to superstores, they are likely to be the first national chain in food retailing.

**FRAGMENTED**   The food retail industry is not highly concentrated. The top five retailers have less than 37 percent of market share. Wal-Mart has the highest market share with 12.1 percent; Kroger has 9.6 percent; Albertsons and Safeway each have a little over 6 percent; and Costco has 2.1 percent.[3] The battle among food retailers is based on price. The specialist retailers such as Whole Foods and Trader Joe's are taking themselves out of the price wars and instead focusing on unique products and the shopping experience. I remember the first time I went into a Whole Foods store in an urban location in San Francisco. They had valet parking. The smell of the store was incredible—baked bread, brewed coffee, exotic flowers. The person who took me there said that the store was known as a place to take a date, just to enjoy the ambiance. It was a fun and happening place, a far cry from conventional supermarkets.

**SLOTTING ALLOWANCES**   SLOTTING ALLOWANCES are one-time payments a supplier makes to a retailer for initial access to the retailer's store shelves. Historically slotting allowances began when retailers had to reorganize their warehouse every time a new product was added. This would entail repunching all the computer cards to reflect this change. Now that everything is automated, the fee is more closely related to opportunity costs. Opportunity costs in this example means the difference between the revenue generated by this product and the potential revenue that could have been obtained from a rival product.

A typical supermarket is 44,000 square feet and carries about 35,000 SKUs (stock keeping units). SKUs are numbers that identify each separate brand, size, flavor, color, or pack of a product. Slotting fees are paid per unit, per retailer, per metropolitan area. So a company that had 500 stores would charge a much higher slotting fee than one with 100 stores. The range of slotting fees can be great; one study reported a range of from $2,313 to $21,768. A survey of suppliers reported that the nationwide introduction of a new product would require $1.5 to $2 million in slotting allowances.[4] When a supplier pays a slotting fee he will be able to keep the product there for a reasonable amount of time, generally four to six months. Slotting fees themselves do not guarantee a particular placement of a product, just that they will be allowed on the shelf. Essentially when a supermarket agrees to carry a new product they must decide to remove one of their previously carried products. About 80–90 percent of new product introductions pay a slotting fee.

Products that are delivered directly to the store (DSD) instead of going through the retailer's warehousing system are less likely to be charged slotting fees. This is because the retailer does not have to reorder the warehouse. Frozen and refrigerated product categories like ice cream and hot dogs have the highest average slotting allowance per item. Slotting amounts are higher for these products because shelf space is more costly to expand. Also proliferation of frozen products tends to be greater so there is more competition for this space.

There are two theoretical explanations for slotting fees. One explanation is based on **MARKET EFFICIENCY THEORY**. The basis for this idea is that a supplier pays a high slotting fee as a way to **SIGNAL** to the retailer that this product will be successful. If this is true then slotting fees can actually play a positive role in the system. The signaling explanation assumes that manufacturers have better knowledge than retailers about the likely success of new products. The other explanation is the **MARKET DOMINANCE THEORY**. Either suppliers will pay high slotting fees to keep competitors off the shelf, or retailers will demand high slotting fees simply because they can. These fees add to their bottom line, profitability.

**CATEGORY MANAGEMENT**    Category management means that some member of the channel, generally the manufacturer, determines what items will be available. A category is a selection of similar merchandise, for instance, shampoo. The overall purpose of category management is to reduce the number of SKUs in an offering, presenting those that will generate the greatest sales for the category with the fewest offerings. There is an old adage that 20 percent of the merchandise generates 80 percent of sales. Category management fits under this principle. However, since category management is usually done by manufacturers such as Proctor & Gamble, the tendency is to build the category with their own products. The sales figures may show that they have enhanced the revenue of the category; however, the problem is that supermarket consumers purchase a wide variety of SKUs. The store will not know which of the brands a consumer considers not substitutable in their minds. In some instances consumers will not really care if their favorite brand is not available; they will simply substitute another. However, the problem comes up when consumers are very loyal to a brand that is discontinued. In this case the consumer may decide that their loyalty to the store is not as strong as their loyalty to the brand, and they switch stores.

I have had this experience. I like a certain kind of cheese that my local supermarket used to carry. One day they didn't have my favorite brand. I didn't buy another brand because experience has taught me that I really do not like the substitutes. The person behind the deli counter assured me that they were only out of stock and would have my brand next week. I bought the rest of my groceries, but didn't buy a substitute cheese. The next time I returned to the supermarket, they still did not have my cheese. This time the deli person told me that they hadn't gotten a delivery this week. Again I bought my other groceries and left. Eventually I learned that the store would no longer be carrying this cheese, so I switched to another supermarket for all my weekly purchases. I had decided that the cheese was more important than my loyalty to the store. That is a major problem for supermarket retailers. They are not just eliminating an SKU; they are tinkering with the loyalty of their customers.

In the next section, I will look at the functions of retailing in a free market system. Later in Parts III and IV, I will discuss retailing in planned economies; the roles are quite different.

## › THEORY OF DISTRIBUTION IN A FREE MARKET SYSTEM

A free market means that producers are free to produce as much of and whatever they wish. Consumers are also free to purchase as much of and whatever they wish. Matching the needs of suppliers and consumers requires some problem solving and planning. Three basic problems need to be resolved in the distribution of consumer products in a free market system.[5]

1. The need to match specialized production with specific demand (SORTING).
2. The need to resolve spatial discrepancy, transporting the products from the place of production to the place of consumption (SPATIAL CLOSURE).

3. The need to equalize supply with demand over different time periods (TEMPO-RAL CLOSURE).

## Sorting

Matching production with demand is an issue in free markets, but not in planned markets. In a planned market, the government tells each manufacturing facility what it should produce and how much it should produce. The government then tells the manufacturers where the merchandise should be shipped. If consumers want to purchase the merchandise, they are limited to the choices that are available from the government manufacturers. In a planned economy, there is no incentive for factories to produce things that consumers actually want; their only customer is the government. In a free market, if consumers do not like one factory's products, they can choose products from another factory. If a manufacturer does not produce what consumers want, the products will not sell and eventually the manufacturer will go out of business.

Production is often geographically concentrated. Much of the home furniture industry is in North Carolina, while office furniture is produced primarily in Michigan. However, consumers throughout the United States buy furniture for their homes, and offices throughout the United States purchase office furniture. Furthermore, large-scale manufacturers tend to produce a certain type of product for a period, and then produce a different type of product. This is called a production run. Just because a factory produces a particular type of table during January, however, does not mean consumers will want to purchase those tables in January, or at another time during the year. Demand is scattered in time and geography.

Wroe Alderson developed the theoretical concept of SORTING, which I will adapt for a retail example. Sorting includes (1) accumulation, (2) standardization, (3) allocation, and (4) assortment.

ACCUMULATION is the process used to gather up inventory. After Hurricane Katrina hit New Orleans in 2005, the Red Cross asked for blood donations from across the country to bring emergency relief to the city residents. People from Maine to California made a special effort to respond to this request.

STANDARDIZATION involves grouping similar products together for effective distribution. Standardizing the blood donations needed above would mean categorizing them by type—A, B+, O, etc. Standardization is a way of organizing inventory. When you look into an egg carton, you expect all the eggs to be the same size. Eggs are graded by size as large, extra large, and so on. The eggs come from many farmers, but the processing plant puts them together into similar (standard) groups.

ALLOCATION refers to the process of giving the supplies to the end users. During the hurricane, several shelters were created; someone had to make the decision about the amount of supplies to send to each shelter. Some retail stores have allocators on their staff. They do not buy merchandise, but instead determine how much each store will get.

ASSORTMENT is the range of offering that a retailer carries. It might be a customized selection of merchandise to satisfy a specific target customer, or a broad range of merchandise to meet nearly everyone's needs.

Sorting resolves the product discrepancy problem created by specialization of production. A difference between a developing and a highly industrialized economy is the degree to which the distribution infrastructure can do sophisticated sorting. Sorting efficiency is essential for an advanced economy.

An example can help to illustrate the four processes involved in sorting. After a major hurricane struck Florida, a group of logistics experts were sent to the area to set up a relief distribution center. The efforts of the distribution center focused on solving the sorting problem; that is, how to match supply with demand. First, the logistics team needed to establish some standards for medical equipment and food supplies. Sterilized rubber gloves were needed. Blood supplies had to be put into groups: A+, AB, and so on. Baby food needed to be assembled according to different nutritional needs. Next, the team needed to determine who would supply these products. Area hospitals and emergency centers were contacted to accumulate a large amount of the needed equipment and supplies. Once the supply was determined, the team designated relief groups to be sent to different shelters. For instance, one shelter would house people who needed medical help. Another shelter would be for families with young children. The team's allocation and assortment efforts included determining the needs of each center so that diapers and baby food, for instance, would not be sent to centers without young children.

## Spatial Closure

SPATIAL CLOSURE relates to the transportation of products to consumers via a direct market, a central market, or a multistage system. Without the central market, purchasers must make individual trips to each of the potential suppliers (Figure 8.2). A multistage distribution system adds a degree of complexity. However, it is also the characteristic of more advanced economies (Figure 8.3). In this system, the retail buyers act as specialists, assembling the best possible set of merchandise for

**Figure 8.2**
In a single-stage distribution system, consumers must visit each store to purchase products. It takes a long time to do shopping with this system.

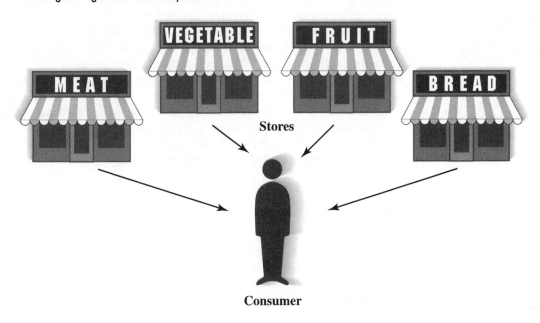

A Single-Stage Distribution System

## A Multistage Distribution System

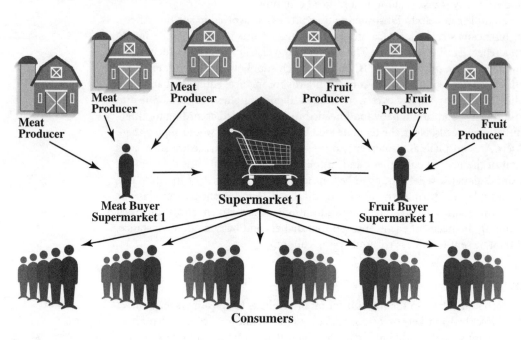

**Figure 8.3**
In a multistage distribution system, specialized retail buyers visit many suppliers and select a wide variety of products for sale. Buyers for the supermarket take over the function of going from one supplier to another. This system greatly streamlines shopping.

consumers. This idea is referred to as the **PRINCIPLE OF MINIMUM TRANSACTIONS**.[6] The introduction of buyers serves to reduce total transactions and is the basic justification for using a multistage distribution structure. In many developing countries, it takes women all day to shop for food. Rather than visit a supermarket where many choices are provided under one roof, she will visit the meat shop, the bread shop, the vegetable shop, and so on. Shopping in these countries is time consuming and inefficient, involving numerous separate transactions. When supermarkets are introduced to developing countries, suddenly it is possible to purchase all the ingredients for a meal in one transaction rather than in five or more.

Intermediaries might be added for a variety of reasons other than just pure efficiency. Bucklin called these intermediaries **SERVICE OUTPUTS**.[7] They include (1) lot size, or the ability to procure small quantities; (2) waiting time, or the length of time it takes following purchases to obtain the actual goods; (3) market decentralization, or the proximity of goods to the buyer; and (4) product variety, or combinations of goods that most closely match demand. These factors help to explain the Japanese distribution system, discussed later in Chapter 12.

### Temporal Closure

**TEMPORAL CLOSURE** refers to the difference between the time when manufacturers produce products and the time when consumers demand products. Products must flow through the distribution system in a timely manner. I have heard estimates that 10 to 20 percent of Russia's food production spoils because of their poor distribution infrastructure.

Consumers in underdeveloped countries, and even retailers, stockpile inventory. In a multistage system, retailers can plan the goods to satisfy demand with a minimum inventory. The relationship of temporal closure to inventory requirements is known as the PRINCIPLE OF MASSED RESERVES.[8] These reserves keep inventory low and associated storage costs down while increasing the consumer's convenience.

In the United States, the current trend is to seek "just in time" delivery systems. Manufacturers deliver merchandise to a retail store precisely as it becomes necessary to replenish store stocks. In this way, retailers can reduce their costs by keeping inventory low. However, a system like this usually creates a backlog, the cost of which is put off on the weaker channel member. As a result, the only retailers who have successfully introduced just in time delivery systems are high volume mass merchandisers who are powerful enough to dictate their own terms.

> SUMMARY

In this chapter, I have discussed some characteristics that help contrast the U.S. retail system with other systems throughout the world. As I talk about these countries in the following chapters, I will point out some similarities. There are some characteristics that apply to all retailing in the United States, others are different for soft goods such as clothing as compared to food retailing. In general the U.S. retail system is one that is largely unregulated. There is little attempt to protect small companies, and as a result the United States has one of the most vibrant small business environments in the world. Only the strong survive. In many European countries the government protects small businesses and as a result they are never forced to find a sustainable strategy. In every retail format there is intense competition, making it difficult for foreign companies to succeed in this market, but also giving consumers a wide range of purchase alternatives.

Chapter 9 focuses on Mexico and Canada, our NAFTA neighbors. U.S. retailers are quite successful in Canada; however, when Canadian retailers have tried to enter the United States, they have not been successful. Several major U.S. retailers have entered Mexico and then pulled out. A major contributor to this initial failure was the devaluation of the peso, which occurred at nearly the same time that U.S. retailers entered that market. Chapter 10's focus is on South America, an interesting continent with large pockets where traditional retailers are the only service providers. Yet in other areas, there is a great deal of competition among local chains and the foreign multinationals.

KEY TERMS

ACCUMULATION
AGENCY THEORY
ALLOCATION
ASSORTMENT
AUTOMOBILE
COMPLEMENTARIES
CONVENIENCE STORES
CROSS DOCKING

HARD DISCOUNT STORES
HYPERMARKETS
MARKET DOMINANCE THEORY
MARKET EFFICIENCY THEORY
PACKAGING
PICK
PRINCIPLE OF MASSED RESERVES
PRINCIPLE OF MINIMUM TRANSACTIONS
SERVICE OUTPUTS
SHOPPING CARTS
SIGNAL
SLOTTING ALLOWANCES
SORTING
SPATIAL CLOSURE
SPECIALTY STORES
STANDARDIZATION
SUPERMARKETS
TEMPORAL CLOSURE
WAREHOUSE CLUBS

## › DISCUSSION QUESTIONS

1. When retail buyers are considered profit centers, they are rewarded for taking procurement risk. However, pay for retail buyers in some countries, such as Japan, is based primarily on seniority. Characterize how you view the buying process to be different based on risk taking or security compensation.
2. An important characteristic of retailers in the United States is their role as assemblers of lines of merchandise. Explain this concept using the central market concept presented in Figures 8.2 and 8.3. Can you use this central market concept to explain why being an independent retailer is somewhat easier in the United States than in countries without permanent markets?
3. Bucklin discussed service outputs such as lot size, waiting time, market decentralization, and product variety. Would wholesalers add or detract from the degree of product variety found in a country? Explain.

## › ENDNOTES

1. "Retailing in the United States." (2004). London: Euromonitor Global Market Information Database.
2. "Retailing in the United States." (2004).
3. Caicco, P., and M. Petrie (2005). "A Rare Moment: U.S. Supermarket Stocks Appear Favorable." CIBC World Markets in Investext September 15, 2005.
4. "Slotting Allowances in the Retail Grocery Industry: Selected Case Studies in Five Product Categories." (2003). Washington, D.C.: Federal Trade Commission.

5. Bowersox, D., and M. B. Cooper (1992). *Strategic Marketing: Channel Management.* New York: McGraw-Hill.

6. Hall, M. (1951). *Distributive Trading.* London: Hutchinson's University Library, p. 80.

7. Bucklin, L. (1966). *A Theory of Distribution Structure.* Berkeley: IBER Special Publications.

8. Hall, M. (1951).

# 9

# MEXICO AND CANADA

## After reading this chapter, you should understand

> Why U.S. retailers are expanding at a rapid rate in both Mexico and Canada.

> How currency devaluation has affected foreign retailers in Mexico, and what strategic decisions these retailers need to adopt to remain competitive.

> Why Mexico's informal retailing sector affects modern retail formats.

> How informal retailing sectors create a sense of place, drawing customers to their location.

> How power centers anchored by foreign chains are creating intense competition for Canadian retailers.

Mexico and Canada, the United States's NAFTA partners, represent very different retailing environments. In Mexico, modern superstores operate in juxtaposition to street vendors and informal merchant markets. Canada, in contrast, offers a retailing environment similar in many ways to that of the United States. Both markets, however, offer many opportunities for foreign retailers seeking to expand their international operations.

Most observers expected that NAFTA would affect the manufacturing industries of member nations more than other sectors of their economies. As a surprise to most, retailing has been affected significantly by NAFTA. Since the early 1990s, foreign-based volume retailers have been entering the Mexican and Canadian markets in even greater numbers. Several Mexican retailers, in turn, have entered joint ventures and strategic alliances with foreign-based volume retailers to gain operational expertise and capital. Most of the U.S. movement of retailers into Canada has been acquisition based.

## › MEXICO

### Country Background

Mexicans have a strong sense of nationalism. Their country's history of revolution has contributed to this sense of unity. Mexicans exalt their pre-conquest native civilization, downplaying the role of the Spaniards in their cultural history.

Highly advanced civilizations developed in central Mexico before the arrival of the Spaniards in 1519. A 300-year colonial period followed. During this time, the native population declined from 28 million in 1520 to little more than 1 million by the end of the eighteenth century. The Spanish rulers excluded from government not only native Indians, but also those persons of pure Spanish descent born in the New World.

By the early nineteenth century, the unrepresented groups were resentful and a rebellion began with the battle cry "Death to the Spaniards." In 1821, Mexico declared independence from Spain. For the rest of the century, different factions fought over who would rule Mexico. The country lost half its territory to the United States.

The Mexican Revolution began in 1910. This developed to a bloody battle to determine who would rule the country. During this time, a movement began to divide up estates of the wealthy elite and distribute the land to landless peasantry. The Mexican government seized control of all natural resources. The political party that emerged from that conflict, the Institutional Revolutionary Party (IRP), remained dominant in Mexican politics until the elections of 1997. Mexico is sometimes called the one-party democracy.[1]

The supermarket chain's level of penetration is much lower in Mexico than in developed countries. Mexico has 83 square meters of supermarket sales floor per 1,000 inhabitants, 5.7 times below the U.S. level. The industry is highly fragmented. Fifty percent of sales still come from traditional formats; however, large companies should gain greater market share as consumers become more price sensitive and automobile ownership increases.[2] Thirty percent of Mexico's population is under the age of 14. This is a sign of great growth potential.

Under NAFTA, Canada and the United States are exempt from quotas in trade with Mexico. This means they can ship unlimited quantities of goods to Mexico and Mexico can ship unlimited quantities back to its two NAFTA partners.

## Department and Specialty Stores

Tables 9.1 and 9.2 summarize the major domestic and foreign retailers in Mexico. Mexico has three major department store chains—El Puerto de Liverpool, Placio de Hierro, and Sanborns. Liverpool and Placia de Hiero have a long history in Mexico. They were both started by French families who moved to Mexico. Liverpool got its name because most of the merchandise the chain sold came from Europe and was shipped through the port of Liverpool. When the merchandise arrived in Mexico, the most prominent feature was the shipping stamp, Liverpool. Both Liverpool and Placia de Hiero have stores throughout Mexico City.

The Zocolo is the central area of a Mexican city. The original stores for Liverpool and Placia de Hierro in Mexico City are located in the Zocolo, right across the street from each other. When I visited the Liverpool store, I found it very disappointing, dark and cramped with unmemorable cheaply made merchandise. The prices were not even low. The Placio de Hierro store across the street had a ceiling reminiscent of Galeries Lafayette in Paris, a dome with stained glass. The merchandise in this store was not as cramped as that at Liverpool, but again nothing was memorable. Imagine my surprise, then, when I visited the other stores of these two companies and found beautiful modern department stores with first-class merchandise and fixtures. These companies alter their store offering based on the clientele living in an area. Although U.S. stores appeal to different target markets, they usually change the name of their offering to maintain their retail image in the minds of consumers.

Liverpool is Mexico's largest department store chain, with 56 stores under the name of Liverpool and Fabricas de Francia. Their format is very upscale, which has made it difficult to compete in the rough economic times that have beset Mexico. To offset the effects of currency changes the company has increased its domestic sourcing. Now over 80 percent of its merchandise comes from Mexico.[3] In 1992, Liverpool entered into a joint venture with Kmart. The venture was unsuccessful, and Kmart pulled out of Mexico in 1997.

Sanborns has stores spread across retail sectors and throughout Mexico. They operate 50 Sears Roebuck stores in addition to a variety of restaurants, drugstores, and bookstores. Sanborns owns music stores under the Discolandia, Mixup, No Problem, and Tower Records banners. Sanborns' early growth was through acquisition but their more recent plans are to grow organically. ORGANIC GROWTH occurs when a company builds its own stores, compared to ACQUISITION, when it purchases stores that are already operating. Sears has operated in Mexico since 1947 under the name Sears Roebuck de Mexico. Sears has greater geographical representation than either Liverpool or Placia de Hierro. In fact, it is really the only national department store chain with stores throughout the country. Sears has a true department store image in Mexico, more upscale than its mass merchandiser image in the United States. Even before the bottom fell out of the Mexican economy in 1994, Sears had begun overhauling the chain's image. It trimmed inventory, lowered

**Table 9.1**
**Mexico—Leading Domestic Retailers, 2004**

| Company | Total Sales and Stores | | | | Global Rank and Penetration | | | Domestic Market | |
|---|---|---|---|---|---|---|---|---|---|
| | Primary Line of Trade | Net Sales ($US Mil) | % Chg Sales | Total Stores | 2004 Rank, Top 200 Retailers Worldwide | Single-country, Regional or Global? | Number of countries | Share of total sales | Share of total stores |
| 1 Wal-Mart de Mexico[1] | Hypermarkets/Supercenters | 12,388 | 11.0% | 696 | — | Single Country | 1 | 100% | 100% |
| 2 Organización Soriana, S.A. de C.V. | Hypermarkets/Supercenters | 3,719 | 14.1% | 138 | 169 | Single Country | 1 | 100% | 100% |
| 3 Controladora Comercial Mexicana | Hypermarkets/Supercenters | 3,329 | 2.2% | 239 | 185 | Single Country | 1 | 100% | 100% |
| 4 Grupo Gigante, S.A. de C.V. | Supermarkets/Grocery Stores | 2,762 | -3.2% | 517 | — | Regional | 5 | 96% | 97% |
| 5 El Puerto de Liverpool | Department Stores | 2,361 | 16.6% | 53 | — | Single Country | 1 | 100% | 100% |
| 6 FEMSA (OXXO) | Convenience Stores | 2,023 | 24.8% | 3,466 | — | Single Country | 1 | 100% | 100% |
| 7 Grupo Sanborns (i.e, Carso) | Department Stores | 1,968 | 10.7% | 580 | — | Single Country | 1 | 100% | 100% |
| 8 Grupo Elektra | Hardlines Specialty Stores | 1,566 | 10.6% | 1,007 | — | Regional | 4 | 93% | 92% |
| 9 Coppel S.A. de C.V. | General Merchandise Stores | 1,388 | 23.9% | 405 | — | Single Country | 1 | 100% | 100% |
| 10 Chedraui | Supermarkets/Grocery Stores | 1,300 | N/A | 101 | — | Regional | 2 | N/A | 95% |
| 11 Grupo Palacio de Hierro S.A. de C.V. | Department Stores | 721 | 11.2% | 9 | — | Single Country | 1 | 100% | 100% |
| 12 Grupo Famsa S.A. de C.V. | General Merchandise Stores | N/A | N/A | 308 | — | Single Country | 1 | 100% | 100% |

[1] Wal-Mart de Mexico is included on the list as an exception because its parent is U.S.-based.

Sources: Retail Forward, company annual reports and published reports

**Table 9.2**
**Mexico—Key Foreign Retailers, 2004**

| Company | Headquarters | Retail Sector | Primary Line of Trade | Global Rank and Penetration | | |
|---|---|---|---|---|---|---|
| | | | | 2004 Rank, Top 200 Retailers Worldwide | Single-country, Regional or Global? | Number of countries |
| Ace Hardware Corporation | United States | Homegoods | Hardlines Specialty Stores | 55 | Global | 70 |
| Alimentation Couche-Tard | Canada | FDM | Convenience Stores | 99 | Global | 7 |
| AutoZone, Inc. | United States | Homegoods | Hardlines Specialty Stores | 123 | Regional | 2 |
| C&A | Belgium | Softgoods | Apparel Stores | 105 | Global | 15 |
| Carrefour Group | France | FDM | Hypermarkets/Supercenters | 2 | Global | 31 |
| Costco Companies, Inc. | United States | FDM | Cash & Carries/Warehouse Clubs | 9 | Global | 7 |
| FASA | Chile | FDM | Drug Stores | — | Regional | 4 |
| H. E. Butt Grocery Company | United States | FDM | Supermarkets/Grocery Stores | 69 | Regional | 2 |
| The Home Depot, Inc. | United States | Homegoods | DIY/Home Improvement Stores | 3 | Regional | 3 |
| INDITEX Group (i.e., Zara) | Spain | Softgoods | Apparel Stores | 110 | Global | 56 |
| Ito-Yokado Co., Ltd | Japan | FDM | Convenience Stores | 6 | Global | 17 |
| Office Depot, Inc. | United States | Homegoods | Office Supply | 54 | Global | 23 |
| OfficeMax, Inc. | United States | Homegoods | Office Supply | 85 | Global | 5 |
| Rallye (i.e., Casino) | France | FDM | Supermarkets/Grocery Stores | 26 | Global | 17 |
| Sherwin-Williams Company | United States | Homegoods | Hardlines Specialty Stores | 161 | Regional | 7 |

Sources: Retail Forward, company annual reports and published reports

average price points, modernized advertising, and hired new buyers to enhance the company's image.

The approach taken was to emphasize a "buy Mexican first" strategy to keep costs down. Simply put, the strategy was to offer merchandise of department store quality with the turnover of a mass merchant. This change took place after the company conducted focus group interviews with customers and found that the store was generally overpriced and out of reach for many of the country's middle-class consumers.

Sears offers the most ample credit plan in Mexico. The retailer gained much of its market share in the United States by extending credit to those who typically would not qualify. Seventy percent of the company's sales come from credit purchases.[4] INFORMAL CREDIT is offered to store customers but it is not based on ability to pay. When I was first married we bought all our appliances from Sears. It wasn't because Sears offered the best price. They gave credit to nearly anyone. We were living in the United States, but during this time period, the early 1970s, credit cards like Visa and MasterCard were not yet available. Nearly every young couple I knew bought their appliances at Sears for exactly that reason. Informal credit is typically found in less developed countries. As a country develops a more formalized credit, this strategy becomes less of a benefit.

J.C. Penney's began operating in Mexico in 1994. Its store in Monterrey at the Plaza St. Agustin is one of its most elegant. In 2004 Sanborns acquired the J.C. Penney stores. The Mexico City store was turned into a Sears nameplate; the others were renamed Sanborns. To place themselves outside the competition with Wal-Mart, Sanborns is upgrading their department store mix by introducing more exclusive and private labels.

Zara entered the Mexican retail market in 1992 with one store; now they have over 100. This makes Mexico Zara's third biggest market, following Spain and Portugal. Zara is planning to increase its sourcing of Mexican-made products. They will use Kaltex to produce clothing, footwear, and crafts that will be sold in the domestic market and exported to those Latin American countries where Inditex does not operate. In Chapter 1 I talked about PREDETERMINED DOMESTICATION. This is when a company enters a foreign market and they make themselves attractive to the host country to avoid political takeover. Two of the components are sourcing products domestically and including local companies in your export efforts.

Mango is collaborating with Palacio de Hierro, an association that is likely good for both. Mango has the hipness; Palacio de Hierro, the elegance.

When Wal-Mart acquired Cifra they also acquired Cifra's Suburbia apparel stores, 53 stores with a focus on low price. Wal-Mart introduced their private label lines Mary Kate & Ashley and G by George. George is the private label line Wal-Mart acquired when they purchased the UK-based ASDA.

Coppel is an apparel and homegoods retailer. The company has 224 stores and 133 shoe stores across Mexico. Customers may use Coppel's direct credit program, which offers extended payment periods to those who have no access to credit cards or other financing. This is another example of where informal credit is being used to build market share.

C&A, a Belgium-based company, has 21 stores in Mexico. They remind me of a less expensive version of the U.K.'s Marks & Spencer. They sell 100 private label lines and plan to expand aggressively throughout Mexico.

## Homegoods Retailers

Mexico has experienced rapid growth in the housing market. With this growth comes a greater need for household appliances and furniture. Mass merchandisers like Wal-Mart have a major part of the market, but a variety of domestic and foreign firms are successful as well. There are two interesting features about the domestic market players. The first is that they use informal credit and easy financing to gain market share; the other is that they offer relatives in the United States the opportunity to purchase merchandise there for delivery in Mexico. They also offer electronic money transfers so that relatives in the United States can transfer money back to family in Mexico.

## Internet Retailing

About one-fifth of Mexicans have Internet access and nearly half of them make online purchases, most of them through Mexican online sites.[5] The biggest online retailer is a copycat of eBay, MercadoLibre (mercadolibre.com.mx). Actually, eBay is now a major stockholder in MercadoLibre. Elektra's online offering is Todito.com, they're targeting the U.S. Hispanic market and its ties to Mexico. Their service ePaid lets Mexican and U.S.-based customers create prepaid accounts for online shopping. These accounts can be used through more than 1,800 branches in Mexico and more than 40,000 in the United States. The ePaid system works like an electronic wallet. Deposited money can be used at more than 50 Mexican chains that work with Todito's web site, or at e-commerce sites of U.S. retailers such as amazon.com, barnes&noble.com, and target.com. Some of these companies deliver only to the United States.[6]

A limitation to online purchasing is the relatively small percent of the population that has credit cards. There are only 11 credit card accounts for every 100 adults. Actually 70 percent of Mexico's population are UNBANKED, meaning that they do not have a bank account.[7] Credit card use has increased by 30 percent a year and is expected to continue this rapid growth.

## Supermarkets and Hypermarkets

Mexico has about 700 stores that offer both groceries and dry goods. Supermarket chains generate only 30 percent of food sales. The rest of these sales occur through mom-and-pop stores or street vendors. *Changaros* (tiny independent shops) and *tianguis* (open markets) make up 60 percent of sales. Because of the predominance of micro-suppliers, the wholesale supply industry is weak. Supermarket managers regard the distribution system as unreliable. The large chains operate their own distribution system with direct links between manufacturers and individual stores.

The retail food sector is an oligopoly. Wal-Mex is the largest retailer in Mexico. Wal-Mex's emphasis on low price has created a price war in the major cities. When I discussed types of competition in Chapter 1, I mentioned that in oligopoly markets in general there will be little price competition because it leads to price wars. This is what occurred in Mexico. Carrefour is a fallout of that price war.[8] Chedraui, a supermarket chain with a strong presence in eastern, southeastern, and central Mexico, purchased Carrefour's 29 stores in 2005. The three Mexican firms Comerci, Gigante, and Soriana are likely to benefit from Carrefour's departure.

**Photo 9.1**
A temporary market is set up on an overpass in Mexico City. This market is adjacent to a suburban subway stop. Overhead costs are minimal for these retailers, allowing them to sell at very low prices. *Courtesy of the author.*

**Photo 9.2**
The temporary market is also a gathering place in the community. Fresh fruits and vegetables are sold here. Camera film is one-third the price paid in a regular store. Many vendors sell prepared food that will be taken home and eaten. *Courtesy of the author.*

## Street Vendors

Street vendors add color to the shopping environment in Mexico. Walking a block without being accosted by merchants selling a variety of merchandise is difficult. Although we generally think of street vendors as a part of the premodern and romantic past in Mexico, they have elevated the practice to a level of great efficiency and productivity. Street vendors take advantage of public space, foregoing the costs of capital investment such as rent. Street vending requires a greater investment of labor relative to inventory, which places a limit on size and necessitates low levels of inventory. These characteristics also contribute to an advantage for street vendors over retail stores: they can be very flexible to market changes.

Because of their location in public space these mobile retailers respond differently to legal and market situations than do fixed retail sites. In many areas of the world, street vending is either illegal or marginally legal. Governments generally write regulatory systems for retailing with fixed retail operations in mind. Fixed location retailers are easier to monitor and regulate. Mobile retailers have different concerns in conducting business. They must watch inventory more carefully to avoid theft. At the end of the day, the inventory must be packed up and stored somewhere. Inventory control takes on a new meaning. Control means of protecting the

**Photo 9.3**
Numerous silver shops are found throughout Mexico. Buyers and sellers haggle over the price. *Courtesy of the author.*

merchandise. Inventory control is labor intensive, and greater trust must be placed in employees. This explains why most street vendors rely on family members only to mind the store. It also limits the growth possibilities of the business.

Street vendors are uniquely suited for sales to pedestrians because they are in the public area. People are less reluctant to stop and inspect a street offering than to step into a store. Vendors are the ultimate purveyors of impulse purchases.

Mexico City has a vibrant street-vending retail sector. There are more than 200,000 vendors in the Federal District alone, which is only half of the entire Mexico City metropolitan area. The number of street vendors has increased since the 1960s. Before that time, the government repressed street vendors, making their operations difficult.

During the 1970s, members of various associations of the blind were given permits to set up metal kiosks at strategic areas within the city. These were perfect sites for taco stands. The blind permit holders and others who received permits through less than legal circumstances soon began leasing their permits to others. Some of these taco stands were even run as a chain of micro-restaurants. Street vendors reemerged in the old areas of the city center in the working-class neighborhoods and in areas behind the National Palace. A retail explosion took place.

Vendors began to specialize in a particular type of trade. In one location, they concentrated on fresh fruits. Another area sold kitchen goods, and another, electrical appliances. The electrical goods area specialized in merchandise that had been smuggled into the country to avoid the high import tariffs then imposed on foreign goods. By 1990, about 20,000 vendors worked in the central areas. Similar magnet markets existed in other areas of the city.

In the magnet markets, the key to success was the concentration of similar products in the same area. An entire street would be devoted to leather jackets, or to fancy

**Photo 9.4**
The Canadian retailer Roots has more than 100 stores in Canada as well as six in the United States and 12 in the Pacific Rim. It specializes in high-quality leather goods, sportswear, and outerwear for children and adults. *Courtesy of Roots.*

dresses. Although you might think that this strategy would reduce an individual vendor's profits because of the overly competitive environment, just the opposite is true. As we saw in Chapter 3, geographical location theories explain that creating a central place draws customers. For customers to travel a distance to inspect one leather jacket vendor is not practical. However, if many leather jacket vendors are located together, potential customers are drawn to the area. These vendors emphasize low margins and rapid turnover, providing an attraction for customers throughout the city who want the best selection and price. Promotion is entirely by word of mouth, reducing the cost structure for vendors as compared to fixed store competitors, who must rely on formal advertising to attract customers.

In residential areas, street vendors followed a different type of marketing strategy. Whereas the magnet markets of the city center tended to be highly specialized, residential street vendors focused on everyday items. Food must be purchased frequently, and transporting food from the city center costs the local customers in terms of time and expense. Street vendors of food in residential areas became very popular.

After the period of street vendor repression ended in the late 1960s, the Mexico City government began to allow tianguis, a special type of street vendor (*tianguis* comes from the word for market in Aztec). As operationalized in Mexico City, tianguis came to mean a market that operated in a circuit, moving to a different neighborhood each day of the week.

The city government required the tianguis to rotate location to reduce the complaints of residents of a particular area who did not want their neighborhoods to be taken over by vendors, but did not mind the inconvenience of having the street hawkers one day a week. Operating in this manner, the tianguistas have the advantage of both a fixed market and a mobile market. Instead of having a single market zone, they now had seven zones. The regularity with which they would appear in an area allowed them to build up an established clientele. They began to operate like the downtown magnet markets, focusing on low profit margin and high turnover.

It became important to organize the market zones and to negotiate with officials. This lead nearly all street vendors to become members of associations that manage the zones like a corporation. Voting was even coordinated to incorporate vendors into the ruling party.

In the 1960s, when street vending was repressed, doing business was physically dangerous and more expensive. When police found street vendors, they would break up their kiosks and confiscate the merchandise. Even if they were not actually destroying the street vendors' kiosks, the police were not inclined to protect them from common criminals. Vendors were easy targets for thieves who knew they would have their daily earnings on their person. When street vending was legalized, the kiosk owners could afford to invest more money in inventory, and they no longer had to fear the threat of arrest or confiscation.

Street vendors have become a sophisticated retail system in Mexico City. Some tianguis may have more than 1,000 vendors that, taken together, equal the same value of goods as a modern supermarket. These neighborhood markets even use layout concepts similar to modern supermarkets. They place key goods, such as meats, dairy products, and other everyday consumer items, at a central location as far away from entrances to the market as possible to draw consumers throughout the market, exposing them to greater amounts of merchandise.

The following example highlights the importance of these informal markets within the Mexican retailing environment. Mexico is known for its silver jewelry. On my last trip to Mexico, I was on a quest for the best price for some jewelry for myself and for gifts to others. As I was planning to interview the major department store managers, I began my search in those stores as well as in specialty stores. One necklace that caught my eye in a fine jewelry store, nicely polished and displayed in a gift box, was $500, more than I wanted to spend. During my 2 weeks in Mexico, I used that necklace as a benchmark comparison.

In Mexico City, I shopped for silver at the Insurgents Market, a type of cooperative in which artisans rent spaces in a building and display their merchandise. Walking through the market can be an unnerving experience for U.S. visitors. Hawkers approach customers, draping silver necklaces around their necks without permission. Everyone promises to give the lowest price and provide the finest quality necklaces. Frequently a shopowner will tell you that he made his jewelry himself. This is probably not true. In fact, all sterling silver in Mexico is stamped with a government-required number registering that the silver is solid sterling and identifying the silver shop and the craftsperson who produced the product.

The person from whom I ended up buying several items, however, did have jewelry that looked different from the other merchandise. It was a welcome change to see what appeared to be some creativity after seeing row after row of identical merchandise, a type of mass production by hand. In Mexico, silver is generally sold by weight, even when it is in the form of finished jewelry. Of course, the price you pay for each gram differs in each store. Several necklace sets at this shop interested me, so I began the negotiation process.

I would make an offer. The shop owner would make a counteroffer. I would say I needed to wait until after I had looked in another shop. He would counteroffer again. Eventually he told me, "Fine, look at other shops; you will not find a better price." He was right. I looked but did not find a better price for that quality of necklace. The next day I went back and purchased the merchandise: three silver necklaces with earrings and one necklace with a bracelet. I purchased all these items for about the same price as the one necklace in the specialty jewelry store. I did not get a fancy store gift box—the items were packaged in fabric bags with a drawstring top—but they were all genuine heavyweight, hand-crafted sterling silver jewelry.

As this example illustrates, the greatest competition for established retailers is from street vendors and informal markets. These forms of informal retailing have very low overhead and greatly reduced tax obligations because of underreporting of income.

## › CANADA

### Country Background

If Canada and the United States are so similar, why have their retail formats been so different? The answer lies in history, location, and legislation. Before the U.S. Civil War, both Canada and the United States had few large population centers. In the early part of the nineteenth century, only twelve U.S. cities had a population of more than 5,000. There was little intracity transportation and discretionary income was low, conditions that restricted the development of the retail industry.

The Civil War created a need for military supplies that actually pushed the United States into the Industrial Revolution. The industrialization process required concentrations of people in cities and the development of transportation systems between cities to bring workers to and from the newly formed factories. These same intracity transportation systems would also later transport customers to large retailers.[9] Industrialization also increased people's disposable income. Wars are generally good for retailing, and the Civil War was particularly good for the development of the retail industry in the United States.

Canada, in contrast, industrialized late and unevenly. The country's demographics hindered its entry into the industrial age. The Canadian population was small and geographically diverse. By the end of the nineteenth century, only three provinces—British Columbia, Quebec, and Ontario—were industrialized.

Seventy-two percent of the Canadian population live within 100 miles of the U.S. border, located between Windsor and Montreal, a strip of 608 miles. This makes cross-border shopping a great concern for Canadian retailers. In addition, Canada has limited market opportunity. There are only eight major population centers in Canada; these centers have 85 percent of the retail market. All of these areas have been overstored and are plateauing. U.S. retailers have been able to exploit economies of scale in their Canadian operations.

The West Edmonton Mall, built in 1981 or 1983, was heralded as the biggest shopping center in the world, until the Mall of America was built in Minneapolis. Some considered it a marriage between retailing and entertainment. The mall has a 15-page directory to help customers find their way to not only stores, but an amusement park, an ice skating rink and hockey arena, a casino, a five-acre wave pool, over 100 restaurants, and a hotel.

I have to admit that huge malls like that leave me cold. There is just too much sameness. I prefer independent retailers who provide greater variety. Canada has a large assortment of small independent retailers. Most cities have special zoning restrictions on large store construction to keep municipal character of the downtown areas. The national specialty chains are generally located in malls and independent specialty stores are found on main streets.

Canada presents an excellent retail marketplace. It has a growing economy, little risk of inflation, and a very stable government system. It is the tenth-largest retail market in the world. That being said, the total retail sales in Canada for 2005 are only slightly less, $269 billion, than the sales Wal-Mart registered in the U.S., about $285 billion.[10] Tables 9.3 and 9.4 summarize the major domestic and foreign retailers in Canada.

## Softgoods Retailers

Hudson's Bay Company is the leading softgoods retailer in Canada. They operate department store formats (Bay Stores), mass merchandise stores (Zellers), and home furnishing stores (Home Outfitters). Sears Canada is the second largest retailer in Canada. Both Hudson's and Sears Canada operate in every population center from coast to coast. In 1999, Sears acquired Canada's largest prestigious department store chain, Eaton's, which had filed for bankruptcy. Sears Canada acquired the assets and brand name with the intention of repositioning the Eaton name within the Sears portfolio. But the Eaton brand name had eroded beyond the point of correction and in 2002 Sears discarded it.

Reitmans is the largest women's apparel retailer with 850 stores; it provides an all-private label line targeting value-conscious consumers. La Senza is the leading lingerie retailer in Canada with stores such as La Senza and Silk and Satin. The company operates more than 200 stores across Canada and licenses stores in Asia, the United Kingdom, the Middle East, and South Africa.

U.S. companies are successful in the Canadian market. Gap operates 102 Gap stores, 16 Banana Republic stores, and 47 Old Navy stores here. It is the largest market for Gap outside its American home.

TJX, an off-price apparel and home furnishings business, operates 168 Winners and 40 Home Sense furnishing stores in Canada. Moores, the Canadian division of U.S.-based Men's Wearhouse, is the Canadian leader in men's clothing.

Probably the most exciting group of retailers in Canada are the international fast fashion retailers—H&M, Zara, Esprit, Mexx, and Mango. The World Trade Organization's (WTO) elimination of apparel quotas in 2005 has allowed them to more easily supply stores in North America with products produced in Asia.

Also like the United States, dollar stores have had tremendous growth since the first one opened in 1998. The first store to open, Your Dollar Store With More, now has 150 stores throughout Canada and they expect to open 30–40 stores per year. Great Canadian Dollar Store operates over 130 franchise outlets. Denninghouse, Canada's largest dollar store operator with 314 Buck Or Two stores in 10 provinces, went out of business in 2005. The only foreign operator of dollar stores in Canada is Daiso Sangyo from Japan.

## Homegoods Retailers

The Home Depot, Best Buy, and Staples are U.S. retailers in this market. Canadian companies such as Rona, Canadian Tire, and Home Hardware are the major competition for the foreign retailers.

**Table 9-3**
**Canada—Leading Domestic Retailers, 2004**

| Company | Primary Line of Trade | Total Sales and Stores | | | Global Rank and Penetration | | | Domestic Market | |
|---|---|---|---|---|---|---|---|---|---|
| | | Net Sales ($US Mil) | % Chg Sales | Total Stores | 2004 Rank, Top 200 Retailers Worldwide | Single-country, Regional or Global? | Number of countries | Share of total sales | Share of total stores |
| 1 Loblaw Companies Limited | Supermarkets/Grocery Stores | 20,134 | 3.9% | 1,577 | 34 | Single Country | 1 | 100% | 100% |
| 2 Empire Company Limited | Supermarkets/Grocery Stores | 9,364 | 10.3% | 1,352 | 81 | Single Country | 1 | 100% | 100% |
| 3 Alimentation Couche-Tard | Convenience Stores | 7,848 | 74.0% | 9,020 | 99 | Global | 7 | 24% | 22% |
| 4 The Jean Coutu Group Inc. | Drug Stores | 7,231 | 142.9% | 2,231 | 107 | Regional | 2 | 18% | 49% |
| 5 Hudson's Bay Company | General Merchandise Stores | 5,431 | −4.5% | 547 | 124 | Single Country | 1 | 100% | 100% |
| 6 Canadian Tire Corp. Ltd. | General Merchandise Stores | 5,018 | 8.2% | 1,078 | 135 | Single Country | 1 | 100% | 100% |
| 7 Shoppers Drug Mart Corp. | Drug Stores | 4,971 | 6.8% | 964 | 136 | Single Country | 1 | 100% | 100% |
| 8 RONA Inc. | DIY/Home Improvement Stores | 3,466 | 22.6% | 550 | 178 | Single Country | 1 | 100% | 100% |
| 9 Home Hardware Stores Ltd. | DIY/Home Improvement Stores | 3,227 | 10.5% | 1,000 | 188 | Single Country | 1 | 100% | 100% |
| 10 Metro Inc. | Supermarkets/Grocery Stores | 2,304 | 7.8% | 650 | — | Single Country | 1 | 100% | 100% |
| 11 The Forzani Group Ltd. | Sporting Goods | 757 | 1.8% | 419 | — | Single Country | 1 | 100% | 100% |
| 12 Pharmasave Drugs Ltd. | Drug Stores | 713 | 7.9% | 340 | — | Single Country | 1 | 100% | 100% |
| 13 North West Company | General Merchandise Stores | 606 | 0.8% | 184 | — | Regional | 2 | 100% | 100% |
| 14 Indigo Books & Music Inc. | Book & Multimedia | 605 | −2.3% | 255 | — | Single Country | 1 | 79.9% | 86.4% |
| 15 The Brick Group | Furniture & Home Furnishings | 464 | 33.6% | 168 | — | Single Country | 1 | 100% | 100% |

Sources: Retail Forward, company annual reports and published reports

**Table 9.4**
**Canada—Key Foreign Retailers, 2004**

| Company | Headquarters | Retail Sector | Primary Line of Trade | 2004 Rank, Top 200 Retailers Worldwide | Single-country, Regional or Global? | Number of countries |
|---|---|---|---|---|---|---|
| | | | | **Global Rank and Penetration** | | |
| Aeon Co., Ltd. | Japan | Softgoods | General Merchandise Stores | 19 | Global | 11 |
| Amazon.com | United States | Homegoods | Non-Store | 111 | Global | 7 |
| Best Buy Co., Inc. | United States | Homegoods | Consumer Electronics & Appliances | 27 | Regional | 2 |
| Circuit City Stores, Inc. | United States | Homegoods | Consumer Electronics & Appliances | 73 | Regional | 2 |
| Costco Companies, Inc. | United States | FDM | Cash & Carries/Warehouse Clubs | 9 | Global | 7 |
| Foot Locker Inc. | United States | Softgoods | Shoe Stores | 126 | Global | 19 |
| HMV Group plc | United Kingdom | Homegoods | Book & Multimedia | 180 | Global | 7 |
| Home Depot, Inc., The | United States | Homegoods | DIY/Home Improvement Stores | 3 | Regional | 3 |
| IKEA AB | Sweden | Homegoods | Furniture & Home Furnishings | 44 | Global | 32 |
| INDITEX Group (i.e., Zara) | Spain | Softgoods | Apparel Stores | 110 | Global | 56 |
| Ito-Yokado Co., Ltd | Japan | FDM | Convenience Stores | 6 | Global | 17 |
| Linens 'n Things Inc. | United States | Homegoods | Furniture & Home Furnishings | — | Regional | 2 |
| Michaels Stores Inc. | United States | Homegoods | Arts and Crafts | 182 | Regional | 2 |
| Office Depot, Inc. | United States | Homegoods | Office Supply | 54 | Global | 23 |
| OfficeMax, Inc. | United States | Homegoods | Office Supply | 85 | Global | 5 |
| Payless ShoeSource Inc. | United States | Softgoods | Shoe Stores | — | Global | 12 |
| PETsMART Inc. | United States | FDM | Pet Stores | 184 | Regional | 2 |
| Sears, Roebuck and Co. | United States | Homegoods | Department Stores | 22 | Regional | 2 |
| Sherwin-Williams Company | United States | Homegoods | Hardlines Specialty Stores | 161 | Regional | 7 |
| Staples, Inc. | United States | Homegoods | Office Supply | 47 | Global | 18 |
| Tengelmann Warenhandelsgesellschaft | Germany | FDM | Supermarkets/Grocery Stores | 23 | Global | 15 |
| Toys "R" Us, Inc. | United States | Homegoods | Toy Stores | 68 | Global | 30 |
| Wal-Mart Stores, Inc. | United States | FDM | Hypermarkets/Supercenters | 1 | Global | 11 |
| Whole Foods Market Inc. | United States | FDM | Supermarkets/Grocery Stores | 165 | Global | 3 |
| Williams-Sonoma Inc. | United States | Homegoods | Hardlines Specialty Stores | — | Regional | 2 |

Source: Retail Forward, company annual reports, and published reports

## Supermarkets and Hypermarkets

The supermarket industry in Canada is led by Loblaws, Provigo, and the Oshawa Group. The industry is highly competitive, a situation that has lead to the use of private label brands. Retailers are trying to gain greater margins and increase market share.

Membership warehouse clubs such as Price Club and Costco have increased the competitive pressure. Traditional food stores have cut prices, promoted private labels, added bulk goods, and tested new store formats. Food and drug combination stores are doing well in this experiment to regain market share.[11]

There are five major differences between the U.S. and the Canadian retail markets. In many ways the Canadian food retailing is more like European food retailing. First is that Wal-Mart operates only discount stores, not supercenters, in Canada. Although they have grocery shelf areas, they do not carry fresh products. The second difference is that Canadian supermarkets operate a wider variety of store formats. A supermarket company might generate nearly a quarter of their sales through the discount-store division. The third difference is concentration. The top three retailers in Canada have over 50 percent market share while the top three in the United States have less than 30 percent. Canadian retail buyers therefore have greater clout with suppliers. Fourth, private label makes up over 25 percent of the total supermarket sales in Canada, compared to 14 percent in the United States. Private label provides significantly higher profit margins for stores. The private label offerings in Canada are also positioned as a high quality offering. The fifth difference is that Canadian supermarkets have been shifting more sales to general merchandise. Loblaw is the leader in this area.[12]

There are also some common issues that face the U.S. and Canadian food retailing industry. The first is the entry of alternative discount formats. Hard discounters such as Lidl and Aldi have been opening stores at a rapid rate in the United States. Hard discounters originated in Europe and governments unwittingly encouraged their expansion through legislature designed to keep large retailers from expanding. Hard discounters are small scale stores, about the size of a convenience store. If Wal-Mart expands its Canadian food retailing option among its formats, they could have a 25 percent market share in Canada in 2010. Including other types of discounters such as Costco would increase the discount part of the market to 75 percent. To meet this challenge, supermarket chains are cutting costs and introducing everyday low price strategies. They are also increasing the use of private label. Loblaws is a world leader in private label, with 25 percent of their total sales and 40 percent of their grocery sales coming from their own label.[13]

With core grocery products that are completely undifferentiated, there is no place to compete except on price. Whether they be hard discount formats or Wal-Mart types, discounters have significant operating cost advantages that make their prices impossible to beat. Supermarkets get their price reputation on the prices they offer on national brands, because that is the only thing that consumers can actually compare. So they discount national brands to the point of having them be unprofitable. In the long run supermarkets will not win the pricing war; the only sustainable advantage for them is to develop private label and to focus on fresh or perishables. This shift will be made even more difficult because retailers only get slotting allowances and supplier rebates on branded merchandise. They will have to forgo vendor allowances, at least in the short run. Currently those vendor allowances account for 90 percent of EBITD (earnings before interest and taxes are deducted).[14]

## International Retailing

Roots outfitted both the U.S. and the Canadian athletic teams in 2002 and 2006. Roots is a Toronto-based company with stores in the United States, South Korea, Taiwan, and China. April Cornell (apparel and housewares), Bata (shoes), Danier (leather goods), and IMAX (big-format Cinemas) all have an international presence. Jean Coutu, Canada's second-largest pharmacy retailer, acquired 252 Brooks drugstores in New England and 1,550 Eckerd drugstores. As a result it is now the fourth-largest drugstore in the U.S.[15] Canada has several apparel specialty store chains such as Le Chateau, Parasuco, Tristan & America, Aldo (footwear), and Couche-Tarde (convenience stores). No new enclosed regional shopping malls have been built in Canada since 1991. If a retailer wants to grow, they have to internationalize or move into a different format. This is an example of a push factor related to locational advantages, discussed in Chapter 2. The PSYCHIC DISTANCE PARADOX applies to some Canadian retailers. This concept means that because the psychic distance between two countries is viewed to be so small, the changes that need to be made for the foreign market are underestimated. Therefore, the failure rate may be higher when moving to a country that has a more similar culture than in movement to a culture that is less similar. Canadian Tire (automotive/housewares), Coles (books), Colour Your World (paints), Loblaws (groceries), Mark's Work Wearhouse (Casual Apparel-now owned by Canadian Tire), Second Cup (coffee), and Timothy's World Coffee all withdrew from the U.S. market because they were not successful. There have been 54 Canadian retail entries into the United States since the late 1980s; of those 26 are still operating there. This is a 48 percent success record, much better than the 20 percent rate found ten years ago.

CoolBrands International went international in 1991 and is now the world's leading frozen yogurt retailer with 5,000 franchised outlets in 82 countries under the names of Swensen's and Yogen Fruz. La Senza (lingerie) has 85 stores in Europe and the Middle East.

In contrast there are more than 100 U.S. retailers operating in Canada. These retailers can actually help the Canadian retailing by providing competition that will encourage them to become more distinctive in their offering.

## Electronic Retailing

Although Canadians spent 25 percent more online in 2003 than in 2004, this figure accounted for only 1.2 percent of retail sales. The major online retailers are Future Shop (electronics acquired by Best Buy), Indigo Books, Amazon's Canadian portal, and eBay's Canadian portal. Sears Canada is the leading online retailer in Canada.

## 〉 SUMMARY

Mexico's retail industry is characterized by a strong informal retail sector that co-exists with modern retail formats. Mobile markets move from one residential area to another, creating a sense of place.

Mexico's retailers have not expanded nationally. Even large companies have a local or regional presence. Most major Mexican retailers have joined forces with foreign retailers. These joint ventures provide Mexican retailers with needed technological advancements. They provide foreign retailers with knowledge about Mexican culture.

Most of Canada's retailers have not developed into national chains. This has made them vulnerable to competition from new format U.S. retailers. Major U.S. chains are represented in nearly every major Canadian city. However, Canadian retailers have been unsuccessful in their attempts to expand into the United States. The learning that occurs when companies nationalize makes these companies very difficult to compete with, especially on their home field. This factor has played a major role in the failure of Canadian retailers to enter the U.S. market.

## › KEY TERMS

ACQUISITION
INFORMAL CREDIT
ORGANIC GROWTH
PREDETERMINED DOMESTICATION
PSYCHIC DISTANCE PARADOX
UNBANKED

## › DISCUSSION QUESTIONS

1. Why are U.S. retailers so eager to move into Mexico and Canada? What factors from Dunning's theory of the eclectic firm (see Chapter 1) would explain this movement?

2. How are retailers affected by the peso devaluation? What strategic changes can a retailer take to reduce the negative effects?

3. The first retailers to move into Mexico and Canada were hypermarkets such as Wal-Mart and Kmart. What makes these operating formats so attractive for these markets? Kmart has withdrawn from Mexico. Can you suggest why they were unsuccessful?

4. Comparatively speaking, there are more U.S. retailers moving into Canada than into Mexico. Using Dunning's theory of the eclectic firm, explain why this is happening.

5. Why is the informal retail sector in Mexico so successful? Will this sector continue to thrive as modern retail formats such as hypermarkets and supermarkets gain momentum?

## › ENDNOTES

1. "Mexico." (1996). *Craighead's International Business.* Detroit, MI: Gale Research, Inc.

2. Zapata, M. (2005). "Mexican Food Retail, The Widening $$$ Gap." Citigroup Global Markets in Investext (November 17).

3. "Retailing in Mexico." (2004). Columbus, Ohio: Retail Forward.

4. La Follette, C. (1993). "Retail in Mexico, 1993." Harvard Business School Case 0-793-144, September 28.

5. "Retailing in Mexico." (2004).

6. "Retailing in Mexico." (2004).

7. "Unbanked Targeted As Mexico Banks Drive Expansion." (2005). Cards International, Lafferty Ltd (April 14).

8. Zapata, M. (2005). "Carrefour: Hasta La Vista . . . Baby." In Investext Citigroup Smith Barney, February 2.

9. Burns, D. and D. Rayman (1996). "Retailing in Canada and the United States: Historical Comparisons." In G. Akehurst and N. Alexander, eds., *The Internationalisation of Retailing*. London: Frank Cass.

10. Retailing in Canada. (2004) Columbus, Ohio: Retail Forward.

11. Coopers & Lybrand (1996). *Global Powers of Retailing*. Chain Store Age—Special Report.

12. Caicco, P. and R. Piticco. (2004). "North American Supermarkets 2005." CIBC World Markets in Investext, December 14, 2004.

13. Caicco and Piticco. (2004).

14. Caicco and Piticco. (2004).

15. Swift, A. (2005). "Drugstore Chain Jean Coutu Working to Upgrade Eckerd Drugstores in U.S." Canadian Business and Current Affairs, Canadian Press NewsWire, September 15.

# 10

# RETAILING IN SOUTH AMERICA

## After reading this chapter, you should understand

> How economic instability affects retailing and the choices consumers make.

> The role that credit plays in retailing in less developed economies.

> The role hyperinflation plays in retailer sourcing decisions.

> How retailers can earn profits on manipulation of monetary transactions.

> How politics of the poor influence how governments view informal retailing.

### › INTRODUCTION

Sadly, in some Latin American countries, democracy still needs succour. This week, Bolivia was in chaos: the president resigned, for the third and seemingly final time, driven out by radical protesters who want the country's gas industry nationalized. They are supported—and, claims the United States, financed—by Hugo Chavez, booted out by its Congress and replaced by his vice-president. In Haiti a United Nations is trying to organize an election amid gang warfare.[1]

South America has recently experienced 10 years of openness and free markets, and is only now returning to LEFTIST control. Leftist is a term used to designate extreme liberal or radical political views such as communism.[2] South America can be characterized as a region prone to a lack of national consensus about the role of government in the economy. Politicians are elected based on broad promises made to the people, only then to find themselves not being able to deliver on those promises. The government has the ability to nationalize industries and capture the production and property, creating chaos. Those whose property is taken naturally don't like it. Foreign investors feel threatened because the government might take over their investment. The appropriation of private property galvanizes opinion in the upper and middle classes that this process needs to be stopped. The excesses are generally stopped by a military crackdown, followed by a period of governing by military leaders. Sometimes the military is not of one mind on this issue and a coup results—one part of the military divides from the other. Box 10.1 summarizes South America's political situation.

South America is a continent of contrasts. On my first trip there I was not prepared for the large number of people descended from European ancestors. I was expecting a much more INDIGENOUS population, and on subsequent trips encountered more variety. Indigenous refers to people who are native to the area. Buenos Aires is a modern city with fabulous restaurunts, interesting shopping, and great entertainment. Buenos Aires has a historic opera house, so I took in a performance while I was there. Although it was 60 degrees the Buenos Aires women wore their furs to the opera. They took their coats off during the performance but put them back over their shoulders for the intermission so they could stroll around and be admired. In contrast, when I went to Asunsion, the capital of Paraguay, I was struck by the number of squatters living within throwing distance of the nation's capital. This type of contrast is found throughout South America.

On one trip to Ecuador, a former graduate student met me at the airport. Smelling something familiar in the air, I asked if they used a lot of heating oil in Ecuador. He smiled and said, "That's not heating oil; it is tear gas." The indigenous people were protesting some government policy so the military cracked down on them. We had planned to drive to my student's hometown about four hours away, but also in protest the indigenous people had cut stripes in the highway to make it impassable. So we ended up flying instead, a really beautiful flight over volcano mountains peaked with snow. When we left the airport parking lot, my student paid the bill with an American dollar. Ecuador began DOLLARIZATION to provide economic stability in their country. Dollarization means that a country actually uses U.S. dollars as their own currency. Ecuador began this practice in 2000. When a country uses another country's currency, they tie their economic situation to the

**Box 10.1**
**Latin America Looks Leftward Again**
*By Juan Forero*

TACAMARA, Boliva

At first glance, there's nothing cutting edge about this isolated highland town of mud-brick homes and cold mountain streams. The way of life is remarkably unchanged from what it was centuries ago. The Aymara Indian villagers have no hot water or telephones, and each day they slog into the fields to shear wool and grow potatoes.

But Tacamara and dozens of similar communities across the scrub grass of the Bolivian highlands are at the forefront of a new leftward tide now rising in Latin American politics. Tired of poverty and indifferent governments, villagers here are being urged by some of their more radical leaders to forget the promises of capitalism and install instead a community-based socialism in which products would be bartered. Some leaders even talk of forming an independent Indian state.

"What we really need is to transform this country," said Rufo Yanarico, 45, a community leader. "We have to do away with the capitalist system." In the burgeoning cities of China, India and Southeast Asia, that might sound like a hopelessly outdated dream because global capitalism seems to be delivering on its promise to transform those poor societies into richer ones. But here, the appeal of rural socialism is a powerful reminder that much of South America has become disenchanted with the poor track record of similar promises made to Latin America.

So the region has begun turning leftward again.

That trend figures heavily in a presidential election being held today in Bolivia, in which the frontrunner is Evo Morales, a charismatic Aymara Indian and former coca farmer who promises to decriminalize coca production and roll back market reforms if he wins. Though he leads, he is unlikely to gain a clear majority; if he does not, Bolivia's Congress would decide the race.

Still, he is the most fascinating candidate, because he is anything but alone in Latin America. He considers himself a disciple of the region's self-appointed standard-bearer for the left, President Hugo Chávez of Venezuela, a populist who has injected the state into the economy, showered the nation's oil profits on government projects aimed at the poor, and antagonized the Bush administration with constant invective.

"In recent years, social movements and leftist parties in Latin America have reappeared with a force that has no parallel in the recent history in the region," says a new book on the trend, "The New Left in Latin America," written by a diverse group of academic social scientists from across the Americas.

Peru also has a new and growing populist movement, led by a cashiered army officer, Ollanta Humala, who is ideologically close to Mr. Chávez. Argentina's president, Néstor Kirchner, who won office in 2003, announced last week that Argentina would sever all ties with the International Monetary Fund, which he blames for much of the country's long economic decline, by swiftly paying back its $9.9 billion debt to the fund.

The leftist movement that has taken hold in Latin America over the last seven years is diverse. Mr. Chávez is its most extreme example. Brazil's president, Luiz Inácio Lula da Silva, by contrast, is a former labor leader who emphasizes poverty reduction but also practices fiscal austerity and gets along with Wall Street. Uruguay has been pragmatic on economic matters, but has had increasingly warm relations with Venezuela. In Mexico, the leftist who is thought to have a good chance to be the next president, Andrés Manuel López Obrador, has distanced himself from Mr. Chávez.

What these leaders share is a strong emphasis on social egalitarianism and a determination to rely less on the approach known as the Washington Consensus, which emphasizes privatization, open markets, fiscal discipline and a follow-the-dollar impulse, and is favored by the I.M.F. and United States officials.

*continued*

**Box 10.1** *Continued*

"You cannot throw them all in the same bag, but this is understood as a left with much more sensitivity toward the social," said Augusto Ramírez Ocampo, a former Colombian government minister who last year helped write a United Nations report on the state of Latin American democracy. "The people believe these movements can resolve problems, since Latin American countries have seen that the Washington Consensus has not been able to deal with poverty."

The Washington Consensus became a force in the 1980s, after a long period in which Latin American governments, many autocratic, experimented with nationalistic economic nostrums like import-substitution and protectionism. These could not deliver sustained growth. The region was left on the edge of economic implosion.

With the new policies of the 1980s came a surge toward democracy, a rise of technocrats as leaders and, in the last 20 years, a general acceptance of stringent austerity measures prescribed by the I.M.F. and the World Bank. Country after country was told to make far-reaching changes, from selling off utilities to cutting pension costs. In return, loans and other aid were offered. Growth would be steady, economists in Washington promised, and poverty would decline.

But the results were dismal. Poverty rose, rather than fell; inequality remained a curse. Real per capita growth in Latin America since 1980 has barely reached 10 percent, according to an analysis of I.M.F. data by the Washington-based Center for Economic and Policy Research. Meanwhile, many Latin Americans lost faith in traditional political parties that were seen as corrupt vehicles for special interests. That led to uprisings that toppled presidents like Bolivia's Gonzalo Sánchez de Lozada and Ecuador's Lucio Gutiérrez; it also spawned demagogues who blame free-market policies for everything without offering detailed alternatives.

The new populism is perhaps most undefined here in the poorest and most remote corner of South America. Mr. Morales promises to exert greater state control over foreign energy firms and focus on helping micro-businesses and cooperatives. "The state needs to be the central actor," he said in a recent interview. But he is short on details, and that worries some economists.

Jeffrey Sachs, a Columbia University development economist and former economic adviser here, says he empathizes with Bolivia's poor and agrees that energy companies should pay higher taxes. But he says Bolivia cannot close itself off to the world. "Protectionism isn't really a viable strategy for a small country," he said.

If Mr. Morales does become president, he might well find that the slogans that rang in the streets are not much help in running a poor, troubled country.

Mr. da Silva, the Brazilian president, acknowledged as much in comments he made Wednesday in Colombia: The challenge, he said, is "to show if we are capable as politicians to carry out what we, as union leaders, demanded of government."

Source: *New York Times*, December 18, 2005, p. 4

---

other country. In this case, Ecuador was able to reduce their inflation rate to the rate in the United States.

REMITTANCES, funds that family and friends living abroad send back to their home country to support their relatives, were estimated to be $40 million (U.S.) in 2004. Only one-fifth of this inflow is transferred through the formal banking system.[2] As I discussed in the chapter on Mexico, many people do not trust the banking system and prefer to keep their resources in cash. The INFORMAL ECONOMIES, street vendors and temporary markets, also operate only in cash. The governments are eager to channel these funds into the formal economy because this drives economic growth by increasing the VELOCITY OF MONEY. Velocity of money is similar to inventory turnover in a retail store. The more you turn over the inventory, the greater use you get of your investment. To encourage consumers to use the formal banking system, the government has promoted the use of electronic payment products such as debit cards, credit cards, and direct funds transfers. Some other examples of policies that governments have used to encourage use of the formal banking systems follow.

> Argentina has made use of direct payroll deposit mandatory for most employees. They have also developed a five-point discount in the country's 21 percent VAT rate for debit cards and a three-point discount for credit cards.
> Brazil has modernized its system for Electronic Express Transfers, enabling customer-initiated direct transfers. A system has been introduced to reach the unbanked with new infrastructure for more than 4,000 communities; paper food vouchers have been replaced with a debit card.
> Chile has improved the efficiency of electronic transactions with a Real Time Gross Settlement System (RTGS) implemented in 2005 and with the connection of the country's ATM networks. Chile has also introduced contactless smart cards for fare payment on the Santiago transit system.
> Venezuela is planning a new RTGS system.

The Latin American economy grew by 5.5 percent in 2004. The region's per capita GDP is estimated to have risen about 4 percent. All Latin American countries except Haiti recorded positive growth rates. Trade exports grew by 22.4 percent and imports grew by 19.5 percent.[3] Since the debt crisis, Latin American governments have reversed decades of economic isolationism that had left them vulnerable. Chile, followed by Argentina, Colombia, Mexico, Brazil, and Peru, privatized state-owned industries, lowered their tariffs, stabilized their currencies, and opened their economies to foreign competition. Mercosur (including Argentina, Brazil, Paraguay, and Uruguay) is the major multinational market in the region. The trade group has been working for ten years to establish better trade links with the European Union and in January 2006, Mercosur began functioning as a common market.

## > ARGENTINA

Argentina is an interesting case because it has moved down the range of socio-economic development. From one of the world's more prosperous countries from 1870 to the mid 1930s, it returned to the state of a developing nation in 1979. Inflation plagued the economy. In the 1990s the country pegged their currency, the peso, to the U.S. dollar, bringing fiscal stability to the country and encouraging a surge of foreign investment. But between 1999 and 2002, Argentina's economy suffered a recession. The early 2000s brought political instability and freezing of bank accounts. In 2002, Argentina moved away from the currency peg to the U.S. dollar and devaluated the peso.

In 2002, consumers lost one-third of their purchasing power in a matter of days. Devaluation brought higher prices (in peso terms), enticed goods producers to concentrate their sales on the export market, forced the disappearance of many lines of products (as well as the re-appearance of older, discontinued products), reduced the size of the packages, increased sales of basic foods, dropped sales in higher-value products, and shifted the sales of foods and beverages from large-

scale hypermarkets and supermarkets towards smaller scale retailers with particular growth in hard discount food retailers.[4]

Investment drives change. Private investment in general, and foreign investment in particular, is drawn into markets where there is little competition and there
is some natural protection due to high transportation costs. This movement is
true for the retailing sector. Food retailers are attracted to emerging markets for
three reasons. First, people in less developed countries pay a higher percent of their
disposable income on food than people in more developed countries, providing a
larger potential market for this product sector. Second, food is not a disposable good;
it is an essential purchase. Although consumers can put off purchases of durables
and most other consumer products, they are unlikely to forego food purchases.
Finally, food is perishable and the costs for transportation are high relative to the
value of the merchandise. This means that competition is local, or it must have a
local presence.

Three conditions which must be present before investment occurs in a sector:
1) government guarantees of the economic climate for businesses, 2) attractive
consumer characteristics, and 3) prospects for market growth. Investors look for
governmental guarantees such as favorable regulations toward business, legal structure, currency stability, and possibility to repatriate profits. Attractive consumer
characteristics could include an increasing standard of living, increased education,
and greater mobility for shoppers. The final necessary element is prospects for future growth. The final element includes things like a market that is over saturated.

From the 1940s to the 1980s Argentina earned a reputation of being hostile to
foreign investment. Government policies would change frequently, and the government threatened repudiation of foreign debt, enforcing legislation that established
forced savings and other types of anti-business legislation. Through its actions the
government internally conditioned business activity. The state nationalized public
utilities during the late 1940s and early 1950s, continuing to own them until the
recent economic reforms. The country went through 50 years of inflation, culmi-
nating in two years of hyperinflation, 1989–1990. Monthly inflation in February 1990
was 195 percent.

CAPITAL FLIGHT plagued Argentina. Investors put their money in foreign bank accounts because they did not trust the economic situation at home. This left little
money for internal investment. Only 25 percent of Argentines use banking services,
a very low figure compared with that of industrialized countries.[5]

## Government Policy

In 2003, the government enacted a law entitled Ley 12573, regulating the opening of
supermarkets and hypermarkets in the province of Buenos Aires. The purpose was
to protect smaller independent grocers. Hard discount stores were able to circum-
vent this law if they opened as franchises. Decree 124/03 changed this; ever since
hard discount outlets, openings have also been regulated.

The return of inflation brought about a debate over price freedom. Consumer
advocate groups have been pressuring large supermarkets and pharmaceutical businesses not to raise their prices. Firms that have increased their prices receive negative publicity. A law passed in 2000 regulated the competitive pricing practices of

the larger retailers and included a code of conduct. The law was designed to control and limit below-cost pricing.

## Retail Location

The economic crisis changed the retail location factor significantly. Argentinian shopping habits have shifted to numerous purchases a week, rather than one large weekly purchase. This practice has made it possible for smaller neighborhood shops to grow in number. The **SHOPPING BASKET** amount, how much consumers spend on a typical transaction, has also decreased. Argentinians have also reduced their out-of-town shopping trips because the amount spent does not justify the transaction costs involved.[6]

## Internet Retailing

Argentinians are avid Internet users and are becoming more comfortable with online transactions. Internet shopping increased by nearly 200 percent from 2001 to 2003. During this time purchases from domestic websites increased almost 300 percent as more Argentinians purchased from providers in their country. Interest rates were lowered substantially, making online transactions more attractive.

The economic crisis made auction sites one of the most important e-commerce tools in Argentina. The possibility for price bargaining online is attractive to consumers. Since 2001 online auction houses Mercado Libre and DeRemate have grown over ten times and have increased both domestic and international sales. An interesting payment system is called Rapipago. The buyer makes a cash payment in person at a Rapipago subsidiary, who then makes the payment to the seller. This way people can purchase merchandise on the Internet without the use of a credit or a debit card.[7]

## Hard Discount Retailers

Eki, Argentina's first hard discount outlet, opened in 1996 when Argentinian consumers were experiencing an economic peak and were consuming top brands at hypermarkets. The outlook for hard discounters was not promising, until 2001, when economic difficulties forced consumers to change their habits and purchase less expensive products in smaller, closer-to-home stores. Because hard discount formats can locate in neighborhood areas and offer very low prices, they now represent the fastest growing outlet type in Argentina and control 6 percent of the supermarket business. Argentinians have also favored private labels, even over branded products similarly priced. This is a bonus to hard discounters. The new law regulating openings for hard discounters has pushed them to expand into the interior of Argentina.

From 1999 to 2003, total sales doubled for hard discount stores. The three leading retailers in the hard discount market are Dia, Eki, and Leader Price. Dia is owned by the Carrefour Group (France), Eki is owned by an investment firm, and Casino Group (France) owns Leader Price.

## Credit

Store cards came to Argentina during the 1960s so retailers could extend personal loans to customers. Later, store cards were combined with credit associations to add formality to the credit application process. C&A was the first retailer to offer a store card, but other companies such as Falabella and Johnson Clothes quickly followed suit. Most store cards operate their own collection branch; exceptions are Wal-Mart, Easy, and Jumbo, which are operated by GE Captial, and Carrefour, which is operated by Banco Cetelem, a bank where Carrefour is a shareholder.

The financial situation in Argentina makes the strategy for store cards a little different. Generally store cards are expensive to administer. Stores FACTOR THEIR ACCOUNTS RECEIVABLE, which means they sell them to outside collection facilities. Factoring your accounts 1) reduces bookkeeping and 2) gives a retailer greater liquidity (money). A retailer becomes freer to do other operational things. Also, because accounts receivable is a better tool for obtaining loans than non-sold inventory, a retailer gets more money for the accounts receivable than they could obtain for an inventory loan.

However, in Argentina, where there is still a rather high interest rate, stores like Falabella and Tarshop have found that these cards help to increase sales, and the FINANCIAL SPREAD will help them increase profits. Financial spread means that a retailer can borrow at a lower rate than they can charge consumers for credit. The difference in the rates can be a major profit machine for the company. C&S is the leader in store credit with a 38 percent value share, followed by Falabella (27 percent).[8]

## Major Retailers

Of the three major retail groups in Argentina, three are foreign. The first is Promodes/Carrefour, which dominates in the food sector. Censosud operates in a variety of sectors such as shopping malls, DIY (Do It Yourself), and hypermarkets. The Casino group operates mainly in the hard discount format.

During the 1990s many multinationals entered Argentina through acquisition. Table 10.1 summarizes the leading multinational groups. Carrefour purchased the Norte-Tia supermarkets and Cencosud purchased the Argentinian Home Depot outlets.

From 2001 to 2002, many businesses closed their doors because of the recession. Additionally, the devaluation of the Argentinian peso meant that those retailers who had debts in dollars had no choice but to close shop. Retailers are increasingly trying to gather some of their revenues in other countries. For example, several food retailers are exporting their meats to Brazil. Other Argentinian retailers are expanding abroad.

Carrefour is the major retailer in Argentina. They entered in 1982 and today have 24 hypermarkets, 141 supermarkets under the Norte banner, and 272 hard discount markets under the Dia name. Carrefour has a policy of paying back ten times the difference if a product can be found elsewhere at a lower price.[9]

## Market Structure and Retailing Practice

Until the mid 1990s, Argentina can be described as having a TRADITIONAL RETAILING SYSTEM. Traditional retail systems are characterized by fragmented markets, long channels, atomistic competition, limited product variety, flexible prices with bargaining, and informal credit. We shall briefly look into these characteristics and try to explain the reason for this market structure.

**Table 10.1**
**Leading Multinational Groups 2003**

| Retail Group | Fascia | Number of Outlets | Subsector |
|---|---|---|---|
| Promodes | Carrefour, Norte, Tia | 437 | Mixed |
| Ahold | Disco, SuperVea, PlazaVea | 237 | Mixed |
| Cencosud | Jumbo, Easy Home Center | 34 | Mixed, DIY |
| Wal-Mart | Wal-Mart | 11 | Mixed |
| Casino | Libertad, Leader Price | 30 | Mixed |

[1]O'Grady, M. (2005). "Brazil Could Turn a Trade Victory into Defeat." *Wall Street Journal* December 10, 2005, p. A19
Forero, J. (2005). "Latin America Looks Leftward Again." *New York Times*, December 18, p. 4.

During the 1970s, 80 percent of the sales in food retailing was done by mom-and-pop stores (*almacenes*). This number fell to 56.4 percent in 1984. Sales for almacenes continued to decline until 1997 when they accounted for only 25 percent of the sales.[10] Market share lost by traditional retailers has been gained by supermarkets.

The almacenes were a main source of self-employment. These small stores are located in residential communities and the owner/operator might live in the same building. Only modest capital was needed to open an almacene, making it an attractive business opportunity for those with little funding. These stores extended INFORMAL CREDIT to customers generally with a repayment of 25 days. Remember, informal credit is not based on a formal evaluation of a person's ability to repay, rather based on the retailer's faith that the loan will be repaid.

## Governmental Guarantees

In 1991 radical economic reforms were introduced, based on the Convertibility Law of 1991. The Argentine government tied the peso at parity to the U.S. dollar. This key reform reduced annual inflation two to four percent, a figure similar to other developed countries. In 1995, inflation dropped to a 50-year low of 1.6 percent. The government eliminated most quotas and reduced tariffs to levels between 0 and 20 percent. The 1991 liberalization opened the country to private business, lowering investment barriers and privatizing state enterprises.

The economic reforms also included a provision allowing foreign firms full repatriation of profits. Foreign investors are not required to register in Argentina, nor do they need any permission to invest and may wholly own a local company.

## ❯ CHILE

Chile is the most successful country in Latin America—politically, economically, and socially. It has the largest GDP in South America, just under $6,000 U.S. dollars. It is estimated that the Chilean economy will grow 5.5 percent during 2005. Unemployment is on a downward trend. However, the President elected in 2005–2006 has leftist convictions, joining Latin America's anti-business, anti-U.S. coalition that includes Cuba's Fidel Castro, Venequela's Hugo Chavez, Uruguay's President Tabare Vazquez, and the Bolivian radical (and friend of the cocaine growers) Evo Morales. It may be farewell adios to the 10-year prosperity that came with free-market and pro-Western ideals.[11]

## Retail Industry Overview

Retail sales in Chile represent 28 percent of Chile's GDP. There are several major trends in the Chilean retail scene. A rapid growth in new selling space, increasing 50 percent between 1999 and 2004, has been mostly in mall developments. Most mall developments have two department stores as chains. The department store industry in Chile is very successful.

Formal retailers are replacing small independent retailers in both the food and nonfood areas. The share of small independent retailers has fallen from 39 percent in 1999 to 30 percent in 2004.[12] Mergers and acquisitions have been extensive during the last five years.

Formal retailers are diversifying to increase their share of consumer expenditure, offering products like credit cards, insurance, and financial and travel services. Chilean retailers have been expanding to other areas of South America, generally Argentina and Peru.

## Food Retail

The Chilean food retail industry has experienced tremendous growth during the last 10 years. During 1995–1999 the industry experienced 12 percent annual growth. This rate slowed somewhat, but still grew by 8 percent during 2000–2004.[13]

The food industry has been leading the mergers and acquisitions activity. International retailers entered Chile in 1998 when Ahold purchased controlling stock in Santa Isabel through its Disco/Ahold joint venture. Carrefour opened its first store in Chile in 2001. However, neither Ahold nor Carrefour were successful. Ahold sold Santa Isabel to Cencosud in 2003, and Carrefour sold their stores to DYS in 2004. This consolidation has left the local market players DYS and Cencosud with 72 percent of the market share in Santiago at the end of 2004. On a national level the four biggest food retailers account for 64 percent of the Chilean market. DYS has 34 percent national market share and Cencosud has a 23 percent national market share.[14] Recently the department store operator has entered the food retail market by purchasing San Francisco.

Chile has 51 cities with populations over 50,000. Cities this size could support a hypermarket; however, DVS, Chile's leading retailer, has a presence in only 22 of these cities. Figure 10.1 shows the selling space per 1,000 inhabitants for a variety of countries.

## Department Stores

The Chilean department store sector is very competitive with four major players: Falabella, Ripley, Almacenes Paris, and La Polar. Cencosud acquired Almacenes Paris in 2005. These department stores target the mid to high socioeconomic segments.

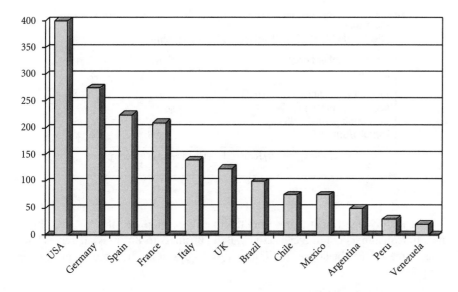

**Figure 10.1**
Formal Food Retail Selling Space per 1,000 inhabitants (sq. m)

Malls in Chile usually have two department stores as anchors. The top three department store chains—Cencosud, Paris, and Ripley—are directly involved in mall development.[15]

Apparel accounts for 60 percent of department store sales and provides a higher margin than electronics or home appliances. Department store selling space increased 8 percent annually from 1999–2004.[16]

Retailers in general, but department stores specifically, have played a major role in credit growth in Chile. Commercial banks have focused on high income clients for their credit cards (American Express, MasterCard, and Visa). Retail companies have taken advantage of this limited positioning and have aimed their sights at a lower socioeconomic group. They are able to use their consumers' credit history in their databases. In 2004 there were 9.5 million active credit cards in Chile; 7.4 million belonged to department stores.[17]

Table 10.2 provides a comparison of the credit situation in Chile and Mexico. One of the ways for department stores to leverage their expertise in providing credit is to expand to other types of retail operations. Cencosud will attempt to maximize the 1.3 million active cards from their recent acquisition of Almacenes Paris into the company's other formats (East and Jumbo). Another attractive scenario is to provide other banking services and insurance. Falabella, Ripley, and Paris have opened commercial banking operations to offer consumer loans, including mortgages.

Sears began operations in Chile in the 1970s. After a couple of years of losses, they withdrew from the country. Likewise, J.C. Penney opened one store in 1995, but were unsuccessful and removed their operatios.

## Internet Retailing

Access to and use of the Internet is growing rapidly in Chile, which has the highest penetration of users in Latin America. About 10 percent of homes have computers, but this number is increasing at double-digit rates each year.

**Table 10.2**
**Private Label Credit Card Penetration, Mexico vs. Chile**

| (As of December 2004) Mexico | | Chile |
|---|---|---|
| Total active credit cards (ACC) (million) | 7.37 | 3.62 |
| ACC/Total population (%) | 46.2% | 3.4% |
| Total credit portfolio (US$m) | 1,883 | 1,636 |
| Portfolio/GDP (%) | 2.0% | 0.3% |

Source: Deutsche Bank, Industry Focus: Retail Chilean Retail (6 July 2005) p. 23

The major department stores were the first to develop websites for B2C (Business to Consumer) commercial activity. B2B (Business to Business) activities have also increased. Falabella uses the Internet to do business with 80 percent of their suppliers.

## Private Label

Private label became increasingly important in both food and non-food products. D&S was the first food retailer to introduce private label in 1995 and from 1998–1999 developing a private label was very important to them. Now they have a private label offering in nearly every product type.

The financial crisis boosted the sale of private label products because they are 20–25 percent less expensive than national brands.

## Government Regulation

The government does not impose any particular requirements on retailing in Chile. The United States and Chile entered into a Free Trade Agreement in 2004. Under this agreement 85 percent of bilateral trade between the two countries was duty-free immediately; the rest of the tariffs will be phased out over the next four years. All trade between the two countries will be duty-free by 2015. Chile has one of the region's simplest and most transparent regulatory systems for trade and business.

## > BRAZIL

Brazil's financial crisis occurred in 1998 and lead to devaluation of their currency, the real, in 1999. In the first phase of an economic stabilization program called the Real Plan (1994–1997), the real was pegged to the U.S. dollar (R$1=US$1).

Before the implementation of the Real Plan, retailers in Brazil focused on financial management during the times of hyperinflation instead of improving operating efficiency. They were able to get large profits from daily interest rate float. Prices were subject to daily, if not hourly, changes.[18] This resulted in consumer's intense price sensitivity. A friend from Brazil said that when they went to a restaurant they would try to pay before they ate because prices would be higher at the end of the meal.

The Real Plan lead to a period of economic stability, requiring retailers to earn money as merchants, rather than speculators. As a result many companies have gone out of business, and there has been intensive consolidation in the industry. During the period of hyperinflation, Brazilians used to buy food on a monthly basis, purchasing a large amount and storing it at home. Since the inflation rate has been reduced people are far more inclined to purchase on a weekly basis.[19]

## Retail Overview

Tables 10.3 and 10.4 summarize the major domestic and foreign retailers in Brazil. From 1998–2000, 12 of the top 20 retailers disappeared through acquisition. There are three major reasons for these acquisitions: 1) they are defensive measures aimed at preventing competitors from getting attractive assets, 2) they are aimed at enabling retailers to move into new geographic regions or to obtain new customers through diversifying their format portfolio, and 3) they are a way to gain economies of scale allowing them to invest in advanced distribution and warehousing assets.[20] Carrefour, Bompreco (Ahold), and Jeronimo Martins were active parties in the acquisition war. One of the most recent moves was taken by Carrefour's acquisition of Se, the country's seventh-largest food retailer, which had been owned by Jeronimo Martins (Portugal). This acquisition gave Carrefour the means to expand rapidly in Brazil.

Consolidation has significant benefits, but it can also have drawbacks. Like Multinational Markets, a consolidated company may look like one big company, but the member companies retain individual identities for a long period of time. CBD centralized their local purchasing in 2001, but left each format to be run separately. Carrefour centralized their buying only to find out that they did not have a distribution network that could handle the additional volume. The result was an embarrassing out-of-stock position.

Most of the consolidation in Brazil has been organized by foreign retailers. One major reason for this is that they have greater access to capital. The depreciation of the real has put a damper on foreign investment. The real was first allowed to float in 1999; it dove to 2.3 to the dollar by the end of 2005. This massive devaluation increased in inflation. Inflation in the retail sector for 2002 was 8 percent; in the wholesale sector, it was about 18 percent. Devaluation and the resulting increase in inflation encouraged manufacturers to focus on exporting. Retailers have taken two stands on the price increases from suppliers: some, like CBD, the operator of Pao de Acucar, have denounced price increases by suppliers and have threatened not to buy from suppliers who increase their prices excessively. Carrefour used the opportunity to stockpile a supply of non-perishables to offset the effects of future inflation.

Depreciation of the local currency makes imported products more expensive; therefore, retailers shift sourcing from imported to domestic goods. The informal market generates about 30 percent of total retail sales. Informal retailers have lower costs because they either pay no taxes or pay lower taxes by underreporting their earnings; also, they do not have any overhead. The government is trying to cut down on this underreporting by requiring small retailers to use a government-mandated software to record all retail transactions. The government inspects the POS machines and will prosecute the retailer if they find that the machines are not operating properly.

**Table 10.3**
**Brazil—Leading Domestic Retailers, 2004**

| | | Total Sales and Stores | | | | Global Rank and Penetration | | | Domestic Market | |
| | | Net Sales ($US Mil) | % Chg Sales | Total Stores | 2004 Rank, Top 200 Retailers Worldwide | Single-country, Regional or Global? | Number of countries | Share of total sales | Share of total stores |
| Company | Primary Line of Trade | | | | | | | | |
|---|---|---|---|---|---|---|---|---|---|
| 1 Companhia Brasileira de Distribuicao (CBD) | Supermarkets/Grocery Stores | 4,294 | 16.3% | 551 | 150 | Single Country | 1 | 100% | 100% |
| 2 Casas Bahia | Consumer Electronics & Appliances | 3,076 | 50.0% | 410 | — | Single Country | 1 | 100% | 100% |
| 3 Globex Utilidades S.A. | Consumer Electronics & Appliances | 1,059 | 22.4% | 339 | — | Single Country | 1 | 100% | 100% |
| 4 Lojas Americanas | Discount Department Stores | 779 | 17.5% | 156 | — | Single Country | 1 | 100% | 100% |
| 5 Angeloni | Supermarkets/Grocery Stores | 256 | N/A | 46 | — | Single Country | 1 | 100% | 100% |

Sources: Retail Forward, company annual reports and published reports

**Table 10.4**
**Brazil—Key Foreign Retailers, 2004**

| Company | Retail Headquarters | Sector | Primary Line of Trade | Global Rank and Penetration | | |
|---|---|---|---|---|---|---|
| | | | | 2004 Rank, Top 200 Retailers Worldwide | Single-country, Regional or Global? | Number of countries |
| Carrefour Group | France | FDM | Hypermarkets/Supercenters | 2 | Global | 31 |
| FASA | Chile | FDM | Drug Stores | — | Regional | 4 |
| INDITEX Group (i.e., Zara) | Spain | Softgoods | Apparel Stores | 110 | Global | 56 |
| J.C. Penney Company, Inc. | United States | Softgoods | Department Stores | 38 | Regional | 2 |
| Leroy Merlin | France | Homegoods | DIY/Home Improvement Stores | 112 | Global | 8 |
| Modelo Continente SGPS (Sonae) | Portugal | FDM | Supermarkets/Grocery Stores | 146 | Global | 2 |
| Pinault-Printemps-Redoute SA | France | Homegoods | Non-Store | 36 | Global | 17 |
| Rallye (i.e., Casino) | France | FDM | Supermarkets/Grocery Stores | 26 | Global | 17 |
| Royal Ahold | Netherlands | FDM | Supermarkets/Grocery Stores | 10 | Global | 18 |
| Sherwin-Williams Company | United States | Homegoods | Hardlines Specialty Stores | 161 | Regional | 7 |
| SHV Holdings N.V. (Makro) | Netherlands | FDM | Cash & Carries/Warehouse Clubs | 163 | Global | 9 |
| Wal-Mart Stores, Inc. | United States | FDM | Hypermarkets/Supercenters | 1 | Global | 11 |

Sources: Retail Forward, company annual reports and published reports

If the government cracks down on informal retailers, unemployment would rise. Informal retailers do not pay the social welfare costs associated with their employees. If they had to pay those wages, retailers would hire fewer employees and/or cut their wages. Also, if the informal retail sector was required to behave like regular retailers, overall prices in Brazil would rise because the competitive prices of informal retailers would not be part of the pricing equation.[21]

## Consumer Credit

Consumer credit increased 161 percent from 1998 to 2002. Brazil has a low savings rate partly because the interest rates are so low. Also, Argentina's financial situation had an effect on Brazil. Argentina's dollar-linked economy suffered with poor performance, which resulted in a depression in the country. This caused the Brazilian real to fall, because multinationals sold local currency and bought dollars throughout South America to protect financial transfers from local subsidiaries to multinational home offices. Also contributing to this financial crisis was the discount rate on Latin American bonds, which forced internal interest rates upward because Brazil is considered internationally as a high investment risk.[22]

During the period of HYPERINFLATION (1985–1995), consumers wanted to leave their liquid funds in interest-bearing accounts. Inflation above 50 percent monthly is hyperinflation. Banks developed a system of financial cards to withdraw money from interest-bearing accounts on a need-to-use basis. Using these cards made Brazilians accustomed to using plastic. Brazilian consumers are now the largest users of credit cards in Latin America; and the country ranks eighth in credit card use worldwide. About 34 percent of the Brazilian population 16 years of age, living in a metropolitan area and making over $150 per month, has a credit card.

## Food Retailing

Brazil's food retail sector includes four major formats: hypermarkets, supermarkets, hard discounters, and informal retailers. Consumers are ranked from A to E, with A being the most wealthy. Hypermarkets focus on B and C consumers; supermarkets aim at B consumers; hard discounters are focused on D consumers; and informal retailers target E consumers. The very wealthiest in Brazil, those in category A, do not shop, but instead rely on servants to purchase food.[23]

Some important trends in Brazilian food retailing are increased use of private label products, development of buying groups among independent retailers, increased demand for organic food for A and B consumers, and an increased emphasis on quality, not just a focus on price. Brazilian consumers also are showing an increased demand for greater customer service; this is true even for low income consumers. There is also a growing demand for home meal replacement, freshly prepared foods ready for eating.[24]

HYPERMARKETS    The leading hypermarket companies are Carrefour, Bompreco, Sendas (Ahold), Wal-Mart, and Extra (CBD). With 224 cities in Brazil and a population of over 100,000, there is a lot of room for hypermarket growth. Each of these cities could support several hypermarkets, yet there are only 250 in the whole country. Because the government does not have any restrictions on large scale store growth, the availability of land for development and the high degree of automobile ownership in Brazil make the environment particularly attractive for hypermarket development.[25]

**HARD DISCOUNTERS**   Hard discounter growth is supported by a saturation of hypermarkets in major cities like Rio de Janeiro and Sao Paulo. Hard discount stores target low-income consumers rather than middle-class shoppers. In this category their major competitors are the mom-and-pop stores, which are particularly vulnerable to low cost offerings like the hard discount formats.

**KEY FOOD RETAILERS**   CBD is Brazil's largest retailer. The company uses several different formats to target a diverse set of consumer needs. CBD makes 70 percent of its sales in Sao Paulo. A quarter of the company ownership is held by Cassino (France). CBD has central buying and about 80 percent of its merchandise moves through distribution centers (DCs) arranged around formats instead of particular types of products. Across its formats CBD is known for excellent customer service and a strong loyalty card program. At Pao de Acucar, the supermarket format with 176 stores, 60 percent of sales come through loyalty members. Extra, the hypermarket chain at CBD, operates 55 stores and accounts for nearly half of CBD sales. Known for its non-food merchandise, Extra is somewhat similar to Target in the United States. Barateiro is the hard discount format, but unlike most hard discounters, Barateiro offers national brands and provides extra service. The store is also larger (25,000 sq. ft. with 20,000 SKUs) than traditional hard discount stores. They offer free home delivery, feeling that even the poorest customers appreciate service. As a result their prices are not competitive with the true hard discounters Dia (Carrefour) and Todo Dia (Wal-Mart) in Brazil.[26]

Carrefour is the second largest retailer in Brazil. Although Carrefour's initial success in Brazil was due to its hypermarket concept, their growth strategy in Brazil involves opening more supermarkets and hard discount stores. Carrefour's hard discount offering is Dia and at 3,000 sq. ft. and 1,000 SKUs, it resembles the true hard discounter. Dia is aimed at low income consumers and offers one leading brand and one private label in most categories. Champion is Carrefour's supermarket concept in Brazil.

Wal-Mart has a great advantage in their superior logistics efficiency and their great access to capital. Even so, Wal-Mart underestimated the amount of adaptation they would need to make in this market. Todo Dia, Wal-Mart's low-priced supermarket concept in Brazil, is bigger than a traditional hard discount format (35,000 sq ft 12,000 SKUs). This format is not doing well.

Casa Sendas is the largest Brazilian-owned food retailer in the country. It is principally in the hypermarket business but also has hard discount offerings.

**NON-FOOD RETAILING**   There are three major apparel retail chains: Lojas Renner, C&A, and Lojas Riachuelo. These retailers have a very small percent of the total apparel market (four to five) as the market is very fragmented. Most of the sales in apparel come from small independent retailers.

Some of the global specialty retailers like Zara, Mango, and Benetton have entered the market, but they have found that the reverse seasonality creates a problem. In the past, Brazilian retailers were content to be six months behind the fashion trends elsewhere; however, this is no longer the case. Brazil is a very fashion-forward area, and it is becoming evident that any foreign retailer or branded supplier that wants to do well in this market will need to adapt their line for the Brazilian market.[27]

Lojas Renner (founded in 1912) was sold to J.C. Penney in 1998. Its focus is A-, B, and C consumers selling in a department store format. After Penney's acquisition the other two Brazilian department stores—Mesbla and Mappin—went bankrupt. Renner purchased many of the large spaces operated by its competitors. In 2005, JC Penney sold its 98 percent ownership in Lojas Renner on the Sao Paulo Stock Exchange. Lojas Renner is the only company in Brazil without a single controlling shareholder; the largest shareholder now only holds just 7 percent of the company.[28]

C&A (Netherlands) is almost exclusively price driven. C&A has 80 stores but does not have a clear positioning statement.

Lojas Riachuelo operates over 70 stores. They sell apparel for men, women, and children, home fashions, and accessories. Most of their merchandise is private label. Their positioning is low price, but high fashion. The company's prototype is Zara, a company that fully integrates its supply chain to achieve efficiency.[29]

## Internet Retailing

Brazil is the ninth-largest Internet market in the world and the largest in Latin America. Their e-commerce is the most developed in Latin America. In 2005, 30 million Brazilians were online on a regular basis, and there are 51 million credit cards in circulation.[30] Internet retailing is very small, particularly considering the large number of Internet users. Only 3 percent of Internet users buy products and services on a regular basis and only 5 percent buy at least once a year. However, 40 percent of Internet users check prices online before visiting a store. Brazil has an excellent postal service, another important infrastructure complementary needed for e-commerce.

## Franchising

Brazil is in third place in number of worldwide franchised outlets, just trailing the United States and Japan. Over 90 percent of these franchises are from Brazil itself. There are three reasons for the high growth in franchising: high interest rates, retail fragmentation, and economic stability. High interest rates make it difficult for a small business to finance its own expansion; it simply cannot afford to expand as rapidly as it would like. In the chapter on franchising, I called this a resourced-based explanation for franchising. A fragmented retail market means that there are few chains to block competition and obtain more favorable sourcing concessions. Economic stability encourages entrepreneurs to invest in themselves rather than looking for employment with someone else.

Brazil does have a franchising law that requires franchisors—or their master franchisees—to provide all potential franchisees with a Uniform Franchise Offering Circular (UFOC), a document that must contain information about the economic and financial health of the franchiser and any information about pending legal disputes.

## 〉 VENEZUELA

Venezuela has experienced a great deal of economic uncertainty the past few years. Retailers have been affected by the general strikes, political and social instability, heightened inflation, and a deflated national currency. There is constant tension between private businesses and government policy. President Hugo Chavez blames the retail sector for causing the strife and has taken measures to punish the industry.

### Retailing Overview

President Chavez relaxed regulations on informal black street markets because this is an important electoral base for the president. This informal black market sells nearly every type of good including food, cosmetics and toiletries, counterfeit designer clothing and accessories, jewelery, and electronic goods, and it undermines the ability of formal retailing to prosper in Venezuela. Although these inexpensive goods are typically not high quality, they enjoy brisk sales. As I discussed in the chapter on retailing in developing countries, the black market stores have the opportunity to be very successful because their overhead is very low.

The Chavez government opened the Mercal grocery stores in 2003 to provide subsidized basic food to low-income Venezuelans. Products such as coffee, sugar, corn flour, milk, oil, and rice are sold in these stores at a 50 percent discount. Originally the stores were meant to be open just for 45 days, but they have proved to be so popular the government is no longer considering shutting them down.[31]

Hugo Chavez was elected president in 1998, running on a revolution platform based on anti-trade, protectionist, and pro-working class efforts. Poor Venezuelans form the core of Chavez's support. He has been in contention with the business community since he took office. The result has been an economic recession (since 2002), brought on by capital flight, business and labor union strikes, political tension, and a decline in the real GDP. [32]

Small independent grocery stores in Venezuela are called *abastos*. These legitimate stores suffer in competition with supermarket chain stores on one end and the informal black market on the other hand. By 2003, retail sales of chained supermarkets passed those of independent supermarkets.

The Chavez government has instituted a variety of measures to frustrate retailers as well as to garner support from the lower income households. Officials have used rhetoric against organized retailers, admonishing them for charging overly high prices. Other measures include opening government food stores, implementing price controls, appending a value added tax, and closing stores that they deem as selling at higher rates than the government approves. The price controls were implemented in 2003, and 60 percent of the products in a supermarket are covered by them.[33] In attempting to stop capital flight, the government has restricted the ability to purchase foreign currency. This affects local manufacturers, suppliers, and retailers.

Twenty percent of the food sold in Venezuela is sold through the Mercal stores.

### Internet Sales

There are several problems plaguing Internet sales in Venezuela. The first problem is related to credit card fraud. Owning a credit card is more expensive in Venezuela than in the United States. The fear of fraud means that most people are reluctant to give credit card details over the Internet. Also, international Internet purchases have been banned since the adoption of foreign exchange control regulations.

### Franchising

Franchising is a growth area in Venezuela. By 2003 there were 3,000 franchises located throughout the country, operated by 180 different companies. About 30 percent of these companies are U.S. based.[34]

### Major Retailers

Of the major retailers in Venezuela, five are foreign and five are domestic. Makro Venezuela is the large store retailer followed by Exito (Colombian). Central Madeirense is the leading domestically owned and operated supermarket chain in Venezuela. Central Madeirense operates 41 supermarkets throughout the country. CADA supermarkets is operated by the Casino Group (France).

## > SUMMARY

The South America legacy is one of volatile contrasts. Economic and political instability have led to retail practices unheard of in other countries. When the value of money changes in double digits between the beginning and the ending of a meal, human nature finds a way to cope with this market phenomenon. In the 1990s much of South America had a golden era of market liberalization and heightened investment interest. In the middle of the 2000s, the dislike of American imperialism has been drawing South American countries back to socialist ties. New elections in South America have yielded support for candidates who call for closer ties to Castro rather than Bush. Argentina paid off their debt to the World Bank in the later days of 2005, many would say to get the International Monetary Fund off their back. Isn't it interesting that while extreme socialistic/communistic views have been extinguished in China and Russia, they have become new thinking in South America?

## > KEY TERMS

CAPITAL FLIGHT

DOLLARIZATION

FACTOR ACCOUNTS RECEIVABLE

FINANCIAL SPREAD

HYPERINFLATION

INDIGENOUS

INFORMAL CREDIT

INFORMAL ECONOMIES

LEFTIST

REMITTANCES

SHOPPING BASKET

TRADITIONAL RETAILING SYSTEM

VELOCITY OF MONEY

## › DISCUSSION QUESTION

1. How does a retail store make money from advancing consumers' credit?
2. If a government gets revenues by collecting taxes from retailers, and informal retailers typically do not pay taxes, why would some governments support informal retailing?
3. What sourcing strategies work well when you have a high degree of inflation?
4. Political and economic instability make local residents reluctant to keep money in a country (capital flight). They also discourage foreigners from investing in a country. How would instability alter the development of retailing in a country?

## › ENDNOTES

1. "Leaders: How to protect Latin American Democracy; The Organization of American States." (2005). *The Economist.* 375, (8430) 10.
2. "Latin America Finance: Electronic Payment Systems Expand." (2005). EIU ViewsWire. New York. November 28.
3. "Latin America: A Dash of Latino Passion." (2005). Brand Strategy. London: September 8, 24
4. "Argentina Country Report." (2004). Euromonitor. Global Market Information Database.
5. Peterson, R. (1996). Argentina-Financial Services ISA 960201. Document #9151, U.S. Industry Sector Analysis, Buenos Aires.
6. Argentina Country Report (2004).
7. Argentina Country Report (2004).
8. Argentina Country Report (2004).
9. Argentina Country Report (2004).
10. Gutman, G. (1997). "Transformaciones Recientes en la Distribución de Alimentos en la Argentina." *SAGPyA,* Buenos Aires.
11. Whelan, J. (2005). "Americas: Chile Could Move Further to the Left As Well." *Wall Street Journal* (Eastern edition) New York, N.Y.: December 9, 15.
12. Lopez-Doriga, J. and J. Rozenbaum (2005). "Chilean Retail: Stepping on Each Other's Toes." Deutsche Band (July 6) in Investext.
13. Lopez-Doriga and Rozenbaum. (2005).
14. Lopez-Doriga and Rozenbaum. (2005).
15. Lopez-Doriga and Rozenbaum. (2005).
16. Lopez-Doriga and Rozenbaum. (2005).
17. Lopez-Doriga and Rozenbaum. (2005).
18. "Retailing in Latin America." (2001). Retail Forward Columbus: Ohio.
19. "Retailing in Brazil." (2004). Global Market Information Database. Euromonitor 1–125.
20. "Retailing in Brazil." (2003).
21. "Retailing in Brazil." (2003).
22. "Retailing in Brazil." (2003).
23. "Retailing in Brazil." (2003).
24. "Retailing in Brazil." (2003).
25. "Retailing in Brazil." (2003).
26. "Retailing in Brazil." (2003).

27. "Retailing in Brazil." (2003).
28. "J.C. Penney Sells Lojas Renner." (2005). Latin American Financial Publications, August 17, DEALS, 4.
29. "Retailing in Brazil." (2003).
30. U.S. Commercial Services Guide to Brazil. (2005). January.
31. "Retailing in Venezuela." (2004). Global Market Information Database Euro-monitor 1–71.
32. "Retailing in Venezuela." (2004).
33. "Retailing in Venezuela." (2004).
34. "Retailing in Venezuela." (2004).

# COMPANY FOCUS II.1.

## WAL-MART

### Patrice Grady, Katherine Harris, Laura Hurrell, Emily Money, AnnaLisa Nelson, Melissa Pinkleman, Crystal Rodes, Todd Sauvola

## Flow Chart:

1991: Mexico (807 stores)
1992: Puerto Rico (54 stores)
1994: Canada (278 stores)*
1995: Argentina (12 stores)
1995: Brazil (293 stores)
1995: Indonesia (Exited)
1996: China (60 stores)
1998: Germany (85 stores)*
1998: South Korea (15 stores)* Exited in 2006
1999: United Kingdom (322 stores)*
2002: Japan (394 stores)*
2005: Costa Rica (130 stores)
2005: El Salvador (59 stores)
2005: Guatemala (119 stores)
2005: Honduras (37 stores)
2005: Nicaragua (35 stores)

## Opening Statement:

Out of 200 global retailers, Wal-Mart is the number one discount retailer, and it continues to grow and dominate the world of retailing. Today, Wal-Mart "has more than 1.3 million associates worldwide and nearly 5,000 stores and wholesale clubs across ten countries. The 'most admired retailer,' according to FORTUNE magazine, it has just completed one of the best years in its history: Wal-Mart generated more than $256 billion in global revenue, establishing a new record and adding more than $26 billion in sales."[2]

## History

In 1962, with few employees, the first Wal-Mart store was opened by Sam Walton in the rural town of Rodgers City, Arkansas. After eight years of hard work, in 1970, Wal-Mart became a public company. Wal-Mart was comprised of eighteen stores with sales of $44 million.[3] The focus was on opening stores in small to midsized towns that could sustain discount retailing.

The next major step in Wal-Mart's expansion was the opening of the first Sam's Wholesale Club in 1983, which grew to be the largest membership warehouse club nationwide. Soon after the success of Sam's, a joint venture was formed in Dallas, Texas, and later renamed as Wal-Mart Supercenter. Currently there are four retail divisions within Wal-Mart: Wal-Mart stores, Sam's Club, Neighborhood Markets, and Supercenters.[4] At a typical Wal-Mart store a consumer could purchase quality, value-priced general merchandise while walking through a pleasant and convenient layout. In contrast, while walking through a Sam's Club, a consumer would still find a broad selection of general merchandise at value prices, but also find large volume items at value prices. The Neighborhood Market stores provide an extra element to customers in addition to general merchandise—they sell groceries and pharmaceuticals at value prices. Finally, the Supercenter format appeals to customers who have a wide variety of needs including general priced merchandise, groceries, and specialty shops like vision centers, Tire & Lube Expresses, and one-hour photo centers. Wal-Mart experienced continued growth in all of these store concepts solely throughout the

---

*Wal-Mart entered these countries through acquisitions (Wal-Mart International Operations 2004).[1]

United States until 1991, when it began its international expansion into Mexico.

## Competitive Advantages

Because Wal-Mart is such a dominating retailer, it excels in the factors of Dunning's eclectic theory. In terms of ownership advantages, the Wal-Mart name alone gives it a competitive edge over other companies because other retailers look to them to learn how to run their companies better. Other asset-based advantages are the selected private labels and licensed brands that Wal-Mart sells, like the George private label it received after acquiring ASDA. Some of the other licensed brands that are seen as valuable and popular to consumers are: Disney, Mary-Kate and Ashley, and McDonald's.[5] Likewise, the way Wal-Mart runs their company gives them many transaction-based advantages that have helped them to internationalize. Offering incredibly low prices and still making a profit is what makes them the world's largest distribution company. They do this by investing early and heavily in the best IT logistics, keeping a price discipline while still passing savings to customers, and having a bargain-seeking purchasing department that is strong and aggressive. In order to keep prices low, they get their merchandise from around the world wherever the costs are low, constituting a strong transactional-based advantage.[6] Wal-Mart's success in international expansion is in large part due to their demand for excellence. Their effective supply chain management system has "changed the face of business,"[7] allowing Wal-Mart to have far lower margins, making them popular in other countries. Another ownership advantage is Wal-Mart's communication infrastructure. They have implemented business critical messaging "to speed the delivery of business information and maximize corporate coordination, while reducing communication costs."[8] This is an effective way for them to communicate with all of their stores, national and international. Wal-Mart's ability to learn by doing, known as tacit learning, is the major reason for their international success,[9] which helped the company expand into Mexico and Canada. After learning from their mis-

takes in those countries, they have been able to expand even further.[10]

Internalization factors also play an important role in Wal-Mart's success. Business critical messaging has enabled them to communicate privately; through this communication system valuable information cannot be accessed by unauthorized parties.[11] Wal-Mart also keeps a lot of secrets due to the fact that they do not franchise or provide licenses for other units. A person can buy and own stocks of Wal-Mart, but he/she cannot own their own Wal-Mart store. Another way Wal-Mart is able to keep its secrets is by requiring their employees to sign a code of ethics document; they are required to continually adhere to updated policies and codes.[12] This code of ethics document states the following:

> "Do not disclose confidential information to anyone outside the company without the express written approval of the People Department or Legal Department."
> "Disclose confidential information to other associates only for legitimate business purposes."
> "Handle all confidential information with care to avoid inadvertent or careless disclosure."
> "Secure or password protects all files or records containing confidential information as necessary to protect the confidentiality of that information."[13]

Wal-Mart has invested in and developed a great system, processes, products, and technology that have made them an industry leader. Their trade secrets must be kept confidential. Wal-Mart does not tolerate the violation of confidentiality or secrecy agreements or the improper acquisition of protected information.[14] For example, in 1999 Wal-Mart filed suit against Amazon for allegedly recruiting employees. In this case, Wal-Mart believed that Amazon had an agenda to use these employees to copy Wal-Mart's secret information systems.[15] Amazon in return filed a countersuit. They accused Wal-Mart of suing to make an example out of the two employees that Amazon recruited. They believe that Wal-Mart wanted to prevent other employees from leaving and doing the same thing.[16] Wal-Mart does its best to take every precaution to keep their company secrets.[17]

Location factors play an extremely important role in Wal-Mart's international expansion. Researching a city's demographics before positioning its stores is critical to a company's success. From their first store opening in Rogers, Arkansas, in 1960, to their first international expansion in 1991, Wal-Mart has been quite successful with the positioning of their stores, and continues to be to this day.[18] Given that Wal-Mart started in small rural suburban areas, their stores tend to locate in areas with lower population densities and lower poverty rates with high incomes.[19] Income is an important factor in measuring the potential retailing expenditure. The higher expenditure may imply longer time periods in the store and more frequent shopping trips. Another positioning technique for Wal-Mart is to locate themselves in areas with less competitive stores. This lets the customers and competitors know that they can stand alone and still be one of the most successful discount stores in the world.[20] These positioning strategies stand true for almost all Wal-Mart stores throughout the world; for example, Wal-Mart's frequent selection of rural locations. However, one unique strategy stands out from the others. The Las Vegas, Nevada, Wal-Mart is different than previous retail strategies for the company because Wal-Mart stores are not located in the postwar regional malls that sought to attract shoppers from throughout a city. Instead, Wal-Mart has developed a unique location strategy of dispersing their stores so they are located within a convenient ten-minute driving radius of residential communities. This multi-nodal strategy provides redundancy and constant visibility on all major corridors and neighborhoods.[21]

As you can see Wal-Mart needs to be very careful when finding a location for its supercenters. Some location strategies pertain only to small cities while other strategies need to come into play while dealing with different areas throughout the world. Wal-Mart always makes a determined effort to adapt to local cultures and become involved in the local community. They have discovered significant growth potential for much greater development worldwide.

## International Expansion

Cultural and geographical proximity both play important parts in the international moves of Wal-Mart.[22] The first three countries that Wal-Mart expanded into were Mexico, Puerto Rico, and Canada. By first entering countries that are located close to the United States and then expanding to countries farther away, Wal-Mart is demonstrating the properties of geographical proximity. Mexico and Canada are both part of NAFTA and free trade is a NAFTA benefit that Wal-Mart is capitalizing on through expansion into these countries which constitute cultural proximity.[23] The advanced infrastructure systems in each country allow Wal-Mart to keep its logistics fairly intact.[24]

Wal-Mart's geographical expansion is shown by its decision to enter geographically close locations and then jump back and forth between different countries. For example, after entering China, Wal-Mart chose to enter Germany. After becoming comfortable in Germany, it continued its European expansion.

Wal-Mart's international growth into the South America region continues with Brazil. While the United States and Brazil are not culturally similar, they are both located close to Mexico. After obtaining knowledge from Mexico, Wal-Mart moved into Puerto Rico.

Wal-Mart first entered countries close to the United States, but then in 1996 they jumped into China. Benefiting from the looser regulations on foreign investment, Wal-Mart began to expand farther.

## Mexico

Wal-Mart internationalized for the first time into Mexico through a joint venture with the Mexican retailer Cifra. This was due to saturation in the United States market. Cifra brought a thorough understanding of the Mexican consumer, which allowed for Wal-Mart's success.[25] Wal-Mart now operates 807 units in 31 states with annual sales of 10.6 billion U.S. dollars, employing more than 100,000 workers.[26]

## Puerto Rico

Due to Mexico's dreary economy, Wal-Mart expanded operations to Puerto Rico in 1992, first opening in Fajardo. Because of Puerto Rico's high rate of unemployment and consumer price inflation, it has had decreased retail sales over the past few years. Therefore, Wal-Mart has had a great opportunity to expand in a market where the consumers are in need of lower prices.[27] Wal-Mart felt that by implementing the same strategy as in Mexico—by cutting prices and increasing productivity—it would provide success in the new market.[28] Wal-Mart also acquired Supermercados Amigo, a supermarket chain in Puerto Rico.[29]

## Canada

Canada's cultural similarities with the United Sates led to Wal-Mart's expansion into Canada. By implementing the same format used in the United States, Wal-Mart currently commands 40 percent of the Canadian discount retail market. It entered Canada in 1994 by acquiring 122 Woolco stores. Even though the cost associated with this acquisition was higher than expected, the retailer still earned a profit within three years.[30] Today, Wal-Mart operates 231 discount department stores and five Sam's Clubs, and employs 60,000 associates.[31]

## Brazil

With an understanding of Latin American culture acquired through tacit learning and success in Mexico, Wal-Mart decided to enter into the Brazilian market in 1995. An attractive market because it is the leading economy in Latin America, Brazil's inflation rate was decreasing. Therefore, purchasing power for lower income consumers was improved. Wal-Mart saw Brazil, with a large population of over 150 million people, as an opportunity to become successful.[32] In March of 2004, Wal-Mart acquired the leading supermarket and hypermarket chain, Bompreco. Bompreco has 118 units and sales have been strong for 15 Supercenters, 10 Sam's Clubs, and two Todo

Dias stores in Brazil. Wal-Mart's presence in Brazil has earned them the reputation as one of the most admired companies in the country.[33]

## Argentina

Wal-Mart also entered Argentina in 1995 with the opening of a Sam's Club in the Buenos Aires area. It now has 4,000 associates who work in the 11 Supercenters and one distribution center throughout five provinces in Argentina.[34] Wal-Mart, the only retailer on the list, received an award as one of the top ten places to work in Argentina. With its increasing consumption of GDP levels, controlled inflation, and open economy, Argentina is a sound market.[35]

## China

Wal-Mart entered into China in August of 1996, opening the first supercenter and Sam's Club in Shenzhen, the fastest growing coastal city in China. Wal-Mart was an attractive retailer to the people of China.[36] In China Wal-Mart tries to cater to local taste by stocking food like dried fish, soy bean milk, and three-snake rice wine.[37]

## Germany

Germany's infrastructure made it attractive for Wal-Mart to expand there in 1998, acquiring 21 units of Wertkauf, a German hypermarket, as well as 74 Interspar hypermarkets. Wal-Mart refurbished the stores and now operates 85 Supercenters. Their operations in Germany have improved inventory levels and have driven excellent customer traffic year after year. However they have negative sales growth and low consumer confidence. Profits have not been as planned, although the outlook for the future is promising.[38]

## United Kingdom

In 1999 Wal-Mart acquired ASDA, Britain's valued food and clothing supercenter. It was an automatic success because ASDA, like Wal-Mart, had an efficient distribution network strategy and followed similar pricing and promotional strategies.[39] Within Europe, the United Kingdom has attracted the greatest amount of U.S. retailers. U.K. consumers have similar tastes and aspirations as those of the United States; they also share similarities in their business culture.[40]

## Korea

Wal-Mart entered into Korea in 1998 through its acquisition of four Makro stores. Makro provides a low-cost pricing strategy and a vast product assortment, like that of Wal-Mart. "In the past traditional supermarkets and department stores were not able to meet the requirements of one stop shopping and shopping as leisure. Consequently huge mass retailers emerged by providing customers with buying large quantities at low cost and one stop shopping."[41] Wal-Mart saw this as an opportunity to become successful with Korean consumers. This is illustrated by being voted the number one discount store in Korea.[42] Wal-Mart now employs 3,000 associates and operates 15 Supercenters.[43]

## Japan

Seiyu, Ltd., a leading Japanese retailer, was purchased by Wal-Mart in 2002; Wal-Mart holds a 37.8 percent stake in the company.[44] Seiyu's new strategy has been shifted toward using everyday low prices and decreasing corporate costs.[45] As with the Korean market, Japanese consumers are looking for low cost goods and one stop shopping, and Wal-Mart provides this commodity. Seiyu employs 30,000 workers and operates 394 supermarkets in Japan.[46]

## Future Growth

Wal-Mart's international division now accounts for approximately one-third of its stores throughout the world. According to a Citigroup report, Wal-Mart is currently looking toward India and Russia as possible areas for their continuing expansion.[47] In addition, Wal-Mart plans to expand into the western part of China. Due to trade restrictions, most of the Wal-Mart stores are located near coastal cities. Recently, the World Trade Organization lifted these restrictions, making it possible for foreign retailers to do business inland,[48] opening up many expansion opportunities for Wal-Mart in China. John Menzer stated that Wal-Mart plans to open 155 to 165 new units in 2005 and 130 to 140 of these stores will be in existing markets. "Relocations of existing stores will account for 30 of these units, while the remainder will represent new operating units for the company."[49] The past growth of Wal-Mart could be perceived as unattainable; however, the company continues to impress the retailing industry with its leading strategies and infinite possibilities.

## Discussion Questions

1. Is the retailer classified as a global retailer or a multinational retailer? Explain its pattern of expansion. What expansion strategy did/is the retailer use/using?
2. Based on Dunning's eclectic theory, how do ownership, locational, and internalization factors play in your retailers' international expansion?
3. What role does cultural proximity and geographical proximity play in the retailers' international moves?
4. Can you predict the retailers' future international expansion?

## Endnotes

1. Wal-Mart International Operations. (n.d.). Retrieved July 22, 2006 from http://walmartstores.com/Globalwmstoresweb).
2. The Story of Wal-Mart (2004).
3. *Hoover's Online.* (n.d.). Retrieved October 17, 2004, from: http://cobrands. hoovers.com/global/cobrands/proquest/ops.xhtml?COID=11600. *Hoover's Online.* (n.d.). Retrieved November 2, 2004, from: http://premium.hoovers.com/ subscribe/co/factsheet.xhtml?ID=11600.
4. Retail Divisions (2004).
5. *Hoover's Online.* (n.d.). Retrieved October 17, 2004.
6. Cote, M. (2004). Eyes Wide Shut. *CA Magazine, 137,* 3.
7. Johnson, A.H. (2002). 35 years of IT leader ship: a new supply chain forged. *Computerworld, 36,* 40.
8. Tarascio, E. (1997). Business Critical Messaging. *Information Management & Computer Security, 5,* 4.
9. Sternquist, B. (1998). International Retailing. (pp 40). New York New York: Fairchild Publications.
10. Sternquist, B. (1998).
11. Tarascio, E. (1997).
12. Security & Privacy. (n.d.). Retrieved October 17, 2004, from: http://walmart-stores.com/wmstore/wmstores/Container.jsp?BV_SessionID=@@@@0636843068. 1101079699@@@@&BV_EngineID=ccchadcmjgijheecfkfcfkjdgoodglh.o&tem plate=PromoFlash.jsp&categoryOID=-8621&contentOID=13949&pagetype= privacy
13. Employee's Code of Ethics. (n.d.). Retrieved October 15, 2004, from: http:// walmartstores.com/wmstore/wmstores/Mainabout.jsp?BV_SessionID=@@@
14. Employee's Code of Ethics. (n.d.). Retrieved October 15, 2004, from: http:// walmartstores.com/wmstore/wmstores/Mainabout.jsp?BV_SessionID=@@@@ 0521107831.1099623350@@@@&BV_EngineID=ccceadcmjgijhdicfkfcfkjdgoodglh. o&pagetype=about&categoryOID=-10626&catID=-8242&template=Display AllContents.jsp
15. Wingfield, N. and A. Zimmerman (2001). Amazon and Wal-Mart Have Discussed An Alliance, But No Deal Is Likely Soon, *The Wall Street Journal,* B6.
16. Anders, G. (1999). Amazon.com Files a Counter Suit Against Wal-Mart. *The Wall Street Journal,* 1.
17. Sternquist, B. (1998). International Retailing. (pp 40).
18. About Wal-Mart (2004)
19. *Show Me the Location.* (n.d.) Retrieved October 17, 2004, from http://gix.esri. com/library/userconf/proc98/PROCEED/TO200/PAP200/P200.HTM
20. *Show Me the Location.* (n.d.) Retrieved October 17, 2004.
21. Wal-Mart Urban (2004).
22. Sternquist, B. (1998). International Retailing. (pp 40).
23. Halverson, R. (1994). Wal-Mart "walks the walk" of a global retailer; eyes all corners *Discount Store News,* 33(23), 95. Retrieved November 2, 2004, from Proquest database.

24. Halverson, R. (1994).

25. Dolan, K. (2004). Latin America: Bump in Brazil. Retrieved September 25, 2004, from: http://www.forbes.com/premium/archives/purchase.jhtml?storyURL=/forbes/2004/0412/076d.html&_requestid=22677.

26. Wal-Mart International Operations. (n.d.). Retrieved October 17, 2004, from: http://walmartstores.com/wmstore/wmstores/Mainabout.jsp?BV_SessionID=@@@@0521107831.1099623350@@@@&BV_EngineID=cccceadcmjgijhdicfkfcfkjd goodglh.o&pagetype=about&categoryOID=-10128&catID=-8242&template=DisplayAllContents.jsp.

27. Levhar/Freidman Inc. (1999). An Island of Opportunity. Retrieved October 12, 2004, from: http://www.findarticles.com/p/articles/mi_m3092/is_1999_Oct/ai_57578925.

28. Weiner, T. (2003). Mexico: Wal-Mart Invades. *New York Times.* Weiner, T. (2003). Wal-Mart Invades, and Mexico Gladly Surrenders. Retrieved September 25, 2004, from: http://www-rohan.sdsu.edu/~rgibson/walmartmexico.html.

29. Wal-Mart International Operations. (n.d.). Retrieved October 17, 2004.

30. Expansion Paradigm Drives Growth. (1999). Retrieved October 20, 2004, from: http://www.findarticles.com/p/articles/mi_m3092/is_1999_Oct/ai_57578924.

31. Wal-Mart International Operations. (n.d.). Retrieved October 17, 2004.

32. Wal-Mart Operations in Brazil. (n.d.) Retrieved November 3, 2004, from: http://www.tristate.edu/faculty/herbig/walmartbrazil.html.

33. Citigroup (October 7, 2004)

34. Wal-Mart International Operations. (n.d.). Retrieved October 17, 2004.

35. DePaulo, L., A. Martin, E. Montel, J. Pogue, and G. Szulick (2000). Wal-Mart Argentina: Taking "Every day Low prices" Below the Equator. Retrieved September 25, 2004, from: http://faculty.fuqua.duke.edu~charvey/teaching/BAL491_2000.- Wm/Wm.ppt.

36. Troy, M. (2002). Wal-Mart to Open Neighborhood Market Store in Shenzhen, China. Retrieved October 12, 2004, from: http://www.findarticles.com/p/articles/mi_m0FNP/is_8_41/ai_85046559/print.

37. Frazier, B. (1998). Wal-Mart. (pp 172-177). New York New York: Fairchild Publications.

38. Citigroup (October 7, 2004).

39. Liang, D. (2003). Big Store Goes Global. Retrieved October 20, 2004, from: http://www.stern.nyu.edu/Sternbusiness/spring_summer_2003/bigstore.html.

40. Anonymous. (1994). New Wave of Transatlantic "power" retailers invading the UK and Europe. International Journal of Retail & Distribution Management, 22 (5), ssi.

41. Lin, M. (n.d). A Comparative Study of Asia Strategy: Wal-Mart verses Carrefour. Retrieved October 12, 2004, from: http://www.google.com/search?hl=en&q=rivero+Part+of+globalization+is+adopting+the+methods+and+customs&btnG=Google+Search.

42. Citigroup (October 7, 2004)

43. Wal-Mart International Operations. (n.d.). Retrieved October 17, 2004.

44. Wal-Mart International Operations. (n.d.). Retrieved October 17, 2004.

45. Iizumi, A. (2004) Seiyu Quits Trading with "Strong Wholesaler". Retrieved October 13, 2004, from: http://nikkeibp.jp/wcs/leaf/CID/onair/nbe/features/307672.

46. Wal-Mart International Operations. (n.d.). Retrieved October 17, 2004.

47. Citigroup (October 7, 2004)

48. Citigroup (October 13, 2004)

49. Expansion Plans. (n.d.). Retrieved November 1, 2004, from: http://www.walmart stores.com:800.

# COMPANY FOCUS II.2

## THE GAP, INC.
### International Expansion
### Michelle Hurd, Kelly Schafer

**Flow Chart:**

> 1969: United States (2,603 in 2005)
> 1987: United Kingdom (132 in 2005)
> 1989: Canada (176 in 2005)
> 1990s: Germany (out in 2004)
> 1993: France (33 in 2005)
> 1996: Japan (85 in 2005)

## Opening Statement

With their classic styles and universal fashion design, The Gap, Inc. has made itself a household name throughout the United States. The Gap, Inc. is classified as a wholly owned subsidiary, which means it is owned entirely by its holding company, or in a sense, itself. The success of the company can be traced back to their basic styles and unique marketing strategy. The Gap was one of the first private label companies to sell its merchandise in its own specialty stores. After The Gap's success in the United States, the company decided to expand their endeavors into other countries throughout the world. In 1987, the first Gap opened outside of the United States—in the United Kingdom—and stores in Canada, Germany, France, and Japan soon followed. Although The Gap operates internationally, domestic sales are its main focus, bringing in 89 percent of total sales in 2003.[1] In this case study, we will provide information regarding The Gap, Inc.'s international expansion into these countries.

The Gap can be described as a global specialty retailer.[2] Not only do they operate under the Gap brand, but they also own the private labels of Banana Republic, Old Navy, and the new retail store of Forth & Towne. The original Gap chains have international stores that continue to expand today. Even with this international growth, The Gap, Inc. remains focused on its domestic markets for growth and success. In the following paragraphs we will outline the Gap's

growth in the United States and its expansion into each individual foreign countries.

## United States

Doris and Don Fisher originally founded The Gap, Inc. in 1969,[3] opening the first store in San Francisco with the goal of creating an atmosphere that was not only easy for the customer to shop in, but one that also provided a wide selection of styles. The Gap provides an extensive variety of high-quality classic and casual apparel. Basic clothing staples such as denim, khaki, and T-shirts dominate the original product line to this day.

Only one year after opening the first store, sales reached more than $2 million and a second store opened in San Jose. With this rapid success, The Gap, Inc. launched its first advertising campaign: the "fall into Gap" slogan was born.[4] Soon after, The Gap went public on the New York and Pacific Stock Exchanges and the company was officially on its way to retail success.

In 1983, The Gap, Inc. acquired Banana Republic in an effort to start expanding its name to a different category of products. At the time, Banana Republic consisted of a two-story travel and safari clothing company. Today, Banana Republic has transformed into a store that offers a sophisticated and fashionable product line. The collections include dress-casual and tailored apparel for men and women, including shoes and accessories. Prices at Banana Republic are higher than those of The Gap.

Shortly after the acquisition of Banana Republic, The Gap, Inc. expanded its traditional product line to include children's clothes. GapKids is still a successful extension of The Gap today.

The late 1980s started the first major expansion of The Gap into international territories. This will be discussed in more detail in following sections. Not long after opening GapKids, the babyGap line debuted in the GapKids store in San Francisco. Now The Gap was appealing to three different generations of shoppers, causing sales to skyrocket. Only two years later, The Gap became the world's second-largest apparel brand.[5]

To appeal to a different consumer demographic, The Gap, Inc. once again expanded its private label and opened the first Old Navy store. Targeting the store to the whole family, they cited "fun, fashion, and value" as their retail strategy.[6] This new store format consisted of men's, women's, children's, and infant's clothing. It also offers accessories, shoes, and personal care items. Old Navy's prices are the cheapest in the Gap fleet of private labels. Adding to the theme of affordability, The Gap, Inc. opened the doors of the first Gap Outlets.

Most recently, The Gap, Inc. has been continuing its growth domestically. Specifically, they launched a new retail format in New York City in August of this year. The store, Forth & Towne, targets women over the age of 35, providing them with the atmosphere of a department store but the quality of an intimate boutique at affordable prices. The product line will offer this group of women versatile styles and a great fit.[7]

To further spur their growth domestically, The Gap, Inc. just recently completed point of sale upgrades.[8] The goal of this new technology is to enhance the customer's experience at The Gap, Old Navy, and Banana Republic. The new system benefits employees as well. Now sales associates can look up out of stock items on the register and print out a receipt for the customer that shows what other stores in the area carry the item. Also, they can look up transactions for returns without customers having to present a receipt. The point of this upgrade, says Calvin Hollinger, vice president of information technology, is to "have a centrally managed system that will inevitably translate into increased sales and a reputation for customer service."[9] The Gap, Inc. is also ready to launch this technology in Japan, with some modifications to meet local needs. The Point of Sales system will pilot in the United Kingdom and France toward the end of 2005.[10]

## United Kingdom

The first Gap store operating outside of the United States was opened in London, England, in 1987.[11] In 1998, The Gap, Inc. planned to open more stores around the United Kingdom to compete head-to-head with its high-street rival, Next.[12] Currently, Gap UK, a subsidiary of The Gap, Inc., operates approximately 140 stores throughout the United Kingdom. Gap UK is looking to bridge the gap between casual European and American fashion with plans to open at least 50 new stores in the U.K., France, and Japan through 2007. The Gap, Inc. is hoping to expand and bring its American parent companies Old Navy and Banana Republic shops to England as well.[13]

## Canada

Canada is The Gap, Inc.'s largest international market, it carries all three main brands.[14] The Gap first opened its doors in Canada in 1989,[15] in Vancouver, British Columbia. Traditionally, the Canadian market is divided into broad categories of men's, women's, and children's apparel, footwear, and accessories. Typically, retailers are active in only a few of these segments, thus leading to a highly fragmented market.[16] Fortunately for The Gap, Inc., they are able to integrate into all the market segments, allowing them to cater to all consumer needs.

In Canada, The Gap, Inc. has followed a trend of opening larger stores. They have used extensive advertising to build brand equity. Also, they have expanded their reach with new store openings, such as Old Navy and Banana Republic.[17]

Old Navy first debuted in the Canadian market in 2001, with twelve stores opening on the same day. Most of the locations were in shopping malls in the province of Ontario. Jonathon Finn, director of public relations and promotions for Old Navy, believes that Ontario "has demographics that will make the retailer a good fit."[18] He added that consumers in the region are fashion and value conscious, which is descriptive of the Old Navy format.

In their newest venture, The Gap, Inc. opened four Banana Republic stores in the province of Quebec in August of 2005.[19] The company felt that they already had numerous customers from Quebec shopping in other Canadian and U.S. stores, so the transition into Quebec was only natural.

## Germany

The Gap, Inc. entered Germany in the 1990s. Germany was the company's smallest international business, with just 10 stores, and it accounted for less than 1 percent of the total company sales. With the focus on international strategy, The Gap, Inc. felt it would be best to relocate their resources to optimize growth in other existing markets.[20] The Gap, Inc. sold its German operations to Swedish retail group H&M Hennes & Mauritz in May of 2004.

## France

The Gap, Inc. first entered France in 1993[21] opening in Paris within the Galeries Lafayette department store as a test boutique. After achieving sales success, The Gap, Inc. decided to open a larger freestanding location. This came after The Gap, Inc. realized their potential market in France was larger than originally thought. French tourists who traveled to the United States were returning to France with suitcases of Gap clothing.[22] They liked the styles as well as the affordability. The Gap clothing fit the tastes of French consumers, who prefer simple, understated, classic sportswear. Upon expansion into France, The Gap, Inc. will include a value added tax to their merchandise as well as custom duties. This will raise the price of The Gap products considerably to make it more competitive in the market. Even with the price increase, The Gap still offers the French a unique variety of apparel not found in other locales.

## Japan

In 1996, The Gap opened its flagship store in the Shibuya shopping district in Tokyo.[23] Upon arrival in Japan, The Gap, Inc. operated as though they were still marketing toward the American consumer. They did not change the format of their product line to ensure success in Japan. The tastes and body structures of Japanese and Americans are quite different. Because of this discrepancy, sales were mediocre at first. After realizing this problem, The Gap, Inc. made the change to "100 percent Japanese fits"[24] and business dramatically increased.

Now that The Gap has officially been in Japan for 10 years, they have become more familiar with and aware of their target customer base. As Andrew Rolfe, president of The Gap's international division states, "Typically the Japanese customer is more fashionable and stylish than their American counterpart—they shop more often and they spend a higher proportion of their disposable income on fashion. It's a market that appreciates quality and it's a market that's not very forgiving if you get it wrong."[25] Given this information, The Gap, Inc. decided that Banana Republic was a natural growth strategy for the Japanese market. American and Japanese teams worked together to tailor merchandise specifically to the Japanese consumer.[26] With this careful planning, Banana Republic opened its doors for the first time outside of North America. To compete with Japanese brands, The Gap, Inc. strategically located themselves in one of the more wealthy neighborhoods. By still offering quality merchandise with affordable prices, Banana Republic was bound for success. Banana Republic also offers customers with a complete wardrobe, whereas Japanese retailers do not, furthering Banana Republic's competitive advantage.

With The Gap, Inc.'s international success, there's no question that they will continue to grow and expand globally.

## Discussion Questions

1. Is the retailer classified as a global retailer or a multinational retailer? Explain its pattern of expansion. What expansion strategy did/is the retailer use/using?
2. Based on Dunning's eclectic theory, how do ownership, locational, and internalization factors play in your retailers' international expansion?
3. What role does cultural proximity and geographical proximity play in the retailers' international moves?
4. Can you predict the retailer's future international expansion?

## Endnotes

1. Global Market Information Database-Statistics (2005). Global Market Information Database from Michigan State University. Retrieved November 12, 2005 from http://www.gmid.euromonitor.com/statspage.aspx
2. Standard's and Poor's Corporate Descriptions, Nov 9, 2005
3. The Gap, Inc. About Gap, Inc. Retrieved November 9, 2005 from www.gapinc.com
4. The Gap, Inc. About Gap, Inc. Retrieved November 9, 2005.
5. The Gap, Inc. About Gap, Inc. Retrieved November 9, 2005.
6. The Gap, Inc. About Gap, Inc. Retrieved November 9, 2005.
7. The Gap, Inc. About Gap, Inc. Retrieved November 9, 2005.
8. Conti, Samantha. (2004). Gap's Global Tech Strategy is Slave to Fashion, Service. *WWD*, 188(101), 18. Retrieved October 25, 2005 from http://proquest.umi.com/pqdweb?index=0&did=736159961&SrchMode=1&sid=4&Fmt=3&VInst=PROD&VType=PQD&RQT=309&VName=PQD&TS=1131904561&clientId=3552
9. Conti, Samantha. (2004).
10. Conti, Samantha. (2004).
11. The Gap, Inc. (2005). The Gap, Inc.-About Gap, Inc.-Milestones. Retrieved October 25, 2005 from www.gapinc.com/public/About/abt_milestones.shtml
12. The Gap, Inc. About Gap, Inc. Retrieved November 9, 2005.
13. Gap (UK Holdings) Limited. Hoover's Company Records. Retrieved October 18, 2005 from http://web.lexis-nexis.com/universe
14. The Gap Inc. (May 2004). *Global Market Information Database for Michigan State University*. Retrieved November 3, 2005 from http://www.gmid.euromonitor.com/Reports.aspx.
15. The Gap, Inc. (2005).
16. The Gap Inc. (May 2004).
17. The Gap Inc. (May 2004).
18. Old Navy Crosses Canadian Border. (2001 April, 10) *The Chronicle Publishing Company*. Retrieved November 9, 2005 from http://web.lexis-nexis.com/universe?_m=d435832a6dc77473fa1276c7b1be453 . . .
19. Banana Republic Announces Four Quebec Locations and Opening Dates. (2005 August, 10). *Canada NewsWire*. Retrieved November 9, 2005 from http://web.lexis-nexis.con/universe?_m=969ab6b125be44d58d612b678ad46e5 . . .
20. Gap Inc. Announces Plan to Exit Germany. (2004). *PR Newswire*. Retrieved November 9, 2005 from http://web.lexis-nexis.com/universe/document?_m=227a79db36ef15cff9ce48e17a06303b&_docnum=7&wchp=dGLbVtz-zSkVA&_md5=0aef8fce12a2349b9561728e9c1a45a9
21. The Gap, Inc. About Gap, Inc. Retrieved November 9, 2005.
22. LaFranchi, Howard. (1994). Gap Inc. Invades France with Cheap, Chic Clothes. *The Christian Science Monitor*. Retrieved November 9, 2005 from http://web.lexis-nexis.com/universe/document?_m=db9ec6f78221e27adaaaa0a3e6ae b734&_docnum=1&wchp=dGLbVtz-zSkVA&_md5=5b6f81f5bf0ffee29195afcc090366a1
23. The Gap, Inc. (2005).
24. Fensom, Anthony. (2005). Gap Hoping to Turn Japan to Banana Republic. *The Daily Yomiuri*. Retrieved October 27, 2005 http://web.lexis-nexis.com/universe/

document?_m=34106867a1f86de86de696d5c34963d9&_docnum=3&wchp=
dGLbVtz-zSkVA&_md5=e601f62c221385ed2e56b2d33f4e5058 .

25. Fensom, Anthony. (2005).

26. Furukawa, Tsukasa. (2005). Banana Goes to Japan. *DNR*, 35(37), 6. Retrieved
    October 25, 2005 from http://proquest.umi.com/pqdweb?index=0&did=
    910208871&SrchMode=1&sid=2&Fmt=3& VInst=PROD&VType=PQD&RQT=
    309&VName=PQD&TS=1131904285&clientId=3552

# PART III

# Retailing in Europe

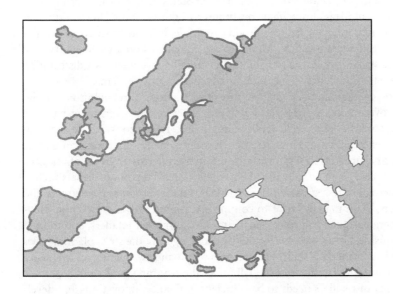

European retailing has been going through a transition in recent years. Retailers are experiencing the same type of consolidation that has already transformed other industries in Europe. The food retailing industry, except in the United Kingdom, is fragmented. Some of the biggest companies are privately held. Takeovers and mergers are occurring in Europe, resulting in greater market concentration held by fewer retailers.

Several characteristics of the retail industry within a country influence the adoption of new logistical technology. These characteristics are (1) scale, (2) concentration of ownership, (3) forms of business, (4) regulation, and (5) profitability. They provide a useful framework for looking at an initial picture of the retail industry in Europe.

The scale of retailing refers to the size of a country's population in relation to its retail sales. Germany and France are two of the most populated countries in Europe; they also have the most concentrated retail industries. Italy has a very unconcentrated retail industry. The Big Four (Germany, France, Italy, and the United Kingdom) account for over 80 percent of the retail sales within the European Union (EU).

Concentration of ownership in retailing is the size of the retailer in relation to sales. Large retailers use efficient logistics systems to capitalize on their economies of scale. These companies are also good candidates for technical innovation. The opposite is true if ownership is highly fragmented. Six of the top 25 retailers in the world are German (Metro, Aldi, Schwartz Unternehmens Treuhand KG, Rewe-Zentral AG, Edeka Zentrale AG & Co. KG, and Tengelmann Verwaltungs und Beteiligungs Gmbh).[1] There are no Italian companies on this list.

Approximately two-thirds of the U.K. stores are independently owned; however, nearly all Italian stores are independents. The United Kingdom averages 165 people per store; Italy, however, averages only 55 people for each store.[2]

Forms of retail business refers to organization. In Europe, retail organizations that are owned and operated as a group are called MULTIPLES. MULTIPLES are synonymous with the idea of chain stores in the United States. Different European countries have different ideas about what constitutes a multiple. In the United Kingdom ten outlets are required to consider a group a multiple. In some other countries, five outlets are considered a multiple. Multiples generally focus on a particular type of merchandise, such as food or electronics. They usually have their own distribution centers where they are likely to introduce innovative logistics systems.

Regulation of retailing refers to government restrictions of retail business activities. Most governments restrict retail activities. The French government has long restricted growth of large-scale retail stores. These regulations are designed to protect small entrepreneurs. However, there is some evidence that larger companies merge with smaller rivals in response, creating an even narrower group of retailers. The laws have also given an unplanned advantage to hard discount formats such as Aldi, who actually are a greater threat to small retailers than supermarkets and hypermarkets. Planning laws refer to commercial zoning restrictions. These planning laws were designed to protect small and medium sized retailers, and to keep the central business district viable. In the United Kingdom, the strict planning laws have pushed supermarkets and hypermarkets to expand by opening convenience stores, which are small enough not to fall under the planning guidelines.

Profitability of retailers needs to be sufficient to finance innovations and development. U.K. food retailing margins have traditionally been higher than those in other parts of Europe. However these margins have decreased recently because of price wars. The dominance of Tesco in the United Kingdom has created a unique market structure. U.K. retailers and Tesco, particularly, have moved private label from an alternative to national brands to a true retail brand, essentially developing corporate branding.

Germany and France represent highly regulated environments where retail expansion is limited to acquisitions. Both countries have laws that restrict the growth of large scale retailers, setting the stage for small format retailers like hard discounters to gain significant market share.

The southern European states are retail laggards. Government planning has contained growth. The emphasis there has been on protecting small and medium sized retailers. Portugal is the exception; they have embraced rapid retail development, increasing the number of shopping malls at a fast rate.

Central and Eastern Europe is the growth engine of Europe. Many Western European retailers have found an environment free of planning legislature. The multinational firms are dominant in most of the major Central and Eastern European capital cities. The continued growth will come from the smaller cities.

The European Union comprises 25 independent states founded to enhance political, economic, and social cooperation. This group was formerly known as the European Community (EC) or the European Economic Community (EEC). The union was founded in 1993; five new members joined in 1995 and ten additional countries joined the EU in 2004–2005. The EU now consists of Austria, Belgium, Cyprus (Greek part), Czech Republic, Denmark, Estonia, Finland, Germany, Greece, Hungary, Ireland, Italy, Latvia, Lithuania, Luxembourg, Malta, Netherlands, Poland, Portugal, Slovakia, Slovenia, Spain, Sweden, and the United Kingdom of Great Britain and Northern Ireland. On October 29, 2004, European heads of government and state signed the treaty establishing a constitution for Europe. This constitution has been ratified by 13 member states and is awaiting ratification by the others. However, this process slowed on May 29, 2005 when the majority of French voters rejected the constitution. Within a few days the Netherlands voters also rejected the constitution.

The final step toward achieving European unification has been the adoption of a single currency system, the euro, by twelve countries (Belgium, Germany, Greece, Spain, France, Ireland, Italy, Luxembourg, the Netherlands, Austria, Portugal, and Finland). Instead of having German marks and French francs, all purchases are made in euros. Achieving a single currency is not as simple as just making the decision to begin printing euros instead of marks. Monetary unification is the process of using one currency throughout the EU countries. The economic environment within each country must be very stable before successful monetary unification can occur. Some countries such as the United Kingdom have opted out of the euro. They want to maintain the right to alter economic situations by altering their fiscal policy.

Countries tinker with their domestic currency to achieve economic objectives. The five economic criteria established by the Maastricht Treaty in 1992 are:

1. Annual inflation must not exceed that of the three best performing nations by more than 1.5 percent.
2. Public-sector budget deficit must not exceed 3 percent of gross domestic product (GDP).
3. Public sector debt must not exceed 80 percent of GDP.
4. Long-term interest rates must not exceed those of the three nations with the best inflation performance by more than two percentage points.
5. The exchange rate has to be kept within normal bands of the European Exchange Rate Mechanism (ERM) for the previous two years.[3]

These economic performance criterion are difficult to achieve. Perhaps you have been to a circus that included a horseback riding act. Two horses canter around the ring side by side while a rider moves from one horse to the other, hangs upside down between them, and generally performs amazing feats. For this act to be performed successfully, the two horses must have the same rhythm in their stride; their legs must extend in unison; and their strides must be equal. This type of harmonizing is required for a country to move from a national currency to a common currency.

Romania and Bulgaria are scheduled to join the EU in 2007, providing that they can meet the terms required by the Treaty of Accession. Turkey is an official candidate to join the EU, but they need to complete economic and social reforms to qualify for membership. Turkey has implemented permanent policies on human rights, abolished the death penalty, granted cultural rights to its large Kurdish minority, and taken steps to solve the Cyprus issue. But the country has faced opposition from France, Germany, Austria, and Cyprus because of its religious and cultural differences. If Turkey joins the EU, it will be the first Muslim country admitted.

Like much of the world, some areas of Europe are experiencing a recession. Most parts of Europe entered the recession later than the United States, and they will probably exit the recession much later. The next four chapters focus on retailing in Europe. Chapter 11 starts with the countries of northern Europe—Great Britain, the Netherlands, and Belgium. Germany and France are featured in Chapter 12. The southern European countries of Spain, Italy, Greece, and Portugal are discussed in Chapter 13. In Chapter 14, the central and eastern European countries, the new Europe, are considered.

## ❯ ENDNOTES

1. 2006 Global Powers of Retailing (2006). Deloitte, January.
2. Cooper, J., M. Browne, and M. Peters. (1991). *European Logistics.* Oxford, UK: Blackwell Publishers.
3. Kamm, T. (1995). "Monetary Chaos Precedes Europe's Single Market." *Wall Street Journal.* July 28, p. A6.

# 11

# RETAILING IN THE UNITED KINGDOM, THE NETHERLANDS, AND BELGIUM

## After reading this chapter, you should understand

> How government regulations affect retail expansion.

> The effect of an oligopoly situation in the United Kingdom and how dominant firms can control and modify the retail system.

> The strategy used by retailers with private label food products in the United Kingdom and how this positioning can be used successfully in other countries.

> Why retailers in the United Kingdom, the Netherlands, and Belgium have expanded internationally.

The three countries included in this chapter share a similar cultural background. The English Channel is all that separates the United Kingdom from Belgium and the Netherlands. Although the three countries do not share a common language, most residents of Belgium and the Netherlands speak a second language, and it is often English. Belgium and the Netherlands are very small countries. They have become world traders to survive. Their major retailers have also expanded internationally, because their home markets became saturated. All three countries have used restrictive legislature to protect small retailers. In Belgium this restrictive legislature makes domestic expansion nearly impossible.

I will start the discussion with the United Kingdom. The retail industry there is large, mature, and stable. The study of retailing occurs at a variety of British universities; some of the best international retailing research has come from professors there. With so much information about retailing available, it can be difficult to select information that distinguishes the industry. I have chosen to focus on the retail characteristics of food and nonfood retailers. The next sections of the chapter discuss retailing in the Netherlands and in Belgium.

## > UNITED KINGDOM (UK)

### Country Background

The United Kingdom is separated geographically and psychologically from the rest of Europe. The Celts arrived on the island about 1000 B.C. Julius Caesar led the Romans to the area in 50 B.C., beginning a period of Roman rule that lasted about 500 years, until the Germanic Anglos and Saxons raided the island and forced the Romans to withdraw. In the centuries that followed, the Danish Vikings attacked the Anglo-Saxon settlements periodically. Then, in 1066 French-speaking followers of William the Conqueror defeated the Anglo-Saxons at the Battle of Hastings. Modern Britain carries remembrances from each of these invading groups. Finally, in the fifteenth century, the people we know today as the English gained control and established the English crown.

The English were great explorers, claiming the world's most extensive overseas empire. They fought the Spanish, the French, and finally the colonies that became known as the United States. At about the time of the American Revolution, Britain was experiencing the first phases of the Industrial Revolution.

The 1900s became the "British Century." Britain became the world's leading manufacturing and trading country. In addition, the British were the dominant world power, creating an empire that at its height encompassed a quarter of the world's land area. By the end of World War II, nearly all of the nations that had flown the British flag became independent nations. However, most have remained members of the British Commonwealth.[1]

The United Kingdom includes England, Scotland, Wales, and Northern Ireland. London is the capital and business center. The major retail centers are Birmingham, in the middle part of the country; Manchester, in the northwest; and Newcastle, in the northeast. Glasgow is the major retail center in Scotland, and Belfast is the center of retailing in Northern Ireland. Because the southeastern portion of the United

Kingdom has greater population density and wealth, most retailers have the bulk of their stores there.[2]

The United Kingdom has experienced low inflation, high employment, and sustained consumer confidence despite the global economic downturn. Economic growth has remained strong in the 5–6 percent annual growth rate. One troubling feature is the level of consumer debt, often fueled by borrowing against real estate. Inflation has remained under 3 percent for the past few years.[3] We will start our discussion with the food retailing situation in the United Kingdom. U.K. food retailers are perhaps the best in the world. They have the power in the distribution system. Private label is prominent in this system. Tables 11.1 and 11.2 summarize the major retailers and foreign retailers in the U.K.

## Food Retailing

The retail industry in the United Kingdom is highly competitive. Retailers operate in an environment of price rollbacks, promotions, and heavy discounts. The industry is engaged in massive consolidation, meaning that there are fewer companies with greater market clout. The most important market trend in the last decade has been the dominance of Tesco. During 2001–2003 they grew 91 percent in terms of sales and 87 percent in profits.[4] Although this company began as a supermarket retailer, their more recent activities have been in the development of a convenience store sector and the movement toward more nonfood sales. Tesco bought the T&S convenience chain in 2002. They plan to develop the 850 chains into T&S One Stop. T&S One Stop stores are primarily neighborhood shops selling candy, news, tobacco, and impulse buys. They will increase One Stop's product offering to include video rental, greeting cards, and gifts. About a quarter of the current T&S One Stop shops will be converted to Tesco's other small format offering, Metro Express. Metro Express is essentially a small format food store carrying a range of grocery items like fresh produce and meats.

Tesco has gained market share by price-cutting across the board, but mainly in food. They are also developing a focus on non-food. Its clothing—Cherokee, Florence + Fred—are some of the fastest growing lines in the United Kingdom.

Tesco gets 80 percent of their sales from the United Kingdom, controlling one quarter of the retail food market.[5] Tesco is developing a worldwide sourcing system with hubs in Bagalore (India), Bangkok (Thailand), and Hong Kong. These hubs are linked through technology, allowing the company to source goods from anywhere in the world and track their progress. Tesco has adopted a development strategy of rapid expansion, not only in the U.K. convenience market, but also internationally. In 2003, Tesco opened 22 hypermarkets in Europe, mainly in Ireland and Central and Eastern Europe, giving the group the largest portfolio of hypermarkets across Central and Eastern Europe.[6] I will discuss their strategy in greater detail in Chapter 14, Central and Eastern Europe.

Tesco Extra is the company's food/nonfood hypermarket concept. Although in the United Kingdom Tesco is predominantely known as a supermarket, their international expansion has been largely as a hypermarket. This model is what they are now introducing into the United Kingdom. Tesco began opening Extra hypermarkets in 1998, and they now have 119. This growth has been accomplished by a

**Table 11.1**
**United Kingdom—Leading Domestic Retailers, 2004**

| Company | Primary Line of Trade | Total Sales and Stores | | | Global Rank and Penetration | | | Domestic Market | |
|---|---|---|---|---|---|---|---|---|---|
| | | Net Sales ($US Mil) | % Chg Sales | Total Stores | 2004 Rank, Top 200 Retailers Worldwide | Single-country, Regional or Global? | Number of countries | Share of total sales | Share of total stores |
| 1 Tesco PLC | Supermarkets/Grocery Stores | 62,274 | 10.5% | 2,365 | 5 | Global | 13 | 77% | 75% |
| 2 J Sainsbury PLC | Supermarkets/Grocery Stores | 27,337 | 4.9% | 727 | 28 | Single Country | 1 | 100% | 100% |
| 3 Wal-Mart (ASDA)[1] | Supermarkets/Grocery Stores | 26,425 | 8.5% | 283 | — | Single Country | 1 | 100% | 100% |
| 4 Wm Morrison Supermarkets PLC | Supermarkets/Grocery Stores | 22,209 | 145.1% | 498 | 33 | Regional | 2 | 99% | 96% |
| 5 Marks & Spencer PLC | Department Stores | 14,133 | -1.5% | 675 | 49 | Global | 32 | 91% | 66% |
| 6 Kingfisher PLC | DIY/Home Improvement Stores | 14,022 | 8.7% | 599 | 50 | Global | 9 | 56% | 57% |
| 7 Dixons Group | Consumer Electronics & Appliances | 12,800 | 7.6% | 1,450 | 56 | Regional | 14 | 69% | 71% |
| 8 GUS plc | Hardlines Specialty Stores | 10,913 | 7.9% | 1,444 | 70 | Global | 4 | 93% | 68% |
| 9 John Lewis Partnership PLC | Supermarkets/Grocery Stores | 8,720 | 5.7% | 192 | 87 | Single Country | 1 | 100% | 100% |
| 10 The Boots Company PLC | Drug Stores | 8,611 | 3.9% | 1,877 | 89 | Global | 11 | 99% | 75% |
| 11 Somerfield PLC | Supermarkets/Grocery Stores | 8,573 | 4.3% | 1,308 | 90 | Single Country | 1 | 100% | 100% |
| 12 Kesa Electricals | Consumer Electronics & Appliances | 7,257 | 5.0% | 800 | 106 | Regional | 6 | 39% | 31% |
| 13 The Co-operative Group | Supermarkets/Grocery Stores | 6,326 | -1.1% | 2,178 | 116 | Single Country | 1 | 100% | 100% |
| 14 NEXT PLC | Apparel Stores | 4,749 | 22.5% | 428 | 142 | Global | 14 | 99.0% | 83.6% |
| 15 Woolworths Group plc | Discount Department Stores | 4,169 | -1.3% | 905 | 155 | Single Country | 1 | 100% | 100% |
| 16 Littlewoods Retail Ltd. | Non-Store | 3,666 | 8.4% | 171 | 170 | Single Country | 1 | 100% | 100% |
| 17 Debenhams plc | Department Stores | 3,488 | 5.1% | 118 | 177 | Global | 12 | N/A | 88% |
| 18 HMV Group plc | Book & Multimedia | 3,456 | 5.1% | 588 | 180 | Global | 7 | 73% | 66% |
| 19 Arcadia Group | Apparel Stores | 3,038 | 0.5% | 2,250 | 197 | Global | 31 | 93.0% | 91% |
| 20 WH Smith PLC | Book & Multimedia | 2,663 | -0.7% | 673 | — | Single Country | 1 | 100% | 100% |

[1] Wal-Mart (ASDA) is included on the list as an exception because its parent is U.S.-based.

Sources: Retail Forward, company annual reports and published reports

**Table 11.2**
**United Kingdom—Key Foreign Retailers, 2004**

| Company | Headquarters | Retail Sector | Primary Line of Trade | Global Rank and Penetration | | |
|---|---|---|---|---|---|---|
| | | | | Top 200 Retailers Worldwide | 2004 Rank, Single-country, Regional or Global? | Number of countries |
| Aeon Co., Ltd. | Japan | Softgoods | General Merchandise Stores | 19 | Global | 11 |
| Aldi Group | Germany | FDM | Discount Food Stores | 13 | Global | 13 |
| Amazon.com | United States | Homegoods | Non-Store | 111 | Global | 7 |
| Bertelsmann AG | Germany | Homegoods | Non-Store | 215 | Global | 22 |
| Borders Group Inc. | United States | Homegoods | Book & Multimedia | 164 | Global | 5 |
| Cora Group/Louis Delhaize | France | Homegoods | Supermarkets/Grocery Stores | 65 | Global | 7 |
| Costco Companies, Inc. | United States | FDM | Cash & Carries/Warehouse Clubs | 9 | Global | 7 |
| Dansk Supermarked A/S | Denmark | FDM | Discount Stores | 100 | Regional | 5 |
| Defense Commissary Agency | United States | FDM | Supermarkets/Grocery Stores | 130 | Global | 13 |
| Fast Retailing | Japan | Softgoods | Apparel Stores | 194 | Global | 3 |
| Hutchison Whampoa Limited | Hong Kong | FDM | Drug Stores | 77 | Global | 18 |
| IKEA AB | Sweden | Homegoods | Furniture & Home Furnishings | 44 | Global | 32 |
| INDITEX Group (i.e., Zara) | Spain | Softgoods | Apparel Stores | 110 | Global | 56 |
| La Senza Corp. | Canada | Softgoods | Other Apparel Specialty Stores | — | Global | 18 |
| Liberty Media Corp. (QVC) | United States | Homegoods | Non-Store | 121 | Global | 4 |
| Mango | Spain | Softgoods | Apparel Stores | — | Global | 76 |
| Metro AG | Germany | FDM | Cash & Carries/Warehouse Clubs | 4 | Global | 29 |
| Mitsukoshi Ltd. | Japan | Softgoods | Department Stores | 98 | Global | 9 |
| Otto Group | Germany | Softgoods | Non-Store | 61 | Global | 19 |
| Pinault-Printemps-Redoute SA | France | Softgoods | Non-Store | 36 | Global | 17 |
| Schwarz Group | Germany | FDM | Discount Food Stores | 12 | Regional | 19 |
| Staples, Inc. | United States | Homegoods | Office Supply | 47 | Global | 18 |
| Toys "R" Us, Inc. | United States | Homegoods | Toy Stores | 68 | Global | 30 |
| Wal-Mart Stores, Inc. | United States | FDM | Hypermarkets/Supercenters | 1 | Global | 11 |
| Whole Foods Market Inc. | United States | FDM | Supermarkets/Grocery Stores | 165 | Global | 3 |

Sources: Retail Forward, company annual reports and published reports

**Photo 11.1**
Tesco's one-stop stores dominate the convenience store market. *Courtesy of Condé Nast.*

combination of new construction and the expansion of existing superstores. Planning permission for superstore extensions/rebuilds is relatively easy to obtain.

Tesco's dominance in the United Kingdom has led some, including Wal-Mart, to call for government intervention in their growth. It is likely that if they made an attempt to acquire another retailer they would be denied this option; however, their

**Photo 11.2**
Tesco Extra combines food and nonfood products in a hypermarket that reflects the company's international expansion goals. *Courtesy of Tesco.*

current mode of growth is to refurbish currently existing stores, bringing them more in line with the hypermarket concept they perfected overseas. Tesco has adopted a variety of formats for the international markets in Thailand, South Korea, and Hungary. They use a four-stage entry process:

Stage 1: Small entry vehicle acquisition. In other words the purchase of an existing company.

Stage 2: New "battleship" Greenfield site hypermarket development program. These are usually high-quality strategic locations. Greenfield development means that they build their own stores.

State 3: Once a critical mass of hypermarkets is achieved, a dedicated supply chain and distribution infrastructure is developed.

Stage 4: Multi-format and in-fill site expansion—smaller hypermarkets, supermarkets, and/or convenience stores (e.g., Express). At this stage there is movement to smaller towns.[7]

Tesco looks for new markets that have most of the following characteristics:

> A stable, consumer-oriented market with good prospects for long-term growth
> A big market with a young/growing population and a growing middle class
> A small entry vehicle acquisition/JV partner to smooth the introduction into the market and help Tesco navigate around the various language, bureaucracy, labor, legal competition, and planning issues
> A liberal planning viewpoint
> A relative lack of organized modern retail competition[8]

ASDA began as a dairy farm, then moved into wholesale and retail outlets for milk and milk products. ASDA (The Associated Dairies and Farm Stores) grew from a few shops into the second-largest food retailer in the United Kingdom. When a new CEO took over ASDA in 1991, he created a classic turnaround story by consciously imitating and borrowing from Wal-Mart. He copied things like

**Photo 11.3**
ASDA reflects the policies, philosophy, and technology of its parent company, Wal-Mart. It has developed from a food retailer into a one-stop shop with non-food products that include a clothing line. *Courtesy of Corbis; photographer: Alex Smailes.*

everyday low price, rollback prices, huddles, greeters, and smileys).[9] Acquired by Wal-Mart in 1999, ASDA has 13 percent market share[10] and represents Wal-Mart's largest international market. George is ASDA's private label and they have begun opening stand-alone George stores to feature the product. Their intent is to make George competitive with the cheap chic fashion specialty retailers like H&M, Zara, and Mango. George apparel line was created by George Davis, who previously launched NEXT and is now revamping the Una brand at Marks & Spencer. In 2004, ASDA announced that they will be creating George Global, designed to take George throughout the world. Just recently the U.K. government approved supermarkets' extended sale of pharmacy products and ASDA will also be investing in this area. Because planning laws have made it difficult for retailers to expand, some companies have been adding mezzanines to their stores to get additional space.[11] Wal-Mart has introduced their information technology systems to ASDA, making them much more efficient. Wal-Mart also has introduced its vendor process, putting immense pressure on suppliers to reduce price. ASDA has adopted a tri-level retailer brand strategy using ASDA, ASDA Extra Special, and ASDA Smart Price to differentiate the three levels of their private offering. Even the George apparel line has been subdivided in the United Kingdom into George, George Collection, and George Essentials to reflect various price points.

Burt and Sparks claim that the real contribution that Wal-Mart has made to ASDA is in the nonfood sector, particularly pharmacy, film processing, and clothing. This sector, in addition to the health and beauty segments, has been strengthened through price reductions and **RANGE EXTENSIONS,** expanding the product line, for instance, a grocery store moving into health and beauty products. Since Wal-Mart's takeover in 1999, prices in the United Kingdom have been lowered. ASDA Wal-Mart has generated a **MARKET SPOILER** effect similar to what Wal-Mart has done in the United States.[12] Through price competition a company requires their competitors to follow suit, essentially reducing the profitability for all players. When I talked about oligopoly market structures in Chapter 1, I said that if price competition is used in a market like this it will create price wars. And that is what has happened.

Sainsbury was once the top retailer in the United Kingdom but now they are in the number three spot, behind Tesco and ASDA. In 2004 they sold their Shaw's chain in the United States to Albertsons. Sainsbury is using this money to develop operations in the United Kingdom. One of the areas where they are developing is a convenience store chain called Local, which is teaming up with Shell gas stations. Sainsbury has also acquired two convenience store chains, Bells (54 stores) and Jacksons (114 stores). They also acquired 14 stores from Morrisons. Sainsbury has replaced its Jeff & Co private label line with a line called Tu, which means "you" in French, Italian, and Spanish.[13]

Wm. Morrison supermarkets acquired Safeway in 2004, making it the fourth-largest supermarket group in the United Kigdom. Safeway had about 480 stores, which is three times the size of Wm. Morrison. They are making a bid to take over Sainsbury's number three spot by aggressive pricing.

These retailers create an oligopoly market situation. They are highly competitive, but until the take over of ASDA by Wal-Mart, they did not have price-focused competition. When Wal-Mart entered the industry they launched a price competition, and the result has been a price war. In the first chapter of this book I talked about the unique aspects of an oligopoly market situation. In general price is not a competitive issue, because the result is a price war. If price is used as a competitive weapon, it would be initiated by the dominant firm. This presents an interesting situation in the United Kingdom, because Tesco is the local dominant firm, but ASDA, backed by Wal-Mart, has the largest pockets world wide. ASDA began the price war, knowing that they had the financial capital to sustain their efforts. This is a unique example of how a company not locally dominant can be an effective price leader because of their power elsewhere.

BP, a major UK oil company, has opened 90 Connect convenience stores attached to their petrol stations (forecourts). They plan to add 300 more shops in an attempt to take market share away from Tesco and Sainsbury. Safeway also launched a new Citystore convenience store format. It is aiming at urban centers and business hubs. Boots is launching a new Work Convenience store format targeting city workers. Supermarket chain Somerfield is acquiring abut 100 forecourt retailers. They have partnered with Martins, primarily a newspaper seller, to develop a combined product offering.[14]

Hard discounters have a small presence in the United Kingdom, which should increase the competitive pressure on price. Both Aldi and Lidl, because of their concentration on a limited number of SKUs, have immense purchasing power. Aldi and Lidl have 700–1,200 SKUs compared to Wal-Mart, which carries 28,000 to 125,000 SKUs. This makes the hard discounter's purchasing per SKU several times that of Wal-Mart. Like Wal-Mart, Aldi and Lidl use this power to get suppliers to reduce their prices.[15]

Marks & Spencer is opening food-only stores in high street locations. There are about 30 of these Simply Food formats. Marks & Spencer has a very good reputation in food. On one trip to the United Kingdom my son and I were staying close to their main Marks & Spencer store. I was busy doing research, so I sent him to Marks & Spencer to pick up something for us to eat. He came back with a variety of prepared meals and tiramisu for dessert. Everything was very good, but the tiramisu was expectional. A couple of days later we decided to do the same thing. This time he returned frustrated; they had sold out of the tiramisu. He said, "Next time we do this I will have to be there earlier to make sure that I get the tiramisu." This is an example of the strategy that Marks & Spencer has used in developing their food offering. Their intent is to sell through the fresh items by the end of the day. My son's reaction is exactly what they want to generate, a feeling that the customer should get there quickly because the best might be gone.

Farmers' markets have been growing in the United Kingdom, largely because of consumers' concerns about genetically modified foods. These markets allow consumers to purchase fruit, vegetables, dairy, meat, and baked goods directly from the producer. Most markets have a requirement that the farmer must be local, usually within 50 miles, and that everything has to be grown by the supplier.[16]

U.K. retailers have upgraded their range of retailer brand, from a traditional low price/low quality positioning to a high quality/value for money retailer brand. This brand is slightly less expensive than the leading manufacturer brand. This repositioning has resulted in the retailer brand being viewed as a brand in its own right. Retailers have also made major investments in new product ranges, packaging, and labeling innovations. The positioning has changed consumer perception of the retailer brand from that of an alternative product option to that of a brand choice option.[17]

## Private Label/Retail Branding

Britain is Europe's largest private label market, with 40 percent of private label sales in Europe. There has been a shift toward premiumisation in private label. Major retailers are developing premium and organic private label. Tesco's Finest and Sainsbury's Taste the Difference have developed a recognition factor comparable to many of the U.K.'s top brands. The distinction between manufacturers' brands and retail brands is becoming blurred. More manufacturers are seeing the value of aligning themselves with a particular supermarket. Proctor & Gamble launched Physique through Tesco, giving the supermarket the exclusive rights to distribute the line. This saved the company millions of pounds in advertising and marketing expenditure because the supermarket promoted the product in-store and through its consumer magazine. Later Unilever struck up a deal with Sainsbury. Both of these examples show how much power the U.K. supermarkets have.[18]

Burt and Sparks make a solid argument that the retailer has become the brand in U.K. food retailing. Retailers invest in a variety of activities which provide "value added" in the eyes of consumers and which align strategic vision with the internal culture and external image.[19] CORPORATE BRANDING is an alignment of vision (top management's aspirations for the company), culture (the organization's values, behaviors, and attitudes—the way employees throughout the organization feel about the company they work for), and image (the outside world's overall impression of the company—including customers, shareholders, media and the general public).[20] Table 11.3 contains a typology of how retail brands develop. The corporate brand is the fifth generation of brand development.

Tesco is an excellent example of a corporate brand. Years ago Tesco was just a supermarket, stocking manufacturer's products. Now they have a distinct position as a major force in their own right, with the brand providing meaning and values internally and externally. Tesco's aim is to "grow a business to create value for customers to earn their lifetime loyalty." The retailer brand product strategy has been transformed (Table 11.4).[21]

The UK has a unique situation in that the food retailers are very powerful, this leads to interesting retailer-supplier relations. In the next few sections I will discuss how this section affects the channel.

## Power and Competition in the UK Food Industry

The top four retailers in the UK control 80% of the retail food sales. Power in the UK distribution system shifted from branded goods manufacturers toward retailers. When retailers begin to compete as brands, instead of just traders it provides them with a variety of important market information and that is power. The UK grocery channel has taken on the characteristics of an ADMINISTERED VERTICAL MARKETING SYSTEM. Administered vertical marketing systems are when there is coordination of the supply chain. Retailers moved away from conventional relationships in which channel members are loosely focused the DYADIC RELATIONSHIPS with the next channel member. Dyadic relationships are pairs of relationships such as retail buyer-supplier, retailer-consumer. The conventional relationship allows for inefficiencies in channel functions and activities by having different functions and activities replicated by various channel members. Relationships in the conventional system are characterized by short-term interactions. Remember when I talked

**Table 11.3**
**Typology of Retail Brands**

|  | 1st Generation | 2nd Generation | 3rd Generation | 4th Generation | 5th Generation |
|---|---|---|---|---|---|
| **Branding form** | Generic; no name; brand free; unbranded | Own label; unsupported own brand | Supported own brand | Extended retailer brand, i.e., segmented retail brands | Corporate brand |
| **Strategy** | Generic | Low price copy | Me-too copy of major brands | Value-added | Corporate positioning |
| **Objective** | Increase margins; provide choice in pricing | Increase margins; reduce manufacturers' power by setting the entry price; provide better-value product (quality/price) | Enhance category margins; expand product assortment, i.e., Customer choice; build retailer's image among consumers | Increase and retain the customer base; enhance category margins; improve image further; differentiation | Produce strong positive identity and practice; first choice for consumers; satisfy stakeholders |
| **Product** | Basic and functional products; commodities | Staple or basic lines with a large volume | Big category products; major sale items | Image-forming product groups; large number of products with small volume (niche) | The corporation and its tangible and intangible attributes |
| **Technology** | Simple production process and basic technology | Technology lagging behind market leaders | Close to the brand leader | Innovative technology and processes | Stakeholder relationship management |
| **Quality/image** | Lower quality and inferior image compared to the manufacturers' brands | Medium quality but still perceived as lower than leading manufacturers' brands; secondary brand alongside the leading manufacturer's brand | Comparable to the brand leaders | Same or better than brand leader; innovative and different products from brand leaders | Quality and consistency throughout the organization |
| **Price position** | 20% or more below the brand leader | 10–20% below | 5–10% below | Equal or higher than known brand | Focus on delivering value |
| **Consumers' motivation to buy** | Price is the main criterion for buying | Price is still important | Both quality and price, i.e., value for money | Better and unique products | Trust |
| **Supplier** | National, not specialized | National, partly specializing to own label manufacturing | National, mostly specializing for own brand manufacturing | International, manufacturing mostly own brands | Innovative partnerships |

Source: Adapted from Laaksonen and Reynolds (1994) and Dawson (2001) for generations 1 to 4.

**Table 11.4**
**Corporate Brand Consumer Relationship Extension**

| Activity | Example | Tesco Example |
|---|---|---|
| Building transaction and information linkages | POS, loyalty cards | Tesco clubcard, Tesco personal finance, Cashback, location maps |
| Extending and deepening infrastructure links | In-store branding, new store formats, new infrastructure | Tesco Extra, Metro, Express etc. formats, Tesco.net, Tesco Direct, Tesco.com |
| Operational links for customers | Consistency of high service performance | "One in front" campaign, "Every little helps," first class service |
| Personal/face to face links | Staff interaction with customers | Service areas, e.g., butchers, customer service desks, customer panels and question time |
| Service or expertise links | 0–800 lines, development of clubs | Baby club, wine club, pharmacy, recipe cards |
| Cementing financial links | Direct financial services | Tesco personal finance, including insurance, pensions, credit cards, Tesco banking |
| Building emotional links | Lifestyle advertising, customer information, trust | Television advertising, finest products, healthy eating leaflets, computers for schools, championing "grey" market goods and reduced brand prices |
| Searching for event links | In-store activities, sponsorship of events, local charity activity | Collection schemes, for sale wall, local event details in store, Millennium Dome sponsorship |
| Have usage links | Convenience products | "Grab and Go" areas, newspaper and lottery areas, 24-hour opening |
| Media communications links | Traditional and Internet | Corporate affairs activities |
| Distribution and availability links | Format development, home delivery, catalogues | Tesco Direct, Tesco Clothing Catalogue, Tesco specialist magazines, e.g., *Vegetarian*, Internet cafes in store, Tesco ISP |

Source: Activity and example columns adapted from Mitchell (1999).

about discrete versus continuous transactions. We refer to discrete transactions as markets and continuous transactions as hierarchies. In contrast, in the administered vertical-marketing system all the channel members are aligned. These types of channels are based on information sharing; they are collaborative and tend to be long term. Administered systems contain power relationships, but the use of power is altered.[22]

An oligopoly such as the U.K. food retailing industry could take on dimensions of a monopoly or duopoly if one or two chains have the market power to maintain their position at the expense of others. Increasing scale used in efficient and appropriate operation and investment provides benefits to consumers. Greater efficiency allows costs to fall across the organization and provides money for further investment. Burt and Sparks refer to this as a CIRCLE OF GROWTH. The circle of growth is driven by scale, investment, and efficient asset use and develops at both outlet and organizational levels. Some companies experience faster rates of sales growth than others; then the circle becomes a SPIRAL OF GROWTH. As the spiral of growth turns

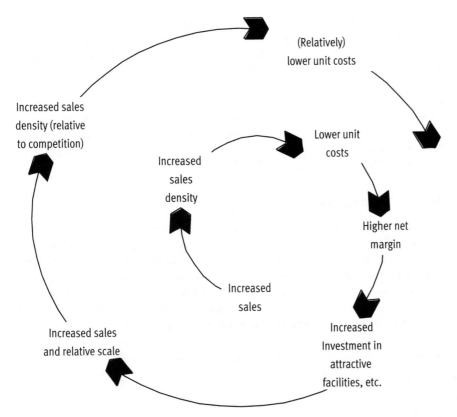

Figure 11.1
The Spiral of Growth

faster, **BARRIERS TO ENTRY** are raised, making it difficult for less competitive organizations to stay on the spiral.[23] It becomes difficult for other companies to enter a market, generally because the costs are too great.

Burt and Sparks go on to explain how U.K. food retailing experienced this phenomenon. Large stores built out-of-town benefit from lower costs because of lower occupancy costs and lower operating and distribution costs that are spread across greater sales. These advantages are in conjunction with being able to provide greater customer benefits such as wider product ranges, easier access and parking, and longer trading hours add to increased sales. Sales increase, sales density (sales per square foot) increase, and unit costs come down, allowing the company to increase their investment in existing and new sites.[24]

## Dominant Chains Market Behavior

Power can allow a dominant chain to manage competition in two directions: **VERTICAL COMPETITION**, achieved through supply chain management, and **HORIZONTAL COMPETITION**, achieved through raising a rival's costs and creating barriers to entry. Like the concept of vertical integration, the concept of vertical competition is achieved from either extending backward to the supply chain, or forward to the consumer. Horizontal competition is directed at firms that are at the same level of the distribution channel; this would be retailer to retailer. Burt and Sparks maintain that these two concepts need to be considered in unison in the case of a market structure like the United Kingdom. One way for a dominant firm to evolve is by using its market power to increase the attractiveness of its offer to consumers while driving up the cost base for competitors. An example of this would be enhancing their physical facilities. The dominant firm would be willing and able to drive up operating costs and take a reduced margin in the short run in the hope of the long-term gain of market dominance. These behaviors then become the industry norm. A dominant firm, or two, can become powerful enough to dictate the competitive behaviors of others, establishing both the competitive agenda and cost structures in the sector.[25] Table 11.5 shows the national market share change from 1991–1999.

## Vertical Competition

The cost of goods sold is the biggest expense for a retailer, accounting for 75–80 percent of U.K. groceries' business sales. After the removal of retail price maintenance (RPM), retailers are free to negotiate supply deals and manage prices and margins. Centralized buying allows retailers to gain greater scope to negotiate deals based on volume. Information management is another important feature of a vertically administered system. Investment in information technology (IT) provides improved monitoring of product movement through the supply chain. This coupled with

**Table 11.5**
**Changes in National Market Share (%) Over Time**

| | Taylor Nelson Sofres data | | | | | | | | | |
|---|---|---|---|---|---|---|---|---|---|---|
| Company | 1991 | 1992 | 1993 | 1994 | 1995 | 1996 | 1997 | 1998 | 1999 | % Change 1991–1999 |
| Tesco | 14.0 | 14.3 | 14.9 | 15.7 | 18.1 | 19.0 | 20.0 | 20.9 | 21.1 | +50.7 |
| Sainsbury | 16.5 | 16.9 | 17.3 | 17.0 | 17.5 | 17.4 | 17.0 | 18.0 | 17.6 | +6.7 |
| ASDA | 8.4 | 8.2 | 8.4 | 8.9 | 9.7 | 10.8 | 11.5 | 12.2 | 12.7 | +51.2 |
| Safeway | 8.0 | 8.1 | 8.6 | 8.5 | 8.4 | 9.0 | 9.4 | 9.5 | 9.3 | +16.3 |
| CR4 | 46.9 | 47.5 | 49.2 | 50.1 | 53.7 | 56.2 | 57.9 | 60.6 | 60.7 | +29.4 |
| Somerfield | 4.6 | 4.4 | 4.8 | 5.2 | 4.9 | 4.5 | 4.5 | 4.3 | 4.1 | −98.0* |
| Kwik Save | 4.3 | 5.3 | 5.8 | 5.6 | 5.5 | 5.5 | 4.9 | 4.5 | — | — |
| Morrisons | 1.8 | 2.2 | 2.7 | 2.9 | 3.3 | 3.5 | 3.4 | 3.7 | 4.1 | +127.8 |

| | IGD data | | | | | | | | | |
|---|---|---|---|---|---|---|---|---|---|---|
| Company | 1991 | 1992 | 1993 | 1994 | 1995 | 1996 | 1997 | 1998 | 1999 | 2000 | % Change 1991–2000 |
| Tesco | 9.9 | 10.1 | 10.4 | 11.4 | 13.4 | 14.2 | 14.8 | 15.2 | 15.6 | 16.2 | +63.6 |
| Sainsbury | 11.3 | 11.9 | 12.1 | 12.3 | 12.2 | 12.2 | 12.4 | 12.2 | 11.8 | 11.5 | +1.7 |
| ASDA | 6.5 | 6.3 | 6.5 | 6.7 | 7.2 | 7.8 | 8.3 | 8.4 | 9.1 | 9.5 | +46.2 |
| Safeway | 7.2 | 7.3 | 7.5 | 7.6 | 7.3 | 7.6 | 7.6 | 7.6 | 7.4 | 7.5 | +4.2 |
| CR4 | 34.9 | 35.6 | 36.5 | 38.0 | 40.1 | 41.8 | 43.1 | 43.8 | 43.9 | 44.7 | +28.1 |
| Somerfield | 4.7 | 4.3 | 4.3 | 4.4 | 4.2 | 4.0 | 3.85 | 6.9 | 6.1 | 5.0 | −36.7* |
| Kwik Save | 3.2 | 3.8 | 4.1 | 4.0 | 4.2 | 4.1 | 3.5 | — | — | — | — |
| M&S | 3.2 | 3.0 | 3.1 | 3.1 | 3.0 | 3.1 | 3.0 | 2.9 | 2.9 | 2.85 | −12.5 |
| Morrisons | 1.7 | 1.7 | 1.9 | 2.2 | 2.4 | 2.5 | 2.5 | 2.6 | 3.0 | 3.3 | +94.1 |
| Waitrose | 1.7 | 1.7 | 1.6 | 1.6 | 1.7 | 1.8 | 1.8 | 1.8 | 1.9 | 2.0 | +15.0 |
| Iceland | 1.3 | 1.5 | 1.6 | 1.7 | 1.7 | 1.7 | 1.6 | 1.7 | 1.7 | 1.7 | +30.8 |

Note: *Somerfield percentage changes based on Somerfield and Kwik Save share in 1991.

centralized distribution and superior logistics systems allows better efficiency gains. The centralized logistics systems of Tesco and Wal-Mart make great use of this strategic tool.[26]

Viewing the channel as a single system, costs can be shifted to the lowest cost provider, such as THIRD PARTY LOGISTICS suppliers. These are specialized companies who provide logistics support to customers. Larger companies reduce the number of suppliers by DELISTING those who cannot add enough benefit, thereby reducing the supplier list to a limited number of dedicated providers. Delisting means that a company is taken off the supplier list. This behavior influences the structure of the supply side of the market through increased supplier dependency and an increase in costs for other suppliers who do not enjoy the economies of scale of the dominant firm.[27]

PRODUCT RANGE ENHANCEMENTS are possible in the vertically administered system because the retailer works in close collaboration with the supplier to provide truly unique retail brands characterized by high quality and innovative products. These enhancements have been a feature of the U.K. retail brands. New product ranges such as ready-to-eat meals have been introduced to the British consumers through retailer brands rather than manufacturer brands.[28]

## Horizontal Competition

In horizontal relationships the dominant firm could use its market power to invest in activities that would grow sales and sales density by appealing to consumers' needs, which would then add to brand building. Some of the ways that a retailer might accomplish this are through 1) above average capital investment programs, 2) service additions, 3) premium labor costs, 4) increased expenditure on promotional spending/brand-building, and 4) customer retention/loyalty card initiatives. Again I refer back to the Burt and Sparks article for a description of these activities.

ABOVE-AVERAGE CAPITAL INVESTMENT PROGRAMS    The development of an oligopoly market situation means that the major retailers are pursuing a similar strategy, opening out-of-town superstores, which can increase costs for all. The stores are competing for the same desirable locations. Having deep pockets, the dominant chain can bid up the costs of these sites, while having the financial strength to pay for them.[29]

SERVICE ADDITIONS    Adding services such as delicatessens, bakeries, pharmacies, post offices, and dry cleaning can add to the attractiveness of the store to consumers. But these services may be costly to add and not yield the sales productivity of other areas. The retailer benefits by locking in the consumer who becomes used to, and expects, this type of service. Likewise the extension of opening hours, perhaps to a 24-hour period, raises the absolute costs to the retailer. A dominant firm can more easily spread these costs over the entire operation. Smaller competitors may feel compelled to add these services without the ability to cost them across a large organization.[30]

PREMIUM LABOR COSTS    The retail industry has been characterized as a low wage and high turnover industry. Companies that are attempting to compete on service need improved training and staff incentives to reduce turnover. The scale economies of the dominant firm allow them to spread these costs over a much larger organization and likely increase the overall market labor costs. An example of this in the United Kingdom is the ability of larger retailers to absorb the recent increases in the national minimum wage, while this has proven very difficult for smaller players.[31]

INCREASED PROMOTIONAL SPENDING ON BRAND-BUILDING ACTIVITIES Retailers have increased their expenditures on promoting their in-store brands, although certainly not at the level of manufacturers. Some of this promotional spending is directly or indirectly funded by manufacturers; however, the dominant retail firms still have the capacity to outspend smaller firms. This investment helps to fuel consumers' expectations that these store brands are superior to those of competitors.[32]

CUSTOMER RETENTION/LOYALTY CARD INITIATIVES The income generated from loyal customers is much greater than that generated from random shoppers. Loyalty cards provide stores with increased information about their customers that can be used to profile and retain customers. But loyalty cards are expensive to administer. Some of the costs of rewards or incentives are funded by suppliers, but these suppliers are much more inclined to invest in loyalty programs with retailers who have sufficient scale. Because of their scale of operations, the dominant retailer is better situated to offset these costs than smaller chains. ASDA and Safeway withdrew from loyalty programs because of the administrative costs.[33]

LOCAL MARKET TRADING RESPONSES Dominant chains bring scale to bear on national or organizational factors, but they can also have an impact on local competition, by putting pressure on competitors' cost structures. Some examples of this would include extending trading hours, payment of above-average labor rates, introduction of service extension, and local competitive pricing such as price leading or matching. The dominant firm has the capacity to absorb these costs because of their scale, but smaller firms generally do not have this capacity.[34]

As the dominant firm in the United Kingdom, Tesco has been controlling the growth spiral. Several firms have found it increasingly difficult to retain their position (Sainsbury, Safeway [now owned by Morrison], and others have fought to stay in the spiral [Somerfield, Iceland]). ASDA had the advantage of Wal-Mart's cash infusion. In the end the market situation may have a duopoly with Tesco and ASDA/Wal-Mart setting the competitive environment. The concentrated market situation and the planning restrictions on building new stores makes it virtually impossible for new entrants to enter the British retail system by any means other than acquisition.[35]

The U.K. food retailing sector is a classic case of retailer power transforming the system. In the next section I consider the nonfood retail sector in the United Kingdom, a sector where many firms dominate.

## Nonfood Retailers

DEPARTMENT STORES The United Kingdom has one of the oldest and most well-established department store industries in the world. Department stores account for 5 percent of total retail sales. Most department stores are in HIGH STREET locations. High Street is the name given to the central business district, an area rather than a single street. This is similar to the American main street. British cities, even those as large as London and Liverpool, have healthy central business district shopping areas.

The department store segment has 24 percent of the total U.K. clothing market compared to 35 percent held by the specialty stores. They also have 18 percent of the DIY market, surpassed only by the DIY specialists with 36 percent of the market.[36]

The large mixed retail sector proved highly changeable during the late 1990s and early 2000s. Mergers, DEMERGERS, talk about mergers, and failed divestments all changed the market. Fenwicks acquired Bentalls department stores in 2001. This has proven to be very successful. Argos became part of the GUS group. Demergers occur when a company exits from a group. Selfridges demerged from the Sears retailing conglomerate in 1998. Debenhams was demerged from the Burton (now Arcadia) Group in the same year. BHS demerged from the Storehouse group in 2000, and Woolworths demerged from Kingfisher in 2001. As a result a large number of the mixed retailers gained their own listing on the London Stock Exchange. Debenhams, Woolworths, House of Fraser, and Selfridges are now listed independently.[37]

Although they have only 26 stores, John Lewis, known for its traditional atmosphere and high quality, is the largest department store group. John Lewis plans to add 10 more stores by 2012, including its first store in Northern Ireland. With 40,000 full and part-time employees, John Lewis is the largest U.K. employee cooperative.[38]

Selfridges and Harvey Nichols, upscale department stores, have also been successful. In the competition for consumers' dollars and with mass merchandisers driving down price, the more upscale strategy of department stores is paying off. Private label is playing an increasingly important role for the mixed retailers. Marks & Spencer has always had 100 percent private label. Argos and House of Fraser focused on branded merchandise but other stores such as Woolworths and Debenhams sell a combination of branded and private label. Marks & Spencer has developed focused private labels such as Per Una designer wear for women and Perfect and Blue Harbour for men. They even have their own cosmetics line, Enhance. Debenhams carries 70 percent private label and their pretax profit increased 123 percent in 2004. They opened 14 new stores and increased their market share by 2 percent bringing it to 16 percent.[39]

In 2005 House of Fraser acquired Jenners and Beatties. Jenners consists of four retail outlets. The primary location is a 130,000-square-feet department store at the opposite end of Princes Street to House of Fraser's 50,000-square-feet store. Jenners is the oldest independent department store in the U.K.; it has been open since 1838. Beatties has 12 department stores. House of Fraser has a portfolio of 67 stores. There are a number of economies that can be achieved by combining these three department store groups. Beatties has operated each store as a separate unit, having buyers at store level. House of Fraser will centralize buying and convert the office space into selling space. Beatties also has a much higher proportion of concession spaces than House of Fraser. CONCESSIONS are areas within department stores that are leased to suppliers. The suppliers decide what merchandise will be presented in that location. Concession sales are similar to the CONSIGNMENT SYSTEM, where a manufacturer puts merchandise in a store and the retailer pays only for the merchandise that is actually sold. The retailer becomes a manufacturer's showroom, providing the physical space. The important thing to remember is that a retailer's primary function is to be an **ASSEMBLER OF LINES OF GOODS**, filtering various merchandise offerings and selecting a subset for its customers. Retailers are gatekeepers for products. When retailers allow manufacturers to decide the merchandise that will be in the store, they give away their most important function. Channel members receive profits based on the value added they provide to consumers. When supplies become the assemblers of the merchandise, they obtain a greater portion of the margin. When suppliers take the risk, they get more margin.

Concession sales at Beatties account for 42 percent of sales compared to House of Fraser's 32 percent. Gross margins in concessions are about 15 percent less than direct purchases. Converting this space to direct purchases could significantly improve gross margin. Private label sales at Beatties is about 5 percent of sales compared to House of Fraser's 10 percent. Again, converting more of the merchandise to private label could significantly enhance margin.[40]

**Photo 11.4**
The food hall at Harrods Department Store looks like a museum. This section is located on the London department store's main floor, next to the accessories and perfumes. *Courtesy of Harrods.*

People who know only one retailer from the United Kingdom probably know of Harrods Department Store. Its semiannual sales are legendary. A visitor to Harrods may imagine bumping into Queen Elizabeth or Prince Charles there. On my first visit, I was surprised by the ambience inside the store. It was more like a museum than a department store. Americans are sometimes surprised that this famous department store sells food. There are other surprises. Midway through my visit to Harrods a group of bagpipe performers marched through the store, playing as they went.

## Other Retailers

Marks & Spencer has had to sell off its financial services business, close its Lifestore concept store, and stop the rollout of its Simply Food stand-alone food format. Marks & Spencer had been well known for its dedication to U.K. suppliers, but to cut costs they are shifting their sourcing to India. They have also reduced their supplier base, enabling them to negotiate better prices. Marks & Spencer has been withdrawing from its foreign markets. You can read the case on Marks & Spencer for a detailed analysis.

Matalan is the U.K.'s most successful fashion retailer. Their product range includes well-known brands, bought and sold at big discounts, similar to U.S. discount department stores. Matalan offers a mix of name brand and private label apparel and home furnishings. Their motto is "high street quality at half the price."

**SPECIALTY STORE CHAINS**    United Kingdom specialty stores have gained worldwide reputations for their aggressive international expansion programs. The Body Shop and Tie Rack, for instance, are so much a part of the American retailing scene that most Americans are surprised to find out they are British companies. Specialty stores in the United Kingdom have the largest market share of any retail format in nonfood items. They focus on a very specific customer target market. These retailers usually use a global expansion strategy, replicating their successful retail format wherever they go.

NEXT is the U.K.'s third-largest clothing retailer. They are rapidly expanding and extending the size of their stores. NEXT has also been expanding internationally, opening a store in Copenhagen and a franchise in Iceland.[41] Marks & Spencer's greatest competition, Next has had double-digit growth for the last few years. They focus on sharp fashions with value-for-the-money proposition.

Arcadia Group attempted a takeover of Marks & Spencer but failed. The group's current strategy is to take market share away from Marks & Spencer. Arcadia Group includes a variety of retail banners including Dorothy Perkins, Miss Selfridge, Wallis, Topshop, Evans, Burton, and Topman.

Poundland is the U.K. version of the dollar store. Its product areas include snacks, confectionery, personal care items, household goods, gardening equipment, pet food, and novelty items. Poundland had to overcome suppliers' initial fears that its form of retailing would damage brands. They have conquered this concern and can now buy directly from manufacturers. They have built up a good rapport with their suppliers because of their ability to order in large volumes. Unlike supermarkets, Poundland's buyers can make rapid decisions, and they are not tied to listing agreements and planograms.[42]

Hennes & Mauritz has 79 stores in the United Kingdom; it is their second-largest market after Germany, who has about 100 stores there. In 2005 H&M teamed up with Stella McCartney to design a women's collection. H&M has over 1,000 stores in 24 countries.[43] You can read more about H&M's internationalization in the case study.

Dixons is the major electronics retailer in the United Kindgom. It operates stores under names such as Currys, PC World, and The Link.

GUS's Homebase home improvement stores are the major competition for B&Q. Homebase is less than half the size of B&Q in sales.

IKEA has 11 stores in the United Kingdom, making it their second-largest market after Germany. To improve performance IKEA's U.K. managing director is decentralizing operations and allowing more decision making to occur at store level.

## Homegood Retailers

Kingfisher is the major homegoods retailer in the United Kingdom. They recently spun off Kesa, their consumer electronics division. Nearly 60 percent of their sales come from B&Q stores in the United Kingdom. Another 25 percent of their sales come from France, where Kingfisher took ownership of Castorama and Brico Depot stores in 2003. Kingfisher has also expanded to China and Russia. The retailer has developed a mini-warehouse format that carries 30 percent more product lines than the old small format and about 60 percent less product than the regular B&Q warehouses. They did this to target 50 new markets that were not large enough to support a full-size B&Q store.[44]

Kesa has about 800 stores across six different banners in seven different countries; each banner is considered a leading player in its country. Comet is second in the United Kingdom behind Dixons; they operate primarily out-of-town stores. France is the leading market with over 400 stores divided between Darty consumer electronics stores and BUT furniture stores.

## Homeshopping

High street retailers dominated the homeshopping operations. Even Littlewoods, one of the founders of homeshopping in the United Kingdom, has retail outlets that are department store sized. All the leading players also offer Internet sales. These retailers have greater access to development capital. Growth is therefore driven by conventional retailers creating additional channels for their high street operations instead of creating new homeshopping businesses. The ease of adding a catalog to the current business, particularly given the advances in retail technology concerning credit and stock control, is very attractive. Many high street retailers generated over 10 percent of their sales through alternative channels. Most of the catalogs are SPECIALOGS, highly focused catalog offerings.

The homeshopping industry has experienced considerable consolidation. Private investors acquired Littlewoods catalog and GUS homeshopping portfolio, which includes Kays and Great Universal. The GUS group has been renamed Shop Direct Group. Compared to newer operators in the sector like La Redoute, the Littlewoods catalog seems old-fashioned and predictable. However many poorer families use the catalog because it offers easy credit. The combined GUS/Littlewoods mail-order business is three times the size of its nearest rival. It also has over half the business-to-consumer parcel delivery business.[45]

The pure catalog business is focused on specialized businesses, often with an artisan or manufacturing base. Furniture companies like Sofa Workshop Direct and Furniture and Sofa Makers offer furniture at much lower prices.

As consumers become more used to clicks, we will likely turn away from the bricks (bricks and clicks is a business model in e-commerce). Growth in sales on the Internet has increased dramatically. The United Kingdom is the second most evolved electronic market; United States is first.

## Internet Retailing

The development of the Internet channel in the United Kingdom is largely the result of substantial supply side research and investment. Growth of Internet retailing was driven by the increased presence of major retail chains. Large chain retailers like WH Smith, Argos, and Next have a major web presence. These well-known high street names provide trust in the format as well as sophisticated logistics systems for product fulfillment. The TV homeshopping network QVC is enhancing its website to update its stock levels in real time so consumers are not able to order something that is out of stock.[46]

Internet retailing was largely launched by the supermarkets, such as Tesco. The major supermarket chains invested a great deal in the development of the supply side of the Internet market. Their wealth allowed them to run the market on their terms. Tesco, Sainsbury, and Iceland are the three leading Internet retailers. They all operate their own delivery service, allowing them to control distribution. Originally they picked merchandise from their physical stores but as the market grew they set up dedicated Internet depots. Now they use both in-store and dedicated depots for distribution.[47]

Tesco is the leading Internet retailer, and even then Internet sales account for only 2 percent of its 2004 sales. But Tesco is still the largest online food retailer in the world. Argos, part of Great Universal Stores, is the second-largest U.K. Internet retailer. Sainsbury's offering Sainsbury's to You has been in operation since 2000, with two dedicated fulfillment depots as well as 53 stores. Amazon.co.uk is the leading U.K. web-only retailer. The company offers around 2.5 million products.[48]

Legislation preventing the opening of new large stores has tightened in the last few years and it is difficult to get permission from planning officials to open new stores.

## Government Regulations

Since 1997, when the new Labor administration came to power, planning permission for new retail development outside town centers has been limited by the government and local planning authorities. Out-of-town shopping center development has come to a standstill as a result of the stiff planning requirements. Town center developments now account for 90 percent of new development. They are doing this in a response to social, economic, and environmental concerns. Retailers who are now limited in expanding outside of town centers are returning to town centers, redeveloping existing stores, and building smaller outlets. In 1999, ASDA (Wal-Mart) started to develop small (10,000–25,000 square ft) supercenters. Other retailers, as I discussed earlier, are turning to convenience stores and smaller neighborhood stores.

The planning regulations have encouraged the supermarket giants to take a new socially responsive approach to expansion. Some of the supermarket chains have teamed up with football clubs so the retailers can build new stores and still be viewed as performing a social function. One example of this is Wimbledon FC's new home in Milton Keys, which is a new 30,000 seat stadium with a 100,000 square foot ASDA Wal-Mart superstore attached.

The number of out-of-town shopping centers has increased dramatically and has adversely affected the downtown areas. Consumer's preference for large stores and one-stop shopping make these centers popular. Additionally, the out-of-town centers generally have longer opening hours and are open on Sunday. Shopping hours in the United Kingdom vary by location. In the city center most shops are open from 9:00 A.M. and to 5:30 P.M. or 6:30 P.M., Monday to Saturday, perhaps having extended shopping hours one or two nights a week, often Thursday or Friday. Many city centers are also open on Sunday from 11:00 A.M. to 5:00 P.M. Most out-of-town centers are open until 8:00 every evening. Some hypermarkets and supermarkets are open 24 hours a day except for Sunday, when by law they can be open only six hours.[49]

Most U.K. retailers have installed point of sale (POS) smart card readers because of new U.K. fraud liability laws. These cards are largely replacing the loyalty cards that had been so prevalent with U.K. food retailers. The new fraud laws make retailers responsible for credit card fraud. Smart cards provide additional protection because they require a PIN number. The United Kingdom is the first country to pass such a law, but Ireland and France are following suit. ASDA is leading in RFID technology, requiring their top 100 suppliers to use the tags. Tesco and Metro also require some portion of their suppliers to use the technology.[50]

The next country in this chapter is the Netherlands. It is a small country so its retailers have had to internationalize to find new markets to fuel their growth.

## > THE NETHERLANDS

The Netherlands has a strong support system for small- and medium-sized retailers. The country also has several retail powerhouses, as the following discussion will reveal. Large retailers in the Netherlands have grown because of early and aggressive internationalization efforts.

### Country Background

The Netherlands gained its independence from Catholic Spain in 1558. Eighty years of bitter struggle had been necessary to establish the new nation. The period after the country's founding has been called the Dutch "Golden Age." During the next century, this small country played a big role in world history. Access to the sea helped it to become a commercial power. The Dutch competed successfully with England and France for overseas markets and colonies. They became rich on trade with the Far East, and for many years they were the only Europeans permitted access to Japan.

The Netherlands were taken over by the French during the Napoleonic Wars, but regained its independence in 1813. From 1815 to 1830, Belgium was included as part of the Kingdom of the United Netherlands. The Dutch were founding members of the Economic Community and have been one of the strongest supporters of closer economic and political union among the European nations.[51]

The Netherlands is the most densely populated country in Europe. Over the years the Dutch government has discouraged the use of new building ground, making organic growth very difficult. The expansion and enlargement of outlets has been restricted through extensive planning restrictions and regulations. In general Dutch retailers still hold the prominent positions in the country; these companies have also expanded at a rapid rate to other countries. Because the home country is so limited, they need to internationalize for growth purposes. The major foreign players are the hard discounters, Aldi and Lidl. Read Box 11.1 for a college student's view of retailing in the Netherlands. Elise Keurentjes was an exchange student here at MSU; she was enrolled in my international retailing course.

## Food Retailers

Ahold started as a small grocer in 1887 but is now the biggest food retailer in the Netherlands. Ahold ranks ninth on the list of the 250 largest retailers in the world. The company operates and franchises stores under the name Albert Heijn. Ahold also has major investments in the United States: BI-LO, Giant Food Stores, and First National Supermarkets. After pulling out of Mexico and Argentina in 2005, they still have operations in the Czech Republic, Estonia, Latvia, Lithuania, Poland, and Slovakia. Heijn, the CEO of this company, is credited with developing self-service in the Netherlands. Before opening self-service stores, he needed to update the packaging industry in his country. Packaging is important to protect merchandise from consumers when self-service is introduced.

Royal Ahold NV is the largest retail operator in the Netherlands. In the late 1990s and early 2000s, the company expanded aggressively in international markets, using acquisition mode (you might want to refer back to Chapter 2, where I discussed the various types of ownership). Investment is when you purchase a very well-run operation and essentially allow the management to continue managing. This is a costly method of expansion, because you are purchasing stores that are well run. In the end it seems like the approach was too costly for Ahold to continue; they have disinvested of most of their ownings in South America and Asia. They still have a presence in Europe, primarily Eastern Europe.

In the Netherlands, Ahold has four major retailing groups. The first is Albert Heijn (AH), which is the top food retailer in the Netherlands. About 30 percent of sales in Albert Heijn comes from private label products. In 1988, Ahold purchased a larger share in the top food wholesaler, Schuitema NV, which operates a large chain of supermarkets, C1000. Ahold also owns the top liquor store chain, Gall & Gall, and a top drugstore chain, Etos. AH XL is Ahold's new hypermarket chain. The hypermarket concept is still in the infant stage in the Netherlands.[52]

On October 20, 2003, Ahold's Dutch subsidiary Albert Heijin started a price war in the Netherlands, lowering prices on more than 1,000 SKUS. Albert Heijn's market share shrank from 27.9 percent in 2002 to 26.7 percent in 2003, and they introduced the price war to bring customers back. These price cuts were immediately copied by other food retailers such as the number two Dutch retailer, Laurus, which operates the Super De Boer, Konmar, and Edah banners. Laurus, like Heijn, had experienced an eroding market share. These top two retailers control 44 percent of the

**Box 11.1**
**Elise Keurentjes**

Every now and then my mom, my sisters and I would go shopping in the city closest to my hometown, about 20 miles away. My mom would park her car at the ice-skating and sports center just on the border of the city. From then we would take the "city bus" which brings us to the center of the city. This partly illustrates the retailing laws that we have in the Netherlands. The sizes of the shops are much smaller in the Netherlands than elsewhere and are very centrally located within cities. Being in the USA right now points that out even more. It's very hard to go to the shops there by car, parking space is rare, except for the food retailers, although many convenience stores are not accessible by car. Industry outside the city is for retail buyers. We have some large retailers such as IKEA (Sweden) and Media-markt (Germany) which entered the country in respectively 1978 and 2000. Mediamarkt is a discounter on electronics and has a format comparable to Best Buy. They sell everything against the lowest prices and gained fast a big market share in electronics. The Mediamarkt shops are only situated in the large cities, close to the center of the city. For convenience and service many people still tend to go to their local electronics store. IKEA is very popular in the Netherlands and in every house you can find an IKEA item; it's something all Dutch people have in common! Another application of these large stores is a hardware store and there are places where different car sellers have their stores together.

Smaller shops also means that the variety of products is much smaller than in shops in the USA. The government in the Netherlands maintains a social system which makes it very hard or impossible for big stores to enter the Netherlands or for present stores to increase their size; space is very limited. The government also tries to protect small shops. The opening hours laws are freer now than a few years ago; 24-hour shops exist these days and shops can open on Sunday a few times a year.

The malls in the Netherlands don't have that many different clothing stores and are not very popular for people to go to, except for people that live close to one. Almost every village has its own convenience store, which is mostly supported by the people living there, since they want to maintain this convenience in their neighborhood. Anyway, many small stores had to close through the years and concentration increases.

Being in the USA points out some differences between retail in the Netherlands and the USA. Having been in many European countries also shows differences within Europe, as we are one of the few countries without a retail format such as Wal-Mart or Carrefour. Consumers in the Netherlands find prices very important, above quality of taste. This changes as people have more to spend and the economy is rising. As a friend of mine said, refills wouldn't work; people would buy the smallest size and bring their own cups and at the end just pay for one. Another thing, I love going to Starbucks. I discovered Starbucks a few years ago in London. Since I've been at MSU I enjoy bringing my books to Starbucks and studying there for a few hours. At my home university this picture is unimaginable. There is no place to get a coffee "to go" except for McDonalds. The students would go someplace at night to study instead. Many question marks arise when I wonder why Starbucks is not in the Netherlands. A market research has shown that the population in the Netherlands wouldn't go there, but let's hope it will enter the Netherlands soon! Typical in the Netherlands are the bruine (brown) cafés. Cafés can be found on every corner of the street; people go there for a coffee, lunch or a beer. The cafés are cozy and people socialize there.

Source: Elise Keurentjes 2006. Written for International Retailing (2nd Edition).

Dutch food retail market. These supermarkets had used high-low pricing, but when the discounters entered the market the price differential became an issue. When the Dutch economy was favorable in the 1990s, customers were not as focused on price, but with the economic downturn in the early 2000s, consumer spending came under pressure. The price gap between Albert Heijn/Super De Boer/Konmar and the discounters increased from 8–10 percent to 15 percent. Albert Heijn forced their suppliers to help absorb some of the price cuts. It is looking more and more like the Netherlands will follow the German and more recent U.K. model where value added retailers are forced to abandon their high quality/high price offerings and make price the long-term focus.[53]

The two German hard discounters Aldi and Lidl have sparked a price war in the Netherlands. No domestic company has really been successful in competing with these hard discounters. And since planning legislature is generally aimed at larger format stores, these two have free rein to open stores.

## Nonfood Retailers

Vendex is the leading nonfood retailer in the Netherlands. The company also has operations in Belgium, France, Germany, Denmark, Luxembourg, and Spain. Vendex derives over three-quarters of their sales from the Netherlands. It operates 15 retail formats with 1,766 stores. The different formats are grouped into six divisions named HEMA, Vroom & Dreesmann (V&D), Bijenkorf, Do-It-Yourself, Apparel, and Consumer Electronics. In 2004, the company underwent some belt tightening, which included reducing 1,800 employees and closing 12 department stores. V&D and Bijenkorf have been losing money for the company. V&D is cutting costs and attempting a complete renewal of styling product offering and branding. They are also introducing a new store concept.[54]

Retail property development in the Netherlands is tightly regulated, and out-of-town retailing takes second place to city center shopping. The Netherlands has half the shopping center development of France or the United Kingdom.

## Government Regulations

The Netherlands has one of the most restrictive legislative environments in the world. Numerous laws and regulations relate to all aspects of commercial operations. A law passed in 1996 allowed retail stores to be open after 6:00 P.M. and on Sundays. Each city has the right to establish their own specific laws. But for retailers, being open more hours carried additional costs through higher labor rates. Although part-time labor is allowed in the Netherlands, adding additional employees can significantly add to labor costs.

The relationship between large- and small-scale retailers is quite good. This may be due to the funding governments provide for research institutes for small- and medium-sized businesses. The research institutes provide small businesses with the type of research information generally available only to larger businesses.

The Netherlands is one of the countries that laid the basis for environmental planning, starting with housing laws enacted in 1901. These laws were designed to improve housing conditions, but they also meant that urban development became subject to national legislation. At first, retailing was not included in this planning, but in the 1930s, shops were included for the first time.[55]

During an economic crisis of the 1930s, many of those who became unemployed looked for a solution in the retail trade. Consumer purchasing power declined, yet the number of shops increased significantly. This led to the first government intervention in the retail industry, the Establishment Law of 1937. This law required that retailers obtain a license, which was only given after proof of competence to run a store was provided. The intent of the law was to improve retail trade, but the actual result was to reduce the number of shops.

After World War II, shopping facilities needed to be rebuilt. The government developed a planned shop hierarchy. The legal framework for the location of shops was formed by a zoning plan. Retail businesses could be established where the zoning plan allowed them. The business location plan of 1954 replaced the old law of 1937. The most significant change in the law was that licenses were tied to specific branches of trade. This kept retailers from responding to changing consumer needs through diversification. The Dutch are famous for reaching consensus; the major trade associations always work together. For the retail sector a special lobby panel was formed between the two major retail associations: NWR (association of small retailers) and RND (association of large retailers). This panel is named Platform Detailhandel; they lobby on behalf of retailers for the following issues:

> accessibility: pertaining to improving accessibility to and within retailing premises
> space development: pertaining to improving possibility for expansion and quality improvement of retail space
> baatbelasting: pertaining to negotiating better and fewer extra municipality fees imposed by retailers
> criminal damages: pertaining to criminal acts that are damaging to retailing businesses, including shoplifting, robbery, and vandalism
> payment systems: pertaining to fees, infrastructure, and regulations on payment and financial systems for retailers.

Value-added tax for nonessential products, which includes alcoholic drinks and most nonfood, is 19 percent. Value-added tax for essential products, which include food and non-alcoholic drinks, however, remains at 6 percent. All retailers in the Netherlands have to abide by one of two major employment acts. The first and most common groups of employment accords are CAOs, which spell out in detail all rules, regulations, and allowances regarding all aspects of employee rights and entitlements, including pay schedules, regulations, and allowances regarding all aspects of employees' rights and responsibilities. An important act was signed in 2003 in response to the economic slowdown; it specified employment issues that were mutually beneficial for both retailers and employees.[56] This is quite a difference from the adversarial nature found in the United States between retailers and employees.

### Internet

The Netherlands is regarded as one of the most technologically advanced countries in the world, with high PC penetration and high Internet use. In 2005 more than 5.8 million Internet users browsed the web for private purposes and 38 percent of these bought something. The demographic characteristics of the Netherlands make Internet retailing conditions unique. The country is one of the most densely populated in the world with the majority of people living in urban areas. One in three households in the Netherlands has a computer.

All leading Dutch mail-order retailers have concentrated their efforts on developing their online businesses because there are synergies to be obtained between traditional mail order and online sales. The leading mail-order retailer, Wehkamp, made 15 percent of their sales on the Internet. A competititor, Neckermann BV, has also been aggressive in generating Internet sales.

Bol.com (Books on Line) is a PUREPLAY Internet retailer, meaning that they do not have a bricks and mortar site, only a web presense. In contrast, Amazon.com does not have a presence in the Netherlands and they do not even have a Dutch website. The Netherlands still operates fixed price maintenance on all books published in the country. This eliminates price competition. The fixed price policy though does not apply to books that are published in other countries.

## Cash & Carry Warehouse Clubs

Sligro Food GroupBV, VEN Groothandelcentrum BV, Metro Cash & Carry, and HANOS Internationale Horeca Groothandel are competitors in this area. All Cash & Carry warehouse clubs in the Netherlands have to operate purely as wholesalers and there is little room for them to move into the country because of the tight planning laws.

## Private Label

Private label in the Netherlands is moving up the quality scale, even beating out the major brands in quality tests. In most large grocery stores, about 70 percent of the shelf space is occupied by A-brands while private labels take up 20 percent and other brands 10 percent. Most retailers are developing three levels of private label—premium, standard, and budget ranges. Hema, a low-end department store, generates 80 percent of sales through their private label.[57]

Belgium, the next country discussed, has government restrictions that are more limiting than those of the United Kingdom or the Netherlands. Retailers from Belgium have expanded internationally, partly to find less restrictive environments and partly because the country is small, leading to early market saturation.

## > BELGIUM

### Country Background

Two thousand years ago, Belgium sat on the border between the Roman Empire in the south and the area controlled by the Germanic Franks to the north. During the Middle Ages, Belgian cities became the wealthiest and the most important trading centers in the world. From the sixteenth to the nineteenth centuries, Belgium was controlled by Burgundy, Spain, Austria, France, and the Netherlands. The country finally gained its independence in 1830. During the European expansion era of the late nineteenth and early twentieth centuries, Belgium claimed vast diamond- and mineral-rich territory in central Africa. This area, formerly known as the Belgian Congo, is present day Zaire. Although Zaire gained its independence in the 1960s, close ties remain between the two countries.

The Germans overran Belgium during both world wars. After World War II, Belgium became a founding member of NATO. Brussels, the capital city of Belgium, is now the headquarters of NATO and the European Community.[58]

## Food Retailers

Belgians spend a fairly high level of their income on food. They have a passion for high quality and great variety. One interesting difference between Belgium and other parts of Europe is that Belgians are large consumers of shelf rather than fresh milk. It is even likely that in a large supermarket you will not find any fresh milk. If you do find some, it is just to meet the needs of foreigners. Food shopping is split between large supermarkets and local stores. There is a high prevalence of local bakers, butchers, fishmongers, and cheese stores. Another form of shopping is the open air market, generally located in one of the city squares.

The use of store cards has increased dramatically. In 2005, 90 percent of the sales made at a Delhaize store are made through the store card. Delhaize has had its Pluscard loyalty card for 11 years but only just started linking it to bank accounts to function as a store card. In 2004, they replaced all the existing cards with smart cards that have integrated personal information for greater security.

Carrefour has the most advanced store card system in Belgium. The Pass card functions as a loyalty card and also as a store card. Customers can pay off the balance in three installments throughout the year without a fee.

Recently there has been a issue about the legality of Belgium's regulations related to loyalty cards. Belgian law prevents businesses from offering a loyalty card with which consumers can accumulate points that can be redeemed for products, services, or price reductions. In reality, loyalty programs in Belgium do offer these benefits; however, there are more restrictions. The bottom line is that this law makes it difficult for international retailers to offer the same loyalty programs in Belgium that they have in place in other countries.

Carrefour (France) is the major food retailer in Belgium. They gained this position when GIB, a former Belgian food retailer, was liquidated and they were able to acquire many of their stores. Carrefour changed the banner of GB hypermarkets to Carrefour but continued to operate the GB banner directly and under licensing agreements. Carrefour also acquired Laurus supermarkets and convenience stores. Kaufhof, the German department store, entered Belgium by acquiring the Inno department stores. The other two major food retailers are from Belgium—Delhaize Le Lion and Colruyt.

Delhaize Le Lion is one of the major food retailers, not just in Belgium, but also in Europe. Delhaize has a majority share holding in Food Lion of the United States.

The segmentation of the Belgian market is similar to the German model of food retailing. The other two models of food retailing in Europe are the French model, dominated by general discounters, and the U.K. model, dominated by quality retailers providing a high level of services. The United Kingdom has become very price driven in the last few years with the market controlled by the two dominant firms. Figure 11.2 illustrates the differences between the models. The old U.K. model is difficult to export because consumers in other countries have become more price sensitized, making the confrontation between the German and French ideas even greater.[59]

**Figure 11.2**
**Different Types of Food Retailing in Europe**

| | U.K. Model | French Model | German Model |
|---|---|---|---|
| **Concentration** | Very high | Rather high | High in discount segment<br>Average in large-scale food retailing |
| **Type of Network** | Branch | Mixed (independent and branch) | Branch for hard discounters<br>Mixed for large-scale food retailers |
| **Marketing Strategy** | Quality | Discount | Discount in hard-discounters<br>Choice in large-scale food retailers |
| **Own Brands** | Corporate Branding | Rather well developed and growing fast | 100% in hard-discount |
| **Countries Involved** | United Kingdom<br>Netherlands<br>Switzerland | France<br>Spain<br>Italy | Germany<br>Belgium |

Source: Dia-Mart—Report in "Les Echos" (1994). Reported in "GIB—Company Report." (February 23, 1996). Credit Lyonnais Laing in Investext [Database on CD-ROM]. Foster City, CA: Information Access. Updated by the author in 2006.

Belgium is one of the first battlegrounds for these two ideologies. Colruyt was the first Belgian retailer to find a solution. Colruyt had less market clout than GIB or Delhaize, so its exposure to the hard discounters makes it even more vulnerable. Colruyt has successfully shown that it could achieve a viable response to hard discount stores with a soft-discount formula based on systematic discounts for brand names.

## Nonfood

Belgians generally shop for non-food products on Saturday. The Belgian retail market remains very traditional with a lack of dominance of chains and the continued popularity of boutiques. Belgians like the more traditional high street shopping rather than the more sterile atmosphere of a shopping mall.

Sales in department stores have shown growth. Kaufhof converted some Inno stores to the Galeria concept, something that has been very successful in Germany. Hema has also had strong growth. Department stores require a large space, which limits opportunities for expansion. Inno has very prominently positioned large stores and does not really plan additional expansion. Inno makes use of a lot of concessions. When products are sold in concessions the manufacturer sends their own sales employees, thereby reducing the wage figures for the company.

## Internet

Mail order has never been very popular in Belgium. Only about half of households have a computer, lagging way behind countries such as the Netherlands and Germany. Amazon.com does not even operate a site in Belgium; if people want to place an order they must use another country's site. Retailers often have a website, but it is most likely for information only and not for ordering. The major food retailers Delhaize and Colruyt offer Internet retailing; Carrefour does not.[60]

## Government Regulations

Belgium has one of the most restrictive laws regulating large-scale store growth. The law is designed to protect small retailers. Retailers can remodel existing stores, but the building of new stores is very difficult. This regulatory environment has deterred international retail groups. If a retailer wishes to set up in business, the impact on other shopkeepers will be analyzed by local authorities. If it is found that the retailer would distort competition, which is nearly always the case, they are denied permission to open.

In addition to this strict planning law, Belgium also has very precise labeling standards. In addition to other information the label must also specify if there are any GENETICALLY MODIFIED ORGANISMS (GMOs), elements whose genetic material was modified in a way not found in nature under natural conditions of crossbreed or natural recombination.

Belgian laws establish maximum opening hours. Most retailers are open Monday to Friday 9:00–6:00. Supermarkets might be open a little later, to 7:00 or 8:00 on Fridays. Bakers, butchers, small grocers, and newsagents can be open on Sunday mornings. Shops of interest to tourists can keep longer hours.

### › SUMMARY

Government involvement influences retailing in the United Kingdom, the Netherlands, and Belgium All three countries have restrictions on large-scale retail development. These laws are designed to favor small-scale retailers, but they have actually provided an unprecedented opportunity for hard discount format retailers. Most of the major food retailers are opening convenience stores because these are one of the few formats that expand relatively unhampered.

Retailers in these three countries have looked outside their borders for expansion opportunities. Expansion in the United States, as well as areas in continental Europe, are attractive options. Lifestyles of people in the United Kingdom, the Netherlands, and Belgium are probably closer to those of the United States than they are to their European neighbors.

### › KEY TERMS

ADMINISTERED VERTICAL MARKETING SYSTEM
ASSEMBLER OF LINES OF GOODS
BARRIERS TO ENTRY
CIRCLE OF GROWTH
CONCESSIONS
CONSIGNMENT SYSTEM
CORPORATE BRANDING
DELISTING
DEMERGERS
DYADIC RELATIONSHIPS
GENETICALLY MODIFIED ORGANISMS
HIGH STREET

HORIZONTAL COMPETITION

MARKET SPOILER

PRODUCT RANGE ENHANCEMENTS

PUREPLAY

RANGE EXTENSIONS

SPECIALOGS

SPIRAL OF GROWTH

THIRD PARTY LOGISTICS

VERTICAL COMPETITION

## › DISCUSSION QUESTIONS

1. Why does the government want to protect small retailers? How does restricting growth in large-scale stores affect the competitive environment in these countries? What retail format has gained the most from these laws?
2. Discuss the role that power plays when you have one or two dominant firms in an industry. Discuss the elements of vertical and horizontal competition.
3. Retailers in the United Kingdom introduced private labels in foods as high value-added products. Retailers in the United States took just the opposite tactic. They introduced private labels as low-cost alternatives to national brands. What factors contributed to retailers in each country taking each route, and what are the long-term effects of each strategy?
4. What are the requirements for corporate branding?
5. Discuss the five generations of private label, corporate branding development.
6. Using Solomon and Tordjman's theory of global versus multinational retailers discussed in Chapter 1, how would you classify H&M and Tesco?

## › ENDNOTES

1. "United Kingdom." (1995). *Craighead's International Business, Travel, and Relocation Guide to More Than 80 Countries.* Detroit: Gale Research.
2. Coopers & Lybrand. (1996). "Chain Store Age." *Global Powers in Retailing.*
3. Retailing in the United Kingdom. (2004). GMID, Euromonitor, October 1.
4. Retailing in the United Kingdom. (2004).
5. Retailing in the United Kingdom. (2004). Columbus, Ohio: RetailForward, September.
6. Retailing in the United Kingdom. (2004).
7. Tesco. (2005). Credit Suisse in Investext. December 12, 22.
8. Tesco. (2005).
9. Burt, S., and L. Sparks (2005). ASDA: Wal-Mart in the United Kingdom. Working paper.
10. Strategic Focus: Retailing in the United Kingdom (2004). Columbus, Ohio: Retailforward.
11. Burt and Sparks. (2005).
12. Burt and Sparks. (2005).
13. Retailing in the United Kingdom (2004). Columbus, Ohio: Retail Forward, September.

14. Retailing in the United Kingdom (2004). GMID, Euromonitor, October 1.
15. Strategic Focus: Retailing in the United Kingdom (2004).
16. Retailing in the United Kingdom (2004). GMID, Euromonitor, October.
17. Sparks, L. (1997). "From Coca-Colonization to Copy-Cotting: The Cott Corporation and Retailer Brand Soft Drinks in the UK and the USA." *Agribusiness,* Vol. 13, No. 2.
18. Retailing in United Kingdom (2004). GMID, Euromonitor, October
19. Burt, S., and L. Sparks (2002). "Corporate Branding, Retailing and Retail Internationalization." *Corporate Reputation Review,* 5, 194–212.
20. Hatch, M., and M. Schultz (2001). "Are the Strategic Stars Aligned for Your Corporate Brand?" *Harvard Business Review,* 79,2, 129–134.
21. Burt and Sparks (2002).
22. Burt, S., and L. Sparks. (2003). "Power and Competition in the UK Retail Grocery Market." British Journal of Management. 14, 237–254.
23. Burt and Sparks (2003).
24. Burt and Sparks (2003).
25. Burt and Sparks (2003).
26. Burt and Sparks (2003).
27. Burt and Sparks (2003).
28. Burt and Sparks (2003).
29. Burt and Sparks (2003).
30. Burt and Sparks (2003).
31. Burt and Sparks (2003).
32. Burt and Sparks (2003).
33. Burt and Sparks (2003).
34. Burt and Sparks (2003).
35. Burt and Sparks (2003).
36. Retailing in the United Kingdom (2004).
37. Retailing in the United Kingdom (2004).
38. Retailing in the United Kingdom (2004).
39. "UK Department Stores Buck Gloomy Trend (2005)." Cosmedias. December 1.
40. House of Fraser (2005). Investec Securities in Investext. September.
41. Strategic Focus: Retailing in the United Kingdom (2004).
42. Retailing in the United Kingdom (2004).
43. Retailer Hopes for a Stellar Performance in Tough Times. (2005). *The Financial Times.* October 25, 17.
44. Strategic Focus: Retailing in the United Kingdom (2004).
45. Retailing in the United Kingdom (2004).
46. Retailing in the United Kingdom (2004).
47. Retailing in the United Kingdom (2004).
48. Retailing in the United Kingdom (2004).
49. Retailing in the United Kingdom (2004).
50. Strategic Focus: Retailing in the United Kingdom (2004).
51. "The Netherlands." (1995). *Craighead's International Business, Travel, and Relocation Guide to More Than 80 Countries.* Detroit: Gale Research.
52. Retailing in the Netherlands (2004).
53. Dut Retail War (2003). Ing in Investtext, October 29.
54. Vendex KBB (2004). Ing Financial Markets in Investext, November.

55. Borchert, J. (1995). "Retail Planning Policy in the Netherlands." In R. L. Davies, ed., *Retail Planning Policies in Western Europe.* London: Routledge.

56. Retailing in the Netherlands (2004). GMID, Euromonitor, July.

57. Retailing in the Netherlands (2004).

58. "Belgium." *Craighead's International Business, Travel, and Relocation Guide to More Than 80 Countries.* Detroit: Gale Research.

59. "GIB—Company Report".

60. Retailing in Belgium (2004). GMID, Euromonitor, June.

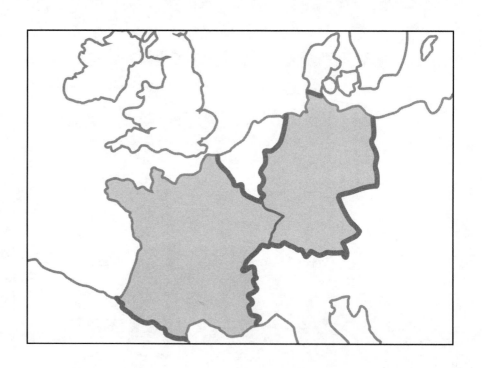

# 12

# RETAILING
# IN GERMANY
# AND FRANCE

## After reading this chapter, you should understand

> How reunification of West and East Germany has affected German retailing.

> Why Germany's concern for the environment and social welfare affects the retail industry and the ability of foreign retailers to enter this market.

> The development of German hard discount food retailers and how this retail format is threatening to take market share from other forms of food retailers throughout the EU.

> How retail competition is altered with a concentrated industry such as Germany's department store sector.

> How French government regulations alter the retailing atmosphere.

> Why French retailers must rely on foreign markets for growth.

In the previous chapter, I mentioned ways in which the United Kingdom, the Netherlands, and Belgium are somewhat similar both geographically and culturally. Although Germany and France are considered middle European countries, they do not have a similar cultural perspective. When these two countries are profiled on high context versus low context dimensions, dramatic differences are revealed: Germany is a low context culture, France is high context. Using Hofstede's dimensions of difference, you can identify the differences between the Germans and the French.

Despite their cultural differences, I have chosen to discuss these two countries together because they have a similar level of retail development. Both countries have been retail innovators. Both countries have well-developed retail sectors with department stores, food stores, and specialty stores that add value and meaning to consumers. Germany is the largest retail market in Europe. France is the second largest. Retailers in both of these countries are internationally active and threaten the competitive environment when they enter a new market. German retailers have been aggressively moving into the former Soviet-bloc countries of Eastern Europe. For some retailers, this means they are reclaiming stores confiscated during the communist takeovers of the early 1950s. French retailers have also expanded very successfully into Spain.

## > GERMANY

### Country Background

Germanic tribes defeated the Roman legions in 9 A.D., halting expansion of the Roman Empire. The German states were again a battlefield during the Napoleonic Wars in the early 1800s. Shortly after this period, the various independent states began the move toward unification. Prussia became the dominant force among these states, leading the emergence of the German Empire. For four decades, Germany dominated the European continent. This was a time of rapid economic and social development for Germans. They surpassed the British and French industrially.

Germans consider the period before 1914 to be a golden age. However, German leaders became a bit too ambitious, leading to conflict with the other great European powers. The result was World War I. Germany's defeat and the collapse of its empire in 1918 left the country fragile and searching for an identity. Economic problems during the postwar years led to extremism and the rise of Adolf Hitler's Nazi Party in 1933. Germany's militaristic expansion culminated in World War II, when the country was again crushed by Allied Forces led by the United States, Britain, France, and the Soviet Union.

The defeated country was divided into occupation zones, which were to be treated as single economic and administrative units under the control of the Allies. By 1948, Soviet ambitions in Eastern Europe led to the Berlin blockade and the division of East and West Germany. A wall was constructed to divide East from West Germany. On September 20, 1949, the three Western allies merged their zones and turned their powers over to a new German government.

A dramatic currency reform stabilized the German mark and a market economy took off. The Federal Republic of Germany joined NATO in 1955, and in 1957, Germany became a founding member of the European Economic Community, now known as the European Union.

East Germany did not fare so well. Until 1989, it remained a Soviet bloc country. In May 1989, Eastern Europe's borders began to open, starting with Hungary. Thousands of East Germans escaped to the West through that route. By October of that year, the East Germans who remained were demonstrating in the streets. Soviet President Mikhail Gorbachev decided not to intervene. In November, thousands of partying Germans from both sides tore down the Berlin Wall, signaling the end of East Germany's isolation from the West. A free German election was held in March 1990, and West German Chancellor Helmut Kohl won the election on a pledge of speedy reunification. On October 3, 1990, the two Germanies became one.[1] In discussing retailing in Germany, it is necessary to review in some detail the single most important event in recent German history, the unification of East and West Germany.

## German Unification

I will never forget that Sunday morning in November 1989. The major news event was the fall of the Berlin Wall. I called my son into the bedroom to watch the TV coverage and told him, "This is history in the making; remember this day the rest of your life." As it turns out there were to be several major events in 1989–1990, and it seems like each one broke on a Sunday morning. I told my son the same thing each time. The first was Tiananmen Square in China in May. Then the Berlin Wall fell in November. The last was the release of Nelson Mandela from prison in February of 1990. There were significant historic events that we had the privilege to witness. Although unexpected, the tearing down of the Wall turned out to be prophetic

**Photo 12.1**
The Berlin Wall divided East and West Germany. In 1989, this wall was torn down, ending official separation of the cities' residents. In 1997, however, there is still a marked difference between East and West Berlin. *Courtesy of AP/Wide World Photos.*

of changes to come in the next few years within the Iron Curtain. The news coverage that day showed people dancing in the streets and even on top of the Wall. It was a celebration of freedom.

The unification of West and East Germany had a great impact on the retailing industry. Before unification, East Germans could buy their consumer goods only from state-owned stores. These stores were concerned with distributing necessities. Luxuries were considered a waste of resources. Because there were few goods to purchase, the East Germans saved a disproportionate amount of their income. When the Wall came down, their pocketbooks came out.

During the first part of 1990, East Germans displayed "CONSUMER TOURISM" as they traveled across the border to purchase merchandise in West Germany. Sales in West Berlin increased 24 percent during the first half of 1991, but were down 10 percent during the second half of that year.[2] Mail-order houses were early beneficiaries of the unified market, as shoppers placed orders from the newly available catalogs. However, East German consumers did not have to wait until new stores were built to shop closer to home. West German retailers filled trucks with merchandise and then took them to the major East German cities, where they parked on the streets and operated as mobile retail units. This temporary measure lasted only until West German retailers could open stores in the former communist territories. Germany started the 1990s with a boom because of the unification. The high level of demand in East Germany created a temporary independence from the global economy. This short-term economic growth, however, was nearly immediately followed by a slump and a recession between 1992–1993. The end of the unification boom was caused by problems in the global economy, increasing production costs, the strong German mark, and issues created by financing the restructuring of East Germany. In the 16 years since unification the economic growth in East Germany has not met expectations.

Most of the investment came from public funding; however, those living in West Germany have also contributed a solidarity tax since 1990, which is used to fund the rebuilding of the East. The integration of the new states with the old states has been socially, politically, and economically painful.[3]

I was in Berlin a few years after the Wall came down. What struck me was the amount of graffiti on buildings. That tells me that there is rage in the city. Many West German citizens felt like they were subsidizing a group of second-class citizens, and many East Germans felt like they were dismissed as being poor relatives. I remember being struck by the difference in subway stations in West Germany and East Germany. West German subway stations were beautiful, filled with fine tile and pretty light fixtures. East German subway stations were dark, dreary places, light bulbs were often exposed. They truly were two different countries. I stayed at a hotel, just on the East German side. The buildings were riddled with bullet holes and many had broken glass, quite different from the orderly and elegant surroundings when you passed over to West Germany.

Germany is still in the midst of social upheaval. As the economy has become globalized, high-paying German jobs have been exported to other countries. The result has been an erosion of the middle class and an increase of lower paying jobs. When Europe achieves monetary union, a major outcome will be a leveling of European wage levels. This will result in a further loss of higher paying jobs in

Germany. There will be a rising number of low-wage earners and a corresponding above-average increase in the number of low-income groups. This trend will favor discounting formats of retail.

Today, Germany has the problem of being overstored, which means that there is too much retail space for the population base. This heightened competition means existing players must work much harder to survive. At the end of the 1970s over 75 percent of retail outlets in cities were small independent shops; currently this figure is less than 25 percent. Most of the outlets in inner cities belong to large chains that can afford the high rents in premium locations. Shopping centers in both out-of-town locations and inner cities have grown in popularity since unification. City planners have focused on shopping centers as the optimum solution to make inner city areas more attractive to consumers and to retain purchasing power.[4] Although Germany has Western Europe's largest population, and is the world's third-largest economy, the economy is in a no-growth position. Part of this is related to the heavy degree of regulations.

## Government Regulations

Germany has one of the most regulated retail environments in Europe. That combined with the tax structure significantly reduces retail spending. Recent tax reforms have reduced the tax rate for the top earners from 51 to 48.5 percent. The lowest rate decreased from 22.9 to 19.9 percent.

The euro replaced the German mark in 2002. The costs of making this transition were borne by retailers because they needed extra cash flow to have a supply of euros during the transition period, as well as German marks. After the introduction of the euro, there was a decline in consumer expenditure that the industry calls the EURO SHOCK. Consumers viewed products as being more expensive when they considered them in euros rather than in marks. Price cutting carried out by the hard discounters such as Aldi had a strong impact on the structure of the grocery retail sector in Germany. Due to the low price structure, German retailers work with some of the lowest margins among the large economies in Europe. This is one of the reasons Wal-Mart has not been very successful in Germany. Leading retailers in Germany routinely work on the type of cost structure Wal-Mart is used to using elsewhere in the world. The introduction of the euro initially had no effect on prices; however, Aldi used the occasion to reduce prices on many of their core products. Some retailers used the euro to mark up prices, but this backfired on them because of the euro shock.[5]

I happened to be in Germany the day the euro was launched. Money machines were shut down for a period of time when the transition was made. Many people I talked with were very sad to see the demise of their beloved German mark. It was like losing a piece of their history and culture.

To keep costs down retailers are heavily dependent on part-time employment. Until 2000 if an employee worked less than 15 hours per week and made less than deutsche marks (DM)630 per month, neither the employee nor the employer had to pay national insurance contributions. However, the government passed a new law that made the employers responsible for the payment of a flat rate of 10 percent for health insurance and 12 percent for pension insurance. This makes part-time employees significantly more expensive. If workers earn less than EUR400 per month they are not required to pay contributions.[6]

Workers in Germany have clout. Part-time workers have the right to determine how many hours they will work, and even *when* they work, regardless of what the employer wants. The influence of trade unions is probably the single biggest obstacle for retailers in Germany. The country has mandated union representation on corporate boards. *Mitbestimmung,* or CO-DETERMINATION, requires that workers and union representatives must hold half of the seats on the supervisory boards of big corporations, giving labor unprecedented power and undermining corporate management. Company executives are unduly influenced by labor, who determines if the executives keep their positions. KarstadtQuelle's troubles can be attributed in part to labor's refusal to remove its chief executive even though shareholders were demanding a change. This law also reduces the attractiveness of Germany as a market for investment because foreign companies taking over German businesses must adopt this policy.[7]

While I was working on this book, I spent some time in Germany conducting research. After completing a series of meetings in Frankfort, I drove two-lane roads back to Munich. I started my trip on Saturday morning. When I stopped to purchase some film a little after two in the afternoon, all of the stores were closed. I had to buy my film at a convenience store attached to a gas station because these were the only places open for business. The Ladenschlussgesetz (shop closing hours' law), put into effect in 1956, stipulates that stores will close at 6:30 P.M. on weekdays, except Thursdays when they can stay open until 8:30, and at 2:00 P.M. on Saturdays (with longer opening on the first Saturday of each month). My scenic tour was even more peaceful than I had expected because the downtown areas were deserted. I imagined that people were at home with their families, and I found this an interesting contrast to life in other parts of the world. Saturday afternoon is one of the busiest days for retailing in the United States and Asia.

Store hours were liberalized somewhat in 2003. The government now allows stores to stay open until 8 P.M. on Saturdays instead of closing at 4 P.M. Stores still remain closed on Sundays and are open from 6:00 A.M. until 8 P.M. on weekdays. Workers receive up to 50 percent more money for working longer hours on Saturday.[8]

The Law Against Unfair Competition includes many of Germany's pricing regulations. For instance, it prohibits businesses with superior market power in relation to small- and medium-sized competitors from pricing below cost, unless the pricing occurs only occasionally and there is an objective justification for it. This law has been particularly problematic for Wal-Mart, who is used to using promotions to gain market share. In 2001, laws prohibiting loyalty cards were repealed. By early 2003 there was approximately one loyalty card per resident, a major increase in a short period of time. One card per resident is about half the level of other European countries.

In 2004, the parliament repealed a law that limited retail sales to a biannual, two-week end of season period. Repealing this law also gave retailers the right to extend discounts to non-seasonal items such as electronics and furniture. Although the law was recalled, more than two-thirds of retailers took part in a voluntary sale during the traditional period.[9] The reason the government had a law restricting sales periods was that they thought sales were confusing to consumers. The government's logic was that people could not keep track of constantly changing prices. Retailers are not allowed to advertise price reductions if they increase and then decrease the price to give the illusion of a price reduction. Retailers are also required to have sufficient stock of the merchandise they are advertising.

In 2002, Germany introduced a law that requires all publishers to fix prices for newly published books, sheet music, and photographic products. Germany has long had a price-fixing system for these products but previously the agreement was between the publisher and booksellers. The European Commission objected to these agreements under the competition law, indicating that they thought fair trading practices were restricted.[10]

Germany has a requirement that levies a deposit on disposable packaging for specific beverages. Cans, glass bottles, and plastic bottles are included under this packaging law. All links in the supply chain are responsible for establishing a collection system. Even exporters are expected to establish this system. The EU feels that this system is a disadvantage to foreign beverage exporters. Disposable beverage packaging sold through vending machines must carry an identifying code number and vending retailers must provide machines to collect empty containers and refund the customer's deposit. If it is not possible to provide a reverse vending machine, the seller must make arrangements through a retailer located in the vicinity to collect the empty containers and refund the money.[11] I have actually seen these recycling containers, but until I started doing research for this book I didn't know what they were. Since 1998, vending machine operators dealing in food and drinks have to certify the quality of their products throughout their supply chain and conform to the "proof of quality" concept.

The packaging laws in Germany are so extreme that some companies chose not to deal with the German market. Many grocery retailers such as Metro and Rewe got rid of disposable packaging. Aldi is introducing its own packaging that works out to be cost effective when being collected and ultimately disposed of. Retail groups are lobbying to try to get this restrictive law changed. Lobbying is also going on to repeal a law that requires all retailers of electrical equipment to charge a deposit on merchandise they sell, and then provide a mechanism for consumers to dispose of the used appliances. Small- and medium-sized businesses contend that this law puts a greater burden on them than on the large retailers.[12]

In 2001, a law called the *Rabattgesetz* was abolished because of an EU directive. The law had prohibited free negotiation of discounts in the retail trade and the *Zugabeverordnung,* which banned the offering of substantial gifts when a purchase was made. Another important aspect of the elimination of these laws is that the EU directive included a country of origin principle that could have severely hampered German retailers' ability to compete. This principle established that within Europe, the laws of the country of the seller determined what was legal. Before this the country of the customer was used to determine what was legal. With the development of e-commerce, companies outside of Germany could offer substantial discounts. The EU has issued a directive that extends the length of guarantee periods that retailers must offer customers from six months to two or even three years.

The German government severely limits land use. The food retailer's association is also lobbying the government regarding a law that limits the size of certain types of retail outlets. They maintain that in the law's present form it gives unfair advantage to hard discounters over supermarkets.[13] The law regulates land use in most urban areas. Regulations limit retailers to a maximum selling space of 700 square meters. Getting the approval to build a big box store or shopping center has been known to take 10 years.

The 95 percent shareholding threshold is a regulation in Germany that gives minority shareholders the right to block transactions except when the majority holds 95 percent or more of the shares. Companies such as ITM, which has majority ownership of Spar, are trying to acquire a 95 percent shareholding so they can reduce the stranglehold of minority investors. ITM wants to sell Spar, but to get this restructuring change they need to acquire the required 95 percent ownership.

In 2005, the German government implemented a new road toll regulation that will add significantly to the logistics costs of retailers and their suppliers. Retailers will face transport cost increases of 3–18 percent depending on the region of the country.[14]

Tables 12.1 and 12.2 summarize the major domestic and foreign retailers in Germany. Germany has 9 of the top 100 retailers. Metro AG is the fourth-largest retailer in the world, operating a variety of formats in 29 countries. Aldi GmbH & Company is number 10, operating hard discount stores and supermarkets in 12 countries. Schwartz Unternehmens Treuhand KG (Lidl) is number 11, operating discount stores, hypermarkets, and supercenters/supermarkets in 19 countries. Rewe-Zentral AG operates in nearly every retail format in 14 countries. Edeka Zentrale AG also operates in nearly every type of retail format in five countries. Number 25, Tengelmann Verwaltungs-und Beteiligungs GmbH, also operates in nearly every kind of retail format in 16 countries. Tengelmann has fallen from number five on the list when the first edition of this book was written in 1998. KarstadtQuelle AG Group ranks number 37 in the world, operating department stores, specialty stores, and mail-order operations in 23 countries. Otto Versand GmbH ranks number 52. Otto operates mail-order systems, specialty stores, and warehouse clubs in 21 countries.[15]

## Nonfood Retailing

The past two decades have brought tough times for German retailers. Department stores have been losing market share since their highlight year of 1980, when they had 7.2 percent share of the retail market. In 1994, they had less than 4 percent. Part of this decline has been due to weak domestic demand for apparel combined with a growing preference for discount and fast fashion. Department stores have shifted either down market or upmarket to counteract discounter's new retail formats. In addition, consumers seem to have become polarized in their expenditures. For everyday products, consumers want to pay the cheapest price, because they regard the products as standard offerings. On the other hand, they shop in high-priced specialty stores for products when they perceive a difference of quality or when the product contributes a prestige attraction. For these reasons, two types of retailers are doing well: retailers such as Aldi that offer low cost with a large element of self-service, and companies like Douglas that sell a full range of products with high service at higher prices. Department stores, caught in the middle, have lost market share.[16]

**Table 12.1**
**Germany—Leading Domestic Retailers, 2004**

| Company | Primary Line of Trade | Total Sales and Stores | | | Global Rank and Penetration | | | Domestic Market | |
|---|---|---|---|---|---|---|---|---|---|
| | | Net Sales ($US Mil) | % Chg Sales | Total Stores | 2004 Rank, Top 200 Retailers Worldwide | Single-country, Regional or Global? | Number of countries | Share of total sales | Share of total stores |
| 1 Metro AG | Cash & Carries/Warehouse Clubs | 70,162 | 5.3% | 2,446 | 4 | Global | 29 | 51% | 71% |
| 2 Schwarz Group | Discount Food Stores | 44,777 | 11.0% | 6,080 | 12 | Regional | 19 | 50% | 46% |
| 3 Aldi Group | Discount Food Stores | 42,506 | -5.6% | 7,517 | 13 | Global | 13 | 64% | 55% |
| 4 Rewe-Gruppe | Supermarkets/Grocery Stores | 40,635 | 1.5% | 11,665 | 14 | Regional | 14 | 72% | 74% |
| 5 Edeka-Gruppe | Supermarkets/Grocery Stores | 38,993 | 1.0% | 14,000 | 16 | Regional | 5 | 95% | 90% |
| 6 Tengelmann Warenhandelsgesellschaft | Supermarkets/Grocery Stores | 35,203 | 5.6% | 7,362 | 23 | Global | 15 | 48% | 72% |
| 7 Karstadt Quelle AG | Non-Store | 16,385 | -6.9% | 220 | 42 | Regional | 19 | 85% | 100% |
| 8 Otto Group | Non-Store | 11,847 | -3.0% | 361 | 61 | Global | 19 | 56% | 38% |
| 9 Anton Schlecker | Drug Stores | 8,209 | 0.8% | 13,750 | 95 | Regional | 9 | 82% | 78% |
| 10 Globus Holding GmbH & Co. | Hypermarkets/Supercenters | 5,320 | 4.3% | 111 | 128 | Regional | 2 | 86% | 86% |
| 11 Bauhaus | DIY/Home Improvement Stores | 4,884 | 7.8% | 180 | 139 | Regional | 10 | 68% | 67% |
| 12 dm-drogerie markt GmbH & Co. KG | Drug Stores | 3,828 | 7.5% | 1,498 | 166 | Regional | 9 | 72% | 47% |
| 13 Norma Lebensmittelfilial-betrieb GmbH & Co. KG | Discount Food Stores | 3,506 | 8.0% | 1,297 | 174 | Regional | 3 | 94% | 90% |
| 14 Dohle Handelsgruppe Service GmbH & Co. KG | Hypermarkets/Supercenters | 2,995 | -14.9% | 223 | — | Single Country | 1 | 100.0% | 100.0% |
| 15 Hornbach Holdings | DIY/Home Improvement Stores | 2,757 | 8.0% | 135 | — | Regional | 8 | 69% | 79% |
| 16 Bertelsmann AG | Non-Store | 2,705 | -4.9% | 600 | — | Global | 22 | 16% | 50% |

Sources: Retail Forward, company annual reports and published reports

**Table 12.2**
**Germany—Key Foreign Retailers, 2004**

| Company | Headquarters | Retail Sector | Primary Line of Trade | 2004 Rank, Top 200 Retailers Worldwide | Single-country, Regional or Global? | Number of countries |
|---|---|---|---|---|---|---|
| | | | | | Global Rank and Penetration | |
| Amazon.com | United States | Homegoods | Non-Store | 111 | Global | 7 |
| C&A | Belgium | Softgoods | Apparel Stores | 105 | Global | 15 |
| Dansk Supermarked A/S | Denmark | FDM | Discount Stores | 100 | Regional | 5 |
| Defense Commissary Agency | United States | FDM | Supermarkets/Grocery Stores | 130 | Global | 13 |
| Delhaize "Le Lion" Group | Belgium | FDM | Supermarkets/Grocery Stores | 32 | Global | 9 |
| Esprit Holdings Limited | Hong Kong | Softgoods | Apparel Stores | – | Global | 40 |
| Groupe Galeries Lafayette | France | Softgoods | Department Stores | 138 | Regional | 2 |
| HSN (InterActiveCorp.) | United States | Homegoods | Non-Store | – | Global | 4 |
| Hutchison Whampoa Limited | Hong Kong | FDM | Drug Stores | 77 | Global | 18 |
| IKEA AB | Sweden | Homegoods | Furniture & Home Furnishings | 44 | Global | 32 |
| INDITEX Group (i.e., Zara) | Spain | Softgoods | Apparel Stores | 110 | Global | 56 |
| ITM Entreprises SA | France | FDM | Supermarkets/Grocery Stores | 8 | Regional | 9 |
| Liberty Media Corp. (QVC) | United States | Homegoods | Non-Store | 121 | Global | 4 |
| Mango | Spain | Softgoods | Apparel Stores | – | Global | 76 |
| Migros—Genossenschaftsbund | Switzerland | FDM | Supermarkets/Grocery Stores | 53 | Regional | 3 |
| Mitsukoshi Ltd | Japan | Softgoods | Department Stores | 98 | Global | 9 |
| Royal Vendex KBB N.V. | Netherlands | Softgoods | DIY/Home Improvement Stores | 134 | Regional | 7 |
| Staples, Inc. | United States | Homegoods | Office Supply | 47 | Global | 18 |
| Toys "R" Us, Inc. | United States | Homegoods | Toy Stores | 68 | Global | 30 |
| Wal-Mart Stores, Inc. | United States | FDM | Hypermarkets/Supercenters | 1 | Global | 11 |

Sources: Retail Forward, company annual reports and published reports

The German department store industry is unique in terms of its concentration. For years, the top four German retailers—Karstadt, Kaufhof, Hertie, and Horten—controlled 90 percent of the department store industry in that country. This is one of the highest concentrations in the world. Besides selling general merchandise, these companies have significant food sales. The two largest companies, Karstadt and Kaufhof, have acquired the two smaller companies, Hertie and Horten. Since Karstadt merged with Hertie, the flagship store of the group is now the famous KaDeWe in Berlin. Founded in 1907, this store became part of the Hertie group in 1927. The original store was demolished in 1943 but rebuilt by 1956. Since 1990, the store has been undergoing a renovation. Twenty percent of KaDeWe's nearly 30 million customers are foreigners.[17] Later the two remaining department store chains merged with strong players in other retail formats. Karstadt merged with Quelle, a major mail-order company. Kaufhof was acquired by Metro, the major cash and carry retailer in Germany, and even the world.

Germany's longtime department store leader, KarstadtQuelle is trying desperately to survive. The two groups joined forces in 1999, and things have gone downhill ever since. The company has diversified past their core competencies and it shows. Domestic business accounts for 90 percent of their sales, and this reliance on the stagnant German economy has proven to be a disaster. In 2004, Karstadt decided to close nearly half of its 180 department stores and to sell non-core assets such as 300 specialty chains, real estate operations, and a chain of fitness centers. Karstadt is taking the nearly 90 department stores still open downscale to create synergies with Quelle and Neckermann mail-order divisions. Karstadt has also introduced a shop-in-shop (concessions) offering YornCasa, featuring innovative products and fixturing.[18]

Esprit, based in Hong Kong but operated out of Germany, reduced its dependence on department stores. They had focused on having concessions in major department store groups, They are also shifting their focus from wholesale trade to retail trade, opening specialty retail stores throughout Germany and Europe. Germany accounts for about half of their total sales, and sales grew 39 percent in 2004. Esprit has more than 1,000 owned and franchised stores in 40 countries. They are positioning themselves as a more upmarket H&M. Like H&M, Esprit produces 12 collections a year.

H&M is the world's largest fast-fashion retailer and Germany is their biggest market. They have nearly 300 stores in Germany, and that market accounts for nearly a quarter of their sales. H&M bought the German operations of Gap (U.S.) in 2004.

Kaufhof Warenhaus was purchased by Metro in 2004. Metro has tried to restore the company, but results have been sad. The company has decided to reverse its long-time policy of using promotions to boost sales, and instead is reaching for a more upscale market. Eighty percent of its stores have been converted to the Galeria Kaufhof concept,[19] dividing sales areas within the store into "shops within a shop." This produces an atmosphere similar to a specialty store with an above-average proportion of higher-quality branded merchandise. This could put them at an advantage compared to low-cost operators. Kaufhof obtained the know-how for this concept when it acquired Horten, the concept's original developer. Horten did not begin to operate department stores until after the war. As a result, the company did not get the best retail sites. This forced it to compete in other ways, including the successful Galeria concept.

Although headquartered in Belgium, C&A derives most of its business in Germany; nearly half of its stores are located there. The company has 11 private label lines and sells 100 percent private label budget apparel. C&A's future expansion is focused largely on Central Europe, especially Hungary and Austria. C&A uses 3D body scanner technology, reading the customer's measurements in less than 10 seconds, for two million measuring points. This technology is mainly used to produce custom clothes for men. They are also perfecting a Bodyguard treatment that uses Scotchlet Reflective technology to produce a fabric which has greater visibility at night.[20]

Mango (Spain), a fast retailer, has made expansion in Germany, where they have 45 locations, a high priority.

## Food Retailing

German consumers have reached the point where brand name products are considered interchangeable. In a government survey, consumers indicated that 85 percent of all consumer goods and 65 percent of all consumer durables received the classification of "good" from consumers. This view of product equality will intensify. Brand names provide added value in very few cases. This makes price a more important parameter and opens the door for no-name products. These no-name products have turned into a product group with the greatest value added.[21]

Food companies have great selling power and great buying power in Germany. This causes a vertical-backward squeeze on food manufacturers. In fact, the food distribution industry is one of the most highly concentrated industries in Germany. More than 60 percent of sales come from 0.3 percent of food distributors.[22]

In contrast, food manufacturers are very small, having one of the lowest concentration ratios of any industry in Germany. This creates an imbalance in the distribution power. The big food distributors are an oligopoly as sellers and an oligopsony of purchasers.[23] OLIGOPSONY means there are few buyers and many suppliers. Food manufacturers have a limited number of companies to whom they can sell. This gives the food retailers a great deal of power. Food retailers are highly integrated, both vertically and horizontally.

Edeka Group is the largest retailer in Germany based on number of stores. It generates 95 percent of its sales in the home market. The group has 14 cooperatives with over 4,000 retail members. This network consists of around 9,000 outlets.[24]

Aldi is the second-largest food retailer. They have perfected the hard discount format. The price war between Aldi and Schwarz Group's Lidl have cut away at Aldi's market share. With the domestic market so competitive, Aldi has focused on the international market. In 2005, Aldi began to accept debit cards, ending a long-term commitment to cash-only payments.

Rewe is the third-largest food retailer. Like Edeka, the company is a cooperative. It focuses primarily on supermarkets, but also has hard discounters. Rewe also operates DIY, electronics, and apparel specialty stores.

Schwarz group has two discount giants, Lidl hard discount stores and Kaufland hypermarkets. Lidl trails Aldi in Germany but is a leader in other parts of Europe, operating in 18 countries with plans to be in all 25 EU countries. Kaufland has a superior logistics system to Lidl. It pays 70 percent of its invoice volume through EDI.[25]

## Television Shopping

Television shopping is a growth area in Germany. The biggest teleshopping companies are HSE (Home Shopping Europe) and QVC, although leading retailers like Metro and KarstadtQuelle are also using television shopping as part of their multichannel formats. Nearly 70 percent of HSE's customers and over 75 percent of QVC's customers are over 50 years of age. The most popular items being sold are jewelry, home electronics, and beauty or wellness products.[26]

## Retail Technology

Germany is one of the leaders in retail technology. All the leading retailers have websites, and some companies like Otto and KarstadtQuelle have 30 to 40 sites. Otto's main website, otto.de, started in 1995, and now sells 100,000 articles from its main catalogue. Shopping24.de, an online shopping mall selling products from 30 different countries, opened in 1997.[27]

In 2003, Edeka Nord developed a TRACEABILITY system for beef. You can track the product from origin to point of consumption, from farm to shop. DNA analysis is used to confirm the information. This kind of system could greatly increase consumer trust, and it provides a high value-added service.[28]

Metro has developed the Future Store. It is an amazing combination of the highest technology and RFID information tags. RFID (RADIO FREQUENCY IDENTIFICATION) tags can contain vast amounts of information. I was at the National Retail Federation convention when Metro first launched the Future Store, setting up a prototype at the conference. We were each given a set of headphones to hear the presentation. We were also given an RFID handset reader that we used to decipher the information from the tags. Bar codes do not include any information of inherent interest to consumers. But RFID tags provide information related to individual items. Therefore, SMART SHELVES that can read RFID information can also allow consumers to trace the production path of the product. Smart shelves have small sensors that read the RFID tags, sensing when the inventory needs to be replenished, or noting if merchandise is past selling date. The Future Store also had a weighing system where a digital camera was used to sense the product being weighed and then calculate the price automatically from the information on the RFID tag. The actual Future Store is located in Rheinberg, Germany. The system will be tested in the next five years before a decision is made about further implementation of this high-tech equipment for supermarkets.

Another important feature of RFID technology is that the data held on the tag can be updated after the original data has been loaded. This provides a great deal of flexibility for the channel system provider. Unlike scanning data, RFID technology does not have to be in the line of sight of the bar code reader, which means that consumers in a supermarket can have a whole cart of merchandise scanned at once. Tags can be read through nonmetallic materials; approximately 60 tags can be read at once. Products tagged with RFID technology can provide volumes of data to consumers. For wines that could include an encyclopedia of information about where the grapes were grown, or vitaculture history and the calory count for each glass of this wine. Reducing distribution costs can reduce price to the ultimate consumer; however, there are likely other applications that can enhance consumer satisfaction and lead to consumers' requesting RFID technology. Unfortunately, partway through my technology tour the system stopped working, so we had to imagine what the experience would be like. Even with the technical flaws I was hooked.

Both Metro and KarstadtQuelle use e-procurement in their organizations. KarstadtQuelle uses auctions for procurement, estimating that they have saved 10 percent by using this method. In 2002, KarstadtQuelle carried out over 1,000 auctions, primarily on electronic products. The advantage of auctions is that they provide great transparency, particularly related to price. They are very quick and you do not have to depend on the expertise of one particular buyer. KarstadtQuelle is sharing data via the GlobalNetXchange (GNX), which will facilitate the collaborative process of planning and forecasting inventory needs.

### Private Label

Private label has grown in all areas of German retailing. Originally retailers did not think that private label was important because it had such a highly developed pricing system, but competition from the hard discounters has convinced them that it is necessary. Aldi is the company that deserves the most credit for developing private label competition in Germany. Over a 30-year period they have developed a reputation of producing a superb private label line and for dispelling the low-quality stigma attached to private labels. Aldi is a market leader in high-quality products, including champagne. One German friend told me that when Aldi first opened up, few respectable people would be seen in the store. But they have been won over by the quality of the private label offerings and the rock bottom prices.

All large German grocery retailers have introduced private labels. Tengelmann, a privately held company, has over 1,000 private label products. Originally the private label offering in German grocery stores was considered inferior to the national brands, but the retailers have upgraded their offerings. Now most German consumers feel that private label products are on par with national brands. Most retailers have even segmented their private label offering, providing tiers of quality or special private lines like organic.

### ⟩ FRANCE

### Country Background

France has always been a crossroads of Europe. Julius Caesar conquered the region, which he called Gaul. It was a part of the Roman Empire for 500 years. With the collapse of the Roman Empire, a tribe of people called Franks moved in. In the ninth century, this area was the major component of the Frankish empire created by Charlemagne. The Franks intermarried with the Gallo-Roman population they ruled and became Romanized themselves, giving a Romanized version of their name to the country, France.

France was one of the first European countries to move from feudalism to a nation state. French armies were the most disciplined of any in their day, warring with England and others countries. During the rule of Louis XIV (1643–1713), France was the premier power in Europe.

Louis, however, was overambitious, which led to financial difficulties for France in the eighteenth century. A bad economy and popular resentment against the rich led to the French Revolution of 1789–1794. Interestingly, the French revolutionaries were inspired by the revolution of the American colonies against England a decade earlier.

France had 26 changes in government between 1946 and 1958. By the time Charles de Gaulle became prime minister in 1958, government instability had lead the country, and it had come close to a military coup.[29]

France has one of the oldest and most diverse retail networks.[30] It is the home of both the department store and the hypermarket format. France is Europe's second-largest retail market, after Germany. Although France and the United Kingdom have about the same population, French consumers purchase over half as much again as consumers in the U.K. market. The country is also known for identifying a good idea and transmitting that idea throughout the world. For the French, inspiration begins with the arts and finds practical application in the way they do business.

Tables 12.3 and 12.4 summarize the major domestic and foreign retailers in France. France can claim seven of the top 100 retailers in the world.[31] The French hypermarket format has spread throughout the world. Carrefour is the second-largest retailer in the world, operating hypermarkets, discount, convenience, and specialty stores in 35 countries. In 1999 they merged with Promodes, another French company that at the time ranked 16th in the world, having hypermarkets, super-markets, cash-and-carry, and convenience store formats in seven countries. Seventeenth in the world is Auchan, operating hypermarkets in 12 countries. Casino is 26th. It operates hypermarkets, supermarkets, and convenience stores in 19 countries. PPR Group (formerly Pinault-Printemp-Redoute) is 39th. This company uses mail order, department stores, supermarkets, and specialty stores in 29 countries to obtain its sales volume.[32] French retail companies are some of the most international in the world. Their international expansion can be explained in large part by the governmental restrictions in their home country.

## Nonfood Retailers

France is a country with many regions that maintain a strong identity. Originally, retail chains developed in regional areas. These regional chains are now giving way to national chains. Nearly 75 percent of France's population lives in urban areas, with 9.3 million people in Paris alone. The market is considered saturated. Thus, instead of opening new stores at home, the French majors are closing unprofitable stores at home and moving into foreign markets.[33] Construction costs are lower and competition less severe in their selected foreign markets. Additionally, in 1997 two important pieces of legislature made expansion within France nearly impossible and limited the profitability of retailers operating there. These two situations have pushed French retailers even more than before to seek international markets.

There have been some notable failures in French company expansion. Galeries Lafayette opened a store in New York City that did not prove successful and was closed. Carrefour's initial entry into the United States was not successful, and the company needed to withdraw. French hypermarkets have learned that their export

**Table 12-3**
**France—Leading Domestic Retailers, 2004**

| Company | Primary Line of Trade | Net Sales ($US Mil) | % Chg Sales | Total Stores | 2004 Rank, Top 200 Retailers Worldwide | Single-country, Regional or Global? | Number of countries | Domestic Market Share of total sales | Share of total stores |
|---|---|---|---|---|---|---|---|---|---|
| 1 Carrefour Group | Hypermarkets/Supercenters | 101,235 | 3.2% | 11,080 | 2 | Global | 31 | 49% | 33% |
| 2 ITM Entreprises SA | Supermarkets/Grocery Stores | 47,264 | 13.8% | 7,247 | 8 | Regional | 9 | 71% | 47% |
| 3 Auchan Groupe | Hypermarkets/Supercenters | 37,371 | 4.7% | 2,560 | 18 | Global | 12 | 61% | 21% |
| 4 Centres E. Leclerc | Supermarkets/Grocery Stores | 34,969 | 4.3% | 1,538 | 24 | Regional | 6 | 95% | 97% |
| 5 Rallye (i.e., Casino) | Supermarkets/Grocery Stores | 29,630 | 0.9% | 9,417 | 26 | Global | 17 | 81% | 78% |
| 6 Pinault-Printemps-Redoute SA | Non-Store | 19,662 | 8.4% | 962 | 36 | Global | 17 | 49% | 83% |
| 7 Système U | Supermarkets/Grocery Stores | 18,266 | 6.5% | 849 | 39 | Single Country | 1 | 100% | 100% |
| 8 Cora Group/Louis Delhaize | Supermarkets/Grocery Stores | 11,316 | 5.3% | 775 | 65 | Global | 7 | 71% | 37% |
| 9 LVMH | Other Apparel Specialty Stores | 9,627 | 7.7% | 1,693 | 76 | Global | 56 | 17% | 16% |
| 10 Leroy Merlin | DIY/Home Improvement Stores | 6,841 | 14.6% | 791 | 112 | Global | 8 | 57% | 79% |
| 11 Groupe Galeries Lafayette | Department Stores | 4,931 | 1.0% | 520 | 138 | Regional | 2 | N/A | 100% |

Sources: Retail Forward, company annual reports and published reports

**Table 12.4**
**France—Key Foreign Retailers, 2004**

| Company | Headquarters | Retail Sector | Primary Line of Trade | Global Rank and Penetration | | |
|---|---|---|---|---|---|---|
| | | | | 2004 Rank, Top 200 Retailers Worldwide | Single-country, Regional or Global? | Number of countries |
| Aldi Group | Germany | FDM | Discount Food Stores | 13 | Global | 13 |
| Amazon.com | United States | Homegoods | Non-Store | 111 | Global | 7 |
| Anton Schlecker | Germany | FDM | Drug Stores | 95 | Regional | 9 |
| Bertelsmann AG | Germany | Homegoods | Non-Store | – | Global | 22 |
| C&A | Belgium | Softgoods | Apparel Stores | 105 | Global | 15 |
| Dixons Group | United Kingdom | Homegoods | Consumer Electronics & Appliances | 56 | Regional | 14 |
| Groep Colruyt | Belgium | FDM | Supermarkets/Grocery Stores | 125 | Regional | 2 |
| Grupo Eroski | Spain | FDM | Supermarkets/Grocery Stores | 113 | Regional | 2 |
| IKEA AB | Sweden | Homegoods | Furniture & Home Furnishings | 44 | Global | 32 |
| INDITEX Group (i.e., Zara) | Spain | Softgoods | Apparel Stores | 110 | Global | 56 |
| Karstadt Quelle AG | Germany | Softgoods | Non-Store | 42 | Regional | 19 |
| Kesa Electricals | United Kingdom | Homegoods | Consumer Electronics & Appliances | 106 | Regional | 6 |
| Kingfisher PLC | United Kingdom | Homegoods | DIY/Home Improvement Stores | 50 | Global | 9 |
| Mango | Spain | Softgoods | Apparel Stores | – | Global | 76 |
| Matsuzakaya Co. Ltd. | Japan | Softgoods | Department Stores | – | Global | 2 |
| Metro AG | Germany | FDM | Cash & Carries/Warehouse Clubs | 4 | Global | 29 |
| Migros - Genossenschaftsbund | Switzerland | FDM | Supermarkets/Grocery Stores | 53 | Regional | 3 |
| Mitsukoshi Ltd | Japan | Softgoods | Department Stores | 98 | Global | 9 |
| Norma Lebensmittelfilialbetrieb GmbH & Co. KG | Germany | FDM | Discount Food Stores | 174 | Regional | 3 |
| Office Depot, Inc. | United States | Homegoods | Office Supply | 54 | Global | 23 |
| Otto Group | Germany | Softgoods | Non-Store | 61 | Global | 19 |
| Rewe-Gruppe | Germany | FDM | Supermarkets/Grocery Stores | 14 | Regional | 14 |
| Royal Vendex KBB N.V. | Netherlands | Softgoods | DIY/Home Improvement Stores | 134 | Regional | 7 |
| Schwarz Group | Germany | FDM | Discount Food Stores | 12 | Regional | 19 |
| Staples, Inc. | United States | Homegoods | Office Supply | 47 | Global | 18 |
| Takashimaya Company, Limited | Japan | Softgoods | Department Stores | 84 | Global | 5 |
| Toys "R" Us, Inc. | United States | Homegoods | Toy Stores | 68 | Global | 30 |

Sources: Retail Forward, company annual reports and published reports

efforts are more successful in central Europe and Latin America, where retail development lags behind other areas.

The first department store, Bon Marché, appeared in Paris, and France has remained a leader in the department store sector for 130 years. Traditional department stores are having a difficult time today in France. Department stores have not streamlined their distribution systems like their hypermarket counterparts.

The French department stores have been caught in a positioning squeeze. During the economic downturn, they stocked more modestly priced merchandise. Then discounters entered the market, providing lower prices for the same merchandise. The higher department store overhead did not allow them to compete with discounters on price. However, by repositioning for a more upscale market, the department stores should be helped in the long run.

Galeries Lafayette, PRR (formerly Pinault-Printemps-Redoute), and LVMH are the leading softgoods retailers. Galeries Lafayette has a joint venture with Casino to develop the Monoprix chain. It is one of the few French retailers that can compete with the fast fashion companies like Zara and H&M. Monoprix, an upscale discount format, accounts for about one-third of total sales for Galeries Lafayette. Galeries Lafayette has also been expanding in several new concepts such as lingerie and the Maison Lafayette home furnishings and design store.

PPR is Europe's largest nonfood retailer. About half the company's sales occur in France where they trade under the names of Printemps department stores, Citadium and Made in Sport sporting goods stores, and Madelios menswear stores. They also have seven luxury brands of the Gucci group. The Printemps stores generate nearly half of the company's sales.[34]

LVMH (Louis Vuitton Moet Hennessy) sells some of the world's most famous luxury brands, sold through company-owned boutiques. The group also ownes DFS (duty free shops), the Sephora cosmetics chain, and Le Bon Marché and Samaritaine department stores.

**Photo 12.2**
Galeries Lafayette in Paris on Boulevard Haussmann located next to Au Printemps and across the street from Marks & Spencer. The historic Paris Opera House, setting for the *Phantom of the Opera* story, is across the street. This is the premier retail location in Paris. *Courtesy Condé Nast.*

**Photo 12.3**
Several European
countries, including France,
allow mark-downs only
twice a year. The length of
the sale periods is also
prescribed by law. *Courtesy
of the author.*

Specialty chains are taking market share away from traditional department stores. Nearly all of the foreign retailers entering France are specialty store chains. Part of the reason for this is that the *Loi Royer* law (discussed later in the chapter) does not cover smaller-sized retailers. Specialty stores also seem to address the unique French lifestyle. Mango, Zara, Esprit, and H&M have 8 percent market share of the apparel market in France. All of these companies have over 50 stores in France and consider it a major market for expansion. Etam Development is a French company competing in the fast fashion area.

## Food Retailers

The main food retailing groups (the independent companies, Intermarché and Leclerc, and the integrated groups, Carrefour-Promodes and Casino) have 64 percent of the total selling space of supermarkets and hypermarkets in France.

Carrefour was the first retailer to develop the hypermarket concept, opening its first store in France in 1963. In 1973, it expanded to Spain and in 1975, to Brazil. Carrefour focuses its expansion efforts on countries where modern retailing is not established. In these countries, hypermarkets are a new concept. They attract customers with their large range of food and nonfood product lines and competitive prices. The company now has over 10,000 stores in 36 countries. Unfortunately this concentration on foreign expansion has seriously affected their effectiveness at home. Although Carrefour derives one-half of its sales and two-thirds of its profits from the domestic market, they have been struggling at home because of a weak French economy, competition from hard discounters, and government price regulations. Carrefour has responded by increasing the presence of its hard discount formats, Ed and Dia. As a result sales at Carrefour's hard discount and supermarket formats showed double-digit sales growth. However, the hypermarket format sales

**Photo 12.4**
This Carrefour cosmetics section offers customers a huge selection. Carrefour is the French company credited with developing the hypermarket format. *Courtesy of Condé Nast.*

were stagnant. Carrefour launched a private label brand called Number One that undercut discounter's prices by 7 to 10 percent.[35]

Centres E. Leclerc is the second-biggest retailer in France, behind Carrefour. Leclerc is a cooperative. Their main business is a supermarket chain but they also operate hypermarkets and specialty stores. The company has a brand of private label called Eco+, which has 850 products.

Auchan operates hypermarkets under the company name and supermarkets under the Atac banner. In 2004 Auchan opened Chronodrive, a drive-thru outlet where customers can choose from more than 4,000 products. Customers can either give their order through an electronic terminal at the drive-in or order online in advance. They have also opened a discount food concept called Les Halles d'Auchan. It is a large format, 4,500 square meters, that focuses on fresh foods and private label products in a warehouse-style presentation. They can open this large scale format because they are converting previously existing stores.[36]

ITM Enterprises is a cooperative of independent merchants called musketeers, who operate under nine banners in six channels. Most of the outlets in France are known as Intermarché, Ecomarché, or Relais des Mousquetaires grocery stores. The company also has over 300 Netto hard-discount stores in France and has a majority stake (97 percent) in Spar Handels AG of Germany. In 2004, ITM introduced the Top Budget label with a line of 300 products.[37]

Casino operates supermarkets, hypermarkets, discount stores, and convenience stores in 19 countries. The group has over 6,700 outlets in France. They have nearly 1,000 hard discount outlets, mainly operating under the names Frarnprix and Leader Price.

Systeme U is a cooperative that mainly operates in rural areas and smaller cities. Their formats include hypermarkets, supermarkets, and convenience stores.

Aldi was the first to launch the hard discount format in France and others have been scrambling to compete or replicate what they are doing. Aldi has over 600 stores in France. Lidl, the other major German hard discounter, entered the French market later than Aldi, but has taken over their lead and now has over 1,000 stores.

Both companies have been helped by the law restricting the opening of stores over 300 square meters because they are both small-scale format stores.

Carrefour has been held up as the textbook example of a multinational company. A multinational company expands internationally, using a decentralized control system. Since 1994, however, Carrefour has been reversing this strategy, moving to centralize its operations. The major benefits of this reversal are in purchasing. By having a larger common product range, the company can centralize negotiation of purchasing terms to obtain better prices. Logistics are also enhanced with centralized control. More uniform product ranges results in cost savings that can lead to increased use of warehouses and loading platforms. This system is more productive than delivery directly to the stores. Centralization allows the company to use data-processing capabilities. This allows Carrefour to manage supplies and inventory, leading to just-in-time delivery and centralized payment of invoices.

## Government Regulations

France, like most European countries, has laws restricting large-scale retailers' expansion. These laws have made expansion in France difficult. The newest laws make domestic expansion almost impossible for large stores.

France has operated under the *Roi Loyer* since 1973. Government officials are now making the retail planning laws even tighter. Currently all retailers are required to obtain a permit. This law has been applied for 20 years. It is a part of the general European concern over the degradation of city centers when retailers are not kept within those locations.

French regulators recently amended the law to lower the size requirement for which a permit is needed. They will now require that stores get approval. The law is viewed as an anti-hypermarket measure that appeals to small retail representatives. However, the law will also greatly affect foreign discounters and category killers that pose a competitive threat to hypermarkets. Discounters had been adapting to the 300–square meter limit and were expanding their numbers. The French hypermarkets may favor this law and view it as a protection from discounters.[38]

Despite the restrictive legislation related to opening hypermarkets and supermarkets in France, large-scale food retailers have grown rapidly during the past 20 years. This growth has been at the expense of traditional stores, such as neighborhood stores, department stores, and general stores. Hypermarkets and supermarkets have 58 percent of the food retailing business and more than 31 percent of the specialty retailing trade in France.[39] The restrictive legislation helps the large-scale businesses that are currently operating in France. Hypermarkets in France operate at a very large scale, which means that start-up costs are very high. It takes between six and eight years for a store to break even when it is this large. This is a barrier to entry for newcomers.

## Sales at a Loss

In 1997, I conducted a series of interviews in France regarding retailer-supplier relationships. Several people mentioned that the 1997 French pricing law called *Loi Galland* was creating friction between French retailers and their suppliers. Spain has passed a law very similar to this French law. Like planning laws that regulate the opening of large-scale retailers, I found that many European countries have laws regulating retail pricing and retail price reduction practices.

In some countries there are no special regulations covering pricing. Denmark, Germany, Spain, Italy, United Kingdom, and Sweden have quite liberal pricing laws. However, in other countries SALES AT A LOSS, as the practice is called, are strictly prohibited. Sales at a loss are not actually selling the merchandise below cost, but selling it BELOW INVOICED COST. Invoice may not be actual price to the retailer because a retailer might receive year-end discounts due to volume or for special promotions that the retailer launches for the supplier. The director of France's major retail trade organization explained it to me using this diagram.

### Four Different Prices

| | |
|---|---:|
| Base cost (Supplier's charge to the retailer or list price) | 100 |
| Discount depending on purchasing terms (delivery or length of time before retailer must pay for the merchandise) | −10 |
| Invoiced price (called net price) | 90 |
| Conditional discounts, including the yearly volume discount | −5 |
| Net/net price | 85 |
| Commercial cooperation costs (in store promotions, etc.) | −10 |
| Real purchasing costs | 75 |

The net price appears on the invoice sent by the supplier to the retailers. However, it might be that the net/net price including the yearly volume discount is really what they will pay for the merchandise. The retailer issues an invoice to charge the supplier with the commercial corporation costs. Those expenses will be reimbursed. The real costs to the retailer for the products are the net/net price, the price after they have received discounts for volume.[40] France's new law requires that the retailer sell for the invoice price.

Because of this law, at least theoretically, the hypermarkets would need to increase the selling prices on very discounted items. This would reduce the price difference between hypermarkets and supermarkets and would make supermarkets more attractive. On the other hand it could make margins across the board higher and consumers will be hurt. The measure is politically motivated, partially to protect small retailers and more specifically to reduce the attractiveness of the hard food discounter prices.

This law will also make development of private label products more attractive to retailers. Shortly after the law passed, manufacturers began to realize that the predictable response of retailers would be to go in the direction of private label.[41]

Belgium was the first to make it illegal for a trader to offer products at less than what the product is invoiced, or will be invoiced in the event of resupply. Certain exceptions are made for special sales such as end-of-season sales and sales when the company is going out of business. Portugal's laws require that sale of an item cannot be lower than the supplier's purchase price plus the tax on the sale.

Luxembourg's law Article 20 makes these exceptions when goods can be sold at lower than invoice price. Promotional prices outside seasonal and clearance sales are authorized when you have the following conditions: 1) any advertisement of price reductions must clearly state the promotional nature of the offer, 2) the date from which the reduced price is applicable must continue to be shown throughout the period of the offer, and 3) reference may be made to former prices, provided the prices were applied previously on the same premises to identical products for a continuous period of at least two months immediately preceding the date from which the reduced price is applicable. Seasonal sales can occur only twice a year, at the beginning of the winter and summer seasons, and can last only one month at a maximum. Clearance sales are allowed only if the business is closing, moving, or has had an accident that damaged the merchandise.

## 〉 SUMMARY

Germany is best known as the home of hard discounters and a heavily concentrated department store sector. The most memorable event in the country's past two decades has been reunification, which had a major impact on retailing in Germany. Almost immediately it brought astronomical increases in sales for West German retailers located close to the former border. These sales were from the East Germans who came to spend money they had hoarded for years, as they waited for the chance to purchase better quality goods. In the long term, unification has had important consequences for retailing. It opened a new country for West German retailers' expansion prospects, just when these opportunities appeared saturated. As a result, German retailers have not been particularly interested in expanding outside Germany. Once these growth opportunities slow, however, a sleek and efficient retail machine can be expected to move into eastern Europe, led by German retailers, armed with knowledge gained through opening up the former East German trade area.

French retailers also found expansion opportunities blocked within their home market. The answer for hypermarkets was to move south, primarily to Spain, but also to Portugal and Italy. France and the southern Mediterranean countries share a Latin-based culture, and the French view these countries as culturally similar.

## 〉 KEY TERMS

CO-DETERMINATION
CONSUMER TOURISM
EURO SHOCK
INVOICED PRICE
OLIGOPSONY
RFID
SALES AT A LOSS
SMART SHELVES
TRACEABILITY

## 〉 DISCUSSION QUESTIONS

1. Discuss how Germany's "green laws" affect retailers. Do these laws make it easier or harder for retailers from other countries to enter the German market?
2. How are the German hard discount food retailers different from other food retailers in Europe? What cultural changes would need to take place to make the German hard discounting format attractive in the United Kingdom?

3. Why would the two largest department store groups in Germany acquire the next two largest retailers? What would you expect from an industry that has such a high degree of concentration?

4. Why do you think French hypermarkets have been so successful in southern parts of Europe, and even Mexico and South America, but not successful in northern parts of Europe or the United States?

5. A law in France stipulates that retailers cannot sell at a loss; would a retailer ever want to sell below cost? What are the effects of such a law?

6. In Germany the law stipulates that employees get an equal share on the board of directors. How would this affect decision making within the firm? What are the long-term implications?

## ❯ ENDNOTES

1. "Germany." (1995). *Craighead's International Business, Travel, and Relocation Guide to More Than 80 Countries.* Detroit: Gale Research.

2. Karstadt Annual Report (1991).

3. Retailing in Germany. (2004). GMID Euromonitor, April.

4. Retailing in Germany. (2004).

5. Retailing in Germany. (2004).

6. Retailing in Germany. (2004).

7. Retailing in Germany. (2005). Columbus, Ohio: Retail Forward, January.

8. Retailing in Germany. (2005).

9. Retailing in Germany. (2005).

10. Retailing in Germany. (2004).

11. Retailing in Germany. (2004).

12. Retailing in Germany. (2004).

13. Retailing in Germany. (2004).

14. Retailing in Germany. (2005).

15. 2006 Global Powers in Retailing. (2006). Stores, January Section 2.

16. Oppenheim Finanzanalyse GMBH, October 2, 1995. Kaufhof Company Report.

17. *Retail News Letter.* (1995). No. 425, June, p. 2.

18. Retailing in Germany. (2005).

19. Retailing in Germany. (2005).

20. Retailing in Germany. (2005).

21. "Retailers: Germany—Industry Report." (1996).

22. Marfels, Christian (1991). "Concentration and Buying Power: The Case of German Food Distribution." *International Review of Retail, Distribution, and Consumer Research*, vol. 2, No. 3, pp. 233–244.

23. Sternquist, B., and M. Kacker. (1994). *European Retailing's Vanishing Borders.* Westport, CT: Quorum Press.

24. Retailing in Germany. (2005).

25. Retailing in Germany. (2005).

26. Retailing in Germany. (2004).

27. Retailing in Germany. (2004).

28. Retailing in Germany. (2004).

29. "France." (1995). *Craighead's International Business, Travel, and Relocation Guide to More Than 80 Countries.* Detroit: Gale Research.

30. "Corporate Intelligence on Retailing." (1997). *The European Retail Handbook.* London: Corporate Intelligence on Retailing.

31. "2006 Global Powers of Retailing." (2006). Stores, January Section 2.

32. Coopers & Lybrand (1996). *Global Powers of Retailing.* Chain Store Age–Special Report.

33. Coopers & Lybrand (1996).

34. Retailing in France. (2004). Columbus, Ohio: Retail Forward.

35. Retailing in France. (2004).

36. Retailing in France. (2004).

37. Retailing in France. (2004).

38. *Retail News Letter.* (1995). No. 432, February, p. 4.

39. Hoare Govett Securities, LTD, April 24, 1995, Docks de France—Company Report.

40. Carrefour-Company Report UBS Research Limited, March 13, 1997, in Investext.

41. Personal Interviews, France, July 1997.

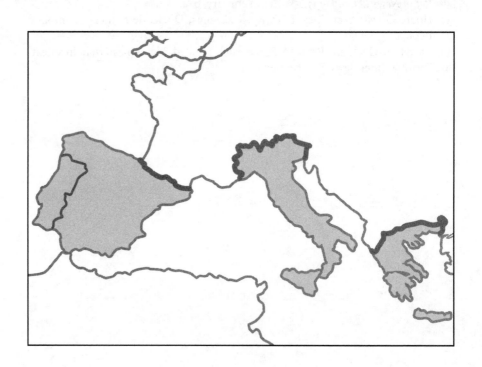

# 13

# RETAILING IN SPAIN, ITALY, GREECE, AND PORTUGAL

## After reading this chapter, you should understand

> How traditional retailers remain strong in these countries, and the changes that will need to take place before modern retail chains dominate.

> Why retailers from more developed countries and saturated markets are expanding aggressively into these areas.

> How retailers gain by using negative cash flow for expansion and be able to predict how this practice affects high growth versus low growth retailers.

> How restrictive laws, such as those in Italy, affect retailing and the impact these laws have on consumers, local retailers, and foreign retailers.

Spain, Italy, Greece, and Portugal form the old new Europe. Birth rates have declined throughout Europe, but the decline in population has been much slower in the south than in the north. This shift in population creates opportunities for retailers. Retailing in the Mediterranean and southern European countries is less developed than retailing in the rest of Europe. Most retailers in this part of Europe are mom-and-pop stores. Countries such as Spain and Italy have 26 stores per 1,000 inhabitants compared with France or the United Kingdom, with eight or nine per 1,000.

Women are less likely to work outside the home in these regions, although this is changing rapidly. This has two effects: lack of dual earning capacity keeps household incomes low and women have more time to shop, making technological conveniences less important. Retail competition is just beginning to intensify, led by foreign retailers who are entering this region as their own countries become saturated. French retailers have followed this pattern, expanding aggressively into Spain.

## › SPAIN

### Country Background

Spain's history is one of repeated invasions. Celtic tribes came from the north. Phoenicians and Greeks arrived from the south. Romans incorporated "Hispania" into their empire. They introduced the Roman language, laws, and culture, and later Christianity. When the Roman Empire collapsed in the fifth century A.D., Germanic tribes plundered their way through Spain. Finally, the Moors from North Africa swept up through Spain conquering nearly the entire country. The Moors introduced Islam, and under their rule, a rich civilization arose. Cities were prosperous. The environment attracted brilliant writers and great philosophers. With Jews, Christians, and Moslems contributing, Spain became a center for arts and learning for all three cultures. This was in sharp contrast to the rest of Europe in the Middle Ages.

The Moslems gradually fell back in Spain as the strengthening Christian kingdoms of the north pressed forward. The Christians finally took Granada, at the southern tip of Spain, in 1492. That year also marks the beginning of Spain's expansion into the New World, with the voyage of Christopher Columbus, financed by the Spanish monarchs. The next century was Spain's golden age. Its holdings in America produced great wealth. By the end of the century, however, the nation had exhausted itself with war and immigration of people and resources to the New World. Spanish supremacy had ended.

Spain fought a civil war in 1936. It gave aid to the Axis powers during World War II but did not declare itself part of the conflict. Spain's political system underwent a major change in the 1970s when the country passed a constitution approved by popular referendum and sanctioned by its king.[1] During Franco's reign Spain was a closed society in both cultural and economic terms. It was only after 1975 that economic liberalization took place. The top six retail businesses account for 23.5 percent of retail sales. The dominant firm El Corte Ingles accounts for only 7.6 percent of sales. The market is very fragmented.[2]

Today, Spain belongs to the youth. It has the largest percentage of persons under the age of 25 in Europe. Many visitors from around the world visit Spain to experience its unique culture in the one remaining affordable environment in Europe.

**Photo 13.1**
El Corte Inglés is Spain's largest retailer. This store is one of several located in Mexico City. The stores are full-scale department stores, offering a complete range of hard and soft lines. *Courtesy of the author.*

Spain's GDP grew an average of 3 percent over the last few years; this growth combined with relatively low unemployment and inflation have made for very positive economic conditions.

Retailing in Spain follows a different pattern than that of northern Europe. Most stores close between 2 and 5 P.M. for lunch and the siesta hour. Shops do not open in the morning until 10:00 or 10:30 A.M. They stay open until 8:00 or 10:00 P.M. Nearly 40 percent of a retailer's sales is generated during the weekend. Sunday is just as important a shopping day as Saturday. The most popular time to shop is after 6:00 P.M., when 50 percent of sales takes place. Restaurants do not open until 8:30 P.M. and do not begin to fill until 10:00 P.M. Prime time TV starts at 10:30 P.M.

My son accompanied me to Spain on several trips. On the first trip he was a typical 15-year-old, always hungry. We ended up eating at a McDonald's-type fast food outlet several evenings because he simply could not wait for the restaurants to open at 8:30. The few times he could last until the formal dinner hour, we were surprised to see families with young children dining out together, often at midnight.

Spain is one of the least saturated markets in Europe. Because of the potential consumer demand, it is viewed as one of the most attractive retail markets in Europe. Spanish retailing has changed rapidly since the 1970s. The Spanish retail market skipped several predictable development stages to progress from outdated to ultramodern retail forms. This means the family food shop was replaced with the giant hypermarket without passing through the intervening stages of supermarket or variety store.

Several U.S. companies, such as Federated, Woolworth, and Sears, attempted to enter the Spanish market. They failed and were forced to leave. In 2004 Marks & Spencer threw in the towel and sold their stores to El Corte Inglés. The biggest success story to date has been the French hypermarkets' entry into Spain. French hypermarkets are found throughout Spanish suburbs. During the 1960s, only one Spaniard in a hundred owned a car; now, about one in three has a car. This has contributed to hypermarket growth. Shoppers coming to the hypermarket purchase a volume of merchandise that cannot be transported without an automobile.

Although Spain still has a very fragmented retail market it is expected to develop rapidly. The three major trends over the next few years are likely to be retail concentration and internationalization, modernization and expansion; and quality over price. The top 28 retailers in Spain are made up of 19 non-specialists (18 of which were food-led), three apparel specialists, two leisure goods specialists, two furniture specialists, and two electrical appliance specialists. This gives you an idea of the low penetration of large retailers in Spain. Spain has been used to being the poor relative of Western Europe, but this is changing. GDP in Spain has increased from 76 percent of the European Union average in the mid 1970s to 88 percent of the average now. Spain's joining the EU stimulated a period of intense trade reform. They also were helped from significant EU development funding channeled toward improving its infrastructure. Monetary policy underwent a series of changes as the economy gradually opened up, shifting its focus to price stability. Spain was among the first countries to introduce the euro.[3]

On my first visit to Spain, I took the train from Bordeaux, France, to Barcelona, Spain. As I crossed the border on the rim of the Pyrenees Mountains, I was reminded of the barren American southwest. The buildings, roads, and vegetation seemed to come right out of a Zane Grey novel. However, arrival in Barcelona brings the visitor right back to the present day. Barcelona is as sophisticated as any other great European city. The city hosted the Summer Olympics in 1992, and in preparation for this event cleaned up its shorefront and beautified its public spaces. Throughout the city, wide boulevards open onto lovely parks. Tables 13.1 and 13.2 summarize the major domestic and foreign retailers in Spain.

## Nonfood Retailers

**DEPARTMENT STORES**    El Corte Inglés is the largest retailer in Spain. Founded in 1940 as a small clothing store, the company now has over 50 department stores and 32 hypermarkets (Hipercor) found in the main population centers. Until 1994, El Corte Inglés had a competitor, Galerias Preciados, with 31 department stores. The groups had long been rivals. Galerias Preciados was the uncontested market leader until the 1960s, when the company was sold several times, tumbling each time further into decline. El Corte Inglés acquired Galerias Preciados in late 1994.

After El Corte Inglés purchased Galerias, the company entered 13 new cities. Interested in developing specialist formats, El Corte Inglés strategically positioned a toy store to compete with Toys " Я " Us. El Corte Inglés is a private group and avoids publicity. The company uses a high degree of vertical integration and is a leader in retailing technology.[4]

As the only remaining department store chain in Spain, El Corte Inglés has 89 percent of the department store industry. They also have the most successful Internet sites, selling 12 percent of Spanish Internet transactions. The company is held in very high esteem by Spanish customers. Their strategy is simple: provide everything for everybody, right across the social scale. For example, the company sells computers to the government and gas-powered domestic appliances to homeowners increase gas consumption.

**Table 13.1**
**Spain—Leading Domestic Retailers, 2004**

| | | Total Sales and Stores | | | Global Rank and Penetration | | | Domestic Market | |
|---|---|---|---|---|---|---|---|---|---|
| Company | Primary Line of Trade | Net Sales ($US Mil) | % Chg Sales | Total Stores | 2004 Rank, Top 200 Retailers Worldwide | Single-country, Regional or Global? | Number of countries | Share of total sales | Share of total stores |
| 1 El Corte Ingles | Department Stores | 17,443 | 7.7% | 390 | 40 | Regional | 2 | 98% | 99% |
| 2 Mercadona | Supermarkets/Grocery Stores | 10,908 | 21.5% | 862 | 71 | Single Country | 1 | 100% | 100% |
| 3 INDITEX Group (i.e. Zara) | Apparel Stores | 7,053 | 23.6% | 2,244 | 110 | Global | 56 | 46% | 59% |
| 4 Grupo Eroski | Supermarkets/Grocery Stores | 6,641 | 6.1% | 1,582 | 113 | Regional | 2 | N/A | 98% |
| 5 Caprabo | Supermarkets/Grocery Stores | 3,490 | 20.2% | 622 | 176 | Single Country | 1 | 100% | 100% |
| 6 Mango | Apparel Stores | 1,313 | 5.3% | 768 | — | Global | 76 | 27% | 30% |
| 7 Grupo Cortefiel | Apparel Stores | 1,139 | 5.5% | 1,100 | — | Global | 37 | 76% | 56% |
| 8 Miquel Alimentacio Grup S.A. | Supermarkets/Grocery Stores | 1,024 | 6.9% | 477 | — | Single Country | 1 | 100% | 100% |
| 9 Mundo Gadisa | Supermarkets/Grocery Stores | 1,016 | 7.0% | 422 | — | Regional | 2 | N/A | N/A |

Sources: Retail Forward, company annual reports and published reports

**Table 13.2**
**Spain—Key Foreign Retailers, 2004**

| Company | Headquarters | Retail Sector | Primary Line of Trade | Global Rank and Penetration | | |
|---|---|---|---|---|---|---|
| | | | | 2004 Rank, Top 200 Retailers Worldwide | Single-country, Regional or Global? | Number of countries |
| Aldi Group | Germany | FDM | Discount Food Stores | 13 | Global | 13 |
| Anton Schlecker | Germany | FDM | Drug Stores | 95 | Regional | 9 |
| Auchan Groupe | France | FDM | Hypermarkets/Supercenters | 18 | Global | 12 |
| Bauhaus | Germany | Homegoods | DIY/Home Improvement Stores | 139 | Regional | 10 |
| Bertelsmann AG | Germany | Homegoods | Non-Store | 215 | Global | 22 |
| C&A | Belgium | Softgoods | Apparel Stores | 105 | Global | 15 |
| Carrefour Group | France | FDM | Hypermarkets/Supercenters | 2 | Global | 31 |
| Centres E. Leclerc | France | FDM | Supermarkets/Grocery Stores | 24 | Regional | 6 |
| Defense Commissary Agency | United States | FDM | Supermarkets/Grocery Stores | 130 | Global | 13 |
| Dixons Group | United Kingdom | Homegoods | Consumer Electronics & Appliances | 56 | Regional | 14 |
| IKEA AB | Sweden | Homegoods | Furniture & Home Furnishings | 44 | Global | 32 |
| ITM Entreprises SA | France | FDM | Supermarkets/Grocery Stores | 8 | Regional | 9 |
| Karstadt Quelle AG | Germany | Softgoods | Non-Store | 42 | Regional | 19 |
| Kingfisher PLC | United Kingdom | Homegoods | DIY/Home Improvement Stores | 50 | Global | 9 |
| Leroy Merlin | France | Homegoods | DIY/Home Improvement Stores | 112 | Global | 8 |
| LVMH | France | Softgoods | Other Apparel Specialty Stores | 76 | Global | 56 |
| Metro AG | Germany | FDM | Cash & Carries/Warehouse Clubs | 4 | Global | 29 |
| Mitsukoshi Ltd | Japan | Softgoods | Department Stores | 98 | Global | 9 |
| Office Depot, Inc. | United States | Homegoods | Office Supply | 54 | Global | 23 |
| Otto Group | Germany | Softgoods | Non-Store | 61 | Global | 19 |
| Pinault-Printemps-Redoute SA | France | Homegoods | Non-Store | 36 | Global | 17 |
| Royal Vendex KBB N.V. | Netherlands | Softgoods | DIY/Home Improvement Stores | 134 | Regional | 7 |
| Schwarz Group | Germany | FDM | Discount Food Stores | 12 | Regional | 19 |
| Staples, Inc. | United States | Homegoods | Office Supply | 47 | Global | 18 |
| Tengelmann Warenhandelsgesellschaft | Germany | FDM | Supermarkets/Grocery Stores | 23 | Global | 15 |
| Toys "R" Us, Inc. | United States | Homegoods | Toy Stores | 68 | Global | 30 |

Sources: Retail Forward, company annual reports and published reports

**SPECIALTY STORES AND VARIETY STORES**    There are several successful chains in Spain. Inditex group ranks number 10 overall by turnover in Spanish retailing. They specialize in clothing and footwear retailing. The company chains include Zara, Massimo Dutti, Pull & Bear, Bershka, Stradivarius, and Oysho. The company is vertically integrated. Inditex's flagship brand, Zara, has been expanding rapidly in international markets. They might be considered one of the BORN GLOBAL international retailers who began international expansion before saturating the home market. Zara is a FAST FASHION or disposable chic retailer, dependent on very rapid sell through of inventory to create an emotional response in consumers. If they don't buy the product now, it will probably not be there later. Zara owns their own production factories.

Cortefiel is Spain's second-biggest clothing manufacturer and retailer. This company was founded in 1950. They operate seven chains: Cortefiel, Springfield, Women's Secret, Milano, Don Algodon, Douglas, and Pedro del Hierro. Cortefiel is expanding in the main European markets. They are expanding internationally with all their brands so that they can achieve economies of scale in distribution and purchasing.

## Food Retailers

The most significant trend in retailing in Spain is the shift from small food specialists to food based non-specialists like hypermarkets, supermarkets, and hard discount formats. More women have entered the work force (38 percent are working), and the pace of life in general has sped up in Spain, making one-stop shopping attractive. Consumers are more likely to go for one-stop shopping at a supermarket or hypermarket rather than make individual trips to the various specialists such as butchers, greengrocers, fishmongers, and bakeries.

There are four major hypermarket groups in Spain. Two of the four are associated with French companies. In 2001 Carrefour (Pryca) merged with Promodès (Continente), causing a higher degree of concentration in the grocery trade by creating Centros Comerciales Carrefour SA. As a result of the merger the government forced Centros Comerciales Carrefour to divest various outlets including 12 hypermarkets. Carrefour accounts for 43.7 percent share in the hypermarket subsector. Carrefour also operates Dia hard discount format in Spain. In 2005, Carrefour launched a new supermarket concept in Spain, Carrefour Express, to replace Carrefour's existing Champion brand of supermarkets. Carrefour's Spanish budget subsidiary Dia recently launched a similar concept, Maxi-Dia, which will also sell consumer goods.[5] The other French retailer is Auchan, who operates Alcampo. Hipercore is a Spanish hypermarket chain owned by El Corte Inglés. Eroski began as a Basque worker cooperative in 1969 and is now the second-largest player in terms of outlets and the fourth in terms of turnover. The group has 65 hypermarkets and 1,650 supermarkets.[6] Market share for these companies is Carrefour Alcampo (18.4 percent), Hipercor (17.3 percent), and Eroski (13.7 percent).

Mercadona SA is the third-largest retailer in Spain, but it is the country's fastest growing. The company operates on a national scale with 750 supermarkets. Ahold (Netherlands) and Lidl (Germany) are also active in the Spanish food market. Ahold operates supermarkets and Lindl operates a hard discount format.

### Internet Retailing

Price is a significant driver in Internet sales. Most of the Internet retailers in Spain provide significant discounts on products purchased online. They are able to do this because of the cost savings generated through automation of operations such as order taking, order processing, and fulfillment. Household appliances and consumer electronics ranked second in terms of sales. This includes large white goods (refrigerators, cleaning and cooking appliances). Internet sales seem to be suitable for these products because there are strong manufacturer and brand values. Since reliability and quality are most important to customers it isn't necessary to see the actual products; instead they focus on technical specifications and price. Because these are big ticket items, any price savings is important. One advantage of Internet retailing compared to bricks and mortar stores is that you can offer all sizes and models in a range, contrasted to high street retailers who are constrained by special concerns. Internet retailers also offer comprehensive return policies. PURE PLAY Internet retailers, those who do not have an acutal physical store, are rare in Spain.[7]

El Corte Inglés is the leading Internet retailer (elcorteingles.es). They offer a full range of products from their department store, grocery, and hypermarket operations. CC Carrefour is Spain's second-largest Internet retailer. Its operations are geared around two sites, its food business (alimentacion.carrefour.es) and its electronics and leisure goods (carrefourocio.com).

Foreign retailers expanded into Spain because there were few legislative restrictions on large-scale retail growth. However, the environment has changed somewhat in recent years, and government regulations are becoming an important consideration.

### Government Regulations

The Spanish parliament passed a law in 1999 that allowed stores to lengthen their opening times and allow hypermarkets to extend their weekly hours open from 72 to 90. The Sunday Trading Act allowed hypermarkets to progressively increase Sunday openings by an extra Sunday a year with the maximum level to be decided at the city level.[8] Regions have some autonomy. In some provinces, stores cannot be open any Sundays or holidays.[9]

At one point the government proposed a tax on large selling units to promote the modernization of small-scale traditional retailing. Part of the plan is to encourage small shopkeepers to take early retirement at 55. They would be paid a stipend if they closed the business, rather than selling it. The money to pay this stipend would come from all retail units of more than 2,500 square meters.[10]

### › ITALY

### Country Background

According to legend, the city of Rome was founded by Romulus in 753 B.C. By the dawn of Christianity, the Roman Empire covered most of the known world, including Europe south of the Rhine and Danube Rivers, Great Britain, Romania, the north coast of Africa, and the Middle East. Five centuries later, the empire was in decline. Like Spain, the history of Italy is also one of repeated invasions. Individual city-states flourished, but the Italian provinces did not form a united front until 1861. The relative recentness of the founding of the Italian state may explain why its people usually identify themselves by province, saying "I am a Sicilian," or a Sardinian or a Lombard first; an Italian, second. Many people, although they speak Italian outside the home, still speak provincial dialects to family members.

Under Mussolini and the Fascist Party, Italy allied itself with Germany during World War II. The last king of Italy, Umberto II, abdicated in 1946 following a referendum on the question of whether the country should be a monarchy or a republic. Despite frequent changes of government, Italy has enjoyed excellent growth in modern times. The country joined the European Community (EC) in 1957.[11]

There have been changes in the retail industry, such as the deregulation of licenses. The retailing sector is dominated by small independent retailers and is highly fragmented. Supermarket chains are increasing their market share. Tables 13.3 and 13.4 summarize the major domestic and foreign retailers in Italy.

## Nonfood Retailers

Italy has a variety of nonfood retailers. Department stores, variety stores, and chains of independent stores have strength in regional locations. Northern Italy is one of the most developed and affluent areas in Europe. The contrast between Northern and Southern Italy is striking. Yet it was only after the late 1980s that modern shopping centers and national multiples began to appear. The Byzantine structure of Italian distribution has discouraged foreign retailers from entering the market. However, since the 1990s, the largest Italian groups have been seeking foreign participation in developing hypermarkets, superstores, and shopping malls, mainly as out-of-town development. The Italian firms' knowledge of the retail regulations has reduced the risks for these newcomers.[12]

Italy has a declining birth rate and a rising age profile, which reduces the demand for clothing and leisure-related products. As a result, Italian clothing chains such as Benetton and Stefanel have had to expand outside the country. They are also exploring the older age groups as a potential market.

**DEPARTMENT STORES**    There are only two department store chains in Italy: La Rinascente and Coin. La Rinascente was originally established in 1865 in Milan. It operates stores in several formats—for the upscale market it is La Rinascente; the mid-market has Upim department stores, Supermarcati SMA, and Cityper supermarkets, Auchan and Citta Mercato hypermarkets, and Punto SMA convenience stores. Like El Corte Inglés, La Rinascente is ubiquitous. Analysts often say that the department store industry is in decline. However, La Rinascente manages to have good operating margins of 5.5 percent.[13] This is much better than France's Printemps or Galeries Lafayette and Germany's Karstadt and Kaufhof chains. La Rinascente has developed a niche as a quality, value-for-money player.

La Rinascente is Italy's largest and most diversified retail company. Its largest department store in Piazza Duomo, Milan, accounts for 9 percent of the company's

**Table 13-3**
**Italy—Leading Domestic Retailers, 2004**

| Company | Total Sales and Stores | | | | | Global Rank and Penetration | | | Domestic Market | |
| --- | --- | --- | --- | --- | --- | --- | --- | --- | --- | --- |
| | Primary Line of Trade | Net Sales ($US Mil) | % Chg Sales | Total Stores | | 2004 Rank, Top 200 Retailers Worldwide | Single-country, Regional or Global? | Number of countries | Share of total sales | Share of total stores |
| 1 COOP Italia | Supermarkets/Grocery Stores | 14,014 | 2.7% | 1,276 | | 51 | Regional | 2 | 100% | 100% |
| 2 CONAD | Supermarkets/Grocery Stores | 8,814 | 10.9% | 3,144 | | 86 | Single Country | 1 | 100% | 100% |
| 3 Esselunga S.p.A. | Supermarkets/Grocery Stores | 5,197 | 3.6% | 125 | | 132 | Single Country | 1 | 100% | 100% |
| 4 Gruppo PAM S.p.A. | Supermarkets/Grocery Stores | 3,176 | 7.5% | 521 | | 191 | Single Country | 1 | 100% | 100% |
| 5 Gruppo Lombardini | Supermarkets/Grocery Stores | 2,009 | 6.2% | 667 | | — | Single Country | 1 | 100% | 100% |
| 6 Finiper | Hypermarkets/Supercenters | 1,990 | 5.0% | 24 | | — | Single Country | 1 | 100% | 100% |
| 7 Benetton Group S.p.A. | Apparel Stores | 1,952 | -3.0% | 5,060 | | — | Global | 120 | 51% | 43% |
| 8 Gruppo Coin | Apparel Stores | 1,334 | -14.6% | 371 | | — | Regional | 2 | 98% | 92% |

**Table 13.4**
**Italy—Key Foreign Retailers, 2004**

| Company | Headquarters | Retail Sector | Primary Line of Trade | Global Rank and Penetration | | |
|---|---|---|---|---|---|---|
| | | | | 2004 Rank, Top 200 Retailers Worldwide | Single-country, Regional or Global? | Number of countries |
| Anton Schlecker | Germany | FDM | Drug Stores | 95 | Regional | 9 |
| Auchan Groupe | France | FDM | Hypermarkets/Supercenters | 18 | Global | 12 |
| Carrefour Group | France | FDM | Hypermarkets/Supercenters | 2 | Global | 31 |
| Centres E. Leclerc | France | FDM | Supermarkets/Grocery Stores | 24 | Regional | 6 |
| Defense Commissary Agency | United States | FDM | Supermarkets/Grocery Stores | 130 | Global | 13 |
| Dixons Group | United Kingdom | Homegoods | Consumer Electronics & Appliances | 56 | Regional | 14 |
| dm-drogerie markt GmbH & Co. KG | Germany | FDM | Drug Stores | 166 | Regional | 9 |
| IKEA AB | Sweden | Homegoods | Furniture & Home Furnishings | 44 | Global | 32 |
| INDITEX Group (i.e. Zara) | Spain | Softgoods | Apparel Stores | 110 | Global | 56 |
| Karstadt Quelle AG | Germany | Softgoods | Non-Store | 42 | Regional | 19 |
| Kingfisher PLC | United Kingdom | Homegoods | DIY/Home Improvement Stores | 50 | Global | 9 |
| Leroy Merlin | France | Homegoods | DIY/Home Improvement Stores | 112 | Global | 8 |
| LVMH | France | All Programs | Other Apparel Specialty Stores | 76 | Global | 56 |
| Mango | Spain | Softgoods | Apparel Stores | — | Global | 76 |
| Metro AG | Germany | FDM | Cash & Carries/Warehouse Clubs | 4 | Global | 29 |
| Mitsukoshi Ltd | Japan | Softgoods | Department Stores | 98 | Global | 9 |
| Otto Group | Germany | Softgoods | Non-Store | 61 | Global | 19 |
| Pinault-Printemps-Redoute SA | France | Homegoods | Non-Store | 36 | Global | 17 |
| Rewe-Gruppe | Germany | FDM | Supermarkets/Grocery Stores | 14 | Regional | 14 |
| Schwarz Group | Germany | FDM | Discount Food Stores | 12 | Regional | 19 |
| SPAR Austria Group | Austria | FDM | Supermarkets/Grocery Stores | 88 | Regional | 5 |
| Staples, Inc. | United States | Homegoods | Office Supply | 47 | Global | 18 |
| Tengelmann Warenhandelsgesellschaft | Germany | Homegoods | Supermarkets/Grocery Stores | 23 | Global | 15 |

Sources: Retail Forward, company annual reports and published reports

**Photo 13.2**
The Galleria is a dome-covered shopping center in Milan, Italy. This center is in the heart of Milan, sharing the square with the major cathedral. *Courtesy of WWD.*

total sales. Forty-three percent of total sales are in food, and 57 percent are in non-food. When J. C. Penney departed from Italy, the company sold its chain of stores to La Rinascente.

Thirteen percent of sales for La Rinascente are own label. The gross margin on own label is 25 percent, compared with 15 percent margin on national brands and 17 percent on premier brands. Hard discounters entering the market will increase the growth of the premier brand market and may force La Rinascente to follow suit to remain competitive. La Rinascente advertises a low price for national brands. Advertising a price for own label and premier brands is not effective because these labels do not have a universal comparison.[14]

The acquisition strategy used by La Rinascente benefits the company by (1) instantly increasing market share in the more mature supermarket sector without adding to industry capacity, (2) bypassing planning hurdles, (3) completing national coverage, and (4) improving the company's purchasing power.[15] The company generates 90 percent of its operating profit and 68 percent of its sales from food.

The other department store retailer is Coin. Found throughout Italy, Coin also owns clothing chain stores, such as Oviesse, and manufactures clothing. Coin began in 1916 and is one of the biggest nonfood retailers in Italy, offering one of the widest product ranges. A network of shops was brought to the company with the acquisition of the Oviesse, Bimbus, and Standa stores. In 2003 Coin sold the Bimbus fascia to Preca Brummel.

**NATIONAL CHAINS**    Benetton is the best-known Italian chain, with operations in more than 100 countries. Its sales are primarily in franchised outlets. The company begins its expansion by manufacturing in the target country and licensing a local entrepreneur to operate a test outlet. If the results are satisfactory, Benetton will create a 50:50 joint venture with the licensee to increase capacity and establish a production pattern. Benetton's strategy consists of limiting owned fixed assets and maintaining in-house control of the crucial stages of production, such as cutting, dyeing, and quality control. Benetton's expansion is based on subcontracting. Seventy percent of production used to be done in Italian cottage industries, where labor costs are lower. However, in 2005 they announced that much of their sourcing would be shifted to India. The products manufactured in India will be distributed in Southeast Asian countries.[16]

Benetton does not charge a franchisee fee. The company's profits come strictly from sale of the products. The company produces two collections each year, about 1,500 styles in 40 colors. Color is very important to Benetton's success and is very dependent on fashion trends. One strategy that Benetton has used to reduce costs is by developing a special dyeing system. The finished products are dyed, not the fabric, allowing the company to customize colors by country.

**HYPERMARKETS**    Italy has one of the most fragmented retail sectors in Europe. This provides unparalleled growth opportunities for retailers who can consolidate existing supermarket capacity and develop the hypermarket and DIY sectors. Hypermarkets have significant growth potential in Italy. In terms of hypermarkets per population, Italy lags behind every major European country. Even if the number of hypermarkets were to double in Italy today, the density ratio per million inhabitants would be about the same as that of Spain. La Rinascente has the greatest market share in hypermarket and home improvement outlets.

Some aspects of the Italian market are much like the Spanish market. La Rinascente's closest competitors are the Spanish hypermarkets Pryca and Continente and their French parent, Carrefour/Promodès. Immature retail markets characterize both the Spanish and Italian markets. Expansion opportunities are available through hypermarkets and commercial centers, extended supplier credit days, and financing by negative working capital.

## Food Retailers

Italians spend a larger percent of their income on food than most other Europeans. They also have lofty expectations for high-quality food. Fresh food is very important to them so they shop more frequently than other Europeans. Also there is somewhat of a backlash against supermarkets and hypermarkets and a preference for specialty stores.

The introduction of private label started very slowly in Italy but now it is expanding at a rate comparable to other EU countries. One of the most important considerations is to use the U.K. positioning for private label "best value for money" since the Italians are so concerned about food quality.

Food retailing in Italy is dominated by supermarket chains managed by three main players—Coop, Conad, and Carrefour. Dominated, however, is a relative term because these three have only 8 percent of the total sales. Coop and Conad are cooperatives. Auchan-Rinascente have a partnership to develop shopping centers in Italy.

The food markets in central and southern Italy are not saturated. There are very few hypermarkets, large-scale supermarkets, and discount stores. There are no warehouse club formats in this area.

NEGATIVE WORKING CAPITAL means that a retailer relies on money owed to its suppliers for expansion. This *capital* provides operating funds only if a company grows. In Italy, accounts are given 100 days to pay so the use of the negative working capital is very important. It inflates the stock position while absolute levels of borrowed cash owed to suppliers decreases, creating a reversal of the negative working capital advantage. This situation causes smaller, overexpanded retailers to fund part of their acquisition buyout and their daily working capital commitment through interest-accruing bank finance.

Large retailers such as CC Carrefour in Spain are also using negative working capital. However, these companies are rapidly expanding. Their aggressive store-opening programs drive sales. These companies also have state-of-the-art information transfer systems that decrease stock holding times and provide efficient retailer response to nonperforming product lines.[17]

The Spanish and French retailers have proven that an investment in information technology and a tighter logistics chain can enable them to control suppliers and maximize their profits. They do this by trading off the best financial returns to be earned either through cash owed to suppliers (in periods of high interest rates) or through rebates used to bolster gross margin and operating cash flow to the detriment of lower financial returns (in periods of lower interest rates). The Spanish retailers have discovered that putting cash flow gains back into the business provides the best return on operating or negative working capital.

La Rinascente is more cautious and refuses to invest suppliers' cash into expanding the business. The company uses operating cash flows to fund expansion. It is true that expanding in Italy is much more difficult than expanding in Spain. Even if La Rinascente wanted to follow an aggressive expansion campaign funded through negative capital, it would not be possible. The La Rinascente group has low yielding assets in the nonfood sector. Risking trade capital could enhance the return on assets in higher yielding organic expansion of food retailing activities, which represent 90 percent of the group's pretax profit compared with 68 percent of sales.[18]

Buying groups have become popular in Italian retailing; they allow retailers to pool their purchasing power. Chains are getting together to develop buying groups, just like independents are pooling their resources for greater purchasing power. The major buying groups are Intermedia (Rinascente, Pam, Conad, Rewe—2,802 outlets), Mecades (Interdis, Sisa, Despar—2,322 outlets), Coop Italia (Coop, Sigma—1,159 outlets), Esd Italia (Esselunga, Selex, Agora—968 outlets), and Carrefour Italia (Carrefour, FIniper, Il Giante—722 outlets).[19]

The slow development of franchising in Italy has been hampered by government intervention. Franchising is an efficient operating mode for Italy since most franchise operations are relatively small format retailers. Most franchising in Italy is the master franchising type. That way the master franchiser has the task of dealing with governmental authorities.

Hard discount is the fastest growing retail format in Italy. It is likely that as traditional shopkeepers become caught in price competition, they will view hard discount as an alternative and will reconfigure their existing stores into hard discounters. This strategy is bound to fail, however, because the hard discount success formula is based on volume and economies of scale to compensate for the low margin.[20]

## Internet Retailing

Around one-third of Italy's homes have an Internet connection; about one-fifth have a connection at their office. Italy has rather low Internet penetration by European standards. Many Italian Internet users access the Internet by using a dial-up connection at home. Broadband is in its infancy, and any kind of electronic shopping is not likely to be successful until there is broader access to it. Retail sales on the Internet have been increasing at about 13 percent per year. The top eight Internet retailers accounted for only 4 percent of sales. The top six Internet retailers are CLICKS AND MORTAR operators, meaning that the company is not a pure Internet retailer, but also has a physical store.

## Government Regulations

Italian retail legislation makes the process of opening a new store arduous. The government designed Law 426/1971 to protect the interest of small retailers. Under this law, municipalities create a plan for the development of retailing within a community, deciding the amount of sales area needed to serve consumers for each product category. The law does not limit the number of stores in a particular format, for example, department stores or specialty stores. Instead, limitations are imposed based on the product they sell. The Products List contained 14 product categories, such as fish stores, book stores, and gift stores. New shops can be opened only if there is a shop space available according to the retail master plan in the area. Although changing the master plan is possible, it requires much lobbying.[21]

Things have gotten a bit better. The law was reformed (with Law 121/1987, Law 241/1990, and modified by Law 537/1993); finally the latest legislation has introduced the most important liberalization, referred to as the Bersani legislative reforms. For stores that are smaller than 250 square meters in communities of 10,000 or for stores that are smaller than 150 square meters in cities with fewer than 10,000, to open, transfer, and upsize a business, the retailer can just give their plans to Town Hall. An authorization is still needed for larger stores and it can be difficult to get, being based on consideration of urban needs and environmental impact. Now retailers can choose to be open up to 13 hours per day between the times of 7:00 A.M. and 8:00 P.M. Stores can be open eight Sundays per year excluding the December holidays. However, in the art and tourist cities the city determines if the retail store can be open.[22]

Italy also does not allow chains in the pharmacy sector. Each entrepreneur can have only one outlet. The number of pharmacies in Italy is regulated by an "organic plant" (Law 362/1991, Article 1), which sets the ratio of one pharmacy for every

4,000 residents in a town with more than 12,500 population and one for every 5,000 inhabitants in towns with less than 12,500.[23] I'm not sure why the Italian government considers pharmacy retailers so dangerous that they need to be handled like this.

Retail owners must also learn about running a business and the products they will sell. An owner of a gift shop in Florence explained how the system works. She told me that someone who wants to open a retail store must take a training program and a qualifying certification examination. The examination will include sections on business operations and specific details related to the product the retailer will sell. This gift shop owner sells handblown glass, silverware, and crystal. Her qualifying examination would cover these product areas, making sure that she knows product-specific information that she can pass on to her customers. She was very surprised that in the United States, you could just decide to open a business, or decide to sell one product one day and another product the next day. Her store had opened in space that had not had a store in it before, so gaining approval was not so difficult. The only other gift store in the area was about five blocks away and was currently closed for several weeks to allow the employees to take their summer vacation. When the gift shop owner's competitors returned from summer vacation, the gift shop owner would close her shop and she and her employees would go on holiday.

In the United States, franchisees pay an up-front fee to the franchiser, and the franchisee pays a continuing franchise fee that is a percentage of the franchisee's sale. Neither of these business practices is commonly used in Italy. The franchiser makes its income from sale of products to the franchisee.[24] This is the system I described earlier for Benetton.

### > GREECE

### Country Background

Greece is the birthplace of Western civilization. The ancient Greeks developed the ideas of justice, liberty, and law that serve as the basis for Western society. Following the collapse of the Roman Empire, Greece continued to play an important role as a center of the Byzantine Empire. When the Turks captured Istanbul in 1453, Greece became a province of the Ottoman Empire. In 1821, Greece began a War of Independence, which became a popular cause for the best minds of the Romantic Age of Europe. Independence came in 1827.

Greece sided with the Allies in World War II. The country was invaded by Italy in 1940 and occupied by Germany in 1941. Greece emerged from the war with several possessions given to it by Italy. After the war, pro-Western forces and communists fought a bitter and bloody civil war. It lasted until 1949, when Greece emerged as a democracy.[25]

Greece hosted the 2004 Athens Olympic Games. The construction and improvement of infrastructure brought Greece's GDP growth to the highest among EU countries. Consumers have low purchasing power; there is an underdeveloped transportation infrastructure; and large-scale retailers are almost nonexistent. Greece has more retail outlets per capita than any other EC country and a greater absolute number than Britain, which has five times the population. Similar to outlets in Italy, the average store employs fewer than two employees. Greece has less than 50 people per square kilometer, compared with the European average of 151 people. Retail activity is concentrated in major urban centers. The infrastructure needed to support modern retail systems—roads, railways, electrical power, and communications equipment—is not present.

There are many infrastructure problems, primarily in the transport area. Moving people or merchandise from one area to another is difficult. In Greece, the average travel time needed to reach a major economic center is more than six hours, compared to the European Union (EU) average of four hours. Goods are transported almost exclusively by independent trucking companies. Greece has benefited from EU financial support, but with the entry of the New Europe to the EU it will be more difficult to secure these funds. Greece remains one of the poorest countries in the EU having a purchasing power of only 69 percent of the average for the rest of Europe.[26]

Here are only 12 square meters of shopping space per 1,000 Greeks compared to the European average of 161 square meters. The total area for shopping malls in Greece is comparable to what is found in Slovenia and Romania. Shopping malls first appeared during the 1980s but were a commercial failure and were converted to office space. Recently an attempt was made to try again. The 17,000-square meter Sanyo Shopping Center in Maroussi, Athens, was developed by the Carrefour-Marinopoulos Group. Although the hypermarket is doing all right the other stores performed poorly and most were closed.

The 18 biggest Greek retailers represent only 23 percent of total retail sales. Organized chains only account for only about 35–40 percent of sales in Greece; this figure can be compared to 70 percent in the more developed areas of the EU.[27] The major retailers are supermarkets and hypermarket chains, but they control little of the total retail sales. Traditional retailers are the most prevalent. Greek lifestyle reinforces the need for customers to have personal interaction with the people they are buying merchandise from. It is the interaction rather than an emphasis on saving time that is important. Open air markets operate once a week in most neighborhoods. There has been a rush of mergers and acquisition, primarily in the supermarket area. Discounters and hypermarkets have had some growth in Greece; these are mainly operated by multinationals.

## Food Retailing

Fresh products such as vegetables, fruits, fish, and livestock are assembled around production by agricultural cooperatives. Some products are consumed locally; the rest are sold to wholesale resellers. The products are transported daily by road to the central markets of urban areas. Small and medium transport companies operate the limited number of trucks. The central markets act as major distribution centers for the urban areas and surrounding rural areas. The products are then sold to consumers by local shops. A central feature of Greek shopping is the traditional convenience store called *bakaliko*.

Supermarkets/cash-and-carry outlets account for the largest food sales. Carrefour-Marinopoulos operates the largest retail sales area of hypermarkets and supermarkets in Greece. The leading 25 companies control 80 percent of the market. Discounters are rapidly increasing their market share in Greece; Dia Hellas and Lidl are the market leaders.

## Government Regulations

Some regions of Greece such as Crete and Messologi ban the opening of big department stores and supermarkets. This is to protect domestic commerce that is threatened by multinationals. For outlets larger than 2,000 square meters, a district committee has to review the request and determine what effect it will have on the local industry. Time and again Carrefour and Praktiker were denied permission to build the 6,000 square meters they had wanted and instead had to settle for stores that fall under the 2,000-square meter requirement.[28] Like many European countries, Greece has a law forbidding supermarkets from selling below cost. Carrefour has been fined a number of times for abusing this policy.

Shopping hours are regulated to protect employee rights. Only outlets in tourist areas are allowed to be open on Sunday. The government also regulates the periods when retailers can have sales, limiting them to twice a year. The winter sales period is January 15–February 28; summer sales are held from July 10–August 31. If retailers hold sales outside of these periods they can be fined up to 3 percent of their gross income.[29]

Portugal is the final country discussed in this chapter. Greece and Portugal have quite different retail characteristics. While Greece has remained more traditional with few shopping centers, Portugal has embraced new retail development. They both share a very limited department store industry. Portugal just recently opened its first department store, El Corte Inglés from Spain.

### > PORTUGAL

## Country Background

Celts were the original inhabitants of Portugal, which was subsequently invaded and ruled by Romans, Germanic tribes, and Moors from North Africa. Portugal was liberated from the Moors during the twelfth and thirteenth centuries, becoming a Christian kingdom. It gained independence from Spain in the late fourteenth century.

The early success of Portugal was tied to the sea. One of the country's explorers, Vasco da Gama, was the first to round the Cape of Good Hope. He later became the first European to visit India. Portugal established colonies in the Canary Islands, the Azores, Brazil, and Ceylon. But between 1580 and 1640, Spain retook Portugal, claiming its empire of colonies.[30]

The Portuguese population is concentrated on the coast. The major retail centers are Lisbon, in the south, and Oporto, in the north. The Lisbon region accounts for 21 percent of Portugal's population. More than 60 percent of Portuguese are employed in service industries. Lisbon has the highest purchasing power in the country. Metropolitan areas suffer from congestion and rising costs. Oporto, the industrial development area in Portugal, has 16 percent of the country's population and is an area of high purchasing power. Lisbon and Oporto are connected by a major highway, and most of the Portuguese industries and people are located between these two cities.

Portugal joined the EC in January 1993. As a requirement for membership, the country had to eliminate trade barriers. Agricultural imports surged in from other

EC countries. Subsequently, foreign price competition in fresh fruits and vegetables from Spain, France, and Holland has led to closure of fruit and vegetable producers.

The overall health of the Portuguese economy is very good. So good that it has been an attractive immigration destination for Eastern Europeans.

## Retailing in Portugal

The Portuguese retail industry is in transition, moving from the traditional, fragmented environment to an industry dominated by multinational multiples. Shopping centers are rapidly covering the country, offering attractive environments for retailers to set up shop. These new shopping centers are more up to date than shopping centers in other parts of Europe. In 2003, Portugal had 62 shopping centers measuring more than 5,000 square meters. The centers are located out of town to facilitate shopping and they are developed around lifestyle attractions like multiscreen theaters, cultural centers, and food courts. The key specialist brands like Zara, Massimo Dutti, FNAC, and SportZone are represented in the centers. The major supermarket and hypermarket chains are beginning to have a dominant role and there has been major consolidation in the industry. As happens everywhere, discount operators have proven popular. The hard discount formats drive down price and make the entire industry more competitive. Sonae is the leading shopping center developer and is also the leading retailer in Portugal.

In 2001, El Corte Inglés entered the Portuguese market. They have experienced excellent sales, with 15 percent growth in their first year of operation. They are essentially the only department store in Portugal.

## Internet Retailing

Only 31 percent of households have Internet connections in Portugal. Of this number only 13.2 percent of private Internet users and 5.3 percent of company users have purchased something over the Internet. Although Portugal has a high level of credit card usage, consumers are still reluctant to make purchases, fearing that their financial transaction will not be safe. Instead most people use the Internet to price search and as a pre-purchase source of information. The use of the Internet is increasing rapidly but is still a miniscule factor in Portuguese retailing.

Continente Online owned by Sonae is the leading electronic retailer. The company makes home delivery including delivery afterhours, an important service because Portugal does not yet have door-to-door delivery service. Home delivery is an important complementary to the development of electronic shopping. The second-largest online retailer is Global Shop SA, a pure play retailer. The company started up with a B-C orientation, but later changed their strategy to B-B.[31]

## Government Policy

Government policy in Portugal discriminates against large-scale retailers. In 1997, a law was passed that limited the opening of large supermarkets and hypermarkets; this law was designed to reduce the power of large stores. In 2001, the government approved a law that limits Sunday opening hours of large supermarkets and hyper-

**Photo 13.3**
Private car ownership is important for hypermarket growth. Without cars, consumers purchase only what they can carry home. When cars are available, the average amount spent per customer increases. This hypermarket is Ahold's first venture in Portugal with Jerónimo Martins Retail (JMR). *Courtesy of Ahold.*

markets, but does not affect small and medium retailers. Stores are considered large if they are 4,000 square meters and sell nonfood or are 2,000 square meters and sell food. The government has encouraged partnerships between Portuguese companies and foreign multinationals.[32]

## Food Retailing

The leading retail groups in Portugal are Sonae, Jeronimo Martins, Carrefour, and Grupo Auchan. The two major hard discount companies—Lidl and Dia/Minipreco, part of the Carrefour group—entered the Portugal market in the 1990s. The stores are primarily located in the metropolitan areas in a retail format that competes with traditional retailers, but because they are smaller format stores, they fall under the rigid planning laws. Lidl has slightly larger stores in more peripheral locations but Dia/Minipreco has smaller stores in more central locations. Lidl used organic growth while Dia generally occupies pre-existing buildings.

Sonae, founded in 1959, is the largest retailer in Portugal and is the only company to operate over a variety of sectors. The company began as a wood products business and didn't diversify into retailing until the 1980s. Sonae expanded its business in 1996 to other European countries including Spain and the United Kingdom, as well as Canada, Brazil, and South Africa. Its biggest foreign market is Brazil, where it is one of the top four retail players. Sonae owns Portugal's leading supermarket/hypermarket chain, Modelo Continente hypermarkets, Modelo supermarkets, and

Modelo Bonjou supermarkets. In the nonfood sector they operate Worten (household appliances and electronic equipment), Vobis (computers), Modalfa (clothing and footwear), SportZone (sports equipment), MaxMat (building and DIY), and MaxOffice (printing and copying). Sonae owns 36 shopping centers, making it the largest operator and giving it a significant advantage over competitors in getting prime locations.

Jerónimo Martins group, the second-largest food retailer, was founded over 200 years ago. They operate Feira Nova hypermarkets, Pingo Doce, a supermarket chain, and Recheio, a cash and carry operation. Jeronimo Martins is also the leading food retailer in Poland with its Biedronka fascias. Private label accounts for 11 percent of sales.

Carrefour is the third-largest retailer in Portugal, with sales growth in the double digits. Carrefour operates hypermarkets and Dia/Minipreco hard discount stores.

The fourth-largest food group is Pão de Açúcar, operated by Auchan of France. This group includes Jumbo, a hypermarket and supermarket group.

## > SUMMARY

When I wrote the first edition of this book the retailing environments of these three countries were much more similar. Now there are striking differences. Spain and Portugal have emerged with many modern retail formats, including a shared department store experience, El Corte Inglés. Italy is in the middle of retail development, still hanging on to some very restrictive government regulations that make operating there difficult, but easier than in the 1990s. The laggard is Greece, who still has a relatively undeveloped retail system and seems to be dragging its heels in modernization.

The southern European countries of Spain, Italy, Greece, and Portugal are vastly different from their northern European neighbors. Average income and education level are much lower. Transportation infrastructures are not well developed, and traditional retailers sell most of the products.

Increasingly, foreign retailers are capturing markets. Their experiences at home have put them in a position to provide competition where little existed before. French hypermarkets have been particularly successful.

Italy represents one of the most regulated retail environments. City planners there control the mix of retail establishments, making it difficult for new entrants. There may not be much impetus to change this heavy regulation.

## > KEY TERMS

BORN GLOBAL

CLICKS AND MORTAR

FAST FASHION

INFRASTRUCTURE

NEGATIVE WORKING CAPITAL

PURE PLAY

> ## DISCUSSION QUESTIONS

1. In several of the old new European countries there are only one or two department stores. What explains this concentration?
2. What geographical factors have impeded the development of national chains? How has this lack of development positioned local retailers for the onslaught of foreign competition?
3. Retailing in these countries appears to leapfrog through retail transitions without passing through the normal stages expected as a country develops. What retail groups will suffer because of this?
4. What explanation can you give for the restrictive laws used in Italy? How do these laws affect (a) consumers, (b) local retailers, and (c) foreign retailers?
5. In several of these countries, retailers use negative cash flow. What is this and how does it affect high growth retailers versus low growth retailers?

> ## ENDNOTES

1. "Spain." (1995). *Craighead's International Business, Travel, and Relocation Guide to More Than 80 Countries.* Detroit: Gale Research.
2. Retailing in Spain. (2004). GMID Euromonitor, May.
3. Retailing in Spain. (2004).
4. *Retail News Letter.* (1995). No. 426, July, p. 17.
5. "Carrefour Launches New Store Concept in Spain." (2005). *Financial Times*, November 7.
6. Retailing in Spain. (2004).
7. Retailing in Spain. (2004).
8. Retailing in Spain. (2004).
9. *Retail News Letter.* (1996). No. 432, February, p. 16.
10. *Retail News Letter.* (1995).
11. "Italy." (1995). *Craighead's International Business, Travel, and Relocation Guide to More Than 80 Countries.* Detroit: Gale Research.
12. "Corporate Intelligence on Retailing." (1997). *The European Retail Handbook.* London: Corporate Intelligence on Retailing.
13. Rinascente. (2002). Giubergia UBS Warburg in Investext October 22.
14. Lehman Brothers Limited, December 11, 1995, La Rinascente—Company report.
15. Lehman Brothers Limited (1995).
16. "Bennetton Plans to Expand Outsourcing from India." (2005). Global News Wire-Asia Africa Intelligence Wire, November 7.
17. Lehman Brothers Limited. (1995).
18. Lehman Brothers Limited. (1995).
19. Retailing in Italy. (2004). Columbus, Ohio: RetailForward, May.
20. Retailing in Italy. (2004).
21. Pelligrini, L., and A. Cardani. (1992). *The Italian Distribution System.* Report prepared for the OECD Study on Distribution Systems, University of Bocconi, March.
22. Retailing in Italy. (2004).
23. Retailing in Italy. (2004).

24. Ishani, M. (1996). *Franchising in Italy. Franchise Update.* Web Services by Los Trancos Systems, LLC.
25. "Greece." (1995). *Craighead's Country Reports.* Detroit: Gale Research.
26. Retailing in Greece. (2004). Columbus, Ohio: RetailForward, July.
27. Retailing in Greece. (2004).
28. Retailing in Greece. (2004).
29. Retailing in Greece. (2004).
30. "Portugal." (1995). *Craighead's Country Reports.* Detroit: Gale Research.
31. Retailing in Portugal. (2004). GMID. Euromonitor June
32. Retailing in Portugal. (2004).

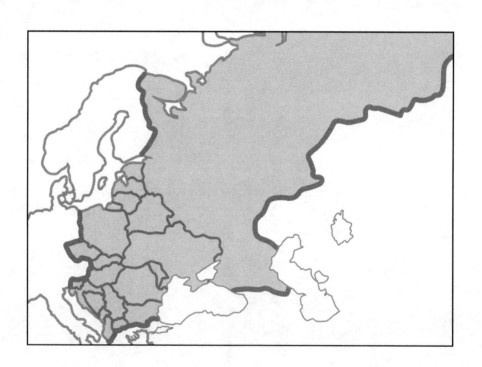

# 14

# RETAILING IN CENTRAL AND EASTERN EUROPE: THE NEW EUROPE

## After reading this chapter, you should understand

> The role retailing played in a planned economy and how this limited innovation in the industry.

> How the Marxist philosophy "From each according to his ability, to each according to his needs" is used to plan product distribution in planned economies.

> That even in planned economies, the informal market always operates under a demand economy, whether it is illegal (black market) or legal (free market).

> How consumers who are accustomed to a scarce supply of products view the market differently than consumers who have operated in a system of plenty.

> The strategies that foreign retailers are using in Central and Eastern Europe.

Central and Eastern Europe offer the type of less-regulated environment Western European retailers have had difficulty finding. Many Western European countries have regulations that restrict the expansion of large-scale stores, place limits on the hours of operations, and severely restrict laying off employees during economic downturns. Although Central Europe does not have these restrictions, which should make it an attractive retail market, countries such as Albania, Romania, and Bulgaria are considered 20 to 25 years behind the West economically, and they remain unattractive markets for retailers.

There are, however, four countries among the former Soviet bloc nations that are of interest to retailers: Hungary, the Czech Republic, Poland, and Russia. These countries have removed price controls and welcome foreign investment.

You cannot understand how much retailing has changed in these countries without understanding what retailing is like under a planned economy. A **PLANNED ECONOMY** is one in which the government determines what goods will be produced, where they will be produced, and where they will be sold. Planned economies generally have **BLOCKED OR NON-CONVERTIBLE CURRENCIES,** meaning they cannot be bought or sold in the world market. The government keeps them within the country to control how people spend their money. The country gets hard currency (convertible) by selling products to the outside world and through the currency brought in from foreigners. A convertible currency is desirable because it allows companies to trade with the whole world rather than just source domestically or resort to barter.

In the first part of this chapter, I will describe how retailing operated in the former Soviet bloc countries under the old system. This background section will be followed by a discussion of the four major countries within this group and their retail industries.

## ❭ RETAILING UNDER A PLANNED ECONOMY

Under the Soviet-era planned economic systems, retailing and wholesaling were controlled by the Ministry of Commerce. This government agency determined what products factories could produce, where they would sell them, and their price. Prices were fixed and often stayed the same for decades. Price competition did not exist. If products had different prices in different stores, it was a marking error, not a strategic action.

In such a planned economy the merchandise price was based on how necessary the product was, not how much it cost to produce. A necessity such as bread would have a very low, subsidized price. I say subsidized because the product was often priced lower than it cost to produce it. A luxury product would be priced very high to discourage purchases. In the United States, in contrast, products are priced based on the costs to produce the product, plus expenses and a planned profit. The idea of pricing a product based on production costs seems very strange to people living in planned economies. The basic Marxist philosophy of "From each according to his ability, to each according to his needs" is reflected in the low cost of necessities, and the relatively high cost of luxuries.

I remember reading a newspaper article on bakers in Moscow shortly after Russia removed price controls. They had no idea what to charge for their bread. The ingredients used in making the bread came from state-owned factories, and the bakers did not pay for them. A baker's job was simply to mix and bake. After much confusion about what to charge for the bread, they decided they would all charge the same price—the price they had charged before price liberalization.

In planned economies, retailing is believed to serve a negative role of fostering useless competition and unnecessary desires in consumers. I often use the term PARASITIC to describe how planned economies feel about retailing. Parasitic means that they believe the industry draws resources by creating unnecessary wants in consumers.

In planned economies, both state stores and cooperatives were under the direction of the Ministry of Commerce. Store merchandise came from government sources required to charge government prices. STATE-OWNED STORES were located in the more urban areas and sold a larger proportion of nonfood items. COOPERATIVES were most prevalent in rural areas and sold both food and nonfood merchandise. In some countries, such as the German Democratic Republic (the former East Germany), Poland, and Hungary, private individuals were allowed to have shops, but the shops had to charge the same prices as state-owned stores for products. Private shops had to get their merchandise from the government and had to sell this merchandise for government-established prices. These independent stores had little advantage. The government wholesale organization handled the physical distribution of merchandise. Wholesalers were organized by main product groups such as staple foods, fresh fruits and vegetables, furniture, and clothing.[1]

Shopping was not easy under the planned economic system. Shoppers waited in a variety of lines. After entering a store a shopper would likely wait in one line to request a product or to check the price of a product because many products were stored behind counters, out of customer reach, under the watchful eye of a stern salesclerk. If the shopper decided to buy something, for instance a pork chop, the salesclerk would then give the shopper a bill. The shopper would take the bill to another counter and, after again standing in line, would pay for the pork chop, receiving a receipt that would need to be taken to a third line, where the shopper would wait to pick up the pork chop. This procedure would be repeated for other categories of merchandise. As you can imagine, shopping required a big time commitment. Often shoppers would wait in line only to find out that the store was sold out of the item they wanted. They then had to go to another store and repeat the process.

The government pricing system kept prices artificially low. There was little incentive to increase supply, so consumers competed for the existing, limited supply by standing in line. Some observers estimate that the average Soviet consumer spent two to three hours per day waiting in line. This affected worker productivity. When news of a scarce item became available, workers would simply walk off their jobs to go stand in line, waiting for the chance to purchase the item.

The waiting in line phenomenon attracted the interest of several academic studies. One study of Polish consumers found that lines formed for many products and services, including those for which there was no shortage. Lines were more widespread for foods than for non-food products. The longest lines were for meat. Three of the eight meat lines at one department store studied contained more than 100 shoppers.[2]

Products were scarce, in part because the government put highest priority on supporting the military-industrial complex. When goods became available, access often depended on a network of contacts or luck (stumbling upon them).[3] Consumer products were viewed as frivolous. The situation was compounded by hoarding behavior, as consumers tended to purchase any products they encountered, regardless of their immediate needs. People did this because they were never sure when they would encounter the products again.

Daily shopping was the practice during this era in central and eastern European countries. On each visit to a store, a consumer would buy a few items, generally five to ten. A survey conducted in 1992 showed that 46 percent of the respondents agreed with the statement: "We have only enough money to purchase food products".[4] Stores were small and filled to excess. Crowds were sometimes controlled through shopping basket distribution. Baskets would be issued to those who entered the shop, including family members shopping together. When the limited supply of baskets was exhausted, no more people were allowed to enter until someone exited.[5] Self-service was not available. Even when shops began to offer self-service, a guard would monitor the entrance, admitting only a specified number of customers at a time.

Customer service was and still is very poor. Salesclerks were rude to customers. Most stores used a RESPONSIBILITY SYSTEM, under which the clerks in a shop were collectively responsible for theft. This contributed to a service approach of "guarding" the merchandise from consumers and often keeping it in glass containers.

In market economies, advertising plays an important role in communicating product availability to consumers. This type of information source was not available to consumers in the planned economies. Advertising didn't need to create demand for products since demand was not considered a factor in product production.

The old systems have been changing, rapidly in some countries and not so rapidly in others. The leaders in this change are Hungary, the Czech Republic, and Poland. Several issues evolve when a country moves from a planned to a free market. People often cannot change as rapidly as markets. The next section will explore these issues.

### › MOVING FROM A PLANNED TO A FREE MARKET

PRIVATIZATION is the process of transferring ownership of businesses from the government to individuals. Two main types of privatization have been occurring in central and eastern Europe. In the first type, vouchers are distributed to citizens, giving everyone a share in state-owned companies. Citizens can then sell or trade these vouchers to other citizens. In the second type of privatization, companies are sold directly with domestic investors given priority.

Each country has approached privatization in a different manner. Poland began with sell-offs to company management. However this proved to be very slow, so the government moved to mass privatization. In mass privatization, companies are given investment funds and the public is able to buy shares in the funds. Hungary has used sell-offs, hoping that this strategy will foster efficient management. It has had limited success. The Czech Republic and Russia have concentrated on the voucher system, which makes the transition faster.[6]

Sell-offs to company management have some advantages and some problems. To begin with, the companies are faced with major repayment schedules. They typically have five or ten years to repay the debt. This leaves little capital for operating expenses, modernization, or product development. These companies typically must look for outside investors. This is an advantage for outside investors, who now do not have to negotiate with the state government. The investment is quicker and easier, and money is not diverted to government coffers. The employees are shareholders so they also gain additional control over the operation of their business.

Another way to gain entry to the central European market is by starting a business from scratch. This is called a **GREENFIELD OPTION,** which here is the same as organic growth. The company is building the stores from the beginning, not acquiring other retailers. The meaning of greenfield in this instance is different from the meaning used in the discussion of retailing in the United Kingdom. In that chapter, we discussed greenfield sites—areas that have not been developed and are being held as green areas in an attempt to prevent or reduce urban sprawl.

Schultz, Belk, and Ger provide some observations about market privatization and the effect on consumers in countries that are undergoing this change:[7]

1. Changes are occurring at an incredible speed.
2. It is likely that the changes will continue to occur in equally dramatic terms over the next decade or more.
3. There are escalating consumer aspirations and expectations that are as yet unmatched by the available and affordable consumer goods.
4. Differences exist between the small stratum of consumers for new and expensive luxury goods in these countries and the majority who still are barely able to afford essentials. This is the truest in Turkey, China, Romania, Vietnam, and India.
5. Many consumers in these countries lament the disappearance of their previous economic system. There is clearly dissatisfaction with some aspects of current marketization.
6. There is a powerful influence from images of Western or American consumption and the good life. These global images are primarily obtained from exposure to tourists, travel to neighboring countries, advertising, and mass media.
7. Local conditions continue to exert strong and unique influences in these cultures despite the increasing influence of global images.
8. There is no single adequate theoretical framework that seems to account for the changes taking place. However, there is agreement that the factors of global consumption orientations, information diffusion, and local cultural transformations will be important in any such theoretical framework.
9. There are negative as well as positive consequences of the changes that are occurring. Although the negative consequences are most dramatically illustrated by Croatia and the disintegration of Yugoslavia, the results of marketization were always two sided, with new consumer desires accompanied by uncertainty, confusion, and frustration in daily consumer life.

The economy of shortage formed consumers' needs and aspirations in the Soviet-bloc countries. Satisfying the need for food overcame all other needs in the planned economies. Products that were neither needed nor desired were purchased and hoarded. Consumers could use these hoarded goods to obtain needed goods later, through **BARTERING.** Bartering means that you exchange goods rather than pay for things with currency. Luxuries were generally not available. If they were available, the price was exorbitant.

In Poland and Russia, however, consumers also purchased through an informal economy. The unplanned economy depended on theft from state sectors for inputs of materials, labor, time, and machinery.[8] The unplanned economy resolved problems created by the planned economy, such as shortage of necessary goods. The government avoided cracking down on the unplanned economy because it released some consumer discontent created by the economy of shortage. Consumers would obtain products through social networks and would reciprocate with special favors. Vodka, canned ham, and chocolates were favorite commodities used to bribe government officials.

When consumers' consumption aspirations are not met, hostilities can erupt. Armed conflict became a daily event in the former Yugoslavia when Serbian and Croatian forces re-inflamed centuries-old ethnic rivalries. The following passage from a book about market development in Yugoslavia and Croatia gives a sense of the disappointment and rage that accompanies unmet expectations.

> . . . a genie offers three wishes. For his first wish, the Englishman asks for a cottage overlooking the English Channel. The Frenchman requests a vineyard and a chateau with enough rooms to house his mistresses. When the (Slav) is asked, he hesitates for a long time. Finally he points to his neighbor and says. "My neighbor has a goat. I don't have a goat. Kill my neighbor's goat." (And then proceeds to assist the genie in not only killing his neighbor's goat but his neighbor's wife, children, family, friends, and all their relations, so destroying a generation and himself in the process.)[9]

According to ETHNIC RESOURCE COMPETITION THEORY, increased rivalry over scarce and valued rewards in the political, economic, and social arenas will exacerbate conflict between groups in society.[10] The more visible the differences between groups, the greater the violence and hostility. Rivalry and hostility will be justified by attributing product acquisition to corruption. Interviews conducted in Croatia confirmed this theory. When citizens pointed out a seaside villa they said, "They stole it from the people. How else could they build a house on their salary?"[11] This same kind of justification was used during the Holocaust in Germany.

ASPIRATION GAP results when there is a difference between what consumers think they should have and what they do have. People suffer disillusionment if their aspired standard of consumption is much less than the actual potential value of their acquisitions. As countries marketize, consumers are exposed to advertising and television programs that intensify their product aspirations.

In this section I will use the term CEE to refer to both Central and Eastern Europe. Ten new countries joined the EU in 2005. These countries are Cyprus, Czech Republic, Estonia, Hungary, Latvia, Lithuania, Malta, Poland, Slovakia, and Slovenia. Although they have officially joined the EU they are not part of the euro yet. To meet the monetary union requirements they have to accomplish the five criteria discussed in the overview to these chapters on Europe. Meeting the requirements will be very difficult to do, and could take much time. In this chapter I will separately discuss three of these countries: Czech Republic, Hungary, and Poland. I will also include a discussion of Russia; although it is not a part of the countries slated for EU membership, it presents an interesting retail country.

## > OVERVIEW OF RETAILING IN CENTRAL AND
## EASTERN EUROPE (CEE)

From the previous discussion you should understand that there were essentially no modern retail structures in the CEE countries. What has happened has been amazing. Expansion by foreign-owned retailers has been explosive. The first wave of investment came in the mid-1990s in Poland, the Czech Republic, and Hungary. Large-scale food retail multiple formats have been quick to emerge. In contrast, retail foreign investment in Russia didn't take off until 2001. The existing black market economy in the CEE countries will be reduced as all goods are officially invoiced with **VAT**, which stands for value added tax, revenue that the governments collect on all sales. If they have the capability to collect this tax, all governments are interested because it gives them revenues for growth. Also, as food safety becomes more important sales will naturally gravitate to modern formats, which have a reputation for excellent hygiene standards.

Metro has had the most experience in CEE; almost 18 percent of their group sales come from this area. Over the last seven years CEE sales for Metro have increased 14 percent compared to the 7 percent growth they experienced elsewhere. Over 75 percent of their sales come from the cash and carry format with smaller amounts being derived from its other formats such as Real, its hypermarket format (14 percent), Media Markt, its consumer electronics division (7 percent), and Praktiker, its home improvement format (7 percent).

Metro usually uses its wholesale cash and carry format for market entry because their customers are the small domestic retail stores and restaurants, complementing wholesale and retail structures within the country. Metro strategically enters a market when competition is low. Entry at this early stage allows them to study the market before others arrive. Metro is currently in eight of the CEE markets. Their approach is to study the market for a year before entry, determining what commercial areas will be profitable. Metro generally uses their medium-sized junior format (5,700–9,500 square meters). Typically 90 percent of their products are sourced within the country.[12] Using the negative working capital model explained in Chapter 13, Metro uses payments owed to suppliers to fund future growth. Metro's negative working capital (NWC) is about 10 percent of sales. If an average store has sales of euro50m and the investment for a new store is euro15–20, it means that three newly opened stores can finance a fourth. Metro expects to break even after two years and gain maturity after three or four years. Metro's private label sales in the CEE are 9–10 percent compared with 15 percent in Germany, its home market.[13]

Tesco generally uses a large-scale format such as a hypermarket (5,000 square meters) rather than their supermarket format to gain the best economies in a new market. The company focuses on establishing a large number of stores in a short period of time to gain decent volumes. With 10–15 hypermarkets in an area they set up a central distribution center, with immediate benefits. They then focus on top-line growth and market leadership. Tesco's major advantage is their experience with a wide variety of formats from hypermarkets to convenience stores; once they have a market presence they can diversify. This flexibility is important when they face CEE countries that are beginning to regulate large-store growth.[14]

The first country to be discussed is Hungary. I was in Hungary five years ago. Budapest has a rich history which it is just beginning to recapture.

**Photo 14.1**
A woman shops for irons in a Tesco supermarket in Prague, Czech Republic. Czech consumers are benefiting from a strong local currency and rising wages, and have a per capita GDP only slightly behind European Union member states Spain, Portugal, and Greece. Tesco, a U.K.-based supermarket chain, is among the biggest foreign retailers in the Czech Republic. *Photo by Sean Gallup/Getty Images.*

## 〉 HUNGARY

### Country Background

Hungary gained independence in 1867 as part of the Austro-Hungarian empire. After the Allied victory in World War I, the empire was dissolved and Hungary lost two-thirds of its territories. Hungary entered World War II on the side of Germany. The citizens of Hungry declared a republic in 1946, but the next year the Hungarian Communists took power with the help of Russian occupying forces. Soviet forces put down several revolts. In 1968, a sweeping reform of the national economic system replaced central planning and allowed individual enterprises relative autonomy. This economic liberalization and political tolerance made Hungry a maverick among the Soviet-bloc countries. By opening its borders with Austria in May 1989, Hungary became a catalyst in the unraveling of Communist rule in Eastern Europe.

Hungary's approach to the privatization of the retail trade has been different from that used in Poland or the Czech Republic. Those two countries tried to remove the state influence as quickly as possible. The Hungarian authorities had a specific strategic plan. Hungary's approach focused on three objectives: (1) to create a market structure similar to that found in Western economies, (2) to raise revenue that could be used to finance the state budget deficit, and (3) to exert effective governmental control over the privatization process.[15]

Today Hungary is considered one of the most important CEE countries. Its 2006 GDP is nearly $12,000; only Slovenia and the Czech republic are higher. The population is similar to the Czech Republic and is exceeded in this region only by Poland and Russia.

## Retailing in Hungary

Hungary is Tesco's best CEE for market share and profitability. It was the first CEE country they entered, getting in very early in 1994. It was the first market Tesco was able to build to the scale necessary to be competitive. Tesco is the market leader holding 15 percent market share. They are experiencing double-digit increases. As the hypermarket industry becomes saturated they are prepared to use smaller formats for continued growth. Carrefour is the number two market leader. They also entered in 1994 with their cash and carry format, a year later adding Praktiker and a year after that Media Markt. They have about 8 percent of the grocery market.

The next country I will discuss in this chapter is the Czech Republic. This country experienced a land rush when foreign companies raced to get properties. Its retail industry is more developed than most in the region.

## › CZECH REPUBLIC

### Country Background

The Czech First Republic lasted from 1918 to 1938. This was the golden age of modern Czechoslovak history. The country enjoyed a prosperous democracy with a lively intellectual and artistic life. However, nationalist tension within Czechoslovakia (conflict between a German minority and the Czechs and Slovaks majority) made it vulnerable to the international rise of Nazism, which brought the republic down in 1938. After World War II, Czechoslovakia regained its freedom from the Nazis briefly, only to lose it again to the Communists, who ruled the country for four decades. The party's rule collapsed in late 1989.

Before World War II, Czechoslovakia was considered to be one of the most developed and sophisticated European countries. Culture flourished and the retail system was similar to that in France and Germany. After the communists came to power in 1948, they brought all elements of the private sector economy under government ownership. Predictably, they regarded retailing as an unnecessary function. In 1989 and 1990, internal revolutions caused the fall of communism in Czechoslovakia. The transition was so peaceful they termed it the Velvet Revolution. Vaclav Havel, a prominent playwright, was elected to be the country's first president. In 1993, Czechoslovakia divided into two countries, the Czech Republic and Slovakia. The Czech Republic has a population of 10 million, twice that of Slovakia. Both countries are democracies. They sometimes refer to the 40-year experiment in socialism as "a long, hard and distressing road from capitalism to capitalism."[16]

Today the Czech Republic, along with Poland and Hungary, is considered one of the lead economies in CEE. At $13,000, its GDP is 10 percent higher than Hungary's and 51 percent higher than Poland's.

### Retailing in the Czech Republic

Prague reminds me of a young Paris. The city center, Nove Mesto, was founded in 1348 by Charles IV, but the current city is vibrant and young. Handblown crystal is one of the best buys in Prague. During my first visit, I decided to purchase some crystal. There are dozens of crystal shops in each shopping area. I wanted to purchase some handblown glasses with a black tulip base. Many stores sold this particular style, so I decided that it would be worth my time to do a price comparison. The prices did vary.

I wove my way through the city on a Saturday afternoon, conducting research for this book and doing my price study of the crystal. After visiting about a dozen stores, I determined that the lowest price to be found was at one of the major department stores. I noted that the store closed at 5:00 P.M. I knew that none of the stores in Prague would be open on Sunday, and I was leaving early Monday morning to go back to Germany. My purchase would need to take place before the store closed. My book research had taken me to the other side of the city. I decided that I had better take the subway to the department store and arrived there at 4:45, only to find the store had closed early. I hurried up a side street I had visited earlier, which I knew had many shops selling the tulip-style glasses. The first store I came to was closed. I went to another; it was closed. Shops were closing literally moments before I could get to them, and they were all closing before their posted closing time of 5:00 P.M. Finally, I found a shop that was still open. It did carry the glasses, but as I recalled from my earlier, and more leisurely comparison shopping, its prices were the highest I had encountered. By this point, it did not matter. I bought them anyway. I learned two things that day. First, Prague stores no longer use the fixed price system. Second, retailers, even large retailers, open and close at their convenience, not being bound by a responsibility to consumers.

The current retail structure in the Czech Republic is very price competitive with discount chains leading the downward price drive. Germany's Schwarz Group (Lidl) is the leader in the market, operating both discount hypermarket format (Kaufland) and Lidl discount stores. Metro operates Cash & Carry markets here and has excellent profits. Tesco is third in the market, but they are struggling because of being forced to go head to head with Metro and Lidl. Tesco's aggressive strategy includes accelerated store opening to be able to achieve economies of scale. Ahold increased its presence in the Czech Republic with the acquisition of Julius Meinl supermarkets. Their major problem is trying to differentiate between supermarkets and the more price-driven discounters in the minds of consumers by focusing on value rather than just price. Carrefour is a small player in the Czech market, having just 15 stores.[17]

The third country I will discuss in this chapter is Poland. Poland entered marketization with a fury; the term "shock therapy" is often used to explain how rapidly the country moved from a fixed price system to free market equilibrium.

## > POLAND

### Country Background

Poland is the second-largest country in central or Eastern Europe, after Russia. The country is named for the Polane, a Slavic tribe that lived in the area more than 1,000 years ago. The name Poland is derived from a Slavic word meaning plain or field, and it aptly describes the country of flat plains and gently rolling hills.

Once, Poles ruled an empire that spanned most of central Europe, but foreign powers conquered Poland, and the land was divided up. Before World War II, Poland was mainly agricultural with 75 percent of its people living on farms. In the post-war years, the country became a leading industrial nation. Poland did not become an independent republic until 1918. After World War II, Poland had a Communist government and became part of the Soviet bloc, COMECON.

Poland has gone through three phases of planned economy. The first phase, lasting through the mid 1950s, involved highly centralized planning. This included the establishment of output objectives for production and strict control over price and margins for the narrow range of goods the government allowed to be produced. The second phase, between the late 1950s and early 1970s, included substantial decentralized planning. Socialist companies could occasionally make their own production and assortment decisions. Price remained centrally controlled. During the third phase, from the mid 1970s through the late 1980s, greater flexibility was permitted to enable socialist enterprises to supply consumers with the goods they wanted, although pricing was still done in a centralized manner.[18]

The change from socialism to capitalism assumes that the planned economy will increasingly decentralize into private hands, and that the unplanned economy will be absorbed into the overall market economy. Poland has a history of capitalism. Throughout the late 1940s the private sector of Poland was responsible for about 70 percent of the country's gross national product (GNP). From the late 1940s to the early 1960s, however, the government confiscated all businesses. This process has been reversed and the large state enterprises have been privatized.[19]

## Retailing in Poland

The economic transformation in Poland has been affected by the consumer perception of the transition process. There are three cultural-historical antecedents associated with this change. First is the socialist legacy. Consumers have been conditioned to wait for the government to tell them what to do. Under the socialist system, people were trained to await orders and to avoid personal initiatives. There was no reward for performance, so the work ethic was weak. A popular saying in Russia about the former government-run business system was, "They pretend to pay us and we pretend to work."

Tables 14.1 and 14.2 summarize the major domestic and foreign retailers in Poland. The second cultural-historical antecedent is the aspiration gap. As noted earlier in this chapter, this refers to consumers' perceptions of a discrepancy between the goods and quality of life that they believe they should have and what they can achieve. Often, unrealistic beliefs sharpen the aspiration gap about how others live. In less-developed countries, reruns of *Dallas, Dynasty,* and *Santa Barbara*—U.S. evening TV soap operas about extraordinarily wealthy families—have set the stage for people to think that is how all Americans live.

The third antecedent is the consumerization process. The change to a capitalist market must be integrated into other aspects of the economy. The Polish people had little experience as a consumer- or demand-oriented culture. Thus, for the market to function effectively, consumer knowledge needs to increase.

The Polish grocery market is still highly fragmented, although it is being supplied with world-class retailers. Tesco and Metro are the market leaders. Jeronimo Martins from Portugo (Biedronka discount chain) and Schwartz Group (Kaufland) are also players. Each group has only about 4 percent market share. Poland was the

**Table 14.1**
**Poland—Leading Domestic Retailers, 2004**

| | | Total Sales and Stores | | | Global Rank and Penetration | | | Domestic Market | |
| | | Net Sales ($US Mil) | % Chg Sales | Total Stores | 2004 Rank, Top 200 Retailers Worldwide | Single-country, Regional or Global? | Number of countries | Share of total sales | Share of total stores |
| Company | Primary Line of Trade | | | | | | | | |
|---|---|---|---|---|---|---|---|---|---|
| 1 Eldorado S.A. Group | Supermarkets/Grocery Stores | 311 | 26.7% | 423 | — | Single Country | 1 | 100% | 100% |
| 2 POLOMarket | Supermarkets/Grocery Stores | 258 | 24.8% | 146 | — | Single Country | 1 | 100% | 100% |
| 3 Komfort | Hardlines Specialty Stores | 203 | N/A | 114 | — | Single Country | 1 | 100% | 100% |
| 4 Piotr i Pawel | Supermarkets/Grocery Stores | 187 | 27.0% | 26 | — | Single Country | 1 | 100% | 100% |
| 5 LPP S.A. | Apparel Stores | 125 | 43.6% | 158 | — | Regional | 8 | 90% | 77% |
| 6 Bomi | Supermarkets/Grocery Stores | 69 | N/A | 14 | — | Single Country | 1 | 100% | 100% |
| 7 Berti | Supermarkets/Grocery Stores | 41 | 22.0% | 20 | — | Single Country | 1 | 100% | 100% |
| 8 Jedynka | Supermarkets/Grocery Stores | N/A | N/A | 19 | — | Single Country | 1 | 100% | 100% |
| 9 ALDIK | Supermarkets/Grocery Stores | N/A | N/A | 21 | — | Single Country | 1 | 100% | 100% |

Sources: Retail Forward, company annual reports and published reports

Table 14.2
**Poland—Key Foreign Retailers, 2004**

| Company | Headquarters | Retail Sector | Primary Line of Trade | Global Rank and Penetration | | |
|---|---|---|---|---|---|---|
| | | | | 2004 Rank, Top 200 Retailers Worldwide | Single-country, Regional or Global? | Number of countries |
| Anton Schlecker | Germany | FDM | Drug Stores | 95 | Regional | 9 |
| Auchan Groupe | France | FDM | Hypermarkets/Supercenters | 18 | Global | 12 |
| C&A | Belgium | Softgoods | Apparel Stores | 105 | Global | 15 |
| Carrefour Group | France | FDM | Hypermarkets/Supercenters | 2 | Global | 31 |
| Centres E. Leclerc | France | FDM | Supermarkets/Grocery Stores | 24 | Regional | 6 |
| Dansk Supermarked A/S | Denmark | FDM | Discount Stores | 100 | Regional | 5 |
| Hutchison Whampoa Limited | Hong Kong | FDM | Drug Stores | 77 | Global | 18 |
| IKEA AB | Sweden | Homegoods | Furniture & Home Furnishings | 44 | Global | 32 |
| INDITEX Group (i.e., Zara) | Spain | Softgoods | Apparel Stores | 110 | Global | 56 |
| ITM Entreprises SA | France | FDM | Supermarkets/Grocery Stores | 8 | Regional | 9 |
| Jeronimo Martins | Portugal | FDM | Supermarkets/Grocery Stores | 159 | Regional | 2 |
| Kingfisher PLC | United Kingdom | Homegoods | DIY/Home Improvement Stores | 50 | Global | 9 |
| Leroy Merlin | France | Homegoods | DIY/Home Improvement Stores | 112 | Global | 8 |
| Mango | Spain | Softgoods | Apparel Stores | – | Global | 76 |
| Marks & Spencer PLC | United Kingdom | Softgoods | Department Stores | 49 | Global | 32 |
| Metro AG | Germany | FDM | Cash & Carries/Warehouse Clubs | 4 | Global | 29 |
| Office Depot, Inc. | United States | Homegoods | Office Supply | 54 | Global | 23 |
| Otto Group | Germany | FDM | Non-Store | 61 | Global | 19 |
| Pinault-Printemps-Redoute SA | France | Homegoods | Non-Store | 36 | Global | 17 |
| Rallye (i.e., Casino) | France | FDM | Supermarkets/Grocery Stores | 26 | Global | 17 |
| Rewe-Gruppe | Germany | FDM | Supermarkets/Grocery Stores | 14 | Regional | 14 |
| Royal Ahold | Netherlands | FDM | Supermarkets/Grocery Stores | 10 | Global | 18 |
| Schwarz Group | Germany | FDM | Discount Food Stores | 12 | Regional | 19 |
| Staples, Inc. | United States | Homegoods | Office Supply | 47 | Global | 18 |
| Tengelmann Warenhandelsgesellschaft | Germany | FDM | Supermarkets/Grocery Stores | 23 | Global | 15 |
| Tesco PLC | United Kingdom | FDM | Supermarkets/Grocery Stores | 5 | Global | 13 |

Sources: Retail Forward, company annual reports and published reports

first target for Western grocers moving into the CEE. They might have entered too quickly. Poland has had a sluggish economy and high unemployment, resulting in losses for most of these retailers for a long time. However, the market is not saturated and a wave of consolidations will likely leave the winners more profitable.[20] The major cities in Poland do seem to be saturated in the hypermarket segment. Growth in this area will need to take place in smaller cities because the largest cities (Warsaw and Krakow) cannot support many more.

Ahold found that applying the same standards they used in the Netherlands did not lead to success in Poland. They sold their hypermarket business to Carrefour and Real. Ahold's supermarkets have proven to be more successful than hypermarkets in Poland. Carrefour's acquisition of Ahold's hypermarkets has made them the second-largest hypermarket player in Poland. In Poland, Carrefour uses a flexible strategy, using large hypermarkets in large cities, slightly smaller ones (6,000–8,000 square meters) in medium-sized towns and supermarkets.

Metro got into the Polish market in 1994 using their Cash & Carry format. Three years later they introduced Real and a year after that Praktiker and Media Markt. They lost money in the hypermarket business but their Cash & Carry probably offset that loss. Tesco has experienced disappointment in the Polish market, but things should be looking better as they are able to gain scale. They entered this market in 1995 and it takes time to gain the scale needed to be successful.[21]

The introduction of hypermarkets has changed consumers' shopping patterns. Trading hours changed as well, with most shops being open on Sunday. Shopping became a form of leisure activity, particularly on Sundays. Priests have noticed a drop in church attendance; it seems they have some competition for people's time.

New stores of 2,000 square meters and larger are now subject to local authority regulations. This will dampen growth and give the current market players a great advantage in being early movers.

The last country to be discussed in this chapter will not be joining the EU anytime soon, but its market potential is so great that it would be a shame to leave it out.

## > RUSSIA

### Country Background

By 1800, the Russian empire reached from Poland in the west to Alaska in the east. Following the defeat of Napoleon in 1812, Western ideas caught the attention of Russian intellectuals. The Russian Revolution against the czarist system occurred in 1917. A provisional government assumed power, but it was overthrown in a Communist coup led by Vladimir Lenin. Lenin's death in 1924 precipitated an internal power struggle from which Josef Stalin emerged as the absolute leader. From the 1930s to 1953, the Stalinist regime killed tens of millions of people in purge trials, mass executions, and mass deportations to slave labor camps. In June 1941, Hitler invaded the Soviet Union. After sustaining great losses, the Soviets were able to resist the Germans. After Stalin's death in 1953, Nikita Khrushchev was elected first secretary of the Communist Party. Khrushchev presided over Moscow's cruel suppression of Hungary and aided the communist revolution in Cuba. In Russia, he relaxed censorship over literary works and released thousands of prisoners from the infamous Gulag, the labor-camp system in Siberia.

In March 1985, Mikhail Gorbachev assumed the leadership of the Soviet Union. He introduced perestroika and glasnost as the new forms of Soviet economic and foreign policy. Russia is the least developed of the CEE countries with a GDP of only $4,000, but the size of its population makes it extremely attractive. A political coup in August of 1991 brought about the shift to a market economy.

## Retailing in Russia

Tables 14.3 and 14.4 summarize the major domestic and international retailers in Russia. It is easy to see why the Russian people might want to return to a planned economy. They are disillusioned. Visitors can see the problems as they approach the central subway stations in Moscow, where people are selling personal items. This type of selling has gone on for years, although it is illegal. In a letter from Moscow, one observer made this note:

> I was in the passage between Revolution Square and Nikolskaya Street when suddenly the hundred or so women standing along the wall began to flutter and then melt into the crowd in a kind of wave; in an instant, a "market" had disappeared. The reason was the approach of two policemen, whose arrival had been silently signaled down the whole queue. The police strolled into a shop to admire some computer games, the objective of their demarche, and pretended at least to be unaware of the dispersal they had caused. Fifteen seconds had not passed before the hundred sellers and their goods had emerged from the crowd and were back to the wall. There is a Russian saying to the effect that no matter how often one scatters the crows they will just circle and roost again. The roles had been played out.[22]

The black market was the most efficient consumer product distribution system in Soviet Russia. A wider variety of products and services were available through black market transactions than through official channels of distribution. Even today over 50 percent of fast-moving consumer goods go through these informal channels. Thirty percent are sold by small food stores and only 16 percent are sold through modern retail systems. So the chief competitors for modern retailers are the street vendors. But many of these goods are counterfeit, which is a real problem in Russia. A study by the Coalition for Intellectual Property Rights found that 93 percent of those surveyed had encountered counterfeit goods.

The major department store in Russia, GUM, is located in Moscow. GUM originated as an open-air market for bakers, spice merchants, tanners, hatters, and cloth makers. In 1888, the city government and the merchants incorporated a company, the Great Merchant's Galleries, with the shopkeepers as the majority shareholders. A competition was held to find an architect to design the Galleries' home. The winner, architect Alexandre Pomerantsev, designed a three-part shopping gallery with exterior turrets and glass ceilings. After the Russian Revolution, the gallery was nationalized and for many years it served as office space. In 1953, the Soviet government decided to create GUM, the Russian acronym for state universal store.

The flagship store has a prime location just opposite the Kremlin, in a structure that looks like a French railroad station. The GUM store is twice as large as Bloomingdale's 59th Street flagship store in New York. It draws 250,000 shoppers a

**Table 14.3**
**Russia—Leading Domestic Retailers, 2004**

| Company | Primary Line of Trade | Total Sales and Stores | | | | Global Rank and Penetration | | | Domestic Market | |
|---|---|---|---|---|---|---|---|---|---|---|
| | | Net Sales ($US Mil) | % Chg Sales | Total Stores | | 2004 Rank, Top 200 Retailers Worldwide | Single-country, Regional or Global? | Number of countries | Share of total sales | Share of total stores |
| 1 Pyatyorochka | Discount Food Stores | 1,108 | 45.8% | 442 | | — | Regional | 3 | 98% | 97% |
| 2 Tander | Discount Food Stores | 968 | 69.1% | 1,019 | | — | Single Country | 1 | 100% | 100% |
| 3 M.Video | Consumer Electronics & Appliances | 962 | 85.0% | 50 | | — | Single Country | 1 | 100% | 100% |
| 4 Perekriostok | Supermarkets/Grocery Stores | 660 | 76.8% | 95 | | — | Single Country | 1 | 100% | 100% |
| 5 Uniland | Discount Food Stores | 560 | 55.1% | 99 | | — | Single Country | 1 | 100% | 100% |
| 6 Sedmoi Kontinent | Supermarkets/Grocery Stores | 496 | 45.0% | 77 | | — | Single Country | 1 | 100% | 100% |
| 7 Lenta | Cash & Carries/Warehouse Clubs | 451 | 57.1% | 7 | | — | Single Country | 1 | 100% | 100% |
| 8 Kopeika | Supermarkets/Grocery Stores | 372 | 60.5% | 63 | | — | Single Country | 1 | 100% | 100% |
| 9 L'Etoile | Cosmetics/Health & Beauty | 300 | 76.5% | 396 | | — | Single Country | 1 | 100% | 100% |
| 10 Paterson | Supermarkets/Grocery Stores | 250 | 78.6% | 56 | | — | Single Country | 1 | 100% | 100% |
| 11 Arbat Prestige | Cosmetics/Health & Beauty | 234 | 15.8% | 22 | | — | Single Country | 1 | 100% | 100% |
| 12 Starik Hottabych | DIY/Home Improvement Stores | 223 | 27.6% | 37 | | — | Single Country | 1 | 100% | 100% |
| 13 Sela | Apparel Stores | 96 | 20.0% | 401 | | — | Regional | 11 | 83% | 87% |
| 14 TsUM | Department Stores | 52 | 44.0% | 1 | | — | Single Country | 1 | 100.0% | 100.0% |
| 15 GUM | Department Stores | 38 | −35.7% | 1 | | — | Single Country | 1 | 100% | 100% |
| 16 Soyuz | Consumer Electronics & Appliances | N/A | N/A | 80 | | — | Single Country | 1 | 100% | 100% |

Sources: Retail Forward, company annual reports and published reports

**Table 14-4**
**Russia—Key Foreign Retailers, 2004**

| Company | Headquarters | Retail Sector | Primary Line of Trade | Global Rank and Penetration | | |
|---|---|---|---|---|---|---|
| | | | | 2004 Rank, Top 200 Retailers Worldwide | Single-country, Regional or Global? | Number of countries |
| Auchan Groupe | France | FDM | Hypermarkets/Supercenters | 18 | Global | 12 |
| Edeka-Gruppe | Germany | FDM | Supermarkets/Grocery Stores | 16 | Regional | 5 |
| IKEA AB | Sweden | Homegoods | Furniture & Home Furnishings | 44 | Global | 32 |
| INDITEX Group (i.e., Zara) | Spain | Softgoods | Apparel Stores | 110 | Global | 56 |
| Karstadt Quelle AG | Germany | Softgoods | Non-Store | 42 | Regional | 19 |
| Leroy Merlin | France | Homegoods | DIY/Home Improvement Stores | 112 | Global | 8 |
| LVMH | France | Softgoods | Other Apparel Specialty Stores | 76 | Global | 56 |
| Mango | Spain | Softgoods | Apparel Stores | — | Global | 76 |
| Metro AG | Germany | FDM | Cash & Carries/Warehouse Clubs | 4 | Global | 29 |
| Rewe-Gruppe | Germany | FDM | Supermarkets/Grocery Stores | 14 | Regional | 14 |
| Tengelmann Warenhandelsgesellschaft | Germany | FDM | Supermarkets/Grocery Stores | 23 | Global | 15 |

Sources: Retail Forward, company annual reports and published reports

**Photo 14.2**
A Russian street scene
featuring open vegetable
carts and an enclosed
kiosk. *Courtesy of Patricia
Huddleston.*

day, including 20,000 foreign visitors.[23] The business part of GUM is privatized.
The building is listed as a historical monument owned by the government of the
Russian Federation, so the building itself cannot be privatized. GUM leases the prem-
ises from the Moscow government. The lease, signed in 1992, expires in 2042.

Today Gum accommodates 440 boutiques for top fashion designers and world-
class brands from 60 countries. Escada, the 26-year-old Italian fashion house, recently opened a shop there.[24]

Russia is the fifth-largest grocery retail market in Europe. The food market is
also very fragmented, with the top five retailers holding only a 5 percent market
share. However, food retailing is the fastest-growing segment in the Russian retail
market. Currently Russians spend over 40 percent of their income on food.[25]

The organized retail market consists of supermarkets, discounters, hypermarkets,
and cash and carry. Although most of the discount operators are domestic, the
other retail formats are mainly foreign based. There have been significant barriers
to entering the Russian market, primarily the difficulty of getting licenses and the
uncertainty of the real estate market. Like in many formerly planned economies,
the ownership of land is questionable, and the government reserves the right to
reacquire land that someone might have thought they freely owned.

Foreign retailers such as Metro, Auchan, Ramenka, and Rewe have successfully
entered the Russian retail market and now hold the dominant market share in the
hypermarket segment. This segment has the highest revenue growth rate. Metro is

the sales leader. Pyaterochka is second with a supermarket format, then Magnit, also with a discount format. Next is Perekrestok (supermarket), Seventh Continent (supermarket), Lenta (cash and carry), Ramstor (hypermarket), Kopeika (discount), Auchan (hypermarket), and Dixi (discount). None of the major chains have anything more than a regional presence and the size and cultural diversity of Russia suggest that it will be decades before anyone does.

In Russia supermarkets continue to be the most important organized food supply and there are no true hard discount formats. Metro is the major foreign player with its cash and carry format. Auchan, Edeka, and other local retailers have opened hypermarkets in the past three years. There is likely to be a great deal of foreign investment in the next few years because of the large markets and strong growth potential. The focus of foreign investment has largely been in St. Petersburg and Moscow, but an increasing amount of growth will come from the provinces. The low penetration of modern retail formats relative to Poland and Hungary makes this market really attractive.

The overall leading food retailer in Russia is Pyaterochka, which recently made its IPO. IPO refers to Initial Public Offerings the first time a company's stocks are offered for sale. The company leads the supermarket sector with nearly 500 stores, mostly in Moscow and St. Petersburg. The company uses a more limited line of SKUs and locates much closer to people's places of residence. Again the food retail market in Russia is very fragmented, with the number one and two market leaders Pyaterochka and Metro each having only about 1.5 percent market share.

## 〉 SUMMARY

Under planned economies, prices of products are low but goods are scarce. Until the principles of supply and demand take effect there will be skyrocketing inflation and product shortages. Planned economies comprised of state-owned stores and cooperatives never had to be accountable for product sales. Sales employees were accountable for theft, under the responsibility system, but they were not responsible for sales and profits.

Of the countries discussed in this chapter, Russia has the longest and hardest road ahead as it struggles to make the transition to a free-market economy. The other eastern European countries had a recent history of capitalism. Communist rule did not begin in Hungary, the Czech Republic, and Poland until after World War II. Thus, one can find citizens who remember what life was like before the centrally planned economy. In Russia, which became a Communist nation in 1917, people do not remember what it was like to have a free market.

The planned market experiment in Russia and the Soviet bloc failed. Hungary was the first eastern European country to open the door to market reform. Germans tore down the wall dividing West from East. Much work has been done in the last ten years to rebuild their economies.

This chapter concludes Part III on retailers in Europe. Our attention now turns to Asia. There are some obvious similarities between Eastern European countries and the People's Republic of China (PRC). The PRC is also in the process of moving from a planned to a free market system. The country's state-owned stores are being turned over to private owners. This move to a market economy is made easier by the involvement of retailers from Japan, Hong Kong, and Taiwan. Their role is similar to that of French and German retailers in Eastern Europe. In the case of the PRC, the move is from East to West. In Europe, the move was from Western Europe to Eastern Europe.

We are witnessing a natural experiment, the first time countries have changed from planned economies to free markets. Each country is approaching the transition in a different way. In the end, they may be able to tell us whether an approach such as Poland's "shock therapy" or China's "putting a toe in the water" makes the transition easier.

## > KEY TERMS

ASPIRATION GAP

BARTER

BLOCKED OR NONCONVERTIBLE CURRENCY

COOPERATIVES

ETHNIC RESOURCE COMPETITION THEORY

GREENFIELD OPTION

IPO (INITIAL PUBLIC OFFERING)

PARASITIC

PLANNED ECONOMY

PRIVATIZATION

RESPONSIBILITY SYSTEM

STATE-OWNED STORES

VAT

## > DISCUSSION QUESTIONS

1. Under a planned economy, retailing is considered to be a nonproductive activity. Why would market planners have this attitude?
2. Use ethnic resource competition theory to explain why consumers would try to disguise consumption.
3. How could American TV shows like *Dallas* and *Dynasty* affect consumers in these marketizing economies? If your explanation did not include the concept of aspiration gap, look back over the discussion of that concept and reframe your discussion.
4. Why do we say that the informal economy is the market system that operates under a demand economy? When the informal market system is illegal (black market), how are prices for goods in that market affected?

## > ENDNOTES

1. Seitz, H. (1992). "Retailing in Eastern Europe: An Overview." *International Journal of Retail and Distribution Management,* Vol. 20, No. 6, pp. 4–10.
2. Turban, J. (1977). "Some Observations on Retail Distribution in Poland." *Soviet Studies,* Vol. 29, pp. 128–136.

3. Huddleston, P., and L. Good. (1998). "The Price-Quality Relationship: Does it Hold True for Russian and Polish Consumers?" *The International Review of Retail, Distribution and Consumer Research*, 8,(1) 33–51.

4. Institute for Socio-Political Researches of Russia (1993). "How are you, Russia?" Moscow Analytical Center in Dixon D.F., and E. Polyakov. (1997). "Physical Quality of Life Indicators in Post-Stalinist Russia." *Journal of Macromarketing.* 17 (1), 39–55.

5. Davies, B., and R. Schmidt. (1991). "Going Shopping in Poland: The Changing Scene of Polish Retailing." *International Journal of Retail and Distribution Management.* Vol. 19, No. 4, pp. 20–27.

6. KPMG—International (May 1996). Central Europe. *Microsoft Internet Explorer.*

7. Schultz, C., R. Belk, and G. Ger., eds. (1994). *Research in Consumer Behavior: Consumption in Marketizing Economies.* Greenwich, CT: JAI Press.

8. Sampson, S. (1991). "May You Live Only By Your Salary! The Unplanned Economy in Eastern Europe," *Social Justice,* Vol. 15, No. 3/4, pp. 135–159.

9. Goldman, M. (1991). *What Went Wrong with Perestroika,* New York: W.W. Norton and Company, p. 116.

10. Samarasinghe, S.W.R. de A., and R. Coughlan. (1991*). Economic Dimensions of Ethnic Conflict.* New York: St. Martin's Press.

11. Pecotich, A., N. Renko, and C. Shultz (1994). "Yugoslav Disintegration, War, and Consumption in Croatia." In C. Schultz, R. Belk, and G. Ger, eds., *Consumption in Marketizing Economies.* Greenwich, CT: JAI Press, pp. 1–27.

12. Eastern European Retailing. (2005). WestLB/Eurostat GMID Euromonitor

13. Eastern European Retailing. (2005).

14. Eastern European Retailing. (2005).

15. Earle, J., R. Fryman, A. Rapaczynski, and J. Turkewitz. (1994). *Small Privatization: The Transformation of Retail Trade and Consumer Services in the Czech Republic, Hungary and Poland.* Budapest: Central European University Press.

16. Drasny, T. (1992). "Retailing in Czechoslovakia, Retailing in Eastern Europe." *International Journal of Retail & Distribution Management,* Vol. 20, No. 6, pp. 30–33.

17. Eastern European Retailing. (2005).

18. Lofman, B. (1994). "Polish Society in Transformation." In C. Schultz, R. Belk, and G.Ger, eds., *Research in Consumer Behavior: Consumption in Marketizing Economies.* Vol. 7, 1994. Greenwich, CT: JAI Press, p. 30.

19. Lofman. (1994).

20. Eastern European Retailing. (2005).

21. Eastern European Retailing. (2005). WestLB/Eurostat GMID Euromonitor

22. Fenster, E. (1995). "Letter from Moscow." *Small World,* Vol. 1, No. 6, November/December, p. 10.

23. Raper, S. (1992). "Moscow's GUM Gearing for Growth." *Women's Wear Daily,* September 9, p. 24.

24. Weathersby, W. (2005). "The Ansorg Design Team Imbues Moscow's Escada Shop with Sparkling Light Bringing a Flair to Red Square. *Architectural Record* August 1 (1993), 156.

25. Russian consumer goods sector. (2005). ING Equity Research in Investext, September.

# COMPANY FOCUS III.1

## H&M

Laura Asher, Meredith Chiarelli, Elizabeth Matthies, Jennifer Mummert, Ashley Nagy, Hilary Newcomb, Beth Roszatycki, Stacey Wilson

### Flow Chart:

1947: Sweden (122 stores as of March 2006)

1964: Norway (78 stores as of March 2006)

1967: Denmark (56 stores as of March 2006)

1976: United Kingdom (103 stores as of March 2006)

1978: Switzerland (52 stores as of March 2006)

1980: Germany (289 stores as of March 2006)

1989: Netherlands (73 stores as of March 2006)

1992: Belgium (49 stores as of March 2006)

1994: Austria   (52 stores as of March 2006)

1996: Luxembourg (7 stores as of March 2006)

1997: Finland (27 stores as of March 2006)

1998: France (72 stores as of March 2006)

2000: Spain (50 stores as of March 2006)

2000: USA (91 stores as of March 2006)

2003: Italy (11 stores as of March 2006)

2003: Czech Republic (12 stores as of March 2006)

2003: Poland (27 stores as of March 2006)

2003: Portugal (7 stores as of March 2006)

2004: Canada (11 stores as of March 2006)

2004: Slovenia (2 stores as of March 2006)

2005: Hungary (1 store as of March 2006)

2005: Ireland (4 stores as of March 2006)

### From Hunting to Fashion

H&M was founded in 1947 in Sweden by Erling Persson[1] and is still a prospering global company. The store began as a women's clothing store called Hennes and later bought the men's hunting and clothing store Mauritz. They decided to drop off the hunting line but keep the men's clothing, creating Hennes and Mauritz.[2] H&M has had one centralized objective since opening the first store—fashion,

price, and quality.[3] The company has done an exceptional job keeping up with changing trends in the past five decades.

### Global Expansion

One of the top global retail companies in Europe and the United States, H&M currently owns and exclusively runs more than 1,134 stores in 22 countries.[4] Neither joint ventures nor franchising plays a role in their expansion strategies. Each of H&M's stores is a wholly owned subsidiary of the H&M Corporation, a significant method when expanding a global company because it doesn't give up any of the company's production secrets or business formats.

H&M is considered a strong retail firm, which gives them a choice of where and when they choose to expand. They can expand with their initial business format and plan, or they can modify it to each country that they enter. Because they are a global company, H&M chooses to keep their products and formats uniform in every market that they enter, in the belief that there will be a consumer in each market who will associate with their products, merchandise, and retail format.

As can be seen from the timeline, H&M first expanded into Norway in 1964, Denmark in 1967, the United Kingdom in 1976, Switzerland in 1978, and Germany in 1980. To this day, Germany is H&M's largest market. They also recently purchased 10 German stores from Gap Inc., all of which have prime locations, enhancing their market share even more.[5] Dunning's theory of ownership advantages plays a major role in their early expansion into these countries. They use asset-based ownership advantage, which revolves around their reputation of high quality, high fashion, and low cost.

## A World of Technology

In 1980 H&M also began to expand store formats to not just specialty stores, but offered mail-order shopping, which is available today in Sweden, Norway, Finland, and Denmark.[6] This mail-order market has increased their presence in the retail industry. Once H&M's mail-order business began, their entry into new countries came faster and closer together. They next expanded to the Netherlands in 1989, Belgium in 1992, and Austria in 1994. Their form of centralized management became more crucial within the operations of the company. Each policy needed to be implemented simultaneously throughout the corporation so that each subsidiary ran effectively with the key objectives in mind. An example of centralized management within the individual stores is the re-stocking from 7 A.M. to 9 A.M. on Tuesdays and Fridays;[7] no matter if you are in Paris or Chicago. Centralized management's application of Dunning's theory of transaction-based ownership advantage helped the expansion of H&M.

## Location Location Location

H&M and other global retailers continually increase the frequency of their expansion into other countries. They are not limited to places that are close to them geographically. Geographic proximity of their expansion patterns becomes less and less important due to their centralized management and consistent retail format. In 2000, H&M created a frenzy in the United States when they opened their first store in New York City. Today there are over 70 H&M stores in the States. Other countries H&M has currently entered include Portugal (2003), Poland (2003), the Czech Republic (2003), Canada (2004), Ireland (2005), and Hungary (2005).[8]

H&M has a goal of expanding into new countries every two years.[9] In recent years, they have surpassed their expectations. They also want to grow approximately 15 percent each year.[10] However, it is not their strategy to obtain first mover advantages. When H&M entered the Polish and Czech market in 2003, many of their competitors had already entered those markets three or four years earlier. Yet they believed they entered those markets at just the right time.[11] H&M waited until they thought those countries would enter the European Union, which would make it easier to sell clothing between the countries, and would also give them a common monetary unit. Many people believe that H&M is missing the boat by not expanding into China, Japan, or Russia, but they are choosing to wait until the time is right, especially when their current markets of Europe, United States, and Canada have yet to be saturated.[12] There are still some areas in Europe that can allow further expansion, such as Germany, France, Spain, Italy, the United Kingdom, and Poland; however, Austria, the Netherlands, and Scandinavian markets are at a very mature stage.[13]

## Size Really Does Matter

H&M's strategy of quick expansion has created several problems. After their first successful store opened on Fifth Avenue in New York, they decided to open larger stores than in Europe. This was an immense mistake. H&M opened stores that were far too big in seven or eight malls.[14] One store was 5,400 square meters; now the top floor is empty.[15] Once they realized their error, they opened much smaller stores. Another problem occurred when H&M entered malls with stores such as Express, Wet Seal, and Old Navy.[16] It was hard for H&M to compete when the malls were dominated by other chain stores. H&M learned from their mistakes and now their approach is to open stores in upscale malls and downtown centers.[17] They are seeking to find cities with similar segments of upper-income consumers, and they enter countries with stable economic and political environments. This concept also goes back to the pattern of expansion for global companies.

## Not Just Your Average Woman

Another example of how they use a global expansion strategy is the creation of new private label lines within each store. Within each category of their merchandise assortment their products are made to H&M's specifications and not sold in any other retail stores. Their women's department consists of five different concepts. H&M has very trendy merchandise that can be supplemented with their more basic items. L.O.G.G., Legion of Graded Goods, features high quality, durable products with a classical look. The L.O.G.G. Sport line consists of modern and practical sportswear. The BiB line offers plus size merchandise, with the same H&M high fashion. This line carries both staple goods as well as very trendy items. The newest H&M private label, The Mama line, is designed for pregnant women who don't want to sacrifice chicness during pregnancy. Women's clothing is complemented by those basic items such as underwear, nightwear, socks, as well as accessories such as jewelry, sunglasses, belts, and purses.

## Men Can Be Fashionable, Too

The men's department maintains high fashion, quality, and affordable price, offering tailored garments such as wool suits, pure cotton shirts, and silk ties.[18] The L.O.G.G. brand is also available for men and is focused on functional sportswear. The men's department is also supplemented with accessories, socks, and underwear.

## Don't Forget the Teenagers

H&M has also created a teenage department called Divided, which offers fashionable products for both sexes. This department is very trendy and consists of denim, street wear, partywear, and a large array of accessories. H&M also has a children's department; this line combines safety and functionality with fashion.[19] H&M recently came out with a new brand of jeans called &denim. Launched throughout the world in September 2005, the collection is made up of 100 different styles of jeans each season for both men and women.[20]

## The Finishing Touch

H&M also created their Beauty Box brand, a full line of cosmetics consisting of makeup, hair and body products, and other accessories.[21] Using H&M's current theme of global strategies, they have entered into an agreement assuring that the products, contents,

packaging, and labeling meet the requirements of safety and quality within the European Union.[22] This has allowed H&M to expand into more countries with greater ease because they don't have to alter or change their products within each country entered.

Their sole use of private label has also provided another asset-based ownership advantage of Dunning's theory. Generally private labels have long lead times, which prevents them from producing high-fashion goods with a short life cycle. This, however, is not the case with H&M.

## Fast and Furious

H&M enhances their position in the market with their quick lead times. Because of their efficient inventory management systems, they are able to provide their customers with products quickly. Since H&M doesn't have their own factories, they rely heavily on feedback from stores, and their 700-some independent external suppliers.[23] Their 21 production offices act as the mediator between the buyers and suppliers, making sure that buyers place their orders with the correct supplier, products produced are of the right quality at the right price, and suppliers conform to the company's standards for working conditions. Production offices are also responsible for checking and testing sample garments, a huge factor in decreasing lead time.

## What Have Your Suppliers Done for You Lately?

Choosing the right supplier is important to ensure efficiency in transporting the merchandise. In the past few years, H&M has been able to cut back the average lead time by 15–20 percent.[24] They are able to move a garment from the designer to the hanger in only 20 days[25] because of advancements in the buying process. Reducing lead times and flexibility allows the store to restock the best-selling merchandise quickly; it also reduces the risk of buying the wrong products.

H&M has two main collections each year, spring and fall. The many sub-collections within each season enable customers to find new products in the store at all times.[26] With new shipments daily, customers constantly see merchandise they have never seen before.[27] H&M is able to order their predictable goods further in advance and then order their trendy, unpredictable goods later in the season since they require very short lead times. Controlling every stage in their logistics chain, H&M acts as the importer, the wholesaler, and the retailer. They currently use backward vertical integration within the distribution network, which also allows for direct control of the market and their customers.

H&M's stock is handled primarily within the company but they contract transportation to third parties. Once the goods arrive to each country's distribution center, they are inspected and then allocated to a store or a centralized stockroom. Information technology (IT) is an important tool that allows individual stores to stay connected with logistics and procurement departments as well as with the central warehouse. The company is able to follow sales of each item from the central department, an intelligent procurement system. H&M is continuously developing their IT, which helps to support the entire logistics chain.[28] Their superior logistics provide another example of their transaction-based ownership advantage.

## Bring the Designers to You

H&M has also had great success with the company's in-house design team, which quickly responds to changing trends and designs clothing resembling apparel created by more expensive designers.[29] The company can predict the trends in terms of color, fabric, and design up to one year in advance of its revealing.[30] Currently, the company employs 95 designers, most of them women, in Stockholm, who create merchandise for men, women, teens, and children.[31] Inspiration is drawn from street trends, films, flea markets, TV, music videos, and the runway. Any type of vulgar or sexist expressions are strictly prohibited by designers.[32,33]

## High-Tech Creativity

With so many in-house designers working closely together, ideas and trends are constantly being thought up and reinvented. It did not begin this way. Margareta van den Bosch is H&M's design director; she runs the White Room, the center of design operations in Stockholm. When van den Bosch was appointed in 1987, the company was buying collections from Southeast Asian agents whose merchandise didn't flow well together.[34] She put together a design team who now have access to computerized design software and color-matching programs that only billion-dollar international companies possess.[35] Computers are available at every workstation so workers can quickly access these programs or look up the latest runway trends, giving these designers a leading edge in fashion.

## Cost-Efficient Fashion

H&M is recognized globally for trendy, upscale clothing that mimics top designers at an affordable price. To keep the cost of apparel low, the company has few middlemen and a large volume of products and materials are bought at one time. There is a deep knowledge and understanding of what goods should be bought and from where, and at every stage there is a sense of cost-consciousness.[36]

Middlemen are the people employed by the company to help import products to the retailer from the factories that manufacture the goods. Their job requires them to communicate between the factories and retailers to solve any problems that may occur. Furthermore, they search for other factories that may be able to produce what the company wants, make sure the quality of the products is up to par, and in some cases purchase raw materials for the company.[37] With fewer middlemen, H&M can keep the price of its products lower because less money is needed to pay salaries.

Being an apparel company, H&M is a labor-intensive industry. Companies rely on people to make their products for them and generally diseconomies of scale occur. As the company gets larger and produces more products, more workers must be hired to keep up with the demand, ultimately increasing costs. However, H&M owns no manufacturing plants and the products they receive are from suppliers.[38]

When orders are placed they are in such large quantities that economies of scale occur instead, and the money the company saves on production is passed along to the consumer.[39]

H&M has been in business for more than five decades, so its employees have a vast and thorough sense of the fashion industry. With that experience comes the knowledge and understanding of where to buy particular products that will be the most beneficial to the company. Currently, H&M receives its products from about 700 suppliers and the majority of orders are placed in Europe and Asia.[40] Where an order is placed affects the price of the product, the time of transportation, regulations on importing items, and quality inspections. In China, for example, productivity is high and cotton and fabrics are being purchased in greater amounts, therefore keeping the cost of the finished product low.[41] H&M also has suppliers in Cambodia. These factories focus on treating their employees justly and paying them adequately. The Garment Manufacturers Association of Cambodia estimates that the government adds taxes of about 10 to 12 percent to the cost of production. These higher taxes increase the prices of the production and clothing and make it harder for Cambodia to compete with other countries that have lower production costs.[42] Due to numerous complaints about these taxes, government officials have increased the channels of distribution by reducing the number of approvals needed for exports.[43] By limiting these approvals, the company can lower the cost of production.

### CEO's on a Budget

H&M also holds a high degree of cost-consciousness led by Chairman Stefan Persson. He makes certain that overheads are low by limiting expenses not just for sales personnel, buyers, or designers, but for all employees. You won't find employees flying business class or taking taxis unless it's an emergency.[44] Employee mobile phones have been banned since the 1990s and only a limited number of key employees have cellular phone privileges.[45] Business executives are not excluded from this method of cost control either; only a few of them have secretaries.[46]

One final reason that H&M can produce less costly apparel is due to the weakening of the U.S. dollar. Many Asian countries have their currency tied to the value of the dollar and as the exchange rate decreases, so does the cost of purchasing products manufactured in those countries.[47] With much of H&M's clothing being produced in Asia, purchasing costs are lower.

### Disposable Fashion

Luxury brands such as Prada and Louis Vuitton are going to have a hard time competing with the disposable fashion that H&M is pumping out of their stores in high volume. Not only does H&M create clothing that is chic and fashionable, but they also do it at the most affordable prices around. Imagine Chanel designs at Old Navy prices. It doesn't seem logical, yet Europe's most fashionable chain is doing just that. H&M uses its unusually fast lead times to restock their stores and keep fashion at the ultimate level. Bringing in limited edition items exclusively creates a feeling of urgency that filters throughout all of the 1,134 of stores worldwide.

### Now You See It, Now You Don't

H&M uses a marketing ploy to create the perceived need that you must buy the fashion item before it sells out, never to return.[48] H&M isn't the only retailer that is jumping on the trend to create a "massclusivity" of limited-edition items solely created to generate heat and sell out immediately.[49] Manhattan stores reported sellouts hours after introducing new limited-edition clothing lines in flagship stores. H&M has created a new breed of shoppers. Fitting room lines might be a 15–20 minute wait, so rather than waiting, shoppers try things on in the aisles. A feeling of frenzy and urgency exudes from every pore of every H&M store. Clothing is torn off the racks and thrown about, giving employees a run for their money to keep up with the cleanup. The excitement is contagious, and if stores had a pulse, this one would be off the charts.[50] Even the most conservative shopper will get her hands into the mix.

Older shoppers looking for disposable fashion are one of the main targets for H&M. Experienced shoppers with years of experience shopping in designer boutiques such as Prada or Louis Vuitton consider H&M a favorite. Affluent consumers are just as likely to shop at a Target or an outlet mall as they are at Barneys.[51] Cross-shopping, which could involve wearing a Gap T-shirt and Abercrombie jeans with Chanel shoes, has become a huge trend. Even the most well-to-do shopper won't turn down a good bargain. Pricing their clothes so low is what gives H&M their huge advantage over fashion-forward designers like Chloe or Club Monaco. Designs will be similar but price points can't even be compared.

Upwards of 100 in-house designers keep watch on trends around the world in order to keep up with demand. Their fast production rate of three to four weeks beats the six-month average it takes a high-fashion designer to send items out onto the floor. Vogue editor Anna Wintour calls this trend a "seasonless cycle" for fashion.[52] Even top designers like Escada are coming up with midseason fill-ins to keep up with trends. When shoppers enter an H&M store they know that everything there is going to be the latest fashion, closely resembling creations they would see on a designer runway.

### *Real* Designers for *Real* Fashion

The designs in H&M not only resemble the works of designers; they *are* the work of designers. H&M brought in Chanel's acclaimed designer Karl Lagerfeld last November to introduce a new trend for the store. Lagerfeld's newest line, exclusively found in H&M stores, opened in Paris last September. This is a new approach to disposable fashion that is being copied by stores such as Target and TopShop, a British retail chain. Fashion designer Isaac Mizrahi has created a permanent line of clothing and footwear that can only be found in Target stores. Guest designers including Mussien Chalayan and Sophia Kokosalaki have created lines for Britain's TopShop.[53]

Karl Lagerfeld's exclusive line lasted only hours in some Manhattan stores last fall. Knowing that the designs were a limited offer shoppers snatched them up, not paying over $150 for anything. Chanel is a leader in the fashion industry and anything produced by Lagerfeld was deemed fabulous and worth every penny. His name brought even more recognition to the global giant.

After Lagerfeld's success in 2004, H&M hired highly influential designer Stella McCartney to introduce a 35-piece line for H&M that came out in November 2005. A limited number of hand-embroidered coats were produced by McCartney and most likely sold out within hours.[54] H&M may well do a new line launch every fall.

### Don't Break the Bank

Seeing such a big name in such a low-priced store makes the average woman feel like she is getting something original and fashionable that won't empty her bank account. Buying such high-fashion items can often be too expensive when they are worn only a few times and are then deemed out of style. H&M puts most of its time and energy into turning out cutting-edge clothing at a price the masses can not only easily afford, but can also afford to throw out when fashion demands changes.[55] This is where the term "disposable fashion" comes from. When something is in such high demand a woman might be willing to pay just about anything for it. At H&M she doesn't have to.

### Fashion Clusters

H&M learned early on in their expansion that they need to use other similar clothing retailers to draw attention to their new store. As H&M expands even more into the United States, they are doing so with the central place theory strategy. This occurs when a company takes advantage of their competitor's location by adding to the attraction of the location by making it a central place for shoppers. When competitors share a market area, it may seem detrimental to their business when in actuality, it is highly beneficial. The location already has the appeal of the other retails, so it draws in more shoppers and provides a convenient location to make numerous stops while shopping.

Manhattan has proven to be an ideal place to try out this theory. In 2004 H&M opened a new location catty-corner to Zara's, another similar European retailer, in the newly constructed Bloomberg Tower, which also houses Manhattan's second Home Depot. Zara's decided to do the same thing back to H&M by building a new store right across from H&M's Fifth Avenue flagship store. Other neighbors in this area include Aldo and Bloomingdale's flagship store. It appears that European-style retailers are popping up in clusters all over the city. H&M usually creates freestanding stores, however. In the Eaton Centre, Toronto's largest mall, they had a separate wing built to accommodate their new store in a prime location.[56]

The Bloomberg Tower's H&M store is using a new format that more likely resembles a boutique than big box. There is an emphasis on small tables and hanging wall displays to keep shoppers in particular sections of the store. This is different than most retailers, who use a more linear manner of merchandising on rectangle racks and tables.[57] Most stores are designed around a white atrium, with theatrical lighting, loud pulsating music, and dramatic photography that extends up through the whole structure. Very little furniture decorates the space; they let the merchandise speak for itself. This mod, chic look screams high fashion. H&M seizes the reality that what's in today will not be in tomorrow.[58] Cutting-edge advertising is also used to promote their fashion-forward merchandise for new store openings. When a new designer is brought in, the opening will often include a DJ, dancing, and free T-shirts.

## Multi-Channel Surfing

Creating ads that are clear and simple, H&M's advertising department informs their customers of what is new. Their stimulating atmosphere inspires customers to create their own look.[59] They do this through not only their print ads, but with their window displays and mannequins as well. H&M's advertising is all done in-house and is centrally based in Sweden. Since they use centralized practices within their corporation they have chosen to comply with the codes issued by ICC regarding all of their advertising techniques used throughout the world. Complying with these standards allows H&M to use one ad for all of their markets. They use many different channels, including stores, billboards, the Internet, catalogues, press, and television.[60]

## Do You D.A.R.E To Keep Your Models Off Drugs?

H&M aims at portraying a healthy and positive image. They do this through all aspects of their corporation, from their clothing line to their advertisements. H&M had hired Kate Moss to be their spokesperson for their new Stella McCartney line, but after the publication of some photos of the model using cocaine, H&M dropped her from the advertisements.[61] H&M is against all drug use/abuse and works with many drug prevention programs and organization. By dropping Moss from the ads they were sending a message of healthy and ethical behavior.

## We All Walk the Catwalk

H&M generally features high-fashion icons in their ads. Much of the culture in the United States deems thin and elegant to be beautiful; the European market even more so. H&M promotes these images within their ads using slim, chic runway models. They are attempting to play on the cultural universal of aesthetics to set a certain standard of beauty and meaning with their product lines and to enhance sales to these types of consumers. For example, a previous advertisement used a catwalk theme print and an outdoor ad campaign with supermodels Heidi Klum, Carmen Cass, and others. Store windows were designed to give the feel of a runway show in progress.[62]

They use these models as change agents to influence the consumer and create a sense of significance to their clothing line. Another recent H&M ad is one of their biggest in history, a 15,200-sqare-foot billboard on the scaffold of the historic Flatiron Building in New York City. H&M is trying to spread the idea that their fashion is for everyone, and by doing so, they target everyone who can see the giant billboard.[63]

As a global retailer, H&M has a wide and diverse target market, yet they are able to use their advertisements globally. They use a uniform global expansion plan as well. H&M started off as a single store selling only women's clothing products and has transformed itself into a global giant selling men's, women's, women's plus sizes, children's, lingerie, and beauty products. Although only 22 countries have been expanded into, their worldwide growth potential is exponential.

## Discussion Questions

1. Is the retailer classified as a global retailer or a multinational retailer? Explain its pattern of expansion. What expansion strategy did/is the retailer use/using?
2. Based on Dunning's eclectic theory, how do ownership, locational and internalization factors play in your retailers' international expansion?
3. What role does cultural proximity and geographical proximity play in the retailers' international moves?
4. Can you predict the retailer's future international expansion?

## Endnotes

1. Larenaudie, S.R. (2004, February 9). Inside The H&M Fashion Machine. *TIME Magazine*. Retrieved October 23, 2005 from http://www.time.com/time/2004/style/020904/article/inside_the_h_m_fashion_01a.html
2. finance.yahoo.com (2005)
3. www.hm.com (2005)
4. www.hm.com (2005)
5. Gap Inc.: Retailer to Sell German Stores to H&M for Undisclosed Sum. (2004, February 6). *Wall Street Journal* (Retrieved October 23, 2005 from Proquest).
6. www.hm.com (2005)
7. Larenaudie, S.R. (2004).
8. www.hm.com (2005)
9. Capell, K. (2002). *Hip H&M*. Retrieved October 28, 2005 from www.businessweek.com/print/magazine/content/02_45/b3807010.htm?chan=mz
10. Hjelt, P. (2004). *H&M: Success In The U.S.* (Retrieved October 27, 2005, from Proquest).
11. Hjelt, P. (2004).
12. Hjelt, P. (2004).
13. H&M Spreads Wings Over Europe-Despite US Slow-Burn. (2004, November 4). Business and Finance Magazine. (Retrieved 23 October, 2005 from LexisNexis).
14. Hjelt, P. (2004).
15. Capell, K. (2002).
16. Yang, D.J., Marcus, M.B., Morrow, J., and Hawkins, D. (2000). Buying—The Swede Smell of Success. *U.S. News & World Report*. (Retrieved 23 October 2005).
17. Capell, K. (2002).
18. www.hm.com (2005)
19. www.hm.com (2005)
20. www.hm.com (2005)
21. www.hm.com (2005)
22. www.hm.com (2005)
23. www.hm.com (2005)
24. Databank Consulting (no date)
25. Larenaudie, S.R. (2004).

26. Databank Consulting (no date)

27. Larenaudie, S.R. (2004).

28. Databank Consulting (no date)

29. Sauer, A.D. (2002, January 14) *H&M-Hot & Mod.* Retrieved October 23, 2005 from http://www.brandchannel.com/features_profile.asp?pr_id=51

30. H&M.com, From Idea to Store

31. Capell, K. and Khermouch, G. (2002, November 11). Hip H&M. *Business Weekly Online.* Retrieved October 30, 2005 from http://www.businessweek.com/magazine/content/02_45/b3807010.htm

32. Capell, K. and Khermouch, G. (2002).

33. Larenaudie, S.R. (2004).

34. Larenaudie, S.R. (2004).

35. Larenaudie, S.R. (2004).

36. H&M.com, Our Philosophy

37. Keeping the Work Floor Clean. (1998, December). Retrieved October 24, 2005 from http://www.cleanclothes.org/codes/floorchain.htm

38. Larenaudie, S.R. (2004).

39. Larenaudie, S.R. (2004).

40. H&M.com, From Idea to Store

41. Montlake, S. (2005, May 12). Cambodia Pitches Sweat-Free Wear. Retrieved October 24, 2005 from http://www.csmonitor.com/2005/0512/p06s02–woap.html

42. Montlake, S. (2005).

43. Montlake, S. (2005).

44. Capell, K. and Khermouch, G. (2002).

45. Capell, K. and Khermouch, G. (2002).

46. Larenaudie, S.R. (2004).

47. "Cheap Dollar" (2005)

48. Boorstin, J. (2005). What's in Fashion This Fall? Scarcity. Fortune, 152(4), 19. (Accessed 11 October, 2005 from Proquest).

49. Boorstin, J. (2005).

50. Wilson, M. (2000). Disposable Chic at H&M. Chain Store Age, 76(5), 64–67. (Accessed 1 November, 2005).

51. Wilson, M. (2000).

52. Thomas, D. (2004). When High Fashion Meets Low. Newsweek, 144(25), E26–28. (Accessed 11 October, 2005).

53. Thomas, D. (2004).

54. Boorstin, J. (2005).

55. Wilson, M. (2000).

56. Scardino, E. (2004). H&M expands reach in Manhattan. DSN Retailing Today, 43(22), 5–7. (Accessed 11 October, 2005 from Proquest).

57. Scardino, E. (2004).

58. Wilson, M. (2000).

59. www.hm.com (2005)

60. www.hm.com (2005)

61. Luckhurst, T. (2005, September 25). The Crucifixion of Kate. *Independent on Sunday, The.* (Retrieved 14 October, 2005 from Proquest).

62. O'Loughlin, S. (2004, March 1). Retailer H&M Pounces on Catwalk Ad Theme. *Brandweek,* Vol. 45, Iss. 9, pg. 15. (Retrieved 23 October, 2005 From Proquest).

63. Van Riper, T. (2005). Retailer H&M to Display Huge Advertisement on Flatiron Buildings in New York. *Knight Ridder Tribune News* pg.1. (Retrieved 11 October, 2005 from Proquest).

# COMPANY FOCUS III.2

## ZARA

Aubrey Fry, Ashley James, Krista Briggs, Michael Endres,
Andrea Hargrove, Kalena Marra, Jenn Dion, Rachel Grear

**Flow Chart:**

1988: Portugal (45 Zara, 57 Pull & Bear, 43 Massimo Dutti, 31 Bershka, 25 Stradivarius, 18 Oysho, 9 Zara Home, and 17 Kiddy Class stores in 2005)

1989: United States (17 Zara stores in 2005)

1989: France (88 Zara, 10 Massimo Dutti, 15 Bershka, and 1 Stradivarius stores in 2005)

1992: Mexico (36 Zara, 14 Pull & Bear, 15 Massimo Dutti, 27 Bershka, 14 Oysho, and 1 Zara Home store in 2005)

1993: Greece (35 Zara, 9 Pull & Bear, 6 Massimo Dutti, 11 Bershka, 3 Oysho, and 1 Zara Home store in 2005)

1994: Belgium (17 Zara, 18 Massimo Dutti, 6 Bershka, and 1 Zara Home store in 2005)

1994: Sweden (3 Zara and 3 Massimo Dutti stores in 2005)

1995: Malta (1 Zara, 4 Pull & Bear, and 1 Bershka store in 2005)

1996: Cyprus (3 Zara, 2 Pull & Bear, 1 Massimo Dutti, 2 Bershka, 2 Stradivarius, and 1 Zara Home store in 2005)

1997: Norway (2 Massimo Dutti stores in 2005)

1997: Israel (14 Zara and 12 Pull & Bear stores in 2005)

1998: Argentina (5 Zara stores in 2005)

1998: Japan (16 Zara stores in 2005)

1998: United Kingdom (38 Zara, 7 Massimo Dutti, 2 Bershka, and 1 Zara Home store in 2005)

1998: Venezuela (8 Zara, 6 Pull & Bear, 2 Massimo Dutti, and 8 Bershka stores in 2005)

1998: Lebanon (2 Zara, 2 Pull & Bear, 3 Massimo Dutti, 2 Bershka, 1 Stradivarius, and 1 Oysho store in 2005)

1998: United Arab Emirates (5 Zara, 3 Pull & Bear, 5 Massimo Dutti, 3 Bershka, 3 Stradivarius, and 2 Zara Home stores in 2005)

1998: Kuwait (4 Zara, 3 Pull & Bear, 1 Massimo Dutti, 2 Stradivarius, and 1 Oysho store in 2005)

1998: Turkey (11 Zara, 3 Pull & Bear, 1 Massimo Dutti, 2 Stradivarius, and 1 Oysho store in 2005)

1998: Turkey (11 Zara and 2 Massimo Dutti stores in 2005)

1999: Netherlands (6 Zara, 1 Massimo Dutti, 4 Bershka, and 1 Zara Home store in 2005)

1999: Germany (39 Zara and 4 Massimo Dutti stores in 2005)

1999: Poland (10 Zara stores in 2005)

1999: Saudi Arabia (15 Zara, 7 Massimo Dutti, 4 Bershka, 11 Stradivarius, and 2 Oysho stores in 2005)

1999: Bahrain (1 Zara, 1 Pull & Bear, and 1 Massimo Dutti store in 2005)

1999: Canada (14 Zara stores in 2005)

1999: Brazil (12 Zara stores in 2005)

1999: Chile (5 Zara stores in 2005)

1999: Uruguay (2 Zara stores in 2005)

2000: Austria (7 Zara stores in 2005)

2000: Denmark (4 Zara stores in 2005)

2000: Qatar (1 Zara, 1 Pull & Bear, 1 Massimo Dutti, and 1 Stradivarius store in 2005)

2000: Andorra (1 Zara, 1 Pull & Bear, 1 Massimo Dutti, and 1 Zara Home store in 2005)

2000: Puerto Rico

2000: Jordan (1 Zara, 1 Pull & Bear, 1 Massimo Dutti and 2 Stradivarius stores in 2005)

2001: Ireland (4 Zara, 8 Pull & Bear, 1 Massimo Dutti, and 3 Bershka stores in 2005)

2001: Iceland (1 Zara store in 2001)

2001: Luxembourg (2 Zara and 1 Massimo Dutti store in 2005)

2001: Czech Republic (2 Zara stores in 2005)

2001: Italy (29 Zara, 4 Pull & Bear, 4 Massimo Dutti, 10 Bershka, 9 Oysho, and 2 Zara Home stores in 2005)

2002: El Salvador (1 Zara store in 2002)

2002: Finland (3 Zara stores in 2005)

2002: Dominican Republic (1 Zara store in 2002)

2002: Singapore (3 Zara stores in 2005)

2002: Switzerland (7 Zara, 3 Massimo Dutti, and 1 Bershka store in 2005)

2003: Russia (6 Zara and 2 Pull & Bear stores in 2005)

2003: Slovakia (1 Pull & Bear store in 2003)

2003: Slovenia (3 Zara stores in 2005)

2003: Malaysia (3 Zara stores in 2005)

2004: Hong Kong (2 Zara stores in 2005)

2004: Morocco (1 Zara and 1 Stradivarius store in 2005)

2004: Estonia (1 Zara store in 2004)

2004: Latvia (1 Zara store in 2004)

2004: Romania (1 Zara and 1 Pull & Bear store in 2005)

2004: Hungary (2 Zara stores in 2005)

2004: Lithuania (1 Zara store in 2004)

2004: Panama (1 Zara store in 2004)

2005: Costa Rica (1 Zara store in 2005)

2005: Indonesia (2 Zara stores in 2005)

2005: Philippines (1 Zara store in 2005)

2005: Monaco (1 Zara store in 2005)

Zara's successful expansion strategies and superior business systems have set the standard within the fashion industry for companies worldwide. Zara's achievements stem from their flourishing private label, unbeatable lead times, and dominating logistics systems. Their products sell themselves with trendy and fashion-forward apparel. Zara's fast fashion approach and internalization advantages have made them the profitable retailer they are today and have allowed them to stay a step ahead of competition. One of Zara's greatest achievements has been their international expansion strategy. This approach has kept them competitive and profitable and with continued expansion, and Zara is sure to become a more thriving and lucrative corporation.

## Company Overview

Inditex Group, the parent company of Zara, began as a small fashion company in Spain, but has flourished to become one of the largest fashion distributors in the world.[1] The company currently has eight brands with over 2,500 stores. These brands include Pull & Bear, Massimo Dutti, Bershka, Stradivarius, Oysho, Kiddy's Class, Zara Home, and Zara.[2] Inditex can credit the majority of its company growth to their most profitable and successful brand, Zara, which maintains the highest contribution of their total sales.

Zara first began as a lingerie shop in the city of La Coruña, Spain. Amancio Ortega, the founder and CEO of Inditex, opened the first Zara in 1975. Inditex was not incorporated with Zara in 1985 and then the company became public in the year 2000.[3]

Zara has a major reputation for having a speedy reaction to the fashion world. They often pull items and cancel others that are not selling. Within just three weeks Zara can create a new concept and have it out on the shelves.[4] The company also produces around 11,000 designs each year. This may be as much as five times more than any equivalent retailer would produce. Although this technique quickly raises production costs, it helps save on later markdowns and discounts. "With Zara, because the stock turnover is so fast, you have to get there on day one. It tends to sell out two days later so you have a real chance of being a little bit exclusive."[5] This is quite unusual for a high-fashion retailer.

One technique used by the company includes a limited supply of new products, which gives customers the feeling of exclusivity. This factor also motivates consumers to repeatedly visit the stores, resulting in customer loyalty. Advertising expenditures remain at a minimum. Zara spends a mere 0.3 percent of sales on advertising costs, while their competitors usually spend between 3 and 4 percent.[6]

Zara's many strengths include their finances, brand image, supply chain and logistics, and product category and mix. Zara saves an abundance of money while using their private label. This strategy allows the company to gain a higher profit margin and price their products accordingly. Their strong brand image allows them to spend fewer advertising dollars and focus more money on their strategic supply chain. Their supply chain consists of high response communication channels because all of the stores are electronically linked to the headquarters. In addition, trend spotters and store managers are constantly sending ideas back to the corporate office. This strategy proficiently meets consumer's changing needs. Zara consistently controls all segments of its business model and produces at least 60 percent of their merchandise in-house.[7]

While many companies outsource much of their goods, Zara has kept most of their distribution close to home. Zara's unique approach to the fashion industry has led them to be a "retailer's dream."[8] Direct communication between store managers and their design team allows the company to be on top of fashion trends. Zara's distinctive and effective strategies will only further their success within the fashion industry.

## Zara's International Expansion

The international expansion of Zara began in 1988 when a store was opened in Oporto, Portugal. In 1989 and 1990 Zara opened its first stores in New York and Paris. In the years that followed Zara used a strategy of opening one store per country each year. By the end of 1997, Zara was present in seven European countries, the United States, and Israel. Zara then gained presence in different countries more rapidly and during the years of 1998–2001, 24 countries were added to their international list. By the end of 2001, Zara was the largest and most internationalized of Inditex's chains. Currently Zara has store presence in 60 countries with 858 stores in prime locations of major cities. Zara's international presence confirms the idea that national borders have no barriers for sharing a single fashion culture.[9]

Inditex, the parent company, has often described Zara's pattern of expansion as an oil stain because during expansion, Zara would first open a flagship store in a major city and then after experiencing success, add stores in adjacent areas.[10] Considering that Zara's home base is in Spain, the company looked for nearby markets when deciding to enter into a new country. They also looked for markets that had low barriers to entry.[11] Employees from headquarters executed a macro- and micro-environmental analysis when trying to decide upon a market entry opportunity. The macro-analysis was implemented to focus on local macro-economic variables such as tariffs, taxes, legal costs, salaries, and property prices. The

micro-analysis was implemented to focus on the specifics of the market in question, such as local demand, channels, available store locations, and competitors.[12] These market analyses varied from country to country depending upon the characteristics that were given.

After the employees determined that entry into a specific market would be beneficial for the company, the next step was to determine *how* to enter the market. Zara originally internationalized their company through wholly owned stores. Because Zara's company-owned stores require the most commitment of resources, Zara decided to implement two other modes of market entry: joint ventures and franchises. To lessen the risk, franchises were used as a mode of entry into countries that encouraged franchising, were small, risky, or had cultural differences. In larger, more important markets that had barriers to direct entry, Zara used joint ventures to form partnerships with local entities.[13]

All of the Zara stores in Spain are company owned, while stores in Russia and Finland are franchises. In 2003, Inditex entered the Russian market through a franchise agreement with a European retailer known as Stockmann, who is also Zara's franchisee in Finland. Recent press information informs the public of Inditex's agreement with Stockmann to acquire its 100 percent stake in Zara Russia.[14] This is an example of resource-based theory, where a retailer buys back the franchise after it becomes successful.

By 2002 Zara had 20 stores in Germany and Japan that were managed through joint ventures.[15] In larger countries like China that have high barriers to entry, Zara would have to enter through a joint venture. As a result of the WTO accession, China committed to eliminating its mandatory policy toward foreign investment, which had allowed foreign retailers to enter the Chinese domestic market only through joint ventures with a Chinese business counterpart.[16] Because of this recent change in Chinese law, Zara was able to enter the Chinese market without a joint venture. As of February 23, 2006, Zara entered the Chinese market with a store in Shanghai. Zara also plans to expand to Beijing within 2006.

The marketing strategy of each store varies by country. The first store that opens is usually in a major city. This flagship store is critical to determine the marketing mix based on local demand. Marketing mix depends on a country's climate, trends, and culture. For example, when it's cold in New York during the month of March, Zara tends to sell sweaters or garments made of heavier material. It may be warm in London during this same time period and Zara will sell lightweight garments. Zara must adapt to each country's demand when internationalizing their stores.

Zara's products do not appeal to only one country's standards. Only a small percentage of products vary from country to country. Most of their products are marketable between international borders. Approximately 80–85 percent of Zara designs are sold in every store in every country, while 10–15 percent of products vary from country to country.[17] Products that cannot be sold in one country may appeal to customers in another country.

## Business Systems

Zara relies on their distribution and production methods for continued success in Spain and other international markets. When they began in their home market of Spain, Zara spent next to nothing on advertising, relying more on their logistics system and brand management for success. According to an article in *Brand Strategy,* branding for Spanish corporations has become progressively more important over the past years.[18] Having retailers with a global reputation will allow these companies to seek out more lucrative markets that are similar to Spain's. Zara's has been listed as having the strongest consumer brand in Spain, which has given them the confidence to enter other lucrative markets around the world.[19] One of the biggest challenges that businesses face today is allocating their merchandise in a timely manner while minimizing costs. Unlike their competitors, Zara's centralized distribution system has allowed them to have one of the fastest merchandise turnaround times in the world. Fashionable merchandise needs faster allocation because trends are always evolving and changing. When customers see something modeled on the catwalk, they want to find it in the store the next day. Zara's competition, such as H&M and Gap, produces their goods as much as five months in advance before they deliver them to

their stores. Produced in Spain, Zara's goods have a turnaround time of just three weeks.[20] H&M and Gap produce only 2,000–4,000 items a year. In contrast, Zara's shorter turnaround time allows them to "alter designs and create the 10,000 new styles annually to accommodate the tastes of fickle customers."[21] Zara has recognized that if they do not have their cutting-edge fashionable merchandise in stock, the customer will simply go elsewhere. Similarly, Zara customers recognize that if they come into the store and see something they like, they will have to buy it right away because in a week or even sooner it will no longer be there. This rack time is an efficient way to create a demand, influence Zara's customers to impulse buying, and also allow new inventory to quickly take its place. Customers also know that if they purchase an item the chance of seeing someone else wearing it is very small. Zara designs, produces, and distributes all their own apparel. These methods provide the flexibility to respond to market demands without reverting to the traditional industry pattern of forecasting, planning, manufacturing, and replenishing. Even with the new methods, Zara must also analyze the industry with a traditional approach. Zara has also managed to construct a logistics system that has enabled them to both increase sales and cut costs.

> Short lead time = More fashionable clothes
> Lower quantities = Scarce supply
> More styles = More choice, and
> more chances of success

## Production

Zara begins their journey from the sketchboard to store racks at their single, centralized design and production center at their La Coruña headquarters. Two hundred designers are divided into three lines consisting of women, men, and children, who work very closely to increase the speed and quality of the design process. Market specialists constantly communicate with store managers, who provide efficient feedback regarding the new designs. In addition, they suggest pricing strategies tailored to their particular market. Next, procurement and production planners estimate the manufacturing expenses and available capacity.[22] Zara purchases their fabric in advance, allowing them to quickly respond and produce products that parallel with forecasted trends. The majority of the fabric purchased is in a generic color, which provides Zara with the flexibility to color or print several different fabric designs in a timely and cost-efficient method. Also, the generic color allows Zara to avoid investing in outsourced processes for the final product.[23] As soon as prototypes are selected for production, the designers refine colors and textures on a computer-aided design system. Depending on what the item is and if it is to be made in one of Zara's factories, the company transmits the pieces directly to the relevant cutting machines and other systems in that factory. Bar codes track the cut pieces as they are converted into garments through the various steps involved in production, including sewing operations usually done by subcontractors.[24] It is vital that Zara coordinates their cross-functional teams to work closely together with open communication in order to maintain their fast and efficient production methods.

## Business Systems within the International Markets

Ninety percent of Zara's manufacturing facilities are located in Europe, with the majority being in the northwestern corner of Spain. In addition, Zara has three other smaller warehouses in Brazil, Argentina, and Mexico to help with distribution in South America. Within the European countries Zara's production and logistics systems distribute more than 90 million articles of clothing from its logistics center in the port city of La Coruña. Trucks are then used to transport the merchandise to its European stores, which represents the majority of its retail locations.[25] Once produced, Zara's clothing is sorted in a single distribution center in La Coruña, and then shipped

out in preprogrammed quantities directly to stores. "Twice a week every Zara store receives deliveries triggered by real-time inventory data collected through a network of computer handsets that feed through the Internet into computers in La Coruña. This fancy digital footwork stripped Inditex's inventory level as of January down to just 7 percent of annual revenues, compared with H&M's 13 percent."[26] Merchandise is shipped to stores in small deliveries to avoid overstock. Headquarters keeps in close contact with in-store managers to determine consumer preferences. While some items continue to sell, most of Zara's designs are replaced with twice-weekly deliveries of newer fashionable items from the factory. This process limits the need for inventory and warehouse space; therefore, Zara spends virtually nothing on warehouse costs.[27]

## Distribution within the U.S. Markets

In 1989, Zara expanded into the U.S. market, which also required them to construct a distribution system similar to what they had in the European markets. The only difference occurred in distributing the merchandise overseas. They had to still maintain their time optimization method of delivering goods because they invested minimally in advertising when they entered the U.S. market.[28] Once the goods are produced and sent to the distribution center, the shipment time is planned by time zone; goods are shipped via air so the stores receive the merchandise within one to two days. Although it costs more to ship via airfreight, Zara's merchandise is not marked down; therefore, the gross margin is higher than that for average retailers. Today, Zara's international success and consumer brand recognition continues to rely on their vertically integrated supply chain and production methods.[29]

## Discussion Questions

1. Is the retailer classified as a global retailer or a multinational retailer? Explain its pattern of expansion. What expansion strategy did/is the retailer use/using?
2. Based on Dunning's eclectic theory, how do ownership, locational, and internalization factors play in your retailer's international expansion?

3. What roles do cultural proximity and geographical proximity play in the retailer's international moves?

4. Can you predict the retailer's future international expansion?

## Endnotes

1. Unknown author (2005, Oct. 7). From a chain in Spain to worldwide success. Derby Evening Telegraph. Retrieved on February 12th, 2006 on Lexis-Nexis database.

2. Inditex Group. Press Releases: Inditex reaches an agreement to acquire Zara's franchise in Russia. (Retrieved March 1, 2006 from www.inditex.com)

3. Inditex Group. (2006).

4. Inditex Group. Zara: Who are we. (Retrieved March 1, 2006 from www.zara.com)

5. www.inditex.com (2004, para 6)

6. "Business: The Future of the Fast Fashion: Inditex." (2005, June 18). *The Economist,* Vol. 375, No. 8431, 63.

7. Folpe, J. (2000). "Zara has a made-to-order plan for success." Fortune. New York. 4 September 2000.

8. www.zara.com (July 2004)

9. Inditex Group. Zara: Who are we. (2006).

10. Ghemawat, Pankaj, and Jose Luis Nueno (2003). ZARA: Fast Fashion. Harvard Business Online, product number 9-703-497.

11. Ghemawat and Nueno (2003).

12. Ghemawat and Nueno (2003).

13. Ghemawat and Nueno (2003).

14. Inditex Group. Press (2006).

15. Harvard Business Review (2003).

16. SinoCast China Daily News. Zara To Enter Mainland China Market Soon. (Retrieved March 1, 2006 from LexisNexus Database)

17. Harvard Business Review (2003).

18. "Branding Espana to the Rest of the World" (2004, March). *Brand Strategy,* p. 12.

19. Brand Strategy (2004)

20. Heller, R. (2001). Spanish clothier Zara beats the competition in efficiency—and almost everything else. Forbes Magazine. Retrieved March 10th, 2006 from: http://www.forbes.com/forbes/2001/0528/098.html.

21. Heller, R. (2001).

22. Ferdows, M.K, Lewis A., and Jose A.D. (2005). Zara's Secret for Fast Fashion. HBS Working Knowledge. Retrieved on March 10th, from: http://hbswk.hbs.edu/item.jhtml?id=4652&t=operations.

23. Dutta, D. (2003). Retail at the Speed of Fashion Part II. Retrieved on March 21st, 2006 from: www.3isite.com/articles/ImagesFashion_Zara_Part_II.pdf.

24. Ferdows, M.K, Lewis A., and Jose A.D. (2005).

25. Schapiro, S.A. (2001). Off the Rack. Journal of Commerce, Inc. Retrieved on March 10th, 2006 from Infotrac database.

26. Heller, R. (2001).

27. Schapiro, S.A. (2001).
28. Schapiro, S.A. (2001).
29. Wahlgren, E. (2005). Fast, Fashionable—and Profitable. BusinessWeek Online. Retrieved on March 11th, 2006 from: http://www.businessweek.com/bwdaily/dnflash/mar2005/nf20050310_0805_db039.htm

# COMPANY FOCUS III.3

## MARKS & SPENCER

### Rashad Dunbar Woods, Brandye VanderPloeg, Bethany Lynn Kinner, Allison Marie Reeping, Tyler David Smith, Matthew Roy Church

**Flow Chart:**

| Year | Country | End Year | Number of Stores |
|------|---------|----------|------------------|
| 1973 | Canada | 1999 | |
| 1975 | France | 2001 | |
| 1975 | Belgium | 2001 | |
| 1977 | Philippines | | 13 stores as of 2005 |
| 1979 | Republic of Ireland | | 12 stores as of 2005 |
| 1988 | Hong Kong | | 9 stores as of 2005 |
| 1988 | United States | | 27 stores as of 2005 |
| 1989 | Portugal | 2001 | |
| 1990 | Spain | 2001 | |
| 1991 | Greece | | 35 stores as of 2005 |
| 1991 | Israel | 1997 | |
| 1992 | Hungary | | 5 stores as of 2005 |
| 1993 | Thailand | | 12 stores as of 2005 |
| 1993 | Indonesia | | 11 stores as of 2005 |
| 1995 | Turkey | | 22 stores as 2005 |
| 1996 | Germany | 2001 | |
| 1996 | Czech Republic | | 4 stores as of 2005 |
| 1996 | Malaysia | | 2 stores as of 2005 |
| 1997 | United Arab Emirates | | 4 stores as of 2005 |
| 1997 | South Korea | | 13 stores as of 2005 |
| 1998 | Bahrain | | 1 store as of 2005 |
| 1998 | Abu Dhabi | | 2 stores as of 2005 |
| 1998 | Dubai | | 2 stores as of 2005 |
| 1998 | Kuwait | | 1 store as of 2005 |
| 1999 | Poland | | 3 stores as of 2005 |
| 2000 | Romania | | 2 stores as of 2005 |
| 2000 | Qatar | | 1 store as of 2005 |
| 2000 | Croatia | | 2 stores as of 2005 |
| 2001 | Saudi Arabia | | 10 stores as of 2005 |
| 2001 | India | | 6 stores as of 2005 |
| 2001 | Guernsey | | 1 store as of 2005 |
| 2003 | Oman | | 3 stores as of 2005 |
| 2004 | Slovenia | | 1 store as of 2005 |
| N/A | Bermuda | | 1 store as of 2005 |
| N/A | Gibraltar | | 1 store as of 2005 |
| N/A | Gran Canaria | | 3 stores as of 2005 |
| N/A | Jersey | | 3 stores as of 2005 |
| N/A | Luxembourg | 2001 | |
| N/A | Malta | | 3 stores as of 2005 |
| N/A | Netherlands | 2001 | |
| N/A | Tenerife | | 1 store as of 2005 |

## Opening Statement

Polish refugee Michael Marks laid the groundwork in 1884, from its humble beginnings as a stall in Leeds, for what would soon become an international retailing power.[1] With 70,550 employees worldwide and franchises in over 30 countries, Marks & Spencer's story is well documented through countless reports, books, newspapers, and business reviews (Mergent Online). Through success and disappointments in its global expansion in North America, Europe, Asia, and the Middle East, Marks & Spencer has aggressively maintained their global expansion plans.

As a global retailer, Marks & Spencer uses centralized management, a standard format for its stores, a private label, and rapid expansion into new markets. The company specializes in clothing, food, retail, and financing services (MarketLine Business). Its private label, St. Michael, has been synonymous with the company since its inception in 1928. Recently, they changed the clothing line name to M&S.[2] Marks & Spencer carries an assortment of goods ranging from household goods, women and men's apparel, children's clothing, and produce. In addition, the company generated revenue of $14,544 million USD at the end of the year reported in April 2005 (Mergent Online).

## Competition

Marks & Spencer's main competition comes from Tesco and Sainsbury. Founded in 1914 in the United Kingdom, Tesco currently holds a 13 percent share of the retail market there. In addition, it has locations in Europe and Asia and operates 2,318 stores and employs over 326,000 people worldwide. It currently operates under Extra, Superstore, Metro, and Express. For the year ending February 2004, it achieved revenues of $59,307.9 million. Sainsbury, founded in the United Kingdom in 1864, operates 583 stores there, serving 11 million customers a week. In addition, it operates Supermarkets, Bells Stores, and Sainsbury's Bank (MarketLine Business).

Despite the various stories told about Marks & Spencer, the story of their expansion as a global retailer is left untold. In this case study, we will provide details of its franchising, joint venture, and wholly owned subsidiary strategies used to expand its operations. From global expansion beginning in the 1970s,

closing of stores, struggles to stay profitable, and a proposed takeover bid by billionaire Philip Green, Marks & Spencer faced and continues to face challenges as a global retailer.

## North America

**CANADA**    Marks & Spencer opened stores in Canada in 1973 and in 1975 bought People's Department Store and became Marks & Spencer Canada, Inc., committed to purchasing 70 percent of its clothing and 40 percent of its food products from Canadian manufacturers.[3] The Canadian market was less responsive than expected. At the beginning, Marks & Spencer did not fully understand their new customers. What sold in England did not sell in Canada. The company took a high-handed approach to discrepancies between British and Canadian consumers based on tastes and lifestyles.[4] Marks & Spencer continued to expand throughout Canada from 1972–1999.[5] Continual net losses and an overall poor performance pattern lead Marks & Spencer to announce in May 1999 that the first of its 38 stores would close, with the other 37 closing by September.[6] The company then decided to focus its international expansion in Europe and Asia.[7]

**THE UNITED STATES**    In 1986, Marks & Spencer planned entry to the U.S. market by signing leases for sites in three New York shopping malls with plans to lease a fourth, operating the stores under their Canadian subsidiary D'Allaird's.[8] The retailer then purchased the 47 stores of Brooks Brothers for $770 million, 30 times more than the chain's estimated net profits from 1987.[9] The company opened their new acquisition by targeting new markets, adding a women's line, and catching the attention of younger consumers.[10] It then acquired Kings Supermarkets Inc. for $108 million, reflecting the retailer's resilience on growing in the U.S. market. The New Jersey–established supermarket, known for customer service and fancy merchandise, would be stocking an assortment of the St. Michael private label.[11]

In efforts to concentrate operations in the United Kingdom, Marks & Spencer sold their U.S.-based unit Brooks Brothers in November 2001 to The Retail Brand Alliance Inc. for $225 million.[12] Its King's Supermarkets, now 25 stores, were seen as being limited to New Jersey.[13] Following its sale of Brooks Brothers, Marks & Spencer planned on selling Kings Supermarkets in 2002 for $160 million.[14] The deal fell through, and Marks & Spencer still owns the franchise (DeMarrais, 2004). There are 27 as of 2005.

## Europe

FRANCE    After a disappointing entrance into Canada, Marks & Spencer strived for international success, opening its first wholly owned store in Paris in 1975 on the Boulevard Haussman.[15] Using their locational advantages through cultural proximity, since France is closer to the United Kingdom and shares its European culture, Marks & Spencer even supplied slightly different products to better fit the French tastes. They soon realized the French were purchasing British imports instead.[16]

Marks & Spencer continued to expand throughout France in the next 20 years and by 1990, the company had eight stores there.[17] Marks & Spencer learned from its stores, installing fitting rooms by French request, then liking them so much, they took the idea home to England. In addition, the Paris store taught the company how to do a more productive job of coordinating the display of complementary clothing ranges.[18] In 1992, the retailer predicted to double its amount of stores in the country and to quadruple its sales by 1995.[19] Marks & Spencer grew to 18 stores across France, although at not nearly as promising an outlook. The retailer then began closing stores all over Europe, experiencing great financial difficulties and even losing its triple-A credit rating.[20] By 2001, Marks & Spencer closed all 18 of its retail outlets and cut thousands of jobs, infuriating employees around the country. The trend recurred throughout Europe.

BELGIUM    The first Marks & Spencer store opened in Belgium's capital, Brussels, in 1975, giving the country its first international franchise.[21] In 1983, a second store opened in Antwerp with an area of 2,800 meters.[22] After realizing its success to make clothing and groceries available all at once, Marks & Spencer planned to open its fourth Belgian store at the end of April 1997.[23]

In April 2001, Marks & Spencer announced closure of its Belgian operations as part of a restructuring plan. Legal action was considered by the Belgian government. In June, the government reported they would not prosecute Marks & Spencer after no evidence of broken laws.[24] After debate on setting a date for closures, Marks & Spencer achieved an agreement with trade unions to close the Belgian stores on December 22, 2001.[25]

REPUBLIC OF IRELAND    The Republic of Ireland's first Marks & Spencer store opened in 1979 in Dublin. Currently, there are 12 stores in the country.[26] Ireland has been a well-performing country for Marks & Spencer, continually improving existing stores as well as opening new ones.[27] In 1996 the company had a particularly good year, opening a 67,000-square-foot flagship store. (Canniffe, 1996).[28] In 1997, the third Marks & Spencer store in Cork was remodeled, adding an additional 13,000 square feet.[29]

Although the company does not release store performances for its locations in Ireland, the first six months of 1998 showed strong growth. The expansions made in this year gave Marks & Spencer 40 percent more selling space; performance was accredited to a strong economy and the company's investment program.[30] In 2005 two stores were opened, one in Dublin and the other in Blanchardstown.[31]

PORTUGAL    In 1989, Marks & Spencer entered Portugal. In 1999, the company was forced to close all six of its franchises due to financial discrepancies with franchisee, CRB Lda. Marks & Spencer stated that CRB did not honor its payment system or maintain quality standards. The first two stores were closed due to a downsizing effort, with the rest due to sluggish sales.[32] In April of 2000, two stores reopened.[33] In December 2001, plans to shut down operations in Portugal were complete.[34]

SPAIN    After Marks & Spencer's success in other parts of Europe, they expanded to Spain. With a less developed retail system than the United Kingdom and other markets, it proved a good strategy for the retailer. The first wholly owned subsidiary opened was a 3,000-square-meter store in Madrid in 1990, an ideal location since it is the capital of Spain and the store is in the well-known shopping district of Calle Serano.[35]

Prior to expanding fully into Spain, Marks & Spencer gained early experience by creating shop-in-shop arrangements in two Galerias Preciados department stores. Merchandise is sold in a commissioned sales area,[36] providing a way for them to enter the market and be able to create their own stores through experience. In addition, Marks & Spencer decided to take part in a joint venture with Cortefiel, an international Spanish retailer. They shared stores in Madrid, Seville, and Valencia.[37] In 1999, the company announced it would buy the 20 percent holding from Cortefiel. This allowed the retailer to run the Spanish operation as a wholly owned business, bringing Spain in line with the other Marks & Spencer continental European operations, which were wholly owned as well. The company conducts an ongoing review of all its business operations.[38]

Between 1996 and 1999, Marks & Spencer planned to open more outlets near Barcelona and Madrid, continuing to expand business and increase market share. In 1999, the company decided to improve its strategy in the Spanish market.[39] Giving more decision-making power to its European affiliates, they created exclusive models for clothing and were buying more from Spanish suppliers. In spite of the rapid expansion and plans for growth, trouble began in '99 when Marks & Spencer closed its store in Grancasa de Zaragoza shopping centre.[40] The store did not meet expectations and erred on location. Marks & Spencer began to evaluate its European operations, realizing many lacked performance and incurred losses. In 2001, the retailer closed its nine stores in Spain due to losses and planned on making a sustainable recovery at home.[41] They sold their stores to the country's top retailer El Corte Ingles.

The decision to close in Spain was due to the loss of profit share, aided by a decline in demand of offering from Marks & Spencer. Department stores faced many challenges in the past decade due to specialty retailers, discounters, and category killers.[42] It became more dificult for large, upscale department stores to compete. Many employees and customers were disappointed, while others stated the department store was very expensive and somewhat out of style.

**HUNGARY**    On September 23, 1991, Marks & Spencer signed an agreement to start a franchise division in Copenhagen. The franchise partner was the Hungarian S-Modell Company.[43] In September 1992, Marks and Spencer's first store in Hungary opened in Budapest, with staff trained by Marks and Spencer in sales expertise.[44]

As of 2004 there are six Marks & Spencer stores currently in operation in Hungary. A new store opened in Debrecen in 2004, the first store outside of Budapest. Plans to open new stores in other cities are currently underway by S-Modell.[45]

**GREECE**    In 1991, Marks & Spencer expanded to Greece in a franchising agreement with domestic company Marinopoulos to operate its stores. Combined with Promedes, Marinopoulus is one of the largest retailers in Greece.[46] It is currently a powerhouse in European retail, sharing ventures with France's Carrefour and Spain's DIA supermarkets.

With yearly increasing turnover and potential for more expansion, Richard Sweet, head of Marks & Spencer franchising in London, noted Greece was at the top of his list of performers. Marks & Spencer's performance in Greece is credited completely to Marinopoulos, who have become experts of the market. Knowing that Greek women are fashion conscious, Marinopoulos used influence from the Italian fashion industry. Food is taken straight from the British culture, because food in the United Kingdom is far different from that in Greece, and many consumers like a change in their foods. In 1999, Marinopoulos opened the doors of two of their own supermarkets to offer space for Marks & Spencer's products, allowing the retailer to offer food, lingerie, branded cosmetics, and toiletries in concession areas. Marinopoulos provides all of the financial backing and cultural expertise for the franchise, while Marks & Spencer provides the managerial experience and the merchandise.[47] As of 2005, there are 35 Marks & Spencer franchise outlets in Greece (Marks & Spencer Groups, 2005).

**TURKEY**    Marks & Spencer expanded to Turkey as a global retailer, forming a franchise agreement with Turk Petrol Holdings.[48] It opened freestanding department stores to sell a full range of women's and men's wear under the St. Michael label. Turk Petrol Holdings was selected out of 46 applicants due to its status as a large franchisee in gas stations, office equipment, and Wendy's. Marks & Spencer believed this would be a strategic move, since retailers Carrefour, Ralph Lauren, and Gucci made their entrance previously. The first franchise store was opened in Istanbul in 1995.[49]

Marks & Spencer opened its largest franchise in Istanbul in 1997,[50] a 31,000-square-foot store located in the heart of the shopping district. The deputy chairman of Marks & Spencer stated that part of their international expansion plan was to have large stores in major cities throughout the world, starting in Turkey.[51] Their priority is to provide first-class customer service.

In 1998, they pursued rapid growth in the country. Initially, they did not expect huge demand for the products but in just three years, the retailer increased its number of customers to 70,000.[52] More franchises appeared throughout the large cities of Turkey, primarily around the capital of Istanbul. Marks & Spencer quickly adapted to its changing consumer habits. Turks began shopping in department stores and hypermarket malls, becoming more brand conscious and demanding quality. As of 2005, Marks & Spencer had 22 franchise stores in Turkey (Marks & Spencer Groups, 2005).

**GERMANY**  Marks & Spencer continued its expansion of Europe with entry into Germany in 1996.[53] The first store, located in Cologne, measured 50,000 square feet and operated with six floors offering 1,300 food lines.[54] The store was built in the Schildergasse, Cologne's Oxford Street.[55] At the time, Germany was thought of as the leading European market, with expansion there necessary to be considered a European retailer.[56] Marks & Spencer's unique tradition of not catering to local tastes was evident in their German slogan, "Not a department store—but a world philosophy."[57]

In 1999, four stores closed in Essen, Dortmund, and Wuppertal, as they did not meet the company's needs.[58] The stores were bought for Cramer & Meer as a group. The fourth store was in Frankfurt.[59] German operations closed permanently in 2001.[60]

**CZECH REPUBLIC**  In 1996 the Czech capital, Prague, opened the first two-floor store in the Czech Republic, with plans to expand to other major cities.[61] Marks & Spencer partnered by forming an exclusive master franchise with the Ceska Obchodni Company. The new store sold merchandise such as clothing and

gifts.[62] The store, located in Myslbek Shopping Gallery, had a total area of 2,300 square meters. In 1998, Marks & Spencer opened its second store in Prague. At that time, they hoped to have three more department stores by 2002.[63] As of 2004, there were four Marks & Spencer outlets in the Czech Republic, selling clothing, interior design items and food.[64]

**POLAND**  In April 1999, Marks & Spencer opened its first store in Warsaw, forming a franchise agreement with MSF Polska.[65] Marks & Spencer believed that many stores would follow in Gdansk, Szczecin, Poznan, Wroclaw, Katowice, and Lodz.[66] Located in the Zlota Centre, it is next to one of the more famous Polish department stores, Galeria Centrum. The product mix consisted of men's and women's wear, children's clothing, shoes, and food items.[67]

The launch of the Polish branch was not error-free. The Polish people, with a long tradition of street vendors, demonstrated in front of the store on opening day.[68] Poland does not require a foreign company to form a joint venture with a local business, but Marks & Spencer decided to, believing this to be better than a wholly owned subsidiary.[69] Although taxes and imports are high, 18–20 and 44 percent respectively, Marks & Spencer believes this will be offset by Polish consumers wanting to pay a higher price for better-quality British goods.[70] As of 2005, there are three stores in Poland.

**ROMANIA**  In 2000, a 75–25 percent joint venture agreement between Greek company Marinopoulos and Turkey's Fiba Holding opened the first Romanian Marks & Spencer.[71] The store offered men's and women's clothing, as well as home accessories.[72] A year later, the store was deemed a success, with sales of 1.1 million in the first half of the year, an increase of 30 percent from the previous one.[73] A second store opened in Orhideea shopping complex in 2003. Expectations were high, with 300,000 visitors and turnover of $3.4 million expected.[74] Both stores remain as of 2005.

## Asia

**PHILIPPINES**  Marks & Spencer expanded to the Philippines in 1977, forming a joint venture with Rustan's Department Store, selling ladies intimate apparel and toiletries. After initial success, it opened its first freestanding site, offering a wide variety of products including children's wear, shoes, gift items, and food.[75]

Rustan Marketing Specialists Inc. runs the expansion operation, a spin-off of Rustan's, created in 1997 to handle the operation and expansion of Marks & Spencer in the Philippines. This is done in strict accordance with Marks & Spencer's U.K. standards, a point they stress when franchising.[76] With an unstable economy, the Philippines are problematic, which explains their plan to focus on the U.K. market. There are 13 franchises presently in the Philippines.

**INDONESIA**    Marks & Spencer initially entered Indonesia in 1993. In the fall of 1999, the retailer departed from its final Indonesian store in Jakarta after financial difficulties and political upheaval. As the millennium approached and the new concept of retailing came into place, they re-entered Indonesia in July 2000 due to great market potential. Gill Morton, director of franchising for the Asia Pacific group of Marks & Spencer, entered strong, opening four stores within the first month. They switched from the original St. Michael's brand to a more modern, bold, and youthful line (Marks & Spencer makes it, 2000). There are currently 11 Marks & Spencer franchises in Indonesia (Marks & Spencer Groups, 2005).

**HONG KONG**    In Marks & Spencer's pursuit to internationalize in the Far East, Hong Kong was a desirable market. After acquiring the Brooks Brothers outlets in Japan, this was the next step in their expansion plan.[77] Their reason for this move was to gain greater sourcing of supplies from the region, a departure from the company's former policy of entering into supply arrangements with local stores (Marks & Spencer, 1987). The first store opened in 1988.[78]

After opening the first shop, Marks & Spencer made plans to open its second store in Hong Kong's central business district to further their expansion plans in the British colony. The second store was to be 9,500 square feet in Melbourne Plaza. Penetration continued, as Marks & Spencer wanted more stores in the region. They wanted to expand the size of stores as well. Two of the stores created in 1997 were increased in sales footage by 60 percent; each of the

stores is 23,000 square feet.[79] One is located in the central business district; the other on the Kowloon Peninsula. The expansion was strategic in a variety of ways, increasing their market share within the company as well as aiding the employees and economy of Hong Kong. With the new stores, the regional office would double in size, allowing them to improve benefits of part-time employees. The increase projected a result of at least 400 jobs in 1997.[80]

Marks & Spencer played a vital retailing role in Hong Kong, being its only European department store. The company was successful at positioning itself as a global retailer by sticking to its centralized management, franchises, and private label, St. Michael.[81] Extensive surveys were conducted to determine the perceptions of the different foreign retailers based on work and theories done by Fladmoe-Lindquist. Throughout the years, the company positioned itself in Hong Kong as an upscale, high-quality, conservative and reliable retailer.[82] Another aspect tested was the awareness of country origin and level of self-reference criterion, which is the unconscious reference to one's own cultural values.[83] Results showed that images are slightly blurred when it comes to the origin of the retailer, and that they did not emphasize it as British, but as a European company.[84] With global retailers, there will be a degree of self-reference criterion or cultural awareness, since the values and culture of the company and country are consistent around the world.

While Marks & Spencer's image remained strong and consistent, it faced challenges due to heavy competition in apparel. Zara and Mango are causing a serious brand crisis to Marks & Spencer with their young, innovative strategies. In response to this, the retailer is attempting to revamp its image overall and work on creating a more creative and innovative approach.[85] As of 2005, there are nine Marks & Spencer stores in Hong Kong.

**THAILAND**    Under a franchise agreement with Central Department Store Group, Marks & Spencer began its expansion into Thailand as a 4,000-square-foot store in 1993.[86] Due to the future implementation of the General Agreement on Tariffs and Trade Act, which will eliminate trade barriers on imported products [now being replaced with World Trade Organization (WTO)], Marks & Spencer increased efforts to expand its number of outlets. Its retail prices were 15–20 percent higher than Hong Kong and Singapore respectively. Two more stores were added in Bangkok.[87] In 1996 the largest store opened in Thailand, an 18,000-square-foot outlet, bringing its total retail area in Bangkok to 69,500 square feet.[88]

The new millennium brought change. In 2001, the company renovated its Central Department Store in Lat Phrao, aiming for a more welcoming atmosphere with better lighting and better opportunity to test products in the store.[89] In 2003, instant Thai lunches with coconut rice and Pad Thai noodles became available.[90] A year later, a test concept began at Bangkok's central store, allocating the first floor to women's clothing, beauty, food, and lingerie. Its UK Simply Food franchising theory was modified, opting to export its non-chilled food products. Consumers reacted positively to the concept.[91] As of 2005, there are 12 stores in Thailand (Marks & Spencer Groups, 2005).

**SOUTH KOREA**   Marks & Spencer announced in 1995 plans to expand to South Korea.[92] In 1997, the retailer announced the signing of a five-year distribution deal with BOC, the company responsible for 85 percent of its chilled food in the UK and 20 percent of its clothing, to deliver merchandise to its Korean franchises.[93] D&S Limited, an affiliate of Dae Sung Group, was granted franchising rights, opening two stores in Seoul in 1997.[94] In its entry to South Korea, Marks & Spencer stated it would emphasize clothing, as its food offering is better suited for the United Kingdom.[95] As of 2005, there are 13 Marks & Spencer stores in South Korea.

**MALAYSIA/SINGAPORE**   Robinson and Company, franchisee for Marks & Spencer Malaysia and Singapore, announced plans to open two new stores early in 1996 in Kuala Lumpur. At 8,000 and 12,000 square feet, they took the place of two older, smaller stores of 2,000 square feet each (Lam, 1995). In 1998, Robinson and Company planned on opening its largest, a flagship store of 30,000 square feet. Chief executive of Robinson and Co., Peter Husum, noted this store would be more adaptive of Marks & Spencer's long-term operational goals for franchising in Malaysia and Singapore. Investing over $4 million

on interior design alone, Husum planned to follow the same design for all stores within the area.[96] There are currently two Marks & Spencer stores in Malaysia.

Marks & Spencer turned in a loss for 1998 in Singapore and Malaysia. Husum credited this downturn to the depreciation of the Singapore dollar and a decrease in Asian tourists. He dealt with this problem by making price cuts on average of 20 percent. After this decrease, Husum began working on decreasing cost of goods. The majority of merchandise was shipped from Britain, causing high transportation costs and longer delivery schedules. Robinson combated this by performing more regional transactions to solve the cost and time deficiencies. As of 2005, there are seven Marks & Spencer stores in Singapore.

**INDIA**   Marks & Spencer first entered India in 2001. At this time, the company saw the closing of its businesses in the United States and the culling of stores in Europe. They decided the ideal way to expand internationally was through a network of franchise partners. The company felt that franchisors would provide better understanding of local environments and position the right products in the right market.[97] The first two stores, located in Delhi and Bombay, opened in December of 2001.[98] These stores focused their merchandise on clothing and housewares.[99] They did not have the option of opening their own stores since India still had a ban on foreign-direct investment.

The success of these two stores allowed further development, with six franchises currently in India.[100] In August of 2004, a new sourcing center was set up in Bangalore dealing with apparel.[101] This helps to increase direct operations within the country as well as to provide buyers in the United Kingdom with knowledge on local pricing, tastes, and quality materials.[102] The former regional director of Mandura Garmets, Venu Nair, was appointed to head operations at this new center.[103] Marks & Spencer is buying back the remaining shares it does not own in its Indian operations and converting it into a wholly owned subsidiary. This provides the company complete stake in Marks & Spencer India.[104] This was made possible by a change in India's law allowing retail foreign-direct investment if the retailer sells only private label merchandise.

## Middle East

In 1997, Marks & Spencer believed that expansion into the Arab world would be a calculated step to becoming one of the leading global retailers in volume.[105] The Arab population of 24 million was expected to double in 15 years.[106] Marks & Spencer had not previously expanded into the Arab region due to its Israeli ties. Companies were boycotted for a period of time if associated with Israel. The franchise was an agreement with Al-Futtaim Sons Co., the company in charge of international franchises of Toys "Я" US and Hertz in the region.[107] The franchises focused primarily on selling clothes, with slight modifications to local conditions, since selling food is difficult in different countries.[108]

Al-Futtaim Sons was granted the master franchising rights over Kuwait, Bahrain, Qatar, and Oman.[109] On January 11, 1998, the first store opened in Dubai, a 29,000-square-foot operation located in the trading hub.[110] A second store opened in Abu Dhabi, with up-to-date displays, a ground floor for men's and children's clothing, another floor for women's clothing, and a home furnishing's section and cafeteria. Products such as cosmetics and homewear are available as well.[111] In December, the first store opened in Bahrain at Seef Mall, with 48 employees, 60 percent of whom are Bahrainis. A plan to open a store in Kuwait was scheduled for 1999.[112]

Due to success in the region, the first store opened at the Land Mark Trade Center in Doha, Qatar, in June 2000.[113] In July 2001, Marks & Spencer opened its third store in the United Arab Emirates at Dubai International Airport.[114] Fall 2003 saw the opening of the first Marks & Spencer in Muscat, Oman.[115] In May 2004, the second Dubai store, a 22,000-square-foot site, opened at Wafi City Mall.[116]

Marks & Spencer announced its opening of a new franchise in Saudi Arabia in June 2001. The franchise holder, Al-Faridah Trading Agencies Company, formed when Prince Al-Waleed Bin Talal's Kingdom Holding Company and his partners Fawaz Al-Hokair, Talal Al-Mayman, and Ahmed Al-Shaikh pooled their investments to bring the retailer to their country.[117] As of 2005, there are 10 Marks & Spencer stores in Saudi Arabia (Marks & Spencer Groups, 2005).

The type of license Marks & Spencer uses in its expansion to the Middle East is master franchising, with Al-Futtaim Sons Co. given control over UAE, Dubai, Kuwait, Qatar, Oman and Abu Dhabi, and the Al-Faridah Trading Agencies Company control over Saudi Arabia. Master franchising, a newer form of retail expansion, gives an individual the right to develop a country or region.[118] Due to geographical and cultural differences, Marks & Spencer is applying risk management for master franchising.[119]

## Other Locations

Other locations for Marks & Spencer stores include Bermuda (1), Canary Islands (4), Gran Canaria (3), Malta (3), Tenerife (1), Channel Islands (4), Guernsey (1), Jersey (3), Cyprus (9), Gibraltar (1), and Croatia (2). In the 1960s, M&S opened in Kabul, Afghanistan, but left shortly after.[120] Business in Israel closed in 1997 after 20 years and losses of $1.1 million in the first nine months. The franchisee for Israel was Blue Square Co-op Investments (Sugarman, 1997).

## Conclusion

Marks & Spencer is a global company that specializes in food, clothing, household goods, and retail and financial services with franchises in over 30 countries. The primary formats used to expand its operations internationally are master franchising and joint ventures. Wholly owned subsidiaries are used for its locations in Hong Kong, the Republic of Ireland, and the United Kingdom. Its primary competitors are Tesco and Sainsbury, two U.K. retailers that have in recent years taken market share from Marks & Spencer. Financial setbacks and unprofitable stores in Western Europe resulted in the closing of several of its European operations. Marks & Spencer's current franchise locations are in Asia, the Middle East, and Eastern Europe and in the United States with King's Supermarket stores. Due to the company's recent financial troubles, it is in the company's best interest to focus on its core market in the United Kingdom as well as its successful franchises in developing countries.

## Discussion Questions

1. Is the retailer classified as a global retailer or a multinational retailer? Explain its pattern of expansion. What expansion strategy did/is the retailer use/using?
2. Based on Dunning's eclectic theory, how do ownership, locational and internalization factors play in your retailer's international expansion?
3. What role does cultural proximity and geographical proximity play in the retailers' international moves?
4. Can you predict the retailer's future international expansion?

## Endnotes

1. *Marks & Spencer—The Company—Who We Are. Our History* (n.d.). Retrieved October 27, 2005 from http://www2.marksandspencer.com/thecompany/whoweare/our history/index.shtml
2. *Marks & Spencer—The Company—Who We Are. Our History* (2005).
3. Kidd, K. (May 29, 1986). Buy-Canadian guideline not raised, UK firms says. *The Toronto Star,* p.E3.
4. Studza, M. (August 20, 1985). "Canadians finding Marks & Spencer." *The Globe and Mail,* p. F10.
5. "Marks & Spencer Announces First Store Closures." (May 20, 1999). *Canada Newswire.*
6. "Marks & Spencer Announces First Store Closures."
7. "Marks & Spencer to Sell Chain in Canada." (March 7, 1996). *DNR,* 7
8. "International Corporate Report." (1986). *Wall Street Journal.* Dec. 30, 1986, p 1.
9. Sternquist, B. (1998). *International Retailing.* New York: Fairchild Publications.
10. Sternquist, B. (1998).
11. Freedman, A. and Marcom J. (Aug 18, 1988). "Marks & Spencer, Expanding Boldly In U.S., Adds Groceries to Its List." *Wall Street Journal,* p. 1.
12. White, E. (November 23, 2001). "Brooks Brothers to Be Sold to Retail Brand, Owner of Casual Corner." *Wall Street Journal,* p. B.1.
13. Beck, E. (September 15, 1999). "Marks & Spencer to Focus on Key Brands—British Retailer To Build More Brooks Brothers, Sell U.S. Supermarkets." *Wall Street Journal,* p. A.25.
14. "Marks & Spencer Sells Supermarkets To D'Agostino Chain." (July 23, 2002). *Wall Street Journal,* p. B.9.
15. Sternquist, B. (1998).
16. Sternquist, B. (1998).
17. Sternquist, B. (1998).
18. Speilman, A. (January 6, 1992). "Marks & Spencer Plans Continental Push." *The Asian Wall Street Journal,* p. 4.
19. Spielman, A. (December 18, 1991). "Minding the Stores: New Euro-Mercants Emerge as Retailing Starts to Cross Borders—In France, Marks & Spencer Learns of Fitting Rooms, Better Display Techniques—Stumbling in North America." *The Wall Street Journal,* p. 1.
20. "Marks & Spencer" (January 18, 1999). *The Financial News,* Sunday Business.
21. Sternquist, B. (1998).

22. "The British Retail Chain Marks & Spencer has Opened its Second Branch in Belgium, in Antwerp." (1983). *Finacieel Economische Tijd.* (4).

23. "Marks & Spencer Opens New Stores—Expansion In Europe." (1997). De *Finacieel Economische Tijd.*

24. Dombey, D., Johnson, J., and Voyle, S. (2001). "Companies & Finance UK—Belgian Cheer for M&S Retailers Court Action Unlikely over Store Closure Plans." *Financial Times.*

25. "Belgian Marks & Spencer, Trade Unions Reach Agreement." (July 5, 2001). *Belgian News Digest.* 10:01

26. Greenwood & Penman (November 5, 2003). "Sorted & the City-Full Marks for Growth." *Mirror,* p.38.

27. Hancock, C. (May 30, 2004). "Irish Growth Market; Business Focus." *The Sunday Times.*

28. Canniffee, M. (September 19, 1996). "M & S May Spend 65M on New Irish Outlets." *Irish Times,* p. 16.

29. "M&S Growing in Cork." (January 29, 1997). *Irish Times,* p.19.

30. Creaton, S. (November 4, 1998). "Group to Continue Expansion in Ireland." *Irish Times,* p. 17.

31. McCaughren, S. (May 25, 2005). "Troubled M&S Sees Profits Slide by 19pc." *Irish Independent.*

32. Burns, E. (November 27, *1999).* "UK's Marks & Spencer to Close Portugal Stores; Franchisee Problems." *Dow Jones International News.*

33. "Marks & Spencer Reopens Stores." (April 4, 2000). *Diario de Noticias.*

34. "Marks & Spencer Delisting from Europe." (December 8, 2001, *The Herald,* p. 16.

35. Sternquist, B. (1998).

36. Sternquist, B. (1998).

37. Sternquist, B. (1998).

38. "Marks & Spencer Gets a Grip on Spanish Operation." (April 20, 1999). *Leicester Mercury.*

39. "Marks & Spencer Changes Strategy Concerning European Affiliates." (November 2, 1999). *Cinco Dias.*

40. "M&S closes its Zaragoza Store and Cuts Managers." (February 25, 1999). *Cinco Dias.*

41. "Madrilenos sad as M&S Says Adios to Spain." (December 15, 2001). *Reuters News.*

42. Sternquist, B. (1998).

43. Hosking, P. (1991). "M&S May Expand Europe Franchises." *The Independent Newspaper Publishing PLC.* p 22.

44. "Britain Marks & Spencer in Business in Budapest." (September 10, 1992). *Hungarian Telegraph Agency; British Broadcasting Corporation.*

45. "Sales of Marks and Spencer Shops In Hungary up 24pc yr/yr In." (July 30, 2004). *Hungarian News Agency (MTI).*

46. "Greek Marinopoulos to Expand in Romania." (May 16, 2003). *Romanian News Digest.*

47. Sternquist, B. (1998).

48. Fallon, J. (March 29, 1994). "Marks & Spencer in Deal to Open Stores in Turkey." *Women's Wear Daily,* p. 13

49. "E.U. Trade/Turkey-3: Pact Would Rid Tariffs, Boost Trade." (December 6, 1995). *Emerging Markets Report.*

50. "Marks & Spencer to Open their Largest Ever Franchise Store." (February 28, 1997). *PR Newswire Europe.*

51. "Marks & Spencer to Open their Largest Ever Franchise Store." (1997).

52. "Marks & Spencer Forsees Rapid Expansion in Turkey." (June 24, 1998). *Turkish Daily News.*

53. "Marks & Spencer to Open First German Store." (January 4,1996). *Reuters News.*

54. "Germans Back M&S formula." (October 19, 1996). *The Grocer,* p.11.

55. Kallenbach, M. (1996, July 31). "Marks & Spencer Enterprise Aiming to Make its Marks in Germany—Analysis." *The Times,* p.27

56. "Marks & Spencer expands into Germany." (March 4, 1996). *Frankfurter Allgemeine Zeitung,* p.14.

57. "Deutschemarks and Spencer—Coronation Chicken, Sandwiches, and Lingerie Hit Germany." (October 11, 1996). *The Times,* p. 11.

58. "Marks & Spencer to Close 6 European Stores." (July 9, 1999). *Reuters News.*

59. "Marks & Spencer to Close 6 European Stores." (1999).

60. "Marks & Spencer Calls it a Day in Germany." (August 14, 200 1). *Retail Week,* p. 1.

61. Robinson, N. (1996). "M&S goes Czech." *The Press Association,* Home News Section.

62. "Marks & Spencer Plans to Open Department Store Chain Here." (1996). *Czech News Agency* (CTK), Business News Section.

63. "M&S Wants to Be Number One." (November 11, 1997). *Access Czech Republic Business Bulletin,* p. 7.

64. "Marks & Spencer Opens Wenceslas SQ. Outlet Today." (September 24, 2004). *Czech News Agency* (CTK), Business News.

65. "Marks & Spencer to Open First Polish Store in Spring." (1999). *Financial Post,* p. C02.

66. "Marks & Spencer Establishes Polish Representative Office." (1997). *Dow Jones & Reuters.*

67. "Retailing: Marks & Spencer Comes to Warsaw." (1999). *The Warsaw Voice,* p 1.

68. "Retailing: Marks & Spencer Comes to Warsaw." (1999).

69. "M&S Heads for Warsaw." (1997). *East European Markets, 17(12).*

70. "M&S Heads for Warsaw." (1997).

71. "Greek Marinopoulos, Turkey's Fiba in Romanian Joint Venture." (November 5, 2000). *Kathimerini*

72. "Marks & Spencer Shop in Bucharest." (May 5, 2000). *Romanian Business Journal.*

73. "Marks & Spencer Chain is Successful in Romania." (August 9, 2001). *Rompres.*

74. "Greek Marinopoulos to Expand in Romania." (May 16, 2003). *Romanian News Digest.*

75. Arceo-Dumlao, T. (2004). "Rewarding Those Who Sell Their Own Products Well." *Philippine Daily Inquirer,* Sec. 8.

76. Arceo-Dumlao, T. (2004).

77. Sternquist, B. (1998).

78. "Marks and Spencer Unveils Next Phase of Asian Expansion." (September 25, 1996). *The Evening Standard.*

79. S.Korea/Marks & Spencer-2: Plans HK Expansion Drive in 1997." (September 25, 1996). *Dow Jones International News.*

80. "S.Korea/Marks & Spencer-2: Plans HK Expansion Drive in 1997." (1996).

81. Sternquist, B. (1998).

82. McGoldrick, P.J., Ho, Sandy S.L. (1992). "International Positioning: Japanese Department Stores in Hong Kong." *European Journal of Marketing,* 26(8,9), p. 61–74.

83. Sternquist, B. (1998).

84. McGoldrick, P.J., Ho, Sandy S.L. (1992).

85. White, A. (August 12, 2005). "Half Measure Won't do for Vanilla Brand." *Media,* p. 18.

86. "Thais get Marks & Spencer." (August 4, 1993). *South China Morning Post (Hong Kong),* p.6.

87. "Marks & Spencer Plans Boost into Thailand." (October 21, 1995). *Bangkok Post,* p. 24.

88. "Marks & Spencer opens largest Thai Store." (October 21, 1996). *Reuters News.*

89. "M&S partner Touts Web Plan." (June 12, 2001). *The Nation (Thailand).*

90. "Food Matters: Instant Thai from M&S." (April 2, 2003). Global News Wire—Europe Intelligence Wire.

91. "Solutions Analysis—M&S Puts New Franchise Store Concept to the Test in Bangkok." (June 18, 2004). *Retail Week,* 23.

92. "HK: U.K.'s Marks & Spencer Plans to Open Korea Stores." (October 10, 1995). *Dow Jones International News,* 6, p. 11.

93. "BOC to Distribute Marks & Spencer Goods in South Korea." (March 10, 1997). *The Independent-London.*

94. "Marks & Spencer Opens Two Stores in Seoul." (April 11, 1997). *PR Newswire Europe.*

95. O'Shea, L. (February 12, 1997). "Marks & Spencer Oates -2: Concentration On Clothing U.MAR." *Dow Jones International News,* 3, p. 46.

96. "Marks & Spencer to Open Second Gulf Store." (July 27, 1998). *Gulf News.*

97. "Marks & Spencer Franchise Stores to Open in India." (August 24, 2001). *Reuters News.*

98. "Marks & Spencer to Expand Indian Operations." (May 11, 2003) *Businessline,* p. 1.

99. "News in Brief Marks & Spencer Moves into India." (December 13, 2001). *Daily Mail.*

100. "Marks & Spencer to Open in India." (August 15, 200 1). *IRP Strategic Information Database.*

101. Kurian, B. (May 11, 2005). "Marks & Spencer Gets Ready for Sourcing Center in Bangalore." *Global News Wire—Asia Africa Intelligence Wire.*

102. Brown, J. and Hall, L. (2005, May 14). "M&S Signals Move to More Direct Sourcing." *Drapers Record,* p.2.

103. Kurian, B. (May 11, 2005).

104. "Marks & Spencer to Buy Out Local Partners." (July 12, 2005). *The Economic Times.*

105. "UK's Marks & Spencer to Open Gulf Stores." (February 6, 1997). *Reuters News.*

106. George, A. (1997, July 17). "Marks & Spencer Launches Middle East Sales Drive

(department store due to open soon in the United Arab Emirates)." *The Middle East.*

107. "Marks & Spencer to Expand into the Arabian Gulf." (February 6, 1997). *PR Newswire Europe.*

108. "UK Retailer Heads into the Gulf." (1997). *Corporate Strategies,* 5(18), p. 8.

109. Nair, M. (November 5, 1997). "Dubai Store to Shape Marks & Spencers Gulf Strategy." *Gulf News.*

110. "Marks and Spencer Makes Its Entry into Arab World." (January, 11, 1998). Agence France Presse—English.

111. "Marks & Spencer Plans Earlier Abu Dhabi Opening." (April 30, 1998). *Gulf News.*

112. "New 'MARKS' Set for Eid Shopping Surge." (December 16, 1998). *Middle East Newslife.*

113. "Marks & Spencer Opens Branch in Doha." (June 18, 2000). *IPR Strategic Business Information Database.*

114. "British M&S Opens New Store in UAE." (July 19, 2001). *Saudi Arabian News Digest.*

115. "Retail Giants M & S and Toys "R" Us in Talk to Open Branches In Muscat." (May 14, 2003). *Global News Wire—Asia Africa Intelligence Wire.*

116. "Marks & Spencer becomes New Anchor Store at Wafi City Mall." (May 20, 2004). *Middle East Company News.*

117. Cadano E.C. and Saudi Gazette Staff. (June 7, 2001). *Saudi Gazette.*

118. Sternquist, B. (1998).

119. Sternquist, B. (1998).

120. "BANDITS, Led Zeppelin . . ." (October 13, 2001). *The Citizen.*

# PART IV

# Retailing in Asia and Australia

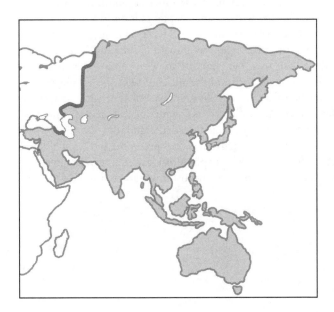

The countries discussed so far in this book share a broad European heritage; although they differ culturally in many ways, there is also some degree of similarity. In Part IV, our focus shifts to Asia; specifically, Japan, Hong Kong, Taiwan, the People's Republic of China, South Korea, India, and Australia. Chapter 15 considers Japan's distribution system, which is nearly opposite the U.S. system. Differences between developed and less developed countries are to be expected. However, it is surprising to see so many differences between two highly developed countries.

In Chapters 16 and 17, I discuss similarities among three groups of Chinese—Hong Kong, Taiwan, and the People's Republic of China (PRC). Hong Kong and Taiwan are populated with immigrants from the PRC. The retail industries in Hong Kong and Taiwan display some characteristics of Japanese distribution and some of American distribution. In July 1997, Great Britain's lease holding Hong Kong expired and Hong Kong reverted to PRC.

The PRC is an interesting retail environment. Until 1992, its government did not allow foreign retailers. Then just a handful of foreign joint ventures were federally approved. This means that the business has been selected as one of two joint ventures in each major city, sanctioned by the national government. There are many more municipally approved joint ventures in the PRC, which means that a city approves the joint venture. For instance, Shanghai, one of the major cities in the PRC, has approved many municipal joint ventures. As part of joining WTO, China has agreed to drastically open its market to foreign retailers.

Before the mid 1980s, the PRC government owned all stores. From the mid to the late 1980s, free market stores gained approval to operate. These were generally very small temporary shops set up to sell excess agricultural products. In the 1990s the government began privatizing state-owned stores. Privatization has proceeded at a very slow rate. The Eastern European countries, in contrast, privatized at a very rapid rate.

Part IV includes several new chapters. Chapter 18's focus is South Korea, a country that shares many retail similarities with Japan. Chapter 19 is on India, to my mind probably the most interesting retail market in the world. India has just approved the first stage of opening their country to foreign investment in retailing. They will not allow retailers who produce their own merchandise to open stores to sell the merchandise in India. So companies like Gap and Zara could get the go-ahead, but companies like Wal-Mart, who sells a variety of brands as well as private label, could not open stores. Chapter 20 is on Australia and its unique retail structure. Since two companies dominate the retail industry there, it's called a duopoly.

Chapter 21 provides a summary of the SIRE2 model presented in Chapter 2 and a discussion of the propositions from that chapter. I use the expansion patterns of several retail companies to illustrate how the propositions can be interpreted.

# 15

# RETAILING
# IN JAPAN

## After reading this chapter, you should understand

> How the Japanese use group affiliation (frame theory) to structure and regulate relationships.

> Why doing well in Japan has been difficult for foreign businesses.

> The details of the Japanese buying system.

> How to use Dunning's theory of the eclectic firm to explain which Japanese retailers will internationalize and where they will go.

> How modern and traditional retail systems coexist in this developed society.

## › COUNTRY BACKGROUND

For much of their history, the Japanese have kept others outside their world. In the fourth century, the title Emperor of Japan was given to a major clan leader. Myth makers added the belief that the emperor was descended from the Sun God, and people soon came to believe in his divinity. This belief continued until Hirohito (the 124th emperor, crowned in 1926) told the Japanese citizens that he was not divine in a proclamation that was part of the surrender agreement after World War II. Today, there are still some Japanese people who believe the emperor is divine.

Many religious and cultural influences came to Japan from China. Traditions that we consider Japanese, such as Zen, the tea ceremony, and bonsai trees, all came from China 1,000 years ago. The Japanese writing system also comes from the Chinese. In 1542, the first Europeans (Portuguese) arrived in Japan. The first Christian missionary, Francis Xavier, came five years later. Will Adam, the first Englishman, entered in 1600; he was followed by the Dutch in 1609.

Japan established trade with the Europeans in the mid-sixteenth century. However, Japanese rulers viewed the rapid spread of Christianity by European missionaries as a threat to their power. They eradicated Christianity in 1639 and expelled all foreigners except the Dutch and Chinese. Foreigners were kept out for the next 200 years.

In 1854, Commodore Perry steamed into Tokyo Bay with a fleet of boats. He demanded that Japan open its ports to trade. Realizing they were outnumbered, the Japanese opened their doors to trade with the United States, Britain, the Netherlands, and Russia. They then began a mad rush to catch up with the industrialized nations. The Japanese were highly successful. They defeated China in the War of 1895. Ten years later, the Japanese did the unthinkable—they defeated imperial Russia.

Japanese leaders were convinced of their ability and right to dominate the world. They annexed Taiwan, took over control of Manchuria from Russia, and overpowered Korea. Japan's support of the Allies in World War I gave the country financial rewards and convinced its leaders that they were destined to lead the rest of Asia to prosperity. A depression in the 1930s, lack of natural resources, and overpopulation led to Japan's expansionist zeal.

Japanese air fleets attacked the United States at Pearl Harbor in 1941. During World War II, the United States destroyed much of Japan's naval power. The war ended in 1945 when the United States dropped atomic bombs on Hiroshima and Nagasaki.

After the surrender, U.S. forces occupied Japan, helping to set up a new constitution. The Americans also helped to construct an industrial machine that would transform Japan's military capabilities to peaceful use. The emperor was retained as a figurehead with no governmental authority or power. Emperor Hirohito died in January 1989, and his son, Akihito, inherited the title.

Japan's subsequent economic growth and development is considered a modern miracle. Once "made in Japan" meant that something was cheap and shoddy; now it is the highest standard of excellence. Economic growth through the early 1970s drove all segments of the retail market in Japan. Department stores had double-digit growth. New retail formats such as supermarkets, general merchandise chains, and convenience stores flourished. It all came crashing down in the 1990s when the economic bubble burst. Incomes flattened. Since reaching a peak in 1998, household spending on food has steadily declined.

Japan is a high context society. Much meaning is derived through the setting of communication, not just the words. I discuss the meaning of high context in Chapter 4. Several years ago, I taught a class in Japan. One of my students gave me a book by Chie Nakane, a well-known Japanese anthropologist. Nakane begins her lesson about the Japanese with two concepts, attribute versus frame orientation.[1]

## › ATTRIBUTE VERSUS FRAME THEORY

Societies that are ATTRIBUTE oriented separate an object into elements, the specific features of a product or person. When all the elements are added together, we get an evaluation of the object or person. For instance, in considering a vacation destination, I would probably evaluate the hotel for price and value, amenities in the area such as beaches or museums, and consider the time and cost expended to reach the destination. In the end some good attributes, such as low cost, might sway me toward my ultimate choice. However, in an attribute-oriented society, assessment of one object does not directly influence assessment of other objects.

In a frame-oriented society, every object is set in an environment—the FRAME of reference—and it is the entire frame that the society evaluates. Suppose an American man and a Japanese man meet at a dinner party. In response to the question "What do you do?", the American would likely respond by mentioning his professional area: "I am a lawyer." The Japanese would likely mention his company: "I work for Isetan." The Japanese response would be the same, whether the person is a maintenance worker or the CEO of the company. Americans cite an attribute: "I am a lawyer." Japanese cite a frame, the setting for attributes: "I work for Isetan."

Figure 15.1 illustrates how two objects—a blind date and a supplier—could be described using an attribute versus a frame perspective. The U.S. version of match.com is rampant with attributes.

Tall, dark, and handsome, SWM, lawyer, seeks sweet but swinging SWF. Must be tall, thin, blond, and tan . . .

## Attribute vs. Frame Orientation

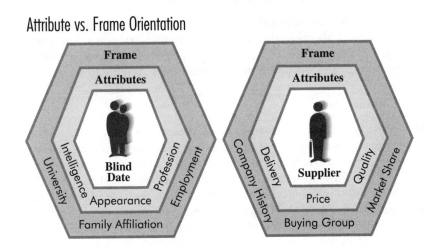

**Figure 15.1**
While attributes are isolated features, frame orientation requires context. Frame features for a blind date might include such information as university attended, family affiliation, and employer. Frame orientation for selecting a supplier might include company history, buying group affiliation and market share. Frame is based on association with others; attributes are individual qualities.

Japanese matchmakers would start with an overview of the blind date's family, company employment, and educational affiliation:

> An oldest daughter of a prestigious Tokyo family, an employee of Sony electronics company, and 2006 graduate of Tokyo University . . .

This information presents three frames: her family, her employer, and her educator.

Attribute versus frame orientation explains in large part why U.S. companies have not been successful in the Japanese market. Consider this scenario. An American handbag salesperson calls on a Japanese retail buyer. The American sells the handbags by highlighting all the features—the fine quality leather, the style, and the competitive price. The salesperson is selling the attributes. These attributes are of secondary consideration to the Japanese buyer. While the American seller is trying to sell the handbags, the Japanese buyer is evaluating the company. He is interested in the reputation of the company in the United States, its market share, and the formal and informal business relationships the company may have with other companies. The Japanese buyer is buying the company within its business frame. Product attributes are important, but only after the Japanese buyer has established the acceptability of the company as a supplier.

The relationship of suppliers to retailers shows evidence of this frame orientation. A Japanese retailer would not change suppliers just because a competitive supplier offered a lower price. Price is important, but the Japanese buyer would likely go back to his supplier and tell him about the lower price offer and expect him to meet it. However, price is very important in the United States. If a lower-priced supplier were available, a U.S. business would likely consider making a change. The frame perspective helps us to understand the following discussion of Japanese cultural tendencies. You are most likely to see these cultural factors in the most traditional forms of retailing, such as department stores, and least likely to see them in institutions like convenience stores. Also remember that whenever you have cultural generalizations there will be exceptions.

## › THEORY OF JAPANESE BUSINESS RELATIONS

The attribute versus frame orientation is an important introduction to Japanese thinking. Shimaguchi goes further in explaining some differences in how the Japanese conduct business. Three concepts that can help us understand Japanese business activities are pseudo-harmonism, eclecticism, and exceptionism.[2]

### Pseudo-Harmonism

The Japanese have a saying: PSEUDO-HARMONISM means that you pretend harmony exists, whether it exists or not. The Japanese want to get along with others, and they suppress feelings and people that ruffle relationships. In business relationships, like personal relationships, there is an attempt to maintain peace and harmony.

In my early days of doing research in Japan, I told a Japanese research colleague that I would like to interview an important woman executive. His response was, "It will be difficult." At the time I thought he was saying, "It will be difficult, but probably can be arranged." As time went on, I never seemed to get any closer to setting up the interview. I realized that when my colleague said, "It will be difficult," what he really meant was, "There is not a chance you will get to talk to this person." Rather than saying no, he just postponed the issue, maintaining harmony.

The same response occurs in business transactions. If a retail supplier is late with a delivery, the retailer might respond graciously, helping the supplier with excuses about why the merchandise was delivered late. There is disharmony; the supplier has not lived up to his end of the agreement; but the retailer will pretend nothing is wrong.

Have you ever fought with a significant person in your life, yet pretended that everything was all right when you went out in public? This is pseudo-harmony. The difference is that in the United States, we save such social protection for our loved ones. In Japan, it extends to business relationships. Japanese business relationships are like intimate family relationships. This designation also applies to the next concept, eclecticism.

## Eclecticism

ECLECTICISM means that decisions are made in a circular manner. In Japan, business solutions often are a compromise or midpoint among the different business options. Decisions are made by consensus. Contracts pass through multiple levels of decision makers, a system known as RINGI. Decision makers affix their seals of approval. These seals are not a signature but a CHOP, a group of characters on a circular seal, which are used instead of a signature in Japan and China. Japanese do not have a custom of signing their name, instead they use a chop for stamping important documents. Japanese children are usually given their chop by their parents. The chop is registered and becomes the equivalent of our signature.

Universities require that you ask research subjects to sign a consent form. The first research survey I was going to conduct in Japan taught me that this would be a problem. Since the Japanese are not used to signing, I couldn't ask them to do that. Affixing a chop is considered more formal than a signature, so that wasn't a good solution. In the end my university approved the idea that if subjects read the consent form and completed the survey, they were providing implied consent.

I have talked with U.S. businesspeople who were very displeased with the outcome of their negotiations with Japanese companies. After carrying out talks with a Japanese team for several weeks, they expected a contract to be signed before they left the bargaining table. In the end, however, the Japanese team said they would need to take the agreement back to Tokyo to have headquarters sign off on it. The U.S. representatives were disappointed, believing they had negotiated in good faith with a Japanese representative who was authorized to make decisions. The Japanese action in this instance is very predictable. Among Japanese, all those involved consider the final agreement, not just the members of the negotiating team.

The next concept is exceptionism.

## Exceptionism

The working method in Japan is EXCEPTIONISM, or the ruleless rule. Rules change with the situation and a flexible, freestyle approach is characteristic. The Japanese rebate system is an example of this absence of rigid rules. Suppliers have discretion rebates. These practices confuse outsiders.

The Japanese government periodically gives the appearance of trying to reduce exceptionism, making rules that are clear to all the market players. Shimaguchi uses the pharmaceutical industry as an example. During fierce competition in the industry manufacturers would provide *tempu* (additional products), a type of rebate. Physicians who placed large orders might receive 200% tempu; that is, two products given to them for every one bought. When the government discouraged this practice, the industry switched to another system, called *okiwasure* (leave and forget). The manufacturer would simply deliver more goods than ordered and then "forget" to correct the error.[3]

Japan's distribution system is a curious combination of a traditional and a modern retail system. The traditional system refers to mom-and-pop stores located close to where consumers live. The department store system is the most traditional of the modern retail formats, which refer to self-service convenience and mass merchandisers using modern distribution technology. Japan has a large number of retail stores per consumer. Its trading partners say Japan's distribution system is closed to outsiders. There is some truth and a lot of fiction in this contention.

I am going to start the discussion with the department store system, which is the most traditional, and then move to the more modern retailing system. The convenience store is a model of a very untraditional system, and it is one of the most successful in the country.

## › RETAIL FORMATS

Tables 15.1 and 15.2 summarize the major domestic and foreign retailers in Japan.

### Department Stores

Japanese department stores have a long history. They are also the most traditional form of retailing. Most department stores have their roots as either kimono shops or railroad terminal stores. KIMONO SHOPS are stores that originally sold textile merchandise. The featured cloth was custom made into clothes (*kimono*) or household items. The oldest Japanese department stores such as Mitsukoshi and Takashimaya began this way. TERMINAL STORES began much later as shops selling everyday items to people going through the train station. This broad classification of kimono versus terminal stores is one basic way to determine the type of department store with which you are dealing. Several present-day stores, such as Tokyu and Hankyu, share a similar ending, *kyu*. This tells you that they began as terminal stores; KYU means the express train line. Another way of classifying stores is as urban versus local.

In the Edo era, Japan experienced a period of security. Manufacturing power increased, causing the economy to grow. The number of merchants increased, and the kimono merchants were the center of this boom. Matsuzakaya originated as a kimono shop in 1611 in Nagoya. Shirakiya, which is now Tokyu Department Store, began in Tokyo in 1662. Mitsukoshi (Echigoya) began in 1673. Daimaru in 1717, Sogo in 1830, and Takashimaya in 1831 were some of the other early retailers. Six of the 10 largest department stores operating in Japan today originated before 1850.

**Table 15.1**
**Japan—Leading Domestic Retailers, 2004**

| | Company | Primary Line of Trade | Net Sales ($US Mil) | % Chg Sales | Total Stores | 2004 Rank, Top 200 Retailers Worldwide | Single-country, Regional or Global? | Number of countries | Domestic Market Share of total sales | Domestic Market Share of total stores |
|---|---|---|---|---|---|---|---|---|---|---|
| 1 | Ito-Yokado Co., Ltd. | Convenience Stores | 56,812 | 2.8% | 29,015 | 6 | Global | 17 | 68% | 42% |
| 2 | Aeon Co., Ltd. | General Merchandise Stores | 36,477 | 20.0% | 6,792 | 19 | Global | 11 | 88% | 69% |
| 3 | The Daiei Inc. | General Merchandise Stores | 13,984 | -8.6% | 1,681 | 52 | Global | 2 | 99% | 100% |
| 4 | Lawson | Convenience Stores | 12,289 | 3.4% | 8,287 | 59 | Regional | 2 | 100% | 97% |
| 5 | Yamada Denki Co. Ltd. | Consumer Electronics & Appliances | 10,193 | 17.4% | 258 | 74 | Single Country | 1 | 100% | 100% |
| 6 | The Seiyu, Ltd. | General Merchandise Stores | 9,538 | -4.0% | 404 | 78 | Regional | 4 | 99% | 99% |
| 7 | UNY Co., Ltd | Convenience Stores | 9,268 | 2.0% | 7,387 | 82 | Single Country | 1 | 100% | 100% |
| 8 | FamilyMart Co., Ltd. | Convenience Stores | 9,232 | 4.6% | 11,501 | 83 | Regional | 5 | N/A | 56% |
| 9 | Takashimaya Company, Ltd. | Department Stores | 8,911 | -3.1% | 24 | 84 | Global | 5 | 100% | 75% |
| 10 | Millennium Retailing | Department Stores | 8,477 | -5.6% | 29 | 91 | Single Country | 1 | 100% | 100% |
| 11 | Mitsukoshi Ltd. | Department Stores | 7,885 | -3.2% | 40 | 98 | Global | 9 | 79% | 47% |
| 12 | Daimaru Group | Supermarkets/Grocery Stores | 6,349 | -2.7% | 81 | 115 | Single Country | 1 | 100% | 100% |
| 13 | ISETAN Company Ltd. | Department Stores | 5,693 | 2.1% | 40 | 120 | Regional | 6 | 93% | 73% |
| 14 | Yodobashi Camera Co. Ltd. | Consumer Electronics & Appliances | 5,342 | 6.0% | 19 | 127 | Single Country | 1 | 100.0% | 100.0% |
| 15 | Kojima Co. Ltd. | Consumer Electronics & Appliances | 4,531 | 3.1% | 229 | 145 | Single Country | 1 | 100% | 100% |
| 16 | Bic Camera Co. | Consumer Electronics & Appliances | 4,222 | 73% | 17 | 153 | Single Country | 1 | 100% | 100% |
| 17 | Edion Corp. | Consumer Electronics & Appliances | 4,050 | 0.9% | 786 | 157 | Single Country | 1 | 100% | 100% |
| 18 | Marui Co. Ltd. | Department Stores | 4,014 | 0.1% | 31 | 158 | Single Country | 1 | 100% | 100% |
| 19 | Izumi | General Merchandise Stores | 3,814 | 4.2% | 116 | 167 | Single Country | 1 | 100.0% | 100% |
| 20 | Life Corp. | Supermarkets/Grocery Stores | 3,576 | 2.8% | 189 | 172 | Single Country | 1 | 100% | 100% |

Sources: Retail Forward, company annual reports and published reports

**Table 15.2**
**Japan—Key Foreign Retailers, 2004**

| Company | Headquarters | Retail Sector | Primary Line of Trade | Global Rank and Penetration | | |
|---|---|---|---|---|---|---|
| | | | | 2004 Rank, Top 200 Retailers Worldwide | Single-country, Regional or Global? | Number of countries |
| Alimentation Couche-Tard | Canada | FDM | Convenience Stores | 99 | Global | 7 |
| Alticor/Amway | United States | FDM | Non-Store | 119 | Global | 80 |
| Amazon.com | United States | Homegoods | Non-Store | 111 | Global | 7 |
| Carrefour Group | France | FDM | Hypermarkets/Supercenters | 2 | Global | 31 |
| Costco Companies, Inc. | United States | FDM | Cash & Carries/Warehouse Clubs | 9 | Global | 7 |
| Defense Commissary Agency | United States | FDM | Supermarkets/Grocery Stores | 130 | Global | 13 |
| HMV Group plc | United Kingdom | Homegoods | Book & Multimedia | 180 | Global | 7 |
| INDITEX Group (i.e. Zara) | Spain | Softgoods | Apparel Stores | 110 | Global | 56 |
| Liberty Media Corp. (QVC) | United States | Homegoods | Non-Store | 121 | Global | 4 |
| LVMH | France | Softgoods | Other Apparel Specialty Stores | 76 | Global | 56 |
| Mango | Spain | Softgoods | Apparel Stores | – | Global | 76 |
| Metro AG | Germany | FDM | Cash & Carries/Warehouse Clubs | 4 | Global | 29 |
| Office Depot, Inc. | United States | Homegoods | Office Supply | 54 | Global | 23 |
| Otto Group | Germany | Softgoods | Non-Store | 61 | Global | 19 |
| Tesco PLC | United Kingdom | FDM | Supermarkets/Grocery Stores | 5 | Global | 13 |
| Toys "R" Us, Inc. | United States | Homegoods | Toy Stores | 68 | Global | 30 |
| Wal-Mart Stores, Inc. | United States | FDM | Hypermarkets/Supercenters | 1 | Global | 11 |

Sources: Retail Forward, company annual reports and published reports

**Photo 15.1**
The Marui department store in Tokyo offers a wide variety of housewares and apparel. The symbol that looks like "OIOI" is the company logo, representing Marui. *Courtesy of the author.*

Echigoya (Mitsukoshi) used some innovative new sales ideas. It was the first company to establish a fixed price, rather than the negotiated prices that had been prevalent earlier. It was also the first company to sell cloth by the piece rather than by the entire roll. A third unique policy was to allow customers to return merchandise. Echigoya became a corporation in 1893. Other stores followed this course.

In these early years, Takashimaya developed a four-point policy: (1) sell good products at lower prices to earn profits, (2) set the right price, with no overcharging, 3) tell customers the good and bad points about products, and 4) treat customers equally, not discriminating against the poor, and not cheating customers.

After Japan opened itself to foreign countries in 1867, kimono shops adopted new ideas that suggested a modern society. They started selling Western clothes. They sent employees on overseas buying trips to buy goods for import and to bring back samples that could then be produced in Japan. They also began to send Japanese goods to international expositions. The birth of department stores was largely influenced by an economic boom between 1894 and 1904.

Department stores enjoyed an era of major prosperity around 1923. They expanded to stock products of all types. By 1910, they began door-to-door and mail-order sales. Innovations such as elevators (1911) and escalators (1914) were added. The stores provided ultimate service such as sending cars to pick up customers and providing home delivery service. The department store became the symbol of modern life in the big city.

The five major buying groups are: Mitsukoshi, Daimaru, ADO (Isetan, Matsuya and Marui), Japan Department Stores Management Association (Seibu stores and affiliates), and High-Land Group (Takashimaya). Each group includes a variety of affiliates. The Mitsukoshi group has more than 50 members yet they operate only 14 stores in Japan.

In 1985, when I first started doing research in Japan, department stores were doing well. The top 10 department stores occupy huge sections of prime city real estate.

Department stores are designed to be cradle-to-grave providers of products and service. The basement level, sometimes there are two of them, sells grocery products. These Japanese stores were the first department stores I had ever visited that sold food. U.S. department stores would never sell food, other than gourmet products, because it does not generate a high gross margin. The ground floor of a Japanese department store would have a layout very similar to a U.S. or European department store. They feature cosmetics, jewelry, and accessories on this floor. The next three to six floors would contain men's, women's, and children's apparel. Additional floors were devoted to housewares, appliances, furniture, and stationary. The top floor would likely contain a restaurant, a pet store, and an outdoors amusement area for children. At one department store in Ginza, I noticed an area where one could select a grave marker and commission the appropriate engraving.

Department stores have an area they call their community college. It is an educational facility where they teach courses. They are not the same type of community college we have in the United States, where students take courses for an associate's degree or take general college requirements and transfer the credits to a four-year institution. The Japanese department store community colleges offer courses in geography, languages, cooking, and flower arrangement. They design the courses to enhance the quality of homemakers' lives and stimulate purchase of supplies from the department store. A few years ago a popular class was "How to hold a cocktail party." Few Japanese consumers have ever given or been to a cocktail party. The department store arranged for teachers who would inform the homemaker students about the tangible and intangible aspects of a cocktail party. The tangible aspects would include how much wine, mixer, and liquor do you need. What kinds of glasses do you use to serve the drinks? Which drinks require an olive; which ones need a cherry? The intangible aspects include how to select people with good communication skills to provide sparkling conversation. The hostess should move around the party, introducing guests to others they might find interesting.

Of course, after learning the skills required to hold a cocktail party, the homemakers will want to hold an actual party. The department store is prepared to offer assistance. Most Japanese homes are too small to hold a reasonably sized cocktail party. The department store can solve the problem by renting some of their fully furnished modern apartments specifically designed for this purpose. The hostess will also need to rent or purchase glasses, flowers, food, and drink. All these things the department stores will arrange. Japanese do not initiate conversations with people to whom they have not been introduced. This can hamper a cocktail party, where the purpose is to engage in conversation. The ultimate cocktail party accessory you can rent in Japan is a friend. For a fee, special agencies provide interesting people you can hire to attend your cocktail party and be your friend.

Department store sales have fallen over the last 10 years and they control a relatively small market share. The department store industry remains fragmented with the top 10 accounting for 50 percent of sales. Takashimaya is the largest department store with 10 percent of the market share. Market share of the other major department stores are Mitsukoshi (6%), Seibu (5.8%), Mauri (5.2%), Isetan (4.6%), Daimaru (4.4%), Matsuzakaya (3.5%), Kintetsu (3.5%), Hankyu (3.2%), and Tokyu (2.6%).

**GIFT GIVING**    There are two **OBLIGATORY** gift giving seasons in Japan. You do not give the gifts out of a sense of sentiment, but because it is socially required. In the two seasons of O-chugen (July or August) and O-seibo (December or January), gifts are given to those to whom you are obligated. This would include your boss, your children's teachers, perhaps the matchmaker that brought you together with your spouse. This gift giving is not reciprocal. You do not expect your boss or your children's teacher or your matchmaker to give you a return gift. Obligatory gifts are practical, not sentimental gifts. Boxes of bar soap, dried fish, and washcloths are traditional gifts. A six-pack of beer is a popular contemporary gift. Fresh fruit in a gift box from a prestigious department store is a popular gift. Department stores set up special display sections to sell these obligatory gifts. They also provide consultants to help young wives select the appropriate gift. Individuals and companies purchase gifts during these seasons; these gifts can account for 40 percent of the department store's total yearly sales. Since the recession, sales during the gift seasons have decreased; however, they are still a major part of department store sales.

## › CHARACTERISTICS OF THE DEPARTMENT STORE SYSTEM

The frame orientation introduced at the beginning of this chapter can help us to understand characteristics of the Japanese retail system. In Japan, retailers and their suppliers work as partners. Generally, the relationship between a buyer and a supplier is very long term. Adding a new supplier is not an everyday event.

### Supplier Support

Suppliers in Japan provide several of the functions handled in the United States by retailers. Suppliers hold merchandise until the retailer needs it, monitoring the stock within a store and replenishing it as needed. Suppliers may restock perishable items, like *bento* or *onigiri*, in convenience stores four times per day. In department stores, suppliers provide salespersons to sell their merchandise. These employees provide the suppliers with important market information. Suppliers provide financial support for remodeling a department store, or for recreating a window display. If a department store needs a new elevator, the store would likely assess its suppliers to have them pay for part of the elevator.

Japanese manufacturers allow department stores to return unsold merchandise. This is a type of CONSIGNMENT system. Manufacturers determine what merchandise will be displayed, hire sales employees to sell the merchandise, and accept return of unsold merchandise. Manufacturers, not retailers, are responsible for the risk of product acceptance. In Japan, retailers became MANUFACTURERS' SHOWROOMS; that is, they function like a real estate leasing agent rather than an assembler of merchandise assortments. They lease the display area in their store to manufacturers. This system gives power to the manufacturers. POWER, in this context, refers to influence in the distribution channel. There are other characteristics of the system that have given retailers power in the past, and the system is changing. Japanese retailers are taking more product risk, moving away from consignment and becoming the channel leaders.

I have been researching Japanese distribution for 20 years. Ninety percent of the articles I read mention the high ratio of retailers and wholesalers to consumers, about twice the ratio in the United States. Japan's critics often cite this as the primary reason foreign manufacturers have a difficult time entering the Japanese system. They

**Photo 15.2**
This mother and child are selecting a toy from a vending machine. In Japan, vending machines are very sophisticated; chilled fresh beef, fancy cakes, and even ladies' lingerie are sold through them. Small stores use vending machines to extend their hours of operation. A liquor store owner might sell five or six different sizes of cold beer, several types of hard liquor, and several varieties of hot and cold *sake* through a vending machine outside the store. *Courtesy of AP/Wide World Photos.*

believe that wholesalers and manufacturers have close interlocking relations and disregard foreign products. KEIRETSU refers to a system of formal business relationships linking financial institutions and manufacturing companies. Although keiretsu relationships are important in Japan, they do not play a major role in Japanese distribution. Retailers and their suppliers are not so purposely linked but rather are linked through mutual obligation.

After conducting hundreds of hours of interviews with department store managers and buyers, I wanted to start talking to their wholesaler suppliers. Throughout the interviews, which we always conducted in Japanese, the buyers would refer to their suppliers. My Japanese colleague and I assumed they meant wholesalers. Weeks before I was to return to Japan for more interviews with wholesalers, my Japanese colleague called and said "There are no wholesalers. All the department store buyers we have been interviewing buy direct from the manufacturer."

We had spent years talking to department store managers and buyers and had not discovered that they buy directly from the manufacturer. We had not even bothered asking, because we thought we knew the answer. Small retailers do buy from wholesalers, but these retailers purchase a small amount of imported merchandise. They are not a viable distribution route for foreign products. The myth of multiple wholesalers is so strong, we did not question it. If we had not set out to interview wholesalers, we might not have found out the truth.

The economist David Flath made a very important contribution to our knowledge about Japan. He studied channel length (number of wholesalers) used in Japan and other parts of the world. He found that if you control for product perishability, there is no difference between channel length in the United States and Japan.[4] For example, fresh fish passes through a lengthy channel in both countries. Japanese people eat a lot of fresh fish, and they value product freshness in a variety of food products. It is this value on perishable products that lengthens the distribution channel, not excessive wholesaler processing.

## The Buyer Is King

Japan is a hierarchical society. When the Japanese exchange business cards, the purpose is not to learn the other person's name, it is to establish the status of the new acquaintance. Without this information, one does not have the necessary information to talk with the stranger, or even to know where one should seat the person. In Japan, people are seated around a conference table in order of their group status.

Relationships have a formal meaning in Japan. They clearly define the role of buyer and seller in Japanese culture. Japanese businesspeople view buyers and sellers vertically. Buyers are superior to sellers. Sellers must conduct themselves in a subservient manner, respecting this difference. U.S. businesspeople view buyers and sellers as equal, having a horizontal relationship. A supplier offers to sell something. If the buyer wants to purchase it, fine; if not, that is fine also.

## Consignment

Japanese retailers and their suppliers have long-term relationships. One part of this relationship is to provide merchandise on a CONSIGNMENT basis. If the merchandise does not sell, it can be returned to the manufacturer for credit. Consignment sales are used in many different lines of merchandise, such as clothing and footwear. In the United States, consignment is used in cosmetics but not in most other product areas. Using consignment effectively spreads the product risk. If merchandise produced by the manufacturer does not sell successfully in the retail store, then both the retailer and the manufacturer share the cost of this product failure. The retailer loses OPPORTUNITY COSTS, the money the retailer would have earned if another, better-selling manufacturer had that shelf space. The manufacturer must absorb the cost of producing the product if it does not sell.

The effect of using consignment merchandise is that merchandise is generally more standard. Manufacturers are less likely to take great product risks because they are responsible for product failure. Effects of the consignment system are presented in Figure 15.2.

## Role of Retail Buyer

In the United States, retail buyers are considered profit centers. U.S. retailers evaluate buyers on how they have increased sales, and profits, on a year-to-date basis. They evaluate buyers on maintained markup, returns, and inventory turnover. If buyers do not purchase merchandise that is saleable, with an adequate maintained margin, the retailer cannot make a profit. Management rewards buyers financially and with promotion for profitable figures. Buyers who do not perform well are demoted or fired.

A different situation exists in Japan. Japanese buyers are rewarded based on seniority not ability and performance. They are not considered profit centers nor are they constantly monitored to determine markup, returns, and inventory turnover. Although most large Japanese retailers do have buyers, these buyers work

**Figure 15.2**
Consignment systems prevail in Japan. Under the consignment system, the manufacturer carries the product risk by accepting the return of unsold merchandise. The consignment system lowers retail margins because the retailer assumes less risk. It also lowers product variety because manufacturers assume the cost of failed innovations, and lowers imported merchandise because of the cost of merchandise returns. The consignment system raises manufacturer margins, because the supplier takes the product risk. It also raises consumer prices because merchandise is not rapidly marked down so it will sell.

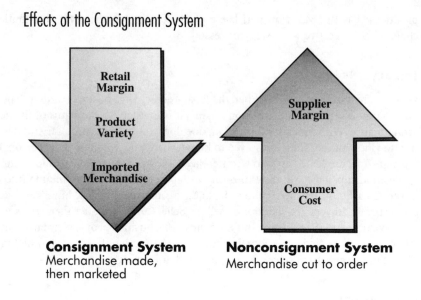

## Effects of the Consignment System

**Consignment System**
Merchandise made,
then marketed

Retail Margin
Product Variety
Imported Merchandise

**Nonconsignment System**
Merchandise cut to order

Supplier Margin
Consumer Cost

Source: Worthy, F. S. "Japan's Smart Secret Weapon." (1991). *Fortune*, August 12, p. 73.

closely with the retail department sales manager and the manufacturer. They serve sort of a public relations role. Purchases are rarely the decision of one individual.

Because of the prevalence of the consignment system in Japanese department stores, many companies do not have buyers. Department managers serve this function. Even in those companies where there is a highly developed central buying office, there is much greater interaction between the buying and selling function in Japan.

Stores control the number of suppliers that can deal directly with them through the issuing of an account number. Only suppliers that have proven themselves obtain a number. I asked Japanese buyers and merchandise managers about the procedure used to approve a new vendor for the stores' buying lists. Their responses were quite similar. The final question is, "Can our current suppliers produce this merchandise?" The bias is against buying from any new vendor, not simply from a foreign vendor.

The Japanese government pressures large retailers to buy more imported merchandise, particularly from the United States. Retailers I interviewed said that they would give preference to a U.S. manufacturer over a new Japanese vendor. Stores' buyers attend foreign products trade fairs to find suitable products.

Negotiations among the department stores focus on nonprice competition. Rather than negotiate price with suppliers, buyers negotiate margin. Margin is 25 percent of sales for domestic merchandise, and 40–50 percent for imported merchandise.

After World War II, a shortage of products in Japan meant that anything could be sold. The suppliers, wholesalers, and manufacturers began to have merchandising power. This supplier's market significantly decreased the merchandising power of department stores. During rapid economic growth, department stores tried to enlarge their stores and increase stock. They became careless about product selection. To ensure access to distribution outlets, manufacturers instigated a consignment system under which retailers could return merchandise that did not sell. This movement to the consignment system significantly reduced the retailers' power in the channel system. Manufacturers also began to send their own representatives to the stores. They did this to make sure the retailer properly represented their products and to provide information about sales volume.

## Buying Methods

Japanese department stores use three types of buying agreements: kaitori shiire, itaku shiire, and uriage (shoka) shiire.

**KAITORI SHIIRE**    In the KAITORI SHIIRE system, there is no return unless the product is bad. The retailer pays for the merchandise in cash, usually one month after delivery. The returns system continues under the euphemism of product exchange. The retailer receives a margin of about 50 percent on sales. If the wholesaler strictly prohibits the return, the department store may move to itaku shiire.

**ITAKU SHIIRE**    ITAKU SHIIRE is the equivalent of consignment sale. Here the risks pass to the department store upon delivery, but payment to the supplier occurs one month following sale to the consumer. Therefore, if the merchandise does not sell, it is returned to the wholesalers manufacturer. If retailers want to put the merchandise on sale, they must receive the approval of the manufacturer or wholesaler. Retailers receive a margin of about 30 percent. In this system, the retailer is responsible for damaged or stolen merchandise.

**URIAGE (SHOKA) SHIIRE**    URIAGE (SHOKA) SHIIRE means, literally, digestion purchase. Product and product risk pass to the department store upon delivery, but payment to the supplier occurs one month following the sale to a customer. Perishable foods are purchased using this system. Uriage shiire began when department stores expanded from the sales of kimono products to perishable foods. Department stores did not have the product knowledge needed to manage the sales of perishable goods. Under uriage shiire, the wholesaler keeps track of sales and pays the retailer about 3 percent of sales.

In a national survey of Japanese department store buyers, we asked the respondents how much merchandise they purchased using the three types of buying systems. Itaku shiire (consignment) was used for 43.27 percent of the merchandise bought. Kaitori shiire (direct purchases) was used for 22.45 percent and Uriage shiire (digestive system) was used for 32.45 percent. This data shows that the consignment system and the return of unsold merchandise is still prevalent in Japanese department stores. The sum of itaku shiire and uriage shiire is 75.7 percent, proving that suppliers take more than 75 percent of product risk in Japanese department stores.

In order for department stores to survive, they need to retake possession of their retail space and move away from the consignment system. Some stores are focusing on private label; for the prestigious names this could be an important step.

## Long-Term Relationships

Trust and interdependence in the channel relationship are not separate elements, but are highly related. Kumar pointed out that trust requires companies to relinquish some of their independence, or, to put it another way, to become more interdependent. The trust and the interdependence in the channel relationship benefits both parties. A study showed that retailers with a high level of trust in their manufacturers or suppliers generated 78 percent more sales than those with a low level of trust. A high level of trust in the relationship also eliminates the necessity of long, detailed contracts. A majority of wholesalers in Japan operate without contracts.

In sum, long-term orientation, interdependence, and trust characterize channel relationships in Japan. I have explained these relationships in terms of behavioral explanations, but there could also be an economically rational explanation. These characteristics, then, should stabilize the channel relationship. As the economy declines and the customers' needs become more unpredictable, the stabilized vertical relationship based on the long-term orientation, interdependence, and trust should benefit both suppliers and retailers. First, there is a cost saving resulting from a stable relationship. Creating a new relationship requires much time, effort, and money from both parties. In other words, the cost of switching channel partners is tremendous. Firms that cooperate most closely with other firms in a vertical relationship obtain the best returns on investment, but establishing such a relationship incurs high implementation cost. Second, a long-term supplier/retailer relationship based on trust creates goodwill and increases the parties' performance. A study showed that retailers who trusted their supplier were 12 percent more committed to the relationship (as measured by their intent to carry the supplier's products in the future) and were 22 percent less likely to have developed alternative sources. As noted previously, the same study showed that retailers with a high level of trust in the manufacturer generated 78 percent more sales than those with a low level. In addition, the long-term relationship realizes its full potential. In a trusting, long-term relationship, the channel members are able to share confidential information, to invest in understanding each other's business, and to customize their information systems or dedicate people and resources to better serve each other. Third, the stabilized relationship increases flexibility among channel members. Interdependency makes the parties interested in maintaining the quality of the relationship. Parties tend to share more information, enabling them to anticipate and respond to each others' needs. As a result, the level of performance and the outcomes the individual members and the channel as a whole can attain are higher. The shared information reduces the uncertainty of channel members, making it possible for them to act more flexibly to reach their goals. Flexibility among channel members enables them to adapt more rapidly to environmental changes in a changing market. The quicker they can respond to these changes, the greater will be their performance and the outcomes.

Under the declining economic environment, it might be reasonable to assume that the traditional characteristics of the Japanese need to change. As previously noted, Japanese buyers are linked to suppliers through long-term business commitments. Most buyers and suppliers have been business partners for decades. They do not base the relationship on price, but instead on mutually beneficial concerns and decision making. Like a family, the partners may argue with each other and voice dissatisfaction with the business relationship, but they remain true to each other.

The relationship situation between suppliers and retailers is not part of the keiretsu system, mentioned earlier. This system, used in manufacturing and in the commodities trade, is a formal linking of businesses. The retailer-supplier link is more informal. However, major retailers belong to specific buying groups. These groups have a financial link with other business partners who, when all things are considered, are the preferred partners for all types of business relationships.

## Sales Employees Sent by Manufacturer (Haken-Shain)

Much of the sales staff in a Japanese department store is not hired by the store, but instead is hired by the manufacturer. In a department store that has 80 percent consignment merchandise, the manufacturers would also send about 80 percent of its sales employees. These sales employees are dressed just like other employees so customers in the store do not know whether the department store or a manufacturer hired the person.

An observer might think the department stores are forcing the manufacturers to provide sales employees, but manufacturers would explain that having their own employees in the store is their most important type of market research. By having their employees talk with customers, the manufacturers receive grassroots information about what customers want. Information is one of the strongest competitive factors in marketing.

## Highly Competitive, But Not Always on Price

Major department stores and mass merchandisers in Japan carry the same merchandise and sell it at the same price. Manufacturers attach a price to products and,

**Photo 15.3**
Fresh strawberries are sold in a gift box as a delicacy. The price is 2,500 yen, about $25 for 12 strawberries. *Courtesy of the author.*

because of the consignment system, can convince retailers to keep the price at their suggested level. If markdowns are to be taken, the manufacturer has the major determination of whether, and when, a markdown will take place.

This pricing system is a part of the larger marketing system in Japan, where most merchandise is produced before demand is known. The Japanese manufacturer determines what merchandise will be made available. The manufacturer's representatives work with retail buyers to determine what merchandise and what volume of merchandise will be offered in each store. If the merchandise does not sell, the manufacturer accepts the return of unsold merchandise. When the merchandise is returned to the manufacturer, it is usually destroyed rather than sold at a reduced price. To reduce the price would erode the price image of the company.

In the United States, in contrast, manufacturers produce merchandise lines that are then shown to retail buyers at markets and trade shows. Buyers review the line and place orders. After the manufacturers review the orders they have obtained from buyers, they decide what merchandise to produce. If they have few orders for a particular model, they will not produce that product. They will tell the retail buyer that an item is not available due to insufficient demand. In Japan, merchandise is made, then sold. In the United States, merchandise orders are taken, and production is based on orders. Figure 15.3 graphically illustrates the difference between how the Japanese and U.S. product development process is carried out. Some stores are using the U.S. method of buying.

The Japanese rebate system is a very good example of eclecticism and exceptionism. A Japanese businessman once told me that when you understand the complex Japanese rebate system, you will understand Japanese distribution.

## Rebate System

Japan's rebate system classifies rebates into six areas: quality rebates, payment debt rebates, target achievement rebates, physical distribution rebates, sales promotion rebates, and special rebates.[5]

QUANTITY REBATES are given to retailers based on order size or total quantity ordered throughout the period. PAYMENT DATE REBATES are given to buyers who pay their bill before a certain deadline. TARGET ACHIEVEMENT REBATES are paid according to how well the buyer has met sellers' agreed-upon targets in areas such as total sales and new customers. PHYSICAL DISTRIBUTION REBATES are given when the buyer helps the seller to process the goods ordered. At the request of the supplier, a retailer may make changes in packaging, putting several items together or dividing items into smaller groups. Inventory burden rebates also fit under this classification for buyers who, at the request of the seller, share the costs of risk and of special inventory. SALES PROMOTION REBATES are refunds paid to the retailer who shares the work or cost of conducting a special sales promotion (advertising, displays, and so on). SPECIAL REBATES are based on the supplier's overall evaluation of how much the retailer contributed to the supplier's business.

There are some important differences between the United States and Japan in how rebates are used. In the United States, rebates are given as immediate discounts. The manufacturer subtracts a quantity rebate on the invoice the retailer receives as a bill. If the retailer pays the bill within a certain time period, they are entitled to

## Product Development Process: United States and Japan

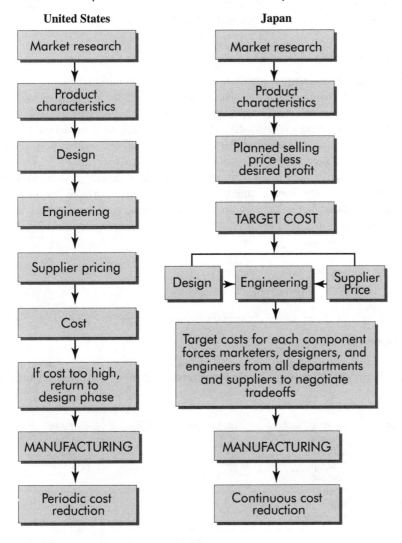

**United States**

- Market research
- Product characteristics
- Design
- Engineering
- Supplier pricing
- Cost
- If cost too high, return to design phase
- MANUFACTURING
- Periodic cost reduction

**Japan**

- Market research
- Product characteristics
- Planned selling price less desired profit
- TARGET COST
- Design → Engineering ← Supplier Price
- Target costs for each component forces marketers, designers, and engineers from all departments and suppliers to negotiate tradeoffs
- MANUFACTURING
- Continuous cost reduction

Source: Adapted from Worthy, F. S. "Japan's Smart Secret Weapon." (1991). *Fortune*, August 12, p. 73.

**Figure 15.3**
The product development process in the United States differs from that in Japan. In Japan, most products are produced and then sold. In the United States, manufacturers produce samples, take orders from retail buyers, and then produce products to fill the orders. Japan uses product engineering for continuous cost reduction.

subtract a payment date rebate immediately. In Japan, they pay the rebates at the end of each accounting period, normally once a year.

U.S. manufacturers generally give sellers 30 days to pay for merchandise. Japanese suppliers generally extend 90 days of trade credit. This longer time in Japan gives the retailer time to sell the merchandise before payment is due, eliminating the need for external inventory financing.

In the next section, I will discuss the retail formats used in Japan. Japan has a well-developed department store sector and strong national specialty store chains.

Food stores range from superstores to mom-and-pop operations. In the 1990s, discount stores began to operate throughout Japan. Brand name discounting occurs only in selected product categories, but it is a growing trend.

## Supermarkets

The supermarket sector is highly fragmented with no national chains. Power is in the hands of manufacturers and wholesalers. The industry is organized into buying groups similar to the department store industry. A summary of the largest supermarket buying groups is provided in Table 15.3. The degree of modernization varies from well-managed modern stores to inefficient players. Food supermarkets accounted for 12 percent of total retail sales.[6]

This segment faces many competitors including general merchandise stores (GMS), department stores selling food, and convenience stores. Supermarkets have not established what value they provide compared to their competitors. To some degree mergers in Japan have been viewed negatively since there is an alliance to the original ownership.

**Table 15.3**
**Largest Supermarket Buying Groups**

| Group Name | Nichiryu | CGC Japan | National Supermarket Association | Nihon Supermarket Association |
|---|---|---|---|---|
| Member Companies | 19 | 220 | 485 | 100 |
| Key Members | Life Corporation<br>Okuwa<br>Heiwado<br>Sanei<br>Izumi<br>Kasumi<br>SunnyMart<br>Inageya | Daimaru Peacock<br>Universe<br>Maruwa<br>Santoku<br>Olympic<br>Raise<br>Belk<br>Mammy Mart | Life Corporation (as CGC) | Yaoko<br>Ecos<br>Maruyo<br>Raise |
| Group Name | Nichiryu | CGC Japan | National Supermarket Association | Nihon Supermarket Association |
| Member Companies | 19 | 71 | 210 | 15 |
| Key Members | Ecos<br>Sunshine Chain<br>Saeki<br>Hinoya | Summit<br>Kansai<br>Supermarket<br>Queens Isetan<br>Maruhisa<br>Otani | Shell Garden<br>Super Daiei<br>Hayashi<br>Shimizu Shoji<br>Kinokuniya | Tokyu Store<br>Okakyu Shojoi<br>Keisei Store<br>Keikyu Store<br>Meitetsu Pare<br>Soteetsu Rozen<br>Tobu Store<br>Keio Store |

Source: JapanConsuming/www.retailforward.com, Strategic Focus: Food Retailing in Japan, July 2003, 13.

Trading houses are taking over some companies. Marubeni has acquired controlling interest in the number two supermarket chain, Maruetsu, which had formerly been controlled by Daiei. The supermarket Summit has been wholly owned by a trading house since 1967.

One new type of differentiated supermarket is called *kokyu super*. They carry very high-quality merchandise, similar to what is found in department stores. Aeon is assuming industry leadership by combining Western retail practices with Japanese business customs. They are putting pressure on their suppliers, especially those providing their Top Valu private label brand.

## General Merchandise Stores (GMS)

The GMS stores were the stars of the 1960s and 1970s with dozens of GMS chains. Today that has been narrowed down to two companies—Ito-Yokado and Aeon (formerly Jusco). Ito-Yokado has taken a cautious road to expansion while Aeon has been rapidly acquiring regional chains. A third player in this market is Daiei. Originally one of the most successful GMS chains, they overexpanded and now are settled with an enormous debt.

In the early 1990s, supermarket sales fell for 21 months in a row. Sales rose during fiscal 1994; however, profits continued to fall. Factors behind the falling unit prices included a stronger yen, cheaper import goods because of deregulation, development of private brands by retailers, and advancement in cost-saving technologies for labor and store expenses.[6]

Wal-Mart's purchase of controlling interest in Seiyu will make them a tough competitor in this area. Wal-Mart's ample financial strength will allow Seiyu to acquire and consolidate smaller, regional GMS operators or make a move for one of the bigger three companies.

## Convenience Stores

Convenience stores were introduced during the 1980s and have been very successful in Japan. Many of them are part of the largest superstore groups. Without realizing it, the Large Scale Retail Store (LSRS) Law gave a competitive push to convenience stores.[7,8] Companies like Ito-Yokado that could not open large-scale stores were able to open convenience stores. Convenience stores in Japan offer the same type of merchandise as those in the United States. Convenience stores provide a merchandise mix based on prepared foods and simple household goods such as cleaning materials, stationery, toiletries, and leisure products such as books and magazines. One difference is that the Japanese convenience store is a major home office connection, often offering photocopying and facsimile services. Stores serve an area of about 500 meters. Nearly all convenience stores stay open 24 hours a day.

The irony is that the large-scale retail store law was designed to protect small- and medium-sized businesses from supermarkets and GMS, but it was actually convenience stores that wiped out the mom-and-pop shops. Characteristics of a convenience (c-store) are:

> Predominantly sell food and beverages
> Small format between 30 and 250 square meters

> Long hours of operation
> Almost all of them operate as franchise
> Heavy reliance on information technology and advanced merchandise and inventory management

Compared with other retail formats c-stores are new to retailing in Japan and can avoid some of the traditional relationships that hold modernization back. The first chains appeared in the 1970s, fueled by The Large Scale Retail Store Law. C-Stores did several things differently in the channel:

> Dealt directly with manufacturers
> Streamlined logistics, usually with cross-docking distribution centers
> Used information to drive merchandising
> Developed their own merchandise
> Controlled their own prices[7]

Seven-Eleven Japan is the largest convenience store chain in Japan. Seven-Eleven's food sales have more than five times the sales of Life Corporation, the largest supermarket chain. Lawson, another c-store, is the number two food sales company in Japan.

C-stores use computer systems to support their operations, employing real-time information for ordering and inventory control. Other than some non-perishable items that are delivered directly to the stores by local wholesalers, products are delivered by manufacturers and wholesalers to distribution centers with cross-docking facilities. The stores then pick up the merchandise and put it on trucks for delivery on their routes to 10 to 25 stores.

The Sogo Shosha trading companies are also expanding into the c-store business. Seiyu sold Family Mart to Itochu in 1999; Mitsubishi acquired a controlling stake in Lawson in 2001; then the am/pm convenience store chain, then a small

**Photo 15.4**
Kimono sales used to occupy a full floor in large department stores. Today kimono are still sold but occupy a smaller area, like a bridal shop. Kimono are worn for traditional occasions, such as weddings, funerals, and New Year celebrations.
*Courtesy of the author.*

**Table 15.4**
**Leading SPAs by Origin and Brand (by wide definition of "SPA" to include all fashion/interiors)**

| SPA Leader | Origin | Main Category | Key Retail Fascias |
|---|---|---|---|
| World | Manufacturer | Apparel | Untitled, Cordier |
| Onward Kashiyama | Manufacturer | Apparel | 23-ku, Gotairiku, Jiyu-ku, Kumikyoku, ICB |
| Itokin | Manufacturer | Apparel | OfuOn, a.v.v. |
| Sanei International | Wholesaler | Apparel | Vivayou, Pearly Gates, Natural Beauty |
| Five Foxes | Wholesaler/Designer | Apparel | Comme Ca+ |
| Flandre | Wholesaler/Designer | Apparel | Flandre |
| Fast Retailing | Retailer | Apparel/Food | Uniqlo, Skip |
| Ryohin Keikaku | Retailer | Mixed | Mujirushi Ryohin, Muji |
| Dan | Manufacturer | Socks | Kutsushitaya |
| Bigi | Wholesaler | Apparel | Bigi, Adieu Tristesse, Moga |
| Mokumoku | Retailer | Apparel | Olive des Olive |
| Sazaby | Wholesaler/Designer | Accessories/Apparel | Sazaby, Agnes B Voyage, Agete, Anayi |
| Bais | Retailer | Interiors/Household | Franc Franc, J-Period |
| Gap | Overseas | Apparel | Gap |
| Laura Ashley | Overseas | Apparel/Home | Laura Ashley |
| Zara Japan | Overseas | Apparel | Zara |
| Mango | Overseas | Apparel | Mango |
| Benetton | Overseas | Apparel | Benetton |
| Eddie Bauer | Overseas | Apparel | Eddie Bauer |

+ : Five Foxes is primarily an apparel chain, but is increasingly diversifying into many categories including food, toys, and restaurants. Each has a different brand based on the Comme Ca prefix: Comme Ca, Comme Ca Ice, Comme Ca Baby, etc.
Source: Japan Consuming/www.retailforward.com, Strategic Focus: Apparel Retailing in Japan, June 2003, 11.

ownership interest in Seicomart. Mitsui has aligned themselves with Ito-Yokado and a supply chain serving both the GMS chain and Seven-Eleven.[8]

## The Apparel Specialty Sector

There are three primary types of apparel specialty shops. The first is an SPA-Specialty Private Label (Table 15.4). These are vertically integrated single brand retail chains. The next is Select Shops, a uniquely Japanese format that has about 60 percent in store brands and about 40 percent in international fashion labels. The fashion labels are used to draw people to the store. The last type is a multi-brand specialty store where the merchandise is fashion or accessories.

SPAs are an important trend that emerged in the 1990s. These shops helped make the transition from manufacturers pushing merchandise down the system to the retailer reclaiming their hold on customers. They do this by producing a private label line. Uniqlo is the Japanese pioneer of this concept. They developed a clear branding story and a model to create pull through the system rather than push. Later in the 1990s apparel groups like World, Sanyo, and Onward began to introduce their own exclusive private label brands under their SPA operations. There are three types of SPAs: 1) manufacturer based (vertically integrated forward), 2) wholesale based, and 3) retailer based (this group includes non-Japanese retail chains such as GAP). The retailers are vertically integrated backward into the supply chain and dictate the product to manufacturers.[9]

Two Japanese SPAs have been successful in overseas markets—Muji (Seiyu Group) and Uniqlo (Uniqlo closed 16 of its 21 stores in the United States). SPAs in Japan include Benetton, Laura Ashley, Eddie Bauer, Gap, Zara, Mango, and Giordano.

## › SUMMARY

Japanese retailing is influenced by unique business practices. The concept of frame is evident in the way decisions are made, relationships are maintained, and merchandise is procured.

The concepts of pseudo-harmonism, eclecticism, and exceptionism help us to understand the complex environment of Japanese businesses. Much of the antagonism between Japan and its trading partners stems from lack of understanding of these important cultural dimensions.

Suppliers in Japan provide extensive support to retailers. They hold merchandise until it is needed at the retail level, a natural just-in-time procurement system. Suppliers accept unsold merchandise returns, sharing the risk of product failure. Retail buyers work with suppliers to determine what merchandise will be offered for sale in the store. Many of the sales employees in large stores are hired and paid by the manufacturer, not the retailer. These sales employees provide an important information-gathering source for manufacturers. Interacting with consumers, these manufacturers' sales representatives gain important information about what consumers want, then relay this information to their employers. This information equals power in the distribution system.

Japan has a highly developed retail system with extensive offerings in most of the format categories. Their department store industry is one of the most developed in the world, offering cradle-to-grave service to their customers.

Although the LSRS Law has been revised, it is still an impediment to domestic expansion. This law, as well as other domestic issues such as intense competition and high cost of land and labor, have influenced Japanese retailers to expand internationally. These retailers have been very successful in expanding throughout Asia and in the next two chapters we will discuss their impact on the Overseas Chinese market and in the People's Republic of China.

## › KEY TERMS

ATTRIBUTE

CHOP

CONSIGNMENT

ECLECTICISM

EXCEPTIONISM

FRAME

ITAKU SHIIRE

KAITORI SHIIRE

KEIRETSU

KIMONO SHOPS

KYU

MANUFACTURERS' SHOWROOMS

OBLIGATORY
OPPORTUNITY COSTS
PAYMENT DATE REBATES
PHYSICAL DISTRIBUTION REBATES
POWER
PSEUDO-HARMONISM
QUANTITY REBATES
RINGI
SALES PROMOTION REBATES
SPECIAL REBATES
TARGET ACHIEVEMENT REBATES
TERMINAL STORES
URIAGE (SHOKA) SHIIRE

## › DISCUSSION QUESTIONS

1. The relationship between Japanese buyers and sellers is vertical. Buyers are considered superior to sellers and therefore are treated in a deferential manner. How would this distinction put foreign sellers at a disadvantage?
2. Americans believe in being explicit with their feelings. We are taught to talk about situations that make us angry. What Japanese concept would this violate?
3. The Japanese government has tried to discourage manufacturers from sending sales employees to work in stores. This is partially due to pressure from the U.S. government, who maintains that this practice is a type of nontariff barrier. The Japanese manufacturers continue to send sales employees to the retail stores, calling them volunteers instead of sales employees. This is an example of one of the Japanese business relationship concepts. Which concept is it?
4. How does using consignment affect the types of products sold? If the system is used throughout Japan, would you expect to find more or less product similarity than in other countries not using consignment?
5. Using Dunning's theory of the eclectic firm, explain how the international expansion issues would affect a company's decision to internationalize. Are these factors related to ownership, internationalization, or locational advantages?

## › ENDNOTES

1. Nakane, C. (1970). *Japanese Society*. Berkeley, CA: University of California Press.
2. Shimaguchi, M. (1993). "New Development in Channel Strategy in Japan." M. R. Czinkota and M. Kotabe, eds. *The Japanese Distribution System*. Chicago: Probus Publishing Co., pp. 173–190.
3. Shimaguchi. (1993).
4. Flath, D. (1990). "Why Are There So Many Retail Stores In Japan?" *Japan and the World Economy*, Vol. 2, pp. 365–386.
5. Taga, T., and Y. Uehara. (1994). "Some Characteristics of Business Practices in Japan." In T. Kikuchi, ed. *Japanese Distribution Channels*. Binghamton, NY: Haworth Press, pp. 71–87.

6. Food Retailing in Japan. (2003). RetailForward, July
7. Strategic Focus: Food Retailing in Japan. (2003). Columbus, Ohio, July.
8. Strategic Focus: Food Retailing in Japan. (2003).
9. Strategic Focus: Food Retailing in Japan. (2003).

## › FURTHER READING

1. Czinkota, M. (1985). "Distribution of Consumer Products in Japan." *International Marketing Review,* Autumn, pp. 39–50.
2. Dawson, J., and T. Sato. (1983). "Controls Over the Development of Large Stores in Japan." *Service Industries Journal,* Vol. 3, No. 2, pp. 136–145.
3. "Department-Store Sales." (1995). *Nikkei Weekly,* July 31, p. 5.
4. "Department Stores Hit Declines in Pretax Profits." (1991). *Nikkei Weekly,* November 2, p. 14.
5. Distribution and Marketing in Japan (Series 3. Retail and Wholesale Distribution). (1985). *Second Workshop on Japan's Distribution Systems and Business Practices.* Tokyo: MIPRO.
6. doRoasrio, L. (1993). "Nihon-Mart." *Far East Economic Review,* September 16, pp. 62–64.
7. Goldman, A. (1991). "Japan's Distribution System: Institutional Structure, Interal Political Economy, and Modernization. *Journal of Retailing,* Vol. 67, No. 2, pp. 154–182.
8. Goldman, A. (1992). "Evaluating the Performance of the Japanese Distribution System." *Journal of Retailing,* Vol. 68, No. 1, pp. 11–39.
9. Goldstein, C. (1988). "The Bargain Hunters." *Far Eastern Economic Review,* May 26, p. 82.
10. Goll, S. (1995). "China's Big State-Owned Retail Stores Form New Ventures with Foreign Firms." *Wall Street Journal,* March 13, p. B5a.
11. Hock, T. L. (1989). "How the Japanese Are Winning the Retailing War." *Asian Finance,* January 15, pp. 26–27.
12. Koji, K. (1998). "Discounting, Upscaling, Refinement." *Journal of Japanese Trade and Industry,* No. 3, p. 27.
13. Larke, R. (1994). *Japanese Retailing.* New York: Routledge.
14. Lein, F. (1987). *Department Stores in Japan.* Tokyo: Sophis University Bulletin, No. 115, p. 10.
15. Matsuzaka, T. (1993). "Garment Maker Tests No-Return System." *Nikkei Weekly,* March 8, p. 8.
16. Murata, S. (1973). "Distribution in Japan." *The Wheel Extended,* Autumn, pp. 4–11.
17. "Supermarkets Ring Up Solid Gains." (1991). *Nikkei Weekly,* November 2, p. 14.
18. Suzuki, T. (1993). "Trade Issues in Distribution." In M. R. Cziinkota and M. Kotabe, eds. *The Japanese Distribution System.* Chicago: Probus Publishing Co., pp. 219–230.
19. Tajima, Y. (1971). *How Goods Are Distributed in Japan.* Shibuya, Japan: Walton-Ridgeway and Co.
20. Watanabe, T. (1994). "Changes in Japan's Public Policies Toward Distribution

Systems and Marketing." In T. Kikuchi, ed. *Japanese Distribution Channels.* Binghamton, NY: Haworth Press, Inc., pp. 17–32.

21. Yamamuro, A. (1994). "Seiyu Steps Gently into Vietnam." *Nikkei Weekly,* August 8, p. 18.

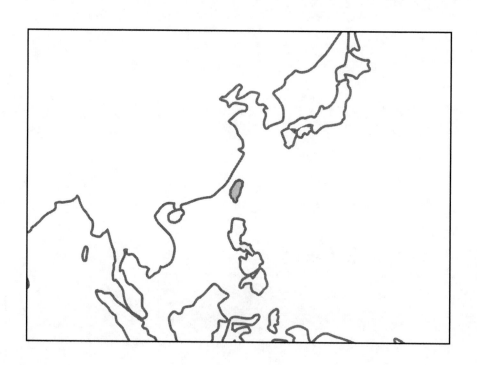

# 16

# IMPACT OF
# OVERSEAS CHINESE

## After reading this chapter you should understand

> How Chinese cultural values shape Chinese business activities and consumer behavior.

> The relationship between the overseas Chinese and mainland China.

> The role Japanese retailers have had on retailing in Hong Kong and Taiwan.

> The difference between Chinese and Japanese methods of retailing.

Many Chinese have left their homeland, mainland China, throughout history. These enclaves of Chinese have started or enhanced new countries with their commercial ingenuity. We credit the Chinese with developing the first system of writing, explosives, and according to some people, even pizza. It should come as no surprise that when Chinese immigrants move away from their home country they take with them a large number of commercial skills and abilities that allow them to be successful in other markets. Chinese immigrants helped to develop the commercial activities of Malaysia, Singapore, Thailand, Australia, and the Philippines. They were the primary ethnic developers of Taiwan and Hong Kong.

The focus of this chapter is the overseas Chinese people, those who live in Hong Kong and Taiwan. Their relationship to the mainland, the People's Republic of China (PRC), is an important factor in understanding the present-day situation in this region. The PRC has always considered Taiwan and Hong Kong its rightful possessions. On July 1, 1997, Hong Kong was returned to PRC control after a long British lease. Ultimately, the PRC is seeking to reunite Taiwan with the mainland as well.

Over the past 20 years, I have spent much time working with Chinese graduate students and interviewing and conducting research with Chinese businesspeople. Gordon Redding, the author of *The Spirit of Chinese Capitalism,* interviewed Chinese entrepreneurs from a variety of countries. His summary provides an interesting overview of the overseas Chinese and their connection to mainland values.

## › CHINESE CULTURAL VALUES

The reason Chinese immigrants have been so successful in so many parts of the country may be partially understood by looking at a group of similar values held by both mainland and overseas Chinese. These values reflect a long-term orientation to the world.

### Man-Nature Orientation

The Chinese regard human beings as a part of nature, and they believe people should not try to overcome or master nature, but rather, adapt in harmony. The following example illustrates the importance of this value. The Regent Hotel is a beautiful building in Hong Kong, on the Thim Shui (Kowloon) side of Hong Kong Harbor. The restaurant has a lovely atrium with glass on three sides. The Chinese man-nature orientation influenced the construction of this building. Originally glass windows were to be on one side only of the atrium, looking into the harbor. However, a Chinese spiritualist was consulted about the building during construction. He predicted the building would have terrible problems if it blocked the exit of spirits from the harbor. According to the spiritualist, the walls of the building would trap the spirits inside. This consultation led the builders to change the structure, making it glass on three sides. In this way, the spirits of the harbor could flow right through the building and not cause trouble.

The Chinese man-nature orientation leads to low expectations toward products. If a product does not meet performance expectations, there is less dissatisfaction because this confirms *yuarn,* the belief that predetermined conditions decide what

**Photo 16.1**
Boat ferries patrol Aberdeen harbor in Hong Kong. A group of Hong Kong residents live on boats, such as those in the rear of the picture. Children swim in the murky water between the boats. Dogs race around the boat decks, and chickens squawk from cages. It is not unusual to see children emerging from a residential boat to go to school in immaculate white starched shirts and sharply pressed gray wool shorts. *Courtesy of the author.*

will happen in life. The Chinese attribute success or failure of a product to fate rather than to the expertise of a particular company. They are, therefore, reluctant to complain about products. Concepts such as consumer dissatisfaction and complaint thus have less relevance in China than in the United States.

## Man-to-Himself Orientation

The concept of man-to-himself orientation refers to how the Chinese view their role in life. Traditional Chinese are raised to believe that they are not worthy. This leads to self-abasement throughout their lives. In Western cultures, for example, a person will say "thank you" in response to a compliment. A Chinese person will say, "I am not worthy of that compliment."

The Chinese are situation oriented and pragmatic. The extended family raises children; this leads to an attitude that is less dogmatic and more flexible. Chinese children learn that the correct response is based on the situation, not on an abstract ideal. In some ways, this corresponds to the Japanese view of frame orientation. The individual alone is not important. It is the environment, the frame, that gives importance to the nature of the individual.

There is an important distinction between the Chinese and the Japanese view of man-to-himself. The ideal for a Chinese person is to be an individual, worthy of respect and reverence. In Chinese culture, entrepreneurs are admired and respected. In Japan, the greatest esteem is given to an individual who is a part of the major group. Working for a large respected corporation conveys respect in Japan, not being an entrepreneur. These differences are very apparent in the way the Chinese and Japanese have made themselves known in world retail markets. Japanese expansion has been through large-scale stores, department stores, and mass merchandisers; Chinese expansion has primarily been in independent family owned businesses. The

Chinese preference for family businesses and the link to clan is further explained by the next concept, relational orientation.

## Relational Orientation

Relational orientation refers to respect for authority. Chinese students respect their teachers and teachers are expected to teach them, not be their friends. Confucius established five cardinal relationships:

> sovereign and minister
> father and son
> husband and wife
> old and young
> between friends

Chinese are expected to act according to the norms prescribed for each instance of interpersonal relations. The king must act kingly, the minister ministerly, the husband husbandly, the wife wifely, the brothers brotherly, and the friends friendly. These relationships are fostered with favors and gifts. The Chinese give gifts for different reasons than the Japanese. The gift should match the income of the giver; this gives face to the receiver of the gifts. Friends should return gifts of comparable or even higher value when possible.

Chinese businesspeople exchange favors when supplying goods on credit without signing any legal documents, believing that the signing of any legal document will end the reciprocity of doing favors. Informal channels of communication are very important in product selection by Chinese consumers. Brand loyalty is very strong, based on previous experiences with a brand. For the Chinese, the past plays an important role in what should happen in the present.

## Time Dimension—Past Time Orientation and Continuity

The past rather than the present or future is the dominant time dimension of the Chinese. Ancestor worship is one part of this dimension, but it is much more complex than this alone. Respect for family is very important. The following proverb illustrates the feeling of most Chinese: "Among the three unfilial duties, to have no heir is the greatest." For a son to leave no heir is a big problem in Chinese cultures, and the concept at the center of the 1993 film *The Wedding Banquet*. A handsome Chinese man is hassled by his mother to get married and provide an heir. He sets up an extensive list of spousal requirements: the bride must have multiple doctorates, be beautiful, musical, and so on. All this is a guise to cover the fact that he is gay and in love with a wonderful male companion. The story is funny, touching, and illustrative of the importance of producing an heir in Chinese culture.

An identification with the past reflects a certain type of time orientation that sociologists call CIRCULAR THINKING. The future is not predictable; therefore, the past is used as the point of reference. In contrast, people in Western cultures use LINEAR THINKING. We believe that what has happened in the past can be used to alter, or change, the future. Linear thinkers believe that one learns from the past to shape the future.

## Activity Orientation

The dimension of activity orientation refers to how people in a particular culture prioritize their actions. For the Chinese, knowing one's place in society is important to group functioning. People's actions convey their knowledge of their position within society. Among Chinese, there is a high degree of moral self-control or self-regulation. The culture has established rules and people are expected to follow these rules. If a person is rich and powerful, that person should do what is expected of someone who is rich and powerful. Likewise, if a person is poor and humble, he or she should do what is expected of someone who is poor and humble. There are five major themes in Chinese behavior, as follows:

1. *All men are born unequal. To the Chinese, the naturalness, necessity, and inevitability of hierarchy is self-evident. An efficient society requires a broadly accepted ordering of people. The alternative to hierarchy is chaos and anarchy, which together are worse than a harsh authority.*

   This view was challenged in mainland China beginning in the 1950s, when the equalizing views of communism were being spread throughout the country. During the Cultural Revolution, students were encouraged to chastise their teachers, and large public demonstrations were held to put into their places those who had been viewed as superior to others. Similarly, nurses were told that they were equal to physicians and that, with only their strong belief in Mao, the leader of the communist party, they could do surgery without any medical training. Many nurses and practitioners followed these beliefs, to the distress of their patients.

2. *The bases of inequality are achievement (usually academic), wealth, and moral example. The last is especially important for commanding political authority.*

   I know a very successful Chinese American who graduated from an Ivy League university and teaches at one of the best universities in the United States. However, in the eyes of his parents, he is not successful because his advanced education has not brought him great wealth. He is only a university professor, not a wealthy company executive.

3. *Laws negotiated by human beings are rigid, artificial, and insensitive to the changing circumstances of life. The judgment of wise and compassionate people is a better way to regulate personal, social, and political relationships.*

   This view corresponds to the British system of law called common law. The United States, in contrast, uses common law that is based on precedence. The basic idea is that law should reflect changes in society. As people's ideas about right and wrong change with societal change, the law should also change. Chinese law is very contextual. Right and wrong is not determined in an isolated situation, but instead is based on the situational constraints.

4. *People exist in and through relationships with others. The goal of socialization is to train children for lifelong interdependence with others by developing skills and values that promote harmony. The family is a fundamental cradle of sure support across time and requires special commitment from its members.*

   Before the civil war in China, this philosophy governed most of human relationships. The Confucian relationships identified earlier governed people's interactions. However, the political changes in mainland China disrupted these philosophical ideals. When the Communists took control of mainland China in 1949, they required that allegiance to family be eliminated. They did this to foster commitment to the greater, larger group. During the Cultural Revolution, families were separated, with various family members sent off to different regions of China. Many families were separated for 10 years. Communist leaders used this technique to diminish the strong bond of family. According to the party, comrades were to be the basic support groups, not family.

5. *The need to master ideographs, the basic symbols of the Chinese written language, reinforces an academic emphasis on memory, attention to detail, and lengthy homework. It also strengthens a predisposition toward perceiving stimuli as whole rather than as collections of parts, and high spatial intelligence.*

This belief continues. Chinese children, both on the mainland and in the overseas communities, are subjected to great amounts of detailed memorized learning. Whereas Western cultures view school success as largely determined by innate ability, Chinese cultures view school success as work or application driven.

## > FLIGHT FROM THE MAINLAND

In 1950, the Chinese city of Shanghai was a booming commercial center. Sections of the city called concessions housed enclaves of foreigners. The French Concession, the American Concession, the Russian Concession, and others essentially determined their own governance. Foreign residents lived in mansions. European-style office buildings line the Bund, the major boulevard, paralleling the harbor in Shanghai. The city was called the Paris of Asia. Today, the architecture along the Bund reflects a mix of European styles, the buildings now housing Shanghai's gov-

**Photo 16.2**
A street scene in busy Tsim Sha Shui, the Kowloon side of Hong Kong Harbor, sometimes called the tourist ghetto. Most corporate offices and the financial district are located on the Hong Kong side. In Tsim Sha Shui, every inch of land is used, and neon lights promote every kind of pleasure and product imaginable. These shops are not selling low-priced trinkets, but expensive watches, jewelry, and designer clothes. *Courtesy of the author.*

ernment offices. At night, as one travels along the Bund, floodlights illuminate the buildings, giving the illusion that things are as they were in 1950.

When the Communists assumed power in the early 1950s, two groups of Chinese citizens left the country. The defeated military group left for Taiwan; the commercial group, for Hong Kong. These two communities have grown and prospered.

## > HONG KONG

### Country Background

Captain Charles Elliot secured Hong Kong Island for England after the Opium War with China in 1841. At the time, Hong Kong was mainly a barren rock, but it was surrounded by a perfect natural harbor. In 20 years, Hong Kong became the center of a thriving opium trade from India. Opium was the major Western export to China. Actually, the Opium War was fought over the right to sell opium to China. The Chinese rulers did not want to allow the British to sell the drug in China. Britain won the war, and with it, the right to expand its opium trade. The British first annexed Stonecutter's Island (Hong Kong Island) and then Kowloon, the community on the other side of Hong Kong Island, in 1860. Today, the two sides are connected by subway, bridges, and the Star Ferry.

In 1898, the Chinese rulers were forced to lease Hong Kong, Kowloon, and the area of the New Territories to the British for 99 years. The British considered the lease a gift; they did not pay any rent. For the Chinese, however, 99 years is a short period in history. In 1997, the Chinese reclaimed their rights to Hong Kong, and it reverted back to mainland China control. The PRC has frequently stated that Hong Kong will continue to function as it has for the past 50 years. Despite these reassurances, many people have their doubts that this will be true.

During World War II, Hong Kong was attacked by the Japanese. The colony surrendered on Christmas Day 1941. The Japanese occupied the area until August 1945. Many Hong Kong families were ruined, and their money converted to yen. After the war, the Japanese debts were discharged by the surrender treaty.

When the Communists took over mainland China in 1949, millions of refugees fled to Hong Kong. They came with the desire to get rich, or stay rich. By the 1980s, Hong Kong and the surrounding areas had become one of the world's wealthiest business centers. There are more Rolls Royces per capita in Hong Kong than anywhere else on earth.

I have spent more time in Hong Kong than in any other city in the world. The city has an excitement—and a smell—that is unique. What is a Hong Kong smell? Describing it is difficult, but forgetting it is impossible. Part of the smell is the harbor. Hong Kong, the city proper, is on one side of the harbor; Tsim Tsui (Kowloon) is on the other side. Both sides of the harbor are considered Hong Kong. The cultural center, the boardwalk, Regent Hotel, Golden Mile, and the Peninsula Hotel are all on the Tsim Tsui side. Mandarin Hotel, Pacific Place, Victoria Peak, and the Hong Kong race track are on the Hong Kong side. Going from one side to the other takes about one minute on the subway, and about five minutes on the Star Ferry.

Shopping is everywhere. Every block is filled with shops, intermixed with fancy hotels and department stores. In small shops, customers bargain for the best prices; in department stores, designer boutiques, and chain stores, the prices are set.

**Photo 16.3**
Wet markets are informal commercial sections that sell fresh fruits and vegetables. Vendors gather together to create a central place. Prices here are lower than in supermarkets or department stores. Products are not refrigerated. *Courtesy of the author.*

Hong Kong is one of the world's leading business and financial meccas. Many businesses have their Asian headquarters here. Hong Kong is also a major tourist destination. Groups of tourists from Japan, Taiwan, and other parts of Asia come to Hong Kong to shop. The average Hong Kong tourist spends $219 U.S. per day. Japanese tourists spend $345 U.S. per day. Over 50 percent of this expenditure is on shopping.[1] Electronics, clothes, and jewelry are sold at rock bottom prices with a vast selection.

Despite assurances by the mainland Chinese government that the free enterprise system will be allowed to continue in Hong Kong for 50 years, there is anxiety about the future. After the June 1989 crackdown on student protesters in Tiananmen Square, many Hong Kong residents had more reason to worry. However, the July 1997 transition was accompanied by fanfare and festivities, as many residents celebrated the end of British rule.

That is the background of Hong Kong. This history plays an important role in how retailing has developed in Hong Kong. It will also affect what will happen in the future.

Hong Kong is a dazzling, confusing, and very exciting place to shop. Take one turn off a major street and you are likely to encounter snake skins dangling from a shop's ceiling and live sea creatures looking at you from water tanks. In sharp contrast are the major global retailers who have locations in Hong Kong. Nearly every major designer label has a shop here. Toys "Я" Us, IKEA, Footlocker, and Benetton have stores scattered throughout Hong Kong.

## Independent Retailers

Open air markets exist for a variety of merchandise. These markets can be an eye-opening experience for Western shoppers. I took my son with me on one of my trips

**Photo 16.4**
Wing On is one of the major department stores in Hong Kong and one of three department store groups (the other two are Sincere and Shui Hing) that was originated and is currently owned by Hong Kong Chinese. The store has remained under Kwok family management since the late 1800s. *Courtesy of the Wing On Corporation.*

to Hong Kong. I had often heard about the jade market, but had never been there. This seemed like an interesting adventure for my son. We took a taxi to the open air market. Arriving a little before the jade market had opened, we took a stroll around the area. Live chickens squawked in cages, live snakes hissed at us from open air pits. We were the only Caucasians in the area. No one spoke English, and we did not speak Chinese.

Then the doors to the jade market opened. This area was covered with a roof, but with only a metal cage around the vendors. We approached a vendor just completing his setup. We were the only customers in the market. I picked up a jade necklace and inquired the price. The vendor did not speak English, but we communicated in the universal shopping language. He held up a calculator and offered a price, first in Hong Kong dollars, then in the U.S. equivalent. It was about $100 U.S. I shook my head and walked away. The man pursued me, clicking out another price on the calculator, $75. I shook my head and walked away. He came after me again, this time pounding out a price of $50. I really was not interested in the necklace and tried to indicate that the price was not the issue. I believed this would stop him. My son was becoming quite upset at this point. He was only 10 years old and did not like this man hassling his mother. The man did not stop; on the next approach, he grabbed my arm and started dragging me back to his stand. He presented the necklace to me again to examine. He then tapped out his price, $20, a steal. Unable to imagine why he had dropped the price so low, I bought the necklace. Later, when talking to a Chinese friend, I found out why the vendor gave me such a great deal. Some Chinese vendors are very superstitious. They believe that their first customer of the day determines how their day's sales will go. To lose a first customer is a bad omen. The vendor offered to sell me the jade necklace at a loss to make sure he got this first sale. Likewise, many vendors believe that their last sale of the day is an omen for the next day's sales. My advice to shoppers is therefore to go early or come late when shopping in the open air markets.

These are the more exotic markets. There are also major shopping centers and shopping districts with full-scale department stores, which are either Chinese or Japanese owned. They carry designer brands, regular national brands, and private label merchandise, all of which are sold at a fixed price.

## Organized Retailing in Hong Kong

As the most competitive retail market in Asia, Hong Kong is home to some of the most powerful retailers on the continent. Dairy Farm and Hutchison Whampoa reign in the food area; Baleno, Espirit, and Giordano star in apparel. All these retailers have expanded throughout Asia. Dairy Farm is particularly well known for the development of convenience stores throughout the area. Foreign retailers in Hong Kong include Jusco (Japan) in general merchandise.

Many retailers, primarily Japanese, have viewed Hong Kong as an assessable laboratory where they can learn how to sell successfully to the Chinese. Their strategy is to start there, where the market is wide open, and then move to mainland China, where the greatest opportunities in the world exist. At one point Japanese department stores in Hong Kong controlled more than 50 percent of the market. Rivalry from Japanese department stores made the industry much more competitive. There have been some changes in the past few years.

Isetan, a Japanese department store, has shifted their focus to mainland China and exited Hong Kong. Seibu, another Japanese department store, opened a spectacular store in Pacific Place, on Hong Kong Island, in 1990. Although the store still has the Seibu name outside, it is now licensed to Dixon Concepts, a retail group that runs many of the luxury specialty stores in Hong Kong. During the 1990s many stores closed because of the spiraling rents. Mitsukoshi closed a store in Tsim Sha Tsui when the landlord wanted to triple the rent. Mitsukoshi exited Hong Kong in 2006, ending 25 years of operating there. Seiyu (Japan) and Ito-Yokado (Japan) operate mass merchandise outlets in Hong Kong. By 1999, rents fell 10.1 percent, reversing the out-of-control rent increases.[2]

During the early years of the 2000s, the number of supermarkets, hypermarkets, and convenience stores increased significantly. However, some outlets of Chinese-style/local department stores, such as Sincere, Wing On, CRC, and Yue Hwa were closed during this time period. The number of department stores in Hong Kong is expected to continue to decrease. Carrefour, the sole hypermarket operator, left the market in 2000. The SARS epidemic of 2003 wiped out many retailers because people stayed home in an attempt to avoid exposure.

Internet retailing has not been very popular in Hong Kong; only 4 percent of Internet users have made an online purchase. Internet sales did peak briefly during the SARS outbreak. Admart was an attempt to break into the Internet market in Hong Kong, but they closed in 2000, leading most retailers to believe that Internet sales are never going to be successful. One explanation for this is the abundant shopping alternatives available to consumers throughout the city.[3]

The leading retailer in Hong Kong is Watson & Co, owned by Hutchison Whampoa, the largest retail group in Hong Kong. Watsons operates the leading supermarket chain, ParknShop, the leading drug store, Watsons, and the leading electrical goods chain, Fortress. Dairy Farm, owned by Jardine Matheson Holdings Ltd, is the second-largest retail group. It operates 7-Eleven convenience stores, Hong Kong's leading convenience store chain and also operates Wellcome, the drugstore chain. Mannings. Dairy Farm is also the franchisee of the four IKEA stores in Hong Kong.

Jusco is the third-largest retailer in Hong Kong. It is a middle-to-low-end department store/mass merchandiser from Japan. China Resources Enterprises Ltd (CRE) is the fourth-largest retailer in Hong Kong; it is a state-owned enterprise of Mainland China. CRE operates a major supermarket chain, CRC Shop, a Chinese medicine chain, CRCare and department store chains, and Chinese Arts and Crafts.[4]

Two supermarket giants, ParknShop and Wellcome, began to aggressively open supermarkets in Hong Kong, each larger than 2,000 square meters.

The Chinese department stores in Hong Kong have a European or American flavor. The opposite is true in Taiwan. Taiwan's Chinese-owned department stores are more oriented to Japanese-style merchandise and layout. In Hong Kong, stores do not use consignment; they use professional buyers, like the United States. Taiwan's department stores, in contrast, use consignment and have either inexperienced buyers or no buyers at all.

**Photo 16.5**
Much of Hong Kong is built on steep hills. This shopping street threads through a busy pedestrian area. Stores extend beyond their structures, capturing part of the busy sidewalk. *Courtesy of the author.*

## › TAIWAN[5]

### Country Background

Taiwan's earliest inhabitants were non-Chinese aborigines. Taiwan became a protectorate of the Chinese Empire in 1206, although migration from the mainland began only in the seventeenth century. The first Chinese immigrants came from the Guangdong and Fujian provinces to escape persecution. Beginning in the 1400s, large numbers of Chinese immigrated from Fujian Province. At that time Taiwan was a prefecture of Fujian Province.

Europeans arrived in the 1500s. The Portuguese explored the area in 1590, calling it Beautiful Island (Isla Formosa). The Dutch, who came in 1624, set up forts on the island. Then Spaniards arrived in the north. In 1641, the Dutch threw the other foreigners out and controlled the island for the next 20 years. By this time, the Ming dynasty of mainland China had been conquered by the Qing dynasty, and the defeated Ming fled to Taiwan. The Ming immigrants soon expelled the foreigners and took the island for their own. Their rule was brief. The Qing dynasty took control of the island in 1683 and held it until 1895. At that time, the island was given to Japan as a result of China's defeat in the Sino-Japanese war. Japan developed and exploited the island, and locals were forced to serve in its army during World War II. After the war, the island was returned to the mainland Chinese.

By 1949, a civil war was raging on the mainland of China. The war was fought between the Nationalists (Kuomintang) led by Chiang Kai-shek, and the Communists led by Mao Zedong. When the Nationalists were defeated, Chiang and more than 1.5 million of his followers took boats across the Formosa Straits to Taiwan. A fleet of U.S. army boats prevented the Communists from pursuing the Nationalists.

The Nationalists, known in Taiwan as the KMT, crushed local organizations, suppressed dissidents, and ruled under martial law until 1986. Chiang was president of the Republic of China (Taiwan) until he died in 1975. He always maintained that he would return to the mainland. His wish was for the two Chinas, the People's Republic of China (mainland) and the Republic of China (Taiwan), to be united. Upon Chiang's death, his son assumed control and began taking greater steps toward a freer country. Martial law was ended in 1987 and a new representative assembly elected at the end of 1991.[6]

### Informal Markets

One of my former graduate students served as my tour guide on my first trip to Taiwan. He took me to a night market, an amazing experience. In one club a gorilla sat on the bar. At an auction, we saw snake blood from a recently slaughtered reptile up for bid. Only men were interested in bidding; they viewed the snake blood as an aphrodisiac, likely to enhance their sex lives. The winning man downed his drink, very happy with himself.

I had told my graduate student that I would like to buy some counterfeit watches to give as gifts. He knew exactly where to go. We approached a street market vendor, and he told her what we wanted. She indicated that we should follow her through a dark alley and up a set of dimly lit stairs. She opened the door to a room filled with watches. One table contained "Rolexes," another had "Cartier." She said something to my student and he translated: "She says that you should look for the watches that say 'waterproof' on the backside, because they are better watches." I said, "For heavens' sake, we're buying counterfeit watches; what makes you think that the stamp on the back is legitimate?" I declared the watches in customs on my arrival back home, the authorities thought that they were so obviously fake that they didn't even care if I brought them back in. Actually they were very good watches, probably had a Timex system, and I wore them for a long time.

## Retailing in Taiwan

On my first trip to Taiwan I stayed at the best hotel there, the Imperial. That night I called my Japanese colleague to discuss our future research. Whenever I said something slightly negative about Taiwan, I was cut off. I redialed my Japanese colleague and began the conversation again, only to be cut off when I criticized Taiwan. I finally called the front desk and asked what was going on. They referred me to the operator, who told me that I had talked for five minutes and that was considered sufficient. I then realized that they were listening to my telephone conversation.

Taiwan has lost many good managers to PRC. Several retailers I talked with mentioned that the person in charge of their buying was from Taiwan. The government implemented the Challenge 2008 scheme, a comprehensive six-year attempt to transform the Taiwan economy. The idea is to make Taiwan the centerpoint of new development by boosting economic growth and environmental protection.

In 2001, Taiwan was overcome with new shopping centers. Within two years the small island was inundated with new shopping areas, and now is overretailed. Still independents, those retailers who are not associated with a chain accounted for 72 percent of retail sales.[7]

Uni-President Enterprises is the leading retail group in Taiwan. The company controls 45% of 7-Eleven, the country's largest convenience store chain, and 40% of Carrefour, the country's leading hypermarket chain. The second-largest retailer is Shin Kong Mitsukoshi Department Store, the most important department store and the most productive.

The Far Eastern Group acquired Pacific Liutong Investment Company to become the major shareholder in SOGO. When I first visited Taiwan in 1987, Sogo department store had just opened in Taipei. The major department store groups were beginning to seek professional assistance from the only professional retailers they knew, the Japanese. I remember being at Sogo at closing, and typical of a Japanese department store, all the employees came to the escalators at closing time and bowed and bid farwell to the customers as they left. Other department stores were scrambling to replicate the modern professional atmosphere created by this Japanese giant. Far Eastern Group includes the Far Eastern Department stores, Ya Tung Department Store Company, Far Eastern Geant Company and Pacific Sogo Department stores.[8]

Unlike Hong Kong, Internet shopping and home shopping are thriving in Taiwan. Home shopping is the second-largest and second-fastest growing alternative shopping channel. Home shopping grew over 20 percent between 1999 and 2003. Internet retailing grew an average of 160 percent per year. These are fantastic growth rates. The success of home shopping has transformed the retailing scene in Taiwan. Many companies have started including catalogue shopping in their existing operations.

**Photo 16.6**
Masked shoppers walk
past the Sogo department
store in Taipei, 10 May
2003. Taiwan's leading
department store Sogo said
it would close for three
days for disinfection amid
the SARS epidemic after
one of its cashiers was
believed to have come
down with the deadly virus.
AFP PHOTO/Sam YEH
(*Courtesy SAM
YEH/AFP/Getty Images*)

Many of these catalogues are distributed through convenience stores, the fastest-growing retail format in Taiwan. Like in Japan, customers place orders, pay for, and pick up merchandise at the convenience store.[9]

Since the liberalization of foreign investment in the retail industry in 1986, modernization of the industry has accelerated. Rubbing shoulders with world class retailers always has a positive effect on local retailers. The first wave of foreign investment was limited to department stores such as Sogo, but the second wave of investment which occurred after 1996 was more diverse. Hypermarkets were introduced by Makro (a joint venture between SHV Holding and Holsgreen Holdings

Taiwan), Carrefour (a joint venture between Carrefour SA and Uni-President Enterprises), Geant (a joint venture between Casino Group and Far Eastern Group), and B&Q (a joint venture between Kingfisher Plc and Test Rite Group). Despite the infusion of foreign retailers to Taiwan the local heavyweights still control the market, albeit through collaborations with foreign companies.[10]

Small independent shops were everywhere. These specialists still account for 87 percent of retail sales. Streets were jumbled, and moving from one place to another took an immense amount of time. McDonald's was one of the very popular restaurants. The small shops sold expensive, low-quality merchandise. The department stores sold Japanese-style clothes, protectively wrapped so that consumers could not spoil the merchandise. Salespersons in department stores lounged on merchandise, ignoring consumers. I had not yet been to mainland China, but later I was to recall the experience of shopping in Taiwan's department stores as being one step up from the mainland Chinese stores. If I were to make a continuum, it would look like this:

Hong Kong—————————————————Taiwan————PRC

Department stores are still the most important channel in mixed retailers; they have about 9 percent of total retail sales and 26 percent of mixed retailer sales. The second and third most important channels are convenience stores and hypermarkets. Both types of outlets are dominated by two major chains. President Chain Store Corporation is the leading retailer in Taiwan. They have the 7-Eleven chain, which has 50 percent of the convenience store market. Presicarre Corporation with its partner Carrefour is the second major retailer, having 36 percent of the hypermarket business. Shin Kong Mitsukoshi Department Store is the third-largest retailer and the best performing department store retailer. This joint venture with the Japanese giant offers a Japanese-styled department store chain with offerings that follow Japanese trends. They have been expanding rapidly, appealing to the higher-end and middle market in Taiwan. Pacific Sogo Department Store is the second-largest department store chain in Taiwan and the fourth-largest retailer in the country. Before Shin Kong Mitsukoshi Department store entered the market, they were the dominant department store chain. Sogo entered the market in 1986 but the competition from Mitsukoshi lead to Pacific Sogo accumulating debts amounting to 81 percent of its assets. They were forced to sell to Far Eastern Group, who now runs the company.[11]

## Government Regulations

In January 2003 the Taiwanese government banned stores from providing free plastic shopping bags to customers. It was the second stage of an environmental policy; the first stage banned plastic shopping bags in government-run stores. The third stage will require that plastic bags be banned in general. There has been strong opposition to this ban.

The Council of Labor Affairs has implemented a number of regulations to improve working conditions. In 2003, an eight-week flexitime policy was implemented. This law requires that standard working hours are eight hours per day for a 6-day week. Employees may not work more than four hours paid overtime a day. Employees are given the option of accumulating hours of work in an eight-week period and combining days off to have an extended weekend or rest period.[12]

## › FUTURE OF THE OVERSEAS CHINESE

Hong Kong and Taiwan will have a major impact on retail operations in mainland China. In each community, foreign retailers, primarily the Japanese, have been testing their retail formats, adjusting their business strategies to bring them in line with what is needed in the larger market, the People's Republic of China. Over the years, I have talked with retailers in Hong Kong about their relationship with the PRC. In the early 1980s, most businesspeople indicated that they did not anticipate much change occurring when Hong Kong reverted to Chinese rule in 1997. After Tiananmen Square in 1989, the view was very different. Many major retailers changed their country of domicile from Hong Kong to other countries, such as Bermuda. Others changed their Hong Kong passports to foreign passports if they had the opportunity.

In the years since Tiananmen Square, the views have softened. Some major retailers who vowed never to enter the mainland market after their stores were confiscated in the 1950s have been courted by the PRC government. The opportunity presented by the vast population of the PRC, combined with relatively weak competition, has made expansion there very attractive for major Hong Kong retailers.

I visited Hong Kong just four months before the July 1, 1997, turnover to China, staying for a week before going on to Shanghai and Beijing. I had expected more change to occur in Shanghai and Beijing than in Hong Kong. I was right. Hong Kong has become a bit duller and Shanghai has become brighter. Shanghai is the new Hong Kong. The interesting and exotic shopping environment I first encountered in Hong Kong is now evident in Shanghai.

## › KEY TERMS

CIRCULAR THINKING
LINEAR THINKING

## › DISCUSSION QUESTIONS

1. Japanese department stores have been very successful in the Hong Kong and Taiwanese markets. Are they successful because they are Japanese? If not, how can you explain this success? Recently, the Japanese department stores have left Hong Kong. Would you expect a similar departure from Taiwan? Why?
2. How do Chinese cultural values help to explain the differences between retailing in overseas Chinese enclaves and Japan?
3. In many parts of Hong Kong and Taiwan, prices are not fixed; buyers and sellers negotiate prices. This does not happen in Japan. Recall the discussion of retailing in developing countries in Chapter 5. When do markets become more formal?

## › ENDNOTES

1. *Statistical Review of Tourism.* (1988). Hong Kong: Hong Kong Tourist Association, p. 41.
2. Retailing in Hong Kong. (2004). GMID Euromonitor, April.
3. Retailing in Hong Kong. (2004).
4. Retailing in Hong Kong. (2004).
5. Adapted and reprinted by permission from Chang, L. D., and B. Sternquist (1993). "Taiwanese Department Stores Industry." *International Journal of Retail & Distribution Management,* Vol. 21, No. 1, pp. 26–34.
6. *Craighead's International Business.* (1996). Detroit: Gale Research.
7. Retailing in Taiwan. (2004). GMID Euromonitor, May
8. Retailing in Taiwan. (2004).
9. Retailing in Taiwan. (2004).
10. Retailing in Taiwan. (2004).
11. Retailing in Taiwan. (2004).
12. Retailing in Taiwan. (2004).

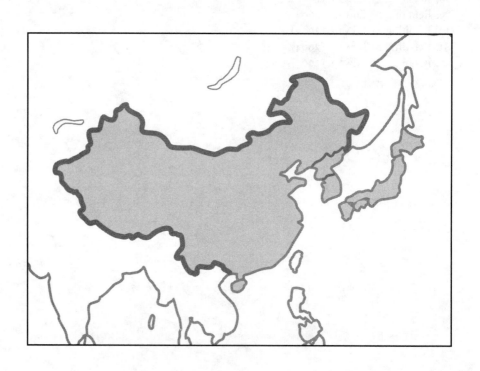

# 17

# RETAILING IN THE PEOPLE'S REPUBLIC OF CHINA

## After reading this chapter, you should understand

> How a planned economy handles the distribution of products.

> How the retailing system in the People's Republic of China (PRC) is similar to distribution in the central and Eastern European countries before marketization.

> The role of state-owned stores in the PRC and how the distribution process has changed since market reforms.

> The rules regulating foreign joint ventures in the PRC and how this affects foreign retailers operating in China.

In this chapter, I will outline how retailing was conducted in China before market liberalization, followed by a discussion of the current retail system. Although foreign retailers are interested in entering this huge market, most are worried about control still exercised by the central government. This is cause for concern. In the last section of this chapter, I will focus on the PRC's joint venture laws and their implications for foreign retailers.

## › COUNTRY BACKGROUND

It is easy to forget that Communism in the People's Republic of China (PRC) is a relatively recent phenomenon in the span of Chinese history. China has a vibrant commercial past. Since the days of Marco Polo, China has been sought as a trading partner by Western nations. Endowed with tremendous riches in natural resources and artistic expression, it was and is a country with tremendous market appeal.

Around the middle of the Ming dynasty (1368–1644) China's economy, consisting of agriculture and the handicraft industry, operated under a capitalist system. The silk and cotton industries were prosperous in southeastern China. Thousands of textile and cotton workshops blossomed, utilizing low-cost labor, and the beginning of a class system emerged. Rather than encouraging these capitalistic enterprises as had its Ming predecessors, the succeeding Qing dynasty (1644–1911) instead placed limits on the size of factories and imposed high taxes on merchants. The Qing dynasty also pursued a closed-door policy to foreign trade, discouraging Chinese merchants from seeking foreign markets. This desire for isolation was reflective of a historical desire for self-sufficiency. The only port the Qing dynasty kept open was Guangzhou, where tea, silk, medicine, and porcelain were traded for woolens, cotton textiles, and spices. Trade was unbalanced, favoring the Chinese exports. British colonialists demanded that China purchase additional British products, or more specifically one prize product of the British, opium. When China refused to cooperate by refusing to legalize the opium trade, the British threatened military force. The Treaty of Nanjing (1842) concluded the first Opium War with Great Britain. China agreed to open the port of Shanghai and four other ports to Western trade. American and West European businesses set up shop in Shanghai. The architecture of the Bund district in Shanghai reflects this European influence.

By 1860, following the second Opium War and a second round of treaties, China had deteriorated into a colonial society. The government was powerless to stop foreign land grabbing and to protect the rights of its citizens. In 1868, a sign posted over the entrance to a new municipal park in Shanghai was a testimony to China's deterioration; the sign read, "No admittance for dogs and Chinese." Thousands of gambling houses, opium dens, and brothels had emerged in the city. It was a mecca for American and European investors. Prosperity was not limited to foreigners. A ruling merchant class of Chinese also emerged.

In the late-nineteenth and early-twentieth centuries, most foreign goods gained acceptance through constant advertising in the modern media. About 200 foreign-owned newspapers and magazines were published in China throughout the nineteenth century. The Chinese publishing giant Commercial Press launched 16 magazines between 1903 and 1937. Radio broadcasting in China dates to 1922. In 1927, the Sun Sun Company, a Shanghai department store, established a station that broad-

**Photo 17.1**
The Shanghai Wing On department store as it appeared in the early 19th century. The owners were Chinese immigrants who went to Australia and then returned to China to open a retail store. In the 1950s, when all commercial property was being converted to state ownership, the store was taken over by the government. *Courtesy of the Wing On Corporation.*

casted market news, current events, and Chinese music. By 1936, Shanghai had 36 Chinese-run stations. Massive department stores with names such as Sincere, Wing On, and Shui Hing sprouted up on Nanjing Road, the major shopping boulevard. These luxury stores were parallel to Macy's and Gimbels in New York and Harrods in London.

The division between the moneyed entrepreneurs and the working class broadened. Starvation, prostitution, and opium addiction were prevalent. The Bund, the beautiful boulevard in Shanghai that surrounds the harbor, was strewn each morning with corpses. China was troubled with civil strife from 1921, leading to civil war. During the first civil war the two major political groups, the Nationalists and the Communists, agreed on a policy of strikes and boycotts that ultimately led to the dispossession of the propertied class and foreigners. During World War II, the two parties put aside their differences and cooperated in the fight against Japanese expansionism. But the end of the war brought renewed hostilities. Eventually, the Nationalists found themselves overpowered and left the mainland to form their own government, the Republic of China, which we know as Taiwan, on the island of Formosa.

On October 1, 1949, Communist leaders and 300,000 citizens gathered in Tiananmen Square, Beijing, to attend the ceremony that marked the formal beginning of the People's Republic of China (PRC). The government set a deadline of January 1956 for the transformation of private businesses to "whole people enterprises." Over the next five years, the state expropriated all of the major industries. The luxurious department stores such as Sincere, Wing On, and Shui Hing were taken over by the Communist government and their names changed to less descriptive terms, such as Number One Department Store and Number Two Department Store. The door between China and the West closed.

**Photo 17.2**
Number One Department
Store is located on nanjing
Road in Shanghai. The
company is the leading
department store in China.
*Courtesy of the Number
One Department Store.*

During the CULTURAL REVOLUTION, from 1966 until 1976, people in positions of authority—government officials, teachers, and managers—were persecuted. In essence the cultural revolution is just the opposite of what the term might seem. It was a period of time when people were encouraged to shun intellectualism and glorify the common man. People from privileged backgrounds were sent to work on farms to learn how to be humble. Families were separated. Eerie sameness, adopted by many as a survival tactic, settled in: everyone dressed alike, thought alike, and shunned anything intellectual. The overthrow of the counter-revolutionary group in late 1976 signaled the beginning of a new historical period in China. The Cultural Revolution was over and socialist modernization became the new focus. The policy line became "emancipating the mind, using the brain, seeking truth from facts, and unity to look forward." This is the paradigm of modern China.

Except for a brief retrenchment following the 1989 Tiananmen Square incident in which Chinese army troops confronted student demonstrators, killing an unknown number of protestors, China has continued to modernize at a very rapid rate. Foreign investment in China increased steadily throughout the 1990s and 2000s. This transition is important to understand so first we will look at what China was like before the reform.

## Before Market Reforms

China is a large and diverse country. Retail market reforms occurred first in the major special economic zones and cities before slowly spreading out to other areas.

I will discuss the retail industry before market reforms in some detail because in most parts of China, the system still exists today. Only in the more economically developed areas has rapid retail modernization occurred.

Beginning in the 1950s, retail sales in China were controlled by the Ministry of Commerce, now known as the Ministry of Domestic Trade. In the prereform system, modeled after the Soviet distribution system, products were categorized into three types. Category 1 included items vital to the national economy and people's livelihood, including products such as rice, cotton, coal, and fuel. The distribution of these products was monopolized by designated state-run units.[1] Category 2 included products such as bicycles, watches, sewing machines, and radios. Industrial ministries controlled the distribution of these products. Category 3 included merchandise considered nonessential; these products were controlled by provincial and municipal governments.

Under this system, known as FENPEI, distribution operated strictly as a case of allocation. The State Planning Commission decided on general production goals for the factories in China. The factories would then be allocated raw materials and told to produce the necessary products. After production, the goods would be shipped to the Ministry of Commerce Central Distribution Centers. In addition to the product orientation, China's distribution system used a three-tier wholesale structure. Three major distribution centers in Tianjin, Shanghai, and Guangzhou served many second- and third-tier distribution centers at the local level. Wholesalers and retailers were owned by the government and served within this allocation function not as market players, but as storage facilities for merchandise.

PRICE CONTROLS were determined on a municipal basis. For instance, Beijing and Shanghai might have different pricing systems based on their local economies and product abundance. This caused problems when I first started doing research in PRC. I would conduct interviews in Shanghai researching the regulated gross margin requirements, and then go to Beijing, where I would be told something completely different.

Originally, there were 146 products under government price control. In addition, 69 products had a REGULATED GROSS MARGIN; that is, the rate was stipulated by the government. Now, except for times of product scarcity, there are no regulated prices or regulated gross margins. The market is relatively free and is likely to continue as such.

This planning system and price controls could be justified when the PRC had an undersupply of merchandise, but they made less sense when merchandise shortages did not exist. During the 1980s, foreign manufacturing firms were allowed to set up joint ventures in China. These joint ventures provided upgraded production technology and product design. The undersupply situation was eliminated. Competition over product quality and efficient distribution prompted changes in the wholesale and retail distribution system.

Governments at the municipal level were given the right to set up and run wholesale activities. Large department stores were also permitted to purchase directly from manufacturers. The control of product pricing was deregulated. Prices could now be negotiated based on quantity ordered and various other considerations. By the late 1980s, China's distribution system contained a variety of wholesale and retail owners. By 1992, STATE-OWNED STORES accounted for just 41.3 percent of total retail sales. COLLECTIVES and private and individual enterprises made up 27.9 percent and 20 percent respectively.[2] By the end of 1995, the distribution was state-owned stores, 30 percent; collective owned, 19 percent; and individual, 30 percent. Joint venture sales in 1995 did not make up even 1 percent of sales.[3] China still has a system of state-owned enterprises albeit it is less important than 10 years ago.

### > RETAIL OWNERSHIP

The Chinese government, like other centrally planned economies, viewed distribution as a nonproductive business activity. In the chapter on Central and Eastern Europe I used the term "parasitic," meaning that it was not productive but rather sucked off resources. Rather than putting money into selling merchandise, it was believed that people should put their efforts into producing the products. As a result, the distribution system in PRC is still inefficient, but it is rapidly being modernized in major cities.

A striking contrast can be seen in how the Soviet Union and China have approached developing a market economy. In the Soviet Union, the political system was changed first. The removal of the Communist Party from power set the stage for transformation of the economic system. The result has been tremendous hardship, including consumer shortages and high inflation. In contrast, the PRC altered the economic system first, moving toward a free market before leaving the political security of a Communist/Socialist system. Unlike the Soviet Union, the PRC has had an abundant supply of merchandise and comparatively low inflation.

Previously, the PRC used a TWO-TIERED MONETARY SYSTEM, very common in planned economies before market liberalization. In the years before 1995, whenever I went to China I would trade my U.S. dollars for Foreign Exchange Certificates (FEC). These notes were printed in currency equivalent to the Chinese People's currency, or RMB. There were some places such as foreign hotels, fancy taxi cabs, and Friendship stores, where only FEC could be used. Some state-owned department stores had luxury floors, or sections of floors, where products could be purchased only with FEC. FEC was actually the preferred method of payment. If I took an inexpensive taxi, or purchased merchandise in a regular state-owned store, I could pay in FEC, but I would receive my change in RMB. I could use this RMB to purchase other merchandise in state-owned stores or ride in inexpensive taxis, but I could not use RMB in foreign hotels, or Friendship stores, or to pay for FEC taxis. Also, when I got ready to leave China, I could get U.S. dollars in exchange for my FEC money, but I could not redeem my RMB for anything. This led to several mad spending sprees in the airport shops prior to departure. Just before my trip in 1995, the dual monetary system was eliminated. Now, everything is priced in RMB, there are no foreign-currency-only stores, and all taxis accept RMB.

What makes China such an attractive market is the size of the population and the rapid economic growth that has occurred since marketization. China's retail sales of consumer goods increased 13 percent in 2005.[4] In a market of 1.4 billion people that translates into the biggest golden egg imaginable.

## Demographic and Geographic Markets

China has more than 30 cities with more than 1 million people, and another 40 cities with over 500,000 people. China's cities are populated with youth; two-thirds of the population are under 40. In the last few years the Chinese government has encouraged home ownership; about 60 percent of urban dwellers now own their homes. But these homes are small, averaging 50–80 square meters (538–860 square feet).[5]

China's GDP has been growing by 8.6 percent since 1994, with 2004's GDP more than double 1994's. This growth has been driving up retail sales of consumer goods by 12.7 percent per year over the last decade, and estimates are that it will increase 15–16 percent in 2006. There is a growing disparity between urban and rural areas in terms of income and consumption growth. In 2004, per capita urban income increased 3.2 times the growth in rural areas. Consumption in urban areas increased from 59 percent in 1994 to 66 percent in 2004, compared to a decrease in the share of rural consumption from 41 percent in 1994 to 34 percent in 2004. Rural people are consuming less of the total consumption dollar and urban residents are consuming more. However, part of this shift can be explained by a movement of people to cities. The natural population growth rate in China has been .8 percent over the last 10 years. Urban population growth rates average 4.7 percent due to population flows from the rural areas. Rural areas will continue to have poor growth rates primarily because of weak purchasing power and poor infrastructure, which translates into high distribution costs. This is a major disincentive for retailers in rural areas.[6] The banking system in China is undergoing reform also. These changes have a major impact on domestic investment in retailing.

## Financial Issues

China's national savings rate is about 40 percent, making it one of the highest of any country in the world. There is no national banking system and no national credit card verification system or payment network, so most credit is local. The closest thing is the Golden Card (Jin Ka) established in 1993. The adoption of this system has been slow and sporadic.

Most financial transactions are through debit cards. These cards can be used for cash deposit and withdrawal purposes as well as for paying retail accounts. These cards have replaced debit ATM cards in China.

Credit cards are becoming increasingly popular. In 2003 the number of credit cards increased 70 percent. The Great Wall card, China's first credit card, was launched in 1985 by the Bank of China. In 1987, the Great Wall became a member of Visa. It was only in 1988 that the first international credit card was issued in China. Even then credit cards did not really become popular, largely because few merchants accepted them. Chinese consumers continued to demonstrate a preference for cash.[7]

## › FOREIGN RETAILERS IN CHINA[8]

The PRC opened its doors to foreign joint ventures in manufacturing many years ago. But, as I have mentioned before, retailing is considered a nonproductive activity in planned economies. Thus, until 1991, foreign retail joint ventures were not allowed. Initially, the government announced that it would approve a limited opening of its retail sector for foreign investors on an experimental basis. Six cities (Shanghai, Beijing, Guangzhou, Tianjin, Qingdao, and Dalian) and five special economic zones (Shenzen, Zhuhai, Shantou, Xiamen, and Hainan) were designated as areas open to foreign retailers. Only two foreign joint ventures would be approved in each of the 11 areas, for a total of 22 foreign joint ventures with state (Beijing-level) approval.

The initial joint venture regulations included several other stipulations. First, the joint ventures could not be majority or wholly foreign-owned operations. Second, they could not be wholesalers. Third, although these state-approved joint ventures could import goods, these goods could not exceed 30 percent of their total sales. The joint ventures would also be required to pay any quotas and licenses if they imported merchandise. At that time, the two-tiered system of foreign exchange, which I described earlier, was still in effect. As a result, the joint ventures had to generate hard currency to pay for any imports. In effect, retailers would first have to produce merchandise, then export and sell it, to obtain currency needed to pay for imports.

These first 22 state approved joint ventures were equity joint ventures, where the partners share the risk. In Beijing, the Luthansa Shopping Center and Dong'an Shopping Center are the two state-council-approved foreign joint ventures. In Shanghai, there are four state-council-approved joint ventures because Shanghai encompasses both the city and the Pudan special economic zone.

A second type of joint venture is one that is locally (municipal level) approved. These ventures, approved by cities such as Beijing, Shanghai, and Guangzhou, have not received approval from the state council. In such cooperative joint ventures, the foreign firm provides all the money and management; the Chinese partner provides the location and local business knowledge. This system has changed since China made agreements to open the retail market in exchange for admission to the WTO.

## New Rules

Although it is helpful to know the history of regulation in China's retail sector because it helps you to understand the most recent change in legislature, it is important to know what the current situation is and how that will impact future retail activity. To meet its WTO commitments, China made a major change in the way it regulates foreign retailers. In 2004 there were over 300 foreign retailers operating in China; this number will likely skyrocket since the more recent liberalization. The central government ministries (MOFTEC and the State Planning & Development Commission) maintain controls on foreign retailers. Typically regional and local governments are delighted to have as much foreign investment as possible to boost their tax base and pay for infrastructure. The newest law covering retailing went into effect December 11, 2004. The Provincial Government needs to send foreign retailers' proposals to the Department of Commerce within one month. The Department of Commerce processes the application and notifies the applicant if the proposal was approved within three months. This is a greatly streamlined system over what had been used before.

The Provincial Government will be allowed to approve on their own 1) foreign investment for fewer than three stores if they are not more than 3,000 square meters each and there are not more than 30 stores total in the PRC owned by the foreign investor; and 2) foreign investment for fewer than 30 stores that are not more than 300 square meters each and not more than 300 stores total in the PRC owned by the foreign investor.[9]

China feels that there has been too much hypermarket development and they want to limit this growth. One of the government policies is to determine if a new retail offering is needed based on a market assessment. This should be a precautionary warning to any company interested in opening hypermarkets in China. The market is not as open or as liberal as you might have been led to believe.

The law also allows foreign retailers to engage in franchising. The foreign retailer has to operate two physical stores in China for one year before operating a franchise system. Companies using master franchise systems need special permission. And they have to have a proven business format to open a franchise. This is essentially the requirement in the United States. A few years ago, the China Chain Store and Franchising Association asked me to give a talk on franchising. This is pretty typical, and of course I said yes. When I told them that franchising was not a particular area of expertise for me, they said that was fine. In the weeks before this engagement I asked a variety of government officials about franchising law in China. No one seemed to know the actual situation. Eventually I found a government official who acknowledged that there was no franchising law in China, and that royalties could not be **EXPATRIATED**. Expatriated means that the money can be taken out of the country, or in this case it couldn't. When I arrived at the venue, I saw that I was a featured speaker at the China International Franchising Association meeting. I gave my talk and later milled around with many foreign companies who had booths in the basement area, trying to attract franchising opportunities. I asked them if they were aware that they could not expatriate profits; none of them knew this. But it didn't seem to diminish their interest in the China market. Sometimes dollar signs cloud your vision. The new Franchise Law passed in 2004 stipulates that profits can be repatriated.

Local competitors have benefited from governmental preferential treatment, primarily by gaining prime locations and having local knowledge. A domestic survey found that local retailers' average sales per square meter are about 70 percent higher than that of the foreign retailers in China.[10]

China still has elements of a planned economy, however. The ninth Five-Year plan focused on regulatory issues such as modernization of retail formats and ownership. The government's Tenth Five-Year plan highlights the development plans for retail chain operations. It contains the following areas:

> Encourage establishment of retail chains to invest in western China through acquisitions, joint ventures, franchising, mergers, and restructuring to consolidate resources and enhance inter-regional expansion.
> Include other businesses in the retail format which have not been the focus of previous plans e.g., 1) new industry includes pharmacies, tobacco, telecoms, and publishing; 2) new services includes property agents, tourism, education/training, car and commercial product rentals, and software development; 3) manufacturers will be encouraged to set up their own retail chains and distribution channels; and 4) development of fast-food chains will be accelerated.
> Embrace more retail formats by accelerating the development of fresh product supermarkets; understand the different formats of convenience stores in various geographical areas; rationally develop big general merchandise stores, professional stores, and specialty stores; restructure traditional department stores

and control the expansion of hypermarkets and warehouse stores by imposing stricter limits on numbers and retail area.

> Develop 5–10 retail chains via mergers, restructuring, and investment to establish them as brands that can compete with the international retailers. Provincial governments must eliminate all road blocks and support this move.
> Accelerate retail chain development by using various ownership/retail formats.
> Promote the development of commercial third-party logistics and distribution centers.
> Improve retail chains' operating efficiency and management quality with the most advanced management skills, point-of-sale systems, MIS, and other methods.
> Encourage local retail chains to learn the latest management and operating skills from foreign companies via different formats.

At the basis of this plan is also a commitment to four key policies: 1) implement regulations to meet WTO commitments; 2) adopt new policies to break away from protectionism; 3) develop training centers to enhance communication between the authorities and retailers; and 4) shift the emphasis from relying on good *GUANXI* to understanding the market and market positioning.[11] But things are always changing in China. As this book went to press the Chinese government announced some major changes. Read Box 17.1 to see the changes.

Tables 17.1 and 17.2 summarize the major domestic and international retailers in China.

A summary of the top foreign retailers' expansion plans is presented in Table 17.3.

I am going to take a moment to explain the concept of guanxi. Much of my research is on buyer-supplier relationships in China. When I started doing interviews on this topic in China I assumed that everyone would say that the personal connections of guanxi would be extremely important because nearly every lay article about doing business in China emphasizes this concept. However, I kept hearing just the opposite. CEOs and retail buyers told me that the days of using personal factors to get merchandise into a store were over. Most companies made every effort to keep their buyers from having a personal relationship with suppliers. They would even go so far as to fire a buyer that accepted gifts. We followed this up with a survey of buyers and found the same thing. It was role performance, not guanxi, that got a supplier on a retailer's shelf.

## Guanxi

Business *GUANXI* is defined as the process of finding solutions through personal connections.[8] I was interested in how this concept impacted the buying system so I conducted a survey; 98 buyers participated. About half of the buyers purchased food and about half purchased non-food. One quarter of the buyers had been in their current position one year or less. Fifty-four percent had been in their position two years or less. Over 80 percent had been in retailing 10 years or less. Seventy percent had been with their current company five years or less. Two-thirds were male and one third was female.

Three main ownership types were identified among participating retailers, namely, state-owned enterprise (SOE), 49.5 percent, privatized former state-owned enter-

**Box 17.1**
**Chinese Rules Could Tie Up Foreign Retailers**

**Proposals Might Add to Cost, Complexity of Building Big Stores**

*By Mei Fong*
*July 17, 2006; Page A6*

BEIJING—China is drafting new rules to regulate large-scale shopping outlets, which could impede the expansion plans of foreign retailers such as **Wal-Mart Stores** Inc. and **Carrefour** SA.

If the rules are finalized, they could raise costs and increase red tape for big retailers by requiring them to file detailed blueprints for proposed new outlets and hold public hearings on the impact on communities.

The rules are under review by China's cabinet, the State Council, and could be released later this year, according to an official at the Ministry of Commerce, which is drafting them. The proposed rules would apply to both foreign and local retailers. But some industry executives say they would be especially cumbersome for large foreign retailers, many of which have been planning major expansions since the liberalization of China's retail industry in early 2005.

Leo Yeung, director of retail services for China at real-estate firm Cushman & Wakefield, said the proposals would make foreign big-box retailers and investors in large malls "consider more carefully their expansion plans" into China's smaller cities and hinterlands.

Despite pilot projects, public hearings on zoning projects are a relatively new concept in China. And in practice, neighborhood committees and citizens' community groups have had little power fighting renewal projects, although they are starting to be more active.

The draft regulations could play to the advantage of local companies like Shanghai-based Lianhua Supermarket Co. and Beijing's **WuMart Stores** Inc. Many Chinese retailers have lobbied the government to address a perceived bias among local governments in favor of well-funded foreign retailers holding brand-name cachet. "We are not going to restrict the development of foreign investors in China," said Wang Yongping, secretary-general of the China Commercial Real Estate Union and a senior adviser to the Ministry of Commerce. "Instead, we just want a more balanced and scientific commercial layout. Foreign companies can no longer get special advantages from the government."

Details of the rules could still change. In their current form, they would consist of two parts, according to Mr. Wang and the Commerce Ministry official. Cities would be required to file detailed blueprints of their commercial plans, including plans for department stores, big supermarkets and other retail outlets in residential neighborhoods.

Retailers applying to build outlets larger than 10,000 square meters would be required to submit to a public hearing, much as they are required to do in some North American and European countries. The hearings would include regulators, industrial associations and academic experts as well as competitors and representatives of local residents.

Pilot public hearings have already been held in some cities since 2003. None has derailed any projects, and they aren't expected to in the future, said Mr. Wang. However, he said, the hearings could result in higher project costs if, for example, local governments require retailers to put in refinements, such as pedestrian tunnels to improve traffic.

Foreign retailers are reluctant to comment on the proposed regulations before details are formally made public. But privately some express concern. "The law is quite cleverly worded because it doesn't explicitly apply to foreign companies, but is based on size, which is where the foreign retailers specialize. So this is hurting them," said one foreign retail executive.

James Zimmerman, vice chairman of the American Chamber of Commerce in China, said in email response to questions that if the proposed regulations "have the effect of unreasonably and unfairly restricting foreign retailers from the market," then China might be setting up a nontariff barrier in violation of World Trade Organization rules, "and we therefore take exception."

*continued*

**Box 17.1** *Continued*

Todd Wang, a Shanghai-based spokesman for Carrefour, said he is aware of the draft rules, but says the company doesn't know the details of the contents. Executives for Wal-Mart couldn't be reached for comment. An official at Shanghai Brilliance (Group) Co., owner of major supermarket chains including Lianhua, welcomed the proposed regulation. "Foreign retailers are always enjoying special favor and treatment from local governments. But the government should protect the national companies better if they want us to grow strong," said the official.

China has gradually liberalized its retail regulations since its WTO entry in 2001. Last year, it ended rules requiring foreign retailers to form joint ventures with local partners, sparking a surge in expansion by foreign retailers. Wal-Mart announced plans to add about 18 stores to the 60 it currently operates in China; Carrefour has plans to add 12 stores to its existing 79. **Best Buy** Co., Germany's Metro Group AG, U.K.-based **Tesco** PLC, and Swedish retailers Ikea and **Hennes & Mauritz** AB also announced plans to open or expand in China.

The proposed regulations are also meant to curb waste, Chinese officials said. In recent years, some of the world's largest shopping malls have been built in China. But many have been unable to convert crowd traffic into robust sales, retail executives say.

If public hearings are effective, the proposed rules could also help preserve local neighborhoods, many of which are being demolished in China's quest to modernize swiftly, especially in preparation for major events such as the 2008 Beijing Olympics and the 2010 Shanghai World Expo. "In the past, the government was very keen to land large-scale projects," said Michael Hart, head of Shanghai research at real-estate consultant Jones Lang LaSalle. "It's refreshing to see concerns about neighborhood preservation."

—Ellen Zhu in Shanghai contributed to this article.

*Source:* Copyright 2006 Dow Jones & Company, Inc. All Rights Reserved

prise (PSOE), 11.1 percent, joint venture with foreign direct investment and domestic organic firm (FJV/ORG), 34.3 percent. Respondents from Shanghai, Wuhan, Beijing, and Guangzhou accounted for more than 70 percent of our sample. The remaining 18 percent span a wide range of locations from coastal cites such as Shantou to inner cities such as Xinjian. Forty-four percent indicated that 100 percent of their company purchases are made through a central buyer. Over 75 percent indicated that imported products accounted for less than 5 percent of what they sell. Their percent of profits from imports accounted for about the same amount.

Twenty percent of the buyers said that 100 percent of the merchandise they purchased could be returned to the supplier. Most of the buyers indicated that 85 to 100 percent of the merchandise they purchased could be returned. About half of the companies use a buying committee.

The following figures show the importance level of six aspects of guanxi among three groups of retailers. The measurement scale used is 1 = not an important factor for the business; 7 = very important factor for the business. We then compared the three types of ownership on buyer's importance rating of each aspect of guanxi. There were no significant differences in buyer's importance rating of each aspect of guanxi with their suppliers across the types of ownership structure. Buyers rated the importance of guanxi below the midpoint with one exception. The FJV/ORG group rated overall guanxi importance slightly above the midpoint. We asked the buyer to evaluate the importance of these role performance factors in general, not

**Table 17.1**
**China—Leading Domestic Retailers, 2004**

| | | Total Sales and Stores | | | | Global Rank and Penetration | | | Domestic Market | |
|---|---|---|---|---|---|---|---|---|---|---|
| Company | Primary Line of Trade | Net Sales ($US Mil) | % Chg Sales | Total Stores | 2004 Rank, Top 200 Retailers Worldwide | Single-country, Regional or Global? | Number of countries | | Share of total sales | Share of total stores |
| 1 Bailian Group | Supermarkets/Grocery Stores | 8,131 | 22.0% | 5,493 | 96 | Single Country | 1 | | 100% | 100% |
| 2 Gome Electrical Appliance | Consumer Electronics & Appliances | 2,885 | 34.0% | 228 | — | Single Country | 1 | | 100% | 100% |
| 3 Dashang | Supermarkets/Grocery Stores | 2,791 | 27.0% | 120 | — | Single Country | 1 | | 100% | 100% |
| 4 Suning Appliance Chains Group | Consumer Electronics & Appliances | 2,671 | 80.0% | 193 | — | Single Country | 1 | | 100% | 100% |
| 5 Beijing Hualian | Supermarkets/Grocery Stores | 1,933 | 18.0% | 68 | — | Single Country | 1 | | 100% | 100% |
| 6 Shanghai Yongle Electric Appliance Co. | Consumer Electronics & Appliances | 1,915 | 62.0% | 108 | — | Single Country | 1 | | 100% | 100% |
| 7 Shanghai Nongongshang | Supermarkets/Grocery Stores | 1,656 | 10.7% | 1,232 | — | Single Country | 1 | | 100% | 100% |
| 8 Beijing Wu-Mart Group Co. Ltd. | Hypermarkets/Supercenters | 1,604 | 56.2% | 608 | — | Single Country | 1 | | 100% | 100% |
| 9 Home World Group | Hypermarkets/Supercenters | 873 | 44.5% | 54 | — | Single Country | 1 | | 100% | 100% |

Sources: Retail Forward, company annual reports and published reports

**Table 17.2**
**China—Key Foreign Retailers, 2004**

| Company | Headquarters | Retail Sector | Primary Line of Trade | Global Rank and Penetration | | |
|---|---|---|---|---|---|---|
| | | | | 2004 Rank, Top 200 Retailers Worldwide | Single-country, Regional or Global? | Number of countries |
| Aeon Co., Ltd. | Japan | FDM | General Merchandise Stores | 19 | Global | 11 |
| Alimentation Couche-Tard | Canada | FDM | Convenience Stores | 99 | Global | 7 |
| Alticor/Amway | United States | FDM | Non-Store | 119 | Global | 80 |
| Amazon.com | United States | Homegoods | Non-Store | 111 | Global | 7 |
| Auchan Groupe | France | FDM | Hypermarkets/Supercenters | 18 | Global | 12 |
| Bertelsmann AG | Germany | Homegoods | Non-Store | — | Global | 22 |
| Carrefour Group | France | FDM | Hypermarkets/Supercenters | 2 | Global | 31 |
| China Resource Enterprises | Hong Kong | FDM | Supermarkets/Grocery Stores | — | Regional | 2 |
| Dairy Farm International Holdings Limited | Hong Kong | FDM | Convenience Stores | 162 | Regional | 8 |
| FamilyMart Co., Ltd. | Japan | FDM | Convenience Stores | 83 | Regional | 5 |
| Fast Retailing | Japan | Softgoods | Apparel Stores | 194 | Global | 3 |
| Hutchison Whampoa Limited | Hong Kong | FDM | Drug Stores | 77 | Global | 18 |
| IKEA AB | Sweden | Homegoods | Furniture & Home Furnishings | 44 | Global | 32 |
| ISETAN Company Limited | Japan | Softgoods | Department Stores | 120 | Regional | 6 |
| Ito-Yokado Co., Ltd. | Japan | FDM | Convenience Stores | 6 | Global | 17 |
| Kingfisher PLC | United Kingdom | Homegoods | DIY/Home Improvement Stores | 50 | Global | 9 |
| La Senza Corp. | Canada | Softgoods | Other Apparel Specialty Stores | — | Global | 18 |
| Lawson | Japan | FDM | Convenience Stores | 59 | Regional | 2 |
| Leroy Merlin | France | Homegoods | DIY/Home Improvement Stores | 112 | Global | 8 |
| Lotte Group | Korea, South | FDM | Department Stores | 58 | Regional | 2 |
| LVMH | France | Softgoods | Other Apparel Specialty Stores | 76 | Global | 56 |
| Mango | Spain | Softgoods | Apparel Stores | — | Global | 76 |
| Metro AG | Germany | FDM | Cash & Carries/Warehouse Clubs | 4 | Global | 29 |
| Otto Group | Germany | Softgoods | Non-Store | 61 | Global | 19 |
| President Chain Store Corp. | Taiwan | FDM | Convenience Stores | — | Global | 4 |
| Shinsegae | Korea, South | FDM | Discount Stores | 122 | Regional | 2 |
| SHV Holdings N.V. (Makro) | Netherlands | FDM | Cash & Carries/Warehouse Clubs | 163 | Global | 9 |
| Takashimaya Company, Limited | Japan | Softgoods | Department Stores | 84 | Global | 5 |
| Tengelmann Warenhandelsgesellschaft | Germany | FDM | Supermarkets/Grocery Stores | 23 | Global | 15 |
| Wal-Mart Stores, Inc. | United States | FDM | Hypermarkets/Supercenters | 1 | Global | 11 |

Sources: Retail Forward, company annual reports and published reports

**Table 17.3**
**Top Foreign Retailers' Announced Expansion Plans**

| Company | Number of stores in China in 2004 | Announced Expansion Plans |
|---|---|---|
| Carrefour | 62 | Champion currently has 8 stores in Beijing and aims to increase this to 40–50 stores in Beijing by 2008 (about 15 new stores per year)<br>Champion will focus on fresh food<br>Carrefour plans to add 4 new stores in Shenzhen in 2006<br>In the next 3 years, Carrefour plans to open 2 or 3 new hypermarkets per year in Guangzhou and 3 or 4 new stores in Hubei |
| Trust Mart (Haoyouduo) | 88 | Trust Mart is seeking a main board listing in Hong Kong<br>Its 2006 target is to reach 100 stores in total |
| Wal-Mart | 43 | Currently has 52 stores in China, and plans to add 6 more by the end of 2005<br>Aims to open 13 new stores in 2006<br>Strategy is to focus on second-tier cities |
| Parkson | 30 | To add 50-60 new stores in the next 4 years by acquisition from its parent and organic growth<br>Strategy is to focus on second-tier cities |
| Lotus | 41 | Aims to reach 100 stores in total in next 2 to 3 years |
| Hymall (Legou) | 31 | Aims to open 10 new stores by 2006 |
| Jinjiang METRO | 23 | Aims to add 40 new stores within the next 3 to 5 years |
| McDonald's | 600 | Aims to add 100 new stores per year |
| Ito-Yokado | 5 | Aims to open 10 new stores in Beijing by 2007<br>Aims to have 12 general stores in total by 2008 (four of which will be in Chengdu)<br>Aims to have 20 hypermarkets in total by 2009 |
| ParknShop | 31 | Aims to add 17 new stores through acquisition from parent and organic growth |
| B&Q | 21 | Targeting 40 stores by 2008, 80 stores by 2009 |
| IKEA | 2 | Aims to add 2 new stores per year to reach a total of 10 stores by 2010 |
| 7-Eleven | 198 | Aims to have 350 stores in Beijing by the 2008 Olympic Games |
| Best Buy | n.a. | May seek acquisition opportunities to enter China<br>Plan to open first store in Shanghai in next 12 months |
| Medicine Shoppe | n.a. | 2008 target is to open 500 stores in China |
| HOLA | n.a. | Aims to have 80 stores in total by 2008 |

*Source:* Various public sources

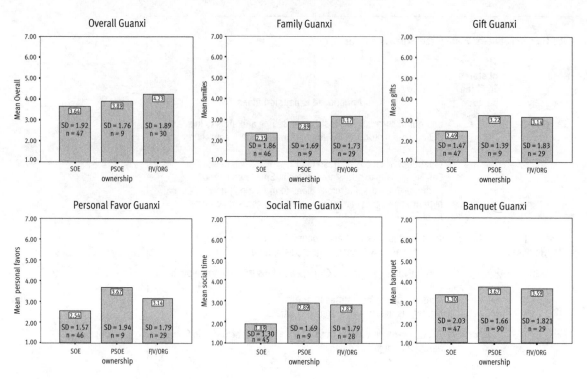

**Figure 17.1**
Six Aspects of Guanxi
Among Retailers

just in relationship to the supplier being evaluated. We measured importance on a 7 point scale with 7 being extremely important. In the following summary we report how many buyers considered the role performance factor as a 6 or 7 on the 7 point scale. In other words how many felt that the dimension was very to extremely important.

1. Product quality (89 percent)
2. Reasonable margin (66 percent)
3. Unique products (65 percent)
4. Delivery of goods (63 percent)
5. Well known/respected brand (62 percent)
6. Level of advertising support (48 percent)
7. Level of slotting fees (33 percent)
8. Level of yearly rebates (39 percent)

Financial assistance provided by suppliers such as slotting fees, yearly rebates, and advertising support were the least important.

These buyers told us about their buying system, process for evaluating new products and vendors, and important features for determining satisfaction with their suppliers. The following are the key points:

> Most of the organizations in the survey use central buying.
> Most merchandise can be returned to the supplier if it does not sell.

> Buyers have little experience in their current position.
> Buyers had little experience with the supplier they were evaluating.
> Product quality, reasonable margin, unique products, good delivery, and well-known brand name were important in selecting a supplier.
> Advertising support, slotting fees, and yearly rebates were much less important.
> Trust, buyer dependence on supplier, supplier dependence on the buyer, and long-term orientation were not significantly different among the three types of ownership.
> The use of guanxi was not indicated to be of great importance, although it was indicated to be of greater importance for FJV/Org than for other types of businesses.
> Market orientation is not significantly different among the three types of ownership structure.

We have focused our discussion on the three types of ownership structure. This type of categorization did not produce any significant findings, leading us to conclude from this preliminary data that the major differences in buyer-supplier relationships are not based on the three types of ownership, but other considerations. This is an important finding, since much Western literature has focused on the perceived weakness of state-owned enterprises or those that are newly privatized. If our results are representative of the industry as a whole the retail state-owned enterprises have been quick in adapting a market based organizational structure. Adopting an organizational structure, however, does not necessarily mean that it has been successfully implemented. Further analysis of this data should help us to determine the results of market implementation.

There are few national brands in China. Most companies operate locally or regionally. Double taxation is another key barrier to retailers expanding across provinces and cities. It is likely that the national government will intervene so that businesses can expand to other regions within China. In the next few sections I will discuss the various segments of retailing in China. The government has been encouraging the former state-owned enterprises to merge into bigger groups so that they can compete with the foreign multinationals. One positive outcome of this move could be the development of retailer brands that are distributed across China. China intends to promote the formation of five–ten national operators in the chain retail sector and further reduce the participation of the State. The government continues to meddle in the development of the retailing sector using town planning and restriction of shop numbers for hypermarkets and warehouse clubs. As part of the central government's Eleventh Five-Year Plan, which began in 2006, they are targeting economic development in second and third-tier cities. Expansion into these smaller cities will require a different kind of management from that in the major cities because the markets are very fragmented and dispersed. In this case the advantage, at least in the short term, will be to local players.[12] Table 17.4 contains a list of the top retailers in China.

I think the Chinese government made a bad call here. Size doesn't necessarily make a retailer more competitive, it is efficiency that matters. In the next section I will discuss the major retailing segments, beginning with the biggest one, Food Retailers.

**Table 17.4**
**China's Top Retailers (2004)**

| Company | Sales (RMB mn) | Growth (%) | Number of stores | Growth (%) | Sales Ranking 2004 | Sales Ranking 2003 | Retail format | Ownership structure |
|---|---|---|---|---|---|---|---|---|
| Bailian Group | 67,627 | 22 | 5,493 | 25 | 1 | 1 | Dept. store/hypermarket/supermarket/convenience store | State-owned |
| Beijing Guomei Electrical Applicancs Group—GOME | 23,879 | 34 | 227 | 63 | 2 | 4 | Home appliances | Private enterprise |
| Dalian Dashang Group | 23,085 | 27 | 120 | 25 | 3 | 2 | Dept. store/supermarket | State-owned |
| Suning Electrical Appliances Chain Store Group | 22,108 | 80 | 193 | 30 | 4 | 8 | Home appliances | Private enterprise |
| Carrefour (China) | 16,241 | 21 | 62 | 51 | 5 | 6 | Hypermarket | Sino-foreign co-operation |
| Beijing Hualian Investment Holding | 16,000 | 18 | 70 | 13 | 6 | 5 | Dept. store/hypermarket/supermarket | State-owned |
| Shanghai Yongle Electrical Appliances | 15,849 | 62 | 108 | 71 | 7 | 12 | Home appliances | Sino-foreign co-operation |
| Jiangsu Suguo Supermarket | 13,880 | 45 | 1,345 | 16 | 8 | 11 | Hypermarket/supermarket/convenience store | Sino-foreign co-operation |
| Shanghai Nonggongshang Supermarket Group | 13,703 | 11 | 1,232 | 2 | 9 | 7 | Hypermarket/supermarket/convenience store/discount store | State-owned |
| Beijing Wumei Investment Goup | 13,277 | 56 | 608 | 17 | 10 | 13 | Hypermarket/supermarket/convenience store | Private enterprise |
| Sanlian Commercial Group | 13,256 | 24 | 254 | 26 | 11 | 9 | Home appliance | Private enterprise |
| Chongqing Commercial Group | 13,113 | 18 | 153 | 16 | 12 | 16 | Dept. store/hypermarket/supermarket/convenience store | State-owned |
| Haoyoudou Management Info. Service (Shanghai)—Trust Mart | 12,000 | 155 | 88 | 226 | 13 | 24 | Hypermarket | Sino-foreign co-operation |
| China Baiseng Food and Beverage Group | 11,869 | 26 | 1,400 | 27 | 14 | n.a. | Western fast-food chain | Sino-foreign co-operation |

| | | | | | | | |
|---|---|---|---|---|---|---|---|
| China Resources Vanguard | 11,014 | 7 | 476 | 2 | 15 | 10 | Hypermarket/supermarket | Sino-foreign co-operation |
| Jiangsu Five Stars Electrical Appliances | 9,379 | 84 | 120 | 25 | 16 | 23 | Home appliance | Private enterprise |
| Xinyija Supermarket | 8,500 | 44 | 58 | 26 | 17 | 17 | Hypermarket | Private enterprise |
| Wuhan Commercial Group | 7,859 | 12 | 39 | 26 | 18 | 14 | Dept. store/hypermarket/home appliances | State-owned |
| Jiangsu Wenfeng Dashijie Chain Store Development | 7,643 | 34 | 506 | 55 | 19 | 19 | Hypermarket/home appliances | State-owned |
| Wal-Mart (China) | 7,635 | 30 | 43 | 30 | 20 | 18 | Hypermarket | Sino-foreign co-operation |
| Yichu Lianhua(China) Chain Store Supermarket | 7,394 | 40 | 41 | 86 | 21 | n.a. | Hypermarket | Sino-foreign co-operation |
| Hefei Department Store Group | 7,300 | 26 | 49 | 32 | 22 | 36 | Hypermarket/supermarket/convenience store/home appliances | State-owned |
| Tianjin Jiashijie Chain Store Commercial Group | 7,225 | 37 | 69 | 41 | 23 | 21 | Hypermarket | Private enterprise |
| Jinjiang Metro Cash & Carry | 6,459 | 15 | 23 | 28 | 24 | 20 | Hypermarket | Sino-foreign co-operation |
| Shenzhen Renrenle Chain Store Commercial Group | 6,200 | 93 | 32 | 113 | 25 | 32 | Hypermarket/supermarket | Private enterprise |
| Wuhan Zhongbai Group | 6,088 | 35 | 330 | 15 | 26 | 26 | Dept. store/hypermarket/convenience store/home appliances | State-owned |
| Beijing Wangfujing Department Store Group | 5,871 | 23 | 15 | 36 | 27 | 25 | Dept. store | State-owned |
| Beijing Jingkelong Supermarket Chain Goup | 5,238 | 13 | 140 | 20 | 28 | 22 | Hypermarket/supermarket/convenience store | State-owned |
| Dongfang Jiayuan | 5,233 | 55 | 22 | 57 | 29 | n.a. | Home furnishing | Private enterprise |
| Qingdao Liqun Group | 5,105 | 49 | 512 | 61 | 30 | 30 | Hypermarket/convenience store | State-owned |

Source: China Chain & Franchise Association

## Food Retailers

In 1991, I visited my first state-owned supermarket. It had a casket-type meat freezer. I asked the store manager if many consumers had freezers. He said no, consumers purchased the meat frozen, took it home, and thawed it. In other words it was a novelty. Today, supermarkets have frozen food sections, selling ice cream, meats, fish, vegetables, and prepared local foods.

China's GDP's growth remained at 13.3 percent. The urban per capita income is 10,990 (US$1,390) for Guangzhou, the richest Chinese city; Shanghai is a little less than that.[13] There is a general observation that every retail format has some requirement of GDP growth. The requirements for supermarkets is a personal GDP of US $800 and convenience store GDP at US $3,000.[14] China reached the required GDP for supermarkets in 2001 but has not reached the level for convenience stores. My interviews with retailers support this conclusion. Most retailers told me that consumers did not differentiate pricing in supermarkets and convenience stores. They expected convenience stores to match the price of supermarkets. In more developed countries consumers realize that they are paying more for the convenience of not having to trek through a large store to get the products they needed; this is the convenience part.

In 1999, the number of hypermarkets was less than 100; however, since that time there has been an explosion of this format. Many domestic firms opened hypermarkets only to find that they could not match the competitive muscle of the foreign companies like Wal-Mart and Carrefour. As a result most of the domestic hypermarket businesses have closed, leaving the foreign competitors alone to fight it out.

Supermarkets have experienced an average growth of 16.7 percent. Two of China's biggest food retailers, Lianhua and Hualian, merged in 2003 into one state-owned company called the Bailian Group. With annual sales of $8 million, it is the biggest retail group in China. The government formed the group to achieve economies of scale, allowing them to compete with the foreign multinationals. Bailian was created from the Friendship Group (Owner of Lianhua Supermarkets), Hulian Group (the parent of Hualian Supermarket), Shanghai Yibai Group (the parent of Shanghai Number One Department Store), and Shanghai Material Group. The group has plans to build 35 shopping malls around the country. At the time of the merger Lianhua was the largest retailer in China, with over 2,000 stores, mainly supermarkets and convenience stores, but some hypermarkets also. Hualin is similar to Lianhua; they had over 1,200 stores at the time of the merger.[15]

Nonggongshang (NGS) is another major food retailer expanding outside their home market of Shanghai. Nonggongshang originated as an agricultural cooperative, known for their ties to the agricultural community, resulting in extremely high-quality produce. This company has a very military approach to training and management. I remember talking with the company's CEO while he explained their boot camp approach to integrating new employees into the organization. When you enter the company's corporate headquarters, you are saluted by a uniformed armed guard.

China's liberalization of the retail sector to 100 percent foreign investment at the end of 2004 has increased the competitive environment in supermarkets, hypermarkets, and convenience stores, often to the disadvantage of local players. Retail sales of consumer goods have grown about 10 percent per year for the last five years. Organized retailing has increased at a rate of 50 percent per year over this time period. Local supermarkets are being pressured to be more efficient to compete with foreign operators who are just now ramping up to their full potential. Beijing is about three years behind Shanghai.[16]

Foreign retailers have received special treatment from local government such as reduced taxes or prime retail locations to entice international retail names. This is likely to continue as the foreign companies expand into the second-tier cities. One advantage that local companies have over foreign ones is in the mergers and acquisition category. They have a better local knowledge and can judge which M&A targets would provide the greatest synergy and what locations have the best growth potential. There is some advantage in getting properties through mergers and acquisitions because it is less expensive to acquire than to build.

Foreign retailers in China have focused on hypermarket formats because they can forego the initial investment in distribution centers. Wal-Mart has two major distribution centers in China now. Carrefour and Wal-Mart entered China in the mid 1990s but were not profitable until 2003–2004. Foreign investors (Carrefour, Wal-Mart, and Metro) in China now rank in the top 10 retailers in the country. China opened the retailing sector to 100 percent foreign investment at the end of 2004. Metro increased its ownership in its Chinese retailing operations from 40 to 90 percent. Wal-Mart owns 65 percent of its Chinese retail operations and Carrefour owns 50–60 percent.[17]

Wal-Mart and Carrefour are the major foreign competitors in China. Carrefour has about twice the sales (RMB 7.8 billion) of Wal-Mart (RMB 3.7 billion), with 61 stores compared to Wal-Mart's 48.[18] However, Carrefour's increase in sales from 2003–2004 was 19 percent compared to Wal-Mart's 35.7 percent. Table 17.5 has a summary of the store distribution for the two chains. Wal-Mart has focused on a value for money proposition and has located in more peripheral areas of cities. Carrefour has focused on fresh produce and typically has locations within city centers. Interestingly, local companies have sort of divided into these two camps with Wumart following the price leader model of Wal-Mart and Lianhua being the fresh produce leader, similar to Carrefour.

In the chapter on Spain, Italy, and Portugal I discussed negative working capital, meaning that the company stretches the payment of inventory and uses that money for expansion. Of the three major local companies, Lianhua has the longest negative working capital (31 days) while Wumart has the highest multiple on a relative measurement basis (Table 17.6). The difference between the inventory days and the payable days is the negative working capital. In this case Lianhua has the longest with 31 days. If you divide the payable days by the inventory days, you get the ratio in the right-hand side. To further consider the use of negative working capital, look at Table 17.7. Both Lianhua and Wumart have franchised, but they have taken a slightly different strategy in the way they handle their franchise operations. Lianhua requires cash payment from their franchise outlets for merchandise purchased; Wumart allows them to buy through credit. Lianhua's extra sales to the franchisees could help Lianhua get a greater increase in supplier discount because of increased volume without having a negative impact on working capital. On the other hand, if Wumart increases its sales to franchisees that could have a negative effect on working

**Table 17.5**
**Hypermarket map for Wal-Mart and Carrefour (Aug 2004)**

| Province | Total no. of Hypermarkets | | Presence | Per city average number | |
| --- | --- | --- | --- | --- | --- |
| | Wal-Mart | Carrefour | No. of Cities | Wal-Mart | Carrefour |
| Beijing | 1 | 6 | 1 | 1.0 | 6.0 |
| Chonqing | 0 | 2 | 1 | — | 2.0 |
| Fujian | 5 | 0 | 2 | 2.5 | — |
| Guangdong | 13 | 6 | 5 | 2.6 | 1.2 |
| Guangxi | 1 | 0 | 1 | 1.0 | — |
| Guizhou | 1 | 0 | 1 | 1.0 | — |
| Heilongjiang | 1 | 1 | 1 | 1.0 | 1.0 |
| Hubei | 0 | 3 | 1 | — | 3.0 |
| Hunan | 1 | 1 | 1 | 1.0 | 1.0 |
| Jiangsu | 1 | 3 | 3 | 0.3 | 1.0 |
| Jiangxi | 1 | 0 | 1 | 1.0 | — |
| Jilin | 3 | 0 | 1 | 3.0 | 0 |
| Liaoning | 4 | 5 | 2 | 2.0 | 2.5 |
| Shandong | 2 | 3 | 2 | 1.0 | 1.5 |
| Shanghai | 0 | 7 | 1 | — | 7.0 |
| Sichuan | 0 | 3 | 1 | — | 3.0 |
| Tianjin | 2 | 5 | 1 | 2.0 | 5.0 |
| Xinjiang | 0 | 1 | 1 | — | 1.0 |
| Yunnan | 3 | 2 | 1 | 3.0 | 2.0 |
| Zheijiang | 0 | 2 | 2 | — | 1.0 |
| Total | 39 | 50 | 30 | 1.3 | 1.7 |

Source: JPMorgan estimates

capital because they are selling on a credit basis. As the competitive environment heats up in China this type of strategic analysis will have a big impact on the profitability of companies.[19]

PriceSmart operated a licensing arrangement in China. PriceSmart executives were on board to run the company in the first few years, but after they left the unwise use of reverse capital brought the company to collapse. Reverse capital works only if the company has increasing sales.

If we consider another indicator of profitability, inventory turns, we see that Lianhua and Wumart are far ahead of their international peers (Figure 17.2). Among Lianhua, Wumart, and Hualian, Wumart has the fastest inventory turn (28 days);

**Table 17.6**
**Inventory and Trade Payable Days in 2003**

| | Inventory days | Payable days | Payable days/Inventory days (x) |
| --- | --- | --- | --- |
| Lianhua | 35 | 66 | 1.86 |
| Wumart | 28 | 55 | 1.98 |
| Hualian Supermarket | 32 | 44 | 1.40 |

Source: Company data, JPMorgan estimates.

**Table 17.7**
**Working Capital Analysis**

|  | 2001 Rmb MM | 2002 Rmb MM | 2003 Rmb MM | 1H04 Rmb MM |
|---|---|---|---|---|
| **Lianhua** | | | | |
| Total current assets | 687 | 1064 | 1957 | 1680 |
| Total current liabilities | 1146 | 1934 | 2479 | 2156 |
| Net working capital plus cash | −416 | −843 | −506 | −562 |
| Net working capital | −461 | −979 | −1056 | −1088 |
| % sales—net WC plus cash (%) | −8.8% | −13.7% | −5.1% | −10.7% |
| % sales—net WC (%) | −9.8% | −15.9% | −10.7% | −20.8% |
| **Wumart** | | | | |
| Total current assets | 362 | 196 | 831 | 1182 |
| Total current liabilities | 387 | 229 | 327 | 419 |
| Net working capital plus cash | 37 | 39 | 632 | 1157 |
| Net working capital | 10 | −75 | 60 | −25 |
| % sales—net WC plus cash (%) | 5.3% | 3.6% | 40.1% | 94.1% |
| % sales—net WC (%) | 1.5% | −6.9% | 3.8% | −2.0% |

Source: Company data, JPMorgan estimates

only Tesco of the United Kingdom has a faster turn.[20] This is an indicator of efficiency but can also have some negative consequences. In an earlier chapter I discussed the consistency of assortment concept, the degree to which consumers hold a store accountable for maintaining an inventory that meets their expectation. An out-of-stock position can result in a loss of business and decreased consumer satisfaction with the company. The ultimate result may be that they take their business elsewhere.

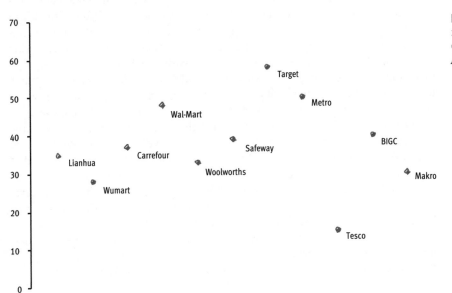

**Figure 17.2**
2003 Inventory turnover days. *Source: Company, JPMorgan estimates.*

Property leases also have an impact on the profitability picture. There has been a significant jump in rental costs. Many formerly state-owned stores were given very low rates on highly desirable properties. Many of these leases are now up for renewal and at today's rental prices, it is having an impact on their profitability. New store leases are often 20 percent more expensive than existing store leases; however, when an existing store needs to renew their lease it might double. This makes it very difficult to anticipate profits. New stores have some advantages that can offset this increase in rentals. When a store opens it is provided with promotional fees from suppliers in addition to slotting fees and product display fees. These are typically a one-time payment that does not recur each year. This supplier payment of fees for the new store opening can push the new store into profitability the first year, but will not be sustainable in the long run. Department stores who received a long-term lease, like Parkson, have actually turned the rental increase to their advantage by renting concessions in their store at high rates, essentially ARBITRAGING the difference between their low, long-term lease with the short-term concessions rents.[21] Arbitrage is when you sell/lease an asset in another market to take advantage of price differentials. In the past, retailers typically leased properties, minimizing their investment requirements and allowing them to expand rapidly. The focus was on organic growth rather than acquisition. However, with the shortage of good locations and the sharp rise in rental prices, retailers are seeking to buy the properties. This creates an interesting cycle. Purchasing the property may cut into their profitability—combined with more intensive competition and eroding margins this will make marginal retail chains targets for mergers from more competitive retailers, thereby contributing to the market consolidation.

Wumart is the largest supermarket chain in Beijing. They have a 9–10 percent market share in that area,[22] with hypermarkets, supermarkets, and convenience stores in Beijing and Tianjin. The trademark *Wu Mei* means "things beautiful/good" and it is owned by Wumart's founder, Dr. Zhang Wenzhong. I talked with the Wumart founder shortly after he opened his first store. He told me that he had founded the company following the Wal-Mart model. When I first visited him his company was in a quansit-type building in Beijing. The atmosphere was bare bones for Wu-Mart. The shelving was straight out of the 1960s. Several years later I visited their company headquarters, a stylish new building, with a sign on their wall tracking their growth with their model and idol, Wal-Mart. Wumart's founders seized early opportunities by signing long-term leases for plants or warehouses of non-performing state-owned enterprises and turning these into supermarkets at a very low cost. Wumart is now the largest supermarket in Beijing. Hypermarkets account for a quarter of Wumart's revenue in 2004. Wumart also has supermarkets that account for 60 percent of their sales. Wumart acquired 12 supermarket outlets in Tianjin from Japanese operator Daiei; they are in the process of renovating 10 of the stores and integrating them into the Wumart system. Two of the stores will be closed because of poor performance. Wumart also has convenience stores in Beijing and Shanghai. The total number in Beijing is about half the number in Shanghai. The Shanghai municipal government has designated convenience stores as an "ENCOURAGED RETAIL FORMAT," another example of the continued government influence in retail development. The government will facilitate the approval of licenses for convenience stores at a more rapid rate than other types of retail development.

Wumart also owns a 49 percent stake in Beijing Chongwenmen Vegetable Market Wumart Supermarket (Beijing Chongwenmen). In 2004, Wumart acquired controlling interest in Beijing Chaoshifa, a formerly state-owned organization and major supermarket chain.[23] The convenience store industry in China is in a state of flux. Operators are having a hard time convincing consumers that paying for convenience is worth the extra price. Only one-fifth of the convenience store outlets in China are profitable. Foreign experts in this area, like Japan's Family-Mart, are likely to be the successful players. As Seven-Eleven is expanding in 2006, they plan to open 350 stores by 2008. It is likely they will transform the convenience store sector.[24]

Although it is still viewed as an attractive market, Shanghai is approaching saturation. Wal-Mart is opening three superstores there. I visited the first store in October 2005. Within 10 minutes on opening day, the 1,300 pushcarts and 3,000 shopping baskets were in use.[25] It was an impressive store with a wide selection of fish and fresh produce. My Chinese counterparts agreed that it was an attractive store to visit. Wal-Marts in China are usually two floor operations and this one was no exception. The upper floor was devoted to non-food items. I saw one interesting item that was on display. Traditional Chinese toilets sit on the ground and people squat to use them. What I saw at Wal-Mart was a folding device, like a camping stool, that the occupant could sit on, rather than squatting to use the toilet. It was marketed for older people with stiff joints or the infirm. That is a good example of how Wal-Mart has adopted their inventory to fit the Chinese market.

Chinese government officials love Wal-Mart, who used the classic strategy of predetermined domestication when they entered the country. In Chapter 3 I talked about this strategy that companies should use when they move into a new country. It included sourcing from the domestic country and involving locals in key management positions. In 2005, Wal-Mart spent 22 billion U.S. dollars on Chinese goods, an increase of 20 percent over the previous year.[26] The government loves Wal-Mart not so much because they are a great retailer, which they are, but because they buy so much.

Companies are using acquisitions for expansion. Tesco has acquired a 50 percent ownership in Hymall, which operates 25 hypermarkets in China, 10 of which are in Shanghai. Some companies are moving into smaller cities. Jinjiang Metro is opening 12 outlets of which 60–70 percent will be in small cities. Wal-Mart is opening a major store in Maoming, a small city in West Guangdong Province. They also opened a new store in Taiuyuan, Northwest Shanxi Province.

China has had department stores since the late 1800s. They are the oldest and most traditional retail format in the country. They were originated by overseas Chinese and today the best performing department stores are foreign, mainly overseas Chinese companies.

## Department Stores

Parkson Department Stores is operated by the Malaysia-based Lion group, the leading department store group in China. They have 39 department stores in 26

**Photo 17.3**
State department stores used to sell all merchandise behind counters. Much of the merchandise is still sold in this manner. Customers must ask to see a product. Sales employees were held responsible for product losses so they "guarded" merchandise to protect it from customers. *Courtesy of the author.*

mainland cities.[27] They focus on mid-to-up-market customers who seek trendy merchandise. To meet government regulations they have opened stores with over 30 different joint venture partners in China. Now that the regulations have been relaxed, it is likely that they will move to simplify their ownership structure, perhaps buying out the joint venture partners.

Pacific Department store is owned by Far Eastern Group from Taiwan. It was one of the earliest foreign department stores to open in China.

Number One Department Store is the major Chinese player. They are now part of the Bailian/Everbright group. I remember visiting the Number One Department Store on my first trip to China. It was a rainy day in March 1989. I came in a side door with heavy plastic drapes over the door in an attempt to keep the interior warm. The floor was covered in mud from the heavy traffic of people. I stood back and watched for a moment as people entered. Slipping on the mud they grabbed at merchandise counters to brace themselves, then leaving the merchandise covered with mud. In those days all merchandise was sold behind counters. Salesclerks were downright nasty to customers. The government even went so far as to ban salespersons from using some phrases (Box 17.2 has some of the banned statements). Today customer service is greatly improved.

Number One department store is now a very modern two-building facility. The main store is on Nanjing Road, the heart of the traditional shopping street. Number One has been losing sales to Parkson and Pacific over the years, but being part of the state-government-sanctioned Bailian group may help it. The government wants the group to be successful so it will likely have favorable treatment.

Two Japanese department stores operate in China. Isetan has five stores and Takashimaya has one store. Isetan entered the market as the upscale retailer they

**Photo 17.4**
*SHANGHAI, CHINA:*
Passersby walk past the Hua Lian Department Store in downtown Shanghai, 12 May 2004. The board of directors of Shanghai Hua Lian and Shanghai No. 1 Department Store Co. have approved a plan to merge the two firms through a stock swap, state press reported. AFP PHOTO/LIU Jin. *Courtesy of LIU JIN/AFP/Getty Images.*

were in Japan, but they have subsequently repositioned somewhat further downscale to match the spending abilities of their clientele. Several Hong Kong department stores such as Wing On and Sincere entered the mainland market, but subsequently had to withdraw. The next section features the most prevalent type of retailer in China, the specialty store.

**Box 17.2**
**Service With Some Bile**

*By Seth Faison*

Shanghai—It may be hard for many Americans to imagine under what circumstances a sales-clerk might actually say to a customer, "Stop shouting, can't you see I'm eating?" But in China, it is common for clerks to abandon their post without notice, and to ignore—or even insult—customers who happen to come along.

One of the legacies of Communist rule has been atrocious service. For years such workers could justify their laziness by decrying attentive service as bourgeois. They could rest assured they would not be fired for performing badly. Managers, too, had few incentives to motivate their staff to do better.

Now market economics are taking over, and with competition emerging, things are changing, even service. But improving service one step up from bad still leaves the customer with pretty bad.

There is a surplus of pretty bad service in any number of Chinese stores, airports, and hotels. But a year ago, as part of a nationwide politeness campaign, the Chinese Government began enforcing a strict policy aimed at reining in the hostility common at the counter. Just a few months ago, it published a list of 50 phrases that are banned from use at any service counter.

"Didn't you hear me, what do you have ears for?" is one such forbidden phrase. "Are you finished talking?" is another. Both hint at the animosity that often erupts at the counter.

If one measure of China's progress toward a functioning economy is a program in which store managers actually demand that their staff be courteous, another is how hard it is to change an old system when the authorities rely mostly on a campaign in the newspapers.

Still, the publication of a list of 50 officially banned phrases offers a clue to understanding how bad service is, rather than a reflection of any genuine effort to improve it.

"Buy it if you can afford it, otherwise get out of here," speaks to the impatience that salesclerks are loathe to hide. "What can I do? I didn't break it," echoes the reluctance to take responsibility for a store's faulty products.

Wang Dao, deputy office director at Shanghai's Number One Department Store, one of the stores chosen to lead the campaign, said: "These phrases were chosen because they are so common. Otherwise why would we pick them?"

A ban on such phrases is unlikely to work in any comprehensive way, since the authorities who are so good at policing dissidents are not yet as strict in the service industry. The Chinese have become inured to political campaigns, too, knowing they must heed them in the short term but that enthusiasm will wane after a while.

So far now, many salesclerks are at least pretending to treat the politeness campaign earnestly.

"It's very serious," said Lin Gan, a 45-year-old salesclerk at the electronics counter in the Number One Department Store. "We're not allowed to stand around in groups of more than two. We're not allowed to fold our arms. And, of course, we have to watch what we say."

One floor down, however, in the men's garment section, six salesclerks were huddled, all arms folded, chatting away while two customers tried to get help.

"Okay, okay, what do you want?" one salesclerk, Ye Ping, said finally, skating close to one of the banned phrases.

"I've been in this store 38 years," said Ms. Ye after the customer left without buying anything. Queried about her attitude, she replied, "I've worked hard all these years. I don't see why we are always asked to do better."

Mr. Wang said his store was serious about the campaign and enforcing it with fines and dismissals.

How many of his 2,000 clerks have been fired since the store began its strict policy a year ago?

"No one yet," Mr. Wang said.

**Box 17.2** *Continued*

How many have been fined?

"It's hard to give an exact number," he said.

Mr. Wang added hopefully: "Change is not going to come overnight. It's going to take some time."

### Hey, Rude Clerks: No. 49!

In China, store clerks were so predictably rude that the government banned 50 of their choicest phrases:

1. Hey!
2. Old man.
3. Hey, soldier!
4. Country bumpkin.
5. Darkie (refers to dark-skinned Chinese).
6. What does it have to do with you?
7. Who told you not to look where you're going?
8. If you don't like it, go somewhere else.
9. Ask someone else.
10. Didn't you hear me? What do you have ears for?
11. Take a taxi if you don't like the bus.
12. Get out the way, or you'll get killed!
13. That's just the way things are!
14. I don't care whom you complain to.
15. Are you finished talking?
16. If you're not buying, what are you looking at?
17. Buy it if you can afford it; otherwise get out of here.
18. Are you buying or not? Have you made up your mind?
19. What are you yelling about? Wait a while.
20. Don't you see I'm busy? What's the hurry?
21. Hurry up and pay.
22. I can't solve this. Go complain to whomever you want.
23. I don't know.
24. I just told you. Why are you asking again?
25. Don't stand in the way.
26. I have no change. Wait here,
27. Why didn't you choose well when you bought it?
28. Go ask the person who sold it to you.
29. If you don't like it, talk to the manager.
30. Time is up, be quick.
31. The price is posted. Can't you see it for yourself?
32. No exchanges, that's the rule.
33. If you're not buying, don't ask.
34. You're asking me. Whom should I ask?
35. Stop shouting. Can't you see I'm eating?
36. It's not my fault.
37. We haven't opened yet. Wait a while.
38. What are you doing? Be quick.
39. I'm not in charge. Don't ask me so many questions.
40. Didn't I tell you? How come you don't get it?
41. I have no change. Go get some yourself.
42. Don't push me.
43. If you want it, speak up; if you don't, get out of the way.  Next!

*continued*

The major department store in Beijing is Wangfujing Department Store, with 16 wholly owned and holding companies. It runs a variety of department stores including Beijing Department Store, Beijing Dong'an Plaza, Beijing Chang'an Market, Beijing Shuangan Mall, Beijing Haiwen Wangfujing Department Store, Guangzhou Wangfujing Department Store, Wuhan Wangfujing Department Store and Changju Wangfujing Department Store, and Wangfujing Mansion. In 2006, they purchased 25 percent stake in Seven-Eleven Beijing. Seven-Eleven Beijing is a joint venture between Seven-Eleven Japan and Beijing Shoulian Commercial Group. They have around 30 convenience stores.

China is sprucing up in preparation for the 2008 Olympics; one of the things they want to offer is world-class shopping. Mitsukoshi's Taiwan-based joint venture Xinguang Mitsukoshi Baihuo is opening their first store in Beijing in 2006, operating under the name Shin Kong Mitsukoshi. The Mitsukoshi name may be changed to Shin Kong Hualian Department Store. Harrods (US) and Galeries Lafayette (France) are also in negotiations to open stores in Shanghai before the Olympics. Galeries Lafayette opened a store in Beijing in 2000 but folded within a year. They obviously think the time is now ripe to try again.[28]

## Specialty Stores

Several Hong Kong-based companies are very active in the China market. Tex-winca Holding Limited has opened over 2,000 Baleno and S&K stores in China. Its Chinese sales account for two-thirds of the company's total retail sales. Giordano is another Hong Kong-based retailer that is very active in China, operating over 600 Giordano stores and 50 Bluestar Exchange stores. Giordano was one of the earliest foreign companies to enter China. Esprit, another Hong Kong retailer, has nearly 100 stores and concession areas in over 500 department stores.

Mango has 20 stores in China, operating under the name MNG because another company had already registered to use the desired name, a fairly typical occurrence in China. Another common problem is that originally the company had to use the exact name they used when they filled out the Chinese application to open a business. Carrefour used Chinese characters for the phonetic pronunciation of their name, so later the government would not allow them to use Roman letters on their store sign. Eventually Carrefour was allowed to use their original name.

## Homegoods

DIY (do it yourself) retailers have a challenge in China because they don't tend to like to do it themselves. They feel it is beneath them, and since labor is so inexpensive they find it more attractive to hire someone. But they will BIY (buy it yourself) and hire someone else to do the work. Since homeownership is increasing so rapidly this is a booming market.

Kingfisher (UK) has B&Q stores scattered throughout China. They are the market leader. They have two formats, a 160,000-square-foot store for larger cities like Shanghai, Beijing, Shenzhen, and Guangzhou and a 100,000-square-foot store for second-tier cities with a population of more than two million.[29]

Home Mart is the second-largest DIY chain; it is part of the state-run Friendship Group. Friendship Group is part of the Bailian group, so Home Mart is likely to benefit from this association. Their strategy is to target second- and third-tier cities of one million or more across China.[30]

IKEA has a store in Beijing and a store in Shanghai. I visited the store in Beijing last year and was surprised to see people sleeping on the sofas and chairs. I'm not talking about one or two but literally dozens of people. Store management didn't seem to mind one bit. IKEA is very popular for its trendy styled and moderate-priced furniture, especially among the younger generation in China.

## Home Appliance Retailing

The penetration rate for home appliances in China is low compared with other Asian nations. For instance, in Taiwan the penetration rate for air conditioners is 85 percent and of home computers, 59 percent, but in China the rate is 70 percent for air conditioners and 34 percent for computers. Improved living conditions in the urban areas as a result of housing reform means that more people will invest in things for the home. Housing reform has given rise to a property-owning boom. The average size of a home in China is 24 square meters in cities and 75 square meters in the country per household. It is expected that will increase to 80 square meters in the next few years, establishing a market for home appliances. Figure 17.3 shows the home appliance penetration rates in urban China.

The big department stores are beginning to withdraw from home appliance retailing. This is pretty predictable. As discount organizations such as Gome come into the sector, the department stores cannot compete. This has happened in nearly every developed market. As a discount format captures market share, others withdraw. For example, Shanghai's No. 6 Department store used to be Number 2 in the market. In 2005 they announced their withdrawal from home appliance sales. Although consolidation is happening quickly, the top seven players account for only about 20 percent of the electrical appliances and consumer-electronic areas.[31]

This sector is different from the supermarket and hypermarket segments. There are virtually no foreign competitors. Major domestic players have made it difficult for foreigners to enter by establishing extensive networks of stores and distribution centers, controlling the market by improving their supply chains and strengthening ties with domestic manufacturers. Gome has a national distribution system; Suning and Yongle have regional presences.[32]

China's 1.4 billion population is attractive by any definition, but their one-child policy makes the market even more interesting. Limiting population has given

Units per 100 households

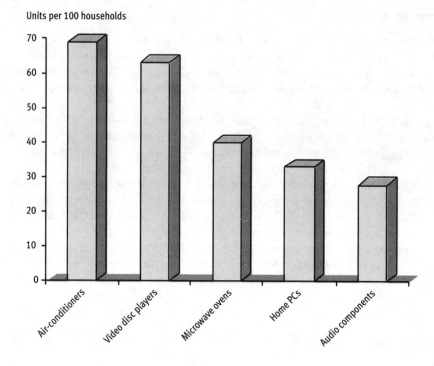

**Figure 17.3**
Home Appliance Penetration Rates in Urban China, 3Q04 (units per household)
*Source: State Statistics Bureau, Smith Barney.*

families much greater disposable income and the tendency is to pour resources into that little bundle of joy, the Little Emperor.

## China's Little Emperors

Virtually every Chinese person under 27 years of age is a single child, accustomed to having been indulged by his or her family. China's one-child policy has been highly successful in controlling its population. Although women can have more than one child, they pay a high fine and face social ostracization from work colleagues. The type of job you have also determines how acceptable it is to have several children. If you work for the government it is highly unacceptable; you are expected to set an example for others. On the other hand, some wealthy Chinese view having more than one child as a status symbol. Fines for having a second child can be up to five times the family's annual income. The offender's taxes are raised and they no longer receive free health care for the child. Interestingly, though, if a Chinese citizen has a child in another country, they are not held to this one-child policy. They will, however, have to pay for the education and medical care of the child born in another country. The government does allow farmers to have two children if the first child is a girl. Recently the government has made some changes in this policy, allowing two people who were single children to have two children. Also, if two divorced people marry they can have an additional child. The one-child policy has produced what is called the 4-2-1 syndrome, where four grandparents and two parents focus all their attention on one child. A recent survey of 7,000 Chinese youngsters showed that 60 percent felt miserable during their childhood. This policy has an impact on retailing because of the great consumption focus on what is called China's Little Emperor, the spoiled single child.[33]

## › SUMMARY

The PRC is in the process of liberalizing its retail trade. Until 1991, foreign joint ventures were not allowed in the country. Today, the government is playing a major role in determining how much foreign retail investment it can tolerate.

A striking contrast can be seen in the ways the Soviet Union and the PRC have approached the challenge of developing a market economy. In the Soviet Union, the political system was changed first, then the economic system. The result has been tremendous hardship, including consumer shortages and inflation. In contrast, the PRC has altered the economic system first, moving toward a free market before leaving the political security of a Communist/Socialist system. Unlike the Soviet Union, the PRC has had an abundant supply of merchandise and comparatively low inflation. It is a unique experience to witness the change of a country from a planned to a free market economy. The PRC has gone full circle: from capitalism to communism in the 1950s; from market planning to the beginnings of a free market in the 1990s; from free market to planned and back to free market in only 50 years.

## › KEY TERMS

ARBITRAGING

COLLECTIVES

CULTURAL REVOLUTION

ENCOURAGED RETAIL FORMAT

EXPATRIATED

FENPEI

GUANXI

PRICE CONTROLS

REGULATED GROSS MARGIN

STATE-OWNED STORES

TWO-TIERED MONETARY SYSTEM

## › DISCUSSION QUESTIONS

1. Why would a government consider retailing a nonproductive activity?
2. The change from guarded merchandise to self-service is an important change in retailing. We think of self-service as a way to reduce expenses; customers help themselves, therefore a store needs fewer sales employees. However, in the PRC, the change to self-service is not implemented to save money. What advantages do consumers have in a self-service environment?
3. Why would foreign franchisors enter a country that has not established franchise laws?

4. Using Dunning's theory of the eclectic firm, described in Chapter 2, can you explain why Japanese retailers have been attracted to the PRC? Why would Japanese retailers be more likely to enter this market than U.S. or European retailers?

## › ENDNOTES

1. Hong Kong Trade Development Council Research Department. (1994). *Retail and Wholesale Distribution of Consumer Goods in China.* Hong Kong: Hong Kong Trade Development Council.
2. Hong Kong Trade Development Council Research Department. (1994).
3. *China Statistical Yearbook.* (1996) Beijing: China Statistical Publishing House.
4. "China's Retail Sales of Consumer Goods up 13 Percent in 2005." (2006). *Financial Times* Information. Global News Wire January 4.
5. Retailing in China. (2004). Columbus, Ohio: RetailForward.
6. China's Retail Sector Seeking Growth Amid Intense Competition. (2005). Citigroup Smith Barney in Investext. June
7. Retailing in China. (2004). GMID Euromonitor, September.
8. Adapted and reprinted with permission from Sternquist, B., Z. XX., Qiao, and Y. Chengmin. (1995). "China: The Planned to Free Market Paradigm." *International Journal of Retail and Distribution Management,* Vol. 23, No. 12, pp. 21–28.
9. Ling, A. (2004) China Retailing 2005: a new age. Deutsche Bank, in Investext December 7.
10. China's Retail Sector Seeking Growth Amid Intense Competition. (2005). Citigroup Smith Barney in Investext. June.
11. China Retailing 2005: A New Age. (2004). Deutsche Bank in Investext December 2004, 9.
12. China Microscope Retailing the Challenges Ahead. (2005). Credit Suisse in Investext December 9.
13. "Guangzhou Comes Atop 5 Cities by Per Capita Income in H1." (2005). *Financial Times.* October 2005.
14. Retailing in China. (2004). GMID Euromonitor, September.
15. Retailing in China. (2004). Columbus, Ohio.
16. China's Retail Sector Seeking Growth Amid Intense Competition. (2005).
17. China's Retail Sector Seeking Growth Amid Intense Competition. (2005).
18. Hooke, P. (2005). "Profile-China's Retail Sector." *Asia Pulse,* September 30.
19. China Supermarkets: Size Does Matter (2004) JPMorgan Asia Pacific Equity Research in Investext November 30.
20. China's Retail Sector Seeking Growth Amid Intense Competition. (2005).
21. China Microscope Retailing the Challenges Ahead. (2005).
22. China's Retail Sector Seeking Growth Amid Intense Competition. (2005).
23. China's Retail Sector Seeking Growth Amid Intense Competition. (2005).
24. China's Retail Sector Seeking Growth Amid Intense Competition. (2005).
25. "Innovation Sharpens Chinese Retailers' Competitive Edge." (2005). *Financial Times,* December 14.
26. "Wal-Mart, Metro to Buy More From China." (2005). Xinhua News Agency. November 9.

27. "Parkson Jockeys for China Retail Market." (2005). Comtex News Network, November 28.

28. "Harrods, Galeries Lafayette Turn Eyes to Shanghai." (2005). *SinoCast China Financial Watch.* October 27.

29. Retailing in China. (2004). Columbus, Ohio.

30. Retailing in China. (2004). Columbus, Ohio.

31. China's Retail Sector Seeking Growth Amid Intense Competition. (2005).

32. China's Retail Sector Seeking Growth Amid Intense Competition. (2005).

33. "Little Emperors Under Pressure." (2005). *The Irish Times.* September 20, p. 15.

# 18

# RETAILING IN SOUTH KOREA

Byoungho Jin and Brenda Sternquist

## After reading this chapter, you should understand

› The role that Korean's Chaebol has played in the development of retailing.

› How an export-driven economy prioritizes industry development.

› What generalizations you can make about a highly concentrated retail market.

› How a Confucian culture affects what goods will be consumed.

› The effect of Yon-go relationships on business.

## 〉 COUNTRY BACKGROUND

Ever since South Korea (from now on, Korea) was unified in the seventh century, the country boasts of having a single language (Korean) and consists of only one tribe (called Han). Korea was under Japanese power for 35 years and liberated in 1945 when Japan surrendered during World War II. After the Korean War (1950–1953), the country divided into North, known as the Democratic People's Republic of Korea (DPRK) and South, known as the Republic of Korea (ROK).

Korea has seen a spectacular economic growth over the last four decades. From being the "Hermit Kingdom" closed years to foreign countries it has now become the 11th-largest economy in the world. Despite being a third of Japan's size and population, the country earned its reputation of "Four East Asian Tigers" (Korea, Hong Kong, Taiwan, and Singapore). This success is owed mainly to consecutive five-year economy development plans initiated by Korean government during President Park Chung Hee's regime (1961–1979). Korea is now leading the world in mobile phones, digital electronics, and telecommunications and is a home to world-rank companies—Samsung Electronics, LG Electronics, Daewoo Electronics, Hyundai Motors, Kia Motors, and more.

## 〉 UNIQUE FEATURES OF KOREAN RETAILING

### The Chaebol Group

You may not understand Korean economy without first knowing the role of CHAEBOL (pronounced *Jae Bol*), a Korean term for large, conglomerate family-controlled business groups. Chaebol began to form in the early 1960s and has been able to grow because of the government's special favor. Korean government in the 1960s was anxious to modernize the country and chose to concentrate their efforts on a small number of large companies.[1] The government used the Chaebol group to execute their economic development plans. The government provided the blueprints for industrial expansion, and the Chaebols realized the plans. Many people accept that Chaebol contributed a great deal to the economic growth of South Korea. The Chaebol is similar to Japanese keiretsu (the successor of the zaibatsu), but it is controlled by the founder's family members while Japanese keiretsu is controlled by professional corporate management. The top 10 Chaebol groups in 2002 included Hyundai, Samsung, LG, SK, Hanjin, Lotte, Daewoo, Kumho, Hanhwa, and Ssangyong, in descending order.[2]

Another important characteristic of Korean Chaebol is that they have many subsidiary companies in diverse industries within their group. For example, Samsung is known for cell phones and cameras, but in Korea you will also see Samsung security company, Samsung heavy industry company, Samsung building company, and so on. In almost every industry, including retail, you will find the name Samsung. Samsung runs a discount store named Home Plus, a joint venture with Tesco, the British retailer. For Americans, Hyundai means Hyundai motors, but Hyundai has subsidiary companies in building construction, heavy industry, and security. Hyundai is also very active in retail industry, owning a department store and home shopping channel. Lotte group is very active in retail business and operates in almost every retail format in Korea, running a department store, a Mart (discount store), LG 25 (convenience store), LG Supermarket, and LG home shopping channel. Knowing the concept of Chaebol is important as the Chaebol dominates Korean retail industry just as they represent large portions of Korean heavy industries and manufacturing sectors.

## Export-Driven Economy and Manufacturer's Power

Korea has an EXPORT-DRIVEN ECONOMY, meaning that their primary focus is on producing merchandise to sell to other countries. For a long time Korea would allow merchandise to be imported only if it were to be used in the production of products to be exported. This is no longer the case, but the focus of Korea is still on developing export markets. In Chapter 3, I talked about how the government or state plays a role in developing industry strategy; this has been the case in Korea. The government prioritized industries that could be important for exports. In this way, the Chaebol were designated as powerful groups that could help lead Korea's economy out of the developing stages. Korea is only half the size of Florida's peninsula and is endowed with very few national resources. The Korean government is keenly aware of these disadvantages and considers export the only way they can be competitive. From the 1960s, Korean government has supported the export sector of all countries, and this resulted in very powerful world-rank manufacturers. Retailing sector was considered only as instigating excess consumption and speculation in real estate; therefore, it did not receive government supports. Compared to manufacturing sector, retail industry was weak and ineffective, thus, Korean government protected its retail industry from foreign competition and finally fully liberalized its retail market in 1996 after four stages of gradual opening starting in 1988. Korea was the last to open its doors to foreign retail investment among the Four Tigers of Asia.

This dominance of powerful manufacturer in Korea created unique retail features —the consignment system and intensive use of manufacturer's franchised sales outlet. The concept of consignment system in department stores is the same as in Japan. Retailer's essential function is planning and buying merchandise for consumers, presenting the merchandise, and handling unsold merchandise. Korean retailers had not had opportunities to learn these functions when manufacturers were ready to sell their goods to the retailers. Therefore, manufacturers, not retailers, do most of the retailers' job: deciding product assortments, dispatching sales associates to department stores, presenting their goods under consignment system, and handling unsold merchandise. The retailers' job under the consignment system is to rent sales spaces to manufacturers and decide which manufacturers need to be tenanted, just like U.S. mall managers.

Korean retailers have been less developed than manufacturers to the extent that manufacturers organize distribution channels themselves. Instead of relying on wholesalers and retailers, manufacturers sell their goods directly to consumers largely through their FRANCHISED SALES OUTLET. This concept is similar to exclusive dealership in the U.S. car industry. Manufacturers provide goods and assist other functions (e.g., presentations and promotions), but the store owner may carry only the manufacturer's goods in return for these services. These franchised sales outlets are popular in the car (100 percent), electronics (90 percent), clothing (80 percent), and food/beverages industries (70 percent) in Korea. This system increases the cost of physical distribution and limits the merchandise assortment.[3] Overall the consignment system and franchised sales outlet were developed when manufacturers had power. Ironically, these systems still dominate and work well even though Korean department stores and discount stores now have power over manufacturers.

## Highly Concentrated Retail Market

Tables 18.1 and 18.2 summarize the major domestic and foreign retailers in South Korea. The Korean retail market is HIGHLY CONCENTRATED by major players (Table 18.3), most likely from the Chaebol group. The three big players in Korean department stores are Lotte Department store (the Lotte group), Shinsegae department store and Hyundai department store (Hyundai group). These three accounted for 68 percent of Korean department stores in 1999 and 75 percent in 2002. This concentration and ownership by Chaebol is no different in discount stores and home shopping channels. The largest discount players are E-mart (Shinsegae, a subsidiary of Samsung), Home Plus (a joint venture of Samsung and British Tesco), and Lotte Mart (Lotte group). These three discount stores shared 50 percent of the market in 2001 and increased to 55 percent in 2002. The Big Three in convenience stores are Family Mart (Bokwang Family Mart Co.), 7-Eleven (Donghwa Industry company, now taken over by Lotte group), and LG 25 (LG group), holding 70 percent of the market share as of 2002. In the home shopping channel, three major players are also owned by Chaebol group—CJ home Shopping (Cheil Je Dang Group), LG home shopping (LG group), and Hyundai home shopping (Hyundai group). While department stores, discount stores, and home shopping network occupy less than 30 percent of Korean retailing (Table 18.4), it is interesting to see how the concentration percent is increasing by year.

## High Number of Retail Stores

As Table 18.2 shows, small mom-and-pop stores account for more than two-thirds of retail market share. This explains why only 2.2 people are working in a retail store on average. In 2000, there were 694,000 retail establishments. This indicates 15.1 retail stores per 1,000 people. Compared to other countries this figure is very high: Japan (13.2), United States (6.1), United Kingdom (1.9), and Germany (1.9).[4] You will observe many small stores in residential areas in Korea, especially in Seoul, the capital city. Within working distance, you will find many small stores selling particular items, such as bakery, video rental shop, restaurant, hair salon, drugstore, grocery store, dry cleaner, school supply store, etc. When I lived in Seoul, it was not uncommon for me to see two or three stores selling the same goods from the bus

**Table 18.1**
**South Korea—Leading Domestic Retailers, 2004**

| Company | Total Sales and Stores | | | | Global Rank and Penetration | | | Domestic Market | |
| | Primary Line of Trade | Net Sales ($US Mil) | % Chg Sales | Total Stores | 2004 Rank, Top 200 Retailers Worldwide | Single-country, Regional or Global? | Number of countries | Share of total sales | Share of total stores |
|---|---|---|---|---|---|---|---|---|---|
| 1 Lotte Group | Department Stores | 12,490 | 18.2% | 2,171 | 58 | Regional | 2 | N/A | N/A |
| 2 Shinsegae | Discount Stores | 5,686 | 12.2% | 86 | 122 | Regional | 2 | 98% | 97% |
| 3 GS Holdings | Supermarkets/Grocery Stores | 2,973 | N/A | 2,103 | — | Regional | 2 | N/A | 100% |
| 4 Hyundai Department Stores | Department Stores | 1,462 | -9.2% | 11 | — | Single Country | 1 | 100% | 100% |

Sources: Retail Forward, company annual reports and published reports

**Table 18.2**
**South Korea—Key Foreign Retailers, 2004**

| Company | Headquarters | Retail Sector | Primary Line of Trade | Global Rank and Penetration | | |
|---|---|---|---|---|---|---|
| | | | | 2004 Rank, Top 200 Retailers Worldwide | Single-country, Regional or Global? | Number of countries |
| Aeon Co., Ltd. | Japan | FDM | General Merchandise Stores | 19 | Global | 11 |
| Alticor/Amway | United States | FDM | Non-Store | 119 | Global | 80 |
| Carrefour Group | France | FDM | Hypermarkets/Supercenters | 2 | Global | 31* |
| Costco Companies, Inc. | United States | FDM | Cash & Carries/Warehouse Clubs | 9 | Global | 7 |
| Dairy Farm International Holdings Limited | Hong Kong | FDM | Convenience Stores | 162 | Regional | 8 |
| Defense Commissary Agency | United States | FDM | Supermarkets/Grocery Stores | 130 | Global | 13 |
| FamilyMart Co., Ltd. | Japan | FDM | Convenience Stores | 83 | Regional | 5 |
| Hutchison Whampoa Limited | Hong Kong | FDM | Drug Stores | 77 | Global | 18 |
| Ito-Yokado Co., Ltd. | Japan | FDM | Convenience Stores | 6 | Global | 17 |
| LVMH | France | Softgoods | Other Apparel Specialty Stores | 76 | Global | 56 |
| Marks & Spencer PLC | United Kingdom | Softgoods | Department Stores | 49 | Global | 32 |
| Otto Group | Germany | Softgoods | Non-Store | 61 | Global | 19 |
| Tesco PLC | United Kingdom | FDM | Supermarkets/Grocery Stores | 5 | Global | 13 |
| Wal-Mart Stores, Inc. | United States | FDM | Hypermarkets/Supercenters | 1 | Global | 11* |

Sources: Retail Forward, company annual reports and published reports
*Withdrew in 2006

**Table 18.3**
**Sales Volume and Market Share Changes of the Big Three Department Stores**

|  | Unit: Million US$, % | | | |
| --- | --- | --- | --- | --- |
|  | 1999 | 2000 | 2001 | 2002 |
| Lotte | 3,192 | 4,229 | 4,824 | 5,765 |
| Hyundai | 2,279 | 2,665 | 2,911 | 3,157 |
| Shinsegae | 1,168 | 1,394 | 1,808 | 1,883 |
| Total | 6,639 | 8,289 | 9,543 | 10,805 |
| Market share by the Big Three | 66 | 72 | 74 | 75 |

Sales excluding Value-Added Tax
Source: Hyundai Research Institute of Distribution. (as cited in Kim et al. (2003), p. 45.)

stop to my home, which is less than half a mile. These stores are mostly run by family members, so their service level and price competition are easily imaginable. This, of course, is convenient to consumers, but their retail productivity could not be higher than the country with less dense retail stores. In fact, this partly explains why Korea's labor productivity in the distribution industry (this includes retail industry) is the lowest among OECD countries. The labor productivity of the Korean distribution industry is approximately 34 percent of Japan, 29 percent of the United States and 34 percent of France.[5]

## Confucian Influence in Business Contexts and Yon-go

CONFUCIANISM came to Korea from China in the fifth century. Table 18.5 shows Confucianism and its impact on management practices in Korea. Confucian values permeate every aspect of Korean society to a great extent, not just for consumers, but also for business contexts. Confucianism articulates five ethical codes that govern one's relationships to superiors, parents, spouse, elders, and friends.[6] Even though Confucianism came from China, its influence there has been reduced since communism. I visited China last summer and was a bit shocked to see a young

**Table 18.4**
**Market Share by Various Retail Formats, 1992–2001**

|  | (unit: %) | | | |
| --- | --- | --- | --- | --- |
|  | 1992 | 1995 | 1998 | 2001 |
| Department Store | 7.2 | 10.7 | 11.5 | 12.7 |
| Discount Store | — | 0.9 | 5.8 | 8.5 |
| Supermarkets | 4.6 | 3.8 | 3.9 | 3.0 |
| Non-store Retailing | 1.0 | 1.5 | 2 | 4.7 |
| Mom-and-Pop Stores | 87.2 | 82.2 | 75.8 | 69.8 |

Source: Korea National Statistical Office and Industry Sources. (as cited in Kim et al. (2003), p.10)

**Table 18.5**
**Confucianism and Its Impact on Management Practices in Korea**

| Confucianism Values | Relationships Between: | Organizational Values | HRM Practice |
|---|---|---|---|
| Eui ( justice, fealty) | King-Subject Employer-Employee | Loyalty; benevolence | Lifetime employment |
| Hyo (filial piety) | Parent-Child | Respect, harmony | Seniority system |
| Byul (separate roles) | Husband-Wife Man-Woman | Hard work ethics | Paternalistic management |
| Suh (order) | Elder-Younger | Obedience | Centralized authority |
| Shin (trust) | Coequals | Collectivity | Yongo-based management |

Lee, H.-C. (1998–1999). "Transformation of Employment Practices in Korean Businesses." *International Studies of Management and Organization*, 28(4), p.29.

man sewing at a clothing factory just like young women. This is unimaginable in Korea. Men are supposed to be superior to women and men should not do women's work. It is uncommon to see women managers in Korean retailing industry. This clear distinction between men and women is changing these days, but is still very prevalent in most of Korean society.

Among many Confucian influences, YON-GO relations are important to understanding Korean business culture. Yon-go literally means a special social relationship or connection based on family ties (*hyul-yon*), schools (*hak-yon*), and birthplaces (*ji-yon*).[7] You will see similar social relationships in countries where Confucian influence prevails. Korean Yon-go is similar to Chinese Guanxi. But Yon-go is different from Guanxi in that it is based on more specific ties such as family, schools, and birthplace and cannot be changed by a person's efforts. Guanxi is a broader relationship that you can earn and accumulate through your efforts. For example, if a Korean meets another Korean at a gathering and knows that they attended the same college (*hak-yon*), then they feel pretty close without sharing other things. Sometimes Korean people want to know another person's family origin in genealogical table and his/her birthplace to get closer. This type of relationship also exists in the United States; however, one cannot get a special favor because of these ties. If other things are equal, Koreans may give a favor to the person who has Yon-go with them. This is the case in retail industry, too. When one buyer knows a supplier went to his school, assigning contracts and getting large orders may become a little bit easier. However, Korean government and retailing industry alike are aware that this practice deters fair competition, so they have developed policies that hinder special benefits because of Yon-go. If a high-ranking government officer gives special favors to a person because of Yon-go, it is pretty shameful and becomes a huge issue.

## Extremely Demanding and Fashion-Conscious Consumers

Korean consumers are notorious for being demanding. As a manager of a multinational company operating in Korea once confessed to me, "Once we can satisfy

Korean consumers, then we are sure of our success in other countries, too." A more extreme case can be found in the Korean cosmetic industry. Korea's beauty market ranks number 7 in the world, and Korea serves as a test marketplace for multinational cosmetic companies due to its choosy and hard-to-please consumers. Especially Lancome, the well-known French cosmetic company, tests Korean women's reaction for a new item and then starts to sell in Japanese market. One scientist in the Lancome laboratory said, "We see Korean women leading the taste of Asian women and eventually controlling the world's taste. Currently the Asian influence, such as Zen, is leading the Western market, too."[8] These sophisticated, demanding consumers create demand condition, a factor among Porter's four national competitiveness factors. This factor refers to the nature of home-market demand for an industry's product or service.[9] Porter views that in countries where the domestic buyers (either industrial buyers or consumers) are the world's most sophisticated and demanding, companies are forced to meet high standards, to upgrade, and to respond to tough challenges, thus naturally becoming the world's leader in the industry.[10] Therefore, having demanding and sophisticated consumers is a kind of luck for the retail industry. These consumers force Korean retailers to challenge themselves continuously, leading them to be world's best.

Korean consumers are also extremely anxious to be trendy. Due to their Confucian heritage, they are sensitive about their appearance. They believe they lose FACE if they are not properly dressed in a public setting. The concept of face is similar to that in China and Japan. To keep face, they dress well especially in public settings, thus exhibiting higher fashion consciousness and brand loyalty.[11] This tendency is not just confined to fashion goods. With a country of 45 million people, trend moves really quickly in Korea. For example, when I first began teaching in the United States in 2001, the typical cell phone used in small town Oklahoma was the one used about seven years ago in Korea. When I visited Seoul in summer 2002, I wore pants that look perfectly fine in the town where I live. I was surprised and a little bit embarrassed to find I was the only one wearing long pants touching the floor in Incheon International airport. Almost all Korean women around my age wore cropped pants in the airport. So I got a pair of cropped pants and wore them when I returned to the States. I was the only one wearing that pants style in Oklahoma airport. Many reasons can explain this fast diffusion. Seoul is a heavily populated city with one-third of South Koreans living there, so new innovations are easily observed by Korean consumers, compared to other loosely dense cities. Confucian influence also explains why Korea consumers tend to conform to others. Deviation is dangerous (see Chapter 16) as they believe it breaks the harmony of the in-group.

## Retail Overview

Korean retail industry accounts for 9 percent of GDP and 18 percent of employment. The industry's share of GDP is only 27 percent of manufacturers due to Korean government's export-oriented policy.[12] However, its employment is equivalent to that of manufacturers.[13] The employment in manufacturing sector has steadily reduced due to increased production overseas, while the employment in retailing sector has continuously grown during the last decade. Department stores share a larger portion of the Korean retail market (12.7 percent), after mom-and-pop stores (69.8 percent), followed by discount stores (8.5 percent), non-store retailing (4.7 percent), and supermarkets (3 percent).[14]

## 〉 DEPARTMENT STORES

### Brief History and Current Status of Korean Department Stores

The first department store in Korea was Mitsukosi, run by Japanese in 1916 when Korea was under Japanese rule. The first department store run by Koreans was Hwa-Shin department store in 1931; however, this store no longer exists. Mitsukosi was taken over by Donghwa after the Japanese withdrew from Korea. Samsung took over this store and re-named it Shinsegae in 1963, which literally means new world. During the 1960s to 1970s, many Korean department stores emerged. Lotte opened in 1979 and Midopa, Cosmos, and Shinshin started their business during this time. These stores are all clustered in Myung-Dong, the downtown of Seoul, near City Hall. Korean department stores flourished and achieved great growths during the 1980s in terms of sales volume, number of stores, services, and management practice. National economic growth, increased urban populations, the housing boom in metro cities to cater to these populations, and the Seoul Olympic games in 1988 all contributed to this growth. Hyundai group joined retail business by starting their first department store in Apgujong-dong, a newly developed wealthy area of Seoul in 1985.

During the 1980s, the Korean department store industry started to represent Korea's modern retailing. Roughly only two retail formats existed in Korea until the mid-1990s, department store (modern) and small mom-and-pop stores (traditional). Annual sales growth from 1983 to 1993 was 26.1 percent, far exceeding average retail growth rate of 12.3 percent.[15] However, this growth came to a halt when the Korean retail market was fully liberalized to foreign companies in 1996. Discount stores began to operate as a new retail format by Korean retailers as well as multinational retail companies. The financial crisis in Korea in late 1997 made another big change. In April 1998, 15 second-tier department stores went insolvent.[16] These stores were largely merged and acquired by Lotte and Hyundai department stores. From that time, Korean department stores started to form competition among the big three—Lotte, Hyundai, and Shinsegae—and their oligopoly was strengthened. As mentioned, these big three are a part of the Korean Chaebol group and occupy 75 percent of Korean department stores (Table 18.3). As of 2002, there are 90 department stores operating in Korea, all of them owned and managed by Koreans (Figure 18.1).

### Unique Features of Korean Department Stores

Most items in Korean department stores are sold by the consignment system, except fresh vegetables. This consignment concept is the same as Japan's. Other unique features are as follows.

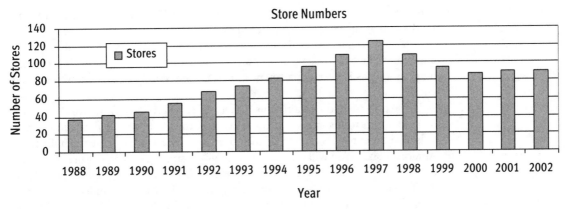

Store Numbers

**Figure 18.1**
Number of Department
Stores By Year. *Source:
Korea Chamber of
Commerce and Industry
Hyundai Research Institute
of Distribution. (as cited in
Kim et al. (2003, p. 51)*

**CARRIES MANY AND VARIED GOODS**   The department store in Korean literally means "store that carries many and varied goods." As with Japanese department stores, Korean department stores carry food and beverages, furniture, home appliances, etc. (Table 18.6). Due to space constraints, the typical Korean department store consists of six or seven floors. Typically the first floor sells cosmetics, luxurious imported goods, and shoes; second and third floors carry women's fashion. The fourth floor is assigned to men's clothes; fifth, to sportswear and athletic shoes; sixth, to home appliances and furniture. The top floor is usually a food court and/or a culture center.

Clothing accounts for the majority of department store sales: 44.4 percent of their merchandise in 1997, 55.3 percent in 2002. This increase is partly because of competition from newly introduced discount stores and conveniences stores around the mid-1990s. As food and beverage items were sold at cheaper prices in discount

**Table 18.6**
**Composition of Merchandise in Korean Department Stores**

| Categories | (unit:%) 1997 | 2002 |
|---|---|---|
| Clothing | 44.4 | 55.3 |
| Food & Beverage | 22.3 | 15.1 |
| Kitchenware | 3.5 | 2.6 |
| Home Appliances | 6.1 | 4.9 |
| Furniture & Interior | 4.1 | 3.4 |
| Shoes & Accessories | 15.7 | 15.4 |
| Other | 3.9 | 3.3 |
| Total | 100 | 100 |

Source: Korea Chamber of Commerce and Industry, 1998, 2003.
Reorganized by the author based on Kim et al. (2003), p. 72.

stores, Korean department stores began to focus more on fashion items. Instead, food and beverage items were reduced in 2002.

U.S. department stores do not carry food simply because its profit is not big enough. While this is also true in Korea, Korean department stores will keep these items as long as Korean department store is perceived as "carrying many and varied goods."

This concept also explains this variety of services offered by Korean department stores. A food court, typically located on the top floor of a department store, sells all different types of cuisine, including Korean, Japanese, Chinese, Italian, and American pizza. You will also find a bank, gift wrapping corner, culture center that typically teaches life-long types of education, such as art, calligraphy, home décor, etc. Recently, to attract more consumers, the top floor even included a swimming pool, fitness center, beauty salon, café, and art exhibition hall. These facilities are usually found in a shopping mall in the United States. However, the shopping mall concept is not popular yet in Korea because only one or two shopping malls exist. Even though Koreans call some retail complexes shopping malls, they are not anchored by department stores or discount stores like in the States. Therefore, for most Koreans, a department store is not just for shopping. It is a place for meeting friends, learning new trends and information, exercising, and entertaining themselves. It is typical for me to meet friends at the top floor of a department store because it is conveniently located (usually connected to a subway station), and offers a lot of activities to do together with friends—shopping, eating, chatting, even having our hair done.

**CARRIES VERY LUXURIOUS BRANDS**   The perception of department stores among Korean consumers is unique. If a brand in a department store is considered as well known, the store becomes an important vehicle in promoting the manufacturer's brand image. Korean manufacturers believe that it is essential for them to be in major department stores to promote their brands.[17] Accordingly, competition among manufacturers who want to open their own brand sections in department stores is extreme.

This high-end image has been reinforced recently. The competition with discount stores results in moving department stores toward more high-end so that they do not overlap their merchandise and price ranges. Because of this reason, the Big Three department stores compete with each other to include more high-end luxurious brands. Now it is typical to see Cartier, Ferragamo, Prada, Gucci, A. Testoni, Christian Dior, Louis Vuitton, and Celine on the first floor of these stores. The array of expensive brands near the store entrance creates a luxurious store image. Probably because of this reason, the general merchandise stores (GMS) concept is not appealing to Korean consumers. They go to department stores for high-quality goods and shop for everyday groceries and necessities at discount stores.

## Discount Stores

**BRIEF HISTORY AND CURRENT STATUS OF KOREAN DISCOUNT STORES**
Discount store retailing in Korea has expanded rapidly since the first discount store was introduced in 1993 by one of Korea's leading retailers, Shinsegae. The Discount

store concept is well accepted by Korean consumers, partly due to a financial crisis in 1997, which made Korean consumers seek lower-priced value merchandise.[18] The discount store segment accounted for 8.5 percent of the total retail market as of 2001, but it is forecasted to grow an average of 30 percent annually over the next few years, compared to 7–8 percent growth for department stores.[19]

Korean discount store retailing encompasses various formats, such as membership wholesale clubs (MWC), hypermarkets, and supercenters. The most successful discount retail format in Korea has been the "hypermarket" or "supercenter," a place where shoppers can buy food as well as household consumer products at one time. Membership wholesale clubs are not appealing to Korean consumers because they typically buy small quantities frequently. Buying large volume at a deep, discounted price is not attractive to them. Also small housing cannot accommodate large shelf space to store the bigger volume.

As of 2002, 230 discount stores were operating in Korea, including multinational ones (Figure 18.2). This includes Costco (United States, entered in 1994), Carrefour (France, entered in 1996), Home Plus (a joint venture of Samsung and British Tesco, formed in 1999), and Wal-Mart (United States, entered in 1998 by acquiring Makro), as well as domestic discount stores, E-mart (Shinsegae group, started in 1993), and Lotte Mart (Lotte group, former name was Magnet, started in 1999). Wal-Mart and Carrefour exited in 2006.

Korea is the one of the few countries in the global marketplace in which local discounters outperform multinational discounters.[20] It was thought that retail liberalization in 1996 would allow multinational retailers to aggressively erode local markets. However, E-mart, a local discounter, has kept the top position for several years. Three discount stores currently wholly owned by foreign companies Carrefour, Wal-mart, and Costco accounted for only 25.8 percent of total discount store sales in 2001. The remaining 74.2 percent were accounted for by domestic discount stores E-mart, Lotte Mart, and Home Plus. E-mart alone controls 51 stores and shares 30 percent of the discount store market in Korea; second rank Lotte Mart shares 14 percent of the market.[21] Table 18.7 shows top 5 major discount store operators' sales revenue and their net profit.

**Table 18.7**
**Top Five Major Discount Store Operators in Korea**

| Company | Store Name | Number of Stores | Sales Revenue Million US $ | | % Change | Market Share |
| --- | --- | --- | --- | --- | --- | --- |
| | | | 2001 | 2002 | | |
| Shinsegae | E-Mart | 32 | 4,734.80 | 6,082.80 | 28.5 | 30 |
| Lotte Shopping | Lotte Mart | 51 | 4,372.40 | 5,444.30 | 24.5 | 14 |
| Carrefour Korea | Carrefour | 25 | 957.50 | 1,145.50 | 19.6 | 10 |
| Samsung Tesco | Home Plus | 21 | 1,059.20 | 1,789.00 | 68.9 | 13 |
| Wal-Mart Korea | Walmart Supercenter | 15 | 474.8 | 622.9 | 31.2 | 5 |

Source: Reorganized by the author based on Kim et al. (2003), p. 10.

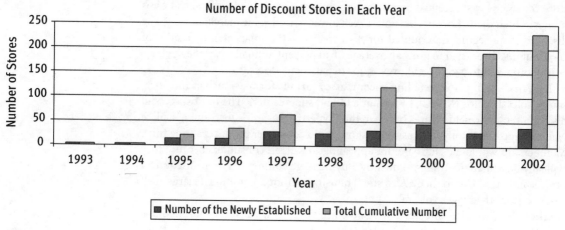

**Figure 18.2**
Number of Discount Stores
by Year. *Source: Korea
Chain Store Association.
(as cited in Kim et al.
(2003), p. 89)*

## Unique Features of Korean Discount Stores

Many reasons attributed to the success of E-mart and Lotte Mart over multinational discounters. The major reason is that domestic discounters comprehend the Korean consumers' tastes and shopping habit really well.[22] One example would be E-mart's creation of a shopping environment more suitable to Koreans' physical characteristics by adjusting the height and size of display racks and shopping carts.[23] The best example would be all varieties of fresh vegetables, fruits, and an instant cooking corner at discounted price. Korean consumers value freshness. They tend to buy groceries every day. E-mart accurately meets these needs. You will see very fresh vegetables and fruits delivered to the store just hours after being picked. I miss this freshness in the States. Seeing withered veggies at discount stores or supermarkets is nonsense in Korea.

If you stop by the instant cooking corner in any domestic discount store, you can request any ingredients and they'll make a dish for you within 10 minutes. Each corner cooks various traditional dishes and snacks upon request, right in front of customers, then wraps the dish for customers to take out.[24] To maintain freshness, leftover ingredients and dishes are typically discarded or sold at deep discounted prices on a daily basis. Some price-conscious Korean wives go to the store around store closing time to get this real deal. Korean people do not like to eat prepackaged frozen meals, so it is typical for Korean wives to cook a meal from scratch. Sometimes this is a burden for Korean consumers, and this instant cooking corner totally solves this problem. I remember shopping at domestic discount stores rather than the one operated by multinational discounters solely to enjoy these fresh dishes. Their success is such that retail practitioners and government officials from neighbor countries including Japan, China, Singapore, Taiwan, Philippines, and Vietnam, visit the stores to learn their success factors. Even the president of Target visited a local E-mart store recently and expressed a special interest in the instant cook corner. E-mart has had more than 70 formal visits of Japanese retail-related groups since 1999. The number is greater if unofficial visits are included.[25, 26]

**MEETING DEMANDING CONSUMERS BY HIGH-SERVICE LEVEL**    Hard-to-please Korean consumers are also well served in discount stores. High quality at low price is not enough. Regardless of retail formats, a pleasant shopping environment and friendly service are essential to satisfy choosy Korean consumers, who have long been accustomed to department stores.[27] To cater to these consumers and strive in fierce competitions, domestic discounters started to offer many other service stores under the roof just like department stores. This includes a free kids lounge, dry cleaners, ATM machine, flower shop, drug stores, banks, and nail care shop, in addition to the fancy food court. Discounters also use luxurious interiors and provide better-quality customer service as well as Everyday Low Price (EDLP). For a more upscale image, Korean domestic discounters also have started allocating larger space for well-known fashion brands. Apparel accounted for 9 percent of discount sales in Korea in 1999,[28] and apparel sales of Samsung-Tesco (Home Plus) were expected to account for 20 percent of total sales in 2001.[29] These services have become standard. Multinational discounters are now adopting localization to catch up domestic players. Aware of this competitive service of domestic discounters, Carrefour recently opened a large store in the complex of World Cup Stadium (of World Cup 2002 fame) and provided one-stop service with a food court, beauty salon, and even a movie theater. Carrefour is even offering a community center, free cooking classes, English lessons, and more in a recently opened store.[30]

**NOT JUST FOR PRODUCT ACQUISITION BUT FOR FAMILY ACTIVITIES**
Shopping at a discount store was basically assumed to be for a solely utilitarian purpose: product acquisition. But one recent study found that Korean discount shoppers visit the stores not only to purchase products for "value for the money" (i.e., utilitarian), but also to seek distraction from everyday routine life (i.e., diversion) and to enjoy being in crowds (i.e., socialization).[31]

Before the introduction of discount stores, basically women shopped. Now you will see many Korean families, especially young married couples with children, who shop at discount stores. Shopping at discount stores is no longer a chore for Korean families. It is a fun event that every member in the family can do together. A neat and spacious atmosphere with varieties of food is perfect for them to enjoy half a day on a weekend.

For Korean consumers, being able to shop at modern discount stores may provide them with feeling some kind of achievement, especially for middle-income customers, the major target markets in Korea. Before, lower-income shoppers generally bought staple goods in small neighborhood shops or general markets. Today not only middle-income groups but also lower-income shoppers can shop at discount stores.

**PRIVATE BRAND IS POPULAR IN DISCOUNT STORES**    Private brand was initially introduced by Korean department stores but realized only minimum success. However, private brand in discount stores has been a huge success. PB products in Korean discount stores currently generate approximately 8 to 10 percent of total sales.[32] E-mart pioneered in developing private brands. HomePlus introduced a private clothing brand and succeeded enough to sell the brand countrywide. Both HomePlus and Carrefour have numerous private brands in processed foods and electric home appliances.[33] Private brand success is important to Korean retailers as this is the first time that consumers have bought less familiar brand names.

## Convenience Stores

BRIEF HISTORY    The first three convenience stores in Korea started their business in 1989 by making joint venture or license agreements with global convenience operators. These stores include 7-Eleven (7-Eleven Japan/Donghwa Industrial Company, taken by Lotte in 1994), Lawson (Dairy Mart American/Taein Distribution Co.; Kolon group acquired Taein in 1995; merged by 7-Eleven in 1999), and Circle-K (US Circle-K/Hanyang group, changed its name to C-Space after expiration of a licensing agreement in 1998). In 1990, Family Mart (Family Mart Japan/Bokwang Co) and Mini Stop (Mini Stop Japan/Daesang group) joined this industry. In the same year, LG 25 (LG group) opened the first convenience store by Koreans without affiliation with foreign company.

Domination by a couple of players is even worse in the convenience store sector than in department and discount stores. Big Three convenience store players Family Mart (25.1 percent), 7-Eleven (24.7 percent), and LG 25 (19.9 percent), dominate approximately three-quarters of Korean market share (Table 18.8).[34]

As of 2002, there are more than 5,680 convenience stores in Korea. The industry reached its market saturation here in about 15 years. In particular, the population/store index, an indicator of saturation level, in Seoul, reaches approximately 5,000 persons per convenience store, almost the same level as in the United States or Japan.[35]

One of the biggest reasons for this saturation would be that many convenience store businesses in Korea are run by franchise agreement. A store can be opened and managed relatively easily and can generate decent and stable profits without sophisticated management skills. Current unstable employment also added to this trend. Employment was once considered lifelong; layoff was uncommon in Korea. However, these days many Korean companies evaluate employees based on their performance, so moving to another company and scouting by a personnel management company becomes common. Consequently, early retirees often invest their retirement assets to convenience stores.

UNIQUE CHARACTERISTICS OF CONVENIENCE STORES IN KOREA    Unlike the United States, convenience stores in Korea are independently located near residential areas (41 percent), business and office areas (36 percent), subway or railroad stations (15 percent), and near high schools and colleges (8 percent).[36] Among 12 players of convenience stores in Korea, only two, OK mart and Joy mart, are operated together with a gas station, the typical format of a U.S. convenience store. Same as Japan, convenience stores are almost always open 24 hours seven days a week, even during Korean Thanksgiving (*Chu Seok*) and on New Year's Day (*Sul Nal*). For Koreans, convenience store means a place you can shop anytime. Along with the typical merchandise assortment, telephone cards, lottery tickets, photo processing, and ATM machines are basic. If you run out of cell phone batteries in Korea, go to a convenience store. You can charge your cell phone at a reasonable price. If you have not had breakfast, you can pick snacks on your way to

Table 18.8
Number of Major Supermarkets by 1995–2002

| | | | | | Unit: Million US $ | | | | | |
|---|---|---|---|---|---|---|---|---|---|---|
| Brand | Established | 1995 | 1996 | 1997 | 1998 | 1999 | 2000 | 2001 | 2002 | Share % |
| Family Mart | 1990.10 | 320 | 362 | 473 | ´493 | 529 | 646 | 903 | 1,429 | 25.1 |
| 7-Eleven | 1989.5 | 114 | 129 | 165 | 171 | 252 | 672 | 1,001 | 1,403 | 24.7 |
| LG25 | 1990.12 | 290 | 361 | 476 | 496 | 546 | 622 | 780 | 1,128 | 19.9 |
| Mini Stop | 1990.11 | 193 | 189 | 175 | 180 | 189 | 255 | 406 | 677 | 11.9 |

Source: Reorganized by the author based on Kim et al. (2003), p. 160.

the office. If you don't have time to each lunch, choose ready-to-eat meals such as lunch boxes, sandwiches, and GimBap (Korean style of California roll). You can even pay your phone and insurance bills in most convenience stores, even after the bank is closed (Koreans pay their bills at a local bank; now they can use the Internet). The highlight of the convenience store service is their holding Internet-ordered goods for you. This service benefits everybody involved—consumers, delivery companies, and convenience stores. Consumers do not need to be home to receive their ordered goods. Delivery companies can save their cost. Convenience stores can increase customer satisfaction and be insured of more visits from consumers. This is feasible because so many convenience stores exist around every neighborhood.

## Supermarkets

Korean supermarkets carry approximately 80 percent food and 20 percent non-food. Many supermarkets in Korea are not part of a national (or regional) chain. Back in the 1970s, supermarket meant a modern grocery store, as opposed to the traditional wet market. Because of this, Korean people still call small independent mom-and-pop stores around neighborhoods supermarkets. So supermarket in Korea could mean either small independent neighborhood store that focuses on groceries, or large (but a lot smaller than discount stores) corporate-led national chain stores. This book focuses on national chain supermarkets.

The first supermarket in Korea, New Seoul Supermarket, started in 1968, but the second supermarket did not appear until the mid 1970s. In 1971, the first supermarket chain, Saemaeul ("new village") Super Chain, started its business with eight stores.[37] During the 1980s and 1990s, supermarkets replaced traditional marketplaces due to increasing apartment complexes in Seoul. However, in the late 1990s major supermarket chains, such as Hannam super chain and Haitai distribution, went bankrupt due to financial crisis and fierce competition with discount stores.[38] Now Big Three chains operating in Korea as of 2002 include LG supermarket (LG group, owns 66 stores nationwide), Top Mart (Seowon distribution, mainly in Busan area, owns 39 stores), and Hanhwa Mart (Hanwha group, owns 26 stores).[39]

The supermarket in Korea is relatively underdeveloped because discount stores expanded aggressively (now numbering 230 stores), accommodating one-stop shopping with attractive merchandises and super services. This competition with discount stores grew even worse. As they reached saturation and could not find big lots to build new discount stores, Lotte Mart started to open smaller-size discount stores (or Super-Supermarket) called Lotte Lemon in residential districts of Seoul's metropolitan area. As of 2002, there were nine Lotte Lemon stores. This super-supermarket targets consumers within five minutes' walking distance. Joining the fray, E-mart opened the same concept of super-supermarket named E-mart Everyday. Discount store shoppers typically drive to the store because of the volume they need to carry, while a supermarket shopper usually walks to the store and buys a small quantity frequently.

Supermarket companies find new ways to compete with discount stores. An example is delivery of ordered goods. Supermarket shoppers walk to a store and shop; the store delivers the goods purchased within a couple hours with no fee. Supermarket companies believe that consumers buy more if they don't have to carry their purchases home.

## Home Shopping

Home shopping is very appealing to Korean consumers. The first TV home shopping, "39 shopping," started in 1995 and then later changed its name to CJ home shopping. LG home shopping followed in 1999. LG and CJ are the major players of TV home shopping in Korea; they ranked first and second, respectively, in 2001. These two players also have catalog and Internet sales, making them multichannel retailers.

## Internet Shopping

Korea has a high potential in the Internet market. It ranks world's third in Internet use, just after the United States and Canada,[40] and the world's first in broadband penetration. More than 20 out of every 100 Koreans have broadband Internet access (i.e., highspeed network, such as ADSL or VDSL) at home.[41] There were 2,896 Internet shopping malls in Korea at the end of 2002. Among these, specialty malls number about 2,496 and 402 are general malls (Korea Chamber of Commerce and Industry, 2003).[42] Internet shopping malls are also driven by major Korean retail groups. Lotte and Hyundai department stores opened their Internet stores in 1996 and 1997. In 1997, two pure dot com retailers, Hansol CSN (Hansol group) and Inter Park (Dacom company) started Internet sales. After this, Shinsegae and LG all joined Internet business. Except Hansol CSN and Inter Park, major players own multi-channels (i.e., catalogs, TV home shopping, department stores) and utilize their multiple channels to create synergies.

There are many small independent Internet retailers in Korea. Korean people are generally very Internet and technology savvy. Putting a computer together using parts is a piece of cake for many young generations. Selling goods over the Internet is not a big task for them. Many independent Internet retailers run their business with a few people in a small office, sometimes at home.

## > SUMMARY

Due to its export-driven economy, the Korean retail industry has not received substantial support from Korean government, compared to manufacturing industry. In achieving its aggressive economic development plans, several Chaebol (large conglomerate family-controlled business) groups such as Samsung, Hyundai, and LG, have formed. These Chaebol groups not only led the country's economic development and became world-rank manufacturers; they also played an important role in shaping its retail industry. Major retailers in many retail formats in Korea are owned and operated by these Chaebol groups. Two major characteristics of Korea's retail industry include high concentration of major players and a high number of retail stores. For example, three top department stores represent 75 percent of Korea's department store market. However, overall Korea's retail market is highly fragmented, having 15.1 retail stores per 1,000 people on average.

As with other Asian countries, Confucianism influenced every aspect of Korean society. Because of this influence, Korean consumers pay particular attention to their behavior and appearance in public settings. Yon-go is the special connection based on family, school, and birthplaces; however, its influence in business contexts has drastically diminished. Korean consumers are notorious for being demanding and picky and have higher expectations for service. This demand has created diverse, unique services in almost every retail format. For example, delivering ordered goods to home for free from a local supermarket is common.

Korea fully opened its retail market in 1996; however, discount stores and convenience stores are the only channels that multinational retailers expanded to Korea. Contrary to initial expectation, Korean domestic discounters outperform multinational discounters. Currently, e-commerce and TV home shopping channels are gaining in popularity.

## > KEY TERMS

CHAEBOL

CONFUCIANISM

EXPORT-DRIVEN ECONOMY

FACE

FRANCHISED SALES OUTLET

HIGHLY CONCENTRATED

YON-GO

## > DISCUSSION QUESTIONS

1. There are some similarities between the Korean and Japanese systems of business groups. How are the Korean Chaebol similar or different from the Japanese Sogo Shosha? Remember the Japanese Sogo Shosha were business groups discussed in Chapter 15.

2. Convenience stores serve a similar purpose in Korea and Japan, they are somewhat like extended home offices. People can pay bills, pick up merchandise that

has been ordered from catalogues, send a fax, etc. Why do you think that convenience stores have taken on this additional role in Korea and Japan?

3. How does the Confucian culture affect consumers' attitudes and activities? How do you think it would affect business relationships?

4. In Korea supermarkets deliver food to customers' homes without charge. What characteristics of the Korean market make this possible?

## › ENDNOTES

1. Sternquist, B., and B. Jin. (1998). "South Korean Retail Industry: Government's Role in Retail Liberalization." *International Journal of Retail and Distribution Management,* 26(9), pp. 345–353.

2. Haggard, S., et al., eds. (2003). *Economic Crisis and Corporate Restructuring in Korea: Reforming the Chaebol.* Cambridge University Press, p. 41.

3. Sternquist, B., and B. Jin. (1998).

4. Kim, D. H., H. Kim, S. H. Ahn, C. H. Oh, C. Park, I. S. Son, and K. J. Lee. (2003). *Korea's Retail Industry in the New Millennium.* Korea Chamber of Commerce & Industry, Seoul, Korea.

5. Kim et al. (2003).

6. Lee, H.-C. (1998–1999). "Transformation of Employment Practices in Korean Businesses." *International Studies of Management and Organization,* 28(4), 26–39.

7. Lee. (1998–1999), p.30–31.

8. "What Cosmetics Korean Women Are Using." (January 23, 2006). *Chosun Il bo,* A2 (in Korean).

9. Porter, M. E. (1998). *The Competitive Advantage of Nations.* NY: The Free Press.

10. Jin, B., and H-C. Moon. (2006). "The Diamond Approach to the Competitiveness of Korea's Apparel Industry: Michael Porter and Beyond." *Journal of Fashion Marketing and Management,* 10(2), 195–208.

11. Jin, B., and A. Koh. (1999). "Differences Between South Korean Male and Female Consumers in the Clothing Brand Loyalty Formation Process: Model Testing. *Clothing and Textiles Research Journal,* 17(3), 117–127.

12. Sternquist, B., and B. Jin. (1998).

13. Kim et al. (2003).

14. Kim et al. (2003)

15. Sternquist, B., and B. Jin. (1998).

16. Kim et al. (2003)

17. Chung, J.-E., B. Jin, and B. Sternquist. (under review). "Market Orientation, Dependence, and Coercion Effects on Economic and Non-economic Satisfaction when the Retailer Has Power."

18. *Country Commercial Guide* (2002), Korea Country Commercial Guide FY 2002, U.S. Commercial Service, available at http://usatrade.gov/website/ccg.nsf/ShowCCG?OpenForm&Country=Korea (accessed 27 April, 2002).

19. *Country Commercial Guide* (2002).

20. Jin, B., and J.O. Kim. (2003). "A Typology of Korean Discount Shoppers: Shopping Motives, Store Attributes, and Outcomes. *International Journal of Service Industry Management,* 14(4), 396–419.

21. Kim et al. (2003), p.26.

22. Jin, B., and J.O. Kim. (2003).

23. Jin, B., and Y.G. Suh, (2005). "Integrating Effect of Consumer Perception Factors in Predicting Private Brand Purchase in a Korean Discount Store Context." *Journal of Consumer Marketing,* 22(2), 62–71.

24. Distribution Journal. (June 2002). "Asian Countries Eager to learn Korean Discount Stores," *Distribution Journal,* pp. 30–33 (in Korean).

25. *Distribution Journal* (June 2002).

26. Cheil Economic News (October 17, 2005). "Han Ryu in Retail Industry" (in Korean).

27. Kim et al. (2003).

28. *Country Commercial Guide* (2002).

29. *Korea Economic Daily* (August 6, 2001). Apparel in Discount Store Reaches Golden Age." *Korea Economic Daily,* p. 28 (in Korean).

30. Kim et al. (2003).

31. Jin, B., and J.O. Kim. (2003).

32. Jin, B., and Y.G. Suh. (2005).

33. Kim et al. (2003).

34. Kim et al. (2003).

35. Kim et al. (2003).

36. Kim et al. (2003).

37. Kim et al. (2003).

38. Kim et al. (2003).

39. Kim et al. (2003).

40. Ipsos Reid (December 10, 2002). "Internet Use Continues to Climb in Most Markets." Retrieved March 22, 2003, from http://www.ipsos-reid.com

41. OECD (2002, September). "Broadband Access in OECD Countries per 100 Inhabitants." Retrieved March 24, 2003 from http://www.oecd.org/EN/document/0,,EN-document-29-nodirectorate-no-1-39262-29,00.html

42. Korea Chamber of Commerce and Industry. (2003).

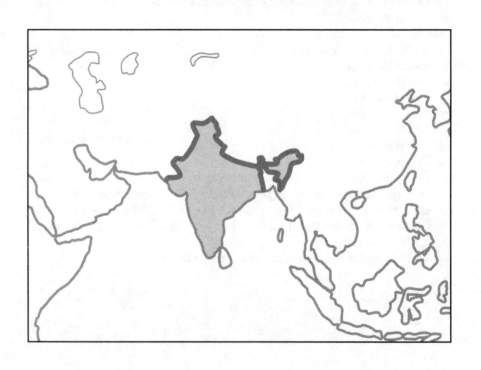

# 19

# RETAILING IN INDIA

Brenda Sternquist and Payal Dupta

## After reading this chapter, you should understand

› What it means for retailing not to have "industry" status in India.

› How the special regulations for transferring goods from one Indian state to another affect retailing.

› How religious practices alter retailing in India

## › COUNTRY BACKGROUND

Europeans discovered India just 500 hundred years ago. Indians calculate their history in millions of years, however; Western scientists and archaeologists credited the oldest civilization in India to 5,000 years. We will briefly trace the history of India with the arrival of the Europeans. A group of 101 subscribers formed the East India Company on September 22, 1599, in England. On December 31, 1600, Queen Elizabeth I gave the company a 15-year charter of exclusive privilege for trade beyond the Straits of Magellan and the Cape of Good Hope. The company's first ship sailed in 1601. Their third voyage, the first to India, arrived at the port of Surat, the chief town of Gujarat, where the first presidency was established in 1629. In 1687, the presidency shifted to Bombay. Meanwhile, the presidency of Madras was established in 1651. Later, the Bengal presidency was established in 1700. The activities of the company were limited to trade only until 1764, when the province of Bengal came under the rule of the company from the Mogul governor.

Being bankrupt, the company sought financial aid from the British government. The Regulatory Act of 1773 provided for a Governor General at Calcutta with supervisory powers over Bombay and Madras. Later, by enacting Pitt's India Act, the British Government virtually took over governing through a Board of Control in 1784. In 1793 the company's monopoly of trade with India was relinquished and by 1813, trade with India was completely open.

Up until 1818 the company's expansion took place within India. Thereafter it penetrated Afghanistan, across the Arabian Sea and the Bay of Bengal, and into Burma. In 1824 all Dutch possessions in India were passed to British by the Treaty of London.

After losing the monopoly over China trade in 1834 at the time of renewing the charter, the company ceased trading altogether. The charter stipulated that the company sold all its properties and possessions in the interest of the shareholders. The last charter expired on June 1, 1874.

Until 1833 the three presidencies were virtually three separate states with separate laws for everything. In that year the first steps towards unification of all British possessions in India were taken. The Governor General of Bengal was renamed the Governor General of India and the Presidency of North West Provinces was created, with the Agra as its headquarters, by dividing the Bengal Presidency.

Following the rebellion in 1857, the British Government directly assumed the rule over India as the Crown Colony in 1858. The Governor General of India became the Viceroy of India, and the President of the Board of Control in London became the Secretary of State for India. In 1935 Aden and Burma were separated from India.

Before leaving, the British created the dominions of India and Pakistan in 1947 by dividing India into two. Several hundred princely states acceded to India and it became a republic in 1950. India took over the French Settlements in India in 1954 and the Portuguese possessions in 1961. In 1972 East Pakistan became Bangladesh.[1]

Before going to India for my first visit in 2003 I didn't have a particular interest in that part of the world. I couldn't have been more wrong. I spent two weeks talking with retailing executives and what I found was amazing. The retail system in India is truly unique. The fact that they have had a total ban on foreign direct investment means that external influences have not modernized the system. In January 2006 the government announced that they would allow retailers who produce their own products in India to open retail stores there. This means that companies like Nike can open stores, but companies like Wal-Mart cannot. I don't think it will be long before Wal-Mart is allowed to open stores in India since in 2004 they purchased over 1.5 billion dollars worth of merchandise from India. The Indian retail market is the eighth-largest in the world, but 95 percent of sales are generated by mom-and-pop stores that are generally referred to as unorganized retailing.[2]

The purpose of my second trip was to attend the wedding of one of my colleagues, so I was thrown into an amazing cultural event. The reception held at an open air rock garden was attended by thousands of guests. There were three live bands and dozens of restaurants catered the food. I noticed that there were armed guards everywhere and asked one of my dinner companions, "Do you have trouble here at weddings?" He laughed and said, "No, the guards are hired by insurance companies to protect the jewelry." I had noticed that the women at this event wore fabulous diamond, emerald, and ruby jewelry. Quite a contrast to the poverty that is the norm for India. My Indian colleague's family provided me with a car and driver for my stay. It was a white Mercedes. He looked like a young Antonio Banderas. Each time he braked at a stop sign, dozens of bony women tapped on our window, begging for money. Many times they carried a child who looked close to death. The driver kept a container full of coins that he distributed to the beggars, who are everywhere. It was nearly impossible for me to walk down the street because I would be the target of beggars who literally stopped me in my tracks.

## ❭ OVERVIEW OF THE INDIAN RETAIL INDUSTRY AND ITS UNIQUE FEATURES

Tables 19.1 and 19.2 summarize the major domestic and foreign retailers in India. The retail industry in India is estimated to be worth $250 billion.[3] There are approximately 12 million retail outlets in India, two-thirds of which are in rural areas. Although there have been significant changes in the business landscape since the economy's liberalization more than a decade ago, the shadow of the LICENCE RAJ (government regulatory intervention) has not completely lifted. For example, the 49 percent limit for foreign direct investment in telecommunication companies discourages global firms from investing in the Indian telecommunications industry in India.[4] This regulatory environment affects the behavioral relationships between channel partners.

The coexistence of organized and unorganized retailers, a differential taxation system, and high import duties lead to the proliferation of a GRAY MARKET. Gray market means the goods are not counterfeit but are not being sold legally, generally meaning they are off the ledger.

The first unique feature dealing with the industry structure is the coexistence of the ORGANIZED RETAILERS (ORs) with UNORGANIZED RETAILERS (UORs). For the purpose of this chapter, the concept of an organization is used as a continuous variable (UORs to the ORs), which can be described in terms of buying power, average size, number of stock keeping units (SKUs), stock turn, and gross margin (see Table 19.1).

The average size, revenues, profitability, and geographical spread of the organized retailer is considerably higher than that of the unorganized retailer. Consequently, the organized retailer leverages its large size and high buying power to source

**Table 19.1**
**India—Leading Domestic Retailers, 2004**

| | | Total Sales and Stores | | | Global Rank and Penetration | | | Domestic Market | |
| Company | Primary Line of Trade | Net Sales ($US Mil) | % Chg Sales | Total Stores | 2004 Rank, Top 200 Retailers Worldwide | Single-country, Regional or Global? | Number of countries | Share of total sales | Share of total stores |
|---|---|---|---|---|---|---|---|---|---|
| 1 Pantaloon Retail (India) Limited | Hypermarkets/Supercenters, | 240 | 64.7% | 68 | — | Single Country | 1 | 0% | 0% |
| 2 RPG Group | Supermarkets/Grocery Stores | 166 | 36.4% | 327 | — | Single Country | 1 | 0% | 0% |
| 3 Shoppers' Stop Ltd. | Department Stores | 118 | 28.8% | 38 | — | Single Country | 1 | 0% | 0% |
| 4 Vivek & Co. | Consumer Electronics & Appliances | 73 | N/A | 52 | — | Single Country | 1 | 0% | 0% |
| 5 Raymond Ltd. | Apparel Stores | 64 | 9.5% | 352 | — | Global | 9 | 7% | 12% |
| 6 Subhiksha Trading Services | Discount Food Stores | 62 | 18.3% | 183 | — | Single Country | 1 | 0% | 0% |
| 7 Trent Ltd. | Department Stores | 50 | 54.7% | 19 | — | Single Country | 1 | 0% | 0% |
| 8 Madura Garments | Apparel Stores | 45 | 10.1% | 309 | — | Global | 3 | N/A | 1% |
| 9 Ebony Retail Holdings | Department Stores | 21 | 17.1% | 8 | — | Single Country | 1 | 0% | 0% |

Sources: Retail Forward, company annual reports and published reports

**Table 19.2**
**India—Key Foreign Retailers, 2004**

| Company | Headquarters | Retail Sector | Primary Line of Trade | Global Rank and Penetration | | |
|---|---|---|---|---|---|---|
| | | | | 2004 Rank, Top 200 Retailers Worldwide | Single-country, Regional or Global? | Number of countries |
| Alticor/Amway | United States | FDM | Non-Store | 119 | Global | 80 |
| Dairy Farm International Holdings Limited | Hong Kong | FDM | Convenience Stores | 162 | Regional | 8 |
| Landmark Group | Dubai | Softgoods | Department Stores | — | Global | N/A |
| Marks & Spencer PLC | United Kingdom | Softgoods | Department Stores | 49 | Global | 32 |
| Metro AG | Germany | FDM | Cash & Carries/Warehouse Clubs | 4 | Global | 29 |

Sources: Retail Forward, company annual reports and published reports

**Table 19.3**
**Characteristics of the Unorganized and Organized Retailers in India (Estimates)**

| Parameters | Unorganized Retailers | Organized Retailers |
| --- | --- | --- |
| Average size (square feet) | 300 | 4,000 |
| Number of stock keeping units | 1,200 | 5,000 |
| Service format | Over the counter | Self service |
| Ambience | Rational | Experiential |
| Sales/square foot. (estimate) | 4,000 | 14,000 |
| Stock turn | 12–18 | 20–25 |
| Gross margin (percentage) | 7–10 | 18–20 |
| Net margin (percentage) | 6–7 | 4–5 |

Source: Kurt Salmon Associates Dec. 2000.

from multiple suppliers. The unorganized retailer has a low buying power and is not able to source from a similar number of suppliers. Therefore, in effect the organized retailer creates a buyer's market with its suppliers while the UOR creates a seller's market.

The second unique feature deals with the taxation policy toward corporate and commercial establishments in India. Due to the differing tax rates between cities, states, and districts, along with the absence of a value-added tax structure for commercial establishments, the UOR does not get captured in the tax system. Therefore, it creates a buyer's market for the UOR and a seller's market for the OR.

The final unique feature that influences the Indian retail industry is the high import duties levied for imported products. This duty structure creates a gray market for supply of certain categorized products (e.g., computer products, stationery).

**Photo 19.1**
Shoppers on a busy street in Khajuraho can purchase all types of merchandise from unorganized retailers. *Courtesy O. Alamany & E. Vicens/CORBIS.*

**Table 19.4**
**Unique Features of the Indian Retailing Industry**

| Unique Features | Organized Retailer | Un-organized Retailer |
| --- | --- | --- |
| Coexistence of the organized and unorganized retailers | Creates a buyer's market | Creates a seller's market |
| Differential taxation system | Creates a seller's market | Creates a buyer's market |
| Existence of a gray market | Creates a seller's market | Creates a buyer's market |

This market is characterized by cash and carry terms and conditions. The organized retailer procures products from a limited number of such gray market firms, thus creating a seller's market. The unorganized retailer creates a buyer's market with its ability to procure from a large number of gray market firms. The above unique features lead to the creation of either a seller's or a buyer's market for the organized or unorganized retailer (See Table 19.4).

## › ADAPTATION OF CONCEPTUAL FRAMEWORK
## TO THE INDIAN RETAIL INDUSTRY

According to the Inter-Organizational Exchange Behavior Framework, the source initiates, implements and reviews the exchange relationship with the target.[5]

### Initiation

The retailer will initiate a search for viable exchange partners. The process may start with people the retailer knows—friends, salespersons or potential business associates—forming the EVOKED SET. Evoked set means the alternative you will consider. The source contacts representatives of the firm in question and discusses the benefits of the exchange. The expected outcome will be EXTRINSIC REWARDS (increase in market share, sales volume, and profits) as well as INTRINSIC REWARDS (psychological pleasure gained by achievement and status within the company/industry). Extrinsic means the external aspects to the unit getting the rewards. Intrinsic means that it is internal to the unit getting the rewards.

Organized retailers prefer long-term associations with their suppliers, which helps guarantee a regular supply of merchandise at the desired quality and acceptable costs. The supplier selection process for the OR is formally structured through negotiations, contractual obligations, and periodic transactions. This is essential for the organizational planning, production, and sales processes to function smoothly. For example, The Radhakrishna group, a Mumbai-based retailer who specializes in food catering and owns the Foodland supermarket, has a roster of about 30 suppliers for dry groceries. Out of these 30, only a few have changed over the past 10 years. The UOR is unable to invest into long-term supplier relationships through a formal process because the sourcing for such retailers is done on a need-to-buy basis through cash-and-carry processes at irregular intervals. Therefore, we conclude that the ORs have a more complex initiation process than the UOR.

For the UOR the initiation process will be more informal—no written documentation, payment by cash against delivery, and a credit period based on the relationship between the UOR and the supplier. Further, the rewards for the UOR will be intrinsic in nature.

The higher the organization of the retailer, the larger its average size, the greater the number of SKUs, the greater the stock turns, and the higher the sales volume and profits (see Table 19.1). A typical example of an OR is Subhiksha, one of Chennai's (southern Indian city) largest supermarket and pharmacy chains.

The behavioral relationships in the form of role expectancies between retailers and suppliers will vary depending on the position of the supplier in the value chain. The supplier can be a manufacturer, distributor, or wholesaler. The relationship differs between UOR and ORs since ORs can leverage their purchasing power to obtain volume discounts.

Due to its size, Subhiksha qualifies for deep discounts since they purchase in bulk directly from the manufacturers or the distributor. Further, FoodWorld, a business of Subhiksha, has many stores across India. It operates out of a centralized distribution center that supports all the stores, simplifying logistics operations and removing the middlemen. As a result, the manufacturer's role changes from a price regulator to a discounter.

The organized retailer can source and procure from a limited number of suppliers due to the taxation policies. An organized retailer can deal only with those suppliers who can issue a legal bill of receipt. Therefore, a seller's market is created for the organized retailer, as they are limited to dealing with legitimate vendors.

In a seller's market, the initiation process is based on the legal status of the supplier. The organized retailer will register and conduct business with the supplier if the above criterion is met. The legal status of the supplier is relevant for the OR but not for the UOR. As a result, there are more legal complexities for an OR.

## Implementation Process

Implementation begins when the exchange of product, services, and information start to take place between the supplier and the retailer. For an OR, a supplier's performance will determine the retailer's dependence and the supplier's power.[6] Further, based on the channel position of each firm, certain norms or rules of conduct can exist in the industry that contribute to each firm's market share, financial strength, and standing in the marketplace (e.g., price maintenance). In India, the manufacturer usually sets the MANUFACTURER'S RECOMMENDED PRICE (MRP) which is printed on the product. MRP is a price at which the manufacturer wants the retailer to sell the merchandise.

Due to a limit on the alternatives for the UOR, the power in the distribution channel relationship rests with the supplier. However, for the OR, the power in the relationship is more balanced. In the retail industry, a large number of manufacturers compete for shelf space, leading to a low bargaining power for the suppliers. Therefore, when the buying power of a retailer decreases, the power tilts towards the supplier and vice versa.[7]

For example, Ravji's, a combination superstore originally based in Ahmedabad, does bulk buying from the manufacturers or their distributors. Daily stock-taking is undertaken and orders are placed according to the predetermined reorder levels.

In the case of Subhiksha, bulk purchases directly from the manufacturers or the distributor qualify for deep discounts. Quick inventory turns also improve the cash flow and reduce operating costs for the company.[8]

NORMS can be defined as expectations about behavior that are at least partially shared by a group of decision makers.[9] In our case, these norms depend on the channel position of the supplier.

DISCRETE exchange norms contain expectations about an individualistic or competitive interaction between exchange partners. The individualistic parties are expected to remain autonomous and pursue strategies aimed toward the attainment of their individual goals. In contrast, RELATIONAL exchange norms are based on the expectation of mutuality of interest, essentially prescribing stewardship behavior, and are designed to enhance the well being of the relationship as a whole.

Compared to the OR, it is easier, less risky, and less cumbersome for the UOR to procure items from the gray market. For the OR, the ratio of risk to profit is higher in this case. As a result, in some product categories, the UOR has higher levels of product innovation. FoodWorld and the *kirana* (mom-and-pop store) grocery store might have the same brands of white flour on its shelves. While the kirana store proprietor can supplement his/her stock of flour with unbranded flour, FoodWorld cannot do so. This is because the unbranded flour comes from the open market, and buying from this market would lead to higher complexity and losses for the OR. For example, FoodWorld would have to package the food, barcode it, and bear transportation costs, which would decrease their profit margin on this product.[10]

## Review Process

This process encompasses an evaluation of the rewards or losses for each firm from the exchange. Both the supplier and retailer make attributes of responsibility for their rewards and/or losses. They use these attributes as cues to ascribe character to each firm, thereby influencing evaluations of personnel and firm performance. The review process of the OR is more detailed and more dependent on technology. For example, Pantaloon has implemented BAAN software through which the concept of category management has been imposed. The key performance measurement parameters for Pantaloon are return per square foot and the individual category profits.

For the OR, the accounting department usually conducts the review process using a prescribed method. For the UOR the review process is done by the owner using an off the record of stock turns as an indicator of rewards or losses.

The role expectancies are high for the OR. When the actual performance fails to meet the expected rewards, frustration and eventual termination of the relationship ensues.

Krishnan, Koelemeijer, and Rao have highlighted a concept called COMMITMENT TO CONSISTENT ASSORTMENT (C2C).[11] By consistency in assortment, they imply a tacit promise by the retailer to carry a given set of brands and sizes over time, assuring the consumer that he/she will find his/her product of choice in that retail store. Retailers who maintain a C2C will not practice opportunistic buying, since this introduces inconsistencies in the product assortment.

The OR usually maintains a wide range for a particular product category, i.e., an OR has commitment to consistent assortment (C2C). Usually, the UOR does not keep the full product range and the products are bought based on the attractiveness of the deals they get; they are opportunistic buyers. Therefore, their product assortment is usually inconsistent and may be termed as SCRAMBLED. The UOR stocks fast-moving items, which maximize the stock turns. (BCCL, 2000–01).

There are a number of reasons the OR does not buy from the unregistered supplier. Unregistered suppliers are those who sell merchandise off record. They do this so that they do not have to pay taxes and can therefore sell for a much lower price. One such reason is that the OR needs to file tax returns at the end of the year and needs a legal receipt of sale that might not always be available from an off the record supplier.

Further, the organized retailer maintains a consistent product assortment for its consumers. In order to maintain this consistency, it needs to be assured of the continuous availability of the product from the supplier. In the case of an unregistered supplier who sells imported products, there is no assurance of product availability. Therefore, these factors create barriers and limit the number of suppliers for the OR.

However, since most UORs do not pay taxes and do carry scrambled merchandise, the choice of suppliers is broader.

As mentioned earlier, due to the legal status of the supplier, a buyer's market is created for the UOR and a seller's market is created for the OR. As a result, the UOR is able to offer lower prices since they do not charge taxes to the end consumer and also have lower operational costs. Since they procure low-priced products from the gray market, the UOR has lower pricing for certain products as compared to the OR.

The organized players have to bear high costs arising from labor, social security to employees, retail outlets at high traffic areas, larger floor space and comfort facilities, such as air conditioning and backup power supply. This puts them at a disadvantage cost-wise compared to the UOR.

The Indian system is very flexible; its food industry is dominated by manufacturers who set retail prices. Also, depending on the level of organization of the Indian retailer from organized to unorganized, the buyer/supplier relationships differ. In 1994 Bandyopadhyay, Robicheaux, and Hill[8] found that relationships between retail buyers and suppliers in India are high from the onset of the business relationship, in contrast to the West, where relationships begin at a low level and may gradually build over time. Larger retailers buy products in bulk and the relationship moves from being more functional (based on solidarity, mutuality, flexibility, role integrity, and trust) to being more price based. Small retailers use their relationships to leverage their discounts. For instance, supermarket margins are typically in the range of 14 to 16 percent resulting in a 3 to 5 percent of sales-before-tax profit. Consequently, Indian retailers negotiate margin rather than price. This system favors private labels where the retailers can establish their own margin base without interference from the manufacturers.

Before large manufacturers introduce new products in India, they conduct extensive consumer research and test marketing. Because there is little price discounting, retail buyers are confident that prices being offered to them are fair. Manufacturers give incentive to dealers and wholesalers, but retailers do not use volume or purchasing power to negotiate discounts. Finally, while there are no slotting allowances given, marketing support is given in terms of promotional allowances and rebates.

Though slotting allowances are not used in India, other forms of trade assistance —promotional allowances and rebates—are in place. In a fixed price system, these types of trade assistance make a significant difference in the retailer's final margin. We expect, though, that the greater the level of supplier role performance, the less important this type of trade assistance will become. Therefore, we predict a negative relationship between a supplier's role performance and the trade assistance required by the retailer.

India has developed a geographically (i.e., state) based supply structure because of the unique tax system within each state. A tariff is charged on merchandise shipped from one state to another, making it costly to purchase merchandise from outside the state of sale. A VAT system should reduce the costs of sourcing outside the state in the long run; however, the current system has been in existence for many years and changes will likely be slow. National manufacturers get around this system by using local agents in each state, a costly practice. Consequently, the geographic differences for branded products are not as high as one might expect.

This section of the chapter describes the impact of the unique features of a developing market on the initiation, implementation, and review process of buyer-supplier relationships. Such an elucidation improves the understanding of behavioral channel relationships across similar countries. In the next section I will discuss market liberalization in India. The environment is unique. To help explain the role of India's government plays I will use the conceptual framework of state as strategist.

## › INDIA'S GOVERNMENT—STATE AS STRATEGIST

Unlike manufacturing, the retail industry is a local industry. As such, it is often the object of government regulations. Governments use regulations to limit imported merchandise, reduce excessive price competition, and protect domestic businesses.

### Ban on Foreign Investment in Retailing

The state has exerted great influence over retail development in India. In January 2006 the Indian government announced that it would allow foreign retailers who produce their own product to also sell their products at the retail level. This gives private label producers entry into the Indian retail sector, but not multibrand retailers such as Wal-Mart. Actually the ban on foreign retailers did not exist until 1997; before that time Dairy Farm entered the Indian market in a joint venture with Food World. Indian consumers see names like Marks & Spencer and Mango around them. What they do not realize is that these stores are licensed outlets, totally owned by Indian nationals. The fast-food industry is considered manufacturing, not retailing, so investment in this industry was liberalized when restrictions were taken off foreign investment in manufacturing. Metro has opened a warehouse club in India; they have been given a license because they say their customers are other companies, not consumers. They were allowed to enter as a wholesaler, not a retailer.

### Lack of Industry Status

Certain industries in India are designated as small enterprise areas; retailing is one of them. Indian businesspeople use the term "denied industry status" to describe

**Photo 19.2**
A child plays in a vat of plastic balls under the careful supervision of an adult outside of a Marks & Spencer store in a new mall. Three new malls opened in 2002, fifteen miles outside of New Delhi in neighboring Gurgaon, Haryana state, and are a big hit with the growing middle class. Locals often spend the day window shopping and eating. India's economy is expected to grow 6–7 percent this year. *Photo by Robert Nickelsberg/Getty Images.*

the position of retailing. This type of government involvement greatly restricts the amount of capital available in the industry. If the ban on foreign direct investment was lifted, then multinational retailers with large amounts of funds could invest in India. Because it lacks industry status the retail industry cannot borrow funds for growth without relying on the asset attractiveness of other parts of the business. For instance, Food World must rely on the assets of its non-food divisions for funding growth. As a part of World Trade Organization (WTO) negotiations, the Indian government agreed to allow foreign participation in the retail industry.

## › CFA

Each province in India collects taxes on merchandise produced in a different province. CFAs are somewhat like bonded warehouses in the United States. Merchandise is brought to these warehouses; taxes are paid if they are from another province, and the goods are distributed from the warehouse. Merchandise that is moved from one province is taxed twice, first in the province where it was produced and second, in the province where it is sold. This type of intrastate taxing system greatly complicates the process of setting up a national chain of retailers, since the buying would either need to be done in each province or exorbitantly high taxes would need to be paid.

India is introducing a VAT to replace the CFA system. Small retailers are concerned about the new system and believe that they will not survive. The VAT system will make it much more difficult to fudge the amount of sales; small retailers have probably been underreporting their amount of sales.

Understanding how and why these government regulations are in place can help us to understand what is likely to happen when India liberalizes its market. Three theoretical perspectives: U VERSUS M MODELS OF MARKETIZATION, hierarchy of government involvement, and four dimensions of state as strategist are the basis for explanation.

## ❯ M-FORM HIERARCHY

The organization structures of Eastern Europe and the Soviet Union were a unitary form based on the functional or specialization principles (the U-form economy). In contrast, the Indian hierarchy has been of a multilayer, multiregional form based mainly on a territorial principle, M-form economy.[12] The M-form structure has been even more decentralized along regional lines during recent reforms with greater authority and incentives for regional governments. India's M-form organization means that there is greater regional independence; each region is relatively self-contained. This decentralization has a long history in India. Organizational characteristics of the U-form are:

1. organization mainly by functional or specialization principles;
2. interdependence between regions is strong and coordination at the top is critical; and
3. the size of enterprises is generally large and industries are very concentrated.

In contrast the characteristics of the M-form are:

1. organization mainly by territorial principle;
2. each region is relatively self-contained and independent;
3. coordination at all levels is important but at the top it is not particularly critical
4. the size of enterprise is generally small and industries are less concentrated; and
5. these characteristics extend to many levels down to the very bottom.[13]

Mihn provides a helpful framework for considering government's role in industrial policy.[14] There are four levels of intervention: general, sector-specific, industry-specific, and firm-specific. The firm-specific policy targets individuals, firms, or groups. In Korea, the targeted groups have been Chaebols, large family based business groups. In China the former state-owned retail groups may receive the same type of preferential targeting.[15] India's privileges are dispensed to businesses with good government connections in a system called the License Raj. Gita Piramal provides insight into this system in *Business Maharajas*.[16]

The heftiest profits came from the High United Value Scheme which the government introduced in 1971, through which polyester filament yarn could be imported against the export of nylon fabrics. This was a game that Mukesh Ambani, chairman of Reliance Industries, already knew how to play. He admits that Reliance Commercial Corporation accounted for over 60 percent of exports under the scheme and was therefore its largest beneficiary. Rumors spread that the scheme had been devised solely for him. At the Mulji Jetha market, polyester was thereafter called *chamak*. Ambani became the *chamatkar*.

## > HIERARCHY OF GOVERNMENTAL INVOLVEMENT

Governments can operate at four levels of intervention: general, sector-specific, industry-specific, and firm-specific.[17] The first level, the general level, refers to a government policy that affects the entire economy. At this level, the government might promote investment, research and development, and efficient resource allocation. At the second level, sector-specific policies target an economic sector, such as manufacturing, through export promotion or import-substitution policies. Many pro-industrialists such as Rodrik view this level of intervention as critical for triggering rapid industrial transition.[18]

Level three, industry-specific policy, aims at specific industries such as steel or chemicals. The fourth level, the firm-specific policy, targets individuals, firms, or groups. Korea and China have used all four levels of government intervention to promote industrial prosperity.[19] It is likely that the India will do this as well.

The four dimensions—authority versus markets, individualism versus communitarianism, security versus prosperity, and equity versus efficiency—will be used to analyze the government's role in India's retailing sector. The Asian economies experiencing rapid economic growth share a pattern of governmental involvement. Japan, Hong Kong, Singapore, Taiwan, and Korea have experienced rapid industrial growth. The governments of Japan, Taiwan, and Korea played a major strategic role in their economic development.[20, 21] Although we can gain some general insights from the development of other Asian countries, the case of India is unique, complicated by the historic movement from a British colony to a democracy. The following section presents dimensions of the state regulatory systems. How does a government influence the market within a country?

## > THE STATE AS STRATEGIST

The state becomes a strategist when it manipulates the commercial environment to achieve objectives. Lenway and Murtha present four dimensions of state (government) organization that affect international economic strategies: domestic policy capabilities, policy networks and the states' domestic autonomy, international autonomy and foreign policy capabilities, and legitimacy and the balance of economic and non-economic values.[22]

### Dimension 1: Domestic Policy Capabilities:
REGULATORY VERSUS DEVELOPMENTAL

Johnson identifies states' influence as regulatory or developmental.[23] Regulatory states have little ability to form economic strategies and few policy tools with which to implement them. Regulatory states are not necessarily heavily regulated; government might take a very laissez-faire approach to business, but the action they do take is institutional and affects all businesses in the same way. The United States and Hong Kong are examples of a regulatory state. There are no specific laws prohibiting foreign ownership in retailing and no requirements for ownership or management participation from country nationals. Countries using regulatory approaches to national economic management assume that the competitive interaction of market forces will ensure economic growth.

Developmental states pursue a strategic or goal-oriented approach to the domestic economy. The Indian government has used a developmental approach. India devised the long-run strategy of focusing on the manufacturing sector. Manufacturing foreign joint ventures transferred important technological know-how to the Indians. However, as mentioned previously, foreign participation in retailing is still not allowed, except if the retailer only sells their own brand products.

## Dimension 2: Policy Networks and the States' Domestic Autonomy: INDIVIDUALISM VERSUS COMMUNITARIANISM

In an individualistic society, the state exists to protect property, enforce contracts, and keep the marketplace open so that competition can be free and vigorous.[24] Individualistic societies believe that firms should compete, and that this competition will lead to overall economic gains. This individualistic theory is expressed in neoclassical thinking such as that of Adam Smith and David Ricardo. Majority decision making rules are associated with individualism. Majority decision-making usually takes the form of a vote and creates winners and losers. Individualism is related to the regulatory forms of governments discussed in Dimension 1.

Communitarian states define and ensure the rights of community members and play a central role in creating consensus to support the direction in which the community should move. Communitarianism can be authoritarian or democratic. Authoritarian communitarian states impose their views in the national interest. Democratic communitarian states charter interest groups and regulate their number by giving them exclusive franchises to represent particular groups, such as labor or industry. These groups are given formal standing and join the state bureaucracies in joint economic decision making. Korea's Chaebols fit this designation. The PRC's central government support for some state-owned retail groups may be an example of democratic communitarian strategy. In India, those with the best government contacts and the greatest likelihood of success are selected for support.

## Dimension 3: International Autonomy and Foreign Policy Capabilities: SECURITY VERSUS PROSPERITY

Security relates to national defense and sovereignty. Prosperity refers to economic well being, either of individuals or the state. Throughout the 1990s, India prohibited most product imports. Only products used to produce exports could be imported. The government put country security before corporate prosperity. India now seeks full membership in the World Trade Organization (WTO); as a result, imports are allowed in nearly all product categories and tariffs have been substantially reduced.

## Dimension 4: Legitimacy and the Balance of Economic and Non-Economic Values: EQUITY VERSUS EFFICIENCY

As countries move through different stages of economic development, they change their views of equity versus efficiency. In early stages of rapid industrialization, countries unambiguously decide in favor of economic freedom and social order. As countries become industrialized, society begins to demand equality, political freedom, and social justice. This challenges the social order and property rights. States that value economic growth more than equitable distribution of the gains sacrifice political freedoms. For example, Singapore has a politically controlled but economically vibrant economy.

These four dimensions can be combined with a vertical organization to clarify government's strategic role in marketization. In the last section I will discuss the current state of retailing in India. India's retail sector is backward, not just by the standards of the developed world, but also in comparison with the developing world.

## > RETAILING IN INDIA

About 70 percent of India's population lives in rural areas. Indian farmers sell some of their production directly to consumers without going through any retail channel. They often attend village markets known as *haats*. Food accounts for 43 percent of the typical Indian consumer's income. The share of food as a percent of income has declined from 47 percent in 1999 to 43 percent in 2003; it is expected that this figure will continue to decline.[25]

India is a country of contrasts. About 260 million Indians (26 percent of the population) live at or below the poverty level. At the same time 280 million (27 percent of the population) are in the upper-middle and high-income classes. This divide between rich and poor touches on all aspects of life.

The largest category of retail businesses are specialized retailers selling food, beverages, and tobacco from fixed retail outlets. These number nearly six million, about half of all retail outlets. The remaining half of all food sales occurs in other types of outlets such as stores that sell food along with other types of necessities (*kirana* stores) and food retailers selling from carts, stalls, and along the roadside.[26]

**Photo 19.3**
Khasis walk from nearby mountain villages to the Central Market in Shillong to sell their crops and hand-made items. A hearty people—they carry loads of over a hundred pounds, for many of the crops are sold by weight rather than by unitary value. *Courtesy of Lindsay Hebberd/CORBIS.*

**Photo 19.4**
Showing various silk materials to customers in one of the many silk shops. Varanasi is famous in India for its high quality of silk products. *Courtesy of Anders Ryman/CORBIS.*

It is not unusual for cows and goats to roam the streets of a major city like Mumbai. I once indicated an interest in where the cows go at night and although my driver didn't speak any English, he understood enough to take me on a side trip. We turned off the major road and after a gut-wrenching trip across a pot-holed series of side streets, he pulled up to an area where dozens of cows were eating their evening meal. It was right in the middle of Mumbai, one of the three major cities in India. The cows had come home to be fed their evening dinner and milked. That milk would then be taken door to door for customers.

Much of retailing in India is not self-service, but full service. Several factors contribute to this. First, the low incomes of shopkeepers makes it difficult to invest in or rent larger shops. Second, the low cost of labor in India means that there is no incentive to economize on labor cost by encouraging self-service. Finally, the limited variety of consumer goods and brands that are available to Indian consumers greatly reduces the need to emphasize display systems or to offer choice. The customer is waited on in most stores. The shopkeeper or his assistant brings out the merchandise from behind the counter to show the customer. My Indian colleague and I entered a small shop that sells traditional Indian shirts. She wanted to purchase a few shirts for herself and her fiancé. They must have taken 30 shirts out of their plastic cases to show her before she finally decided on several. I have to admit that I was beginning to feel a little guilty as I saw the number of shirts that someone would have to refold and put back in the plastic cases. I joked about this to my friend and she just laughed and said, "Labor is so cheap in India; we don't give things like that a second thought."

There are only 14 companies running department stores, and two with hypermarkets. The number of businesses running supermarkets numbers around 400, but only 10 of those can be considered chains. Sales through supermarkets and department stores have been increasing about 30 percent per year. Franchising has also been increasing at a rate of about 14 percent per year. The first modern shopping center, Crossroads, was opened in Mumbai in 1999. However, since that slow start they are popping up everywhere now. Mumbai has near 25 new malls under development. Only three of India's retailers are publicly held—Bata, Pantaloon Retail, and Trent.[27] Most of these retailers have operations only in the southern part of India (the triangle from Mumbai to Chennai and then south to Hydrabad) where retailing is more developed. I have talked to the CEOs for most of these retailers. They are a colorful group, definitely entrepreneurs through and through.

## › MAJOR RETAILERS

Bata is a manufacturer and retailer of footwear. It is the largest retailer in terms of total revenues, but if you exclude franchising revenues then RPG is bigger. In India since 1930, Bata has over 1,500 stores, a third of which are franchised outlets. Bata also sells their footwear to other retailers; this is called DUAL DISTRIBUTION.

RPG Enterprises is the second-largest chain in India. They operate supermarkets known as FoodWorld, music stores (Music World), health and beauty stores (Health & Glow), and a hypermarket (Giant). RPG has an equity collaboration with Dairy Farm International (Hong Kong-based retailer) that began before the ban on foreign direct investment in retailing. The government, however, would not allow Dairy Farm to invest in its hypermarket development because this came after the ban. The RPG group is a leading Indian business group operating in areas such as tire, power, information technology, and communications.

Pantaloon Retail began as an apparel manufacturer. In 1997, they shifted their focus to retailing by setting up their first department store, Pantaloons. In two years they had 14 stores. Then they branched out into hypermarkets, opening Big Bazaar outlets. They are expanding rapidly.

**Photo 19.5**
Pantaloon Retail has successfully opened a series of hypermarkets known as Big Bazaar.
*Courtesy of Big Bazaar.*

**Photo 19.6**
Shopper's Stop is India's oldest department store chain even though it did not open until 1991.

Shoppers' Stop operates the oldest and largest department store chain in India. Even though they didn't open their first store until 1991, they are considered a pioneer. Shoppers' Stop is part of an innovative retail investment group (the K Raheja group) led by a charismatic CEO with great ideas. They were the first in India to introduce information technology systems and the first to introduce loyalty programs and store cards.[28]

The major discount chain is Subhiksha. They sell groceries and medicine. Their stores have no self-service; you tell the workers what you want and they fetch it from the back. These barebones stores keep overhead down.

Viveks is India's largest retailer for consumer durables and home appliances. The group has 40 stores located in the southern part of India.

Lifestyle operates department stores and is known for efficient supply chain management leading to very rapid growth.

Trent, short for Tata Retail Enterprises, is part of the Tata group, one of India's top business conglomerates. The Tata group is involved in nearly every kind of industry including tea plantations. They operate department stores called Westside. Their 11 Westside stores are distinctive because of their high percent of private label. In the next section I will explain why a country as undeveloped as India has such a thriving private label program. It is caused by the market structure.

### › PRIVATE LABEL PRODUCTS

Most department stores and supermarket chains in India are promoting the sale of private label products because they have greater margin and profitability than branded alternatives. Also, remember that most branded merchandise has the MRP (manufacturer's recommended price) and retailers do not have enough economic clout to negotiate lower prices. Essentially they are negotiating a thin margin with the supplier and not being given free rein to make their own pricing decisions. The margins on private label products are 30–50 percent higher than margins on branded apparel.

The four major department stores have a strong focus on private label. Through its Westside department store, Trent sells 90 percent private label. They entered the retailing business in 1998 by taking over the Indian operations of Littlewoods (United Kingdom), which focused on private labels. Their original intent was to have a combination of branded and private label merchandise, but when they discovered the difference in profitability they decided to stay with private labels. Shoppers Stop has about 22 percent private label; however, they also sell branded merchandise. Pantaloons vertically integrated forward to open up department stores; their private label accounts for 80 percent of sales. Ebony's private label sales only account for 3 percent of their sales.[29]

Most supermarkets repackage rice, wheat, sugar, salt, flour, and pulses and consider this a private label. FoodWorld also sells private label products such as pickles, jams, and condiments. Private label for FoodWorld now accounts for about 22 percent of sales. Nilgiris, another supermarket chain, began as a dairy so it had a natural source of private label supply for dairy products. They have increased their private label offering until now; it accounts for just under 40 percent of sales.[30]

## › RELIGION AND RETAILING

Supermarkets in the southern part of India do not sell meat in their main area because cows occupy a sacred place in Hindu beliefs. If sold at all, meat is sold in a separate building. One small supermarket I visited had the meat in the basement. Supermarket operators know that many of their customers would become physically ill at the sight or smell of meat.

Some apartment buildings even promote themselves as meatless homes. Residents are not allowed to have meat in their homes. This is to prevent other residents from having to smell meat being cooked. There are even streets identified in cities where customers are guaranteed not to be confronted with meat.

At McDonald's in southern India, there are no meat-based offerings. Now do you see how religion affects retailing?

## › THE INTERNET

Internet sales are increasing by 69 percent per year, although it is from a very small base. Most Indian families do not own a computer; the majority accesses the Internet from cybercafes. I was surprised at the availability of cybercafes. On one trip I spent some vacation time in Kerala at the very southern part of India. With fabulous beaches on one side and gorgeous mountains on the other, it is sort of like India's Hawaii. I hired a car and driver to take me up to the tea country, a remote and lovely area, and was surprised that even in the remotest of villages there was a sign advertising Internet use.

The largest Internet company is Bazee.com. It is similar to EBay; many of its transactions are auctions. Beginning in 1996, Rediff.com is one of the oldest portals.

It offers shopping in addition to news, information, e-mail services, and entertainment. Indiatimes.com is part of the Times group, India's largest media conglomerate. Fabmail is similar to Amazon, but they also have brick-and-mortar grocery stores in Bagalore.[31]

## › SUMMARY

India has one of the most fascinating retail structures in the world. If India opens up the industry to FDI, the changes will be so rapid that it might be easy to miss the significance that the first department store was opened only in 1991. The first shopping center opened in 1991. The first cash and carry retailer and the first supermarket opened in 1993. This is just amazing.

In the first part of this chapter I discussed the differences between organized and unorganized retailers. Ninety five percent of all sales go through the unorganized retailers; because they are dealing off the books they do not pay taxes and do not give or get receipts. This means they can keep their cost structure very low, selling at prices below the organized retailers.

The next section discussed the role that India's government has played as strategist in market liberalization. They are trying to achieve national objectives by manipulating the market. In a sense they have become a market player. There are four dimensions of state as strategist representing two opposites of a continuum. The dimensions authority versus markets, individualism versus communitarianism, security versus prosperity, and equity versus efficiency are used to analyze the Indian government's role in developing the economy.

## › KEY TERMS

COMMITMENT TO CONSISTENT ASSORTMENT

DISCRETE

DUAL DISTRIBUTION

EQUITY VERSUS EFFICIENCY

EVOKED SET

EXTRINSIC REWARDS

GRAY MARKET

INDIVIDUALISM VERSUS COMMUNITARIANISM

INTRINSIC REWARDS

LICENCE RAJ

MANUFACTURER'S RECOMMENDED PRICE (MRP)

NORMS

ORGANIZED RETAILERS

REGULATORY VERSUS DEVELOPMENTAL

RELATIONAL

SCRAMBLED

SECURITY VERSUS PROSPERITY

U VERSUS M MODELS OF MARKETIZATION

UNORGANIZED RETAILERS

## › DISCUSSION QUESTIONS

1. Like China, India had a ban on foreign investment in retailing unless the retailer sells only private label merchandise. Their reasons for having this ban, though, were somewhat different. What is the motivation for each of these countries to keep out foreign investment in retailing?

2. India's system of requiring VAT to be paid when merchandise crosses a state border provides a great hindrance to the development of national brands; instead most products sold are local. How does this affect retailers who might operate in several states?

3. When would it be preferable to use discrete transactions rather than continuous transactions?

4. When does the government (state) become a strategic market player? What are they hoping to accomplish?

5. Both China and India have an M form of market reform. How does an M form differ from a U form and what kind of industries would you expect to come out of each of these types?

6. How can unorganized retailers in India be competitive with organized retailers?

## › ENDNOTES

1. A Brief History of India by Madhukar and Savita Jhingan, www.stampsofindia. com/readroom/507.htm

2. Bellman, E. and K. Hudson. (2006). "Wal-Mart Stakes India Claim," *The Wall Street Journal.* January 18, A9.

3. Bellman, E. and K. Hudson. (2006).

4. Shukla, S. (2003). "What Will This Man Do in Ten Years?" *Times News Network,* April 18.

5. Frazier, G.L. (1983). "Interorganizational Exchange Behavior in Marketing Channels: A Broadened Perspective. *Journal of Marketing,* 47, 68–78.

6. Frazier, G.L. (1984). "Interfirm Influence Strategies and Their Application Within Distribution Channels." *Journal of Marketing,* 48 (3), 43–56.

7. Chandrasekhar, P. (2001). "Retailing in India: Trends and Opportunities," *Business Line: Catalyst,* February 15.

8. Bandyopadhyay, S., R.A. Robicheaux, and J.S. Hill. (1994). "Cross-Cultural Differences in Interchange Communications: The United States and India," *Journal of International Marketing,* 2(3), 83–101.

9. Heide, J.B. and J. George. (1992). "Do Norms Matter in Marketing Relationships?" *Journal of Marketing,* 56 (2), 32–45.

10. Nanda, M. (2002), "Retailing in India: A Perspective on Scalability of Retail Formats," http://www.indiainfoline.com/bisc/reta.html.

11. Krishnan, T., K. Koelemeijer, and R. Rao. (2002). "Consistent Assortment Provision and Service Provision in a Retail Environment. *Marketing science,* 21(1), 54–73.

12. Qian, Y. and C. Xu (1993). "Why China's Economic Reforms Differ: The M-Form Hierarchy and Entry/Expansion of the Non-State Sector." *Economics of Transition.* 1 (2), 135–170.

13. Qian, Y. and C. Xu. (1993).

14. Mihn, K.H. (1988). "Industrial policy for industrialization of Korea," *KIET Occasional Papers,* 8803, Seoul: KIET.

15. Sternquist, B. and B. Jin. (1998). "South Korean Retail Industry: Government's Role in Retail Liberalization." *International Journal of Retail & Distribution Management,* 26(9)345–353.

16. Piramal, G. (1996). *Business Maharajas.* New Delhi: Penguin Press, p. 27.

17. Mihn, K.H. (1988). Industrial Policy for Industrialization of Korea, *KIET Occasional Papers,* 8803, Seoul: KIET.

18. Rodrik, D. (1995). "Getting Interventions Right: How South Korea and Taiwan Grew Rich." *Economic Policy,* 20, 35107.

19. Auty, R. (1997). "Competitive Industrial Policy and Macro Performance: Has South Korea Outperformed Taiwan?" *The Journal of Developmental Studies,* 33(4), 445–460.

20. Sternquist, B. (1998a). *International Retailing.* New York: Fairchild Books.

21. Sternquist, B. (1998b). "Internationalization of Food Retailers: A Conceptual Model." 1998 International Food and Agribusiness Management Association (IAMA). Conference, Punta del Este, Uruguay.

22. Lenway, S. and T.P. Murtha. (1994). "The State As a Strategist in International Business Research." *Journal of International Business Studies,* 3rd quarter, 513–535.

23. Johnson, C. (1982). *MITI and the Japanese Miracle; The Growth of Industrial Policy: 1927–1975,* Stanford, CA: Stanford University Press.

24. Lodge, G. (1990). *Perestroika for America.* Boston, MA: Harvard Business School Press.

25. Retailing in India. (2004). GMID Euromonitor April.

26. Retailing in India. (2004).

27. Retailing in India. (2004).

28. Retailing in India. (2004).

29. Retailing in India. (2004).

30. Retailing in India. (2004).

31. Retailing in India. (2004).

# 20

# RETAILING IN AUSTRALIA

Patricia Huddleston

## After reading this chapter, you will understand

› What sets Australia's retail system apart from that in other similar, developed countries (e.g., the United States and the United Kingdom).

› What similarities exist between Australian retailing and retailing in other countries.

› How government regulation affects certain retail industry sectors.

› The impact of duopolistic competition on Australia's retail industry.

## › COUNTRY BACKGROUND

Australia is unique in that it is a continent and a country roughly the size of the lower 48 states. While large geographically, its population of 20.1 million people is only 10 percent of the population of the United States. To put this in perspective, Poland is home to a population of 40 million on about 3 percent of the size of Australia's land mass. With a population density of two persons per square kilometer, Australia has one of the lowest population densities in the world. Over 90 percent of its citizens live in urban areas, the majority of which are located along the coastline. With only 6 percent of its land being arable, Australia's interior is primarily desert and considered to be uninhabitable. Comprised of six states and two territories, Sydney and Melbourne are the two largest cities and retail capitals; Perth, Adelaide, Canberra (the capital), and Brisbane are the other major retail centers (see Figure 20.1 for map). Sydney, with a population of 4.2 million and Melbourne with a population of 3.3 million comprise over 35 percent of Australia's total population. Table 20.1 presents selected demographic and economic data for Australia.

Even though Australia is geographically isolated and over 10,000 miles away from Great Britain, it has much in common with Great Britain, as one of its colonies and, to some degree, the United States. Aboriginal people have inhabited Australia since 50,000 B.C. They lived in areas with access to water (near rivers) and coastal plains. Prior to the arrival of the British in the late 1770s, the aboriginal population was estimated at 300,000. The British First Fleet arrived at Botany Bay (New South Wales) in 1787, seeking a place to send an excess of prisoners. Thus, with the arrival of non-aboriginal people, Australia was configured as a penal colony. Australia's geographic distance and isolation created unique challenges in gaining access to supplies for its new inhabitants to sustain themselves, as it took nine months for supply ships to travel from Great Britain to New South Wales.

## › BRIEF HISTORY OF AUSTRALIAN RETAILING

As a penal colony, New South Wales did not need a retail system until several years after settlement in 1787. Convicts and military personnel's food and apparel needs were met by direct imports from England. Once free settlers began to arrive in New South Wales and convicts earned their tickets of leave, the need for a local system of production and distribution arose. One of the earliest shops was founded by one of the emancipated convicts, Simeon Lord, who provided convicts with the opportunity to trade used clothing for tobacco and spirits.[1]

By the 1850s, Sydney had become a major city. The Horderns, one of Australia's first retail families, opened a drapery business in 1824; David Jones, founded by a Welsh immigrant of the same name, is Australia's oldest department store, opened on George Street. It imported goods from a variety of countries and sold them both wholesale and retail. At the same time Sydney was growing, other settlements and retail systems were forming in Hobart (Tasmania), Melbourne, and Adelaide. The Australian gold rush began in 1851 when gold was discovered in Bathhurst. Similar to the California Gold Rush, it created a huge economic and population boom for Melbourne and its environs due to the demand for miners equipment, apparel, and other provisions. The golden era of department store retailing followed, with Melbourne emerging as a retail hub.[2] Prominent department stores evolving from this era

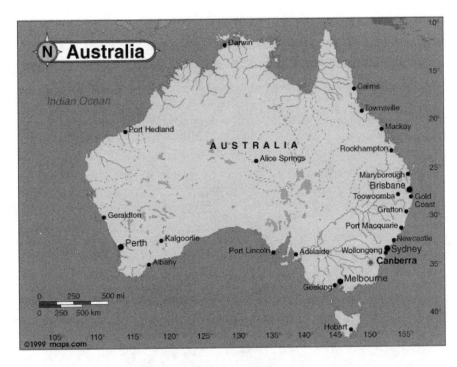

**Figure 20.1**
Map of Australia. *Mergent Online*

included George's—Melbourne, Grace Brothers—Sydney, and Myer's—Bendigo. Like the United States, department stores were the dominant force of city center retailing in Australia until the 1960s. The population shifted from city centers to the suburbs after World War II. The exodus from the city centers spurred the growth of neighborhood and regional shopping centers; department stores anchored these centers.

Self-service was first introduced in 1923 in Brisbane (Brisbane Cash and Carry), but it did not become widespread until the 1950s.[3] Supermarket formats in Australia were inspired by those developed in the United States. The first free-standing supermarket, Coles-Dickens, opened in 1960 in Victoria. 7-Eleven was the first convenience store to enter the Australian market in 1977.

**Table 20.1**
**Selected Demographic Characteristics of Australia**

| High income | Population (millions) 2004 | Area thousands of sq. km. | GNI* per capita | | PPP estimates of GNI* | | Life expectancy at birth (years) | Adult illiteracy (%) |
|---|---|---|---|---|---|---|---|---|
| | | | Dollars 2004 | Avg. Annual growth (%) | International Dollars | U.S. Dollars | | |
| Economies | 1001 | | $32,040 | | | | 78 | |
| Australia | 20.1 | 7700 | $26,900 | 3.5 | $29,200 | $26,900 | 79.8 | a |

a = <5%. *GNI= Gross national income
Source: World Bank 2005

**Photo 20.1**
Sydneysiders shop at a Coles supermarket as shares in Australia's largest retailer Coles Myer Ltd surged more than two percent after it predicted a boost in full-year net profits on the back of higher-than-expected full-year sales, in Sydney 14 August 2003. The Coles Myer group, which includes chains such as Kmart, Officeworks, Grace Bros, Megamart, and Target, said net profit for the 12 months to July 27 was likely to be about 445 million dollars (289.3 million US), up from previous estimates of 425–435 million dollars. *Courtesy WILLIAM WEST/AFP/Getty Images.*

Today, 2.1 million people (22.5 percent of total employment) work in the retail sector.[4] Thirty-five percent of all retail employees work in the supermarket and grocery stores followed by specialty food outlets with 13 percent. Next, an overview of the two major retail groups and their impact on Australian retailing is presented.

## ❭ THE TITANS OF AUSTRALIAN RETAILING

In most developed countries, retail trade is characterized by MONOPOLISTIC COMPE-TITION, which exists when there are many competitors and a great deal of product differentiation. In most Australian retail sectors, monopolistic competition dominates. But the food sector is characterized by a DUOPOLY, a form of oligopoly limited to two sellers. An oligopoly is a form of imperfect competition where there are few sellers, each has the ability to affect market price and each has a great deal of market power.[5] For example, if one store engages in Every Day Low Pricing (EDLP) in an oligopoly, other stores are likely to follow suit. Oligopolistic firms, especially those producing differentiated products, rely upon differences in price, quality, and reliability to promote sales and increase profits. "They attempt to create a very strong awareness among consumers of brands and product reputation," which is the case in Australia.[6]

One of the most unique features of the Australian retail industry is the overwhelming domination of the "Big Two" retail groups, the duopoly of Coles-Myer and Woolworths. Economists acknowledge that an industry is highly concentrated when there is a four-firm concentration of about 60 percent.[7] While estimates vary, Coles-Myer and Woolworths control up to 80 percent of Australia's food and liquor market. By comparison, Wal-Mart controls about 15 percent of the U.S. food market. Coles-Myer and Woolworths exhibit competitive behavior termed RIVALRY OF THE FEW. Rivalry of the few is characterized by firms that have strategic interactions with one another, and make educated guesses about how each other will react to key business decisions. Both Coles and Woolworths have attempted over time to create barriers to entry by creating a differentiated retail mix.

Coles-Myer and Woolworths' competitive behavior has displayed a "me-too" strategy, with one leading and the other following. When each firm has a slightly different market share and different cost structure, price conflicts are not at the forefront of strategic moves. Rather, Woolworths and Coles-Myer have tried to achieve dominance in a variety of ways such as COST REDUCTION AND PRODUCT (BRAND) DIFFERENTIATION. For example, in 1999 Woolworths embarked on a nine-year supply chain transformation called "Project Refresh," designed to establish Woolworths as the cost leader, with a goal of eliminating $6 billion AUD out of its cost structure. Coles-Myer followed suit several years later with its own program, "Operation Right Now."

To create a competitive advantage over Coles-Myer and to strengthen its brand identity, Woolworths entered the petrol (gasoline) market in 1996. This was followed by a joint venture with Caltex, Australia, in 2003 giving them a chain of petrol stations. Coles-Myer was forced to respond with a petrol strategy of its own, but did not do so until 2003, after suffering market share losses.

## 〉 FOOD RETAILING

If you compare food shopping in Australia to the U.S. food shopping experience, particularly in markets where there is competition between hypermarkets, it is rather disappointing. Supermarkets are much smaller, offering less product variety. I often saw evidence of supply chain problems. For example, if I shopped on a weekend, unless I shopped early in the day, I could expect the produce department to be out of key products like lettuce and would either have to do without or go to another store.

## Coles-Myer Group

Coles-Myer is the largest retail group in Australia and is one of the top 25 retailers in the world (see Table 20.2). Coles-Myer's presence is seen across numerous retail sectors and is the largest non-government employer in Australia with over 165,000 employees (7.9 percent of the total retail workforce). Coles-Meyer's portfolio of

**Photo 20.2**
This recent photo shows pedestrians outside a Woolworths store in central Sydney. Roger Corbett, chief executive for Woolworths, Australia's biggest supermarket retailer, announced 20 April 2004 total sales for the first nine months of the year rose 6.1 percent, saying also that subject to current trading patterns being maintained, full year earnings are likely to be up by as much as 15 percent. *Courtesy GREG WOOD/AFP/Getty Images.*

stores looks very much like a "me-too" copy of a number of iconic American retailers with similar names and formats.

Dubbed as Coles-Myer's "big engine," the food and liquor division generates 68 percent of its revenue. This division consists of Coles Supermarkets, Bi-Lo Food stores, Coles Express, Liquorland, and 1st Choice Liquor stores. Coles supermarkets

**Table 20.2**
**Leading Retailers of Australia**

| Retailer | Sales 2004 (A$ Million) | | Stores 2004 |
|---|---|---|---|
| **Coles-Myer** | $32,266.8 | 2650 | |
| **Food and Liquor** | 18014.6 | | |
| Supermarkets | | | 700 |
| Liquor | | | 645 |
| Coles Express | 3177 | | 598 |
| Kmart | 3,799 | | 150 |
| Myer | 3030.7 | | 61 |
| Megamart | 291.7 | | 9 |
| Target | 2851.8 | | 253 |
| Office Works | 1101.9 | | 78 |
| Harris Technology | | | 9 |
| **Woolworths** | $27,934 | 1700 | |
| Food and Liquor | 24,193 | | 708 |
| Free-standing liquor stores | | | 192 |
| ALH/MGW Retail Liquor Outlets | | | 382 |
| Caltex/WOW Petrol | | | 117 |
| WOW Petrol | | | |
| Big W | 2718 | | 120 |
| Consumer Electronics | 886 | | |
| Dick Smith Electronics | | | 164 |
| Dick Smith Electronics Powerhouse | | | 18 |
| Tandy | | | 148 |
| **Bunnings** | 44,474 | 47 | |
| | **Specialty Retailers** | | |
| | **Sales 2005 (A$ million)** | | **Stores 2005** |
| **Angus & Coote (Holdings) Ltd.** | 245.2 | | |
| Angus & Coote | | | 148 |
| Goldmark | | | 124 |
| J's Room | | | 1 |
| **Billabong** | | 64 | |
| **Brazin Ltd.** | 421.32* | 450 | |
| BNT (Bras 'N Things) | 101.6 | | 140 |
| Ezydvd | | | 37 |
| Ghetto & Sport Pty. Ltd | 15.2 | | 39 |
| Sanity, Virgin, IN2 Music | 267.3 | | 234 |
| **Colorado Group** | 471.2 | 407 | |
| Mathers | | | 107 |
| Williams | | | 168 |
| Colorado | | | 93 |
| JAG | | | 29 |
| Diana Ferrari | | | 10 |

*continued*

**Table 20.2** *Continued*

| Retailers | Sales 2005 (A$ million) | Stores 2005 | |
|---|---|---|---|
| **Just Group** | 632.8 | 729 | |
| Just Jeans | | | 284 |
| Jay Jays | | | 212 |
| Urban Brands | | | 1 |
| Portman's | | | 107 |
| Jacqui E | | | 94 |
| Peter Alexander | | | 5 |
| Dotti | | | 26 |
| **Millers Retail Ltd.** | 1120.9 | 1064 | |
| **Apparel** | 463.4 | | 711 |
| Crossroads, Katie's, Miller Fashion Club, 1626 | | | |
| **Discount** | 657.5 | | 353 |
| Go-Lo, Crazy Clark's, Chickenfeed | | | |
| **Noni B. Ltd.** | 97.07 | 174 | |
| **Palmer Corp. Ltd.** | 58.86 | 29 | |
| **Rebel Sport** | 305.43 | 59 | |
| Glue | | | 7 |
| Rebel Sport | | | 52 |
| **Harvey Norman Holdings Ltd.** | 1284.9 | | |
| Harvey Norman | | | 527(franchises) |
| Domayne | | | 14 |
| Joyce Mayne | | | 4 |

are a traditional supermarket with the range of product categories one would expect to find there. Bi-Lo is a discount supermarket with a restricted range of fresh foods and lower service levels than the traditional Coles Supermarkets. To match Woolworths competitive advantage in the liquor market, in 2002, Coles-Myer purchased Theo's Liquor, a large independent liquor chain. Together with Liquorland, these outlets target the mass market. The majority of Liquorland stores are attached to a Coles supermarket.

Coles Express stores offer two formats. In the suburbs they feature fuel and a convenience store product assortment. In the city centers (Sydney and Melbourne), they are a mini-service market with food and other convenience items. Coles Express contributes approximately 15 percent to the food and liquor group revenues. Using a copycat strategy, Coles-Myer entered the petrol market in 2003 to halt loss of market share and compete with the success of the Woolworths model.[8] Coles-Mayer forged an alliance with Shell Australia and now owns a network of over 600 outlets. This alliance has been a profitable move for Coles-Myer.

In 2005, Coles Myer modified its private label product strategy by introducing a three-tiered housebrand, which offer a good-better-best range. Prior to the introduction of this range, branded suppliers were charged slotting fees of $100,000 in order to retain the current shelf space.[9] Currently, housebrands comprise 13 percent of sales, and executives hope that this share will increase to 30 percent of supermarket sales by 2007.[10]

Compared to Woolworths' performance in the food and liquor sector, Coles-Myer has been playing catch-up for several years. It was imperative for Coles-Myer to enter the petrol market, upgrade fresh food assortment, and change consumer perceptions that Coles had higher prices in order to stop losing market share to Woolworths.[11] Historically, Coles-Myer has higher operating costs than Woolworths, thus making it more difficult to be profitable.

Employing a strategy similar to Woolworths Project Refresh, Coles-Myer embarked on a five-year cost-saving measure, with the goal of saving $300 million AUD. Dubbed "Operation Right Now," the anticipated cost savings in increasing supply chain efficiencies has not yet been realized.

## Woolworths

Founded as Wallworth's Bazaar in Sydney in 1924, Woolworths Australia is not, and never has been, related to the now defunct American retailer Woolworths. While Woolworths Australia is the second-largest retailer in terms of sales, it is first in profitability and holds a 28.4% market share in food, liquor, and grocery. The key to its superior performance is their greater concentration in the supermarket and grocery sector.[12] It operates more than 1,700 stores with major brands:

Food and liquor: Woolworths, Safeway, Food for Less, Woolworths Metro, Woolworths Liquor, BWS, First Estate, Dan Murphy's, Plus Petrol, Australian Independent Wholesalers (AIW)
General merchandise: Dick Smith's Electronics, Powerhouse, Tandy, Big W
Other: Woolworths Ezy Banking, Woolworths HomeShop, and Green Grocer

Woolworths/Safeway is the leading food retailer in Australia and accounts for almost 80% of Woolworths revenue. Woolworths initiated several very successful strategic moves that have given it a competitive advantage and cemented its leadership in the food industry. In 1996, they opened their first Petrol Plus outlets, offering petrol discounts to customers spending more than $A30.[13] In 2003, they entered into a joint venture with Caltex Australia to expand their presence in this sector. This forced Coles-Myer to follow suit or permanently cede market share to Woolworths.

Woolworths is recognized for its emphasis on fresh food, reflected in their slogan "The Fresh Food People." The focus on fresh foods has paid off in high market share in this category; fresh foods represent over 25% of Woolworths' food sales.[14] Coles also does a better job in merchandise presentation and cost control. Woolworths also has a private label strategy, with the largest supermarket private label grocery brand (Home Brand) in Australia. There are plans to introduce a premium house brand in 2005. Its ultimate goal for housebrands is to comprise 20 percent of supermarket sales.

Woolworths, with about 13 percent market share in the liquor market, has seized first mover advantage in acquiring the best liquor businesses. Sales from their liquor outlets have contributed to Woolworths sales growth and increased the price competition in this sector. Their four liquor channels are comprised of attached liquor stores at 344 Woolworths/Safeway stores. Dan Murphy's, with 26 units, is touted as having the most extensive assortment in Australia, stocking five times the average product assortment of other liquor stores. First Estate, a free-standing wine store, and 168 BWS (Beer, Wine and Spirits) round out the liquor holdings. Woolworths also owns a 50 percent stake in MGW, a Queensland liquor business.

In 1999, CEO Roger Corbett initiated a nine-year supply chain transformation, Project Refresh, to save $6.9 billion AUD in supply chain costs and establish Woolworths as a cost leader. Components of the Project Refresh initiative encompassed the introduction of electronic stock management, supermarket remodels, and upgrading warehouse management to a forecast-based replenishment system. Woolworths' 31 distribution centers are being consolidated into nine regional and two national distribution centers. By 2009, they plan to invest almost $600 million AUD into information technology to implement the supply chain transformation.[15] Over the past six years, a cost savings of almost 4 percent of sales has been realized.[16]

Besides the Big Two, there are few other competitors in the Australian retail food sector. Until 2005, Foodland Associated Ltd operated 250 supermarkets, franchises, wholesale operations, and department stores throughout four states in Australia.[17] Foodland's 80 outlets in Western Australia, Queensland, Northern New South Wales, and Southern Queensland (operating under the Action fascia) competed successfully against Coles-Myer and Woolworth, and the company was a dominant food retailer in Western Australia because of its geographic remoteness. However, Foodland ultimately did not have the scale necessary to compete with Coles and Woolworths and in 2005 was the target of a takeover bid between Metcash (a South African grocery wholesaler) and Woolworths. These two firms split the Foodland assets in the following manner: Woolworths bought the New Zealand Foodland units and 22 of the 69 Action stores; Metcash acquired Foodland's wholesale business and the remaining retail stores.

Aldi, a privately owned German discount food store, entered the Australian market in 2001 and currently has a store network of 94 stores in three states (New South Wales, Victoria, and Queensland). Aldi runs a lean operation, with a product range of 750 items compared to over 20,000 for Coles and Woolworths. Its plans are to open 30 stores a year, with a focus on the eastern seaboard.[18] "Wherever you can find 10,000 people, we will open a store—but it has to be viable" stated Aldi's managing director.[19] Currently, Aldi has about a 3 percent market share of the Australian grocery market but does not compete with Coles-Myer and Woolworths in the petrol sector. Originally, its presence had forced Woolworths and Coles to lower prices by 4–4.5 percent in stores located nearby, but this effect has leveled off.

## › NON-FOOD RETAILING

### Department Stores

The struggling department store sector in Australia is a mature sector, and is the worst performing sector in terms of profitability. Despite the poor performance, department stores have increased floor space. They look much like a 1970s version of

**Photo 20.3**
Apparel and cosmetics
displays at David Jones
projects an upscale image.
*Courtesy Condé Nast.*

U.S. department stores. They have retained low turnover and low margin product categories such as furniture and small appliances.

Australia has two dominant department stores; David Jones, with 34 outlets, and Myer, with 61. According to retail analysts, the right number for a large department store in Australia is about 30 stores.[20]

David Jones, an up-market department store, founded in 1838, is the oldest department store in Australia. It is believed to be the oldest department store in the world still trading under its own name.[2] It targets the upper- to middle-class consumer and has 34 outlets and a presence in every state in Australia.

The battle for department store market share in Australia is between David Jones and Myer's. David Jones has embarked on several growth strategies to capture market share, with varying degrees of success. It has a reputation for being "home of the designer brands" (a similar strategy to Neiman Marcus in the United States) and is the exclusive distributor of such Australian apparel icons as Witchery and Collette Dinnigan. Recently, it has undergone an extensive remodeling program that has increased sales.

David Jones has a profitable credit card business. While its product strategy is recognized as superior to Myer's, David Jones has also made strategic missteps. An attempt to enter the food business with an up-market grocery chain (Foodchain) was disastrous. David Jones exited this business in 2003, after losing close to $100 million AUD. Because David Jones is leaner, it was able to manage the huge loss on Foodchain. As a more focused operation, they made a good head start on their strategic revamp; thus they are in a much better competitive position than Myer.

Myer department stores, owned by Coles-Myer, was founded in the late 1800s. In 1983, Myer acquired Grace Brother Holdings, a Sydney department store chain. In 2004, they eliminated the Grace Brothers brand and re-launched the Myer brand to be a more serious competitor of David Jones. Myer offers apparel, home goods, small appliances, books, and music. Furniture is being phased out.

With 61 stores, Myer has experienced turmoil and strategic missteps in the last several years. There was a period in which Myer was repositioned to compete with Target and Kmart. An indicator of the Myer's problems was the revolving door of the CEO's office, with four officers in just 10 years. Dawn Robertson, an American, was hired in 2002 to turn the company around. Her goal was to make Myer a house of brands that appealed to women 25–45.[21] She scored a coup when she forged an exclusive partnership with Country Road apparel. Another branding partnership has been established with the Sanity Entertainment group (owned by Brazin, Ltd.). Sanity has developed 60 Virgin concept stores in Myer department stores.

Despite these moves, Myer's performance has been disappointing. Thus, in June 2006, Myer was sold for $1.4 billion AUD to a consortium, led by the private investment firm Newbridge Capital. The Myer family retains a 10 percent stake.

The third traditional department store chain, the 156-year-old Adelaide-based Harris Scarfe with 23 stores, underwent a management buyout in 2001 and embarked on a repositioning strategy. This included introducing a new logo and targeting a younger customer. They have undergone a $10 million revamp of their flagship store and a $5 million investment in point of sale software. They are considering a share market float in 2007.[22]

## Discounters

Kmart (Australia) is not related to the Kmart stores in the United States, but was originally 51-percent owned by Kmart-U.S. In 1978, Coles acquired full ownership of Kmart Australia and in 1994, bought back all the Coles stock held by Kmart Corporation. U.S. Kmart (Australia) is a discount department store with apparel and general merchandise. Located in most major, urban shopping centers, Kmart is Australia's highest volume discount department store. Noted for its unattractive store fixtures and environment, Coles-Myer has invested in refurbishment of 15 of the 167 Kmart stores. Kmart also operates several automotive parts and services formats, including Kmart Tyre and Auto Service, Tyremaster, and Mycare. Kmart has also five Kmart Garden Supercentres.

Target (Australia) was founded in 1925 as a dress and furnishings store in Geelong. It was bought by Myer Emporium Ltd. (Coles-Myer) in 1968 and renamed Linsday's Target Pty., Ltd. Today, Target is the third-largest entity in the Coles-Myer group. Apparel is its major business, but its apparel does not resemble the trendy, edited assortment of its American counterpart (and it is not related to the U.S. store). Target (Australia) has a private label program, sourced primarily in Asia, which contributes significantly to gross margin. Its product assortment is similar to Kmart (Australia).

Target (U.S.) is one of my favorite places to shop, so when I spent six months in Australia, I eagerly anticipated being able to purchase similar merchandise and expected to see a store format that resembled American Target stores. My first experience at Target was to purchase a hair dryer; the one I had brought from the States didn't work. I went to the small appliances section, only to find that six of the eight brands were out of stock. I thought perhaps this was an anomaly, so I returned several days later, but they were still out of stock. I ended up buying a hair dryer at Myer's.

Officeworks, a warehouse format office supply store, closely resembles its U.S. counterparts, Staples and Office Depot. It targets customers with home offices and small- to medium-sized businesses. Cole-Myer's market share in this category is about 12–13%.[23] Officeworks has developed a strong first mover advantage as the category killer in the office supplies market in Australia.[24] Recently, Inkworks, a store within a store concept selling ink and toner cartridges, has been introduced into 17 Officeworks stores.

Launched in 1998, Megamart, a category killer in furniture and electronics, was unable to compete with Harvey Norman's 160 stores and was never profitable. In 2005, Coles-Myer decided to eliminate this unit, selling six of the nine units to Harvey Norman, and closing the other three stores. At the time the first Megamart opened, Harvey Norman predicted: "Coles-Myer will never make a success of either furniture or electrical."[25] His predictions were accurate.

A co-branded credit card was introduced in 2003 to expand their loyalty program and gain a competitive edge over Woolworths. The Coles Myer Source Mastercard offers a 6-cents-a-liter discount on petrol versus 4 cents for Coles/Bi-Lo customers without the card. There is also a loyalty program, Myer one, with more than 600,000 members.

Woolworths competes in the consumer electronics business with three fascia: Dick Smith's Electronics (164 outlets), Tandy (148 company owned stores), and Dick

Smith's Electronics Powerhouse (18 outlets). Recently, the Leading Edge group that operates a national network of 1,300 electronics stores bought out Dick Smith and Tandy retailers, who have severed their relationships with Woolworths.[26]

Woolworths' on-line presence, Woolworths HomeShop, was launched in 2000, right before the dot.com crash. Currently, HomeShop is available only in Melbourne, Sydney, and Canberra. Using a centralized fulfilment center, customers can select from a variety of products available at Woolworths/Safeway stores.

Woolworths seeks to dominate the sectors in which it competes. Their future growth plans include opening 15–25 new supermarkets each year for the "foreseeable future." Big W's presence will eventually expand to 150 stores; the number of petrol outlets will be increased to 470. Increasing market share in the liquor sector will be achieved through the opening of six-twelve Dan Murphy's outlets per year, increasing this business from $2.1 billion per year to $2.5 billion.[27]

Emergence of discount superstore category killers such as Harvey Norman and Rebel Sports is having a major effect on the structure of the Australian retail industry.[28] The open store plans allow employees to supervise a large area, decreasing labor costs; located outside of traditional retail areas, they have low land/rent costs. While price was the initial attraction for consumers, their wide product assortments have proven to be a larger factor as well. Even though the number of outlets in this sector has expanded rapidly, not all entrants have enjoyed success. Cole-Myer's Megamart lost money almost from its inception and was sold by its parent to Harvey Norman.

Harvey Norman is the fourth-largest retail business in Australia by market capitalization and is a pioneer of the warehouse-style furniture and home furnishings formats. Its owner, Gerry Harvey, an iconic figure in the Australian retail landscape, is quick to criticize his rivals and is swift to pounce on the strategic missteps of others, as exemplified by his 2005 purchase of Megamart from Coles-Meyer.

Harvey Norman's reputation was built on being a discount operation in the furniture, housewares, and appliance categories. This company has a unique franchise operating strategy; each store is structured with as many as four separate franchises: electrical, computers, bedding, or furniture. Thus, it is possible that four different franchisees might operate out of one store. Each franchise runs as a separate business.[29] Franchisees are not required to purchase their business, although the company carefully scrutinizes each franchise applicant. Franchisees pay fees depending on sales volume and store location, as well as a marketing fee. Harvey Norman retains control over marketing, purchasing, and pricing. Franchisees have autonomy in staffing and payroll decisions.

Another key to Harvey Norman's success is their location strategy. They own many of their sites and originally, their strategy was to operate at low cost sites away from city centers, to take advantage of low overhead. With increasing competition in these sectors, Harvey Norman cannot sustain its pricing and product range advantages over the long term. Thus, they have gradually increased prices as their location strategy has expanded to include outlets in shopping centers with higher rents. Harvey Norman is reaching the stage where they will saturate the Australian market and are contemplating expansion into Asia and Eastern Europe.

Other financial interests of Harvey Norman include a 55-percent stake in Rebel Sports and Fantastic Furniture. In its acquisition of Rebel Sports, Harvey Norman decentralized management, giving store managers autonomy over buying.

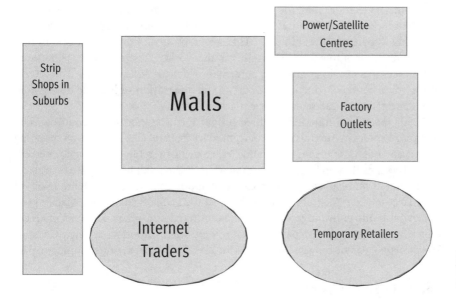

**Figure 20.2**
Typical Struture for
Urban/Regional Retailing[71]

## > STRUCTURE AND LOCATION STRATEGY FOR
## AUSTRALIAN RETAILERS

The previous sections have provided you with an overview of the major players
in food and nonfood retailing. Now I would like to discuss the typical shopping
structure and location strategies for Australian retailers (refer to Figures 20.2 and
20.3 for an overview). Australia has over 900 shopping centers ranging from 5,000

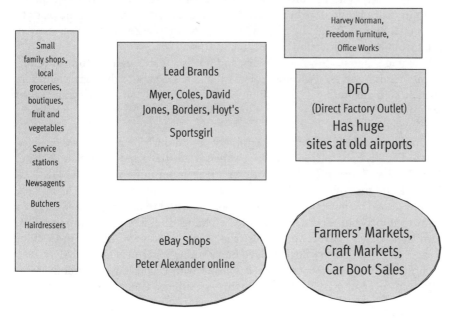

**Figure 20.3**
Typical Struture for
Urban/Regional Retailing[72]

square meters to more than 100,000 square meters, with smaller centers tending to be supermarket based. Stand-alone shopping malls account for 28 percent of retail space, but 41 percent of retail sales.[30] This represents one of the highest penetration rates of retailing of this form of retailing in the world.[31] There are over 38,000 specialty stores in shopping centers, 47 percent of which are independents. The success of shopping centers is due in large part to the integration of lifestyle outlets that include restaurants, cafes, and movie theatres.

Retail space is dominated by three property trusts: Westfield Group owns 43 shopping centers in Australia, a 4.5 percent market share; Gandel owns 28 shopping centers and has a 3.1 percent share; and Centro owns 110 retail centers, a 12.2 percent share. Together they control almost 20 percent of the retail property in Australia.

We are all familiar with large regional shopping malls, and there are many of these large malls in Australia. One of the most profitable is Chadstone Mall in Melbourne, also one of the largest malls in the southern hemisphere. Regional malls are typically anchored by a department store and often a food store (e.g., Coles or Woolworths). Major branded specialty stores also locate in major shopping malls.

## Specialty Store Chains

Several major players in the specialty apparel sector have made strategic acquisitions in the past several years in order to broaden their customer base and capitalize on growth markets (for example, aging baby boomers). Australia has several prominent, publicly held specialty store chains.

Brazin Ltd. operates in two seemingly unrelated product categories: women's clothing and recorded music. Its fascia include: Sanity music, Sanity.com, Bras n' Things, and Aztec Rose (surfwear manufacturer). Sanity Entertainment is a major contributor to its revenue but is experiencing a decline due to Internet piracy. Brazin has capitalized on its ownership of the Virgin music license and has established 60 Virgin concept stores in Myer department stores. In 2005, Brazin acquired its third major music store brand, HMV, from its U.K. parent.[32] There are plans to grow their Bras n' Things chain by adding 25 stores in New Zealand and aggressively rolling out its jewelry chain Diva, BNT, and Dusk.[33]

Colorado manufactures, wholesales, and retails apparel under a number of different brands (Mathers, Williams, Colorado) and has expanded through acquisition. Its success in integrating its acquisitions comes by focusing on acquiring businesses with similar high-end target markets such as Diana Ferrari,[34] an Australian footwear icon acquired in 2002.

Country Road began as a manufacturer of cotton shirts in 1974, and has emerged into a specialty apparel retailer with 42 outlets in Australia and six in New Zealand. They have an international presence with franchised outlets in Singapore, New Zealand, and the Gulf States.[35] Capitalizing on its position as an Australian brand, Country Road manufactures, imports, wholesales, and retails apparel and targets a mid- to upper-end market. Woolworths Holdings Ltd, a South African retailing firm (not related to Woolworths Australia) owns an 88-percent stake in Country Road.[36] In 2004, Country Road entered into a strategic partnership with Myer as an exclusive supplier, terminating its relationship with David Jones. Currently, Myer represents over 30 percent of Country Road's business. Country Road was one of the few Australian retailers to venture into the U.S. market in the late 1980s but closed the stores in 2002 due to poor performance.

Just Group Ltd. specializes in fashions of the moment or fast fashion, as it is termed in the United States. It is one of the largest specialty apparel retailers in Australia and New Zealand. Their retail network, selling 90 percent of its apparel under its own label, includes six retail brands. Just Jeans, its flagship chain, made denim ubiquitous in Australia. It features fashionable casual wear at mid-market price points, targeted at the 16–39-year-old. Originally founded as a one-store operation in 1970, Just Jeans grew over the next 30 years into a multimillion dollar chain. Floated in 1993, Just Jeans remained a public company until 2001. Jay Jay's market niche is value for money, street smart casual apparel aimed at the 16–24-year-old market. There is no direct competition for this store, with great product value, store formats and unisex offer.[37] Jacqui E offers quality and fashionable women's wear at mid-market price points. They target a slightly older customer (30–35) who is overlooked by most Australian retailers. Unlike the other retailers in the portfolio, Jacqui E private label product is sourced domestically. Portman's, acquired in 2002, has a higher fashion brand aimed at the young 20s value-conscious female looking for a balance of career and casual.[38] Urban Brands is Just Group's high street fashion offering of branded apparel. Just Group has recently experienced problems with Urban Brands; sales have not met expectations. They planned to exit this business.[39] Peter Alexander, originally a sleepwear catalogue, has a product assortment that now includes fitness apparel, bed linens, resort wear, and accessories. Dotti, Just Group's latest acquisition, targets the teenage market.

Millers Retail Ltd. was founded in 1993 and has two divisions. The Apparel Division is a women's specialty store group that targets value-conscious women 35+ at the lower end of the market. Miller's Fashion Club, with over 100 stores, is its flagship chain and offers work wear, casual wear, and evening wear. Most of Miller's products are private label (Millers label). Miller's loyalty program (Miller's Club) is a competitive advantage, and has facilitated special promotion offers to its two million member database. Specialty retailers Katies and 1626 were purchased from Coles-Myer in 2000. 1626 targets large-sized women in the value conscious market.

Until 2005, its second division consisted of several discount chains—Discount Variety Go-Lo, Crazy Clark's, and Chickenfeed stores. This division was sold to two private equity firms for $120 million AUD.[40] Miller's took a $50 million loss on the sale, which was motivated by the poor performance of this division. The merger of the Miller Discount Group with the Australian operations of the Warehouse Group will create a significant presence with its 450 stores. The emergence of this new retail group will threaten the dominance of Coles Myer and Woolworths in the discount sector.[41]

## Specialty Apparel Retailers—Privately Held

The specialty apparel retailers discussed in the previous section are publicly held, but several others are worthy of mention because of their unique strategy or established niche as an Australian icon. Established in 1939 as a single store, the Sussan Retail Group owns several apparel chains—Sportsgirl, Suzanne Grae, and Sussan. With sales of over $600 million AUD, it is the largest women's retailer in the Southern

Hemisphere. Each retail entity targets a different age segment. According to CEO Naomi Milgrom, "We almost go from birth to death, now."[42] Sportsgirl is aimed at the 16–24 year old, Sussan, the 24–39 age group, and Suzanne Grae the 39–55 segment.

Sportsgirl was founded in 1948 and had the reputation for selling trendy products. Naomi Milgrom brought Sportsgirl out of bankruptcy in 1999. Even though the firm was close to collapse, it had strong brand recognition, "We took a dead duck and made it sing," says Milgrom.[43] Her goal was to make Sportsgirl "the girls meeting place." Their stores were moved to "hot areas" (near hip, edgy retailers such as General Pants). Sportsgirl has arrangements with record companies to broadcast new releases in the store; their stores have a "chill-out area" with the aim to create destination shops where teenage girls would feel comfortable hanging out on a Saturday afternoon.[44] Sportsgirl's product strategy is similar to that of Zara's "fast fashion," with products delivered weekly. Their products are 100-percent private label, with 90 percent sourced in Asia, and have a product life cycle of two–eight weeks.

Sportsgirl.com.au is one of the hottest retail websites, being constantly reinvented. While you cannot buy merchandise from it, there are contests for trips, cars, fashion, and relationship advice. In 2004 Sportsgirl was recognized as the "Best High Street Brand" by retail industry leaders.

General Pants is one of Australia's edgiest retail stores. Their tagline reads "Best Denim Selection on the Planet." General Pants is a streetwear retailer specializing in urban brands and has created an image of a cool store featuring jean brands that sell upwards of $600. Their friendliness of their sales staff is a competitive advantage; they have the ability to approach customers without seeming pushy. Salespeople are considered to be family members and there are regularly sponsored get-togethers to foster this unique environment.[45] General Pants has developed some signature promotional events including sponsoring a film-making competition producing a *catamagalozine* that features pictures, photos, fashion, and stories that General Pants customers like. One of the nicest shopping experiences I had while in Australia was visiting with the salespeople at General Pants. While I was clearly not the target customer for their hip and edgy fashions, they treated me as if I was their most important customer.

## Electronics

The electronics retail sector is fragmented and rife with competition and includes major national retailers such as Harvey Norman, Woolworths Dick Smith, and Tandy; buying and marketing groups consist of Retravision, Betta Electrical, The Good Guys, Camera House, and Autobarn; national specialty retailers comprise J.B. HiFi, Sanity Entertainment, Strathfield Group, HMV, Video EZY, and Blockbuster, and local independent specialty retailers.

JB Hi-Fi is recognized as an industry leader in electronics retailing. As a specialty retailer of home entertainment products, JB Hi-Fi is positioned as a low-price operator with both stand-alone destination sites and shopping centers. Its strategy is to offer leading brands in each category with a "carefully targeted focus on home entertainment distinctive branding and prominent retail locations."[46] Their stores are literally crammed with merchandise and produce sales per square meter of $25,000. JB HiFi is a formidable competitor in this sector and is poised for future growth. Currently, JB Hi-Fi has 60 stores and has plans to open 100 stores within the next few years. Entering one of their stores is like being on sensory overload—in addition to the overwhelming product assortment, the music and barrage of customers give their stores a high energy level.

POWER OR SATELLITE CENTERS are unenclosed malls situated near large malls such as Chadstone. They are able to capitalize on the infrastructure of the large mall (road and transportation system) yet enjoy lower operating costs. Usually power centers feature two or three big box retailers. I will now provide an overview of some big box retailers typically found in power centers.

Harvey Norman, discussed in the section on discount retailers, had first mover advantage in locating in power centers. Other stores such as Fantastic Holdings, Freedom Furniture, and Rebel Sports also locate in these centers.

Fantastic Holdings Ltd. is a vertically integrated company positioned as a discount retailer. It manufactures, imports, and retails furniture. Its 42 outlets are primarily company owned, although it does have four franchise outlets. Forty percent of sales come from their own production or direct import, with the balance being purchased from third parties. To target a more up-market customer, Fantastic Holdings opened Plush Leather in 2003. There are currently four of these stores with plans to operate a total of 92 stores across Australia.[47]

Employing a similar location strategy to Harvey Norman, Fantastic Furniture stores were originally located in outer suburban areas, but some of the newer stores are being opened in inner suburban areas. Mirroring both of its competitors, Harvey Norman and Freedom Furniture, Fantastic Holdings embarked on an aggressive promotional campaign that included television to build awareness of the Fantastic brand.

Freedom Group, a privately held company, is the largest Australian chain specializing in furniture. It also has a small manufacturing operation. All store merchandise is private label and is sold under the Freedom name. Freedom Group is recognized as a consolidating force in the Australian furniture industry and spends heavily on advertising.

Freedom Group has made several related acquisitions. In 2001, they acquired Capt'n Snooze, a discount bedding retailer, and in 2002, they purchased Bayswiss Emporium. Bayswiss is one of the most unique Australian retail formats, with a product mix comprised of prepared food and homewares; it is the first of its type in Australia. To visualize this format, think about a synthesis of World Market and Panera Bread. It's possible to purchase a wide selection of home goods and then sit down to enjoy an espresso and a sandwich.

Freedom Group is one of the few Australian retailers to expand internationally. It entered the United Kingdom to form a supply and management agreement with Cargo Homeshop, a retailer with similar positioning to Freedom's profile in Australia.

Rebel Sports, a category killer, is the largest retailer of sporting goods in the fragmented Australian and New Zealand sporting goods sector. It has 36 stores in Australia (company owned) and eight New Zealand stores operated as part of a master franchise agreement with Briscoe's (a retail housewares group).[48] Glue, a chain that sells lifestyle and street fashion clothing, is owned by Rebel Sports. Harvey Norman owns 55 percent of Rebel Sports and as majority owner has concentrated on increasing Rebel Sports' profitability. The fragmented nature of the sporting goods industry coupled with the high level of interest in sports in Australia presents growth opportunities for Rebel Sport.

## Home Improvement and Garden

Competitors in the home improvement and garden sector employ a variety of location strategies. The newest megastores are situated in power centers. But often the older, smaller stores are located in strip centers.

There are two major competitors in this burgeoning sector: Bunnings and Mitre 10. Bunnings is the larger of the two, with over 200 stores. Bunnings has been a major force in consolidating the DIY retailing market. Even with the Bunnings influencc, the industry remains fragmented in terms of ownership. There are still opportunities for expansion in this sector.[49]

Similar in format to Home Depot, Bunnings has a 20-percent market share in the home improvement sector. It is owned by Wesfarmer's, a diversified conglomerate, and represents over 30 percent of Wesfarmer's revenue. Its tag line, "lower prices are just the beginning," reflects its emphasis on everyday low pricing (EDLP). In addition to serving the "do it yourself" customer, 16 percent of Bunnings sales volume is generated from the construction trade, for which they have a dedicated trade center in New South Wales. Bunnings was originally a regional competitor in the DIY market. Until it acquired Howard Smith BBC hardware in 2001, it did not have a presence in Sydney.

Even though Bunnings is modeled after Home Depot, its product assortment (45,000 products) reflects differences between the United States and Australia. It carries a wider number of categories but not in the same depth as Home Depot. Additionally, plumbing and electrical are not major categories for Bunnings, as Australian law does not permit do-it-yourselfers to undertake these types of projects.[50] Over 30 percent of the product assortment is focused on garden and associated products, reflecting the Australian passion for gardening.

Bunnings has many core competencies—product assortment, prime locations, and widespread brand awareness. But one of its most distinctive advantages is their employees. They provide an exceptionally high level of service and are unfailingly friendly, polite and eager to assist.

Mitre 10, a hardware cooperative founded in 1959, is similar to Ace Hardware in the United States. Until 1999, it was the largest hardware retail operator in Australia. Its market share in the hardware market has dropped from almost 14 percent in 1999 to about 8.4 percent currently. This loss of market share is due to Bunnings' rapid expansion. Mitre 10 Mega stores are big box DIY stores designed to compete directly with Bunnings. A key strength for Mitre 10 is its owner operators, but this structure has also slowed decision making and access to capital by members.

STRIP CENTERS permeate the suburbs and have developed around catering to different lifestyles. For example, some strip centers appeal to the high fashion shopper (for example, Chapel Street in Melbourne) while others appeal to a café lifestyle (for example, St. Kilda Beach). In the major cities, nearly every neighborhood has a strip center with a grocery store, specialty food providers (butchers, greengrocers), and pharmacies. These strip centers also offer dine in and takeout restaurants. For example, within walking distance of my house in Australia, there were at least six different restaurants to choose from, including Italian, Chinese, Indian, and French. Neighborhood strip malls in Australia often have limited parking and are within walking distance of local residences.

TEMPORARY RETAILERS such as farmers' markets, craft markets, and car boot sales are growing in popularity. Major cities like Sydney and Melbourne offer very large farmer's markets, such as the Queen Victoria Market in Melbourne. There you can buy just about any fruit, vegetable, meat, or fish imaginable and all sorts of souvenirs as well. When my friends from the States came to visit me, the Queen Victoria market was one of the first places I took them.

In addition to these well-established resident and tourist destinations, farmers markets in Australia have been mirroring those in the United States. In 2005, Australia had about 100 farmers markets, compared to just 35 in 1999. Estimated sales were about A$20 million.[51]

## Internet Traders

Australia has an Internet penetration rate of 68.2 percent, nearly equal to that of the United States (http://www.internetworldstats.com/stats6.htm). Retail sales through the Internet have increased from $900 million AUD in 1999 to $8.5–9 billion AUD in 2004, a 900 percent increase since 1999.[52] On-line sales account for 2-5 percent of Australia's retail sales.[53]

Internet retailers face the same challenges as in other countries: high customer acquisition costs, customer preference to see and touch products before buying, and high promotion/marketing expenditures. Australian Internet retailers also have the additional hurdle of competition with international online retailers such as Amazon.com and Barnes&Noble.com.

The most popular Australian e-commerce site is eBay Australia, which hosted over 2.5 million users in 2004.[54] The total value of merchandise sold on eBay (Australia) increased 107 percent to A$600 million in 2004. Over 8,500 Australians use Ebay as a primary or secondary source of income, selling goods ranging from plus size clothing to antiques.[55] Another interesting social phenomenon that has arisen from eBay Australia is the formation of eBay communities, such as the Kowgirls, six women in their late 30s from Queensland and New South Wales, who met through eBay and have now become close friends.[56] The geographic distances between major metropolitan centers in Australia may facilitate the formation of these communities.

Companies that have been successful in this channel include large, traditional retailers such as Coles-Myer, Harvey Norman, and Woolworths. Books, media, financial products, and tickets are product categories that produce high sales volumes.

## Franchises

In Australia, franchises contribute about 10 percent to the total GDP and employ over 600,000 Australians in 64,000 workplaces.[57] Sales in this sector account for over $80 billion AUD. Franchises are regulated by the Trade Practices Industry Code of Regulation.[58] MOBILE FRANCHISES are emerging as an important trend in the Australian franchise sector, with almost 40 percent of all franchised units operating under this type of structure.[59] A mobile franchise is a business based around a product or service that is brought directly to the consumer (for example, Molly Maid cleaning service in the United States) rather than the consumer traveling to the business site.

Some of the best-known Australian franchises include Harvey Norman, Boost Juices, Ultra Tune, Lube Mobile, Priceline, and Baker's Delight. Harvey Norman's unique franchise structure has already been discussed. Boost Juice, a juice bar, has 86 outlets in Australia, with 80 percent operated by franchisees. Ultra Tune and Lube Mobile offer auto services. Ultra Tune opened in 1979 and has 135 drive-in outlets throughout Australia. Lube Mobile uses a mobile model of auto service delivery, going directly to the customer. Baker's Delight has almost 700 bakeries. Franchisees are offered the opportunity to become shareholders, which encourages participation and feedback. Their IT network allows franchisees to log on and see the average prices that other bakeries are paying for ingredients. Baker's Delight has recently expanded into Canada under the name Cob's Bakery. It is committed to communities in which they operate, donating over $25 million worth of bread each year to local causes.

## Pharmacies

One unique feature of Australian retailing is the degree to which the pharmacy industry is regulated by the government. Currently, it is a highly fragmented industry, as ownership is limited to licensed pharmacists, and no pharmacist is allowed to own more than three pharmacies. A legal limit of 5,000 pharmacies can operate in Australia. Pharmacies enjoy a monopoly over prescription medicine and derive a majority of their income from this product category.

Prescription medicine cannot be purchased from any other retail outlet. Supermarkets such as Coles-Myer and Woolworths lobbied the government to reduce ownership restrictions and to allow pharmacies to be installed in their stores. To date, these efforts have not been successful because of the political power of the Pharmacists Guild. Not surprisingly, pharmacists oppose the expansion of pharmacies into supermarkets, alleging that it would drive community pharmacies out of business. Woolworths counters that argument, noting that reduced supply costs would decrease drug prices 25 percent if prescription medicine was sold from supermarkets. While introducing pharmacies into Coles and Woolworths would decrease prices, I believe that it would also result in a marked decrease in service levels currently found at community pharmacies. The local pharmacy near my house provided personalized and friendly service. For example, once I was looking for a skin care product that I used in the States. The staff offered to call the local distributor to see if the product was available. Then, the salesperson called me at home to apologize that this product was no longer being sold in Australia. It was an amazing example of superior customer service.

The inability of supermarkets to open their own pharmacies is viewed by many as hypocritical and in defiance of anti-competition laws. Recently, the Victorian Government drafted laws to relax the regulation of pharmacy ownership and open the industry up to competition from the supermarket chains, but these laws have yet to be ratified.[60]

Two recent pharmacy acquisitions provide evidence of the turbulence in this retail sector. In 2001, healthcare and logistics business Mayne Nickless Ltd. acquired pharmaceutical manufacturer and wholesaler FH Faulding & Co. The latter company owned several well-known marketing groups in the pharmaceutical retailing industry: Terry White Chemists, Chemmart, and the Medicine Shoppe.[61] Second,

Australian Pharmaceuticals Industries (API) recently acquired several prominent pharmacies, including Soul Pattinson Pharmacy and Chemworld. Priceline Pharmacy, a discount pharmacy, was acquired when API bought its holding company, New Price Retail Group. Both of these acquisitions can be viewed as a defensive strategy to increase these firms' retail presence and to counter what is expected to be the eventual introduction of pharmacies into Wooworth's and Coles-Myer supermarkets. The Big Two currently hold about a 20 percent market share in health and beauty and want to increase that share to more than 30 percent by 2010.[62]

## Government and Legal Issues

Only two sectors are heavily regulated. In addition to pharmacies, the other sector heavily affected by legislation is liquor retailing, which is limited to specialty outlets that must hold a license to operate.[63] Overall, there is a low level of government interference in Australian retail trade. Similar to the United States, laws exist to prevent businesses from abusing their market power to the detriment of competition. The Australian Competition and Consumer Commission (ACCC) is the enforcement arm of these laws. Not surprisingly, Woolworths and Cole-Myer's business practices have often been scrutinized by the ACCC. Most recently, there have been allegations that both companies engaged in anti-competitive behavior after their acquistions of businesses in the liquor and service station sectors. However, these allegations were dismissed.

TRADING HOURS are regulated by local governments and vary by state. This can be a confusing issue for consumers, particularly around holidays. For example, in Victoria, Good Friday is a public holiday during the Easter season, thus shops are not allowed to be open. Easter Saturday is also a public holiday, but all shops may be open. Easter Sunday is a non-trading day with special exemptions for some stores. Major retailers with more than 100 employees, such as supermarkets and department stores, are not allowed to be open. On Easter Monday, another public holiday, trading hours return to normal. This confusing system is widely criticized, in particular by the Victorian Retailers Association and Victorian Employers Chamber of Commerce.

Not surprisingly, taxation is another issue that affects retailers. In July 2000, a 10-percent Goods and Services Tax (GST) was introduced, forcing retailers to invest in technology upgrades of their POS systems to track these payments.

## Differentiating Factors of Australian Retailing

As discussed earlier in this chapter, the food sector is dominated by oligopolistic competition. This unique characteristic of Australian retailing, dubbed by one executive the "Big 2 Effect," has had an impact on the retail industry as a whole. This concentration at the top has held back the development of Australian retailing. The domination of Woolworths and Coles-Myer has created a "me-too" sameness effect, with their competitors choosing strategies that emulate the Big 2. According to this executive, because at least 25 percent of Australian retail executives have worked within the Coles or Woolworth paradigm, management style of these two companies has been transferred from company to company. Because innovation is squelched in the Big 2, people don't learn how to innovate. Woolworths and Coles dominate promotional expenditures and number of employees. Because of their size, they have lowered the cost of doing business, but niche retailing, prevalent in the United States has not occurred.[64] The fact that so many Australian retail formats copy existing formats can be directly attributed to the Big 2 effect.

The dominance of three major property trusts (Centro, Westfield, and Gandel Retail Trusts) over shopping centers is another key differentiator of the Australian retail market. To be successful, a retailer must have a presence in major shopping centers. The lack of competition among the property trusts results in rent/sales ratios being almost double what you would see in the United States.[65] Further exacerbating this problem are the low vacancy rates. Retailers have not yet formed alliances to gain power in negotiating with the property trusts, which play one retailer against another. For example, when negotiating with an independent pharmacy, a landlord might threaten to offer Priceline the lease if the independent does not agree to a higher rent. Lease length is also a problem. While five–ten year leases are common in the United States, this is not the case in Australia. The stage is set for almost continuous rent negotiations. There have been examples of 52 percent rent increases in an economic framework of 4–5 percent growth. The trade press has confirmed that high rents are an issue and detract from retailers' profit potential.[66]

The third differentiating factor relates to the recruitment and retention of retail talent. Over 2 million people or 22.5 percent of total employment work in the retail sector.[67] Thirty-five percent of all retail employees work in the supermarket and grocery stores followed by specialty food outlets with 13 percent. Despite the prevalence of retailing as a source of employment, it has not been an industry of first choice for careers, particularly by college graduates. Therefore, retailing has not been able to attract the best talent. Retailers have not developed the right recruitment infrastructure to support growth. For example, in the United States, retailers commonly recruit on college campuses, often with one executive responsible for recruitment. This is not the case in Australia.

## Similarities to the United States

The retail sector in Australia demonstrates a number of similarities to American retailing. First, there is an increasing dominance of multiformat retailers, such as the Just Group and the Sussan Retail Group. Retailers see openings in markets that are poorly addressed and find segments that do not overlap with one another.[68] They then create distinctive brands within the umbrella organization, as Just Group has done with its various retail brands

The Australian retail sector continues to be a hotbed of merger and acquisition activity. Often these activities appear to be motivated by a desire to achieve economies of scale (Warehouse's acquisition of Millers discount chains), to grow (Woolworth's purchase of Dan Murphy's), or to counterbalance the impact of Coles-Myer and Woolworth's (Australian Pharmaceutical's acquisition of New Price Retail).

Vertical integration among apparel specialty retailers with overseas production facilities is increasing and may be driven by falling production costs as well as a recent decrease in apparel tariffs from 25 percent to 17.5 percent. As a result, imported clothing became 6 percent more cost effective than domestically manufactured products.[69] While China dominates Australian apparel imports, Australian retailers are trying to diversify their production from that country. Five major Australian retailers (David Jones, Country Road, Little Label, Target, and Lowe's) plan to open buying offices in Chennai, India.[70]

Private label is an important branding strategy for many Australian retailers and has an impact on retailer profitability. Whether the product category is food or apparel, retailers are seeking differentiation through housebrands. At the other end of the spectrum, exclusive partnerships between retailers and branded manufacturers (Country Road and Myer) are another differentiating strategy for Australian retailers.

## > SUMMARY

Australia's retail system originally evolved out of serving the needs of emancipated convicts and military personnel in Sydney. While geographically as large as the United States, the major retail activity is limited to about six major cities—Sydney, Melbourne, Adelaide, Canberra, Perth, and Brisbane.

Two dominant retail groups in Australia—Coles-Myer and Woolworths Ltd.—have a major impact on the food and liquor, department store, and discount sectors. In particular, the food and liquor sector is very highly concentrated. The impact of the Big 2 has been cited as restricting the level of innovation in retailing.

Australian retailing has several dominant specialty store groups that have diversified to serve several target markets. Over the past several years, there has been a wave of merger and acquisition activity in Australian retailing, primarily to achieve economies of scale or to counterbalance the influence of Cole-Myer and Woolworth's.

## > KEY TERMS

AUSTRALIAN COMPETITION AND CONSUMER COMMISSION (ACCC)
COST REDUCTION AND PRODUCT (BRAND) DIFFERENTIATION
DIFFERENTIATION
DUOPOLY
MOBILE FRANCHISES
MONOPOLISTIC COMPETITION
POWER OR SATELLITE CENTERS
RIVALRY OF THE FEW
STRIP CENTERS
TEMPORARY RETAILERS
TRADING HOURS

## > DISCUSSION QUESTIONS

1. What elements of Australia's retail system set it apart from other similar, developed countries? What similarities to other similar countries are there?
2. How does the dominance of Coles-Myer and Woolworths influence the retail sector in Australia? Discuss major strategic differences between these retailers. Which of the Big 2 would you evaluate as being more successful?

3. What do you think is the underlying motivation for companies such as Just Group, Ltd. to continue to acquire new businesses?

4. Very few Australian retailers have an international presence, yet several have characteristics similar to global retailers (for example, some are vertically integrated). Why do you think so few Australian retailers have internationalized?

> **ENDNOTES**

1. Collins, M. (1991). "A Brief History of Retailing Part 2: The Development of Australian Retailing (1800–1990) in *Australian Retail Readings*, 3(2), 2–22. Monash Distance Education Centre: Melbourne, Australia.

2. Collins. (1991).

3. Collins. (1991).

4. Euromonitor (April 1, 2004). Global Market Information Database: Retailing in Australia. Available http://www.gmid.euromonitor.com/HitList.aspx?geogCode= 0971970299317706493585890&prmLoginType=IPRecognition

5. Samuelson, P. A., and W. D. Nordhaus. (1998). *Economics.* 16th ed. Burr Ridge, IL: McGraw Hill-Irwin.

6. Thompson, A. A. (1985). *Economics of the Firm: Theory and Practice.* 4th ed. Englewood Cliffs, NJ: Prentice Hall.

7. Samuelson and Nordhaus. (1998).

8. Yule, M., and H. Hong. (2003). "Australian Retail: What's in Store for F 2004?" *Morgan Stanley Equity Research—Asia Pacific,* 1–40.

9. Jimenez, K. (2005a, 23 April). "Supermarkets Turn Screws with Own Brands. *The Australian,* p. 3.

10. Hunt, P. (20 April, 2005). "House Brands Muscle In." *Weekly Times,* p. 7.

11. Yule, M. and H. Hong. (2003).

12. Euromonitor (2004, 1 April). Global Market Information Database: Retailing in Australia. Available http://www.gmid.euromonitor.com/HitList.aspx?geogCode= 0971970299317706493585890&prmLoginType=IPRecognition

13. "Why Woolies Is Really No. 1." (January 12, 2004). *MMR,* Vol. 21, p. 60.

14. Yule, M. and H. Hong. (2003).

15. Mills, K. (August 24, 2004). "Retailer's Revamp Reaps Savings." *The Australian,* p. 35.

16. "Woolies Hits 790 M on Super Sales." *ACRS Insights* (September 2005) p. 1.

17. Marketline (2005). Foodland Associated Limited. Available: http://dbic. datamonitor.com/

18. Jimenez, K. (September 1, 2005d). "Small loss for Cut Price Grocer Aldi." *The Australian,* p. 22.

19. Lehman, J. (July 27, 2005). "Aldi Plans to Open 36 Stores in a Year." Nationwide News Pty Limited, p. 24.

20. McCullough, J. (August 20, 2005). "What's Now in Store for Myer?" *The Courier Mail,* p. 26.

21. Lloyd, S. (April 29, 2004). "Back in the Game." *Business Review Weekly,* p. 47.

22. Bawden, T. (June 22, 2005). "Harris Scarfe Eyes Options for Expansions." *The Advertiser,* 40.

23. Euromonitor (April 1, 2004).

24. Jackson, S. (October 28, 2005). "Coles Myer Limited." *Asia Pacific Equity Research-JP Morgan.*
25. Wood, L. (May 14, 2004a). "Megamart Goes Under the Griller." *The Age.*
26. Downie, S. (August 16, 2004). "Getting an Edge on the Giants." *Herald Sun,* 25. "Cutthroat Cut-Price War Goes for Jugular." (March 11, 2004). *The Australian,* p. 48. "Easter trading Rules remain a Farce." (April 6, 2004). *The Age* p. 16.
27. Woolworths Annual Report (2005).
28. Euromonitor (April 1, 2004).
29. Euromonitor (April 1, 2004).
30. Euromonitor (April 1, 2004).
31. Euromonitor (April 1, 2004).
32. "Brazin to Buy HMV Australia for US$3 MLN." (September 29, 2005). *Asia Pulse.*
33. Jimenez, K. (August 24, 2005c). "Ghetto Drags Brazin Down." *The Australian,* p. 23.
34. Euromonitor (April 1, 2004).
35. Euromonitor (April 1, 2004).
36. Jimenez, K. (July 9, 2005b). "County Road Hits Flat Stretch." *The Australian,* p. 35.
37. Roux, G. (March 2, 2005). "Just Group Ltd. Just Fine." *Citigroup Global Markets.* Available: http://pdf.galegroup.com/PDF/getPDF?repNum=10164752&appUI= itweb&date=1135016964&digest=842FD6CFE3938239A50D0E70EEE20179
38. Lloyd, S. (April 29, 2004).
39. "Just Group to Sell Urban Brands Outlets." *ACRS Insights* (September 2004). p. 2.
40. Williams, F. (November 24, 2005). "Wrap: Miller's, Warehouse Sell Aust Discount Variety Business. *Australian Associated Press Pty. Ltd., AAP* Newsfeed.
41. "New Player Threatens Coles." *ACRS Insights,* (November 2005). Woolies, p. 1.
42. Evans, S. (September 9, 2002). "Milgrom Shapes Sportsgirl for a Chain Reaction." *Australian Financial Review,* p. 15.
43. Evans, S. (September 9, 2002).
44. Meagher, D. (March 28, 2003). "Desperately Seeking Sussan." *Australian Financial Review,* p. 62.
45. Huddleston, P.T. (2004). Personal interviews.
46. JB Hi-Fi Limited Prospectus for the offer of 86,592, 912 shares of JB Hi-Fi Limited. (September 18, 2003).
47. Fantastic Holdings Limited (2005). Investor presentation August 25. Available: http://www.fantasticfurniture.com.au/documents/companyinfo/FAN% 20Investor%20Presentation.pdf
48. Euromonitor (April 1, 2004).
49. Euromonitor (April 1, 2004).
50. Huddleston, P.T. (2004).
51. Stevenson, G. (September 23, 2005). "Things Organic." *Nationwide News Pty Limited.*
52. Colley, A. (January 25, 2005). "Online Selling's Not the Portal to Paradise." *The Australian,* p. 27.
53. Colley, A. (January 25, 2005).
54. Colley, A. (January 25, 2005).
55. Pullman, F. (November 18, 2005). "Sales on the bay a lifestyle decision." *Townsville Bulletin/Townsville Sun,* p. 304.

56. Pitelen, T. (June 19, 2005). "For love or Money." *Sunday Telegraph Magazine,* p. 24.

57. Franchise Council of Australia (October 10, 2005). Media Release: "PM Addresses "Dymamic and Job Generating" Franchise Industry. Available: http://franchise.org.au/franchisenews/?fuseaction=info&id=152&ct_id=0&i=2

58. *Trade Practices (Industry Codes-Franchising) Regulations 1998.* Available: http://www.comlaw.gov.au/comlaw/legislation/legislativeinstrumentcompilation1.nsf/0/21A1E712585B40FACA256F71004E4CD8/$file/TradePracIndCodeFran1998.pdf

59. Chow and Frazer (2003). "Servicing Customers Directly: Mobile Franchising Arrangements in Australia." *European Journal of Marketing,* 37, 3–4, 594–613.

60. Forbes, M., and D. Wroe. (April 9, 2004). "Supermarkets get pharmacies hope." *The Age,* p. 3.

61. Euromonitor (April 1, 2004).

62. Jimenez, K. (September 7, 2004). "API Deal Lifts Retail Presence." *The Australian,* p. 23.

63. Euromonitor (April 1, 2004).

64. Huddleston, P.T. (2004).

65. Huddleston, P.T. (2004).

66. Roux, G. (July 21, 2004). "Just Group Ltd.: A Look That Fits." *Citigroup Global Markets.* Available: http://pdf.galegroup.com/PDF/getPDF?repNum=9685452&appUI=itweb&date=1135103380&digest=99DD9096E0188234F9A511C068371764

67. Euromonitor (April 1, 2004).

68. Jimenez, K. (September 7, 2004).

69. McClennan, A., and M. Willoughby. (July 20, 2004). "Just Group Limited: Does This Retailer Have legs?" *JP Morgan Asia Pacific Equity Research.* Available: http://pdf.galegroup.com/PDF/getPDF?repNum=9689532&appUI=itweb&date=1135106306&digest=E4ECB5024AD25902FDE35A3727F86C2B

70. "Five Australian Textile Giants to Set Up Offices in India." (June 9, 2005). *Asia Pulse.*

# COMPANY FOCUS IV.1

## CARREFOUR

### Lindsay Brown, Anne Dovitz, Lauren Greenberg, Christa Larabell, Abi Peterson, Kristen Wilk

**Flow Chart:**

1960: France (1,526 stores)
1969: Belgium (495 stores)
1973: Spain (2,179 stores)
1975: Brazil (390 stores)
1982: Argentina (475 stores)
1989: Taiwán (34 stores)
1991: Greece (447 stores)
1992: Portugal (293 stores)
1993: Italy (411 stores)
1993: Turkey (251 stores)
1994: Malaysia (8 stores)
1994: Mexico (Exited 2005)
1994: Singapore (2 stores)
1995: China (226 stores)
1996: South Korea (32 stores)
1996: Hong Kong (27 stores)
1996: Thailand (20 stores)
1997: Poland (87 stores)
1998: Chile (4 stores)
1998: Columbia (15 stores)
1998: Indonesia (15 stores)
1999: Czech Republic (10 stores)
2000: Slovakia (4 stores)
2000: Japan (Exited 2003)
2000: Qatar
2001: Switzerland (11 stores)
2001: Oman
2001: Romania (4 stores)
       UAE
2002: Tunisia (1 store)
       Dominican Republic

Carrefour, meaning cross roads, is Europe's largest hypermarket retailer. This French retailer's first supermarket was located at an intersection of five roads, giving them their name, Carrefour. Carrefour was born in 1959 when the French Fournier and Defforey families joined forces to develop and own a supermarket.[1] The family's plans were finally realized in 1960 when their first supermarket opened in Annecy, Haute-Savoie, France.[2] Carrefour was the leader and developer of one of retail's most prominent formats, the hypermarket.[3] A hypermarket is a place where the consumer can find everything they need under one roof. "Hypermarkets are huge department stores and supermarket combinations that sell food, clothing, electronics, and household appliances, among other items at a discounted price."[4]

## Industry/Market Entry

In Europe, there are many successful retailing formats including department stores, supermarkets, and specialty stores. As Carrefour invaded the retail frontier, a new format of retailing emerged and is now known as the hypermarket. Soon after Carrefour entered into the market, other companies followed, but no one could top Carrefour's success. Today, hypermarkets are the leading retail format in France.[5]

Small business in France, long supported and nurtured by the French government, began to experience competition from the new hypermarket format. The government began to place laws on the size and expansion of the stores, making it harder for Carrefour to expand their business further into other French cities. France was regulated under the *Loi Royer,* which handles "retail developments of 16,146 square feet or larger in towns with populations over 40,000 people, or 10,764 square feet or larger in smaller cities."[6] This law was used against Carrefour's hypermarkets. In 1996, a new law was developed to lower the size requirement to get a permit for a store, called the *Loi Raffarin.* This law is viewed as an "anti-hypermarket measure that appeals to small retail representatives."[7] Because hypermarkets are usually very large, it is expensive to start a business. It takes six to eight years for a store to break even,[8] which makes it very hard for new businesses to enter the hypermarket format.

Carrefour not only owns and operates hypermarkets, they also have individual supermarkets, hard discount stores, convenience stores, cash and carry, and food service. The market entries into these competitive formats are much more difficult because of market saturation. In order for Carrefour to compete with the other businesses in these markets they "build market share in each country in which it does business by expanding the type of retailing best suited to the local market and by taking advantage of the way the formats complement one another."[9] Carrefour not only uses this strategy to succeed but they also use many more to gain competitive advantage in the market. This is why Carrefour is the number one retailer in Europe and the second leading retailer in the world.

## Management

The foundation of every powerful corporation is a strong management system. Carrefour has perfected its management structure and is working to better enhance those in the positions. There are two main boards that run Carrefour, the supervisory board and the board of management. The supervisory board has the tasks of appointing and dismissing the members of the Board of Management, including their chairmen, and approving any changes in the structures of the group and its capital.[10] The board of management is a body that is strictly appointed by the supervisory board. They are responsible for the general management of Carrefour including financial responsibilities. The board of management is made up of five members: Chairman of the Management Board Jose-Luis Duran; Manager and Director for Human Resources, Communication, and Secretary General Jacques Beauchet; Manager and Director of Dia Javier Campo; Manager and Director of Europe Jose Maria Folache; and Manager and Director of French hypermarkets Guy Yraeta.[11] Under the board of management is the ten-member executive board, which is in charge of operational implementation and management strategies. Over the past six months there has been mass turmoil in the Carrefour management hierarchy.

On February 3, 2005, Carrefour's chairman Daniel Bernard turned in his letter of resignation. Bernard had been the chairman and managing director of Carrefour for more then 12 years, leading Carrefour "though an aggressive global expansion that made it second to Wal-mart."[12] During the last year of his chairmanship, Bernard "lost the confidence of the group's founders and that of its leading shareholder, the Halley family, owing to his failure to stop the decline in the sales of its French hypermarkets."[13] French hypermarkets account for 27 percent of Carrefour's total sales.[14] Bernard did his best to save the lost sales of Carrefour, investing about $391.4 million in price cuts and launching various cost-cutting initiatives.[15] Bernard's efforts did not go unnoticed but it was too late. Since his resignation Carrefour has initiated key restructuring moves in its management system.

Taking over as chief executive officer was José Luis Duran, a 40-year-old Spaniard fluent in English and French. Duran has held many different positions in the Carrefour Company, including being the forerunner and engineer in the turnaround of Carrefour's Spanish operations. Duran has also been chief financial officer for Carrefour. Luc Vandevelde was appointed to the position of non-executive chairman, who is assigned as chairman of the supervisory board. He is 53 and "joined Carrefour's board last year as a representative of the biggest shareholder, the Halley family."[16] Vandevelde is the former chief executive officer for Marks & Spencer and was also the chief executive officer of Promodes before Carrefour acquired it in 1999.[17] He is expected to help jumpstart a turnaround for Carrefour. Since the takeover of Duran and Vandevelde, Carrefour has seen a mass transition. The decline in hypermarket sales has been halted and for the first time in recent years Carrefour's sales have been seen as stable. "Mr. Vandevelde and Mr. Duran are expected to continue with the strategy of investing in price, cutting costs, and refurbishing stores, which seems to have helped stem the decline in Carrefour's home market."[18]

Though the loss of a 12-year veteran was devastating to Carrefour, it seems as though the new team of Jose-Luis Duran and Luc Vandevelde will be extremely effective. As leaders they are also "expected to demand better returns from the group's international assets, a strategy that includes quitting unattractive markets such as Japan."[19] The biggest difference seen thus far between Bernard and the new team is that the change of pace has and will accelerate significantly. For many people who have invested large amounts of time, funds, and heartache, this is great news to hear. Duran and Vandevelde will be giving country managers and store managers greater autonomy, decision making will be faster; bureaucracy will be cut back, and management layers will be stripped out.[20] Carrefour has worked extremely hard to advance their management system and better enhance their corporation. With the transition to the supervisory board and board of management, opposed to a chairman/director overseeing the whole company, Carrefour is more likely to be fast paced, efficient, and profitable.

## Competitors

According to Hoover's, Carrefour's top two competitors are Auchan and Casino Guichard.[21] Although Carrefour is still the leader of the three in France, the other two companies are very similar to it.

Auchan is France's third-largest supermarket chain behind Carrefour and ITM Entreprises.[22] Auchan operates about 356 hypermarkets and over 646 supermarkets with 170,000 employees.[23] In addition, it also has over 1,250 supermarkets that are operating as partnerships or franchises.[24] It operates stores throughout Europe and in China, Morocco, Russia, and Taiwan as well as France.[25] Therefore, not only is Auchan a competitor for Carrefour in France, but also in the countries they have both expanded into. Auchan was once a competitor in the U.S. and Mexican markets, but like Carrefour they also exited in 2003.[26] Auchan has stores of many formats: hypermarkets, supermarkets, home improvement stores, warehouse-style sporting goods stores, consumer electronics stores, and do-it-yourself stores. Their products include groceries, apparel, consumer electronics, fast food, and travel services.[27] Auchan, too, is a multinational company, tailoring its goods to the habits of the customer in each country.[28] Already in many countries besides France, Auchan plans to expand its number of stores in Poland, Hungary, Italy, and Russia. It has recently acquired La Reniscenta, one if Italy's biggest retailers.[29]

Casino Guichard is one of France's biggest food retailers, owning over 9,000 hypermarkets, super-markets, restaurants, convenience stores, and discount stores.[30] It operates hypermarkets mostly under the banner Géant, supermarkets under Casino, Franprix, and Monoprix, restaurants called Casino Cafétéria, Poncholito (Tex-Mex), and La Pastaria (Italian), convenience stores called Petit Casino, Vival, and Spar, and discount stores named Leader Price.[31] Casino's convenience stores are #1 in France and its supermarkets are #5.[32] Casino's primary home is France, but like Carrefour it has also internationalized, with over 2,000 stores in 14 countries, including Brazil, Mexico, Poland, Taiwan, and the United States.[33] Like Carrefour, Casino's supermarkets and hypermarkets are also being hurt by the great success of the discount stores.[34] Each company is losing business to these hard discounters. Casino is a much older company that had much success before Carrefour was even born. It began in 1889 when Geoffroy Guichard married a grocer's daughter and eventually took over his father-in-law's business.[35] By 1900, Guichard had opened 50 stores, and it hit the 100 mark by 1904.[36] Casino grew much like Carrefour and Auchan did, acquiring CEDIS, La Rouche Maridionale, Guyenne et Gascogne, Proxi, and nearly 300 supermarkets and hypermarkets from Rallye.[37] It also acquired over 400 convenience stores from rival Auchan.[38] Casino began its internationalization in the late 1990s, acquiring retailers in Argentina (Libertad), Uruguay (Disco), Colombia (Exito), Brazil (Companhia Brasileira de Distribuicao), and Thailand (Big C), and it also opened its first hypermarket in Taichung, Taiwan.[39] For the future, Casino is setting its sights on the environment. They have formed action plans to reduce their power consumption, manage their water consumption, improve their store waste management, and limit their use of packaging.[40]

## Advertising/Marketing Strategies

With several companies in the market selling essentially the same product, advertising and market share influence what consumers buy. While walking through a hypermarket such as Carrefour, a consumer must make multiple decisions as to what exactly to buy. All of these decisions can be influenced by distinct advertising and market strategies. Carrefour has done a great job of marketing its products and continually tailoring their campaigns to fit each country. With the constant growing hypermarkets, Carrefour has been able to expand its growth.

Carrefour primarily advertises on billboards, in the press, and on television. An important goal for them is to bring about brand awareness through their strategies.[41] Carrefour creates each aid with the consumer in mind. "Chinese have a clear concept of freshness.[42] In a series of outdoor ads for Carrefour China, foods like a tomato, a strawberry and grapes are portrayed as so fresh that they bleed when cut into with a knife."[43]

Carrefour intends to gain market share by increasing the range of products on offer by as much as 15 percent in hypermarkets and by 10 percent in supermarkets. Another main focus will be to employ more staff and lengthen the operating hours in the group's 100 biggest hypermarkets.[44] Through Carrefour's advertising techniques and marketing strategies, they will continually add both more service and value to their company.

## Expansion

In 1963, Carrefour invented a new concept in the grocery store business when they opened their first hypermarket in France.[45] The hypermarket concept offered vast quantities of items at attractive prices to its customers. The hypermarkets were huge stores, in terms of square footage, with multiple checkout registers.[46] The first hypermarket even had a parking lot for customers, which was very forward thinking, since French consumers were used to walking to local markets for their daily grocery store needs.[47]

Carrefour had the innovative awareness that it would be profitable to focus its expansion into countries where modern retailing was not available.[48] Their strategy was to shock new customers with huge stores stocked with gigantic quantities of offerings. This strategy has worked in most of the countries that Carrefour has entered.

Carrefour has been successful in its international expansion efforts because they have relied on diversification of their types of retail stores.[49] Famous for its hypermarkets, Carrefour has also branched out into discount stores, supermarkets, and convenience stores.[50] This strategy allows Carrefour to reach across borders and offer whatever size retail establishment the locale can accommodate.

In 1969, the Promodis supermarkets expanded operations to Belgium, where they were known as Champion supermarkets.[51] Between 1972–1975, the Carrefour chain expanded into Spain. Carrefour even opened its first South American hypermarket in Brazil. When it opened in new countries, Carrefour renamed its hypermarkets.[52]

The Promodis group opened its first convenience store in 1972.[53] By 1977, Promodis grew by introducing a convenience store chain in France called 8 à Huit. The Promodis Company greatly expanded in 1988 when it acquired 128 supermarkets from another company.[54]

Carrefour opened their first hard discount store, ED in Spain in 1979.[55] As Carrefour and Promodis continue to expand, their forward thinking plans become evident.[56] In 1981, Carrefour launched its own payment card called the Pass Card.[57] They also introduced Carrefour brand-name products in 1985. As of 2005, there are 800 products with the Carrefour name.[58]

Carrefour generally sets up a joint venture when it expands into a new country,[59] allowing them to connect with local companies that know the consumers and their tastes. The joint venture also lets Carrefour open shops in regions of the country where they will be likely to succeed.

In 1989, Carrefour hypermarkets branched out into the Asian market, opening their first store in Taiwan. Carrefour greatly added to their expansion efforts in 1991 when they bought out two French hypermarket chains, the Euromarché and Montiaur.[60] This same year, the Carrefour hypermarket in Greece opened.[61]

From 1993–1998, Carrefour expanded rapidly,[62] bringing their hypermarket concept to Italy, Turkey, Mexico, Malaysia, China, Thailand, Korea, Hong Kong, Singapore, Poland, Chile, Colombia, and Indonesia. Promodis also expanded into China.[63]

In 1999, Promodis and Carrefour merged.[64] This business decision made Carrefour the largest European food store chain and the second-largest food store chain in the world.[65] Despite its merger with Promodis, Carrefour further added to its portfolio with 85 Brazilian-owned supermarkets.[66]

The year 2000 brought Carrefour to the Japanese market. Carrefour did much buying, selling, merging, and acquiring throughout 2000–2005.[67] Even though the Asian governments are quite regulatory, the Asian people are quite receptive to the hyper-market shopping experience. Thailand is a country where Carrefour anticipates much expansion during the next few years.[68] In Malaysia, Carrefour hyper-markets account for roughly 10 percent of total retail sales.[69] Malaysia is a good example of where Carre-four stepped in to create a modern retail environ-ment where none had previously existed.[70]

While Carrefour is still in the growth mode, they do have the ability to accept that they may not be successful everywhere.[71] They made a recent business decision to leave the Mexican marketplace. Carrefour pulled out of the United States.[72] The US did not fit the mold of Carrefour's strategic expansion plans. The US was not a country in need of updating to a modern retail environment.[73] Carrefour was merely competition in the land of malls, mega malls, and big box stores.

As of 2005, Carrefour is planning to increase ex-pansion of their convenience stores and supermar-kets.[74] They are not so much interested in expanding into new countries as they are in saturating the countries where they presently do business.

## Growth Options

Juxtaposed to when Carrefour first started its corpo-ration in the 1960s, the years 2005 and beyond will pose much more of a challenge to the now multi-national powerhouse. International markets are filled with more competition and a need for faster com-pany growth. In previous years Carrefour could move slowly, steadily gaining market share without need-ing a plethora of capitol for support. However, in the years to come it will be important for the corpora-tion to move quickly, supporting themselves with a larger financial foundation.[75]

One can expect Carrefour to open stand-alone stores and to invest in land to increase their economies of scale, as well as to continue their strategy of tacti-cal acquisitions.[76] Selling their 29 hypermarkets in Mexico provided some of that extra financial padding that the corporation needs. In addition to selling in

Mexico, during January of 2005 Carrefour sold retail spaces in the Czech Republic, Poland, Slovakia, and Turkey, which included 13 shopping centers and 19 hypermarkets. Selling spaces is another way that the corporation is making more capital available for ex-pansion, even though they plan to lease the space back later.[77] This type of selling and buying back shows that Carrefour is using a resource-based ap-proach to provide for new growth options.

A focal point of growth for the corporation in the upcoming years will be Malaysia. Carrefour has eight hypermarkets there currently, and within the next year they will open at least six more. This in-cludes their ninth hypermarket in Kepong by the end of 2006. The corporation's operating company has also joined forces with Syarikat Pesaka Antah Sdn Bhd (SPA), a company with interests in property de-velopment, information technology, and financial services in Malaysia. This partnership will provide growth of cultural knowledge and allow local goods to enter into the hypermarkets, as well as add extra financial support to the corporation.[78] So, it seems as though Carrefour has learned a lesson from their less-than-profitable solo entry into Japan, which left the normally successful retailer behind in the real es-tate race and disconnected from their consumers.[79] In addition to Malaysia the company will most likely be targeting Thailand, China, and South Korea.[80]

Another growth opportunity for Carrefour will be its new formats. New formats provide a way for a corporation to become a market leader in all sectors of the retail market in a particular country. Carrefour continues to grow their most recent formats, super-markets and convenience stores. However, they are also considering going in the less familiar direction of hard discounting.

Finally, Carrefour will be investing in their home country, where their image has been slightly shaken due to creeping prices. They will be lowering costs and increasing their home product lines in some re-tail formats as much as 15 percent,[81] in the hopes that consumers will more easily find what they need, guar-anteeing a purchase.

## Discussion Questions

1. Is the retailer classified as a global retailer or a multinational retailer? Explain its pattern of expansion. What expansion strategy did/is the retailer use/using?

2. Based on Dunning's eclectic theory, how do ownership, location, and internalization factors play in your retailers' international expansion?
3. What role do cultural proximity and geographical proximity play in the retailers' international moves?
4. Can you predict the retailers' future international expansion?

## Endnotes

1. Hoovers (11/6/2005).
2. Hoovers (11/6/2005).
3. Hoovers (11/6/2005).
4. Proquest (11/6/2005).
5. Sternquist, B. (1998). Retailing in Central and Eastern Europe: Company Focus III.6: Carrefour, International Retailing (pp.401). New York, New York: Fairchild Publications.

   Sternquist, B. (1998). Retailing in Central and Eastern Europe: Company Focus III.6: Carrefour, *International Retailing* (pp. 401–402). New York, New York: Fairchild Publications.

   Sternquist, B. (1998). Retailing in Germany and France, *International Retailing* (pp.306–309). New York, New York: Fairchild Publications.
6. Sternquist, B. (1998). Retailing in Central and Eastern Europe: Company Focus III.6: Carrefour, International Retailing (pp.401). New York, New York: Fairchild Publications.

   Sternquist, B. (1998). Retailing in Central and Eastern Europe: Company Focus III.6: Carrefour, *International Retailing* (pp. 401–402). New York, New York: Fairchild Publications.

   Sternquist, B. (1998). Retailing in Germany and France, *International Retailing* (pp.306–309). New York, New York: Fairchild Publications.
7. Sternquist, B. (1998). Retailing in Central and Eastern Europe: Company Focus III.6: Carrefour, International Retailing (pp.401). New York, New York: Fairchild Publications.

   Sternquist, B. (1998). Retailing in Central and Eastern Europe: Company Focus III.6: Carrefour, *International Retailing* (pp. 401–402). New York, New York: Fairchild Publications.

   Sternquist, B. (1998). Retailing in Germany and France, *International Retailing* (pp.306–309). New York, New York: Fairchild Publications.
8. Sternquist, B. (1998). Retailing in Central and Eastern Europe: Company Focus III.6: Carrefour, International Retailing (pp.401). New York, New York: Fairchild Publications.

   Sternquist, B. (1998). Retailing in Central and Eastern Europe: Company Focus III.6: Carrefour, *International Retailing* (pp. 401–402). New York, New York: Fairchild Publications.

   Sternquist, B. (1998). Retailing in Germany and France, *International Retailing* (pp.306–309). New York, New York: Fairchild Publications.
9. Carrefour's Activities. (n.d). Retrieved November 1, 2005, from http://www.carrefour.com/english/groupecarrefour/activities.jsp

10. Carrefour's Board of Management. Retrieved October 13, 2005, from http://www.carrefour.com/english/groupecarrefour/directories.jsp

11. Carrefour's Management. Retrieved October, 31, 2005, from http://www.carrefour.com/english/groupecarrefour/comiteexecutif.jsp

12. Carrefour CEO ousted. *Business and Industry MMR.* 22(4)-1. issn:0743–5258.

13. Segond, Valerie and Seithumer, Ingrid. Carrefour chairman to step down. *La Tribune.* 3. feb. 2005

14. Carrefour CEO ousted. *Business and Industry MMR.* 22(4)-1. issn:0743–5258. Carrefour ousts CEO, Appoints Former Marks & Spencer Boss. *Progressive Grocer.* 4 Feb. 2005. www.progressivegrocer.com

15. Carrefour CEO ousted. (2005).

16. Carrefour ousts CEO, Appoints Former Marks & Spencer Boss. *Progressive Grocer.* 4 Feb. 2005. www.progressivegrocer.com

17. Carrefour ousts CEO, Appoints Former Marks & Spencer Boss. *Progressive Grocer.* 4 Feb. 2005. www.progressivegrocer.com

18. Hollinger, P. *Carrefour's revolutionary: Going from strength to strength. Financial Times.* London (UK):Dec 4, 1998. p. 13.

19. Hollinger, P. (1998).

20. Hollinger, P. (1998).

21. Carrefour History. Hoover's. 10/25/2005. http://proquest.umi.com/pqdweb?index=3&did=168186271&SrchMode=1&sid=1&Fmt=3&VInst=PROD&VType=PQD&RQT=309&VName=PQD&TS=113167 1610&clientId=3552.html. Carrefour Overview. Hoover's. 10/25/2005. http://proquest.umi.com/pqdweb?index=3&did=168186271&SrchMode=1&sid=1&Fmt=3&VInst=PROD&VType=PQD&RQT=309&VName=PQD&TS=113167 1610&clientId=3552.html.

22. Carrefour History. (2005).

23. Auchan. 10/25/2005. www.auchan.com.

24. Carrefour History. (2005).

25. Carrefour History. (2005).

26. Carrefour History. (2005).

27. Carrefour History. (2005).

28. Auchan. 10/25/2005. www.auchan.com.

29. Carrefour History. (2005).

30. Carrefour History. (2005).

31. Carrefour History. (2005).

32. Carrefour History. (2005).

33. Carrefour History. (2005).

34. Carrefour History. (2005).

35. Carrefour History. (2005).

36. Carrefour History. (2005).

37. Carrefour History. (2005).

38. Carrefour History. (2005).

39. Carrefour History. (2005).

40. www.groupe-casino.fr/agir/?sr=1 &id_art=40001030&lang=en, 10/25/2005

41. Kittikanya, C. (September 27,2005). Muan Thai Life sells policies at Carrefour. *Knight Ridder/Tribune Business News.* Retrieved November 6, 2005. From Lexis-Nexis database.

42. Crain Communications, 2005.

43. Crain Communications, 2005.

44. Carrefour at the crossroads;retailing. (October 22,2005) *The Economist.* Retrieved November 6,2005. From Lexis-Nexis Database

45. Carrefour's Activities. (2005).

46. Carrefour's Activities. (2005).

47. Carrefour's Activities. (2005).

48. Sternquist, B. (1998). Retailing in Central and Eastern Europe: Company Focus III.6: Carrefour, International Retailing (pp.401). New York, New York: Fairchild Publications.

    Sternquist, B. (1998). Retailing in Central and Eastern Europe: Company Focus III.6: Carrefour, *International Retailing* (pp. 401–402). New York, New York: Fairchild Publications.

    Sternquist, B. (1998).Retailing in Germany and France, *International Retailing* (pp.306–309). New York, New York: Fairchild Publications.

49. Sternquist, B. (1998). Retailing in Central and Eastern Europe: Company Focus III.6: Carrefour, International Retailing (pp.401). New York, New York: Fairchild Publications.

    Sternquist, B. (1998). Retailing in Central and Eastern Europe: Company Focus III.6: Carrefour, *International Retailing* (pp. 401–402). New York, New York: Fairchild Publications.

    Sternquist, B. (1998).Retailing in Germany and France, *International Retailing* (pp.306–309). New York, New York: Fairchild Publications.

50. Jitpleecheep, S. (July 19, 2005). Carrefour Seeks new business models: Convenience Stores May Be Next Bangkok Post. Retrieved October 28, 2005, From Lexis-Nexis database.

51. Carrefour's Activities. (2005).

52. Carrefour's Activities. (2005).

53. Carrefour's Activities. (2005).

54. Carrefour's Activities. (2005).

55. Hollinger, P. (January 25, 2005). Hypermarket Hell: A Price War Forces Carrefour To Defend The Home Front The London Financial Times. Retrieved October 28, 2005, From Lexis-Nexis database.

    Hollinger, P. Time for Store Giant to Accelerate Change Strategy. *Financial Times (London, England).* P.28, 4 feb 2005.

56. Ganesan, V. (September 26. 2005). Carrefour on Aggressive Expansion Path Malaysia Business Times. Retrieved October 28, 2005, From Lexis-Nexis database.

57. Carrefour's Activities. (2005).

58. Hollinger, P. (2005).

59. Sternquist, B. (1998). Retailing in Central and Eastern Europe: Company Focus III.6: Carrefour, International Retailing (pp.401). New York, New York: Fairchild Publications.

    Sternquist, B. (1998). Retailing in Central and Eastern Europe: Company Focus III.6: Carrefour, *International Retailing* (pp. 401–402). New York, New York: Fairchild Publications.

    Sternquist, B. (1998).Retailing in Germany and France, *International Retailing* (pp.306–309). New York, New York: Fairchild Publications.

60. Sternquist, B. (1998). Retailing in Central and Eastern Europe: Company Focus III.6: Carrefour, International Retailing (pp.401). New York, New York: Fairchild Publications.
    Sternquist, B. (1998). Retailing in Central and Eastern Europe: Company Focus III.6: Carrefour, *International Retailing* (pp. 401–402). New York, New York: Fairchild Publications.
    Sternquist, B. (1998).Retailing in Germany and France, *International Retailing* (pp.306–309). New York, New York: Fairchild Publications.
61. Carrefour's Activities. (2005).
62. Hollinger, P. (2005).
63. Carrefour Aims For More Expansion This Year. (March 5, 2005). China Post. Retrieved October 28, 2005, From Lexis-Nexis database.
64. Carrefour's Activities. (2005).
65. Sternquist, B. (1998). Retailing in Central and Eastern Europe: Company Focus III.6: Carrefour, International Retailing (pp.401). New York, New York: Fairchild Publications.
    Sternquist, B. (1998). Retailing in Central and Eastern Europe: Company Focus III.6: Carrefour, *International Retailing* (pp. 401–402). New York, New York: Fairchild Publications.
    Sternquist, B. (1998).Retailing in Germany and France, *International Retailing* (pp.306–309). New York, New York: Fairchild Publications.
66. Carrefour's Activities. (2005).
67. Carrefour's Activities. (2005).
68. Jitpleecheep, S. (2005).
69. Ganesan, V. (September 26. 2005). Carrefour on Aggressive Expansion Path, Malaysia Business Times. Retrieved October 28, 2005, From Lexis-Nexis database.
70. Ganesan, V. (2005).
71. Sternquist, B. (1998). Retailing in Central and Eastern Europe: Company Focus III.6: Carrefour, International Retailing (pp.401). New York, New York: Fairchild Publications.
    Sternquist, B. (1998). Retailing in Central and Eastern Europe: Company Focus III.6: Carrefour, *International Retailing* (pp. 401–402). New York, New York: Fairchild Publications.
    Sternquist, B. (1998).Retailing in Germany and France, *International Retailing* (pp.306–309). New York, New York: Fairchild Publications.
72. Sternquist, B. (1998). Retailing in Central and Eastern Europe: Company Focus III.6: Carrefour, International Retailing (pp.401). New York, New York: Fairchild Publications.
    Sternquist, B. (1998). Retailing in Central and Eastern Europe: Company Focus III.6: Carrefour, *International Retailing* (pp. 401–402). New York, New York: Fairchild Publications.
    Sternquist, B. (1998).Retailing in Germany and France, *International Retailing* (pp.306–309). New York, New York: Fairchild Publications.
73. Sternquist, B. (1998). Retailing in Central and Eastern Europe: Company Focus III.6: Carrefour, International Retailing (pp.401). New York, New York: Fairchild Publications.

Sternquist, B. (1998). Retailing in Central and Eastern Europe: Company Focus III.6: Carrefour, *International Retailing* (pp. 401–402). New York, New York: Fairchild Publications.

Sternquist, B. (1998).Retailing in Germany and France, *International Retailing* (pp.306–309). New York, New York: Fairchild Publications.

74. Jitpleecheep, S. (2005).

75. Hollinger, P. *Carrefour's revolutionary: Going from strength to strength. Financial Times.* London (UK):Dec 4, 1998. p. 13.

76. Tienman, R. "Carrefour expands as sales accelerate." *Knight Ridder Tribune Business News.* Washington:Oct 16, 2005.

77. Kiblinger, S.S. "Central European Retail Space Draws Investors Keen to Diversify." *Wall Street Journal (Eastern Edition).* New York, N.Y.:Nov 2, 2005. p. 1.

78. Hun, C.J. Carrefour shifts expansion plans into higher gear. *Business Times.* Kuala Lumpur:May 17, 2005. p. 5.

79. Parker, G. and G. Matthews. "Carrefour Retreat Points Up Pitfalls of Flying Solo Into Japanese Market." *Wall Street Journal (Eastern Edition).* New York, N.Y.:Oct 13, 2004. p. A.14

80. Jitpleecheep, S. (2005).

81. "Business: Carrefour at the crossroads; Retailing." *The Economist.* London: Oct 22, 2005. Vol. 377, Iss. 8449, p. 79. &Fmt=3&VInst=PROD&VType=PQD& RQT=309&VName=PQD&TS=113167 1610&clientId=3552.html.

# PART V

# Regionalization and Internationalization of Retailing

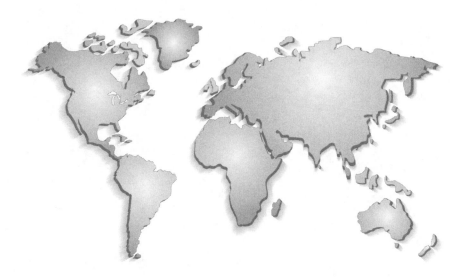

This section consists of a single chapter entitled "Prognosis for the Future." The concepts presented in this final chapter are not new. The first five chapters of this book presented concepts and theories that are used here to construct a framework for predicting (1) which retailers will internationalize, (2) where they will internationalize, and (3) how the pattern of internationalization might vary based on the experience of the retailer.

The macromarketing environment introduced in Chapter 1 forms the basis for Dunning's locational advantages, which relate to how suitable the host country is with respect to the firm's strategies. Dunning's ownership advantages represent the basic reasons why companies pursue international expansion. International culture and human behavior, the topic of Chapter 2, also influences whether a company can adapt to a variety of locations. Multinational companies, one of the two expansion types described initially in the chapter, are able to adapt to cultural differences, unlike the second expansion type, global companies.

Risk is a concept introduced in Chapter 4, on licensing and strategic alliances. When handled directly by a company, international expansion provides great learning. A portfolio of methods for handing situations emerges, giving the retailer tools for further adaptation and expansion. Direct exposure provides the greatest learning, but also presents the greatest financial risk.

Chapter 21 presents the strategic international retail expansion (SIRE) model to join these theories. In using these models, an important first step is to watch and observe whether predicted types of actions occur. It is important to take a medium- to long-term view, as the expected short-term results of some types of expansion will look very positive, but after the initial depletion of resources the effects may be as positive.

# 21

# PROGNOSIS FOR
# THE FUTURE

## After reading this chapter, you will understand

> How to apply Dunning's theory of the eclectic firm, stages theory, and risk theory to predict retailers' methods of international expansion.

> Why franchising and licensing arrangements, although methods for rapid growth, dissipate retailers' ownership advantages.

> Why retailers would select a global versus multinational method for internationalization.

This concluding chapter pulls together many of the concepts and theories intro- duced earlier in this book to provide a model for analyzing and predicting patterns of internationalization by retailers. The first part of this chapter reiterates or expands on content included in Part I of the book, particularly Chapter 2. This restatement of key concepts and theories is necessary to build the framework for analysis presented here.

## ❯ INTERNATIONALIZATION OF RETAILING[1]

Several journals have devoted special issues to the internationalization of retailing. These issues often begin with a discussion of what constitutes retail international- ization. Does retail internationalization exist when a retailer agrees to allow a for- eign retailer to operate under its name in a licensing agreement? Does it exist when a retailer begins to source from international vendors? An important distinction in the discussion was made by Pelligrini,[2] when he developed a scheme to explain paths for growth. Pelligrini identified the search for growth to be related to (1) an attempt to extend the application of a firm's proprietary know-how to extract the implied rents, and (2) an attempt to optimize the scale of operations (economies of scale) or the mix of operations (economies of scope) to reduce costs and increase efficiency. He makes the point that while these actions can be proactive, they can also be reactive.

In this chapter, I will consider only the strategic internationalization of retailing. By this I mean that a retailer purposely considers internationalization options as a part of its overall market expansion strategy. By this definition, international sourc- ing would not be a part of the strategic internationalization of retailing. How- ever, the retailer who allows a foreign retailer to license its company name would be making a strategic internationalization of retailing decision. This retailer would be choosing a low-risk alternative to extend the application of the firm's proprietary knowledge to extract the implied rents. The model of strategic international retail expansion (SIRE) that is the basis for this chapter is presented in Figure 21.1.

This model contains elements of theories described earlier in the book. Dun- ning's theory of the eclectic firm, hereafter referred to as "eclectic theory," focuses on ownership, locational, and internalization factors that influence a company to seek international expansion.[3] The focus of Salmon and Tordjman's theory is on global versus multinational retailers, a distinction based on a centralized versus a decentralized dichotomy.[4] Several researchers have explored the stages theory of international expansion. According to this theory, retailers will begin their inter- national expansion in countries that are culturally or geographically similar to the home country. As they gain experience in each country or region, they move into another area.

Eroglu considers the concept of risk as an explanation of why companies would expand internationally.[5] In her conceptual model, she provides the basis for pre- dicting which firms will seek international expansion because of organizational characteristics such as size, experience, and international orientation.

Hollander notes that much of the impetus for international expansion is inad- vertent and not based on commercial factors.[6] For instance, much of the initial re- tail expansion during the 1960s and early 1970s was the result of decolonization and

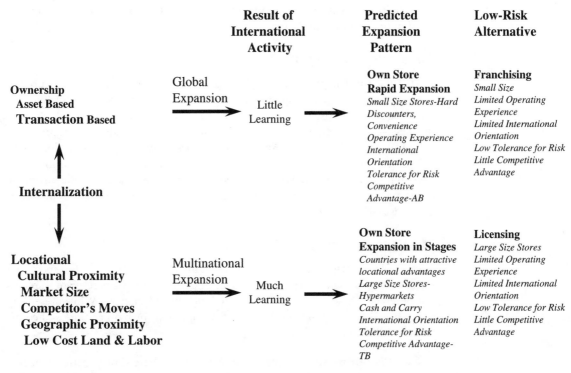

**Figure 21.1**
Model of Strategic International Retail Expansion (SIRE)

post-colonial developments. Other researchers have pointed out, correctly, that retail expansion is often the result of opportunity. For example, a retail owner may have relatives in another location, or may vacation in a particular location, and so decides to open a store there. Most importantly, chain stores have been approached by entrepreneurs in other countries saying that they think one of these stores would do very well in their country, so a franchise is born. This is international expansion, but many retailers do not view the decision to allow a franchise or to develop a licensing arrangement as a strategic decision. They do not view the decision as having an impact on their other market expansion plans. However, such decisions do have an impact. Each time a company enters into a franchising or licensing arrangement or a joint venture, it is renting its unique company assets to others. In doing this, the company needs to consider what it is losing in opportunity costs for internal market expansion.

The remainder of this chapter will explore factors related to the strategic international expansion of retailers, their reasons for expanding internationally, and predictions for where they will go next.

## ❯ ECLECTIC THEORY

Dunning's eclectic approach is recognized as a conceptual framework for explaining foreign direct investment.[7] The model, described in Chapter 2, includes three types of advantages, which influence foreign direct investment. These advantages are ownership advantages (O), locational advantages (L), and internalization advantages

(I). Pelligrini applies the OLI model to retailing and provides some insightful expansion of the locational factor.[8]

## Ownership Advantages

As discussed in Chapter 2, ownership advantages include innovative or unique products or processes a company can use to obtain market power. Included in this grouping are asset-based advantages and transaction-based advantages. Remember that asset-based advantages refer to an organizational innovation or unique products. A private-label line is an example of asset-based advantages. Transaction-based advantages come about because of the way things are done. Gaining economies of scale in production is a transaction-based ownership advantage. Volume buying or economies because of centralized management are examples of transaction-based advantages in retailing.

## Locational Advantages

Locational advantages relate to how suitable the host country is with respect to a firm's strategies. Pellegrini's 1991 work identifies locational issues relevant to retailing. Several of these issues were introduced initially in Chapter 2. While presenting in full here, I have expanded Pellegrini's list, adding my own observations of countries that illustrate these issues.

1. **Cultural proximity.** People in some countries share similar patterns of life. Periodically, I hear that the European country most similar to the United States is Belgium, not the United Kingdom, as many would assume because of the language similarity. Cultural proximity is more important for mass retailers and becomes less significant when retail concepts involve narrowly defined consumer markets that are similar in various countries, i.e., global retailers.
2. **Market size.** Market saturation in the home country is an impetus for foreign direct investment by retailers. Ample space for expansion must be available, particularly if the firm needs to reach a certain size to exploit economies of scale. Legal restrictions governing growth in the home country can be considered a motive for companies to move to foreign locations. Most European countries have stringent requirements that limit large-scale retailers' growth, pushing retailers in these countries to expand outside national borders. Examples of this effect have been presented throughout the book. French hypermarkets dominate the Spanish market. Delhaize de Lion owns the leading supermarket chain in the Czech Republic. German department stores have expanded rapidly into the former East Germany. Japanese department stores have expanded into Hong Kong, Singapore, and the People's Republic of China (PRC).
3. **Competitors' moves.** A first-mover advantage may be lost if competitors enter a foreign market. In general the first major retailer to enter a market will become the market leader. Wal-Mart, Carrefour, Metro, and Tesco often come head to head in major markets. In the chapter on Central and Eastern Europe I discussed Tesco's strategy of entering the market quickly and setting up a presence of 10–15 hypermarkets so they can justify opening a warehouse. Having set up their infrastructure, they then have the market presence to diversify into other formats.

4. **Geographical proximity.** Expanding closer to home reduces transfer costs related to transportation and corporate communication. Geographical proximity is more important for retailers selling private labels that they produce in a central location. It is less important for decentralized companies, because they are allowed to operate as independent units, generally sourcing from within the country.

5. **Low-cost land and labor.** Japanese department stores were lured to Hong Kong by the offer of subsidized land and reduced taxes to make their investment more attractive. By the late 1980s, Japanese stores controlled more than 50 percent of the Hong Kong department store industry. The second stage of the retail leapfrog is now occurring. Isetan opened stores in Hong Kong during the previous decade. These stores are now being closed. Instead, Isetan is opening stores in the PRC. This movement is not strictly due to low-cost land, because the rental cost is very high for good locations in major PRC cities. However, Isetan is likely gambling that prices will soar as others join the retail pioneers in the PRC. This is supported by findings of the Healey & Baker survey.[9] According to this survey, Causeway Bay in Hong Kong had taken over the top position from Pedder Street, also in Hong Kong, as having the most expensive commercial rents in the world, up to $10,000 per square meter. The next most expensive locations were Fifth Avenue, New York; Nanjing Road, Shanghai; and Ginza, Tokyo.

## Internalization Advantages

Internalization has to do with keeping company secrets. All companies have secrets—information that helps to make them unique or successful, or both. The greater a company's ownership assets, the more important it is to protect these assets by guarding company secrets.

In retail franchising, a company sells or leases assets to other firms. Therefore, franchising is a particularly dangerous idea for retailers with strong asset- or transaction-based ownership advantages. Retailing innovations are difficult to defend from imitators. Competitors can freely copy them because there are no patents on retail know-how. Therefore, to maintain a competitive advantage, a retail company needs to internalize its innovations. The only way for a retail company to keep its operating secrets is to open wholly owned subsidiaries in various countries. This is too expensive for many companies, who are forced to franchise their retail innovations to expand rapidly. However, over time these companies may come to regret this decision because they have lost the market opportunity of that area.

Joint ventures offer less protection of secrets than wholly owned subsidiaries, but they are often necessary when entering a different cultural environment or because of government regulations. Many developing countries require that controlling interest of multinational companies rests with domestic ownership.

## › GLOBAL AND MULTINATIONAL EXPANSION

The two major strategic alternatives available for international retail expansion are global and multinational. The characteristics of these strategies are presented in Table 21.1.

| Table 21.1 | |
| --- | --- |
| **Characteristics of Global versus Multinational Strategies** | |
| **Global** | **Multinational** |
| Centralized management | Decentralized management |
| Standard format | Adapted format |
| Rapid expansion | Expansion in stages |
| Private label | National brands and private label |

## Global Retailers

As we saw in Chapter 2, global retailers reproduce a standard product in each country they enter. Generally doing this requires centralized management decision making. Many global retailers begin with decentralized management and then, to gain greater control of their rapidly expanding company, move back to a more centralized management system. Global retailers expand internationally using a standard retail format. Each store looks similar. The products are generally universal. Fixtures look like they belong to the same family. In its early years, The Body Shop allowed its stores to select one of three color schemes. The stores were also free to sell merchandise other than The Body Shop line. However, these freedoms were later eliminated to provide a more unified store image.

Generally global retailers are vertically integrated backward, producing their own private label lines. It is often difficult to determine to what degree the success of a global retailer can be attributed to its retail format and to what degree it is due to the product itself. Because these retailers produce their own private labels, the lead time for product development is longer than for a traditional retailer. However, the fast-fashion retailers have generally turned this generalization around. Mango and Zara have some of the fastest turning inventory available and they have 100 percent private label.

Benetton's distribution system looks like a franchisee system, but the company maintains that because it does not charge royalties or dictate the operating format of individual stores, it is *not* a franchise. The company does not want to be directly involved in the selling phase. Initially, financing was 50–50, with Benetton providing half of the costs and the store owner the other half. Later, the company found that potential store owners were willing to underwrite all the costs of opening a Benetton store.

## Multinational Retailers

In contrast to global retailers, multinational retailers are decentralized, and they alter their offerings based on cultural differences. Companies such as France's Carrefour and Tesco (United Kingdom) are multinational. Expansion of multinational retailers is generally more sporadic than that of global retailers. Table 21.2 details Carrefour's international expansion efforts, listing entries and, more important, exits over the years.[10] Generally multinational retailers concentrate their expansion within a geographic area, filling that area before moving to a new country or region.

**Table 21.2**
**Carrefour's Record of Overseas Expansion in the Hypermarket Format, 1978–1997**

| Year of Entry | Country | Status |
|---|---|---|
| 1969 | Belgium | Out in 1978 |
| 1969 | United Kingdom | Out in 1983 |
| 1972 | Italy | Out in 1984 |
| 1973 | Spain | 54 stores in 1997[a] |
| 1974 | Brazil | 45 stores in 1997 |
| 1976 | Austria | Out in 1979 |
| 1977 | Germany | Out in 1979 |
| 1982 | Argentina | 17 stores in 1997 |
| 1988 | United States | Out in 1994 |
| 1989 | Taiwan | 16 stores in 1997 |
| 1990 | Portugal | 3 stores in 1997 |
| 1993 | Italy | 7 stores in 1997[b] |
| 1994 | Mexico | 16 stores in 1997 |
| 1994 | Malaysia | 2 stores in 1997 |
| 1996 | Thailand | 5 stores in 1997 |
| 1996 | China | 3 stores in 1997 |
| 1996 | South Korea | 3 stores in 1997 |
| 1996 | Hong Kong | 1 store in 1997 |
| 1997 | Monaco | 1 store in 1997 |
| 1997 | Turkey | 1 store in 1997 |

[a] Under "Pryca" name. [b] One store under "Al Gran Sole" name.
Source: Carrefour—Company Report. (March 13, 1997). UBS Research Limited in *Investext* [Database on CD-ROM]. Foster City, Calif.: Information Access; and http://www.carrefour.fr/monde.html

These retailers change their offering based on customer and cultural differences. This strategy requires a great deal of learning. Each country mastered gives the retail firm a broad knowledge base. However, because these companies are decentralized, this knowledge base often remains within each country. After operating as a very decentralized company, Carrefour began to centralize the development of private label lines in Europe. The company had buyers from each of the major countries bring samples of their private label products for certain lines, such as dairy. As a European team, these buyers decided which country would produce the private label ice cream, which would produce the private label orange juice, and so on. The basic question the buyers were asked to address was, "Are country differences significant enough to justify all of these different products?"[11]

### ❯ STAGES THEORY

Learning sets the stage for future investment. For example, U.S. chain stores have learned as a result of their investment throughout this country. This learning may allow them to say, for instance, that moving into Ontario, Canada, will be like moving into Seattle. The ability to make these analogies serves to distinguish those who are able to compete from those who are not.

International expansion can involve different levels of learning. Global companies expand rapidly, using the same standard retail format. They do not learn much about their market environment. Multinational companies change as they move to other countries. Each movement prepares them to move to another location. They arm themselves with an arsenal of stereotypes about doing business in diverse conditions. International expansion can involve different levels of learning. Retailers who franchise or license their format for other retailers obtain little information that will help them in additional markets. For these retailers, the short-term benefits of franchising and licensing fees are what drives their investment.

Multinational retailers expand into locations that they perceive to have greater locational advantages. Wal-Mart, Sears, and Kmart expanded into Mexico because of geographical proximity. In addition, because these companies had many customers in border towns from Mexico, they had a chance to get to understand the Mexican culture before making this move.

French hypermarkets expanded very successfully into Spain. The cultural similarities between France and Spain are viewed as much greater than those between France and other European countries.[12] Today, the French hypermarkets' private label products have become the leading national brands in Spain.[13]

## > RISK THEORY

The reward for risk is margin or profit. Some companies are inherently greater risk takers than others. Eroglu identified some organizational characteristics that help to explain the risk-taking behavior of companies.[14] She believed that a set of organizational and environmental characteristics influenced perceived risk and perceived benefits, two ideas that directly affect the intention to internationalization. The characteristics she places under environment are domestic competitive pressures, external change agent influences, and perceived favorability of the external environment. These characteristics are part of the SIRE model under locational advantages.

The organizational characteristics are firm size, operating experience, top management's international orientation, top management's tolerance for risk, and top management's perception of the firm's competitive advantage. All these characteristics are positively related to whether a retailer will choose international expansion.

In the next section I will restate the propositions from Chapter 2 and provide a brief discussion of how a proposition would be analyzed.

## > RESEARCH PROPOSITIONS

### Propositions Related to Ownership Advantages

P1:    The greater the ownership advantages for retailers, the less likely they will franchise or license.

P2:    The greater the available organizational slack, the greater the likelihood of expanding internationally.

[Ratio of current assets to current liabilities (3-year average before their first international expansion)][15]

P3:   The greater the recoverable slack, the greater the likelihood of expanding internationally.
[Ratio of general and administrative expenses to sales (three-year average before their first international expansion)]

P4:   The greater the potential slack, the greater the likelihood of expanding internationally.
[Ratio of equity to capital (three-year average before their first international expansion)]

## Propositions for Locational Advantages

Multinational Companies (High adaptive-Decentralized)

P5:   Multinational retailers will move to countries with lower disposable income than their home country.

P6:   Multinational retailers will move to countries that have a high positive change in GDP.

$$\frac{\text{(GDP 5 years before expansion-GDP at the time of expansion)}}{\text{GDP R5 years before expansion}}$$

P7:   Multinational retailers will move to countries that have a high positive change in service-value added as % of GDP.

$$\frac{\text{(Service\% of GDP 5 years before expansion-Service\% of GDP at the time of Expansion)}}{\text{Service\% of GDP 5 years before expansion}}$$

P8:   Multinational retailers will first move to countries that are culturally the most similar to their home country. (Hofstede's indicators Home country-Host country for four factors, MvsF, HuvsLU (uncertainty avoidance); IndvsCol; HPDvsLPD)

P9:   Multinational retailers will expand within the country and then will expand regionally within that area (for example, expanding to Brazil and then Argentina and Chile).

P10:  Periodically the multinational retailers will "jump" to a new geographic area and begin the stages form of expansion.

P11:  Multinational retailers will move to countries that are geographically close to the home country initially, then expand to more distant countries (miles from home country to host country).

P12:  Multinational retailers will move to countries with large population bases.

Global Companies (standard format-centralized)

P13:  Global companies will move to the largest/capital cities in a country.

P14: Global companies will not be attracted by population size, income, cultural proximity, or geographical proximity.

P15: The greater the asset-based ownership advantages of a global retailer, the more likely they are to franchise.

P16: The greater the transaction-based ownership advantages of a global retailer, the less likely they are to franchise.

P17: The greater the available organizational slack, the greater the likelihood that global retailers will reacquire international franchisees.
[Ratio of current assets to current liabilities (three-year average before they begin reacquisition)]

P18: The greater the recoverable slack, the greater the likelihood that global retailers will reacquire international franchisees.
[Ratio of general and administrative expenses to sales (three-year average before they begin reacquisition)]

P19: The greater the potential slack, the greater the likelihood that global retailers will reacquire international franchisees.
[Ratio of equity to capital (three-year average before they begin reacquisition)]

The Gap, Inc. can be defined as a global retailer; it has a centralized management, standard format, rapid expansion, and private labels. The Gap's world headquarters are based in San Francisco, California. They have offices around the globe to support store management, operations, and distribution, but the majority of their decision making takes place in the United States. Although the Gap had to adjust their product sizing in Japan, merchandise is standard throughout all of the countries into which they have expanded. The Gap is 100-percent private label branded. They have four different store types including, The Gap, Banana Republic, Old Navy, and Fourth and Towne. They do not franchise or license their stores. They are fully owned and operated by The Gap, Inc. The countries where they located are not culturally similar, nor have they used a stages expansion strategy. They have located exclusively in high-income countries, not countries less developed than the home market. Following the prediction in the propositions, they have not franchised because they want to keep control of their assets.

### Gap Flow Chart:

> 1969: United States (2,603 stores in 2005)
> 1987: United Kingdom (132 stores in 2005)
> 1989: Canada (176 stores in 2005)
> 1990s: Germany (out in 2004)
> 1993: France (33 stores in 2005)
> 1996: Japan (85 stores in 2005)

The company purchases merchandise from more than 700 vendors with facilities in over 50 countries.[16] This creates a very diversified vendor base allowing them to avoid potential problems with product flow because they do not rely on only one manufacturer.[17] Here is an example of how you could analyze one of the propositions.

## P13: Global companies will move to the largest/capital cities in a country.

The Gap, Inc.'s first international expansion was in London, England. London is ranked the twentieth most-populated city in the world with 7,421,209 people.[18] When expanding into Canada, The Gap, Inc. chose to locate itself in the bustling city of Vancouver in British Columbia. Next, The Gap, Inc. entered France. Their flagship store was located in Paris, known for fashion and its numerous tourist attractions. Specifically, six main attractions in Paris draw 23.5 million visitors a year.[19] The Gap, Inc. has also expanded into Japan, the flagship store was located in Tokyo. This particular city is ranked as the fourteenth most-populated city in the world with 8,336,599 people.[20]

## Multinational Retailers

Tesco (United Kingdom) is an example of a multinational retailer. Here is its flow-chart.

| Flow Chart | | | | | |
|---|---|---|---|---|---|
| Year Market Entry | Country | Number of Stores | New Stores Opened in 2004/2005 | Planned Openings 2005/2006 | Details |
| 1924 | United Kingdom (UK) | 1,780 | 114 | 111 | 1) Opened first store in 1929 and now have a total of 1,780 stores through four formats: Express, Metro, Superstore, and Extra<br>2) Over 250,000 employees |
| **Expansion to Europe** | | | | | |
| 1994 | Hungary | 69 | 9 | 14 | 1) First superstore opening in 1997<br>2) Two hypermarkets opened in 2000<br>3) Nine hypermarkets opened in 2004–2005 |
| 1995 | Poland | 78 | 9 | 20 | 1) Invested in Savia, a small retail chain in 1995<br>2) In 1997, Co. acquired a controlling interest in 23 stores in Poland<br>3) In 2000, Co. acquired Madex and Minor food chains<br>4) Built a market leading position employing 18,000 people |
| 1996 | Czech Republic | 25 | 3 | 8 | 1) The first hypermarket in the Czech Republic was opened in Prague—Zličn in 1998<br>2) All stores "Tesco" brand name in 2000 |
| 1996 | Slovakia | 30 | 7 | 6 | 1) In 1999, opened first hypermarket in Slovakia<br>2) In 2003 *Tesco own-brand* was voted the most popular retail brand in Slovakia<br>3) A new fresh food distribution center is operational in May 2005 |

*continued*

| Year Market Entry | Country | Number of Stores | New Stores Opened in 2004/2005 | Planned Openings 2005/2006 | Details |
|---|---|---|---|---|---|
| 1997 | Republic of Ireland | 87 | 8 | 8 | 1) In 1997, Co. acquired the Irish food retailing and related businesses of Associated British Foods plc for £643,000,000<br>2) In 2005, opened first Extra |
| 2003 | Turkey | 5 | — | 3 | 1) The acquisition of five Kipa hypermarkets in 2003 marked entry<br>2) In June 2005, opened first new store |
| Europe | | 294 | | | |
| **Expansion to Asia** | | | | | |
| 1998 | Thailand | 107 | 43 | **83** | 1) In 1998, Co. acquired a controlling interest in Lotus in Thailand from CP Group<br>2) Acquired the Lotus hypermarket chain of 14 stores<br>3) 49 hypermarkets, 46 Express, and 12 Value stores |
| 1999 | South Korea | 38 | 10 | 31 | 1) In 1999, Co. acquired a 51% controlling interest in Samsung Tesco Co. Ltd.<br>2) Next month, Co. increased its holding in Samsung Tesco Ltd. to 81%<br>3) In 2002, Co. increased its holding in the equity capital of Samsung Tesco Co. Limited to 89%<br>4) Second-largest retailer with 31 hypermarkets in Korea<br>5) Seven new Express stores |
| 2001 | Taiwan | 5 | 1 | 1 | 1) Opened first hypermarket in 2000<br>2) They plan to open more than 40 Express stores over in 2006 |
| 2002 | Malaysia | 6 | 1 | 5 | 1) Joint venture with Sime Darby Bhd<br>2) In 2004, double the number of stores |
| 2003 | Japan | 104 | 28 | 15 | 1) Tesco formed a joint venture with C Two-Network in 2003 creating a presence in Japan with 78 convenience stores in the Tokyo area<br>2) Acquire Fre'c, which currently owns 25 supermarket stores |
| 2004 | China | 31 | 31 | 15 | 1) In 2004, acquired a 50% share in the Hymall hypermarket chain through a joint venture<br>2) Six hypermarkets |
| Asia | | 291 | | | |
| Total | | 2,365 | 263 | 318 | |

Their expansion in general fits the propositions. They moved to less developed markets that were culturally similar to their home market before jumping to a new geographic area. Then they expanded operations in that new geographic area before expanding elsewhere. They are using stages theory, building up an area before moving to a new one.

The purpose of presenting a theory and its supporting propositions is to have others evaluate the theory and find flaws with it. That is exactly what I hope will happen because by pointing out errors and omissions, I can continue to adapt the basic framework. That is what theory builders do. So find instances of where these propositions do not work and let the rebuilding begin.

## > SUMMARY

The model presented in this chapter is based on four theories that help to explain strategic retail internationalization. The model is not meant to be descriptive, but instead is presented as a normative model based on the four interconnected theories. No doubt readers can think of global retailers who use franchising and are very

**Photo 21.1**
Even this small store in Vietnam sells Pepsi.
*Courtesy of SN.*

**Box 21.1**
**Firms in China Think Globally, Hire Locally**

*Beijing*

DU LIMIN is living the American Dream—in China. A decade ago, Ms. Du joined Wal-Mart China as an accountant. Today, she is a director overseeing three Sam's Club supercenters and more than 1,500 employees in China for the U.S. retailer, Wal-Mart Stores Inc.

Ms. Du's rise has been replicated across China as multinational corporations fill management positions with local talent. According to Taihe Consulting Co., of Beijing, about 70% of foreign firms' top positions today are filled by Chinese workers. In the mid-1990s, almost all such posts were filled by non-locals.

In recent years, more Chinese have studied or worked overseas, strengthening their English-language and leadership skills and making them more suitable for management positions, executives at multinationals say. "My first choice will always be local," says Niklas Lindholm, human resources director for Nokia Corp.'s Chinese investment unit in Beijing. "We are an international company and we need the variety."

Multinationals in other developing countries also have localized their staff after establishing themselves in a market. Many locals, for example, have moved up through the ranks of foreign corporations in India. These kinds of developments have uncovered a wellspring of new managerial talent and are changing the way global corporations do business locally.

Executives at foreign companies in China say local hires cost less to employ than expatriates and often have a better understanding of the Chinese market. A Chinese manager, on average, has a total compensation package that is only 20% to 25% of that of a hire from a Western country, says Taihe Consulting. Having a local boss also serves as a morale booster, giving career hope to ambitious junior employees.

When multinationals first opened in China in the early 1990s, expatriates filled most mid-level and senior management posts. Locals settled for junior positions. The expats, usually from the company's home country, were valued for their knowledge of corporate culture. Some multinationals would tap managers from Singapore or Hong Kong where they were already established, before they would consider developing local talent.

Chinese managers began gaining ground in the late 1990s. Expats usually had costly relocation expenses, and often they proved less effective than locals as a result of cultural and language differences. Meanwhile, changes in China's labor market—such as the reform of state-owned businesses and restructuring of government offices—freed many experienced managers to take jobs at multinationals.

The trends have helped transform the staff makeup of many companies. At Siemens Ltd. China, a unit of Siemens AG, seven of nine regional managers are Chinese. Richard Hausmann, chief executive of the Chinese unit, says he wants to elevate a Chinese executive to the China operation's six-person board of directors. Three of four regional managers at Motorola Inc.'s unit in China are local Chinese. At FedEx Corp.'s China operations, locals account for 78% of management positions.

Tu Min, vice president of communications at Telefon AB, L.M. Ericsson's China subsidiary, graduated from college in 1992 and took a government job. Three years later, as some of China's best and brightest went to work for foreign companies, Ms. Tu heard about an opening for a translator at Ericsson. She joined the company in 1995, a year after it had set up its wholly owned business in China.

Her supervisor recognized her as a "quick learner" and "cheerful person," and recommended her for a job as a public relations executive, she recalls. After stints in sales and business development, Ms. Tu was promoted to manage the communications department.

Ericsson helped pay for her advanced degrees, including a master's in journalism and an MBA from the company's China Academy in Beijing. Last October, Ericsson promoted Ms. Tu to vice president. Local managers now account for 90% of the firm's middle management posts and half of its senior management.

*continued*

**Box 21.1** *Continued*

Wal-Mart's Ms. Du was also in one of the first waves of Chinese to benefit from localization. A few years after graduating with an accounting degree from a Shanghai college in 1986,
Ms. Du took a job as an accountant in a Chinese cartoon company in the city of Shenzhen,
bordering Hong Kong. When Wal-Mart started recruiting staff for its first China store, which
was set to open in Shenzhen in 1996, Ms. Du applied for a job—although she knew nothing
about retailing and had never heard of Wal-Mart, except that, as a friend told her, it was a big
name in the U.S.

Ms. Du's first job at Wal-Mart was as team leader of the Shenzhen store's finance department. She says virtually all the managers at that time were Westerners or from Hong Kong.
When the store's general manager, who was from Hong Kong, predicted at a staff meeting
that five years later someone from China would head the store, "all of us burst out laughing,
thinking he was telling a joke," Ms. Du recalls.

Ms. Du was named the store's training manager in 1997 and its general manager in 2000.
She became director of Sam's Club in January. Today, local Chinese account for 100% of Wal-
Mart China's middle managers, and 99% of its senior managers.

Stephanie Wong, vice president of Wal-Mart China's personnel division, describes Ms. Du
as "an outstanding performer and one of many success stories at Wal-Mart China." Ms. Du
says one advantage she has as a local Chinese manager is that she can communicate better
with her employees. "They take me as their big sister and they confide their family issues
with me," says Ms. Du, 43 years old. That "is impossible if you're an expatriate."

When SARS hit China in 2003, people were reluctant to go to stores and other public
places. To assuage customers' fears, Ms. Du required staff at the Shenzhen store she was
managing to disinfect shopping carts after use by each customer. Although almost all of
Shenzhen's stores saw a decline in sales volume during the period, Wal-Mart's Shenzhen
branch maintained growth, Ms. Du says.

Ms. Du says for many Chinese, a barrier to advancement to Asia-Pacific or other regional
posts is their lack of knowledge about the rest of the region. "We need to know more about
other countries before heading the regional operations," she says. But China's vast market
is a great training ground, she adds. "Being successful in China, Wal-Mart's Chinese managers surely have a better chance to move up," she says.

—*Cui Rong*

Source: *Wall Street Journal,* February 27, 2006.

successful. However, a long-term evaluation of the success of this strategy is needed.
For instance, although a company may look very successful initially, this success is
predictable; franchising allows the retailer to expand at a rapid rate without massive corporate investment. In effect, franchising is a short-term solution, providing
rapid growth and income.

There are few examples of Japanese companies that offer their company expertise
to a franchising or licensing arrangement. Their orientation is long term. Investors
are prepared to accept long-term corporate growth rather than short-term profits.
U.S. retailers have been eager to engage in franchising and licensing arrangements.
Will they regret this strategy in the coming decades?

Recently I conducted interviews with management at several U.S. national chain
stores. These chains are eager to engage in international franchising opportunities
and potential licensing arrangements. When I asked them if they would be eager to
engage in franchising or licensing in their home market, they indicated that they do

not want to sacrifice control of their retail image and identity, and so are not interested in franchising or licensing at home. There will come a time when their view of the world is like their view of the national market. Yet by then they may have sold their share of these foreign markets to strangers.

Most U.S. manufacturers sacrificed long-term market presence in Japan by entering licensing arrangements with Japanese companies. The names of these U.S. manufacturers were always represented in Japanese stores; however, Japanese companies produced their products under licensing agreements. Years later, when the American companies wanted to have a larger presence in the Japanese market, the Japanese companies blocked them because of the earlier licensing arrangements. In some instances, retailers have used licensing to protect their company interests. For example, Price Club entered Beijing through a licensing arrangement with an equity option. This is the only method of entry into the PRC market that does not require the foreign retailer to contribute a large amount of money. I talked with the Price Club's U.S. manager in Beijing. He had also worked on the Price Club's South Korean licensing arrangement. His job was to set the company up, train local managers, and move on to the next international assignment. Local companies participating in such joint ventures in the PRC were very disgruntled if the company had to absorb high expatriate manager salaries. **EXPATRIATE** managers are managers from foreign countries. The benefit packages these managers receive for foreign assignments can turn a $70,000 middle manager's salary into a $350,000 expense for the company. The benefits package generally includes a housing allowance, education reimbursement for children, and hardship pay. In contrast, the senior managers in the PRC might be paid $6,000. This issue was discussed at a seminar I attended at University of Michigan. The basic recommendation was for MNE to expense the salaries of expatriate managers to the corporate entity, rather than to the national subsidiary. The reason given was exactly the issue that I have heard expressed in many interviews with less-developed country executives: "The expats are just too expensive. They could hire 10 local executives for the price they are paying for the international executive." I think this suggestion is a good one. If the local enterprise does not have to pay for the foreign executive talent, they are more likely to be accepted, and listened to. It is an important lesson in international retailing. Make the local enterprise pay for things that are truly local, and have corporate pay for those things that are likely to add global synergies to the corporate organization. (Read Box 21.1: "Firms in China Think Globally, Hire Locally," from the February 27, 2006 *Wall Street Journal* B1.)

Retailers have moved very slowly in their international expansion activities. Those retailers who have gained a portfolio of strategies for international expansion are poised to make the leap into future markets. Those who have not conducted their own international expansion, but rather, have given their proprietary knowledge to others, will likely begin to contract their expansion into new markets. In the Appendix you will find a summary of many retailers' internationalization efforts.

> **KEY TERMS**

EXPATRIATE

## > DISCUSSION QUESTIONS

1. Which of Dunning's advantages are more important for global retailers? Which are more important for multinational expansion?
2. When is it worthwhile for a retailer to use an investment strategy for internationalization?
3. How does franchising or licensing hurt a retailer?
4. When does franchising or licensing help a retailer?

## > ENDNOTES

1. Parts of this chapter are published with permission from the International Journal of Retail and Distribution Management, 1997.
2. Pellegrini, L. (1994). "Alternatives for Growth and Internationalization in Retailing." *International Review of Retail, Distribution and Consumer Research,* Vol. 4, No. 2, pp. 1212–48.
3. Dunning, J. H. and M. McQueen. (1982). "The Eclectic Theory of the Multinational Enterprise." In A. M. Rugman, ed., *New Theories of the Multinational Enterprise.* Beckenham, Kent: Croom Helm, pp. 79–106.
4. Salmon, W. J., and A. Tordjman. (1989). "The Internationalization of Retailing." *International Journal of Retailing,* Vol. 4, No. 2, pp. 3–16.
5. Eroglu, S. (1992) "The Internationalisation Process of Franchise Systems: A Conceptual Model." *International Marketing Review,* Vol. 9, No. 5, pp. 39–45.
6. Hollander, S. C. (1970). *Multinational Retailing.* East Lansing, MI: Michigan State University.
7. Dunning, J. H. (1981). *International Production and the Multinational Enterprise.* London: Allen & Unwin.
8. Pelligrini, L. (1991) "The Internationalization of Retailing and 1992 Europe." *Journal of Marketing Channels,* Vol. 1, No. 2, pp. 3–27.
9. "International—World Rents and Other News." (1995). *Retail News Letter.* No. 429, p. 1.
10. Compiled from company reports, source unknown.
11. Personal interviews (1994).
12. Personal interviews (1994, 1996).
13. Sternquist, B., and M. Kacker. *European Retailing's Vanishing Borders.* Westport, CT: Greenwood Publishing.
14. Eroglu. (1992).
15. Rhee, J.H. and J.L.C. Cheng (2002). "Foreign Market Uncertainty and Incremental International Expansion." *Management International Review,* Vol. 42, No. 4: 419.
16. Pricetargetresearch.com, October 16, 2005.
17. Global Market Information Database, November 3, 2005.
18. Pubquizhelp.com, November 11, 2005.
19. Gofrance.about.com, November 11, 2005.
20. Pubquizhelp.com, November 11, 2005.

# INDEX

Note: Page numbers in boldface refer to pages that contain definition of terms.